Comparative Criminal Justice Systems

A Topical Approach

PHILIP L. REICHEL

University of Northern Colorado

Prentice Hall Career & Technology
Englewood Cliffs, New Jersey 07632

Library of Congress Cataloging in Publication Data

Reichel, Philip L.
  Comparative criminal justice systems: A topical approach/Philip L. Reichel
    p.   cm.
  Includes bibliographical references and index.
  ISBN 0-13-151937-9
  1. Criminal justice, Administration of—Cross-cultural studies.
I. Title
HV7419.R45   1994
364—dc20   93–4493

Acquisitions Editor: Robin Baliszewski
Acquisitions Editorial Assistant: Rose Mary Florio
Marketing Manager: Ramona Baran
Supplements Editor: Judith Casillo
Cover Design: Mike Fender
Prepress Buyer: Ilene Levy Sanford
Manufacturing Buyer: Ed O'Dougherty
Production Editor: Patrick Walsh

 © 1994 by Prentice Hall Career & Technology
Prentice-Hall, Inc.
A Paramount Communications Company
Englewood Cliffs, New Jersey 07632

Printed in the United States of America
1 2 3 4 5 6 7 8 9 10

ISBN 0-13-151937-9

Prentice-Hall International (UK) Limited, *London*
Prentice-Hall of Australia Pty. Limited, *Sydney*
Prentice-Hall Canada Inc., *Toronto*
Prentice-Hall Hispanoamericana, S.A., *Mexico*
Prentice-Hall of India Private Limited, *New Delhi*
Prentice-Hall of Japan, Inc., *Tokyo*
Simon & Schuster Asia Pte. Ltd., *Singapore*
Editora Prentice-Hall do Brasil Ltda., *Rio de Janeiro*

Contents

Chapter 7
An International Perspective on Courts   **213**

Chapter 8
An International Perspective on Corrections   **265**

Chapter 9
An International Perspective on Juvenile Justice   **311**

Chapter 10
Japan: Examples of Effectiveness and Borrowing   **345**

Appendix
Almanac Information for Countries Referenced   **399**

Index   **435**

Preface

In 1986, the Commission on the Role and Future of State Colleges and Universities reported concern about the deficiency of American students' knowledge of world affairs, of America's role in the international scene, and of other nations' cultures. The Commission recommended that our educational system incorporate a strong international dimension at all levels, from grade school through graduate school. The dramatic political and economic changes occurring around the world, as the final decade of the twentieth century began, suddenly gave the Commission's plea a concrete dimension for anyone who may have viewed it as academics simply crying wolf.

This text is an effort to respond to the concerns expressed in that report. The text is organized in ten chapters that reflect the material and order of presentation typically found in introductory books on the American system of criminal justice. That is, arrangement proceeds from concern with criminal law through examination of police, courts, and corrections. This organization distinguishes the text from other comparative criminal justice books that present detailed information on five or six specific countries. This text contains less detail on the criminal justice system of particular countries, but it provides greater appreciation and understanding of the diversity in legal systems around the world.

A benefit of using the same countries for each chapter would be a sense of consistency and depth in the text. However, not every country offers the same level of contrast in all aspects of its criminal justice system. For example, describing German and French policing results in interesting and specific contrasts. But if the same countries are used to contrast the trial procedure, their similarity makes us less aware of the variation occurring in that process when other countries are considered.

Luckily, there is an alternative means for presenting information on law, police, courts, corrections, and juvenile justice. The organization used in this text follows the belief that comparison relies on categorization. That is, to best understand and explain similarities and differences among things, one must start by categorizing them.

The first chapter provides the rationale for studying other systems of justice and sets down the specific approach used in this text. The second chapter reviews crime as a world problem and sets the stage for consideration of the different ways justice systems are organized in attempts to respond to the crime problem. Chapter 3 presents traditional material on American criminal law so that the reader has a familiar and common base to use in the following chapters. Chapter 4 presents the four contemporary legal traditions and outlines the basic features of each. Chapter 5 continues material in Chapters 3 and 4 by looking at substantive and procedural criminal law in each of the four legal traditions.

The next four chapters cover the topics of policing (Chapter 6), the judiciary (Chapter 7), corrections (Chapter 8), and juvenile justice (Chapter 9). Countries representing Europe, Asia, North and South America, Latin America, Australia, and Pacific islands are included in the coverage. Some make frequent appearances (for example, Australia, France, Nigeria, and Saudi Arabia), while others are less recurrent (for example, Canada, Denmark, Mexico, and Fiji). The text concludes with a concentrated look at the criminal justice system of Japan. This country was chosen for special consideration because it has a history of borrowing from other countries (a point encouraged by comparative studies) and has what many consider to be a very effective criminal justice system. Also, ending the text with an in-depth look at a particular country provides an opportunity to tie together some of the topics and items presented in earlier chapters.

Comparative criminal justice is still in its infancy, but increasing numbers of academics and practitioners are coming to realize that it is a field whose time has come. As more and more textbooks begin to appear, more scholars attempt cross-cultural research, and more practitioners share ideas, comparative criminal justice will advance to levels we cannot yet appreciate. I hope you will find this book to be a positive contribution toward the advancement of this important field of study.

ACKNOWLEDGMENTS

I would like to acknowledge the support I have received from colleagues, both here and abroad, in my attempt to expand my knowledge about comparative criminal justice. At Warsaw University Andrzej Rzeplinski, Monika Platek, and Zbigniew Lasocik provided me with valuable information and kindly arranged tours of Polish prisons and police agencies while I visited their wonderful country. Kurt Neudek at the United Nations International Center in Vienna provided me with United Nations publications that were of great benefit. The opportunity offered me by Al Coox at San Diego State University to participate in the Japan Studies Institute inspired the detailed look given Japan in Chapter 10. At the University of Northern Colorado Lucille Schweers and her staff in the Inter-Library Loan department were able to handle my requests for both easily available and difficult to find publications with speed, efficiency, and friendliness.

The staff at Regents/Prentice Hall has also been wonderfully easy to work with. Editor Robin Baliszewski not only expressed interest in my proposal but was very supportive of the direction I wanted the book to take. The patience shown by Production Editor Patrick Walsh as he walked me through the various stages was greatly appreciated.

Finally, acknowledgment also goes to the reviewers who kindly assisted in the evaluation of the manuscript. The following people gave their valuable time and assistance in helping this book come to publication in a better form than was first submitted. The remaining weaknesses, of course, are my responsibility. Thank you to:

David Neubauer, Ph.D., *University of New Orleans*

Robert J. Homant, Ph.D., *University of Detroit*

Joan Luxenburg, Ed.D., *University of Central Oklahoma*

Joseph W. Lipchitz, Ph.D., *University of Massachusetts at Lowell*

Jan K. Dargel, M.A., J.D., *University of Tampa*

William D. Hyatt, J.D., LL.M., *Western Carolina University*

C. Ray Jeffery, Ph.D., *Florida State University*

*To my wife Eva
and our sons, Scott and Matt*

Chapter 1

Taking an International Perspective

KEY TOPICS

- Reasons for studying foreign legal systems
- How an international perspective can benefit our own legal system and the world at large
- International efforts in law enforcement and adjudication
- Three ways to study foreign criminal justice systems
- Two ways to explain how criminal justice systems work in different countries
- Classification strategies
- How this book is structured

KEY TERMS

authentic strategy	functions/procedures	nonfinancial bail
cash deposit bail	descriptive approach	political approach
classification	historical approach	recognizance
commercial bail	institutions/actors	synthetic strategy
criminalization		

COUNTRIES REFERENCED

Australia	France	Panama
Belgium	India	Russia
China	Japan	South Africa
England	Mexico	United States

The 1981 best-selling novel *Gorky Park*, by Martin Cruz Smith, began with the arrival of Soviet police (militia) at a place in Moscow's Gorky Park, where an officer found three bodies lying in the snow. Chief Investigator Arkady Renko was the head of the Homicide Department of the Moscow Town Prosecutor's office. Upon his arrival, Arkady " . . . suspected the poor dead bastards were just a vodka troika that had cheerily frozen to death. Vodka was liquid taxation, and the price was always rising. It was accepted that three was the lucky number on a bottle in terms of economic prudence and desired effect. It was a perfect example of primitive communism" (Smith, 1981, p. 3).

Arkady was soon given reason to believe that this was not an ordinary case involving equal doses of vodka, jealousy, boredom, and despair:

> Lights appeared from the opposite side of the clearing, shadow trees sweeping the snow until two black Volgas appeared. A squad of KGB agents in plain-clothes were led from the cars by a squat, vigorous major called Pribluda.

> The militia—the police arm of the MVD—directed traffic, chased drunks and picked up everyday corpses. The Committee for State Security—the KGB— was charged with grander, subtler responsibilities, combating foreign and domestic intriguers, smugglers, malcontents, and while the agents had uniforms, they preferred anonymous plainclothes. Major Pribluda was full of rough early-morning humor, pleased to reduce the professional animosity that strained cordial relations between the People's Militia and the Committee for State Security . . ." (From *Gorky Park* by Martin Cruz Smith, © 1981 by Martin Cruz Smith. Reprinted by permission of Random House, Inc., pp. 3–4).

After completing his initial investigation of what turned out to be a gruesome triple homicide, the Chief Investigator typed his preliminary investigation report and took it to the prosecutor's side of the building.

> A prosecutor was a figure of unusual authority. He oversaw all criminal investigations, representing both state and defendant. Arrests had to meet the prosecutor's approval, court sentences came under his review and appeals came from his initiation. A prosecutor entered civil suits at his pleasure, determined the legality of local-government directives and, at the same time, decided the million-ruble suits and countersuits when one factory delivered nuts rather than bolts to another factory. No matter how great or small the case, criminals, judges, mayors and industrial managers all answered to him. He answered only to the prosecutor general (Smith, 1981, p. 17).

Today, the republics of the former Soviet Union have modified versions of the system described in *Gorky Park*. The KGB was succeeded by new organizations like the Russian Agency for Federal Security, but the basic structures and procedures in Russian criminal justice were little changed. American readers of mystery/detective novels set in other countries are still presented characters in jobs different from what we understand to be the role of police and prosecutors.

We would find it hard to believe a story where the CIA "assists" the New York Police in investigating a Central Park murder. We can handle English investigators from Scotland Yard who seem to have more prosecutorial power than we understand, but they are not really different from our image of detectives. Similarly, stories of French police who seem able to enforce laws throughout the country without regard to city or county boundaries may make them appear a bit presumptuous to the American reader.

A goal of this text is to lessen the likelihood that you will be surprised by criminal procedures in other countries as they become known to you. This is not so that you may enjoy a greater variety of mystery/detective novels, but instead supports the increased need for citizen understanding and appreciation of foreign legal systems.

WHY STUDY THE LEGAL SYSTEM OF OTHER COUNTRIES?

Because an international perspective is still unique in American criminal justice curricula, it is important to spend time showing its value. We begin with the premise that contemporary technology has provided a global communications network serving to shrink the world from the perspective of its people. It is a "small world" in terms of common problems! There is every reason to believe that the citizens of the world, through their respective governments and businesses, will become increasingly interdependent. As a result, an international perspective has both provincial and universal benefits. We will discuss these as they relate to criminal justice and from the viewpoint of Americans.

Before continuing, a few words regarding the use of the terms America and American are in order. Some authors are troubled by the use of those terms in sole reference to the United States and its citizens. Such concerns are well founded, since the North American continent is comprised of Canada, Mexico, and Central America, as well as the United States. Further, since the term America does not distinguish either the northern or southern continent, the citizens of South American countries could also be the subjects of conversation. However, despite the insensitivity its usage may encourage, I will use America as specifically referring to the United States. Citizens of other North and South American countries are more easily, and more correctly, identified with reference to their specific country. While the names Canadians, Peruvians, Mexicans, and Panamanians allow us to place a citizen with a particular country, a term like United Statesian does not roll off the tongue so easily. With apologies to our North and South American neighbors, this book uses America and Americans to refer to the United States of America and her citizens.

Provincial Benefits of an International Perspective

To understand better one's own circumstance it is often beneficial to have a point of contrast and comparison. LePaulle noted that there is a tendency to view the law of one's own country " . . . as natural, as necessary, as given by God" when it is more accurately the result of " . . . historical accident or temporary social situations" (quoted in Cole, Frankowski, and Gertz, 1987, p. 19). Such a view makes the system seem uninteresting and not worthy of scrutiny. After all, why should we need to examine and appreciate what amounts to the only game in town?

When we realize that the American legal system is not the only game, it becomes more interesting and more important to scrutinize that system. For example, the rather passive role of a judge in the American trial process takes on new meaning when contrasted with the very active judge under a civil legal system. When we read of socialist civil legal systems making use of private citizens as lay judges, it puts the use of citizens on American juries in a new perspective. In this manner, a knowledge of alternative systems of justice provides a point of contrast. That, in turn, allows the student and scholar a means and reason to gain new insight into a procedure or structure previously viewed as uninteresting and ordinary. A comparative view of legal systems allows us to understand better the dimensions of our own system. "Without such a comparison, we could be led to a false belief in the necessity and permanency of the status quo" (Terrill, 1982, p. 23).

Besides providing new insight and understanding of our system of justice, an international perspective can furnish ideas to improve that system. A technique used in one country to combat crime might be successfully adapted for use in another country. For example, a key ingredient of Japan's police system is the *koban*, or police box. Since policing in Japan is considered to be very effective and efficient, it has been studied and written about in many countries. Some researchers and practitioners have argued that the *koban* system's community-wide deployment of police would be effective in the United States. And, as Chapter 10 discusses at length, some American cities are finding *koban*-like strategies to be very useful.

No society can incorporate another culture's legal system in its entirety and expect it to work. Yet certain aspects of another system—modified to account for cultural differences—may operate successfully in a new setting. It is important to note that potentially transferable ideas come not only from countries at similar levels of development. For example, Americans are becoming increasingly interested in mediation to settle a variety of legal disputes. As anthropologists remind us, mediation and dispute resolution have a long and distinguished tradition at the tribal and village levels in, for example, African countries. To ignore the experiences of those systems is imprudent and elitist.

Universal Benefits of an International Perspective

As we exit the twentieth century, rapid travel and communication are making us painfully aware that crime no longer is confined by the geographical boundaries of individual countries. In the new age of crime, Fooner (1989) sees common murderers and thieves as comparatively less troublesome to society than terrorists, drug dealers, arms merchants, and money launderers. Further, criminality in the twenty-first century seems less apt to prey on private citizens and more likely to victimize communities, governments, and even entire nations.

Such transnational crimes as terrorism, air and sea hijacking, and drug smuggling are serious concerns that beg for a cooperative international response. Inter-nation collaboration is occurring, but the needed action requires a level of teamwork that countries of the world are only beginning to consider. Understandably, cooperation often begins with neighboring countries, since their common border not only presents the problem of intercountry crime, but also provides both reason and opportunity to do something about it. Consider, for example, arrangements between the United States and Mexico, and the bilateral agreements of Belgium.

In 1990, the United States announced guidelines permitting Mexican police to operate in the United States while American drug agents work in Mexico ("Mexico cops . . .," July 1, 1990). Under this reciprocal arrangement, the Mexicans could send into the United States the same number of police the Americans have operating in Mexico. Even that minimal level of cooperation served to raise additional problems regarding the form such inter-nation policing should take (see Lenhard, 1990). For example, should "guest" police be allowed to carry weapons in each others' country? Must pursuing police be uniformed, or can they be plainclothes detectives? Should police be allowed to cross borders only in search of suspects in certain types of crimes? How far into the host country can foreign police proceed? The questions are many and difficult.

An example of the complexity occurred in 1992, when the United States Supreme Court ruled that the U.S. government may kidnap people from foreign countries to stand trial in the United States (*United States* v. *Alvarez-Machain*, 60 LW 4523). The Drug Enforcement Administration (DEA) believed that Mexican physician, Humberto Alvarez-Machain, was a participant in the torture of DEA agent Enrique Camarena-Salazar. The DEA arranged to have the doctor forcibly abducted from his Guadalajara office and flown to El Paso, Texas, where DEA agents arrested him. Mexico was especially upset by the American actions, since the United States and Mexico have an extradition treaty presumably for just such purposes. But Chief Justice William Rehnquist found nothing in that treaty prohibiting the forcible abduction of people from the territory of the other nation.

The Canadian government, which also has an extradition treaty with the United States, filed a brief supporting Mexico's position in the case. Both countries believed the American actions went against fundamental principles of justice and violated international law. After the Supreme Court's decision was announced, Mexico banned all activities by DEA agents in Mexico. Cooperative efforts were resumed (on what Mexican officials called a temporary basis) a few days later, after American officials assured Mexico that no more suspects would be seized across the border. However, the increasing internationalization of criminal behavior suggests that the three largest North American countries will continue to have their cooperative efforts tested as each combats crime within and across its borders.

European countries have an older but still elementary level of cooperation among law enforcement officials. Belgium, for example, has bilateral agreements on limited cross-border powers for national police forces with France (since 1919), Luxembourg (since 1920), the Netherlands (since 1949), and Germany (since 1989). The arrangements fluctuate from providing official sanctioning of regular contacts between police in the two countries to allowing police carrying out their duties in the other country to wear uniforms and service weapons (Geysels, 1990).

As if worrying about national borders were not enough, technology is presenting new challenges to the cooperative spirit of nations. The new Channel Tunnel (Chunnel) between England and France introduces unique concerns for the police in each country. Under a 1992 pact, French and British police will be able to arrest Chunnel travellers in each other's country. Officials in both countries will be able to investigate passengers while the Chunnel trains are moving, but Britain did not agree to let French police carry guns on the trains ("Chunnel Patrol," 1992).

Political changes in central and Eastern Europe will likely increase the ability of people (including criminals) to move more freely from country to country. Lenhard reacts to the opening of European internal borders with the warning that "it is preposterous to allow criminals free passage throughout Europe while pursuing police forces must stop at the border" (1990, p. 3). Major Frans Geysels of the Belgium Gendarmerie would likely agree. He relates the story of former Belgian Prime Minister Paul Vanden Boeynants, who was kidnapped in January 1989. Soon after Vanden Boeynants's release in February 1989, French police arrested the internationally wanted criminal Bajrani Basri. The arrest occurred after detectives had tailed Bajrani's wife from the Netherlands, via Germany, Belgium, and Luxembourg, to France (Geysels, 1990). The ability to trail a wanted criminal through a variety of legal jurisdictions becomes increasingly necessary as criminals become more mobile.

Efforts to open the borders of European Community member countries are being closely watched by various police forces, who express both concern and confidence that security can be maintained. In the former West Germany, for example, over sixty percent of all drug seizures took place at the country's borders. Relaxing border controls means that European police forces must engage in a careful collaboration to compensate for the reduced security accompanying the newly open borders (Rupprecht, 1990). A necessary step in achieving such cooperation in Europe, and among the other countries of the world, is an increased understanding of criminal justice systems in the various nations. In this manner, taking an international perspective toward criminal justice will have definite universal benefits.

APPROACHES TO AN INTERNATIONAL PERSPECTIVE

An author's goal typically instructs the approach used to convey information. A police officer writing her report of a recent arrest tells the story by referring to

Historical Approach	*Political Approach*	*Descriptive Approach*
• What mistakes and successes have already occurred?	• How does politics affect a nation's justice system?	• How is a country's justice system supposed to operate?
• What do earlier experiences tell us about the present?	• How does politics affect interaction among nations	• What are the main components of a justice system?
• How can knowledge of the past prepare us for the future?	• How is a country's legal tradition affected by politics?	• Who are the main actors in a justice system?

Figure 1-1   Approaches to an international perspective.

what she heard, saw, smelled, and touched. That approach is more likely to achieve a prosecution goal than would a report providing biographical information about the suspect without reference to the suspect's behavior at the time of the incident. However, after a conviction, a pre-sentence investigation written by a probation officer would be of little use if it fully described the event resulting in conviction but provided no biographical information about the offender.

The police officer's descriptive style and the probation officer's historical one are both necessary. The two approaches differ in their appropriateness rather than their importance. Similarly, the approach used to present information about criminal justice systems throughout the world will depend on the goal sought. There are at least three ways to study different criminal justice systems (see Figure 1-1). The historical, political, and descriptive approaches afford a structure that we can use to narrow and specify the goal of this text.

Historical Approach

The author of a report on the state of his country's prison system complains about the heavy cost to the treasury of maintaining prisons. Adding to the problem, prison discipline is minimal, and the convicts leave prison more corrupt than they entered. The high recidivism rate may be explained by the prison's failure to instill in its inmates any principles of morality or sense of responsibility. The author goes on to tell of another country's prison system that not only shows a financial profit, but does so under more humane conditions. Prisoners in the second country are placed under severe but uniform discipline, requiring rigorous work during the day and complete isolation at night. The benefits of this inflexibly uniform system include few recommittals to the prison.

We could argue that the author's first country is the United States and the second either has a good public relations official or is a place we should send observers to get ideas on how to improve the American prison system. Actually, the authors were Gustave de Beaumont and Alexis de Tocqueville. The country criticized was their own nineteenth-century France, and the envied system was the American penitentiary structure in 1831 and 1832 (Beaumont and

Tocqueville, 1964). An early nineteenth-century American prison system being coveted as superior to others seems ironic in light of late twentieth-century problems. Yet it is just that type of helpful comparison that the historical approach presents.

Beaumont and Tocqueville toured America when the Pennsylvania and Auburn systems were being touted as solutions to the new idea of imprisonment as punishment. The Frenchmen seemed to initially favor the Auburn system (quite likely for its economic benefits) but by the mid-1840s, Tocqueville spoke before the Chamber of Deputies in favor of the Pennsylvania system (see Sellin's introduction in Beaumont and Tocqueville, 1964). Despite such wavering, there is no doubt that the two travellers to the United States considered either American penitentiary system as superior to others known at the time. Their report to French citizens (Beaumont and Tocqueville, 1964) provides a classic example of the historical comparative approach. After describing its evolution and objectives, the American system is compared to Switzerland's and to France's. The authors explain why they consider the American system superior and suggest reasons and ways to implement it.

Beaumont and Tocqueville used an international approach for what we earlier called "provincial benefits." They wanted to improve their system and looked to other countries for suggestions. Their appreciation of the American penitentiary system's historical evolution made it easier for them to see how that system might apply to the French situation. Today, their report provides a sense of history for American and French prison systems. Researchers wishing to learn from earlier mistakes and successes in each country will benefit from an international perspective incorporating a historical approach.

An understanding and appreciation of history provide the criminal justice student with information about the present and the future. Like all other social institutions, criminal justice changes over time. Ignoring the past will prevent preparation for inevitable change in the procedures and institutions encountered in the future. As Terrill puts it: "The historical approach prepares students to understand and be a part of a world of change" (1982, p. 25). Despite the changes always taking place in any society, the problems faced remain remarkably stable (McCullagh, 1984). The need for security, justice, and freedom are neither the only, nor least, of those problems.

Political Approach

To understand a country's criminal justice system, we must understand its political one. Political and legal philosophies explain how and why a country treats and processes those citizens characterized as deviant (Terrill, 1982). For example, Chapter 6 discusses policing systems as either centralized or decentralized. The specific form taken reflects, in part, political aspects of the country.

As intense proponents of dispersed power, founders of the American republic avoided creating a single law enforcement agency with significant power at either the federal or state level. Police responsibilities were instead decentralized throughout the country and within each state. A reason for decentralization was fear that a large, well-organized police force could be used for misguided political purposes in the same way that the military has been used throughout history.

In 1989, events occurred to remind Americans that caution toward centralized forces is not simply a paranoid response. In December, President Bush sent military troops into the Republic of Panama. Stories of looting and general disorder following the American invasion became more understandable when we learned that there was no independent police force in Panama. Instead, Panama's policing was the responsibility of the same Panama Defense Forces that the American military was fighting. Needless to say, the PDF was unavailable for its civilian police role.

The PDF was constructed in 1983 by combining Panama's National Guard, Air Force, Navy, Canal Defense Force, Traffic Direction, Investigations Department, Immigration Department, and Police Force (Abad, 1989). In this antithesis of American decentralization, Panama consolidated the power of military, paramilitary, and civilian police units and placed the finished product under the authority of the republic's president. In addition, the law creating the PDF gave important functions to the commander-in-chief of the Defense Forces. Since that commander-in-chief, General Manuel Noriega, was the target of the American invasion, Panama had neither a military commander nor police commissioner after American troops arrived.

A first effort of the new Panamanian government was the creation of an independent security organization called the Panama Public Force (in Spanish, *Fuerza Publica de Panama*). The PPF got off to a rocky start with problems in distancing itself from the old PDF, but was striving toward autonomy from the military and paramilitary organizations.

Several political changes began an attempt to move Panama from the corrupt PDF to a corruption-free police force. In attempts to calm the Panamanian people's fears, the PPF was not to have a secret police like the old PDF's G-2 unit. Instead, investigations under the PPF, the citizens were assured, would be conducted by a new investigative police unit (*Policia Tecnica Judicial*) that reports to judicial authorities rather than to enforcement authorities (Sutton, 1990). This technique of linking the investigation of crimes to the judiciary rather than to enforcement personnel is common in several countries we review in later chapters.

A country's political system will influence, if not determine, its policing, court, and corrections system. The political approach recognizes the importance of politics to understanding criminal justice at a national and international level. Like the historical approach, the political approach is not the primary one we will follow, but it is important nonetheless.

Descriptive Approach

A description of how something should operate provides the necessary base for analysis, repair, and revision of that item. Just as it would be difficult to repair a motor without knowing how that motor is supposed to function, we must understand a justice system's stated organization and structure before we can determine how close it comes to that model. Description is the essential first step to comparative criminal justice. The historical and political approaches are also necessary, and will receive occasional attention in this book, but the descriptive approach provides an initial understanding that allows us to gain an overview of a country's justice system so that we can begin to identify similarities and differences among the nations. To that end, this book emphasizes a descriptive approach when presenting information about criminal justice in other countries.

Two tactics are possible when a descriptive approach is selected for a cross-cultural text book. One technique focuses on specific countries and describes the legal system's operation in each country. The result is a text in which the same topics (for example, law, police, courts, and corrections) are described in a separate chapter for each country (for example, England, Germany, Australia, and Japan). This strategy provides depth of coverage and gives the reader a strong background in the systems of several countries.

An alternative technique focuses on specific components of the criminal justice system and describes how different countries implement those segments. The result is a text wherein a wide variety of countries (the four above, plus others) are referred to in separate chapters on such topics as law, police, courts, and corrections. This tactic does not provide the reader with detailed information about any two or three specific countries. Instead, the detail centers on primary components of all systems of justice and uses various countries to highlight the variations.

Since goals of this text include developing a better understanding of the American system of justice and gaining ideas for improving that system, the second technique seems most appropriate. In that manner, we can concentrate on already familiar concepts (that is, law, police, courts, and corrections) but do so by looking at the diversity in executing those concepts. As noted, the trade-off for showing variance is loss of detail by country. However, several countries make appearances in at least two chapters, so readers will have a nearly complete portrait of some places, such as Germany and France.

STRATEGIES UNDER THE DESCRIPTIVE APPROACH

When differences among standard components of criminal justice systems are explored, the descriptive approach can follow two paths. Each tries to explain how criminal justice systems work in separate countries. However, one approach emphasizes the institutions and actors, while the other highlights specific functions and procedures. This text follows the institutions/actors path, but occasionally makes use of the functions/procedures strategy as well.

The Functions/Procedures Strategy

Lynch (1988) believes cross-national research would benefit from a functional rather than organizational or positional description of national criminal justice systems. He argues that there is more similarity of jobs across systems than there is among persons performing those duties. For example, the Gorky Park prosecutor briefly mentioned at the start of this chapter had duties that Americans divide among private citizens, police, and judges, as well as prosecutors. Later in the book we will see that English police have some authority to initiate prosecution of cases. Similar authority in America is reserved for the public prosecutor.

The argument Lynch makes is that all countries require that similar jobs be done—they just assign the duties differently. Ingraham (1987) provides an excellent example of this approach in his descriptive account of the underlying structure common to the procedural systems of France, the former Soviet Union, the People's Republic of China, and the United States. As he puts it: "Nations may differ from one another in the manner of collecting evidence, the way they sift it, refine it, and evaluate it prior to trial, and the way they present it at trial, but they all have procedures to do these things" (Ingraham, 1987, p. 17). The comparison model he develops describes procedures under the headings of intake, screening, charging and protecting, adjudication, sanctioning, and appeal. The result is a concise account comparing the four countries in each of the six categories.

As an example, we will consider the way each of Ingraham's four countries responds to the task of charging a defendant and protecting that defendant against abuse by the accusers. The first concern in this process is the need to protect the defendant against prolonged and unnecessary pre-trial detention. Since Ingraham is not interested in the particular office or person responsible for insuring this protection, he reviews the procedures each country has to accomplish this task.

Police in the United States may detain a suspect for a limited time if there are reasonable grounds to believe the person is, was, or may soon be engaged in criminal activity. Short-term detention at the police station for purposes of investigation is not, however, allowed. After a formal arrest and booking, the suspect should be taken to a magistrate, who advises the defendant of her rights regarding bail and legal counsel. At that point the defendant will be released on money or property bond (or simply on her promise to return at the appointed time for a court hearing), or placed in jail until trial.

The powers of French police to detain accused persons before trial differ somewhat from those in the United States. In cases of "flagrant" felonies and misdemeanors the police may detain a suspect without a warrant for 24 hours so that an investigation can be conducted (Ingraham, 1987). The prosecutor can extend the detention period for another 24 hours upon being shown additional and weighty evidence supporting guilt. The defendant cannot be detained beyond the 24 (or the total of 48) hours unless the prosecutor turns the investigation over to an investigation judge, who can then authorize temporary detention. In order to use temporary detention, the authorized punishment for the alleged offense must exceed two years, there must be reason to believe that the accused would respond negatively in the community (for example, flee, exert pressure on witnesses, or commit new offenses), or that *judicial supervision* is determined inadequate. Rather than relying on the bail system, France allows the defendant to obtain liberty before trial either with or without "judicial supervision." That procedure is a pre-trial release with conditions (for example, do not leave the area, or report at specific times to particular officials) imposed by the magistrate.

Procedures in the former USSR were similar to those in France with two important distinctions. First, the Soviet periods of authorized detention were longer. In certain cases (similar to the French "flagrant offenses"), Soviet police could confine a suspect for 24 hours before notifying the procurator (essentially the prosecutor). The initial restriction could be extended an additional 48 hours while the procurator decided whether to order release or continued "confinement under guard." The second major difference from the French system was the absence of judicial control or supervision of pre-trial confinement (Ingraham, 1987). Rather than requiring a magistrate's approval for confinement under guard (similar to the French temporary detention), the Soviets authorized the person conducting the inquiry (the investigator, the procurator, or the court) to restrain the suspect.

China's 1979 Procedure Law allows public security bureaus to detain a suspect for up to three days. "Special circumstances" allow the initial period to be extended from one to four days. After that extension the prosecutor has three days to approve the arrest or release the suspect. If approved, suspects may be held an additional two months. If the case is particularly complex, pre-trial detention may be extended additional months only as authorized by increasingly higher levels of administrators. Ingraham (1987) identified such alternatives to pre-trial detention as securing a guarantor for the suspect's court appearance, and confinement at the suspect's home under house arrest. It is not clear which cases allow alternatives to pre-trial release, and which actor or agency is authorized to grant the alternatives.

That brief review (paraphrased from Ingraham, 1987) of how four countries protect citizens against prolonged and unnecessary pre-trial detention provides a quick look at the functions/procedures perspective. This approach allows easy viewing of similarities among countries while drawing attention to the basic functions and procedures found in a variety of criminal justice systems. When differences become apparent, they suggest topics of conversation and debate.

For example, Ingraham suggests that by failing to allow limited periods for investigative detention prior to arrest, the United States may not provide suspects with the level of protection we may think we have. His position is that the absence of investigative detention provisions forces American police to initiate the arrest process very early. Once the suspect is arrested and confined, pre-trial release procedures come into play. Because American pre-trial release relies so heavily on bail, arrested persons are frequently too poor to raise the necessary security. As a result, the United States may provide many safeguards against arbitrary and prolonged pre-trial detention, but in practice it operates to deprive poor defendants of that very protection (Ingraham, 1987). We shall offer "food for thought" of this type throughout this text.

The Institutions/Actors Strategy

A functions/procedure strategy, like that championed by Lynch and by Ingraham, clarifies duties and highlights the similarity among countries. However, it may mask important differences among countries, since the stress is on resemblance. Also, while that approach makes it easy to organize and compare a few countries, it becomes more cumbersome when one is working with large numbers and when jumping around among separate nations.

The other approach is to compare countries on the basis of specific institutions and the people charged with accomplishing particular duties. Ingraham emphasizes protection against prolonged and unnecessary pre-trial detention by describing the functions and procedures used in four countries to accomplish that task. He is not concerned with the specific agency or officer responsible for those efforts. The alternative way to approach the topic is to emphasize such institutions as police, courts, and corrections while discussing the assigned duties of people, such as police officers, attorneys, judges, and wardens.

Each approach is reasonable and useful. However, for our purposes, the second technique—the institutions/actors description—is featured because it better enables the viewing of differences and can handle a larger number of countries. The chapters of this book rely on descriptions of institutions and actors, so it is an approach that will soon become very familiar to you. To illustrate the strategy, we can look briefly at how the same topic covered by Ingraham would be addressed by the institution/actor strategy. In this case we will deal with the institution of bail as it operates in one type of justice system.

Arresting a person for a criminal offense sets into motion two conflicting goals. On the one hand, the government agency making the arrest wants to be sure that the suspect will appear at the necessary time and place for a trial regarding the charges. Opposing that goal is the suspect's desire to move freely about, since he has not yet been found guilty of anything, and to assist in preparing a defense to the charges. The extreme ways of responding to this dilemma would involve forcibly detaining the suspect until trial (the seesaw tilts toward the government's goal) or allowing the suspect to roam free until the required court appearance (a tilt in favor of the suspect). For centuries, systems of justice have sought to balance the seesaw and ensure that both goals are met. The justice system with an English heritage (that is, the common law system) developed a procedure called *bail* to equalize the conflicting goals.

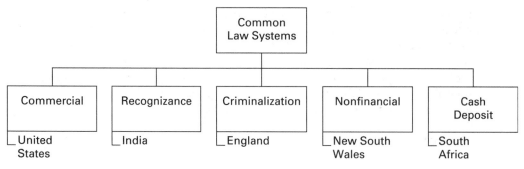

Figure 1-2   Types of bail.

As it developed in eighteenth-century England, bail in criminal cases was by *recognizance*. That is, a person pledges to meet some condition set by the court. In more technical terms, a person recognizes his obligation to a judge to perform a specific act or pay a specified sum for failure to perform the act. Performing the act voids the obligation to pay. In criminal matters, English courts used the idea of recognizance as a means to guarantee a suspect's appearance in court. This was accomplished by finding third parties, called *sureties*, who made financial pledges on the suspect's behalf (Devine, 1989). In that manner, the sureties bore responsibility for the suspect's appearance in court. If the suspect did not show up, the sureties forfeited the previously agreed-upon sum.

Devine (1989) argues that common-law bail systems share a heritage of placing primary responsibility for an accused's court appearance upon the sureties guaranteeing the person's attendance. Five basic types of bail are identified on the basis of the primary surety or security used to insure the accused's presence at trial (see Figure 1-2).

Commercial Bail. Commercial bail, as conducted in the United States, is the first type identified and the one many people already know about. Between the 1800s and the 1960s, American jurisdictions predominantly required criminal suspects to post commercial bail to secure their release (Samaha, 1988). Currently, other programs supplement the use of commercial bail, but it still exists in most criminal courts across the country. The term "commercial" is used because the criterion for pre-trial release is a financial obligation with the court. If the person shows up at the appropriate time, the obligation is voided and the money is returned to the defendant. If the person does not appear, the bond is forfeited and remains with the court.

This type of bail is controversial because of its possible discrimination against economically disadvantaged defendants and its spawning of the criminal justice system actor called a *bondsman*. As bail developed in America, the historical sureties came to be played by third parties willing to take a chance on a defendant in return for an opportunity to make some money. In this manner, a bondsman will advance his or her money to get a defendant released from jail to await trial. In return, the defendant will pay the bondsman a nonreturnable fee of about ten percent of the bail amount set by the court.

Recognizance. The historical *recognizance* system exists today in only a few countries. Bail based on recognizance was abandoned in England in the 1970s, so today the country providing the best example of this approach is India (Devine, 1989). Pre-trial release is allowed, and appearance for trial is secured, by the defendant's acknowledging an indebtedness to the court. If the defendant does not appear or fails to meet other conditions of bail, the stipulated amount "comes due." Since no cash or property is deposited with the court (by the defendant or a third party), the system is not open to criticism of economic discrimination like that directed at commercial bail. Since no cash is involved unless forfeiture occurs, the Indian system is similar to the historical concept of recognizance in English common law.

Criminalization. With the Bail Act of 1976, England replaced the recognizance system with a system of criminal punishment for fleeing. Now the criterion used to allow pre-trial release and secure court appearance is the imposing of a criminal penalty for absconding. Failure to appear at the appointed time means that the defendant is automatically guilty of absconding and may be punished with up to three months' imprisonment, a 2000-pound fine, or both (Devine, 1989). In this manner England also avoids the opportunity for commercial bail bonding, but differently than India does.

Nonfinancial. In a specific attempt to allow release on bail without the possibility of economic discrimination, the Australian state of New South Wales implemented a nonfinancial system. As a result of the Bail Act of 1978, New South Wales courts grant bail to defendants on either an unconditional or a conditional base. Unconditional release is just that—the defendants are told where and when to show up for court, and off they go. If the court believes the defendant may not appear for trial, might commit another crime, or could interfere with evidence, witnesses, or jury, conditions for pre-trial release may be imposed (Devine, 1989). Conditional release might include stipulations regarding the movement of the defendant, requirements to make periodic appearances at a specified police station, or to present one or more persons who testify as to the defendant's likelihood to appear for court.

Cash Deposit. It is possible to have a bail system that uses cash deposits but does not amount to commercial bail. The Republic of South Africa exemplifies such an approach when it deals with persons accused of ordinary, nonpolitical, common-law crimes. The South African approach typically requires a cash deposit to secure pre-trial release. A third party may provide the money but cannot profit financially from doing so. If it seems reasonable to assume that the third party will be indemnified against loss of the money or will gain financial benefit as a result of making the payment, the deposit must be rejected (Devine, 1989). This system discourages the development of professional bail bondsmen despite the reliance on cash deposits.

The description of five forms of bail not only exemplifies the institutions/actors (more institutions than actors) strategy in a descriptive approach but also introduces an important concept used throughout this book. In identifying the five basic types of bail, we made use of classification to compare those types. Each of the five jurisdictions used to show a type of bail also employs other procedures. Financial conditions are possible in New South Wales, England, and India. Both the United States and the Republic of South Africa make use of nonfinancial criteria for pre-trial release. For purposes of discussion, however, we have categorized the jurisdictions according to their primary method of allowing pre-trial release and securing appearance for trial.

This technique of classification serves the primary purpose of adding a sense of order to a seemingly jumbled array of institutions for providing bail. Because of the classification, we have a better grasp of the point and should more easily remember the different ways in which bail can be carried out in common-law systems.

It is possible that we have left out an important bail type that does not fit into any of the five categories. Or maybe additional research will show that we make distinctions where none should be made. That is, maybe there should be only two types instead of five. But that is another benefit of a classification system! It is open to debate, revision, modification, and even complete dismissal. For those reasons, and others noted below, the use of classification seems an appropriate way to approach the discussion of diverse criminal justice systems. Its importance to the remaining chapters requires an elaboration of the classification technique.

COMPARISON THROUGH CLASSIFICATION

In a popular parlor game, one person thinks of a person, place, or thing while others try to guess the object, using no more than 20 yes or no questions. When you consider the infinite number of possibilities, we are quite presumptuous to believe that we can guess, with no more than 20 questions, what object someone is thinking of. However, the fact that questioners are successful enough to perpetuate the game is a sobering thought.

A standard approach for players is to ask questions by setting up categories. For example, after determining that the object is a person, questioners may ask if it is male or female. Additional questioning may identify living or dead, famous or infamous, and eventually narrow down the person's occupation, basis for fame, etc. This process used to identify the object is dependent upon the players' knowledge and use of *classification*.

The Need for Classification

Classification refers to the grouping of individual objects into categories based on the objects' relationships. Through this process of naming and then grouping items into recognizable categories, we order and summarize the diversity that exists in the world. Its importance for operating in society (rather than simply winning a parlor game) becomes apparent upon realizing that survival of early humans must have been aided by an ability to recognize that individual objects shared certain properties. For example, some items were edible, while others made one sick. Some animals were helpful, while others were lethal. The ability to distinguish the category into which a particular item fell certainly made life more pleasant.

The process of classification and the resulting classification systems have been studied most completely by scientists interested in living organisms (see Dunn and Everitt, 1982; Mayr, 1982; Stace, 1989). Terms like *taxonomy* and *systematics* are familiar from biology classes. The concept of classification, however, is helpful and applicable whenever one has to deal with diversity. From the rather frivolous example of playing "20 Questions" we can move to the more practical need of finding a book in the library. Simply mentioning the prospect of searching for a particular book from a grouping of thousands, in no order what so ever, is enough to remind us to be grateful for the Library of Congress's classification system.

Basically, then, there is no argument on the need for classification. Instead, disagreement rests on how to classify, what criteria should be used in the process, and what the ultimate purpose of classification is. We will spend some time responding to these questions, since classification plays an important role in the structure of this text. Our guiding principle will be Ehrmann's quotation: "All comparison proceeds from categorization" (1976, p. 12). The diversity of the world's criminal justice systems requires an understanding of, and appreciation for, the classification process and the resulting schemes.

Classification Strategies

Rather than tackle the difficult issue of how the classification process should take place (interested readers are referred to texts on *macrotaxonomy, mathematical taxonomy, plant taxonomy,* and *biosystematics*), I take the position that each classification strategy has good and bad points. What is "best" in a particular instance depends on the goal sought or the purpose the classification should achieve. It seems more important for our purposes to be aware of what schemes are possible than to argue over which one is superior.

Two ways of classifying are possible (see Figure 1-3). The first is called a *synthetic strategy* resulting in categorization of *artificial groups*. Classification of this type typically has a *special purpose* and attempts to bring order to a confusing array of objects. The terms *synthetic* and *artificial* are used with this

Synthetic Strategies

- Results in artificial groups

- Is based on only one or two aspects of the object

- Resulting classification has a practical or special purpose that brings order to diversity

Authentic Strategies

- Results in natural groups

- Is based on extensive study of the object

- Resulting classification allows some predictivity regarding the group's members

Figure 1-3   Classification strategies.

approach because the ensuing classification is the result of scientists manufacturing a group that categorizes objects on the basis of some criteria of interest to the scientist.

Usually artificial groups are built around only one or two aspects of the object being classified. For example, a telephone book groups people alphabetically within the 26 groups of letters. A book for hikers may group flowers by color, thereby making identification easier and quicker. The classification of library books uses more criteria (for example, subject matter and author's last name) but still is essentially a "pigeonholing" exercise for the purpose of bringing order to diversity.

While synthetic classification strategies have practical applications, such as making it easy to find a phone number, identify a flower, or track down a book, their artificial nature does not allow us to imply or deduce other information about the object. For example, we would not assume that all people listed under "S" in the phone book are females of German heritage just because our friend Helen Schneider is an Austrian woman. Because nothing else about an object is suggested, beyond the one or two characteristics used in the classification process, synthetic strategies have low predictivity.

Authentic strategies to classification provide categorization of *natural groups*. Because this scheme uses a great number of characteristics to categorize objects into groups, it is much more predictive than are synthetic systems. The terms *authentic* and *natural* are appropriate here, because scientists group objects based on factual characteristics shared by members of a group. Unlike synthetic strategies, this approach relies on verified inherent attributes rather than traits assigned or manufactured to meet some purpose that a scientist has. Humans may comprise an artificial group when categorized simply by last name in a phone book. But they are a natural group when classification is based on our broad knowledge of human biology and the inherent characteristics of humans.

The ability to identify natural groups requires extensive investigation of the objects classified and identification of such characteristics as bone structure, nervous system, muscle movement, and the like. For example, when scientists determine that everyone in a group of 100 humans drives erratically after imbibing a certain amount of alcohol, it seems safe to hypothesize that all (or most) other humans (that is, all other members of the same category of living organisms) would be similarly affected. Additional study may require us to revise that initial assumption to allow for variation in size, weight, and so on. Even so, the predictivity when one is dealing with a natural group is greater than is possible with an artificial grouping. We cannot assume that a poison oak leaf is edible just because, like a lettuce leaf, it is green.

It may seem that its predictivity makes an authentic classification strategy superior to a synthetic one. However, each scheme has good and bad points. Predictivity is important and should be sought, but it is not the sole criterion for judging classification schemes. It may be just as important and interesting to know the evolutionary history and relationships among items as it is to make predictions about the attributes of a particular object in a group. Similarly, the currently observable structure of objects in a specific category requires description and understanding regardless of any need to make predictions. These concerns with *historical relationships* and *contemporary relationships* are examples of special-purpose classifications easily handled by synthetic strategies. Predictivity is not a goal of the categorization, so natural groups are not necessary. Therefore, the classification may be sufficiently conducted with knowledge of only one or two characteristics of the objects we are trying to categorize.

Recall, for example, the classification of common-law bail types presented earlier in the chapter. The categorization was determined only on the basis of what form of surety or security was used as the primary means of securing the accused's presence at trial. This categorization resulting from a single characteristic is not helpful in predicting anything about bail in common-law countries. It does, however, suggest interesting historical questions (for example, why did countries sharing a common heritage with England develop sometimes very different techniques?). Similarly, questions about contemporary relationships are generated. For example, since the United States and New South Wales share a common legal tradition, can America be more forceful in initiating nonfinancial bail systems? Questions of this type are addressed in an "Impact" section in this chapter.

The Role of Classification in This Book

The classification of living organisms traces its origin at least as far back as Aristotle (384–322 B.C.). It is not surprising, therefore, that some authentic systems of classification resulting in natural groups and having significant predictivity are found in biology and botany. The cross-cultural study of criminal justice systems does not share such a distinguished history. As a relatively new area of study, comparative criminal justice has not investigated its various "objects" to the extent necessary to provide authentic systems and natural groups. Today, classification in comparative criminal justice is essentially of the synthetic scheme. Synthetic strategies are important, however, because they successfully serve purposes other than predictivity.

Chapters 2 through 9 of this text are organized around particular classification schemes. Some of those approximate authentic systems with a general purpose, but most are the synthetic type having a special purpose (either historical or contemporary). In both cases, you are reminded that classification (of either type) is being used to summarize and make sense of diversity. In addition, any classification system should serve as an aid to memory. Presenting information about a topic via a classification scheme should enable you to visualize and conceptualize the material more easily.

A final note of caution is necessary. Some people tend to view a particular classification as equivalent to a scientific theory. As such, the classification could be proved wrong. Viewing a classification in that manner is inappropriate and incorrect (see Dunn and Everitt, 1982, p. 5). Since it is a creation of reason based on accumulation of experienced data, a classification can be neither right or wrong. It is merely an intelligible summary of information. Its value is determined by its usefulness to others. Importantly, saying that a classification is neither right or wrong is not the same as saying that it cannot or should not be changed. If it ceases to be useful, it should be modified or discarded. "As the needs and knowledge of scientists change so must the system of classification" (Dunn and Everitt, 1982, p. 9).

IMPACT

Each chapter of the text includes an "Impact" section where topics mentioned in that chapter will receive greater attention and where questions raised by chapter material can be addressed. These sections should encourage mental gymnastics suggesting things like links between countries, ideas for improving systems, and ways to encourage more global understanding. This first Impact section takes a closer look at bail.

Ingraham (1987) suggested that, absent an allowable period of investigative detention, American police must use arrest too early. Since many American jurisdictions use commercial bail as the primary means an accused person can secure release from pre-trial detention, early use of arrest means that some poor people may remain in jail. We also read how other countries with a similar legal heritage avoid the use of commercial bail to secure the accused's presence in court. In this section, we consider the problems presented by pre-trial detention in greater detail. We then see how procedures in other countries have been, or could be, introduced in American jurisdictions.

Law professor Alan Dershowitz (July 8, 1987) reminds us in one of his columns about a problem Alice had in Wonderland.

As long as there have been trials, there has been the dilemma of what to do with defendants before the verdict. Even Lewis Carroll's Alice in Wonderland recognized that problem in her discussion with the Queen. Says the Queen: "There's the King's Messenger. He's in prison now, being punished: and the trial doesn't even begin till next Wednesday: and of course the crime comes last of all."

"Suppose he never commits the crime?" asked Alice.

"That would be all the better, wouldn't it?" the Queen responded.

. . .

Alice felt there was no doubting that, "Of course it would be all the better," she said: "But it wouldn't be all the better his being punished."

"You're wrong . . ." said the Queen. "Were you ever punished?"

"Only for faults," said Alice.

"And you were all the better for it, I know!" the Queen said triumphantly.

"Yes, but I then had done the things I was punished for," said Alice. "That makes all the difference."

"But if you hadn't done them," the Queen said, "that would have been better still, better, and better, and better!" Her voice went higher with each "better," till it got quite to a squeak.

. . .

Alice thought, "There's a mistake somewhere." (Alan Dershowitz, reprinted by permission of UFS, Inc.).

In the United States, unlike Wonderland, you are innocent until proved guilty. The problem created by this philosophy was mentioned earlier. While awaiting trial, the defendant is concerned with such things as supporting herself and/or her family; locating witnesses and aiding the lawyer in preparing a defense; and in putting her affairs into order should she be convicted and sent to prison. Members of the community are not anxious to jail (that is, punish) a person not yet convicted of anything. At the same time, the public wants to make sure the defendant appears at trial and refrains from endangering others in the meantime. The concerns are often in conflict, and American jurisdictions seem to fluctuate between which of the two is emphasized.

In the 1960s, concern seemed more directed to the problems of the defendant. Believing that detaining poor people because they could not afford bail violated of the Eighth Amendment stipulation that "excessive bail shall not be required," some reformers sought alternatives to commercial bail. One of those alternatives, release on recognizance, is similar to the system described earlier for India. The American version of ROR was the result of activity by the Vera Institute of Justice, which initiated the Manhattan bail project in the early 1960s. Using a point-weighing system, Institute staff members interviewed prisoners brought in for booking. Based on the accused's responses to questions about his or her "community ties" (length of time in the community, location of relatives, employment, and so on) the staff member would determine whether or not the person was a good risk for release simply on a promise to appear in court as required. The procedure was successful and popular. As a result, it supplements, but does not replace, commercial bail in many American jurisdictions today.

If dissatisfaction with traditional bail procedures in the 1960s seemed to emphasize the concerns of the defendant, a more recent dissatisfaction sides with the worries of the public. A foretelling of the switch occurred as early as 1970, when Congress passed a bill authorizing the District of Columbia to hold defendants without bail if the judge believes they pose a threat to the public safety. The public's perspective was more broadly supported in the 1984 Bail Reform Act, wherein Congress expanded the possible use of preventive detention to federal courts.

By 1987 over thirty states had followed the federal lead and allowed bail decisions to be influenced by a concern for the threat the defendant posed to the community. Finally, in *U.S.* v. *Salerno* (1987) the Supreme Court upheld the Bail Reform Act's pre-trial detention procedure by ruling that it does not violate the Fifth or the Eighth Amendment. The reasoning behind the ruling included the justices' belief that the Act was designed as a regulatory act for purposes of ensuring public safety. It was not meant to be a form of punishment. The decision was not popular with everyone, but the increased use of pre-trial preventive detention will likely continue.

Can an international perspective help us identify other ways to respond to the conflicting interests of the accused and the community? The four alternatives to commercial bail covered in this chapter suggest that there may be other choices. Some alternatives to commercial bail are already being used in American jurisdictions. In addition to the release on recognizance (as in India's system), some American courts provide for a conditional release similar to that used in New South Wales. Most alternatives, however, are consistent with the preference for a financial obligation (see Hall, 1984) and are (like the South African system) simply variants of the traditional American approach.

United States policy makers and the American public seem hesitant to support widespread movement from a financially based pre-trial release system. Even if the pendulum moves from emphasis on pre-trial worries of the public back to pre-trial concerns of the accused, our legal history does not provide many nonfinancial examples from which to reap alternatives. This is why it is important to be familiar with, and willing to borrow from, the experiences of other countries. The dilemma presented by conflicting interests of the accused against those of the community will not go away. But other countries experience the same dilemma. If our goal lies more with protecting the community perhaps we should allow the police to detain suspects for purposes of investigation. The experience of countries like France and Russia in that area may prove quite helpful. If the goal rests with concern for the rights of the accused, nonfinancial systems like those of India and New South Wales may be worthy of closer attention. In either event, an international perspective will be useful.

THE STRUCTURE OF THIS BOOK

The approach this book takes is best reviewed by highlighting the key positions as presented above. First, I use a descriptive approach focusing on primary components of a large number of nations rather than providing a detailed description of a few countries. This topical rather than "country by country" approach loses detail of specific countries but compensates by allowing coverage of a greater number of countries and by more clearly identifying system differences. The particular path followed with this descriptive approach emphasizes institutions and actors rather than functions and procedures. However, historical and political approaches cannot be ignored, nor can descriptive accounts of functions and procedures. But those devices provide only secondary themes here.

To aid in presenting the descriptive information, I use classification schemes built around both synthetic and authentic strategies. The infancy of comparative criminal justice as a field of study requires greater use of synthetic strategies, since these can be built on only one or two criteria. The resulting artificial groups provide a sense of order to the diversity of institutions and procedures in the criminal justice systems we will encounter. Remember to approach the classification in each chapter as a summary of information rather than a scientific theory. In that manner, continuing political and cultural changes occurring throughout the world present opportunities to modify the classification scheme as our knowledge of different systems expands.

One more area of caution must be mentioned. In taking a descriptive approach to presenting information about a variety of countries, there is a distinct danger of providing incomplete information. Sociologists are well aware that social groups and organizations have an informal structure as well as the formal one presented to the public. A police department's organizational chart may clearly show a chain of command flowing from the police chief through bureau chiefs to division chiefs and down to section and unit commanders. What may not be shown is the department's informal policy that allows administrators to bypass a level or two when working on certain tasks or with "old friends." Earlier the procedures used to insure a suspect's right against prolonged and unreasonable detention were described for four countries. It would be naive of us to believe that those procedures, in any of the four countries, are followed to the letter by each actor every day.

The best way to identify and eventually describe the informal structure and relations of a group or organization is through participant observation over a prolonged period of time. Unfortunately, comparative criminal justice is a foundling among scientific fields of study. As a result, it has few participant observation-type research efforts. The absence of knowledge about informal workings should not, however, preclude the use of a descriptive approach. It should only serve to remind us that there is much to learn about criminal justice organizations in our own country as well as those in other parts of the world. At this point, then, the descriptive approach provides information about only the stated workings of criminal justice institutions and actors. But, when you think about it, we would not want to start anywhere else. After all, it is necessary to understand how something is supposed to work before we can even begin to discern how it varies from the model.

There is a final point to make concerning the structure of this book. Actually it is more accurately a point referring to the structure of the world. The last decade of the twentieth century started with dramatic and traumatic world events beginning in the late 1980s. The social, political, and economic changes brought down the Berlin Wall, saw the rise of democracy in former communist countries, encouraged the reunification of Germany and the break-up of the Soviet Union, and essentially insured the world will end the century a very different place than either experts or lay people imagined.

The changes brought opportunities to many people in a variety of occupations, but map-makers comprised one occupational group for whom the events were as frustrating as they were exciting. Throughout the late 1900s, media reported the futility felt by artists responsible for portraying geographic boundaries, encyclopedists attempting to prepare factual entries by publication deadlines, and college professors trying give accurate lectures on the politics of Eastern European countries. Persons interested in comparative criminal justice were placed in a similar predicament. What if a country's justice system is faithfully and accurately described in February only to find that country operating under a different political system in March? If we wait until April to describe the system, who can say that other changes will not occur in May?

During times of rapid geographical change, cartographers continue to make and distribute maps. During times of rapid economic change, economists continue to debate and predict financial issues. Similarly, despite changes affecting government structures and organization, criminal justice scholars continue to describe and analyze justice systems. Actually, the field of comparative criminal justice has an advantage over some other fields, since even rapid political and economic change cannot easily force similarly paced structural and bureaucratic change. For example, changing the former Russian Soviet Socialist Republic's name to Russia and devaluing the ruble happened more quickly than did a structural change in the way policing was provided. It is one thing to replace a country's governing body with the first democratically elected representatives in over forty years and quite another to release all her prisoners and start over with a whole new penal system. In other words, change does not necessarily occur at the same pace in all parts of a country.

In 1991, newspaper columnist Cathy Collison enlisted University of

Michigan professor Ted Hopf to answer a question posed by a 10-year-old Michigan girl. The girl wondered how long it would take the Russian government to form a democracy. She was told the change will take some time. Two of the reasons offered for the slow transition to democracy also explain why drastic changes in the Russian criminal justice system cannot suddenly occur: (1) tradition is hard to overcome, and (2) change is scary (Collison, October 5, 1991).

The comfort of tradition and the threat of change are not conditions unique to the Russian people. As a result, there is a stability in the social institutions of nations that provides a continuity in areas like the police, courts, and corrections. This is not to say that those organizations avoid change. Even when the Union of Soviet Socialist Republics existed, there were changes occurring in such areas as the role of Soviet defense counsel and the way prisons were used. The point is not that criminal justice agencies escape modification. Instead, what appears to be rapid social change affecting all aspects of a country and its people may be the start of a marathon race rather than a sprint. As you read this book's description of criminal justice in various countries, you will undoubtedly find information that is no longer accurate for that country; you may even read about a country that no longer exists in the form described. Such problems are inevitable in today's dynamic world. But, since people and their social institutions tend to find comfort in tradition and anxiety in change, the discrepancies are likely to be ones of detail rather than of the whole.

SUMMARY

This chapter introduces a book describing the different ways criminal justice can operate. That variability is shown by reference to justice systems operating in countries around the world. The study of criminal justice systems in other countries has specific benefits for our own justice system as well as for international relations. The provincial benefits include having points of contrast that allow better understanding and greater appreciation for the American system. In addition, an international perspective can suggest ideas to improve our system. On a broader scale, knowledge of how other countries conceive and implement the idea of "justice" is increasingly necessary. The presence and persistence of cross-national crimes like terrorism, hijacking, drug smuggling, and organized crime networks demand a cooperative international effort. Such an effort is aided when citizens of different countries are familiar with, and try to understand and respect, the institutions and procedures of other countries.

The process of studying assorted criminal justice systems is achieved through at least three approaches. The historical, the political, and the descriptive approaches each use specific methods to understand and explain the diversity found throughout the world. Because we emphasize the descriptive approach, the particular techniques used by that strategy are stressed. Most generally, the goal of this book will be achieved with emphasis on a descriptive approach highlighting the formal workings of organizations and people driving a country's criminal justice system.

The descriptive approach allows for comparison of a number of countries. A problem with that is the overwhelming diversity confronting us as we attempt to find similarities and identify differences among various systems. To aid in the process, each chapter uses a classification scheme that provides order and aids the memory process. The process of classification is achieved through two strategies: synthetic and authentic. Each strategy results in a grouping of objects (artificial or natural groups) having special (the artificial groups) or predictive (the natural groups) purposes.

SUGGESTED READINGS

Ehrmann, Henry W. (1976). *Comparative legal cultures.* Englewood Cliffs, NJ: Prentice Hall.

Ingraham, Barton L. (1987). *The structure of criminal procedure.* New York: Greenwood, an imprint of Greenwood Publishing Group, Westport, CT.

Terrill, Richard, J. (1982). Approaches for teaching comparative criminal justice to undergraduates. *Criminal Justice Review, 7*(1), 23–27.

REFERENCES

Abad, Jaime. (1989). The criminal justice system of Panama, *C. J. International, 5*(3), 11–18.

Beaumont, Gustave de, and Tocqueville, Alexis de. (1964). *On the penitentiary system in the United States and its application in France.* Carbondale, IL: Southern Illinois University Press.

Chunnel Patrol. (1992). *C. J. Europe, 2*(2), 3.

Cole, George F., Frankowski, Stanislaw J., and Gertz, Marc G. (1987). Comparative criminal justice: An introduction. In G. F. Cole, S. J. Frankowski, and M. G. Gertz (Eds.). *Major criminal justice systems: A comparative study* (2nd ed., pp. 15–26). Newbury Park, CA: Sage.

Collison, Cathy. (1991, October 5). Expect democracy in Russia by the end of the decade. *The Denver Post,* p. 2E.

Dershowitz, Alan. (1987, July 8). Punishment before the trial. *The Denver Post,* p. 3C.

Devine, F. E. (1989). Forms of bail in common law systems. *International Journal of Comparative and Applied Criminal Justice, 13*(2), 83–95.

Dunn, G., and Everitt, B.S. (1982). *An introduction to mathematical taxonomy.* Cambridge, England: Cambridge University Press.

Ehrmann, Henry W. (1976). *Comparative legal cultures.* Englewood Cliffs, NJ: Prentice Hall.

Fooner, Michael. (1989). *Interpol: Issues in world crime and international criminal justice.* New York: Plenum.

Geysels, Frans. (1990). Europe from the inside. *Policing, 6*(1), 338–354.

Hall, Andy. (1984). *Pretrial release program options.* Washington, DC: National Institute of Justice.

Ingraham, Barton L. (1987). *The structure of criminal procedure.* New York: Greenwood, an imprint of Greenwood Publishing Group, Westport, CT.

Lenhard, Heinz. (1990). Criminal investigation perspectives on opening the borders. *International summaries—Opening the borders in the European community: Perspectives on internal security.* Washington, DC: National Institute of Justice.

Lynch, James P. (1988). A comparison of prison use in England, Canada, West Germany, and the United States: A limited test of the punitive hypothesis. *Journal of Criminal Law and Criminology, 79,* 180–217.

Mayr, Ernst. (1982). *The growth of biological thought.* Cambridge, MA: Belknap Press.

McCullagh, C. Behan. (1984). *Justifying historical descriptions.* Cambridge, England: Cambridge University Press.

Mexico cops allowed to work in U.S. (1990, July 1). *The San Diego Union.* p. A–2.

Rupprecht, Dirigent R. (1990). The emergence of a European security consciousness. *International summaries—Opening the borders in the European community: Perspectives on internal security.* Washington, DC: National Institute of Justice.

Samaha, Joel. (1988). *Criminal justice.* St. Paul, MN: West.

Stace, Clive A. (1989). *Plant taxonomy and biosystematics* (2nd ed.). London: Edward Arnold.

Sutton, James. (1990). Democratic revival from a despot's totalitarianism. *C. J. the Americas, 3*(2), 1.

Terrill, Richard, J. (1982). Approaches for teaching comparative criminal justice to undergraduates. *Criminal Justice Review, 7*(1), 23–27.

Chapter 2

Crime on the World Scene

There is an understandable tendency for a country's citizens to take a narrow view of the crime problem. Of initial concern is how safe one feels to walk in the neighborhood without fear of bringing harm to yourself or to the now vacant home you just left. The idea that residents of some neighborhoods in every other country may have similar fears is only minimally interesting and certainly not comforting. Even if criminal activities in another country have a direct effect on crime in your neighborhood, your interest may be only slightly increased. After all, the government cannot do anything about "home grown" crime; why should it be able to do anything about crime originating in some other country?

The United Nations has a less cynical outlook on crime as a national and international problem. From its universal, rather than parochial, perspective, the United Nations understands the damaging role crime plays but also sees possibilities for a positive response to the problem. Appreciation of the problem and pursuit of solutions takes the United Nations into the areas of measuring crime, identifying common crime problems, and working toward common solutions. This chapter uses those three themes to lay the groundwork for the rest of the book.

The chapters of this text take a specific look at the variety of ways nations use to respond to crime. In the future envisioned by the popular television shows "Star Trek" and "Star Trek: The Next Generation," there may well be a unified justice system reflecting the values and supporting the laws of the universe. However, the foreseeable future for the planet Earth will likely consist of as many justice systems as we have nations. That is neither inherently bad nor clearly unworkable. But, as noted in Chapter 1, the changes occurring throughout the world require the various nations and their citizens to be at least familiar with the justice systems in other countries. That familiarity can nourish harmony and understanding as sovereign nations face a future where crime and criminals ignore national boundaries. So, before looking at the variety of ways criminal justice systems operate, I will use this chapter to present the larger picture. Once we appreciate the magnitude of the crime problem, we can see how the United States' response compares with the response in other parts of the world.

THE CRIME PROBLEM

This chapter's primary goal is to introduce you to the crime problem in its world context. Since we more typically read, hear, and watch reports on crime in America, it is important to appreciate the problems of other countries. In this way, the remaining chapters, which focus on how countries respond to crime, may seem more appropriate. We begin with discussion of how crime statistics are compiled.

During a barroom fight, John breaks chairs, tables, and glassware, hits George in the face and breaks George's nose, and then tries to get away by stealing a car parked in front of the bar. What crime or crimes did John commit? Although it may be tempting to argue for counting one assault, one destruction of property, and one auto theft, the Federal Bureau of Investigation's Uniform Crime Reporting network tells the police to choose only one crime. That choice is to be the most serious offense occurring during the incident (assault in this case). Of course, the police and prosecutor are not affected by this UCR directive, and John could well be charged with all three offenses. But for crime recording purposes only the assault will make it into the statistics.

Try another example. Yamaguchi Yukio became angry with his wife Noriko and beat her during a domestic quarrel. Noriko died as a result of the beating. What crime, assault or homicide, is tabulated? Given your recently acquired knowledge of UCR recording practices, an answer that ignores the assault and records the homicide is understandable. And if this quarrel had taken place in the United States it would be the correct answer. However, the Yamaguchis live in Kyoto, Japan. In Japan, assault resulting in death is classified as assault rather than homicide (Kalish, 1988).

How about one more? Ladislav Urbanek forces his date for the evening, Irena Svoboda, to have sexual intercourse. Ms. Svoboda dies as a result of the rape. Both rape and homicide are, of course, serious crimes. The UCR requires that homicide be the recorded offense. However, this crime took place in the former Czechoslovakia, and they were not interested in what the UCR requires. For Czechoslovak statistics, the crime was classified as rape, not as homicide (Kalish, 1988).

These examples of differences in recording acts as one type of crime or another should make us wary of comparing crime statistics among countries. However, despite the difficulties there is reason for optimism. As discussed later, with due recognition of the problems when comparing crime data cross-culturally, and with care in terms of the type of comparison conducted, it is possible to comment about crime on the world scene.

There are two main types of statistical information on crime in the United States. The first of these, *offender/offense statistics*, are typically kept by government agencies and range from very specific data, such as "Violent Crime in the United States" (Bureau of Justice Statistics), to data with broader interests, like the "Uniform Crime Reports" (Federal Bureau of Investigation). Those examples happen to be at the federal level, but each state and many city governments have similar data sources and resultant publications. The second type, *victim statistics*, is best exemplified by the "National Crime Survey" (Bureau of Justice Statistics).

The Uniform Crime Reports (UCR) and National Crime Survey (NCS) are the most complete and frequently cited data sources on crime and victimization in the United States. As good as they are, however, they have problems. We will take a few moments to review the goals and difficulties with the UCR and NCS, since the pros and cons here are transferable to data sources in other countries.

The Uniform Crime Reports

The UCR is an incomplete nationwide system of voluntary reporting of offenses that come to the attention of police agencies and departments. Statistics are kept on 29 categories of crime broken into Part I and Part II offenses. The Part I offenses, called *index crimes*, are comprised of the four violent (homicide, rape, robbery, and assault) and the four property (burglary, larceny, motor vehicle theft, and arson) crimes believed most important for keeping detailed information. Information on these crimes, and, when an arrest is made, on the persons believed to have committed them, is provided by police departments throughout the country.

Although providing the data is voluntary, most police agencies willingly participate by sending monthly and/or annual reports to the FBI. As a result, the UCR provides the United States with systematic, nationwide information on crime across the country. Not surprisingly, however, the UCR has some problems. It is important to remember that our discussion of these problems should serve to indicate the difficulty of compiling data on crime in a country. Although the UCR can be criticized, few other countries match the United States' effort at compiling and reporting the crime occurring in the nation. The following criticisms must be interpreted as highlighting universal problems, since every country must deal with reporting and recording obstacles when determining their amounts of crime.

Reporting Problems. Reporting problems with the UCR are very well documented. For the police to know about a crime, and thereby to include it in the police department's tally, the police themselves must see the offense occur or a victim/witness must report the crime to the police. Since only about one-third of all crimes are reported to the police (Report to the Nation, 1983) the UCR is known to underestimate the amount of crime occurring each year. The extent to which crime is underestimated varies (Report to the Nation, 1983) by type of crime (violent is reported more than is personal theft), sex (female victims are more likely to report than are male victims), and age (older victims report more than do younger victims). The dependence of the police on other citizens to report crime makes an accurate count difficult to obtain. But even when the police have been told about a crime, the potential for data problems does not end.

Recording Problems. In countries with a decentralized system of laws and policing, identifying which category of offense has occurred is often very difficult. With its 51 systems of law, the United States presents a real barrier to compiling national data on crime. For example, one state may define forced illegal entry into another's home with the intent to steal something as "burglary." Another state may call the illegal entrance "breaking and entering" and reserve the term "burglary" for the taking of another's property after illegal entrance. The UCR provides police agencies with an instruction manual that helps determine where to categorize each offense according to UCR terminology. The need for such a manual exemplifies the definitional problems in describing crime in numerous jurisdictions with similar yet individual laws.

Political control of crime recording is a reality that must be recognized when one is trying to interpret crime statistics. This may seem particularly true when dealing with statistics from other countries. The old Union of Soviet Socialist Republics provided an extreme example of politics affecting the tracking of crime. The Communist Party of the Soviet Union set itself the task of uprooting all violations of law and order, eliminating crime, and removing all causes of deviance (Shargorodskii, 1964). Complete and accurate criminal statistics would have been a good way to judge the Party's success in that endeavor, but such statistics were unavailable to Soviet criminologists. When statistics were provided, they tended to be so general that no implications or relevant variables could be identified, or so specific that generalities could not be made.

For example, Djekebaev (1975, p. 63) noted that "crimes against the person and the personal property of citizens occur *generally* and displays of hooliganism are *frequent*" (italics added). That information is followed by the similarly general statement that "The theft of socialist property is statistically one of the *leading* crimes" (Djekebaev, 1975, pp. 63–64; italics added). Imagine the difficulty of understanding trends in crime rates or preparing policy with information based on modifiers like "generally," "frequent," and "leading," without having specific numbers to attach.

When Soviet statistics were not couched in gross generalizations, they were presented with such specificity as to remain uninformative. Dubovets (1970), for example, notes that the most widespread crimes of the Byelorussion Soviet Socialist Republic were hooliganism (26.6 percent of all convicted persons), brewing illicit liquor (15.4 percent), theft of private property (11.1 percent), and minor bodily injury and assault (9 percent). From this, Dubovets concluded that crime was basically of a minor character in the BSSR. Simple addition tells us that some 38 percent of the convicted individuals remain to be identified. Since those remaining crimes were not among those Dubovets called "insignificant," we could assume that the 38 percent comprised "serious" crime. But we really do not know what to deduce from these statistics. Since breakdown was provided only for those four crimes, and because no raw numbers were given, we do not know what crimes made up the other 38 percent. Such specific data were about as useless as the general data of Djekebaev.

A role for politics in recording crime is not, however, restricted to totalitarian governments. Imagine how tempted the incumbent sheriff might be during an election year to show that crime had dropped during her years in office. Similarly, the police chief may want to use statistics to convince the city council that his administration has reduced the number of drug offenses after receiving a budget supplement to fight the war on drugs. *Newsweek* (May 16, 1983) reported on an FBI investigation that found Chicago police, believing that superiors wanted a low crime rate, were discarding 14 times more crime reports than were police in other large city departments. The story caused increased scrutiny of police reporting practices in Chicago and, as a result of more accurate recording, crime in Chicago increased 25 percent. In the mid-1970s, the mayor of Cleveland told police that their expected 5 percent salary increase would come about only with a similar percentage reduction in the crime rate. Not surprisingly, the crime rate dropped by an amount even larger than 5 percent (Hagan, 1989).

The National Crime Survey

The first problem associated with the UCR was the underreporting of crime. People had long suspected that the UCR's estimates of crime were below what actually occurred (since it was obvious that not all crime was reported). But not until 1973 was it possible to say specifically that less than half of all crimes are reported to the police. The turning point came with the first annual survey of American households, which questioned people about their own victimization during the preceding year. Since 1973 the U.S. Bureau of Census and the Bureau of Justice Statistics have cooperated in conducting a random national survey of crimes occurring to individuals and businesses. Since the resulting data are based on the report of a person actually involved in the crime, the reliance on police department records is eliminated. Not only are crimes the police knew about recorded, but also those never reported to the police. As a result, we know how crime reporting varies by crime type and the sex and age of the victim, and the reasons given by victims for not reporting crime in the first place (e.g., "Police couldn't do anything," "It wasn't important enough").

Like the UCR, the NCS also has problems. Extended discussion like that given UCR problems is not necessary, since the goal here is simply to provide you with reason for skepticism and caution when approaching crime statistics of your own or any other country. Instead, we simply note some problems that you may have already considered (see Levine, 1976). The accuracy of the NCS depends on the sometimes faulty memory of humans. That is, the victim may not remember if a crime occurred within the last six months (the time period asked about) or nine months ago. Problems of overreporting may occur if people misinterpret events as being criminal (for example, my bike was stolen) when it was not (the bike was forgotten about in the tool shed). Similarly, underreporting is possible because some crimes involve family members or friends, and victims may choose not to divulge the incident.

The NCS provides important information about the actual amount of crime occurring in the country, and about the characteristics of crime victims. As a result, it serves as a nice supplement to the UCR. Each has its own purpose (see Figure 2-1), and together they provide the United States with a rather complete and accurate reporting of the country's crime.

IMPACT

This chapter began with the observation that many people feel that crime, and official response to it, are of only parochial concern. Actually, we have seen

	Uniform Crime Reports	**National Crime Survey**
Offenses measured	Homicide Rape Robbery (personal and commercial) Assault (aggravated) Burglary (commercial and household) Larceny (commercial and household) Motor vehicle theft Arson	Rape Robbery (personal) Assault (aggravated and simple) Household burglary Larceny (personal and household) Motor vehicle theft
Scope	Crimes reported to the police in most jurisdictions; considerable flexibility in developing small-area data	Crimes both reported and not reported to police; all data are available for a few large geographic areas
Collection method	Police department reports to FBI or to centralized state agencies that then report to FBI	Survey interviews; periodically measures the total number of crimes committed by asking a national sample of 49,000 households encompassing 101,000 persons age 12 and over about their experiences as victims of crime during a specified period
Kinds of information	In addition to offense counts, provides information on crime clearances, persons arrested, persons charged, law enforcement officers killed and assaulted, and characteristics of homicide victims	Provides details about victims (such as age, race, sex, education, income, and whether the victim and offender were related to each other) and about crimes (such as time and place of occurrence, whether or not reported to police, use of weapons, occurrence of injury, and economic consequences)
Sponsor	Department of Justice Federal Bureau of Investigation	Department of Justice Bureau of Justice Statistics

Figure 2-1. How do UCR and NCS compare?. *Source:* M. W. Zawitz, (ed.) (1988) *Report to the Nation on Crime and Justice*, 2nd ed. Washington, D.C.: Bureau of Justice Statistics.

that crime is increasingly widespread, ignores national boundaries, and is taking new forms that require international cooperation among justice agencies. In other words, transnational crime and the reaction to it have significant consequences for citizens of every country. To appreciate the current and potential reactions to the problem, this chapter's impact section looks at international response to transnational crime.

Conceivably, the future may include an international corrections system with prisons, community correctional facilities, and cooperative ventures in prison labor. Already there are agreements between some countries to provide probation-like supervision for persons sentenced by other nations. The areas of policing and adjudication, however, seem more likely arenas for an international response to crime. Existing efforts in these areas exemplify the type of inter-nation cooperation that transnational crime and criminals are fostering.

International Policing Efforts

The idea of international cooperation in police activities was first introduced in 1914 (with the French as primary advocates), but the onset of World War I postponed action. Attempts were again made in 1923 (Austrian instigation this time), and headquarters for the International Criminal Police Commission (ICPC) were established in Vienna until the Second World War caused suspension of activities. Finally, in 1946 the French offered a building in Saint-Cloud (near Paris) for the reestablishment of a headquarters. The ICPC continued to grow and in 1955 was renamed the International Criminal Police Organization (Interpol). By 1990 Interpol, which had outgrown its Saint-Cloud building, moved to new facilities in Lyons, France.

One of the most curious aspects of Interpol's status is the organization's very legitimacy. It is not based on an international treaty, convention, or any similar document. The multinational group of police officers who drew up its constitution never submitted it to their respective governments for approval, authorization, or ratification (Fooner, 1989). Despite questionable legality, Interpol is treated as a legitimate organization by most governments of the world. Nations must apply for membership, appoint delegates, pay dues, and abide by the organization's rules. With recognition now from such prestigious organizations as the United Nations, the Council of Europe, the Organization of African Unity, and the Pan-Arab Social Defense Organization, Interpol remains a legal curiosity but stands on firm ground.

Interpol's structure consists of four parts: the General Assembly, the Executive Committee, the General Secretariat, and the National Central Bureaus. Representatives from the member nations meet yearly as the General Assembly and thereby provide the organization's supreme authority. The delegates elect officers, vote on admitting new members, approve the budget, and set policy. Decisions made by the General Assembly are implemented by the Executive Committee, which is comprised of 13 members from the General Assembly itself. Most of the action, however, occurs in the General Secretariat and National Central Bureaus (NCB).

The office of the General Secretariat has ultimate responsibility for Interpol's various activities. This section is administered by the secretary general, who serves a five-year term after selection by the General Assembly. The secretary general is responsible for the technical and administrative staff assigned to Interpol, administers the budget, and supervises the permanent departments at the headquarters.

On an organizational level equal to the General Secretariat is the National Central Bureau (NCB) network. But despite its equal status on the organizational chart, the NCBs have primacy in terms of making the multinational police cooperation system work (Fooner, 1989). Each member nation of Interpol (around 150 of them) must provide space, supplies, and personnel to serve as a liaison for Interpol communication and to handle requests from other member countries. Since each country controls its own NCB, they differ widely in size, personnel, and level of activity.

Each NCB has three responsibilities: (1) to maintain open channels to all police units in its own country; (2) to maintain connections with the NCBs of all other member countries; and (3) to maintain liaison with the General Secretariat (Fooner, 1989). In this manner, the NCBs provide a contact point in each member nation to allow the coordination of international criminal investigation. Interpol is not a force of international detectives with worldwide jurisdiction, but instead "an international clearinghouse and data bank for member nations" (Stead, 1983, p. 157). Operating through the NCB network, any police officer or agency in a member country has access to global policing services when faced with a problem involving foreign jurisdiction.

Determination of the appropriate police agency to serve as a country's NCB is not difficult in countries with centralized systems. With greater decentralization there is some difficulty in identifying the best agency to serve as the NCB. In the extremely decentralized United States, it would be practically and politically unsuitable to name a state or local police department as the country's representative to Interpol. Instead, the United States turned to its federal level agencies to find America's NCB. As a result, the United States' NCB is in Washington, D.C., where it exists as a separate agency within the Department of Justice (Simpson, 1984).

The involvement of the United States in Interpol increased dramatically during the 1970s and 1980s (Fooner, 1989; Simpson, 1984). In 1981 the NCB established an Economic and Financial Crime Unit to respond to the growing problem of domestic and international financial crimes. An Anti-Terrorist Unit was created in 1983 to evaluate information regarding terrorist activities and determine if such information would help other member countries. Similarly, a Fugitive Unit attempts to augment existing fugitive tracking programs through coordination of information exchange (Simpson, 1984).

Today's increased use of computerization and automated electronic communications systems makes the US-NCB one of Interpol's strongest units (Fooner, 1989). American efforts provide a Computer-Assisted Foreign Language Translation System, which can receive radio messages and scanned documents in French or Spanish and then disseminate them in English. Also, a computerized Case-Tracking System assembles all investigative and case material as a data base providing quick access to crime and criminal information.

The United States' commitment to Interpol continues today as each state sets up a point of contact in their police system to handle all requests involving international matters. The need for such a system is the result of increasing internationalization of crime and the sheer volume of foreign nationals now living in, or visiting the United States. To respond to these situations, Sweatman (1989) believes it is becoming increasingly apparent that even local police need an international channel of communication available at their level. As a result, even the decentralized police system in America is participating at a local level in a multinational effort in policing.

COMPARING CRIME RATES

Since every country has similar difficulties in recording and reporting its own crime figures, crime rate comparison among countries is problematic. Industrialized countries like Japan, Australia, Canada, Germany, and Great Britain have their respective versions of the general data like the Uniform Crime Reports and more specific figures like the Justice Department's *Correctional Populations in the United States*. As a result, there is an understandable tendency to compare, contrast, and even rank the various countries in terms of general and specific crime rates (see Figure 2-2).

If the data in Figure 2-2 were used by authors of the increasingly popular "Best Places to Live" type of books, the industrialized countries would not fare very well. But this is exactly why such cross-cultural comparisons are frowned upon by many researchers—and even more so by government officials. The United Nations expressed that concern in this manner: "Member States are increasingly recognizing the importance of comparative work for cross-national purposes, but require reassurance that the data reported will not be used for any international numerical `ranking'" (1990a, p. 7).

Consider again the countries noted in Figure 2-2. These data from the International Criminal Police Organization, Interpol, reflect each country's response to a request for the total number of penal offenses detected by or reported to the police. The result includes such differences as the type of activities recorded (for example, are traffic offenses included?) and variation in the inclusion or exclusion of offenses by juveniles. Even if all countries agreed that offenses by juveniles should be included, there is no agreement on the ages comprising the category "juvenile." Add difficulties like these to the recording problems mentioned earlier and we can appreciate how dangerous cross-cultural rankings can be.

There are very good reasons why numerical rankings based on crime data should be undertaken only with caution. Some primary reasons are differences in

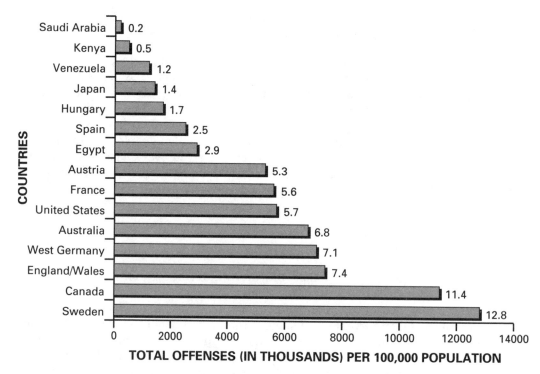

Figure 2-2. 1988 crime rates (in thousands) in selected countries. *Source:* Interpol. (1987/1988). *International Crime Statistics.* Lyons, France: ICPO—Interpol General Secretariat.

the legal definitions of crime and in the ways countries report and record crime. Also, the efficiency of criminal justice agencies is likely to make a difference. High rates of recorded crime in some countries may reflect the "real" crime occurring, or it may reflect efficient and thorough systems for reporting and recording crime. Similarly, countries reporting low crime rates may actually have little crime, or the low rates may simply reflect system inefficiency. In this manner, crime statistics probably tell us as much about a country's justice organization as about its crime rate (United Nations, 1990a).

The danger in emphasizing problems when crime data are compared is to imply that nothing can be gained from gathering and analyzing such information. That interpretation is wrong; researchers have found several types of questions that cross-national crime data can appropriately address. For example, Bennett and Lynch (1990) and the United Nations (1990a) agree that whereas crime surveys cannot reliably be used to rank countries, they are appropriate for assessing the direction of change in crime over time and across nations. Other researchers have used comparative crime data to look at violence cross-nationally (Archer and Gartner, 1984; Messner, 1980); to explain the evolution of criminality over the last 200 years (Shelley, 1981); and to identify common features among countries with low crime rates (Adler, 1983). Like all provocative research, these studies have been criticized (see Beirne and Messerschmidt, 1991; Groves and Newman, 1989), but they are also recognized as important contributions to the growing area of comparative criminology.

Crime Data Sets

A difficulty for anyone interested in comparing crime data is to identify a single source containing crime information for nations around the world. Currently, four sources provide the best available statistics on crime throughout the world: Interpol, United Nations, Comparative Crime Data File, and Correlates of Crime. The first two sources provide data sets compiled by specific organizations, while the other two data sets are from the work of independent researchers. The World Health Organization could also be included with these four, but their statistics are only for homicide, whereas the others include a greater variety of crimes.

Since 1950, the International Criminal Police Organization, Interpol, has biennially provided annual data on crime and criminal justice in a number of nations throughout the world. The actual sample size varies with each publication, but in a recent survey 86 countries provided Interpol with crime-related statistics (Interpol, 1987–1988). The United Nations also relies on member nations to voluntarily provide crime data. Three surveys have been completed and the United Nations now has compiled three data sets covering five-year periods: 1970–1975, 1975–1980, and 1980–1985 (this last survey includes some 1986 data).

The two private efforts to collect cross-national crime data provide researchers with the Comparative Crime Data File (Archer and Gartner, 1984) and the Correlates of Crime data set (Bennett, 1990). The Comparative Crime Data File is based on information from the authors' international correspondents, who provided data on 110 nations and 44 international cities. Data in the Correlates of Crime file cover 52 nations from 1960 through 1984.

Each of the four data sets provides interesting and useful information, but each has its own strengths and weaknesses. The Interpol data are the most frequently used, and the most often criticized, but in a study by Bennett and Lynch (1990) the Comparative Crime Data File, Interpol, and United Nations data sets were found to be statistically similar for cross-sectional and longitudinal descriptive studies. This important finding suggests that the use of any one of the three data sets should provide valid information on items like assessing the direction of change in crime over time and across nations. To provide such information, I use reports from the Interpol and the United Nations surveys.

Interpol Data.   Figure 2-3 shows the crime rates for five offenses and total crimes in 25 countries. These statistics, which are based on data collected by the police in Interpol member countries, are reported on a standard form that is given to each member country. The offense types are divided into seven general categories (murder, sex offenses, serious assault, theft, fraud, counterfeit curren-

Country	Murder	Sexual Offenses*	Assault	Theft	Drug	Total Offenses
Australia	4.5	55.6	369.6	5491.2	n/a	6773.2
Austria	1.8	37.4	1.6	2505.3	65.3	5288.2
Canada	5.4	108.2	130.5	5133.1	232.9	11414.8
Chile	6.5	32.6	112.5	748.4	15.5	1309.4
Denmark	5.2	55.4	140.2	8524.9	253.2	10500.4
Egypt	1.5	0.4	0.7	39.1	20.7	2939.0
England/Wales	2.0	52.8	305.4	5534.1	15.5	7395.6
France	4.6	37.6	76.3	3569.1	85.8	5619.1
Hungary	3.8	13.7	51.9	1021.9	0.8	1747.8
Iraq	1.4	9.8	2.6	2124.2	1.1	2410.8
Ireland	1.0	11.1	2.9	2238.0	1.2	2529.0
Italy	2.2	1.5	33.0	2085.2	54.1	3297.9
Japan	1.2	3.8	17.5	1159.9	1.8	1430.3
Kenya	4.8	8.1	70.6	86.1	48.1	485.5
Norway	2.0	33.9	36.3	3936.4	147.6	5220.4
Philippines	36.9	3.0	51.7	80.7	n/a	316.5
Saudi Arabia	1.1	21.9	32.2	70.5	35.6	200.5
Scotland	10.0	99.3	133.6	6206.8	102.3	16796.2
South Korea	1.3	29.5	19.6	229.3	4.4	2229.3
Spain	2.3	15.0	25.2	1948.2	61.1	2519.4
Sweden	7.2	62.3	37.6	7629.6	362.2	12836.6
Switzerland	2.3	46.5	48.9	4336.8	283.2	4988.0
United States	8.4	37.6	370.2	5248.0	n/a	5664.3
Venezuela	9.1	39.3	155.0	867.1	28.9	1158.3
West Germany	4.2	60.0	102.7	4382.8	138.8	7114.0

*This category includes all types of sexual offenses except in the Philippines and the United States, where only the "rape" rate is counted.

Figure 2-3.   1988 crime rates (per 100,000 population) in 25 selected countries. *Source:* Interpol. (1987/1988). *International Crime Statistics.* Lyons, France: ICPO—Interpol General Secretariat.

cy, and drug offenses). Some categories are further subdivided. For example, rape is a subcategory under sex offenses and acts like robbery and auto theft are subcategories under theft. In a final category, data were requested on the total number of offenses detected by or reported to the police (this is the category used in Figure 2-2). This "Total Offenses" category is expected to be greater than the sum of the seven specific categories, because those seven are not likely to have covered all offense types in any particular country.

The crime rates provided in Figure 2-3 show a considerable range under each offense category. Again it is tempting to rank the countries by murder rate, theft rate, and so on. It is to be hoped that the preceding warnings will prevent you from succumbing to that trap. If we had data from other years for these countries we could comment on trends within the country and on long-term patterns differentiating countries. Instead, the single year data offered in Figure 2-3 are most useful as a thought provoker. Interpol provides data from other years, so it is possible to conduct cross-sectional and longitudinal studies with this data set. The United Nations statistics are also used for that purpose, so we will take this opportunity to discuss that data set.

United Nations Crime Data. In 1990, Cuba played host to the Eighth United Nations Congress on the Prevention of Crime and the Treatment of Offenders. This Congress, which meets every five years at a different location throughout the world, provides delegates with an opportunity to discuss issues related to crime and punishment. At the Eighth Congress, researchers presented statistics and analyses of the third United Nations crime survey covering the period 1980–1985. The following comments are based on information from those reports (United Nations, 1990a, 1990b).

Between 1975 and 1985, the total amount of reported crime grew at a world-wide average of five percent each year. That rate could not simply be attributed to population growth, which averaged under two percent annually. The escalation in crime was especially high during the last five-year period, which had an increase of 23 percent compared to an 11 percent increase during 1975–1980. In addition to the general increase, most individual categories of recorded crime also grew. The sharpest increases were in drug-related crimes and robbery.

Although recognizing the problems of comparing countries on the basis of crime rates, the United Nations researchers did find an intriguing variable to highlight. After categorizing the responding countries into either developed or developing, as had been done in both the first and second surveys, a certain trend seemed evident. In all three surveys, developed countries report a higher incidence of theft. The researchers suggest that the broader availability of material goods in developed countries might offer more opportunities to steal. Certainly there are other interpretations for such a finding. The point is that cross-cultural comparison of crime rates does not require country-by-country comparison or ranking. Instead, the rates can be used to compare groupings of countries linked together by common characteristics.

Victimization Data Set

For reasons similar to those giving rise to the National Crime Survey in the United States, several other countries are making use of victimization studies to supplement their own police-based statistics. Since official crime statistics from police sources require victims to report an offense, there is concern that cross-national comparison of crime statistics may compare reporting habits as much as crime incidents. We know, for example, that in many countries the likelihood that a crime will be reported to police is affected by such things as the seriousness of the offense (see Skogan, 1984), but we do not know how cultural differences may affect crime reporting from one country to another. Do cultural differences make Italians more or less likely to report theft than are Saudi Arabians? Are Colombians more or less likely to report assaults than are Canadians? At this point we cannot answer such questions. But attempts at data gathering that is

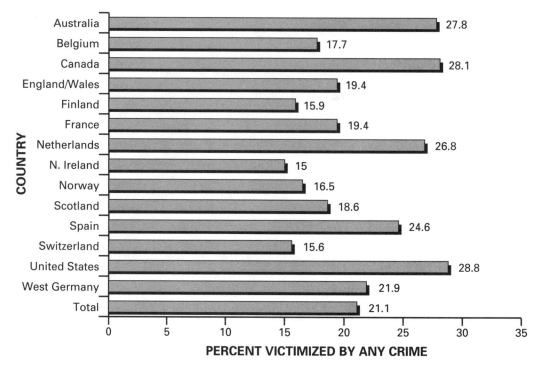

Figure 2-4. Overall victimization rates for all crimes (1988). *Source:* J. Van Dijk, P. Mahew, and M. Killias (1990). *Experiences of crime across the world.* Boston: Kluwer Law and Taxation Publishers.

similar to the National Crime Survey have begun, and comparative researchers are gaining more information about crime from the victim's perspective.

During 1989, 14 nations (see Figure 2-4) participated in a standardized international survey of victimization in their respective countries. This independently organized event was under the direction of Inter/View (the Netherlands) and is fully reported by van Dijk, Mayhew, and Killias (1990). Of the several interesting findings from this 1989 International Crime Survey, we consider those related to offenses against vehicles, robbery, assaults, and overall victimization.

Overall victimization rates (see Figure 2-4) were highest in the United States where 28.8 percent of the respondents said they had been victimized during 1988. Closely following were Canada (28.1 percent) and Australia (27.8 percent). Citizens reporting the lowest incidence of victimization were those in Northern Ireland (15.0 percent), Switzerland (15.6 percent), and Finland (15.9 percent). Not surprisingly, the overall rates tended to reflect the rates for specific offenses in each of the 14 countries.

Generally, countries with higher rates of vehicle ownership had higher levels of offenses involving these vehicles. So the availability of targets seems the best explanation for the amount of vehicle crime. This point is clearly made upon considering differences in thefts of automobiles, motorcycles, and bicycles. The risk of having a car stolen was highest in France (2.3 percent), Australia (2.3 percent), and the United States (2.1 percent); motorcycle/moped/scooter thefts were highest in Switzerland (1.2 percent) and bicycle thefts were highest in the Netherlands (7.6 percent). In each instance, the countries reporting high vehicle victimization also have high ownership of the same type vehicle. Van Dijk *et al.* (1990) note that countries where car thefts were low reported high bicycle thefts. They suggest that offenders stealing out of need for temporary transportation will make do with a bicycle if there are enough of them around.

The link between high ownership rates and high crime rates also presents itself when robbery offenses are considered. Here, however, the link is not between what the victim owns but instead what the offender possesses. Robbery was most often reported in Spain (2.8 percent) and the United States (1.9 percent), but the weapon of choice shows interesting differences. On average, the offender used a knife in 20 percent of the robberies in the 14-country sample. But in Spain, 40 percent of the robbers used a knife. In the United States, on the other hand, the comparatively high robbery rate typically involved the use of a gun. On average, 8 percent of the robbers in all 14 countries used a gun during the offense. In the United States, 28 percent of robbery offenders used a gun. That high percentage of gun-point robberies in the United States corresponds with survey findings on gun ownership in America. Specifically, Americans were much more likely to own guns (29 percent) than were citizens of other countries (average of 6 percent).

The highest rates of assaults and frightening threats were in the United States (5.4 percent), Australia (5.2 percent), and Canada (4.0 percent). Citizens of European countries fared much better; the average for their continent was only 2.5 percent (ranging from Switzerland's 0.5 percent to the Netherlands' 3.4 percent).

Van Dijk *et al.* (1990) compared the results of the victimization study with those using police statistics and found some similarity. The two types of measures were especially close on automobile thefts, but there was poor correspondence for robbery, assault, and sexual offenses. Generally, however, the two measures reported similar levels of crime (for example, both types report more auto thefts than robberies) but differed on the amount of crime. They conclude that for comparative purposes, survey victimization rates may be a more valid measure than police statistics when the burden of crime on a country's citizens is measured.

We must not conclude that police statistics have methodological problems while victim-based measures are free of similar difficulties. For example, the International Crime Survey found that victimization most often occurred, regardless of the country, near the victim's own home or elsewhere in the local area. Only some 4 percent of the victimizations occurred while the respondents were outside their own country. Interestingly, the Swiss provided an exception; 16 percent of their reported incidents took place outside Switzerland. This point becomes methodologically important because victimization rates in Switzerland may overstate the actual vulnerability of the Swiss in their own country. Just as police-based statistics may overstate the crime rate in popular tourist areas having a low native population, victim-based statistics may overstate the rate in countries with well-travelled citizens. This is just one of several problems presented by victimization studies. Just as police-based statistics are useful as long as we remember their limitations, the victim-based measures are welcome additions for comparative criminology, but they are not a methodological solution.

IMPACT

International Adjudication Efforts

After the 1985 hijacking of the Italian ship *Achille Lauro* and the murder of American Leon Klinghoffer, great frustration was felt across the United States about not being able to bring the terrorists to justice in this country. Efforts were made to extradite the terrorists from Italy, but the complex rules of international law made it unlikely that U.S. courts would get a chance at the defendants. The predicament was complicated because both Italy and the United States had firm legal ground for bringing charges. The crimes occurred aboard an Italian ship in international waters, so the law of Italy obviously applied. However, under piracy laws, people who seize ships for criminal purposes are considered international outlaws and can be prosecuted by any country wishing to do so. In addition, the 1984 antiterrorism law passed by Congress made it a crime punishable by life imprisonment to take an American citizen hostage anywhere in the world (Serrill, October 21, 1985). Additional obstacles would be presented if the United States filed charges that could result in the death penalty should the terrorists be found guilty. Italy, like several other European countries, forbids extradition to a country where the defendant could be executed.

Eventually, an Italian court convicted several Palistinian men on charges of hijacking and of kidnapping for terrorist ends. The presumed mastermind of the hijacking, [Mohammed] Abul Abbas, and his two top aides were tried and convicted in absentia. Their life imprisonment sentences were the harshest possible under Italian law. But Klinghoffer's confessed killer and two others, who were present in court, received sentences ranging from 15 to 30 years (Jenkins, July 11, 1986). American officials continued efforts to bring the hijackers to justice in the United States, but in November 1987 the Justice Department withdrew its arrest warrant for Abbas ("Justice Dept. Drops . . .," April 18, 1988) and accepted the Italian conviction, even though Italian officials had still been unable to find Abbas and carry out the sentence.

The American decision to drop the arrest warrant recognized the difficulty of several countries seeking justice against the same suspect. Even if Italy and the United States both agreed to take their turn at the hijackers, another problem would have to be considered, since a 1984 United States–Italian extradition treaty prohibits double jeopardy.

The United Nations has proposed several model treaties to increase international cooperation in combatting transnational crime (United Nations, 1990d). The Model Treaty of Mutual Assistance, for example, would encourage member states to help each other in criminal matters that transcend country boundaries. Countries could arrange to transport criminals from one country to another to give evidence in criminal prosecutions or to assist in a criminal investigation. Similarly, mutual assistance could encourage countries to share evidence required for investigation or trial in a member state's justice system.

While the transporting and sharing of witnesses and evidence is important, a bigger hurdle may be the extradition of suspects and defendants to foreign countries. The Model Treaty on Extradition (United Nations, 1990d) builds on existing treaties by providing a wider basis for extradition arrangements and making it easier for the requesting country to show cause that the suspect or offender should be relinquished to their custody. Provisions for a temporary surrender that allow persons to stand trial in another country and then to be returned to serve the sentence in their own country are proposed as potentially effective when dealing with major drug rings. Regardless of the specifics chosen, it is becoming increasingly apparent that effective prosecution of transnational offenders requires a modernized and more flexible conception of jurisdiction.

One way around the problem of jurisdiction would be the establishment of a criminal court with global authority. In 1989 the United Nations General Assembly asked the International Law Commission to examine the possibility of establishing just such a court. An international criminal court could, it is argued, competently and efficiently deal with several international crimes without worrying about jurisdictional problems (United Nations, 1990d). Its authority would be restricted to a list of international offenses agreed upon in advance by participating nations. The difficulty of getting countries of the world to relinquish traditionally state authority to a new international body became very clear during the United Nations debate on this topic. The various countries accepted the need to develop international legal means to solve the problem of transnational crime. They also recognized that establishing an international criminal court, if feasible, would enhance the efficiency of the international criminal justice system. But, despite the apparent benefits, the countries also realized that the issues were very complex and required significantly more study. Despite the optimism of some futurists, and even the acquiescence of pragmatists, a fully empowered international criminal court remains a vision.

Current efforts at international policing and adjudication fall short of what officials deem necessary to effectively fight transnational crime. But given the diversity of cultures, governments, and nations, these first attempts are admirable nonetheless. It is unlikely that the world's nations will ever adopt identical laws in areas beyond very specific acts like terrorism or perhaps some drug-related crimes. International unification of the police, courts, and corrections processes seems even less likely than consolidation of laws. However, unification is not the only alternative to a structure of scattered and distinctive justice systems. It is also possible that nations can achieve harmony among their police, courts, and corrections mechanisms. Cole *et al.* (1987) believe that harmonization (that is, elimination of major differences by minimizing existing legal obstacles) has great potential as countries cooperate to fight transnational crime. Achieving such harmony requires each country to understand and appreciate the operation of legal systems beyond their own. Studies in comparative criminal justice strive to achieve exactly that kind of goal, and the remaining chapters of this book provide a step in that direction.

CRIME TRENDS AND CRIME THEORIES

Crime has economic, social, and personal costs everywhere it occurs. As the incidence of crime rises, governments must use more and more of their budgets to respond to the crime problem. Such financial costs are especially burdensome for developing countries, but even developed countries feel the financial hardship brought by crimes like smuggling, financial fraud, and currency manipulation, as well as the more traditional crime types. High as the financial costs are, the social and personal suffering brought by crime may be even higher. Crime can eat away at the moral order, may provoke fear among citizens, and can certainly be damaging to people's well-being. An understanding of crime trends and the development of explanations for criminality are areas where comparative criminology may prove very beneficial.

Crime Trends

The United Nations crime surveys, especially the one covering 1980–1985, are especially helpful in identifying trends that show a growing internationalization of crime. Broadening the definition of criminal acts to include acts that are harmful but may not be illegal, the United Nations identifies five clusters of transnational crime: (1) internationally organized crime, (2) terrorism, (3) economic offenses involving more than one country, (4) crimes against cultural heritage, and (5) crimes against the environment. Crimes and other harmful acts falling into these clusters have been increasing around the world and show no indication of subsiding in the near future.

Internationally Organized Crime.   There is a tendency to consider organized crime as bound to specific countries. For example, the Italian Mafia, the American Cosa Nostra, and Japanese Boryokudan exemplify criminal syndicates linked to particular territories. But in the last few decades, organized criminality has increasingly shed its parochialism and is less confined by national boundaries. Expansion of such illicit activities as drug trafficking and sexual slavery to new markets in developed countries presents significant economic opportunities for organized crime. With the emergence of new markets in Eastern European countries during the 1990s, the continued internationalization of crime seems inevitable.

Advantages of organized crime include providing an effective distribution system for illegal goods and services. As the market for such goods and services expands beyond a criminal organization's original territory, it is simply good business for that organization to similarly expand its distribution. International expansion can mean that the organization members involve themselves in activities in another country, such as the involvement of Japanese Boryokudan (also called the *yakuza*) in Brazil and Korea (Kaplan and Dubro, 1986). More commonly, however, crime syndicates in one country develop relationships with those of one or several other countries. In that way, for example, drugs like heroin, cocaine, and marijuana reach the United States from sources as diverse as Colombia and Afghanistan.

Drug trafficking is one of the most visible activities involving organized crime on an international basis. The innumerable actors, efficiently organized division of labor, production and distribution systems that are national and international in scope, and a multinational political base combine to make drug trafficking an underground empire (Martin, Romano, and Haran, 1988). The emerging opportunities for criminal activity in the new countries of Eastern and Central Europe are apparently too good for many crime organizations to ignore. For example, Colombia's powerful Cali drug cartel did not wait to seek access into possible Czechoslovakian and Polish markets. In October 1991, Czechoslovak authorities seized 100 kilograms of cocaine that had been hidden in a truckload of Colombian coffee (Castro, December 16, 1991). The coffee was traced to a Polish ship that had stopped in Colombia, so Polish officials also got involved. Their investigation discovered another 100 kilograms of cocaine sitting in a Warsaw warehouse.

Drugs provide only one of organized crime's illicit goods and services. Other activities especially suitable to a network of criminal alliances include trafficking in weapons, industrial secrets, migrant labor, female and child prostitution, works of art, and even human organs (United Nations, 1990d). The resulting individual, social, political, and economic damage in developed countries is significant, but it is easy to ignore the destruction that organized crime activities can cause in developing countries. As the United Nations (1990d) points out, organized crime in developing countries may infiltrate public administration and political structures (including the armed forces), can undermine the democratic process, and may distort a society's ethical norms.

International Terrorism.   The United Nations defines international terrorism as "terrorist acts, the author or authors of which plan their actions, are directed or come from, flee to and seek refuge in, or otherwise receive any form of assistance from a country or countries other than the one in which the acts themselves take place" (1990c, p. 6). Such activities increased from about 125 in 1968 to around 850 in 1988 before declining to some 530 in 1989 (United Nations, 1990d). Casualties followed a similar pattern by increasing from just over 240 in 1968 to a peak of 2900 in 1987 before declining to about 1080 in 1989.

There are no universally accepted statistics on terrorism, but those kept by the United Nations provide a broad picture of a criminal activity that is expanding in scope. During the 20 years from 1968 to 1988, terrorist incidents showed interesting geographic changes. In 1968, 32 percent of the incidents took place in North America, but in 1987 the percentage dropped to zero. Conversely, terrorist acts increased in the Asia/Pacific region from 0.8 percent in 1968 to 20.8 percent in 1987. In 1968, 68 percent of the terrorist incidents took place in either Latin America or North America. In 1987, 65 percent took place in the Middle East, or the Asia/Pacific area.

Changes in the targets of terrorism also shows interesting developments in this form of crime (see Figure 2-5). Diplomatic and government personnel accounted for over 52 percent of the terrorist targets in 1968, but only about 17 percent in 1987. Instead of seeking out diplomatic, government, and military officials, post-1984 terrorists targeted business people and other civilians. In this manner, terrorists tried to make their acts sensational enough to attract publicity and to make individual citizens collectively responsible for the policies and actions of their government.

In addition to the harm to specific victims of terrorism, this form of international crime increases tensions between countries, dramatically influences national and international politics, and impacts the economy (for example, tourism) of even those countries not directly involved.

Economic Crimes.   Economic crimes of an international type can be divided into those benefiting a corporation and those benefiting an individual (United Nations, 1990c). The first category of harmful acts or crimes includes activities that maximize, maintain, or obtain economic profit for multinational corporations. Typical of such acts is transnational corporate bribery, wherein company officials persuade government or business personnel in foreign countries to behave favorably toward the corporation (Beirne and Messerschmidt, 1991). While the transaction may benefit specific people or companies in each country, it is also likely to harm other citizens through increased prices, decreased wages, and exploitation of an already impoverished populace.

The quest for corporate profit also results in transnational corporations "dumping" on a country certain products banned or not approved for sale in another country. Contraceptive devices, lethal drugs, toxic pesticides, and other items have been sold or distributed to a variety of countries and have harmed

Year	1968	1970	1975	1980	1981	1982	1983	1984	1985	1986	1987
Total incidents	125	309	382	532	496	477	485	598	785	774	831
By region											
Africa, Sub-Saharan	0.0	3.6	6.3	4.7	3.8	3.4	4.1	7.5	5.5	2.6	3.5
Asia/Pacific	0.8	7.8	5.8	5.5	3.0	5.9	7.6	4.5	5.4	9.9	20.8
Eastern Europe and USSR	0.0	0.3	0.5	0.6	1.4	1.0	0.4	0.2	0.3	0.0	0.1
Latin America	36.0	41.4	17.5	24.8	22.6	20.1	24.9	13.9	15.2	20.5	13.0
Middle East	14.4	12.9	18.3	22.2	19.6	10.7	22.1	34.3	45.5	46.5	44.5
North America	32.0	8.1	15.4	6.4	6.3	6.7	1.9	0.8	0.5	0.3	0.0
Western Europe	16.8	25.9	36.1	35.9	43.3	52.2	39.0	38.8	27.8	20.2	18.1
By type											
Bombing	66.4	40.5	51.0	42.3	50.8	55.3	51.2	50.7	48.4	59.2	56.9
Armed attack	16.8	11.0	13.6	31.8	20.6	14.8	15.1	23.3	17.1	16.7	15.7
Arson	9.6	18.1	11.3	8.6	9.4	15.2	9.5	9.7	12.4	14.3	18.0
Kidnapping	0.8	13.9	14.7	3.0	4.9	6.5	8.1	7.7	10.6	6.1	6.4
Skyjacking	2.4	5.8	1.0	1.5	2.4	1.0	1.2	1.7	0.7	0.2	0.1
Other	4.0	10.7	8.4	12.8	12.0	7.1	14.9	7.0	10.8	3.4	2.9
By target											
Business	17.5	15.7	28.0	17.3	15.3	23.0	13.2	22.9	23.5	24.9	20.0
Diplomat	31.7	29.5	28.0	36.4	38.3	33.8	33.5	18.5	9.4	10.1	7.6
Government	20.6	20.0	6.9	8.7	7.0	5.9	10.0	11.7	9.5	10.9	9.2
Military	2.4	5.9	3.5	8.6	9.1	11.5	16.2	7.4	6.9	6.0	8.7
Other	27.8	28.9	33.7	29.0	30.3	25.8	27.1	39.5	50.6	48.0	54.5
Number of victims											
Total	241	336	782	1569	972	883	1904	1279	2042	2321	2905
Dead	34	127	266	507	168	128	637	312	825	604	612
Wounded	207	209	516	1062	804	755	1267	967	1217	1717	2293

Figure 2-5. International terrorist incidents, 1968–1987 (Percentage of total). *Source:* United Nations (1989). *Report on the World Situation* (Table 44, p. 165). Economic and Social Council (sales number E.89.IV.1). New York: United Nations. Used with permission.

thousands of people (Beirne and Messerschmidt, 1991), especially in Third World countries.

The second category of economic crimes is those benefiting an individual. For these offenses, private persons represent their international activities as perfectly legitimate when in fact the intent is to defraud individual investors, public or private institutions, or governments. Sometimes with the help of organized crime, these individuals operate to launder money, smuggle, provide prostitutes, make weapons deals, assist in the "adoption" of children, and manipulate investments. The result is harmful to the citizens and social structure of both developed and developing countries.

Crimes Against the Cultural Heritage. Patrimonial crimes violate a country's heritage through the unlawful procurement or acquisition of archaeological and artistic objects that are classified as part of the cultural legacy of a country. We do not often think of such thefts as particularly frequent nor in the context of international crime. However, the number of such incidents has increased in recent years so that today systematic theft and even simple plundering by occasional thieves threaten the cultural property of nations (United Nations, 1990b).

The most destructive pillaging occurs in developing countries with the spoils being sent to the developed countries. Since World War II, the United States has been cited as "the largest single buyers' market for stolen or illegally exported cultural property" (Greenfield, 1989, pp. 236–237). But other countries certainly take part—and some with little sign of guilt. For example, the National Gallery of Scotland includes a statement in its catalogue of Spanish and Italian paintings that the gallery's *El Medico* by Goya was stolen from the Royal Palace in Madrid in 1869 (Greenfield, 1989).

The problem is neither new nor only recently recognized. In 1970, the General Conference of the United Nations Educational, Scientific and Cultural Organization (UNESCO) adopted a Convention on the Means of Prohibiting and Preventing the Illicit Import, Export and Transfer of Ownership of Cultural Property. By mid-1989, 66 nations had accepted or acceded to the Convention, but only three of those were developed countries (United States, Canada, and West Germany). Since developed countries are the most important markets for the cultural objects, their nonaccession to the Convention has limited its impact on illicit traffic.

Even if a significant number of developed countries accepted the UNESCO Convention, it is questionable whether such regulations can have an impact. Both France and the United Kingdom, for example, have problems with the Convention's position on the return of cultural items to the claiming country. Should France return the Venus de Milo to Greece? Should all the Egyptian mummies in museums throughout the United States, and elsewhere, be returned to Egypt? Should the Natural History Museum in London have to return the skull of the Middle Stone Age, Broken Hill Man, to Zambia, where miners discovered it in 1921? Because there is no time limit on how long the protected items must be in a territory for a state to claim it for the national heritage, and given the very imprecise phraseology as to what is protected, it is unlikely that developed countries will change their position on existing international regulations.

Despite what may be reasonable concerns regarding existing regulations, we cannot lose sight of the breadth and growth of this problem. UNESCO estimates that more than 50,000 art objects were smuggled out of India during the 1980s (Greenfield, 1989). Turkey, which has been called an "open-air museum," has some 200,000 monuments, 10,000 tombs, and 3,000 ancient cities providing a supermarket for looters (Walsh, November 25, 1991). Drawing the world public's attention to the problem is a necessary first step, and one that is being slowly taken. *Time* magazine underscored the crisis by noting:

> The art of the world is being looted. From New York to Phnom Penh, from ancient ruins in Turkey to up-to-date museums in Amsterdam, precious records of human culture are vanishing into the dark as thieves steal with near impunity (Walsh, November 25, 1991, p. 86).

Possibly, as crimes against the cultural heritage are more often committed against such developed countries as those in Europe and North America, patrimonial crimes will receive a more concerted response. But since museums are more abundant in prosperous countries, the poorer nations continue to serve more as suppliers than preservers.

Environmental Crimes. The opening of Eastern Europe and continued development in other parts of the world present a challenge for environmentally sound economic and social development. Unfortunately, it is a challenge that is not easily met, since problems worldwide are so serious that some consider offenses against the environment to be crimes against humanity (United Nations, 1990b). Air, water, and land pollution cease to be an exclusively national problem when the result reaches beyond the initiating country's borders. The massive use of chemical herbicides, detergents, and inorganic fertilizers, and the careless and indiscriminate disposal of poisonous and radioactive industrial waste, exemplify new forms of transnational crime.

Environmental offenses, as, for example those that result in damage to the ozone layer and acid rain, present situations that challenge the traditional and narrowly interpreted concepts of sovereignty and criminal responsibility. The harm caused to the environment threatens life and property around the world, not stopping at the offending country's borders. As a result, some argue that response to such offenses should no longer fall within the jurisdiction of a single country. The alternative, however, is not at all clear. Delegates at the Eighth United Nations Congress on the Prevention of Crime and the Treatment of Offenders considered actions ranging from new laws to reparation for damages. As with many other problems at national and international levels, there is more agreement on the goal than on how it should be achieved.

Crime Theories

Knowledge of national and international crime trends is appropriately followed by an interest in explaining them. Such mental gymnastics, which are the domain of comparative criminology, actually fall outside this book's focus. Our interest in comparative criminal justice systems is more concerned with the structures and procedures nations use to deal with offenders than with how those countries explain the criminal's behavior and crime's occurrence. Of course, there is necessarily some overlap in those interests. Countries with high and low rates of crime may require different justice systems. Similarly, different justice systems may partially explain why one country has a higher crime rate than another. In either event, explanations for criminal behavior and of the distribution of crime are inevitably linked to a society's method of social control.

A thorough examination of how criminological theory is applied to cross-cultural and international crime statistics is not possible in this book. However, it is important and intriguing enough to warrant some attention. Just to give you an idea of how some theorists use comparative analysis I will highlight the variables of religion, socioeconomic factors, and the role of the situation. Keep in mind, however, that this exercise simply exemplifies the point; it is not meant to be a review essay covering the research that considers possible links between these variables and crime.

Religion. It is popularly believed that religion's promotion of a morally correct life-style will likely provide a negative correlation between religiosity and criminality. That is, individuals living a morally correct life should have a low crime rate. Studies over the last several decades provide contradictory evidence on the link between religiosity and crime or deviance, but a study by Stark, Kent, and Doyle (1982) set a standard to which more recent studies respond. That research was not comparative in nature, but it took a position that intrigued and encouraged comparative studies.

Stated most simply, Stark *et al.* (1982) found that in communities where religious beliefs are strong, the resultant moral values suppress the delinquency rate. The key point is the emphasis on "community." Stark *et al.* take an ecological perspective and argue that "religion only serves to bind people to the moral order if religious influences permeate the culture and the social interactions of the people in question" (1982, p. 7). This concept of religion "permeating the culture" is the element that comparative criminologists find intriguing.

The Kingdom of Saudi Arabia is a country where religion permeates the culture. More specifically, Saudi Arabia operates under the guidelines of the laws of Islam as provided in the writings, statements, and deeds of the prophet Muhammad. Islamic law (the *Shari'a*) provides not only the country's legal system, but is effectively the standard governing all individual behavior and social relations. In other words, the *Shari'a* (religion) permeates Saudi culture and society. In this sense, Saudi Arabia presents a unique opportunity to test the hypothesis that criminality will be low where a culture of religiosity is strong. Though neither were designed to test that specific hypothesis, studies by Ali (1985) and Souryal (1987) provide data relevant to the general point.

Both Ali (1985) and Souryal (1987) note the difficulty in comparing crime rates in Saudi Arabia to rates in other countries. In addition to methodological problems mentioned earlier, Saudi Arabia presents two rather unique obstacles. First, *Shari'a* allows, and even encourages, nonlegalistic response to misbehavior. Criminal complaints are often resolved through arbitration even before a police record is made (Souryal, 1987). That practice obviously means that crime is underreported in official statistics. Even homicide statistics are probably higher than official counts, since the *Qur'an* condones punishment by the victim's family under a feuding model rather than a court system (Groves, Newman, and Corrado, 1987).

The second methodological problem when one is working with Saudi statistics comes from the kingdom's use of the Arabic lunar calendar based on an Islamic year (*Hijri*). Instead of the 365 days in a Gregorian calendar year, a *Hijri* year has only 354 days. In addition, a *Hijri* year usually overlaps with two Gregorian years, so any seasonal effect on crime may be confused when one undertakes cross-national comparison of crime statistics. Both Ali (1985) and Souryal (1987) are well aware of these problems and try to accommodate them. We will first look at Ali's findings.

Ali compared criminal statistics in Saudi Arabia for the Islamic year 1401 (basically November 9, 1980 to October 29, 1981) with 1981 statistics for the United States generally and Ohio specifically. He found Saudi Arabia's rate (per 100,000 population) for all reported crime was 159 compared to a rate on the seven UCR Index crimes of 5625.9 in the United States and 5284 in Ohio (Ali, 1985). He also compared specific crimes (taking definitional problems into consideration) and found that both violent and property offenses in Saudi Arabia were far below those in the United States. Ali attributes the lower Saudi crime rates to a "profound internalization of Islamic religious values among Saudi people . . . (and to) a firm and uncompromised implementation of the Islamic penal code" (1985, p. 54).

Souryal's (1987) comparison was more global in nature. He contrasted official Saudi statistics from 1970–1975 with world rates of reported offenses as found in the First (1970–1975) United Nations survey of crime rates. Saudi Arabia fared well in the comparison with a murder rate about one fourth that of the combined world rate (that is, 1 per 100,000 compared to 3.9 per 100,000). For property crimes, the combined world rate was 908.5 compared to the Saudi rate of 1.4, while the world rate for sex offenses was about five times the Saudi rate (24.2 to 5).

In an attempt to isolate the role of *Shari'a* as distinct from Middle Eastern culture, Souryal also compares Saudi Arabia crime rates with those in neighboring Islamic countries. He argues that while the other countries are influenced by Islamic law, only Saudi Arabia uses the *Shari'a* as its sole legal system. Criminal justice in other Arabic countries is influenced by things like codification and precedent through their dealings with other nations. Saudi Arabia's leadership in the use of orthodox *Shari'a* law provided one variable to set it apart from neighboring countries. Comparison of Saudi crime rates with rates in other Islamic nations may reflect any effect the *Shari'a* has on criminality.

As with the combined world data, the Kingdom of Saudi Arabia appears to have a crime rate lower than Arabic countries incorporating state law. For the categories of murder, property crimes, and sexual offenses, the Saudi rate consistently fell below that of six other Arab countries. Souryal highlights the comparison with Kuwait, which is culturally, ethnically, and religiously similar to Saudi Arabia. The primary difference between the countries, for Souryal, is that Saudi Arabia applies *Shari'a* law to crime while Kuwait does not. The average Saudi murder rate from 1970 through 1979 was 0.482 per 100,000 population compared to Kuwait's rate of 3.05. Similar results are found for property crimes (7.44 in Saudi Arabia and 111.90 in Kuwait) and sexual offenses (3.2 for the Saudi's and 28.05 for Kuwait).

Souryal concludes that incidents of crime under *Shari'a* law in Saudi Arabia are far fewer than those in the world generally and are even below the rates of similarly situated Arab countries. Both Ali (1985) and Souryal (1987) suggest that the penetration of religion (that is, the *Shari'a*) throughout Saudi society is an important variable in explaining the low crime rates. In this manner, the researchers seem to support the Stark, *et al.* (1982) claim that crime and delinquency are suppressed in communities where religiosity is strong.

Socioeconomic Factors. One of the exciting, and irritating, things about criminology research is the way that results can vary depending on the type of analysis conducted and the variables used. For example, Groves *et al.* (1987) also studied the link between religiosity and crime, with Islam exemplifying cultural permeation. Unlike Souryal (1987), these researchers assumed that Islamic cultures can be grouped together whether their legal system is solely *Shari'a* or also incorporates state law. Their resulting comparison is on combined crime rates between 14 Islamic countries and 33 non-Islamic countries. Saudi Arabia is not included among the Islamic countries in this sample, which uses the countries responding to the first United Nations crime survey (1970–1975).

Groves *et al.* (1987) found significant differences in the theft and fraud crime rates, with the non-Islamic rate being roughly ten times greater. Although not significant, data for robbery and drug abuse were in a similar direction. What sets the Groves *et al.* study apart from Ali (1985) and Souryal (1987) is its reluctance to claim that Islamic religion suppresses crime. Instead, they look for other variables that may explain the noted differences. Their investigation took them to the per capita Gross Domestic Product indicator, which shows a country's level of economic development. Inclusion of that variable eliminated all significant effects of Islamic religion in explaining crime rate variation. Groves *et al.* conclude "that it is high level of economic development that is strongly related to high crime rates, rather than Islamic religion being related to low crime rates" (1987, p. 500).

Shichor (1990) also looked at the relationship between crime and socioeconomic factors from a cross-national perspective. He predicted that socioeconomic change leads to a degree of anomie wherein a country's people feel that there are no guidelines for their behavior. If problems of individual adjustment to the changing social situation creates opportunities and conditions for crime, Shichor reasoned, increased socioeconomic development should be accompanied by an increase in property crime. Simultaneously, socioeconomic indicators should be negatively related to violent crime, since those types of offenses are usually more prevalent in rural societies. He used Interpol's International Crime Statistics to test his reasoning.

Homicide (representing violent crime), larceny (representing property crime), and the total volume of crime comprised Shichor's dependent variables. The independent variables were population size and change (developing nations have a rapid population increase), public health (for example, infant mortality rate, number of hospital beds), and communication/education (for example, number of newspapers and education expenditures). Upon applying these variables to 44 nations, Shichor concluded that "homicide rates were negatively correlated with indicators of modernization, while larceny and total crime rates showed a positive relationship with them" (1990, p. 74). As one explanation, Shichor suggests that availability of material possessions increases with economic development. When that availability is accompanied by increased cultural emphasis on having those possessions, an increase in property offenses seems to naturally follow. Also, compared to developing countries, modern countries likely have more efficient law enforcement, more accurate recording methods, and citizens who more willingly report crimes. Each of those factors may help explain why an increase in property crime rates seems to accompany modernization.

The Role of the Situation. Both religion and socioeconomic factors provide a macrolevel analysis of cross-national crime data. Some researchers are also interested in more microlevel investigations as they attempt to identify patterns in the spread and distribution of crime. LaFree and Birkbeck (1991) provide just such an analysis in their look at situational characteristics of crime.

Working on the assumption that crime is more likely to occur in some situations than in others (that is, crime is "situationally clustered"), LaFree and Birkbeck (1991) considered situational variables present when specific personal contact crimes were committed. The cross-national aspect of this study results from their taking victimization samples in the United States and in Maracaibo, Venezuela. The authors freely admit to significant differences between the two samples (one of a country, the other of only one city in a different country), but they argue that for their purposes the differences become a strength. Since their goal was to test the generalizability of hypotheses about situational characteristics of crime, diverse samples yielding similar patterns could only make the argument more potent.

Upon comparing data for the crimes of assault, robbery, and pickpocketing in the United States and assault, robbery, and property snatching in Maracaibo, the authors found some interesting similarity. In both countries, assault typically involves single victims, private locations, men, and offenders acquainted with the victim. Similar correspondence occurred for robbery, which, in both samples, involved public domains, lone victims, strangers, and incidents taking place outside buildings. Finally, pickpocketing and property snatching shared the variables of involving a lone victim who is a stranger to the offender, and occurring in a public place (LaFree and Birkbeck, 1991).

If other investigation continues to show cross-national similarities in crime "situations," comparative criminologists will have provided valuable information to such fields as victimization studies. More specific to our purpose, LaFree and Birkbeck remind us that microlevel analysis of cross-national crime data is as appropriate and possible as the macrolevel studies using variables like religion and socioeconomic conditions.

Both macro- and microlevel investigations provide an opportunity to test the applicability of criminological theory to crime in places other than the theory's country of origin. That is an important activity, since the alternative results in criminological ethnocentrism, wherein criminological concepts and generalizations about one society are assumed to apply to all others. A preferred approach for comparative criminology might be what Beirne (1983) calls *methodological relativism*. That strategy allows an observer to design cross-cultural generalizations while at the same time maintaining respect for cultural diversity. But whether it is ventured to achieve a general theory of crime, merely to test a theory's generalizability, or is undertaken to modify theories for different cultures, cross-national study of crime is an important endeavor. However, since this book's focus is on response to crime, rather than on its occurrence and distribution, the topic of comparative criminology must be set aside.

SUMMARY

This chapter sets the stage for the rest of the book by presenting crime as a worldwide problem requiring a reaction from nations individually and collectively. Problems in preparing crime statistics are noted, but as long as the user is aware of the limitations such statistics have, the various crime and victimization data sets provide useful information.

Cross-national crime statistics are especially useful in identifying trends in certain crime with international impact. The five clusters of such crimes are: internationally organized crime, terrorism, economic offenses, crimes against the cultural heritage, and crimes against the environment. The statistics are also useful to test and develop crime theories. The variables of religion, socioeconomic factors, and the role of the situation are offered as examples of comparative analysis making use of cross-cultural data.

The chapter's Impact sections look at specific efforts in international policing (Interpol) and ideas about increasing international adjudication efforts. In both areas the United States has a vested interest in the direction such efforts take since Americans, like other citizens of the world, are increasingly affected by criminals who ignore national boundaries.

SUGGESTED READINGS

Adler, Freda. (1983). *Nations not obsessed with crime.* Littleton, CO: Fred B. Rothman.

Fooner, Michael. (1989). *Interpol: Issues in world crime and international criminal justice.* New York: Plenum.

Shelley, Louise. (1981). *Crime and modernization.* Carbondale, IL: Southern Illinois University Press.

van Dijk, Jan J.M., Mayhew, Pat, and Killias, Martin. (1990). *Experiences of crime across the world.* Boston: Kluwer.

REFERENCES

Adler, Freda. (1983). *Nations not obsessed with crime.* Littleton, CO: Fred B. Rothman.

Ali, Badr-el-din. (1985). Islamic law and crime: The case of Saudi Arabia. *International Journal of Comparative and Applied Criminal Justice, 9,* 45–57.

Archer, Dane, and Gartner, Rosemary. (1984). *Violence and crime in cross-national perspective.* New Haven: Yale University Press.

Beirne, Piers. (1983). Generalization and its discontent: The comparative study of crime. In I. L. Barak-Glantz and E. H. Johnson (Eds.), *Comparative criminology* (pp. 19–38). Beverly Hills, CA: Sage.

Beirne, Piers, and Messerschmidt, James. (1991). *Criminology.* San Diego: Harcourt Brace Jovanovich.

Bennett, Richard R. (1990). *Correlates of crime: A study of 52 nations, 1960–1984* (computer file). Ann Arbor, MI: Inter-university Consortium for Political and Social Research (distributor).

Bennett, Richard R., and Lynch, James P. (1990). Does a difference make a difference? Comparing cross-national crime indicators. *Criminology, 28,* 153–181.

Castro, Janice. (1991, December 16). Eastern Europe's new bad guys. *Time, 138* (24), 15.

Cole, George F., Frankowski, Stanislaw, J., and Gertz, Marc G. (Eds). (1987).

Major criminal justice systems: A comparative study (2nd ed.). Newbury Park, CA: Sage.

Djekebaev, U. S. (1975). Crime in socialist society and its principal features. *Soviet Sociology, 14,* 62–85.

Dubovets, P.N. (1970). Research on crime and crime prevention in the Byelorussian Soviet Socialist Republic. *International Review of Criminal Policy, 28,* 43–48.

Fooner, Michael. (1989). *Interpol: Issues in world crime and international criminal justice.* New York: Plenum.

Greenfield, Jeanette. (1989). *The return of cultural treasures.* New York: Cambridge.

Groves, W. Byron, and Newman, Graeme. (1989). Against general theory in comparative research. *International Journal of Comparative and Applied Criminal Justice, 13,* 23–29.

Groves, W. Byron, Newman, Graeme, and Corrado, Charles. (1987). Islam, modernization and crime: A test of the religious ecology thesis. *Journal of Criminal Justice, 15,* 495–503.

Hagan, Frank E. (1989). *Research methods in criminal justice and criminology* (2nd ed.). New York: Macmillan.

Interpol. (1987–1988). *International crime statistics.* Lyons, France: ICPO—Interpol General Secretariat.

Justice Department drops warrant in Achille Lauro hijacking. (1988, April 17). *Washington Post,* p. A20.

Kalish, Carol B. (1988). *International crime rates.* Washington, DC: Bureau of Justice Statistics.

Kaplan, David E., and Dubro, Alec. (1986). *Yakuza: The explosive account of Japan's criminal underworld.* Reading, MA: Addison-Wesley.

LaFree, Gary, and Birkbeck, Christopher. (1991). The neglected situation: A cross-national study of the situational characteristics of crime. *Criminology, 29,* 73–98.

Levine, James P. (1976). The potential for crime overreporting in criminal victimization surveys. *Criminology, 14,* 307–330.

Martin, John, Romano, Anne, and Haran, James. (1988). International crime patterns: Challenges to traditional criminological theory and research. *Criminal justice research bulletin* (Monograph Vol. 4 No. 2). Huntsville, TX: Sam Houston State University.

Messner, Steven F. (1980). Income inequality and murder rates. *Comparative Social Research, 3,* 185–198.

Serrill, Michael S. (1985, October 21). In pursuit of justice. *Newsweek,* p. 29.

Shargorodskii, M. D. (1964). The causes and prevention of crime. *Soviet Sociology, 3,* 24–39.

Shelley, Louise. (1981). *Crime and modernization.* Carbondale, IL: Southern Illinois University Press.

Shichor, David. (1990). Crime patterns and socioeconomic development: A cross-national analysis. *Criminal Justice Review, 15,* 64–77.

Simpson, John R. (1984). Interpol—Dedicated to cooperation. *Police Chief, 51*(6), 31–34.

Skogan, W. (1984). Reporting crimes to the police: The status of world research. *Journal of Research in Crime and Delinquency, 21,* 113–137.

Souryal, Sam S. (1987). The religionization of a society: The continuing application of Shariah law in Saudi Arabia. *Journal for the Scientific Study of Religion, 26,* 429–449.

Stark, Rodney, Kent, L., and Doyle, D.P. (1982). Religion and delinquency: The ecology of a 'lost' relationship. *Journal of Research in Crime and Delinquency, 19,* 4–24.

Stead, Philip J. (1983). *The police of France.* New York: Macmillan.

Sweatman, Beverly. (1989). New dimensions for international law enforcement: INTERPOL/State. *C. J. International, 5*(1), 14–15.

United Nations. (1990a). *Third United Nations survey of crime trends, operations of criminal justice systems and crime prevention strategies* (A/CONF.144/6). Vienna, Austria: UN Crime Prevention and Criminal Justice Branch.

United Nations. (1990b). *Crime prevention and criminal justice in the context of development: Realities and perspectives of international co-operation* (A/CONF.144/5). Vienna, Austria: UN Crime Prevention and Criminal Justice Branch.

United Nations. (1990c). *Proposals for concerted international action against forms of crime identified in the Milan Plan of Action* (A/CONF.144/7). Vienna, Austria: UN Crime Prevention and Criminal Justice Branch.

United Nations. (1990d). *Effective national and international action against: (a) organized crime; (b) terrorist criminal activity* (A/CONF.144/15). Vienna, Austria: UN Crime Prevention and Criminal Justice Branch.

van Dijk, Jan J.M., Mayhew, Pat, and Killias, Martin. (1990). *Experiences of crime across the world.* Boston: Kluwer.

Walsh, James. (1991, November 25). It's a steal. *Time, 138*(21), 86–88.

Chapter 3

An American Perspective on Criminal Law

KEY TOPICS

- Development of law in America
- The division of labor in society
- Essential ingredients of justice systems
- General characteristics of criminal law
- Major principles of criminal law

KEY TERMS

actus reus	mechanical solidarity
conflict approach	*mens rea*
concurrence	penal sanction
consensus approach	politicality
crime control model	presumption of guilt
due process model	presumption of innocence
factual guilt	procedural criminal law
legal guilt	specificity
mala prohibita	substantive criminal law
mala in se	uniformity

COUNTRIES REFERENCED

United States

As explained in Chapter 1, this book uses categorization and classification to describe various legal systems. However, to get to the point where classification is helpful, it is desirable to identify a basic foundation for all legal systems. After this is done, subsequent classification proceeds in a more logical fashion because it flows from a single source. To that end, this chapter centers on the basic components of any justice system: delineating the laws and specifying the manner of enforcement. The former, called *substantive law*, and the latter, *procedural law*, provide the common ingredients and basic foundation of any legal system. The way in which a society achieves the two objectives yields the variety found among the world's justice systems.

While our primary interest is studying that variety, we must remember that a benefit of an international perspective is a more accurate perception of our own legal system. Obviously, that position works only if our own system is sufficiently understood so that similarities and differences become apparent. It is assumed that readers of this text have more than a lay person's comprehension of the American system of criminal justice. Because of that assumption, detailed information about police, courts, and corrections in the United States is minimal. However, it is not so easy to assume that each reader has a similar level of knowledge regarding criminal law. Introductory level text books in criminal justice, for example, provide several chapters on American police, courts, and corrections. Those same books, however, seldom contain more than one chapter concerning criminal law itself. That is rather ironic, since it is criminal law that gives those other topics their "reason for being." Ironic or not, specifics of criminal law are seldom as well comprehended as are the terms and processes associated with American policing, adjudication, and punishment.

This chapter must accomplish two tasks. First, it needs to provide information helpful in establishing a common understanding of the basis for the American system of justice. Second, we must clearly understand and appreciate the essential ingredients of all justice systems: substantive and procedural criminal law. The second goal also relies on the American system as its explanatory vehicle since, in cyclical fashion, appreciation of other systems requires understanding of how our own operates. We begin the first task by looking at the history of criminal law in the United States and by developing a clear perception of its main components. This background will make it easier to see how today's system is similar to or different from historical America and contemporary foreign countries.

THE DEVELOPMENT OF LAW IN AMERICA

One of two perspectives usually orients discussion of criminal law's development in America. The consensus model argues that criminal laws evolved as a natural representation of the values and morals of American citizens. The conflict model suggests that criminal laws are the result of maneuvering by special interest groups to protect themselves, their position in society, and their property.

The Consensus Perspective

Figure 3-1 shows the results of a national survey that asked people to rate the severity of one type of crime in comparison to others. If you passed this list among your friends, family, and neighbors, and they each agreed with the ranking, you will have found an example of the consensus perspective. This approach believes that criminal law is a reflection of widely held beliefs and values in the society. Therefore, a country's criminal law represents social agreement (consensus) about what behavior is undesirable and deserving of punishment. An important base for this approach is the work of French sociologist Emile Durkheim (1964).

Durkheim, who wrote in the late 1800s, studied the nature of the social bonds holding people together in groups. He hypothesized that the division of

Figure 3-1. Ranking of offenses by severity score. *Source:* M. E. Wolfgang, R. M. Figlio, P. E. Tracy, and S. I. Singer, (1985). *The National Survey of Crime Severity.* Washington, D.C.: Department of Justice, Bureau of Justice Statistics.

72.1   A person plants a bomb in a public building. The bomb explodes and 20 people are killed.

52.8   A man forcibly rapes a woman. As a result of physical injuries, she dies.

47.8   A parent beats his young child with his fists. As a result, the child dies.

39.1   A factory knowingly gets rid of its waste in a way that pollutes the water supply of a city. As a result, 20 people die.

13.3   A person, armed with a lead pipe, robs a victim of $10. The victim is injured and requires hospitalization.

13.0   A factory knowingly gets rid of its waste in a way that pollutes the water supply of a city.

12.0   A person gives the floor plans of a bank to a bank robber.

11.8   A man beats a stranger with his fists. The victim requires hospitalization.

10.8   A person steals a locked car and sells it.

10.3   A person operates a store where he knowingly sells stolen property.

9.7   A person breaks into a school and steals equipment worth $1000.

9.6   A person breaks into a home and steals $1000.

9.4   A public official takes $1000 of public money for his own use.

8.3   A person illegally gets monthly welfare checks of $200.

8.0   A person steals an unlocked car and sells it.

7.7   Knowing that a shipment of cooking oil is bad, a store owner decides to sell it anyway.

7.5   A person, armed with a lead pipe, robs a victim of $10. No physical harm occurs.

7.3   A person beats a victim with his fists. The victim is hurt but does not require medical treatment.

7.3   A person breaks into a department store and steals merchandise worth $1000.

6.2   An employee embezzles $1000 from his employer.

6.1   A person cheats on his Federal income tax return and avoids paying $10,000 in taxes.

3.6   A person steals property worth $100 from outside a building.

3.3   A person picks a victim's pocket of $10.

1.9   An employee embezzles $10 from his employer.

1.7   A person is a customer in a place where he knows gambling occurs illegally.

1.1   A person disturbs the neighborhood with loud, noisy behavior.

0.8   A person under 16 years old runs away from home.

0.6   A person trespasses in the backyard of a private home.

labor (the number of different jobs done by different persons) in a society gave society its order, harmony, and solidarity. As a measure of that solidarity, Durkheim chose the type of law expressed in the society. Law, he believed, could be either repressive (the wrongdoer must suffer or lose something) or restitutive (attempts to return the wrongdoer to a productive societal role). The type of law used in a society depends on society's solidarity.

Durkheim argued that the primarily rural and agrarian early societies required little division of labor. Everyone had a similar job (for example, farming) and as a result had similar beliefs and values. After all, if an economic, political, or educational condition favored one farmer, it was likely to favor the others. Because of this similarity of ideas, beliefs, and values, the members of the society agreed on what behavior was good or bad. That agreement provided a strong base for social solidarity which, in this type of society, Durkheim called "mechanical." Their law was repressive, because it reflected those commonly held values. Anyone violating the norms offended each member of society.

With development of society comes an increase in the division of labor. Instead of everyone farming, some people are now bankers, merchants, and factory workers. No longer is a particular economic or political condition that benefits one person necessarily going to benefit all the others. The differences among the members of this "organic solidarity" society do not, however, mean that their society lacks cohesion. The specialization brought by the division of labor means that people are no longer self-sufficient. Now they must depend on each other for items they no longer own or produce. Because their cohesion comes from interdependence instead of commonly held beliefs, their law does not require repression of the wrongdoer. In fact, the offender may still be a necessary part of society. Restitutive law is more appropriate here, because the offender can be returned to society and fill a productive role.

Whether operating under mechanical or organic solidarity, citizens are in agreement concerning what behavior is appropriate in society. That consensus comes from the similarity of people in homogenous societies and the interdependence of people in heterogenous ones. In other words, villagers agree about the appropriateness of the laws in their community, because those laws reflect the villagers' commonly held values. Conversely, city dwellers may have values that differ from one another, but they remain in general agreement about the laws, because they understand that those norms keep society cohesive despite the friction brought by contrasting beliefs.

The Conflict Perspective

Look again at Figure 3-1 and consider what penalty might be attached to each example. If we assume that a society will punish more harshly those crimes it finds most serious, we can expect the level of punishment to decline with the severity of the crime. Interestingly, that assumption does not always hold true. Colorado, for example, punishes a public official taking $1000 of public money for his own use (severity ranking 9.4) at the same level (8-year maximum sentence) as a burglar who broke into a department store and stole $1000 of merchandise (severity ranking 7.3). A store owner knowingly selling bad cooking oil and a person who steals $100 in property from outside a building could both receive a maximum Colorado sentence of one year, despite the difference in their perceived severity (7.7 for cooking oil and 3.6 for theft).

That exercise is not really an appropriate use of the national survey, but it does suggest interesting questions. Why don't our punishments more closely correspond to our perception of the seriousness of crime? Why is criminal behavior by public officials and merchants punished similarly to that of burglars and thieves, despite the perception that illegal behavior by public officials and merchants is more serious? While we might find "consensus" among the public regarding the ranking of crimes, why is that consensus not reflected in the level of punishment for the offenses? If there are inconsistencies in the punishment–severity link, are there also inconsistencies in the enforcement–severity link? That is, are the offenses of public and corporate officials responded to differently than those of "street criminals?"

Those are the kinds of questions asked by theorists taking a conflict approach to the origin of criminal law. Conflict theorists believe that criminal law reflects the norms and values of particular groups of people, rather than values and norms shared by all society members. They view society as organized more on power, force, and constraint than on common values. Also, the unequal distribution of political influence means that some groups find it easier to pass laws and protect their interests. The conflict approach presents its position in several historical studies.

Chambliss (1964) used the conflict perspective to study the laws of vagrancy as they developed in England during the fourteenth century. His research linked those laws to the Black Plague, which struck England around 1348 and decimated the population. The great number of deaths reduced the supply of cheap labor just when serfdom was beginning to break down and peasants began to flee from the manor. Chambliss suggests that the vagrancy law enacted in 1349 had the purpose of forcing laborers to accept employment at a low wage to ensure that landowners had an adequate supply of cheap labor. The passage of that crisis placed the laws into dormancy until around 1530. At that time came an increased emphasis on commerce and industry. Again the vagrancy laws came into play. But now, they locked vagrants up, instead of putting them to work, since their idleness suggested potential criminality. Chambliss argues that the formulation of and later changes in the vagrancy laws were the result of efforts by powerful interest groups.

Michalowski (1985) explains the development of American criminal law from a conflict perspective. He notes that most of the prosecutions in the colonies were for offenses against the church or morals. The interest groups influencing our earliest laws, therefore, were religious ones. Yet Michalowski makes an interesting point by suggesting that what appears simply a moral concern at first also may have social order aspects. For example, the crimes of fornication, insolence, and disobedience appear only of moral concern until we remember that such behavior could cause serious problems for the elite in the colony. Besides being an act against God's will, fornication could add fatherless children to the community's economic burden. Insolence and disobedience were forms of immorality, but laws against such behavior protected the economic order by legally obliging servants and slaves to be subservient to their masters.

Colonial punishment exemplifies even more obvious economic links. In colonial Virginia, hogs were a more important source of income than were sheep. The laws reflected that prominence by making theft of hogs more serious than theft of sheep. In Maryland, it was a capital offense to burglarize a tobacco (an economically important crop) warehouse, but most other forms of burglary were not punishable by death (Michalowski, 1985).

After the American Revolution, our country experienced a steady rise in prosecutions for property crimes and a corresponding decline for moral offenses. With Massachusetts as an example, Michalowski notes that prior to the Revolution, over half the prosecutions were for moral offenses while 13 percent were for property crimes. By 1810, theft alone had increased to 50 percent of all prosecutions, while offenses against morals had dipped to scarcely 0.5 percent. A reason for this change, Michalowski argues, was a change in the interests to be protected. The Revolution placed elite property owners and entrepreneurs in control of the new government, and the interests they wanted protected were more economic than moral in nature.

Consensus and Conflict

Many people find aspects of both approaches to the origin of criminal law appealing. Cole (1986), for example, suggests that each can be of use. Laws prohibiting acts that are *mala in se* (bad in themselves), like murder, rape, and assault, seem best explained by consensus, since they can be found in most Western societies. Other laws are *mala prohibita* (bad because they are prohibited) like vagrancy and such so-called "victimless crimes" as gambling and prostitution. They seem better explained as a result of interest group manipulation. From this perspective the most reasonable position may be to say that some laws originate in social conflict but perpetuate through consensus.

Whether you accept a consensus, conflict, or combined view of how criminal law developed, the next concern must be more precise. That is, what is specifically created when we develop "criminal law?" That question's answer requires that attention be turned to the second task of this chapter: identification of a justice system's essential ingredients.

ESSENTIAL INGREDIENTS OF JUSTICE SYSTEMS

Two problems need resolving before any society can implement an institutionalized pattern of criminal justice. First, the laws must be delineated. Next, the manner of enforcement must be specified. As noted at the start of this chapter, the way a society resolves these problems involves the essential ingredients of any legal system. These activities are of equal importance and provide a sound basis for diagraming the basic foundation of legal systems. But simply stating the existence of this foundation is not sufficient. To allow comparison and contrast, it is necessary to examine those ingredients more closely. That examination is aided by identifying key features of each ingredient.

Figures 3-2 and 3-3 illustrate the essential ingredients and their key features in terms of a justice paradigm. As those figures show, an institutionalized pattern of justice rests on the definition of rules (substantive law) and the determination of their enforcement (procedural law). In turn, delineation of rules specifies the requirements to be met for something to qualify as a law and the criteria used in deciding if a particular behavior is criminal (see Figure 3-2). The first condition, requirements to qualify as a law, can be called the *general characteristics* of law. The second condition, determining if a particular behavior is criminal, comprises the *major principles* of law. Importantly, both the general characteristics and the major principles are discussed here in terms of law in Western nations. Although it hints of ethnocentrism, such tunnel vision is necessary at this point to assure us of having a common base from which to view the law and legal systems in other countries.

Just as we can analyze two aspects of the definition of laws, we can also bifurcate the manner in which the rules are implemented (see Figure 3-3). The rules can be activated to emphasize repressing rule violation (crime control model) or to contain the system's level of intrusion into the citizen's life (due

Figure 3-2.   Substantive law.

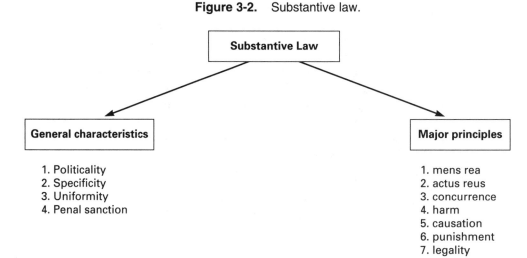

Crime Control Model	Due Process Model
Assumes freedom is so important that every effort must be made to repress crime.	Assumes freedom is so important that every effort must be made to ensure that government intrusion follows legal procedure.
Seeks to make decisions that will identify factual guilt.	Seeks to make decisions that will identify legal guilt.
Follows rules that emphasize the repression of criminal activity.	Follows rules that emphasize containing the government's level of intrusion into citizens' lives.
Emphasizes efficiency of action (i.e., speed and finality).	Emphasizes legitimacy of action.
Requires a high rate of apprehension and conviction by early exclusion of those not likely to be guilty.	Insists on a formal, adjudicative, adversarial fact-finding process even though such restraints may keep the process from operating with maximal efficiency.

Figure 3-3. Procedural law.

process model). As Packer (1968) presents those two models, they are less bound to specific legal systems than are the characteristics and principles of criminal law. Therefore, the comments below about procedural law are applicable to a wider range of legal systems than is the following analysis of substantive law.

Substantive Criminal Law

An interest in the manner in which definitions of criminal behavior evolve is a concern of substantive law. *Black's Law Dictionary* defines substantive law as "that part of law which creates, defines, and regulates rights." The penal or criminal code of each state provides examples of these laws.

The Criminal Code of Colorado, for example, defines Robbery as:

(1) A person who knowingly takes anything of value from the person or presence of another by the use of force, threats, or intimidation commits robbery.

(2) Robbery is a class 4 felony. (*Criminal Code of Colorado*, 1981).

Georgia, on the other hand, has this definition:

(a) A person commits the offense of robbery when, with intent to commit theft, he takes property of another from the person or the immediate presence of another:

(1) By use of force;

(2) By intimidation, by the use of threat or coercion, or by placing such person in fear of immediate serious bodily injury to himself or to another; or

(3) By sudden snatching.

(b) A person convicted of the offense of robbery shall be punished by imprisonment for not less than one nor more than 20 years. (*Criminal Code of Georgia*, 1982).

Notice that in addition to defining (at different lengths) what constitutes the crime of robbery, the statements also specify what punishment will be attached to that crime. A class 4 felony in Colorado requires a sentence of at least two but no more than eight years. Although both states are defining the crime of robbery, the definitions and punishment vary. Despite the differences, both are examples of substantive law, because they each serve two purposes: (1) they define the behavior subject to punishment by the government, and (2) they specify what the punishment will be for those committing that offense.

Such definitions are not easily arrived at. Many criteria must be met before a definition qualifies to be a criminal law. Even more standards are necessary before a specific act is considered to be criminal. Consider, for example, the development of the law of theft. As explained by Hall, the law of theft provides an example of how something comes to be defined as illegal, and emphasizes how the definition can change over time.

Hall notes that prior to the fifteenth century the crime of theft essentially referred to the taking of property without the owner's consent. Today, it has a broader meaning and encompasses acts wherein property was lawfully obtained but then appropriated for the taker's own use (for example, swindling, embezzlement, misappropriation). The turning point came in the English "Carrier's Case" of 1473. The defendant (the carrier) was hired to carry certain bales (probably wool, cloth, or both) to Southampton. "Instead of fulfilling his obligation, he carried the goods to another place, broke open the bales and took the contents. He was apprehended and charged with a felony" (Hall, 1952, p. 4).

Today, the felony charge of theft seems only reasonable. Then, however, common law recognized no criminality in a person who came legally into possession of an item and then converted the item to his own use. The reasoning behind such a position was that the owner of transported goods was responsible for protecting himself by employing trustworthy persons. If his trust turned out to be misplaced, it was unfortunate but not illegal. After all, trespass (unlawful interference with a person's property) was an essential part of the definition of theft. It seemed impossible for a person to commit trespass upon items he possessed.

Despite what would appear to be an ironclad defense, the court eventually found the defendant guilty of larceny. The verdict was based on reasoning by Justice Choke (one of three justices hearing the case), who argued: "I think that where a man has goods in his possession by reason of a bailment he cannot take them feloniously, being in possession; but still it seems here that it is felony, for here the things which were within the bales were not bailed to him, only the bales as an entire thing were bailed" (quoted in Hall, 1952, p. 9). In other words, the defendant had legal possession of the bales but not of the contents of those bales. The defendant could have sold the bales intact or left the bales unopened in his house, but when he opened them and took the contents, he committed a felony.

Hall suggests that this new interpretation of what constitutes larceny was a result of changing social conditions and pressing social interests. Specifically, Hall notes political and economic conditions that preceded and possibly influenced the outcome of the Carrier's Case. First, consider the political conditions. The King at the time was Edward IV, who, like his predecessor Henry VI, occasionally "consulted" with judges before they handed down a decision. Hall reviews the comments of several chroniclers of the time and concludes that Edward IV was likely to interfere with decisions made at several court levels.

With these political considerations, Hall also emphasizes important economic ones. The Carrier's Case occurred at a time when the economic structure of England was dramatically changing. Alteration of the manorial system and the destruction of serfdom preceded England's movement to a situation where more than 3000 merchants were engaged in foreign trade as the sixteenth century began. Hall suggests that it would be hard to believe that, as the old feudal structure based on agriculture gave way to a new order based on industry and trade, the king would be standing by as a casual observer. Edward IV, supportive of merchants and of trade relations with other countries, was himself a merchant engaged in many private ventures. With this background, and because the merchant "stolen" from was foreign, Hall believes that Edward IV had good reason to use this case as one requiring his "consultation" with the justices.

Hall draws it together in the following manner:

> We are now in a position to visualize the case and the problem presented to the judges as a result of the legal, political, and economic conditions described above. On the one hand, the criminal law at the time is clear. On the other hand, the whole complex aggregate of political and economic conditions described above thrusts itself upon the court. The more powerful forces prevailed—that happened which in due course must have happened under the circumstances. The most powerful forces of the time were interrelated very intimately and at many points: The New Monarchy and the *nouveau riche*—the mercantile class; the business interests of both and the consequent need for a secure carrying trade; the wool and textile industry, the most valuable, by far, in all the realm; wool and cloth, the most exports; these exports and the foreign trade; this trade and Southampton, chief trading city with the Latin countries for centuries; the numerous and very influential Italian merchants who bought English wool and cloth inland and shipped them from Southampton. The great forces of an emerging modern world, represented in the above phenomena, necessitated the elimination of a formula which had outgrown its usefulness. A new set of major institutions required a new rule. The law, lagging behind the needs of the times, was brought into more harmonious relationship with the other institutions by the decision rendered in the Carrier's Case (1952, p. 33)

The difficulty in defining something as criminal has led some legal theorists to explain substantive criminal law by reference to its general characteristics and its major principles. A review of those characteristics and principles allows us to appreciate the complexity of our legal system.

General Characteristics of Criminal Law. Four conditions comprise the general characteristics of Western criminal law: politicality, specificity, uniformity, and penal sanction (Sutherland and Cressey, 1978). If any of these four is not present, the activity prohibited or required cannot be called criminal. *Politicality* refers to the fact that only violations of rules made by a government authority can be crimes. Rules can be made by many groups and individuals. A basketball coach can tell her players what time they must be in their dorm room; an employer can tell his employee what to wear to work; a teacher can require students to prepare a paper following a certain typing format. If players, employees, and students violate those rules, they may be subjected to punishment for having done so. They have not, however, committed a crime, since a governmental authority did not make the rules.

For people to know in advance what particular behavior they must do (for example, in some states citizens must come to the aid of a police officer upon request) or refrain from doing (for example, shoplifting), criminal law must be *specific*. Korn and McCorkle (1959) relate an example of a case (*McBoyle* v. *United States*, 283 U.S. 25, 1931) in which the defendant had his conviction of interstate transportation of a stolen airplane set aside. The trial court convicted McBoyle under a statute prohibiting the taking of a motor vehicle or "any other self-propelled vehicle." Because of the airplane's relatively recent invention, the Supreme Court believed such words as "self-propelled vehicle" still brought to many people's mind a picture of vehicles moving on land rather than through the air. Since the legislature had not specifically included airplanes in the statute, their theft was not prohibited. In a 1945 Virginia case (cited in Hall, 1960, p. 39) a court set aside a charge of disorderly conduct on a bus because the statute specified only car, train, or caboose. While each of these examples may cause some people to wince at the "technicality" of the law, it is important to consider Justice Holmes's remarks in the McBoyle case:

> It is reasonable that a fair warning should be given to the world in language that the common world will understand, of what the law intends to do if a certain line is passed. To make the warning fair, so far as possible the line should be clear (cited in Korn and McCorkle, 1959, p. 103).

Criminal liability should be *uniform* for all persons despite social background or status. The definition of a crime should not allow one kind of person to commit the act without blame while legally sanctioning a different category of person for the same behavior.

Finally, to qualify as criminal law there must be some punishment that the government will administer. Without a *penal sanction* the rule becomes more of a guideline than a crime. It may seem strange that a government would try to make some behavior criminal without providing a punishment for that behavior, but it has happened. For example, some states define adultery as a crime but provide no criminal punishment for its occurrence. Since it can be used in civil court as a basis for divorce, the states believe that it serves a purpose. The following definition of criminal law incorporates each condition:

> A body of specific rules regarding human conduct which have been promulgated by political authority, which apply uniformly to all members of the classes to which the rules refer, and which are enforced by punishment administered by the state (see Sutherland and Cressey, 1978, p. 6).

As neat and concise as all that sounds, it is obvious when we look at our criminal laws that the above is an ideal definition. Further, it is an ideal relating more generally to Western legal systems and to the American system particularly. There is no requirement that "law" in general needs to be specific or have a sanction before citizens of some society view it as law. Similarly, politicality becomes problematic when, for example, a revolutionary tribunal enforces its decrees. Even uniformity is breached in the United States when we direct laws to specific categories of people, such as prohibiting some citizens from disobeying authority figures, skipping school, or leaving home, because they are under a certain age.

Despite such problems, these criteria are appropriate and a generally fair description of what constitutes criminal law in much of Western society and in several other places as well. For our purposes, they provide a context and terminology that will be helpful as we look at other legal systems.

Major Principles of Criminal Law. There are different criteria to be met in deciding if a particular behavior is criminal. Something that is often hard for the lay person (and even criminal justice employees) to understand is why or how a defendant who seems so obviously guilty can avoid prosecution. At times an explanation lies in the absence of one or more of the following conditions. Jerome Hall (1960) has suggested seven criteria as comprising the major principles of Western law: *mens rea*, act (*actus reus*), concurrence, harm, causation, punishment, and legality. Mueller summarized these by suggesting that crime refers to legally proscribed (legality) human conduct (act), causative (causation) of a given harm (harm), which conduct coincides (concurrence) with a blameworthy frame of mind (*mens rea*) and which is subject to punishment (punishment) (Hall and Mueller, 1965).

The requirement for a guilty act (*actus reus*) reminds us that having bad intentions is not enough. Behavior is criminal only (with exceptions noted below) when the individual acts in a prohibited way or fails to act in a required way. In addition, that behavior must be linked in a causal way to some harm considered detrimental to social interests. Consider the following illustration. Suppose that John poisoned Bob with every intent to kill him. Bob is taken to the hospital, where he recovers from the poison but dies of the antidote. Although John's overt act was the necessary first link in the chain of events culminating in Bob's death, it was not John's act that caused the harm (death). Instead, another event (administration of the fatal antidote) intervened between that first link and the final result. John could, of course, still be guilty of several other crimes, such as assault or maybe attempted murder. But, as Korn and McCorkle (1959) point out, this principle has been the basis for successful appeals in homicide cases where victims died of negligent medical care instead of the bullet that caused the need for the care in the first place.

The requirement for a guilty mind (*mens rea*) can be difficult to understand because of confusion between motivation and intent. A young boy may be motivated to take food from a grocery store without paying because his family is starving. Although some see that as an acceptable motivation, the criminal law cares only about the boy's intention. His intent, clearly, was to steal. His motivation may be considered by the store owner, police, prosecutor, and judge as they decide what action to take. But as far as criminal law is concerned, the boy intended to take another person's property without paying and has therefore stolen.

The existence of a harmful act and the presence of *mens rea* are not enough to show that a crime has occurred. It also must be shown (with exceptions noted below) that there was fusion of intent and conduct (that is, concurrence). Consider a strange case that Hall (1960) relates. In 1896 an Ohio medical student tried to kill a young woman with whom he had been having an affair. He gave her a large dose of cocaine in Ohio, believing the cocaine would kill her then and there. He then took what he believed to be her dead body into Kentucky, where he decapitated it. Medical evidence established that the woman had been alive at the time of the decapitation in Kentucky. A Kentucky court found the man guilty of murder (*Jackson v. Commonwealth*, 100 Ky. 239, 1896), but Hall makes a point relevant to our discussion. An argument can be made that there was no intention to kill or injure a human being at the time of the decapitation, since the man believed that the woman was already dead. Hall suggests that since the court believed the defendant thought she was dead when he decapitated her, the court should have found that the *mens rea* did not concur with the actual killing. On that basis, Hall believes, the court decision was wrong, since it violated the principle of concurrence.

As we look over these seven conditions for crime, it becomes easier to appreciate the difficult job that attorneys, judges, and juries sometimes have in determining if and how these things fit together. As if the task were not difficult enough, there are some exceptions to those conditions that may come into play. For example, we modify the requirement that a harm must be caused by some behavior, so *attempts* and *conspiracy* are themselves crimes. Also, the requirement of *mens rea* is modified in strict liability cases, which consider the individual responsible despite intent. Most strict liability laws concern public welfare offenses (sale of adulterated food, violations of building regulations), but some relate to serious felonies (Hall, 1960). An example would be the felony-murder rule found in some states. If a death occurs while the offender is committing a felony, that offender may be held criminally responsible for the death even if there was no intent on his part to kill the victim.

Despite those instances of strict liability, intent is an essential part of our legal conception of criminal responsibility. In cases where intent is absent, the defendant is not criminally responsible for an act that would otherwise be a crime. For example, many of us would not define as criminal a five-year-old child who opens the mailboxes in his apartment complex and throws his neighbors' mail into his wagon to empty later in the sandbox. We also might question a legal system that brings charges of assault against a woman who caused great physical harm to a man trying to rape her. In each example our objection seems based on the belief that the child and the woman were not responsible for the acts, though they may have constituted a crime. We may even smile with a sense of self-satisfaction that we live under a system where such behavior can be excused or justified in appropriate cases. Problems arise, however, when presenting cases not so clear-cut. What would we think if that boy had been 10 instead of 5, or maybe 15? What if the man were unarmed, smaller, and physically weaker than the woman, yet she chose to protect herself by shooting him? The question of responsibility in these situations will not result in as much agreement among us. The Model Penal Code (American Law Institute, 1985) notes seven generally recognized defenses based on absence of criminal intent (see Figure 3-4). Each state will phrase the defense in its own way and may not even have all seven. One, insanity, is commonly found and provides a good example of one way to approach the question of responsibility.

Under Anglo-Saxon law and well into the thirteenth century, the mentally deranged were treated much like any other criminal. Eventually "insanity" was accepted as a condition negating blameworthiness. But deciding what constituted insanity remained a problem. The "wild beast test" developed in the thirteenth century was among the first methods used. It said that a madman was one "'who does not know what he is doing, who is lacking in mind and reason, and who is not far removed from the brutes'" (Hall, 1960, p. 475). The first long-lasting criteria for determining insanity came in 1843. In that year a court found Daniel M'Naghten not guilty of murdering of Edward Drummond because M'Naghten was suffering from delusions. Specifically, M'Naghten felt pursued by several enemies including Sir Robert Peel, who was England's prime minister at the time. M'Naghten killed Drummond while believing that Drummond was actually Peel. The public outcry in response to the acquittal resulted in a request by the House of Lords for the judges of the Queen's Bench to present their views of the insanity defense. Their response, considered by the judges to be a restatement of existing law rather than an innovation (Hall, 1960), was called the M'Naghten rules. They established a "right from wrong" test with the following necessary to show insanity: (1) At the time of the crime the defendant was operating under a defect of reason so as to be unable to know the nature or quality of the act, or (2) If the defendant was aware of the act's nature, he did not know the act was wrong (see Moran, 1985).

Section 2.04. Ignorance or Mistake
1. Ignorance or mistake as to a matter of fact or law is a defense if:
a. the ignorance or mistake negatives the purpose, knowledge, belief, recklessness or negligence required to establish a material element of the offense; or
b. the law provides that the state of mind established by such ignorance or mistake constitutes a defense.
2. Although ignorance or mistake would otherwise afford a defense to the offense charged, the defense is not available if the defendant would be guilty of another offense had the situation been as he supposed. In such case, however, the ignorance or mistake of the defendant shall reduce the grade and degree of the offense of which he may be convicted to those of the offense of which he would be guilty had the situation been as he supposed.
3. A belief that conduct does not legally constitute an offense is a defense to a prosecution for that offense based upon such conduct when:
a. the statute or other enactment defining the offense is not known to the actor and has not been published or otherwise reasonably made available prior to the conduct alleged; or
b. he acts in reasonable reliance upon an official statement of the law, afterward determined to be invalid or erroneous, contained in (i) a statute or other enactment; (ii) a judicial decision, opinion or judgment; (iii) an administrative order or grant of permission; or (iv) an official interpretation of the public officer or body charged by law with responsibility for the interpretation, administration or enforcement of the law defining the offense.
4. The defendant must prove a defense arising under Subsection (3) of this Section by a preponderance of evidence.

Section 2.08. Intoxication.
1. Except as provided in Subsection (4) of this Section, intoxication of the actor is not a defense unless it negatives an element of the offense.
2. When recklessness establishes an element of the offense, if the actor, due to self-induced intoxication, is unaware of a risk of which he would have been aware had he been sober, such unawareness is immaterial.
3. Intoxication does not, in itself, constitute mental disease within the meaning of Section 4.01.
4. Intoxication that (a) is not self-induced or (b) is pathological is an affirmative defense if by reason of such intoxication the actor at the time of his conduct lacks substantial capacity either to appreciate its criminality [wrongfulness] or to conform his conduct to the requirements of law.

Section 2.09. Duress.
1. It is an affirmative defense that the actor engaged in the conduct charged to constitute an offense because he was coerced to do so by the use of, or a threat to use, unlawful force against his person or the person of another, that a person of reasonable firmness in his situation would have been unable to resist.
2. The defense provided by this Section is unavailable if the actor recklessly placed himself in a situation in which it was probable that he would be subjected to duress. The defense is also unavailable if he was negligent in placing himself in such a situation, whenever negligence suffices to establish culpability for the offense charged.
3. It is not a defense that a woman acted on the command of her husband, unless she acted under such coercion as would establish a defense under this Section. [The presumption that a woman acting in the presence of her husband is coerced is abolished.]
4. When the conduct of the actor would otherwise be justifiable under Section 3.02, this Section does not preclude such defense.

Figure 3-4. Model penal code defenses to crime. *Source: Model Penal Code*, Official draft. Copyright 1985 by The American Law Institute. Reprinted with the permission of the American Law Institute.

Section 2.13. Entrapment.
1. A public law enforcement official or a person acting in cooperation with such an official perpetrates an entrapment if for the purpose of obtaining evidence of the commission of an offense, he induces or encourages another person to engage in conduct constituting such offense by either:
a. making knowingly false representations designed to induce the belief that such conduct is not prohibited; or
b. employing methods of persuasion or inducement that create a substantial risk that such an offense will be committed by persons other than those who are ready to commit it.
2. Except as provided in Subsection (3) of this Section, a person prosecuted for an offense shall be acquitted if he proves by a preponderance of evidence that his conduct occurred in response to an entrapment. The issue of entrapment shall be tried by the Court in the absence of the jury.
3. The defense afforded by this Section is unavailable when causing or threatening bodily injury is an element of the offense charged and the prosecution is based on conduct causing or threatening such injury to a person other than the person perpetrating the entrapment.

Section 3.02. Justification Generally: Choice of Evils.
1. Conduct that the actor believes to be necessary to avoid a harm or evil to himself or to another is justifiable, provided that:
a. the harm or evil sought to be avoided by such conduct is greater than that sought to be prevented by the law defining the offense charged; and
b. neither the Code nor other law defining the offense provides exceptions or defenses dealing with the specific situation involved; and
c. a legislative purpose to exclude the justification claimed does not otherwise plainly appear.
2. When the actor was reckless or negligent in bringing about the situation requiring a choice of harms or evils or in appraising the necessity for his conduct, the justification afforded by the Section is unavailable in a prosecution for any offense for which recklessness or negligence, as the case may be, suffices to establish culpability.

Section 3.04. Use of Force in Self-Protection.
1. Use of Force Justifiable for Protection of the Person. . . . the use of force upon or toward another person is justifiable when the actor believes that such force is immediately necessary for the purpose of protecting himself against the use of unlawful force by such other person on the present occasion.
2. Limitations on Justifying Necessity for Use of Force.
a. The use of force is not justifiable under this Section:
i. to resist an arrest that the actor knows is being made by a peace officer, although the arrest is unlawful; or
ii. to resist force used by the occupier or possessor of property or by another person on his behalf, where the actor knows that the person using the force is doing so under a claim of right to protect the property . . ..
b. The use of deadly force is not justifiable under this Section unless the actor believes that such force is necessary to protect himself against death, serious bodily injury, kidnapping or sexual intercourse compelled by force or threat; nor is it justifiable if:
i. the actor, with the purpose of causing death or serious bodily injury, provoked the use of force against himself in the same encounter; or
ii. the actor knows that he can avoid the necessity of using such force with complete safety by retreating or by surrendering possession of a thing to a person asserting a claim of right thereto or by complying with a demand that he abstain from any action that he has no duty to take. . . .

Section 4.01. Mental Disease or Defect Excluding Responsibility.
1. A person is not responsible for criminal conduct if at the time of such conduct as a result of

Figure 3-4.   (continued)

mental disease or defect he lacks substantial capacity either to appreciate the criminality [wrongfulness] of his conduct or to conform his conduct to the requirements of law.
2. As used in this Article, the terms "mental disease or defect" do not include an abnormality manifested only by repeated criminal or otherwise antisocial conduct.

Section 4.10. Immaturity Excluding Criminal Conviction; Transfer of Proceedings to Juvenile Court.
1. A person shall not be tried for or convicted of an offense if:
a. at the time of the conduct charged to constitute the offense he was less than sixteen years of age [in which case the Juvenile Court shall have exclusive jurisdiction]; or
b. at the time of the conduct charged to constitute the offense he was sixteen or seventeen years of age, unless:
i. the Juvenile Court has no jurisdiction over him, or
ii. the Juvenile Court has entered an order waiving jurisdiction and consenting to the institution of criminal proceedings against him.
2. No court shall have jurisdiction to try or convict a person of an offense if criminal proceedings against him are barred by Subsection (1) of this Section. When it appears that a person charged with the commission of an offense may be of such an age that criminal proceedings may be barred under Subsection (1) of this Section, the Court shall hold a hearing thereon, and the burden shall be on the prosecution to establish to the satisfaction of the Court that the criminal proceeding is not barred upon such grounds. If the Court determines that the proceeding is barred, custody of the person charged shall be surrendered to the Juvenile Court, and the case, including all papers and processes relating thereto, shall be transferred.

Figure 3-4.   (continued)

From the 1850s to the 1970s the M'Naghten rule was the primary means for determining insanity in the federal and most state courts in the United States. Some states supplemented M'Naghten with an "irresistible impulse" test that assumed that people may have known their act was wrong but they could not control the impulse to commit it. Sometimes called the "policeman-at-the-elbow" test, the irresistible impulse modification accepts the "right versus wrong" concept but understands that persons may have such a compulsion to commit a crime that they would do so even if they knew the act was wrong and a police officer was present and watching.

Today less than 20 states still use the M'Naghten rule (with or without the irresistible impulse modification), whereas nearly half the states follow the definition adopted by the American Law Institute. This ALI test (also called the Brawner rule from *U.S.* v. *Brawner*, 1972) is section 4.01 of the Model Penal Code (see Figure 3-4). Under this standard, a criminal defendant is not responsible for acts resulting from a mental disease or defect wherein the actor lacked substantial capacity either to appreciate (rather than "know" under M'Naghten) the wrong of his ways or to conform his conduct to the law.

The difficulty of deciding whether a lack of criminal responsibility is best linked to not knowing right from wrong, to mental disease or defect, or to irresistible impulses, is a continuing problem. Since the much-criticized verdict finding John Hinckley, Jr. not guilty by reason of insanity in the attempted assassination of President Reagan, the federal government and many states have sought modification and even abolition of insanity defenses. At the federal level, the Insanity Defense Reform Act of 1984 set a new criterion for determining insanity in federal criminal trials. In many ways it is a return to the M'Naghten rules, since the defendant must be shown to have been unable to appreciate the wrongfulness of his acts. But it also borrows from the ALI test in linking the inability to appreciate wrongfulness to a severe mental disease or defect. In another important modification of previous standards, the Insanity Defense Reform Act requires that the defense prove insanity. Previously, the burden of proof fell on the state to show that the defendant was sane. Now, in the federal courts, defendants can be required to prove their insanity, thus making such a plea more difficult.

Some states have adopted the new federal guidelines, but others have chosen to make the insanity defense even more difficult, or even impossible. In 1982 Idaho provided an example of the latter position when it abolished the insanity defense (Geis and Meier, 1985). By 1988, two other states (Montana and Utah) had followed Idaho's lead (Department of Justice, 1988). Under the Idaho statute defendants can be examined before trial to determine if they are fit to proceed to trial. If not, they are placed in a mental facility until such time that they can adequately participate in their defense. Defendants found fit to go to trial are subject to only two kinds of verdicts: guilty or not guilty. If the defendant is found guilty, his or her mental condition can be considered for sentencing purposes (Geis and Meier, 1985).

When one country interprets the importance of intent and criminal responsibility in such a variety of ways, we must expect similar variation among nations. Although the substantive law in each country invariably addresses such issues as responsibility, there are differences in how that concept is interpreted and incorporated. If we remember the example of the insanity plea and its variations in the United States, we will be better able to understand differences in issues of substantive law under other legal systems.

Procedural Criminal Law

Substantive criminal law was conveniently divided into its general characteristics and major principles. Similarly, as Figure 3-3 describes, procedural criminal law also has two components. However, while general characteristics and major principles theoretically carry equal weight in substantive law, the bifurcation of procedural law results in two components that are unlikely to be found in equal proportion. Instead, procedural criminal law is likely to emphasize one philosophy over the other at any given time.

The Due Process Model and Crime Control Model were described by Packer (1968) as separate value systems competing for priority in the operation of the criminal process. While neither is said to correspond to reality or represent a best approach, they are effectively used to understand the operation of the process. In that manner, the models provide a technique for discussing a variety of criminal justice systems. Since neither model is deemed better than the other, procedural law in different justice systems can be described without making value judgments. Chapter 5 takes exactly that approach. However, as noted earlier, gaining an international perspective is benefited by establishing a parochial base. Therefore, we will see how Packer's models help us understand American procedural law so that we can more fully appreciate the workings of procedural law in other countries. We begin by reviewing aspects of the American Constitution that relate to the criminal process.

Constitutional Provisions for the Criminal Process. After creation of the new Constitution of the United States, some framers expressed concern that the document contained the seeds of a tyranny by government. Discussion focused on adding a bill of rights to restrict the powers of the new federal government. Thomas Jefferson favored such a declaration of rights when he wrote to James Madison:

> Let me add that a bill of rights is what the people are entitled to against every government on earth, general or particular, and what no just government should refuse. . . (Boyd, 1955, p. 440). The inconveniences of the Declaration [of Rights] are that it may cramp government in it's (*sic*) useful exertions. But the evil of this is short-lived, moderate, and reparable. [The absence, however, of a Declaration is] permanent, afflicting, and irreparable (Boyd, 1958, p. 660).

The proponents' voices were so strong that the first Congress to meet following the adoption of the new Constitution submitted 12 amendments for consideration by the states. Ten of those were ratified by 1791 and they have become known as the Bill of Rights. For purposes of criminal law, the Fourth, Fifth, Sixth, and Eighth Amendments have particular relevance. The others are not unconnected to criminal law, but typically have a more tangential link. For example, the First Amendment references to restrictions on religion, speech, press, assembly, and petition has been the source of controversy in trial proceedings (conflicts between a free press and a fair trial) and confinement of prisoners (may a satanist practice his religion while in prison?).

In the interest of focus, we will highlight only the Fourth and Fifth Amendments. The Sixth (providing for such things as the right to a speedy and public trial before an impartial jury, and for the assistance of counsel) and the Eighth (prohibiting excessive bail, excessive fines, and cruel and unusual punishment) are relevant to procedural law but involve topics more appropriate for other sections of this book. However, before addressing the Fourth and Fifth Amendments, there is one other to note. When drafted, the U.S. Constitution was not intended to protect individual citizens from the unfair enforcement of *state* laws. In the spirit of states' rights, and with greater fear of the federal government than of the state government, citizens expressed interest in controlling in the closest thing they had to a monarch and Parliament. That the Bill of Rights limited only the federal government was made most clear by Chief Justice Marshall in the *Barron* v. *Baltimore* (1833) decision:

Had the framers of these amendments intended them to be limitations on the powers of state governments, they would have imitated the framers of the original Constitution, and have expressed that intention. . . . These amendments demanded security against the apprehended encroachments of the general government—not against those of the local governments (quoted in Cole, 1986, p. 92).

That view held until after the Civil War, when protection of citizen rights gained new concern and attention. The Thirteenth Amendment abolished slavery, but in response to continued violation of rights, Congress adopted the Fourteenth Amendment in 1868. The portion of the amendment affecting criminal justice reads: "No State shall . . . deprive any person of life, liberty, or property, without due process of law. . . ." Since the amendment's adoption, the meaning of the phrase "due process" has been a point of controversy. One resolution rests on the theory that the provisions of the Bill of Rights are *incorporated* into the due process clause of the Fourteenth Amendment and therefore applicable to the states as well as the federal government. This legal theory has served as the basis for many U.S. Supreme Court decisions. The Court selectively has made certain Bill of Rights stipulations binding on state governments. In this manner, the U.S. Supreme Court can tell any state how to proceed (due process) when trying to deprive a citizen of life, liberty, or property. Because of the Fourteenth Amendment the procedural conditions of the Fourth and Fifth Amendments must be followed by state governments in criminal proceedings.

The Fourth Amendment says, "the right of the people to be secure in their persons, houses, papers, and effects, against unreasonable searches and seizures, shall not be violated, and no warrants shall issue, but upon probable cause, supported by oath or affirmation, and particularly describing the place to be searched and the persons or things to be seized."

Importantly, this amendment does not prohibit *all* searches. Only those that are unreasonable are not allowed. The problem becomes one of defining "unreasonable" and, by implication, "reasonable." Since the 1960s, the United States Supreme Court has dealt with the question in the context of "searches and seizures" by the police. One type of police procedure governed by the Fourth Amendment would be the stopping and frisking of a citizen. In *Terry* v. *Ohio* (1968), for example, the U.S. Supreme Court held that police could stop and search three men whom the officer had observed prowling in front of some store windows. The search produced guns on two of the men, and the justices said the search was a *reasonable* precaution for the officer's safety. Further, after lawfully arresting a person, the police may conduct a "search incident to the arrest" to include the surrounding space in which a suspect could reasonably be expected to obtain a weapon or destroy evidence (see *Chimel* v. *California*, 1969).

Independent of, yet associated with, the Fourth Amendment is the judicially developed regulation known as the "exclusionary rule." In the 1961 case of *Mapp* v. *Ohio* the U.S. Supreme Court held that state courts must, just as the federal courts had been doing since 1914, exclude from trial any evidence obtained in violation of the privileges guaranteed by the U.S. Constitution. Such violations have come to include such things as an absence of a warrant, lack of probable cause to arrest, or the use of a defective warrant. In addition, under the "fruits of the poisonous tree" doctrine, evidence generated by or directly obtained from an illegal search also must be excluded. The primary purpose of the exclusionary rule was to deter police misconduct or, when misconduct occurred, to return the "case" against a suspect to its position prior to the violation.

It is not comforting to hear about the release of an "obviously guilty" person because the evidence gathered against him cannot be used at trial. This is particularly troublesome when the violation is something trivial, such as an incorrect warrant form. One result of efforts to modify the exclusionary rule has been a "good faith exception," which the U.S. Supreme Court put forth in *United States* v. *Leon* (1984). The Court ruled that evidence obtained through an illegal warrant need not be excluded at trial if the police can show that they got the evidence while reasonably believing they were acting according to the law. The extension of the good faith exception to include warrantless cases has not been decided by the Court, but in 1988 the House of Representatives added such an exception to the Omnibus Drug Initiative by a 259 to 134 vote. Its impact has yet to be tested, but it does reflect a public desire to continue movement away from a strict application of the exclusionary rule.

According to the Fifth Amendment, "no person shall be held to answer for a capital or otherwise infamous crime, unless on a presentment or indictment of a Grand Jury . . . nor shall any person be subject for the same offense to be twice put in jeopardy of life or limb; nor shall be compelled in any criminal case to be a witness against himself, nor be deprived of life, liberty, or property, without due process of law. . . ."

Obviously, there are several aspects of the Fifth Amendment that relate to procedural criminal law, but we will consider only that section regarding compelled self-incrimination. Consistent with the adversarial process and its requirement that the state must prove the defendant's guilt, the protection against compelled self-incrimination links to the Fourth Amendment's prohibition against unreasonable search and seizure and the Sixth Amendment's right to counsel. In the context of the Fifth Amendment, self-incrimination is interpreted more specifically in reference to whether a confession was voluntary and not coerced, and whether due process was followed while a confession was obtained. This second point, the process followed in obtaining a confession, was addressed in a 1966 U.S. Supreme Court decision.

On the evening of March 3, 1963, an 18-year-old girl was abducted and forcibly raped in Phoenix, Arizona. Ten days later, police arrested Ernesto Miranda at his home, took him to the police station, and placed him in a lineup. The victim immediately identified Miranda, who was then placed in a room and interrogated by the police. After two hours of interrogation, Miranda signed a confession, admitting that he had seized the girl and raped her. At the trial, defense counsel pointed out that the police did not tell Miranda about his right to counsel and to have counsel present during the interrogation (a point decided earlier in *Escobedo* v. *Illinois*, 1964). Miranda was convicted, but on appeal the U.S. Supreme Court overturned the conviction (*Miranda* v. *Arizona*, 1966) and ruled that the confession (self-incrimination) could not be used, because the police did not tell Miranda of his right to remain silent. The Court specified the procedural safeguards to be followed before statements made during a custodial interrogation can be used against the defendant. Those safeguards have become known as the *Miranda* warnings. In general, individuals who are in police custody, and are being interrogated, must be advised of their rights before any statement they make can be used against them. Police custody refers to the restraint of a person's freedom in any significant way. Interrogation refers to questioning initiated by law enforcement authorities to elicit an incriminating statement.

IMPACT

Two topics were chosen for discussion in this chapter's Impact sections. Each deals with the area of procedural criminal law and highlights issues important in later chapters. The first concerns the question of whether or not due process rights considerably restrict prosecution efforts. The second (on p. 85) presents one way of viewing due process rights in other countries.

Restricting Prosecution Through Due Process

Since the 1960s, critics have complained about the hands of police and prosecutors being tied by the proliferation of "rights for the criminal." Although the "criminal's rights" are also the Bill of Rights, it is important that the public feels justice is being done. In 1988 a special panel of the American Bar Association issued a report on the effect of such constitutional protections as the *Miranda* warning and the exclusionary rule. Prosecutors and police did not believe that Fourth Amendment rights, or their protection via the exclusionary rule, are a significant impediment to crime control (American Bar Association, 1988). Instead, those interviewed believed the police training required to become familiar with Fourth Amendment protection has promoted professionalism in police departments across the country. The number of cases lost because of the exclusionary rule was "modest" with estimates between 0.6 percent and 2.35 percent. The figures are highest for drug cases (for example, 7.1 percent), but the exclusionary rule causes few violent crime cases to be lost.

Similarly, neither police nor prosecutors believe the restrictions imposed by the *Miranda* decision are troublesome. Reading a suspect his or her rights does not prevent police from obtaining statements from those suspects. And prosecutors have not found that *Miranda* hampers the prosecution of cases. The police still obtain confessions, and prosecutors dismiss only a few cases because of *Miranda* problems.

As concerns were expressed in recent decades over the exclusionary rule, displeasure was also voiced with the *Miranda* decision. Advocates of a "get tough on crime" policy favored modifications to the *Miranda* warnings that would allow police more flexibility to accept statements by suspects. For example, a statement volunteered by the individual, that is, one in which there is no questioning by officers and which the individual freely makes, does not require *Miranda* warnings. Generally, on-the-scene questioning is also exempt, since at this stage the investigation has not reached an accusatory phase. In *New York* v. *Quarles* (1984) the Court included a "public safety" exception to *Miranda*. In situations where there is an immediate need to protect the public safety, the Court decided that this need takes precedence over the suspect's Fifth Amendment privilege against self-incrimination.

More recently, in *Colorado* v. *Spring* (1987), the Court reinstated the murder conviction of John Spring, who was arrested on firearms charges during a hunting trip. Not knowing that the police also suspected him of murder, Spring waived his right to remain silent. The Colorado Supreme Court ruled that his statements to police could not be used against him, since he should have been told, before waiving his rights, that they would ask about the murder. The U.S. Supreme Court disagreed, saying "the Constitution does not require that a criminal suspect know every possible consequence of a waiver." The Court will continue to explain, modify, and refine the *Miranda* ruling as more situations present themselves. And as it does so, we will continue to see the pendulum swing between competing philosophies that stress control of crime and those that want to regulate the actions of justice officials. The resulting controversy between those philosophies is the basis for Packer's distinction between crime control and due process.

Decisions like those in *Escobedo*, *Miranda*, and *Mapp* seem to support a due process model to the extent that they restrict police behavior in favor of protecting citizen rights. The trend toward a more conservative public and U.S. Supreme Court in the 1980s and 1990s brought increased complaints that rights of "criminals" were more protected than were rights of "law-abiding citizens." That opinion reflects a position of the crime control model.

Crime Control Model. Under the authority of the Fourteenth Amendment, the U.S. Supreme Court has tried to stipulate the requirements of due process when government action is taken against a citizen. The result is American procedural law. Analysis of the form that law takes is aided by Packer's earlier mentioned models. The procedural law can emphasize efficiency of action (Crime Control Model) or legitimacy of action (Due Process Model).

The value system underlying the Crime Control Model assumes that repression of criminal behavior is the most important function performed by the criminal process (Packer, 1968). The primacy of this function is necessary to ensure human freedom and allow citizens to be secure in person and property. The criminal process guarantees this goal of social freedom by efficiently operating to screen suspects, determine guilt, and appropriately sanction convicted persons.

To operate successfully, the Crime Control Model requires a high rate of apprehension and conviction following a process that emphasizes speed and finality. Packer (1968) compares the model to an assembly-line conveyor belt moving an endless stream of cases to workers standing at fixed stations as they perform their respective operations and move the case to a successful resolution. Speed of the conveyor belt is kept high as long as there are no ceremonious rituals cluttering the process and slowing advancement of the case. Speed is also achieved when the cases are handled in a uniform and routine manner. In this sense, the Crime Control Model is appropriately identified as an administrative, almost managerial, model (Packer, 1968).

An emphasis on finality means reducing chances to challenge the process or the outcome. Borrowing his metaphor, we can point to the problems created when assembly-line workers are constantly subjected to review and second-guessing by supervisors. These interruptions while doing your job are bad enough, but imagine the damage to "finality" when workers are constantly having returned to them products presumably finished several weeks or months earlier. The metaphor is, of course, transparent. An efficient criminal process means that as a case proceeds from victim/witness to police, then to prosecutor, each "worker" performs his or her job in a speedy manner without fear of later veto.

A successful conclusion under the Crime Control Model is one that excludes, at an early stage, persons apprehended but not likely to be guilty, while securing prompt and lasting conviction of the rest. Packer uses the concept of "presumption of guilt" to describe the orienting attitude toward those not excluded because of probable innocence. The presumption of guilt is important in the Crime Control Model, because it allows the system to deal efficiently with large numbers of cases. This model expresses confidence in the screening process used by police and prosecutors when they release the "probably innocent" suspects and sustain action against the "probably guilty" ones. That is, after determining sufficient evidence of guilt to permit further action, all subsequent activity directed toward suspects is based on the view that they are presumed guilty (Packer, 1968).

Packer warns us not to think of presumption of guilt as the opposite of the presumption of innocence. These concepts are different, rather than being opposite ideas. Specifically, the presumption of innocence is a concept directing authorities about how they are to proceed—not what they are to believe. That direction includes a warning to ignore their belief (that is, presumption of guilt) while processing (where they presume innocence) the suspect/defendant. Since the presumption of guilt is simply a prediction of outcome, authorities can believe suspects are "probably guilty" while treating them as if guilt remains an open question.

It is apparent in this review of the Crime Control Model that the early, administrative fact-finding stages are of utmost importance. Subsequent stages of adjudication should be as abbreviated as possible to ensure speed and finality.

Due Process Model. If the Due Process Model were put in charge of the assembly-line conveyor belt formerly run by the Crime Control Model, one of the first changes would be an increase in the number and frequency of quality control inspection points. The speed and finality used by the Crime Control Model to achieve its goal is seen by the Due Process Model as inviting abuse of governmental power. Built upon concepts like the primacy of the individual and the limitation of official power, the Due Process Model insists on a formal, adjudicative, adversarial fact-finding process. If this means that the process is slowed down and lacks finality, then so be it. As Packer says: "Precisely because of its potency in subjecting the individual to the coercive power of the state, the criminal process must, in this model, be subjected to controls that prevent it from operating with maximal efficiency" (1968, p. 166).

One way to implement its antiauthoritarian values is with the doctrine of legal guilt. Legal guilt can be distinguished from factual guilt in the following manner. Police Officer Williams observes Peter Jones run up to Virginia Spry and grab Virginia's purse and then run down the sidewalk. Officer Williams, the fastest runner in the department, catches Jones from behind, places him under arrest, and begins questioning him about the robbery. Jones immediately admits to the criminal act and, with the corroborating observation by Officer Williams, we can safely say that Jones is in fact guilty of the crime. Under the Crime Control Model, this "presumption of guilt" would result in a rapid and final determination of guilt. However, under the Due Process Model, emphasis is on the manner in which a government official (initially, Officer Williams) used her authority to intrude in the life of Peter Jones. The officer's actions are appropriately reviewed to determine their legality. If it is determined, for example, that Jones's confession was extracted without being informed of his right to remain silent, the confession cannot be used against Jones. A result of losing the confession as evidence may mean that the case against Jones is dropped or lost in court. According to the Due Process Model, Jones was not "legally guilty" of the purse snatching, since rules designed to protect him and to safeguard the integrity of the process were not in effect. Factual guilt may be apparent or even legitimately known, but legal guilt must be validly decided via the previously determined process.

There is a tendency to suppose that the values of the Due Process Model are opposite those underlying the Crime Control Model. That position would be incorrect, since it implies that the Due Process Model is uninterested in repressing crime. Instead, the differences are best seen with reference to procedure rather than outcome. Cole (1986) distinguishes the values of each model in the following manner: The Crime Control Model assumes that freedom is so important that every effort must be made to repress crime, while the Due Process Model assumes that freedom is so important that every effort must be made to ensure that criminal justice decisions are based on reliable information. Each model seeks to guarantee social freedom. One does so by emphasizing efficient processing of wrongdoers, while the other emphasizes effective restrictions on government invasion in the citizen's life. Who is the greater threat to our freedom? The criminal trying to harm us or our property, says the Crime Control Model. The government agents like police officers and prosecutors, says the Due Process Model. Both criminals and government agents can invade our interests, take our property, and restrict our freedom of movement. Social freedom requires that the law-abiding citizen be free from unjustifiable intrusion by either criminals or by government agents. Unfortunately, it does not appear possible to achieve both goals simultaneously. One is emphasized at the expense of the other, but neither can be identified as qualitatively better. While we may have an individual preference of one over the other, it would be unfortunate and incorrect to attribute intrinsic superiority to our choice.

IMPACT

Due Process Rights in Other Countries

Procedural protection for citizens is not solely an American idea. Each country and each legal tradition require some level of due process when the government confronts an accused. So far this chapter has not used a classification scheme to present cross-cultural information. But then the chapter's discussion has centered only on American concepts. At this point, however, the benefits of classification come into play.

Cingranelli and Wright (1986) conducted a content analysis of State Department reports on the human rights practices of most foreign countries. The authors looked at how a country's government fared in providing five justice system traits: pretrial guarantees against unreasonable searches, arbitrary arrest or imprisonment, arbitrary abduction, the use of torture, and the fairness of the trial itself. For example, under their research methodology, governments were classified as violating the right to a fair trial if they did not allow the accused to hire his or her own lawyer or if the judges were not impartial and independent of the regime in power.

The resulting classification developed around two primary variables: extensiveness of due process protection, and the consistency with which the law is implemented. The authors evaluated nations as either "not providing" due process, or offering it at "very extensive," "extensive," or "moderate" levels. In addition, the authors understood that governments could vary in extending these provisions. Therefore, they further categorized countries as implementing their law in either a "consistent" or "inconsistent" manner.

The resulting eight-cell typology is based on 1980 activities so there have been changes in some countries' classification. This is particularly true of countries like Poland, East Germany, Rumania, and Czechoslovakia, which experienced dramatic political and economic changes starting in 1989. Cingranelli and Wright (1986) said that they would be surprised if a reclassification resulted in major changes (for example, movement between consistent and inconsistent, or an up or down movement of more than one category) of more than 10 percent of the nations in the sample. With that warning in mind, Figure 3-5 provides an instructive typology of criminal justice systems.

There is a tendency to try to identify other common characteristics among nations in each group. Do all the Western nations or industrialized countries group together? Can we identify one or two cells where all the developed countries gather, while developing nations assemble in other cells? Are there clear cell distinctions between countries that followed a socialist philosophy in 1980 and those that were historically linked to the common-law tradition as started in England? Questions like these are the stuff from which comparative criminal justice is made. But to answer them we must understand the differences and similarities among various systems, and identify the ways systems can be grouped according to those differences and similarities. We begin that quest in the next chapter with a classification of the legal systems themselves.

SUMMARY

An understanding of basic criminal law concepts is important for appreciating any country's legal system. This chapter used terms well-known to many of you, so we can begin the journey to other countries with familiar baggage. The development of criminal law in America was viewed from both a consensus and a conflict perspective. Knowledge of those perspectives will be of assistance as we look in the next chapter at how different legal systems developed.

The chapter also highlighted two essential ingredients to any justice system: substantive law and procedural law. The former concerns the definition of rules, while the latter specifies their enforcement. Each has two aspects that help us better to understand their operation. Substantive criminal law is made up of general characteristics that allow identification of some act as criminal, and major principles that determine if a particular behavior is criminal. Procedural criminal law is implemented through either a Crime Control Model or a Due Process Model. Although each seeks to ensure the social freedom of citizens, they emphasize different, and often conflicting, ways to achieve their goal.

This chapter emphasized American perspectives, mechanisms, and terminology to provide a common base on which future chapters can build. As we begin to focus on criminal justice in other countries, it is important to set aside our understandable biases that America's way of doing things is the only reasonable or correct way. Such ethnocentrism hinders our ability to understand and appreciate alternative systems. In the end, we may well conclude that the United States has the best of all possible justice systems. But such a judgment should be based on a knowledge of the alternatives and not simply on blind faith.

The Implementation of Law is:

Due Process Protections Are:	Consistent	Inconsistent
Very Extensive	Australia, France, Mongolia Austria, Gambia, Netherlands Barbados, German FR, New Zealand Belgium, Greece, P. New Guinea Canada, Iceland, Saint Lucia Costa Rica, Ireland, Senegal Cyprus, Israel, Solomon Islands Denmark, Italy, Norway Dominica, Japan, Sweden Egypt, Luxemburg, Switzerland Fiji, Malta, Western Samoa Finland, Mauritius	Hungary Bahamas Dominican Republic Jamaica Portugal Spain Trinidad/Tobago United Kingdom
Extensive	Bhutan Botswana Central African Empire Sri Lanka Equatorial Guinea Maldive Islands Saudi Arabia Tunisia	Brazil, Oman Ecuador, Panama Gabon, Peru Ghana, Rwanda Honduras, United Arab Emirates Lebanon, Venezuela Mexico, Zaire Morocco, Zambia Nigeria
Moderate	Bahrain, Quator Bangladesh, Sao Tome & Principe Cape Verde Islands, Seychelles Guinea-Bissau, Sierra Leone Ivory Coast, Singapore Jordan, Swaziland Kuwait, USSR Malaysia, Zimbabwe Rhodesia	Algeria, Taiwan Colombia, Tanzania India, Thailand Republic of Korea, Turkey Nepal, Yemen, Arab Republic Nicaragua, Yemen, People's DR Surinam, Yugoslavia
Not Provided	Kenya Lesotho Malawi Niger Sudan	Afghanistan, Cuba, Libya Albania, Czechoslovakia, Madagascar Angola, Djibouti, Mali Argentina, El Salvador, Mozambique Benin, Ethiopia, Pakistan Bolivia, German DR, Paraguay Bulgaria, Grenada, Philippines Burma, Guatemala, Poland Burundi, Guinea, Romania Kampuchea, Guyana, Somali Rep. Cameroun, Haiti, South Africa Chad, Indonesia, Syria Chile, Iraq, Togo China, Korea, PR, Uganda Comoro Islands, Laos, Upper Volta Congo Republic, Liberia, Uruguay Vietnam

Figure 3-5. A typology of criminal justice systems. *Source:* David L. Cingranelli and Kevin N. Wright (1986). "Measurement of cross-national variations in the extensiveness and consistency of due process," *Policy Studies*, 15, p. 106.

SUGGESTED READING

American Bar Association. (1988). *Criminal justice in crisis*, (Report by the Special Committee on Criminal Justice in a Free Society). Chicago: Author.

Cingranelli, David L., and Wright, Kevin N. (1986). Measurement of cross-national variations in the extensiveness and consistency of due process. *Policy Studies Journal, 15*, 97–109.

Hall, Jerome. (1960). *General principles of criminal law*. Indianapolis: Bobbs-Merrill.

Packer, Herbert. (1968). *The limits of criminal sanction*. Stanford, CA: Stanford University Press.

REFERENCES

American Bar Association. (1988). *Criminal justice in crisis* (Report by the Special Committee on Criminal Justice in a Free Society). Chicago: Author.

American Law Institute. (1985). *Model penal code: Official draft and explanatory notes*. Philadelphia, PA: Author.

Boyd, Julian P. (Ed.). 1955. *The papers of Thomas Jefferson* (Vol. 12). Princeton, NJ: Princeton University Press.

Boyd, Julian P. (Ed.). 1958. *The papers of Thomas Jefferson* (Vol. 14). Princeton, NJ: Princeton University Press.

Chambliss, William J. (1964). A sociological analysis of the law of vagrancy. *Social Problems, 12*, 45–69.

Cingranelli, David L., and Wright, Kevin N. (1986). Measurement of cross-national variations in the extensiveness and consistency of due process. *Policy Studies Journal, 15*, 97–109.

Cole, George. (1986). *The American system of criminal justice*. Monterey, CA: Brooks/Cole.

Department of Justice. (1988). *Report to the nation on crime and justice*. Washington, DC: Bureau of Justice Statistics.

Durkheim, Emile. (1964). *The division of labor in society* (G. Simpson, Trans.). New York: Free Press.

Geis, Gilbert, and Meier, Robert F. (1985). Abolition of the insanity pleas in Idaho: A case study. *The Annals of the American Academy of Political and Social Science, 477*, 72–83.

Hall, Jerome. (1960). *General principles of criminal law* (2nd ed.). Indianapolis: Bobbs-Merrill.

Hall, Jerome. (1952). *Theft, law and society*. Indianapolis: Bobbs-Merrill.

Hall, Jerome, and Mueller, Gerhard. (1965). *Cases and readings on criminal law and procedure*. Indianapolis: Bobbs-Merrill.

Korn, Richard, and McCorkle, Lloyd. (1959). *Criminology and penology*. New York: Holt, Rinehart and Winston.

Michalowski, Raymond. (1985). *Order, law, and crime*. New York: Random House.

Moran, Richard. (1985). The modern foundation for the insanity defense: The cases of James Hadfield (1800) and Daniel McNaughtan (1843). *The Annals of the American Academy of Political and Social Science, 477,* 31–42.

Packer, Herbert. (1968). *The limits of criminal sanction*. Stanford, CA: Stanford University Press.

Sutherland, Edwin, and Cressey, Donald. (1978). *Criminology*. Philadelphia: J. B. Lippincott.

Chapter 4

Legal Traditions

KEY TERMS

canon law	particularization
codification	points of law
Corpus Juris Civilis	precedent
custom	principle of analogy
equity	*qadi's*
feudalism	*Qur'an*
ijtihad	Roman law
issues of fact	Russian law
legal system	*Shari'a*
legal tradition	*stare decisis*
Marxism–Leninism	*Sunna*
mazalim	written code

COUNTRIES REFERENCED

China	Roman Empire
England	Russia
France	United States
Mexico	

The legal systems in today's world can be divided among four families or traditions. Each legal tradition has unique elements that influenced its development and form. This chapter identifies some of those foundations for each tradition. Then, with that new understanding and appreciation of each tradition, we compare the legal families in terms of cultural, substantive, and procedural components.

A clarification of terminology is necessary before presenting material in this chapter. For purposes of organization and classification it is desirable to collapse categories into as few types as reasonable. For example, discussion of the legal system in every country of the world is clearly unreasonable. Similarities exist, but the emphasis on sovereignty and nationalism means the legal system (that is, legal institutions, procedures, and rules) in one country is not exactly duplicated in any other. However, although countries do not duplicate "legal systems," they often share "legal traditions" (Merryman, 1985, pp. 1–3).

A legal tradition puts the legal system into a cultural perspective. It refers to deeply rooted and historically conditioned attitudes about things like the nature of law, the role of law in society, how a legal system should be organized and operated, and the way law is or should be made, applied, or perfected (Merryman, 1985). From this perspective, it is possible to identify a much smaller and more manageable number of units. In doing so, however, we must not forget the variability of systems within the traditions. England, New Zealand, and New Jersey share a common legal tradition but do not have identical legal systems. Similarly, France, Germany, and Italy have their own legal systems but can be grouped in the same legal tradition along with the separate legal systems of Argentina and Brazil.

Today, comparative legal scholars identify three or four legal traditions (some call them legal families). This number has not been consistent throughout history, and some formerly prominent legal traditions no longer even exist. We will concentrate our efforts on four contemporary traditions but must first mention some historically significant ones.

In 1928, law professor John Henry Wigmore published a three-volume work on the evolution of the various legal systems. A 1936 version not only revised and expanded the information, but also incorporated the three previous volumes into one library edition. This prototype of comparative legal studies still

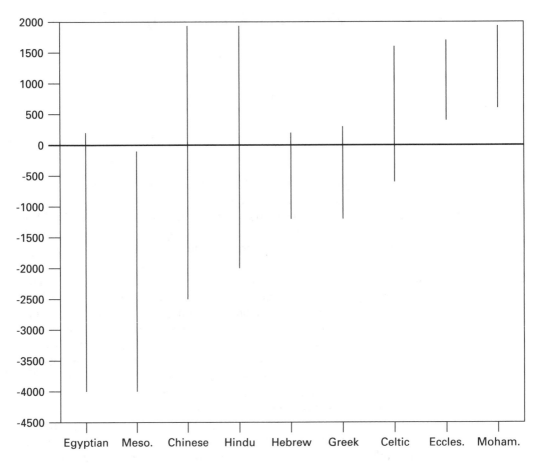

Figure 4-1. Duration of legal systems.

sets the standard for comprehensive coverage. Wigmore (1928) believed there had been 16 legal systems in the world: Egyptian, Mesopotamian, Chinese, Hindu, Hebrew, Greek, Roman, Maritime, Japanese, Mohammedan, Celtic, Germanic, Slavic, Ecclesiastical, Romanesque, and Anglican. By 1936, Wigmore saw six systems as having completely disappeared as legal structures (Egyptian, Mesopotamian, Greek, Hebrew, Celtic, and Ecclesiastical). Five survived as hybrids (Roman, Germanic, Slavic, Maritime, and Japanese). The Chinese, Hindu, and Mohammedan remained essentially unmixed, and the two newest (Romanesque and Anglican) were hybrids. To provide a sense of history and development, Figure 4-1 graphs the duration of the nine systems not considered hybrids that Wigmore recognized in the mid-1930s.

It is not my purpose to provide support, criticism, or updating of Wigmore's classification scheme. Instead, his work presents a brief review of some ancient legal systems. A momentary retreat to before the time of Christ will instill an appreciation for the maturity of the idea that law is an instrument for social organization. If, in the process, we produce a sense of humility, that also will be good. After all, in some ways our contemporary legal systems have existed for less time than others have been extinct.

The Egyptian legal system extends back as far as 4000 B.C., but it was especially well organized by the Fourth Dynasty (2900–2750 B.C.). By that time, the Egyptian king ruled as a theocrat with divine authority coming from the Sun-God Osiris through his son Horus. In this manner, the source of law and justice was divine but moved by way of the king, who appointed chief judges.

As sole legislator, the Pharaoh provided codes that set down the proper behavior of his people. The particular procedures for implementing the codes were more likely handled by the chief judges. Disputing parties brought their case before the judge, who listened to their oral arguments. The trial judge was expected to "Be quiet while (listening) to the words of the petitioner. Do not treat him impatiently. Wait until he has emptied his heart and told his grief" (Wigmore, 1936, p. 30).

In its over 4000-year existence, the Egyptian legal system obviously passed through many stages. Unfortunately, its legacy is not always well remembered. The discovery of a 250 B.C. bail bond for a jail prisoner's release, and a recognition of women's independence and equality with men in some legal relations remind us that we more "modern" citizens may be mere revisors instead of innovators.

In the region between the Euphrates and Tigris rivers (basically Iraq today), the Mesopotamian civilization emerged and fought off successive waves of conquest until the arrival of Persians and Greeks in the centuries before Christ. The legal system developed by these traders emphasized commercial law and provides reasonable examples of today's deeds, partnerships, and other contract forms.

The most notable achievement of the Mesopotamian legal system was the Babylonian law called the Code of Hammurabi. King Hammurabi's (circa 1792–1750 B.C.) code is one of the first known bodies of law. The laws, engraved on stone tablets, emphasized property rights and spoke to such issues as theft, ownership, and interpersonal violence.

The Hebrew legal system started with Moses receiving the two tablets of stone and the recording of the first five books of the Bible (known as the Torah, or Ancient Law). That first period (about 1200–400 B.C.) was followed by the Classic period (300 B.C.–100 A.D.) in which rabbis developed the law. The Talmudic period (200–500) saw the consolidation of records and was followed by the Medieval period (700–1500) of private codes and commentaries. Finally, the Modern period (1600–1900) saw the Hebrew language and legal system relegated to secondary standing as Jews became more linked to national (territorial) norms. Actually, Wigmore (1936) suggests that the Hebrew system ended as a strictly legal system with the end of the Classical period. After 100 A.D., Hebrew law was replaced in Palestine by Roman rule and since then Jewish law has operated mainly as local custom and as ceremonial and moral rules.

Writing before the 1949 establishment of a communist People's Republic of China, Wigmore (1936) identified the Chinese legal system as the oldest continuing legal system. It has now followed the way of other pre-Christian era systems and lives only in a borrowed format. Possibly more so than in other systems, the Chinese legal system relies heavily on a philosophy of life. Specifically, the belief in a law of nature wherein all parts harmoniously adjust to each other was basic to Chinese law and justice. The implications of such a philosophy were provided great clarity through the words of Confucius (551?–479? B.C.)

The Confucian philosophy emphasized a government of men rather than of laws. The government will flourish with the right men but will decay without them. A result of that perspective was a situation where a single official directly ruled each province or locality. That magistrate, or governor, would collect taxes, serve as chief priest, provide moral guidance, and dispense justice. The Emperor in Peking kept the governor in office as long as law and order prevailed and the people remained content and prosperous.

Law and order among content and prosperous people was best achieved, according to Confucius, through moral force and the rule of reason. Strict technical rights and insistence on principle were deemed inappropriate and unnecessary under the Chinese system. Instead, compromise was the goal to achieve and mediation or arbitration (in today's terminology) was the means to that end. Operating without lawyers, the accused, accuser, and witnesses were questioned by the magistrate. In his efforts at dispensing justice, the judge was expected to operate from the position that nothing is so important that it cannot be compromised for human welfare, comfort, or dignity. With convictions like that, the Chinese joined the Egyptians, Mesopotamians, and Hebrews in providing the world a foundation for continually evolving legal systems.

TODAY'S FOUR LEGAL TRADITIONS

As that review suggests, the decision to place the various legal systems into categories is easier than deciding how many categories to use and what to name them. Some scholars suggest that there are just two legal traditions: one based on private ownership of property, individualism, and liberalism, and another supporting more collective and socialistic goals (Cole, Frankowski, and Gertz, 1987). Others use three groupings that are often called common law, civil law, and socialist law traditions (see Cole et al., 1987; Merryman, 1985). Finally, Rene David (David and Brierley, 1985) identified four legal families: common, civil, socialist, and religious/philosophical.

I have decided that the classification strategy most useful for this text is one using four legal traditions. The result follows David's format but specifies Islam as the fourth type. That modification seems appropriate, because the movement toward Islamic fundamentalism is impacting world economics and politics to such a degree that we need to understand better this important part of Islamic society. Also, of the contemporary religious and philosophical doctrines, Islam most clearly presents a separate legal system. Of the other three (common, civil, and socialist), the American reader is most familiar with the common legal tradition, since the United States falls into that general category. The civil tradition, oldest of the four, is today's primary competitor with the common legal tradition and can be found in some format throughout the world. The socialist legal tradition is both the youngest of the four and may be the first of the four to die out. However, even in a weakened state, the socialist tradition has influenced the countries where it appeared in a manner not easily tossed aside. As such, it deserves our attention and consideration as we review the major legal traditions in today's world.

Common Legal Tradition

Although not the oldest, the common legal tradition provides a familiar base for discussing the history and essential features of a legal tradition. After covering that more native material, we can move to less familiar traditions.

The Romans occupied Britain from about 50 A.D. to the start of the fifth century. However, only the groundwork for the Roman law (civil law tradition) had been laid at that time. By the time the *Corpus Juris Civilis* was published (533 A.D.) the Romans in Britain had been pushed out by Germanic tribes like the Saxons and the Angles. St. Augustine's efforts at converting Britain to Christianity (597 A.D.) provided some Roman influence in terms of church law, but this early period served mainly to provide a base for a separate legal tradition called common law.

The common legal tradition developed from several subtraditions. Those include feudal practices, custom, and equity (see Figure 4-2). An overview of each provides information helpful in understanding the basics of common law.

Feudal Practices.   The primary political and military system of the Middle Ages (about 500 A.D. to 1450) was feudalism. Under this system, a lord provided vassals with land in exchange for military and other services. By the 1200s, when feudalism was in decline, several layers of feudal relations existed. For example, the vassals of an important baron (the vassals' lord) were in turn the lord of their own vassals. Obviously, not everyone could be a landholder. Someone had to do the work necessary for keeping the lord (at whatever level) viable. A variety of peasant villagers provided this service in their role as agricultural workers in the lord's estate or manor.

Inevitably, differences arose between vassals at various levels, between vassals and their lords, and among villagers in a manor. Before the Norman Conquest (1066) of England, a nonfeudal Anglo-Saxon political system provided dispute settlement through assemblies of freemen sitting in shire and hundred courts. Upon his arrival in England, William the Conqueror (1066–1087) chose not to abolish the existing Anglo-Saxon process. Instead, he set up an orderly government with stern enforcement of royal rights. A new system of royal courts was developed with primary interest in settling disputes of landholders. For example, a baron (beholding to his lord the king), presided over disputes between the baron's vassals. In doing so, the baron drew upon the advice of his other vassals (the disputants' peers) in arriving at a judgment. Failure by a vassal to answer an order to appear (summons) in court could result in the lord's reclaiming the vassal's land.

Disputes among the villagers were deemed more appropriately handled by the lord of the manor than by a royal court. If the manor court was unavailable or inappropriate, villagers could turn to traditional shire or hundred courts. In this manner, England retained Anglo-Saxon influences on her legal system into the early twelfth century. Even after William, law under Henry I (1100–1135) was mostly Anglo-Saxon and administered at a local level according to widely varying regional custom (Plucknett, 1956). Even so, the administrative machinery, such as royal courts, placed by William I and Henry I provided the base for a common law dominating the realm. The realization of a common law occurred with Henry II (1154–1189) and allows us to turn to custom as the next subtradition of common law.

Custom.   Henry II saw the reign of his predecessor, Stephen (1135–1154) as a period without law and troubled by civil war. Henry's grandfather, Henry I, on the other hand, ruled over a more orderly kingdom. In addition, in the one hundred years since the Norman Conquest, both royal courts and the separate system of church courts had grown and become involved in many jurisdictional disputes. Henry II sought to return order to the kingdom and to solve disputes between state and church courts. One of his efforts resulted in the Constitutions of Clarendon (1164), which listed customs said to be the practice during the reign of Henry I. The 16 articles forming the Constitutions provided custom as a basis for building order and served to declare the proper relation between church and state. This importance of custom must be elaborated.

The principal element in most premodern legal systems was custom. Not surprisingly, custom was an essential aspect of court decisions under Anglo-Saxon law and the English feudal process. Importantly, however, custom was not always consistent by geography or by social standing. Local village customs settled disputes among peasants and other villagers. Occasionally, those customs contradicted the habits of vassals, lords, and other freemen. Plucknett (1956) notes that village customs in England frequently kept a woman's property free from her husband's control and allowed her to enter into contracts on her own. Bourgeois custom did not allow such behavior by women. This point becomes important because the common legal tradition was built upon only one of these custom types. Specifically, common law was the custom of landholders as accepted and interpreted by the royal courts. It is appropriate to keep this point in mind as we discuss custom's role in the origin of common law.

According to Blackstone (I *Comm* 53-54), legal custom is ancient (no one can remember its beginning); continuous (it has never been abandoned or interrupt-ed); peaceable (it has the common consent of those using it); reasonable (in terms of "legal" reason); certain (ascertainable); compulsory (it is not obeyed at option); and consistent (one custom cannot contradict another). As complete as that might sound, we must still consider the question of how custom is determined. One way to decide if a custom met the criteria for being a good legal custom was the jury system. Presumably, if a freeman's peers settle a dispute by using princi-ples that reflect common and immemorial custom, the decision exemplifies com-mon law. Or, as Blackstone put it: "The only method of proving, that this or that maxim is a rule of the common law, is by showing that it hath been always the custom to observe it" (I *Comm* 68).

The origin of common law in custom makes *precedent* a basic concept in the common legal tradition. When stated as a policy, precedent is called *stare decisis*, which means courts are expected to abide by decided cases. But, we must be careful here not to imply that presixteenth century courts had anything even resembling the modern principle of precedent or policy of *stare decisis*. The dis-tinction is best handled by referring to the work of medieval judge Henry de Bracton. Bracton saw the courts of his time (mid-thirteenth century) as foolish and ignorant corruptors of doctrine, deciding cases by whim instead of by rule (Plucknett, 1956).

In an attempt to return to the rule of law, Bracton reviewed the original plea rolls (immense in number and weight, and without index) from the courts. He used those documents to research legal principles and then to identify cases as historical evidence for the accuracy of his statements. Note that this process was different from studying cases and deducing rule of law from them. For Bracton, a case can illustrate a legal principle and provide proof that the principle was once applied; but the case is not in itself a source of law (Plucknett, 1956). In other words, Bracton was searching for evidence of custom, and that custom could be identified through reference to several cases. As a result, court decisions were governed by custom, not by the case or cases cited as proof of that custom.

The movement to citing prior cases as binding (that is, the movement to precedent in its modern sense) instead of simply showing custom, began in the sixteenth century. Still, it was the seventeenth century before the practice became established. Specifically, decisions of the Exchequer Chamber (where the judges were the state Chancellor and the Treasurer) were held to be binding on other courts. Even so, the process was not really entrenched until the nineteenth century brought a strengthening of the House of Lords and the organizing of a single court of appeals. Therefore, custom is not only an important component of com-mon law, but it also allows precedent and *stare decisis* to become essential features.

Equity.   The early history of equity (from the Latin *aequus*, meaning "fair" or "just") links it to the subtraditions of feudal practices and custom. Yet it differs from those because of its eventual standing as a separate legal system both con-flicting and cooperating with common law.

In the early stages of development, the king was in constant contact (usually through his council) with the various judges and courts across the country. In an informal manner, cases moved from court to court with little difficulty and without excessive regard to jurisdictional boundaries. Judges, in close cooperation with the king's council, had considerable discretion, especially in procedural matters. With the fourteenth century came significant elaboration of the judicial system responsible for implementing the common law. As a result, the contact between monarch and judge became infrequent, and the court's discretion in handling matters was correspondingly reduced. By the mid-1350s we find courts refusing to bend procedural rules, even in a sense of "fairness," and instead declaring that judges are bound to custom and to taking a strict definition of statute (Plucknett, 1956).

Not surprisingly, a result of inflexibility in the royal courts led to unhappy people who were unable to obtain justice or expressed shock at the solution given. These people turned to the king and asked him to add fairness to the law. The king's agent in such matters was the chancellor, who had responsibility for guiding the king's conscience. Traditionally, the chancellor was also a church official, but with the growth of the office and expansion of responsibilities, laymen came to be appointed chancellor in the fourteenth century. Simultaneously, then, we find a combination of judges isolated from the king while another royal office, with direct access to the monarch, is strengthened. The outcome of these events was the institutionalization of equity as an important aspect of law in England.

The chancellors decided conflicts between law and morals based on morality rather than technical law. Therefore, in Chancery court, decisions were based on the equity of the case without concern for the procedural necessities (David and Brierley, 1968). By the fifteenth century, the chancellor was essentially an autonomous judge deciding cases in the name of the king. This situation did not always sit well with common law judges. To appease them, the fifteenth- and sixteenth-century chancellors often called upon the judges to explain a point of law.

The cross-pollination of ideas, between common law courts and Chancery courts, benefited both. Common judges learned that technicalities were not an

Figure 4-2. Developmental subtraditions in the legal traditions.

Common tradition	Civil tradition	Socialist tradition	Islamic tradition
• Fuedal practices • Custom • Equity	• Roman law • Canon law • Codification	• Russian law • Law as artificial • Marxism–Leninism	• Shari'a • Witnesses and oaths • Extensions

excuse for reaching obviously wrong decisions, and the chancellors came to understand better the law and its application. In addition, Chancery courts aided common law courts by providing relief to procedural and substantive defects in the common law system. Plucknett (1956) identifies such faults as slowness, expense, inefficiency, technicality, antiquated methods of proof, and suspicions of volunteer witnesses as particular areas where Chancery courts helped common law courts.

Having one court system existing primarily to correct the defects of another court system is not desirable in perpetuity. Something had to give. Over the centuries, the rules of equity became as strict, consistent, and "legal" as those of the common law. The growth and formalization of equity finally provided an opportunity to unite the two legal systems, and in 1875 a Judicature Act removed the formal distinction between the two courts. Common law was now complete. From a historical base (feudal practices), the common legal tradition had basic principles (custom) and a sense of fairness (equity).

Civil Legal Tradition

Because the phrase *civil law* is familiar to American readers, it is necessary to distinguish the term from its use in reference to a legal tradition. In its more typical usage in the United States, civil law is set against criminal law because it deals with private wrongs instead of the social wrongs handled by criminal law. In that manner, civil law deals with such matters as contracts, ownership of property, and payment for personal injury. But in its original meaning, civil law referred to the code of laws collected by the Roman emperor Justinian. The *Corpus Juris Civilis* set the stage for subsequent law not only with Justinian's successors but eventually with Napoleon and his *Code Civil* (*Code Napoleon*) as proclaimed in 1804. The use of civil codes as a legal tradition spread across Europe and to such places as Quebec, Canada, and South America. As a result, in much of the world, the term *civil law* brings to mind a legal tradition based on written codes, not a specific type of law dealing with private wrongs. Since our concern throughout this book is with criminal justice systems, we will have no need to use civil law in reference to those laws regulating individual disputes. So, when you read about civil law systems and civil legal traditions, place it in the context of a code of laws as first developed for the Roman Empire.

Just as the common legal tradition developed from several basic subtraditions, the civil tradition has its own underpinning (see Figure 4-2). Specifically, we look at the role played by Roman law, canon law, and codification.

Roman Law. Civil law's claim of being the oldest contemporary legal tradition rests on its link to Roman law. In turn, Roman law was the result of statutes, edicts of magistrates, and the interpretations of jurists (Kolbert, 1979; Watson, 1970).

Three legislative bodies created Roman law statutes. The *comitia centuriata* and *comitia tributa* enacted statutes known as *lex* (a collection of laws). The *concilium plebis* enacted *plebiscitum*, a law passed by the common people. These laws were binding only on the average citizen unless the Senate made it binding on the nobility and senators. The earliest form of written Roman law dates to 451 and 450 B.C., when a council of 10 men inscribed 12 bronze tablets with specifics concerning the rights of Roman citizens. These Twelve Tables were approved as *lex* by the *comitia centuriata* in 450 B.C. They provided the basis for private rights of Roman citizens, consisted mainly of ancient custom, and concerned procedure more than substantive law. For example, the opening passage of the Twelve Tables states, "If a man is summoned to appear in court and does not come, let witnesses be heard and then let the plaintiff seize him. If he resists or absconds, the plaintiff can use force. If he is ill or too old, let the plaintiff provide a beast to bring him: but if he declines this offer, the plaintiff need not provide a carriage . . ." (quoted in Kolbert, 1979, p. 13).

Superior magistrates, especially the praetor, of Rome issued edicts that initially identified how magistrates planned to fulfill their duties. For example, complaints between Roman citizens were taken to the Urban Praetor, who handled cases of Roman *jus civile* (private law). By issuing edicts at the start of his term, the praetor could identify the principles he would follow during his one year in office. Although the edict was valid only for that praetor's term, a tendency developed for praetors to borrow from their predecessor's edict. This certainly is different from *stare decisis* in common law, but it does suggest an early means of attaining consistency in procedure (Watson, 1970). A more appropriate link between the praetor and common law refers to a means for attending to fairness. In this manner, the edicts became a body of law known as the *jus honorarium*, which was to Roman law what equity was to common law (Kolbert, 1979). The advance notice of procedural rules he would follow allowed the praetor to give the process a sense of fairness.

Finally, Roman law was the result of interpretations by jurists. Under Roman law, the jurists were more like what we would consider statesmen knowledgeable in the law. They were not lawyers or legal practitioners in the modern sense. The emperor would confer upon certain jurists the right or privilege of giving written opinions on cases. Those opinions would become binding on the parties in the dispute. Because jurists also could write on imaginary cases, there came to be an extensive, and often contradictory, collection of legal opinions on a variety of cases. At this historical point, the emperor Justinian enters and provides one of the most important legal documents in the civil legal tradition.

Justinian became emperor in 527, succeeding his uncle Justin. As one of his first acts, he charged 16 experts with examining the existing juristic writings and refining the massive bulk of material then serving as Roman law. The resulting *Corpus Juris Civilis* was meant to eliminate incorrect, obscure, and repetitive material. Further, it was to resolve conflicts and doubts while organizing the

remaining material into some systematic form (Merryman, 1985). At its completion in 533, the *Corpus Juris Civilis* stood as the sole authority for the laws and
juristic writings.

Interestingly, most of the material in the *Corpus Juris Civilis* was over 300
years old and therefore predated Christianity. Emperor Constantine (275–337)
was the first Roman emperor to become Christian, and Theodosius (346–395)
made Christianity the sole religion of the empire. Obviously, Justinian's compil-
ers had access to some 200 years of ecclesiastical law that they chose to ignore.
While church law did not have much impact on Roman law, it was an important
factor in the development of the civil legal tradition.

Canon Law. The Roman Catholic church developed canon law to govern
the Church and the rights and obligations of her followers. As Roman civil law
comprised the universal law of the worldly empire, canon law was the universal
law of the spiritual realm (Merryman, 1985). Civil courts administered Roman
civil law, while ecclesiastical courts managed the canon law.

The primary source providing the specifics of canon law were the various
decretal letters. These decrees were authoritative papal statements concerning
controversial points in doctrine or ecclesiastical law. Basically, any matter the
papacy considered relevant to the well-being of the whole Christian body public
was potential subject matter for a decretal letter. The decretal letter had official
and binding force and in essence was a judicial verdict signifying appropriate
behavior and thought.

With the Church claiming jurisdiction over the entire life of Christians,
potential conflict with the state was inevitable. In fact, the papacy and the government in Constantinople were in serious conflict from Pope Leo I (440–461)
onward. By Pope Gregory's time (590–604), canon law had secured a foothold in
the legal system of the empire. Ullman (1975) suggests that a main reason for this
ascendancy of canon law was its flexibility. With Gregory, canon law operated as
a living law, providing a written system of law for contemporaries. The Roman
law, as codified in the *Corpus Juris Civilis*, stood in stark contrast with its cen-
turies-old standards. Canon law developed from real situations in the current
time period, and was flexible enough to absorb features of other systems, like
those of the Germanic tribes.

By the ninth century, both Roman law and canon law had experienced their
heyday. Germanic and other invaders provided modifications as the empire collapsed, but by the eleventh century each reestablished itself as superior systems.
Law became a major object of study at Bologna and other Italian universities, and
Italy became the legal center of the Western world (Merryman, 1985).

Scholars from many countries came to study the *Corpus Juris Civilis* and, as
a result, it provided a base for a common law of Europe (*jus commune*). This situation prevailed until the fifteenth century, when the idea of national sovereignty
gave rise to national law. The foundation had been laid, however, and Roman

civil law, and canon law to a lesser extent, remained a large part of the legal systems in Western Europe.

Codification.   The components of the civil legal tradition have relied primarily on written (codified) laws. Though not fully realized until the *Corpus Juris Civilis*, Roman civil law had a tradition, dating back to the Twelve Tables, of laws as binding because they were authorized and recorded. Canon law supported the codification principle through papal decrees. Codification became so entrenched that in 319 Emperor Constantine could declare: "The authority of custom and long usage is not slight but not to the extent that it will prevail against reason or against statute" (quoted in Kolbert, 1979). Roman law and canon law provided a tradition of codification that, in turn, emphasized a revolutionary nature of law and stressed its written form.

When Justinian announced the *Corpus Juris Civilis* his goal was to abolish all prior law. When the French codified their law in the Code Napoleon, all prior law in those areas was repealed. Of course, both *Corpus Juris Civilis* and the Code Napoleon had principles of prior law incorporated in the new codes. But, in each case, and by implication in all cases of codification (Merryman, 1985; Sereni, 1956), the codes received their validity not from a previous incarnation, but from their incorporation and reenactment in the new code.

The relevance of codification's revolutionary nature becomes clearer when contrasted with common law. For example, Merryman (1985) notes that codes exist in common law jurisdictions (see, for example, the codes of Louisiana and California); but they are not based on the ideology or cultural reality supporting similarly appearing French or German codes. Specifically, codes under common law do not abolish all prior law in their field (that is, they are not revolutionary). Instead, they claim to perfect and supplement it. The view of civil law codes as replacing, instead of extending, prior law more appropriately distinguishes the civil and common traditions than does the presence of codes themselves.

Besides its revolutionary nature, codification is distinguished by its written form. Some people argue that civil law is distinct from common law because it is written, whereas the latter is unwritten. This distinction is, at best, misleading. Actually, the distinction between written and unwritten law has little to do with the recording of law in written documents (Postema, 1986). Unwritten law exists in the customs of the community and is binding by that fact, regardless of whether someone wrote it down. Written law, on the other hand, exists and is binding because it was enacted by a recognized authority (for example, a monarch or a legislature) following formal procedures.

Codification gives civil law a revolutionary character and written format that adds to its separate identity among legal families. Upon combining those features with the historical links to Roman and canon law, we have the basic ingredients of the civil legal tradition.

IMPACT

The United States is among the countries identified with the common legal tradition. But the lack of surprise with which you read that statement distorts the role played by the civil tradition in America's history. The Impact section of this chapter looks at civil law's influence in America so that we can appreciate the influence one tradition can have on another. We could easily reverse emphases and show how civil law is becoming more like common law; socialist law is returning to some of its civil tradition roots; Islamic law is borrowing from all three traditions. However, the purpose of Impact sections is to address chapter-related topics that may affect the American situation.

English colonists to America brought with them an understanding of common law, yet the English were not the only, nor even the first, people on the new continent. Native Americans had complicated forms of government that predated by many centuries the arrival of the English. Indian tribes had traditional courts that did not enforce a set of laws but oversaw a system of private settlement in a fashion that today we call mediation. Despite the variability of tribes, a system of private settlement of individual criminal offenses was nearly universal among Indian tribes (Deloria and Lytle, 1983). The goal was to mediate the case to the satisfaction of all parties and emphasized restitution and compensation over retribution. Unfortunately, some would argue, American law ended up reflecting European tradition instead of the indigenous precedent.

Rivaling the English for a foothold in the area that would eventually become the United States were the Spanish and the French. Spain established the first permanent white settlement (St. Augustine, Florida in 1565) and the first continuing capital city (Santa Fe, New Mexico in 1610), while English settlers located their first permanent settlement in 1607 at Jamestown, Virginia. In doing so, the Spanish and English predated the French, who claimed the entire Mississippi River valley in 1682 before founding the French colony of Louisiana in 1699. In terms of legal traditions, then, the area that would become the United States was presented with both common and civil law opportunities. Giving Spain her due, we concentrate here on Spanish and Mexican influences on American legal systems.

The province of New Mexico was part of Spain's vast holdings in the western hemisphere. All police and judicial powers in the New Mexico province fell to the Spanish governor, who conducted colonial affairs for the monarch. As chief of police and chief jailer, the governor's enforcement power was officially carried out by soldiers, other officials he could appoint, and, especially, the local *alcalde* and *alguacil*. These latter two positions help highlight the civil legal tradition Spain was following in her colonies.

Upon establishment of the New Mexico province, Spain provided the capital city (Sante Fe) with a municipal government called a *cabildo*. The *cabildo*, as a source of law, made local law and tried court cases. Citizens elected its four members, who, in turn, chose *alcaldes* to serve as city managers or mayors. Their special distinction, however, was that the *alcalde* also had judicial powers (Prassel, 1972; Spanish History Museum, 1988). They served as a combined mayor/judge and were assisted by the Spanish counterpart to a constable—the *alguacil*.

Similar positions developed in what was to become Texas. In 1823 and 1824, at the colony of San Felipe de Austin, Stephen Austin combined the Spanish and English systems so that each justice of the peace had a constable. Austin also created an appointed post of sheriff, and by 1831 a community patrol to maintain law and order was operating. Prassel (1972) believes that this patrol was the first working local police agency in the English-speaking West.

The proved leadership and local acceptance of the *alcaldes* and *alguacils* required the Americans to take these positions into consideration as they attempted to transform Spanish–Mexican law to a system more in accord with English common law. Typically, this was handled by transferring the persons in those posts to the new positions dictated by the new government form. In those new positions, they were expected to help implement the still developing American system of justice. Traditional systems are not, however, easily tossed aside. After the Mexican War (1848), the "new" judges in New Mexico frequently cited civil law when deciding cases (Friedman, 1973).

While adjusting to positions like the *alcalde* and *alguacil*, some jurisdictions were more forceful in their desire for infusion of common law. A particularly sought-after feature was the right to a trial by jury. Spanish and Mexican law did not allow for a jury, and many settlers versed in common law saw its absence as a shortcoming. This was particularly true in Texas, where Americans began moving after the Louisiana Purchase (1803).

By 1827, with the majority of Texas still part of the empire of Mexico, the procommon law voices succeeded in having trial by jury in criminal cases added to the constitution for the Mexican state of Coahuila and Texas. However, the strong influence of the civil tradition resulted in a jury of seven men elected for one year with decisions based on majority rule rather than unanimity. That jury could also question the defendant and his counsel and would set the penalties in the case (Markham, 1951). Even significant modifications in 1834 left a jury system that appeared strange to common law eyes. The new panel of 12 men was to judge the facts of the case and the rules of evidence, could differ with the judge, and would reach their decision with a vote of eight jurors.

After it achieved independence from Mexico (1836), Texas retained aspects of the civil law tradition but increasingly turned toward English common law as the system for Texas's future. Finally, in 1840, civil law was abolished by statute and the common law took hold in the Republic of Texas.

California was another seat of Spanish–Mexican influence. Even after receiving statehood (1850), California was feeling the impact of centuries under a civil legal tradition. For example, upon their arrival in California, Americans found Mexican lawmen called *jueces de campo*, or judges of the plains. In 1851, the California legislature repealed all prior laws with one exception—the statute relating to judges of the plains (Ruiz, 1974). Mexican law required all cattle runs or drives passing through a city, town, or village to be inspected for brands and ownership by the judges of the plains. Those judges could arrest suspected cattle or horse thieves and take them to the nearest magistrate. In the absence of any English equivalent, the California legislature gave this Mexican law enforcer the same powers as a sheriff, constable, or police officer.

The judge of the plains exemplifies the difficulty in directly applying English common law to such a different culture. Settlers in the American frontier had to stretch their imagination when applying the ancient customs and traditions of eleventh-century England to the cattle drives and gold rushes of the nineteenth-century West.

The civil law tradition inclined some areas to recognize the usefulness of law codes. Miners' codes served as bodies of law in Western mining camps from Colorado to California. These rough but workable rules and processes provided a means to record claims, to decide whose claim was first, to settle disputes among claimants, and to enforce decisions of miners' "courts" (Friedman, 1973). Answers to such questions were not easily identified in English common law.

Actually, the legal problems confronting the frontiersmen were not new in America. The difficulty of applying English common law to the American situation was apparent with the start of colonization. But without a Spanish or French legal tradition in New England, the colonists were unsure of alternatives to English common law. Even so, early colonial law was in part a codified law (Friedman, 1973) reflecting a traditional Puritan belief in the importance of the written word and the role of the Bible as a source of law.

Despite flirtations with codification and the civil tradition, the legacy followed by American legal systems has been that of the common law. Admittedly, Louisiana did more than flirt with civil law. Louisiana Codes of 1808, 1825, and 1870 borrowed heavily from the French Code Napoleon. As a result, Louisiana judges decide cases (private more than public law) chiefly on the basis of codes rather than prior decisions. The complicated history of the civil law in Louisiana (nicely reviewed by Tucker, 1956) reminds us that aspects of the civil tradition have helped shape a specifically American legal system.

Undoubtedly, one area in which law in America (and indeed in all common law countries) has become more civil-like is with the increased reliance on statute as an important source for law. However, even when the legislature plays a primary lawmaking role, we view the resulting statutes in a special way. As Sereni explained: "The content of statutory provisions is not authoritatively established unless and until they have been construed by the courts" (1956, p. 66). For example, the U.S. Congress can pass a law prohibiting the burning of the American flag. In a country where codification prevails, the courts would be obliged to find all flag burners guilty and apply the appropriate punishment. Because of the common legal tradition in the United States, a law prohibiting flag burning is not "authoritatively established" until the courts accept it as such. So, despite the obvious increase in statutes as a source of law, countries following the common legal tradition are still distinguished from their civil tradition cousins in terms of the power courts have to evaluate the legislature's work.

Socialist Legal Tradition

This legal tradition is the newest of the four discussed here. Its roots, however, are as deep as those of the other three. Not all comparative legalists believe that the socialist legal family constitutes a separate tradition. The historical link between civil law and law in socialist countries leads some to believe that these legal systems are simply a modification of the civil law tradition (see Quigley, 1989, for a particularly persuasive argument). However, I side with David (David and Brierley, 1985), Hazard (1969), and Merryman (1985), who are among those believing that a close look at law under socialism clearly identifies distinctions warranting a separate category for a socialist legal tradition. Admittedly, political and economic changes beginning in 1989 have modified the legal system in many former socialist countries. Other countries, such as Cuba, Vietnam, and the People's Republic of China, were less affected by challenges to traditional socialism. The result is a legal tradition category with several legal systems implementing shared characteristics in a variety of ways. That is why we use the term *legal tradition* rather than *legal system*.

To identify a separate socialist legal tradition, we must begin with the development of Soviet law. In this process, we must remember that just as the civil legal tradition owes part of its existence to a political entity no longer existing (that is, the Roman Empire), the socialist legal tradition is traced to the former Soviet Union. As such, the legal system of the Union of Soviet Socialist Republics provided the philosophical, and sometimes technical, base for a socialist legal tradition. As socialism spread, other countries set up a new legal system borrowing from the Soviet model but placed in their own cultural situation. So the components of Soviet law (Russian law, a view of law as artificial, and Marxism–Leninism) became the basic elements of the socialist legal tradition (see Figure 4-2).

Russian Law. In 395 the Roman Empire divided into eastern and western parts. The civil legal tradition was more closely tied to Rome and the Western

Empire, although influence from the eastern section via Justinian was immense. Russian legal history borrows more from the Eastern or Byzantine Empire. This is primarily because Russia's contact with the eastern "Romans" did not occur until the tenth century. By then, Byzantine law, as a historical extension of Roman law, was becoming more closely linked to canon law.

As with all legal systems, customary norms oriented the initial legal effort of Russians. With the conversion to Christianity around 989, custom was reduced to writing so, in the Byzantine tradition, it could be related to the influence of the Church. Of the various princes becoming involved in recording laws, Grand Prince Iaroslav the Wise (1015–1054) is credited with compiling the first Russian Code of Laws. Iaroslav's *Pravda* is a brief document based on customary law with emphasis on penal law (see the English translation by Vernadsky, 1947). A crowd of independent states made up Russia until Mongol invaders destroyed Kiev in 1240 and made Russia part of the Mongol Empire. The Mongols were primarily interested in maintaining power and collecting taxes, and produced little change in Russian life. They also, however, prevented Russian contact with the new ideas dramatically changing Western Europe during the Renaissance in the 1300's and 1400's.

The Russian princes surviving under Mongol domination still played the roles of judges and rule makers in their principalities. Russian law near the close of the fifteenth century was essentially a series of private collections consisting of princely enactments and, secondarily, of customary and Byzantine law (Zigel, 1974). Control by Mongols essentially ended by 1490, and in 1497 the Grand Prince of Moscow issued a new Code of Laws for all territories subject to Moscow. This Code was a digest of the earlier laws and the first formulation of the basic principles of a new monarchical regime. One of those principles gave the Grand Prince, soon to be called the *czar*, authority to decide how his various lords must judge in their courts (Vernadsky, 1947; Zigel, 1974).

With the reign of the czars came the firmly established idea of law as reflecting the will of a monarch. Customary law was still relevant, since princes and czars felt no need to establish rules for everyone and for all situations. That is not the same as believing that customary law limited their power. Instead, princes and czars simply felt no challenge to their authority if customary law was used to handle disputes in which they had minimal interest. The indifferent attitude of rulers toward firmly establishing a countrywide Code lasted until 1832. Before that date, attempts to modernize Russian law are more accurately described as efforts to consolidate and explain than to reform and redesign. But in 1832 a codification of Russian law was finally established and in 1855 a Penal Code was created. Though late by Western European standards, Russia finally had a written law.

Law as Artificial. The English came to appreciate the rule of law as binding because it recognized immemorial custom. The Romans and Western Continentals came to appreciate the rule of law as binding because it was appropriately authorized and recorded. The Russians never came to appreciate the rule of law at all. This is not meant to be a disparaging statement. It is simply recognition of a difference in the Russian attitude toward law compared to the attitude toward law held by other Europeans. As an old Russian proverb expresses it: "Law is like a wagon tongue, it goes wherever you turn it" (Reshetar, 1978, p. 250).

On the Continent and in England, people considered law a natural complement to morality and a fundamental base for society. This idea did not take root in Russia. David and Brierley (1985), suggest that this is partly due to the absence of Russian jurists and the late appearance of a Russian university (1755) and a Russian legal literature (mid to late nineteenth century). Perhaps more important is the point that written law was foreign to Russian mentality. Law was deemed the arbitrary work of an autocratic sovereign, a privilege of the bourgeoisie, and therefore of no import to the common person. Russians took for granted that the sovereign was above the law. The impact that this view of "law as artificial" had on the Russian people becomes clearer as we move to the role played by Marxist philosophy. A basic tenet of Marxism–Leninism is that under communism the need for law will wither away. That concept would likely have been difficult for twentieth-century British, French, or Germans to understand. But in Russia, where law had been essentially ineffective and artificial for hundreds of years, people found the concept neither surprising nor unreasonable (cf. David and Brierley, 1985).

Interestingly, Chinese history reflects some traditions similar to those in Russia. Clark (1989) points out that the Chinese people have never been treated very well by their governments and, as a result, the citizens are not inclined to wholeheartedly trust and respect government of any type. Since law was provided by those very governments, the Chinese also came to view it as rather artificial. As a result, Chinese reaction to misbehavior has a long tradition of being handled in an informal (that is, nongovernmental) manner by the people most directly involved in the violation.

In several of the remaining chapters we will see examples of this Chinese preference for grass-roots handling of crime. It will be good to remember that China (arguably the best contemporary example of the socialist legal tradition) shared some historical and cultural features with the Russians. That common heritage may partly explain why a socialist legal tradition, with its concepts like "Law as artificial," was more acceptable to China's people.

Marxism–Leninism. The Bolshevik revolution (November 7, 1917) provided the primary ingredient for a separate socialist legal tradition. To this point, the history of Russian law, and even the idea of law as artificial, could have provided the background for yet another country joining the civil legal tradition. However, the communist revolution in Russia forced her legal development to take a different path.

Marx and Engles had proposed a scientific socialism based on their understanding of laws ruling the development of society and humanity. In Russia, Vladimir Lenin became absorbed in the study of Marxism and, after the Bolshevik victory, Lenin was appointed head of the new Soviet state. Unfortunately, neither Marx nor Lenin had provided real specifics about establishing a legal system once a communist revolution occurred. Instead, general principles had to suffice for about five years until codification occurred. Meanwhile, courts loyal to the working class were instructed to apply the old imperial codes as interpreted by the revolutionary consciousness of the judges.

The primary principle directing the new Soviet law was the idea that law is subordinate to policy. Law was a means to be used by the leaders to achieve some desirable end. It was not an absolute value dictating the leader's conduct. But the history of law in Russia meant that the people did not see this idea as necessarily original. Since law is artificial, it may just as well be subordinate to policy as it was in the past to the will of princes and czars.

The policy to which law is subordinate places the rights of the collectivized economy and the socialist state above the idea of law or the rights of an individual. Socialists view this subordination to policy as an improvement. While agreeing with bourgeois-democratic revolutions that claim all people are equal before the law, the Marxist adds that law is sacred to the bourgeois because it is his design, enacted with his consent, and exists for his benefit and protection (Terebilov, 1973). With all that going for him, the socialist asks, why wouldn't the capitalist believe that the rule of law is supreme?

In 1992 one of the first examples of the potential for damaging consequences when following a "law is subordinate to policy" course was made public ("Russia's system . . . ," April 25, 1992). Andrei Chikatilo, a 56-year-old former schoolteacher, was tried in a Russian court for raping, slaying, and partially cannibalizing 53 victims. The case attracted attention not only because of its gruesome nature, but also because it highlighted some of the defects of the former Soviet legal system. For example, following a policy of placing ideology above public safety, residents of the town where the murders (which started in 1978) occurred were not warned for more than five years that a maniac was killing young women and children. Further, Soviet authorities now admit that, in an attempt to solve the crimes and stop the killings, they executed the wrong man before Chikatilo was arrested near a murder scene in late 1990 ("Russia's system . . . ," April 25, 1992).

The Chikatilo case is an extreme example (and not one that could happen only in a socialist legal system), but it does accentuate types of problems that might develop when law is used by leaders to achieve some desirable end rather than as an absolute value dictating the leader's conduct. By seeing law as a tool, rather than an absolute value, Lenin argued that law could well serve the purposes of socialism. And despite examples like the Chikatilo case, those purposes are presumed to benefit society. More specifically, socialist law—and this is clearly a distinguishing feature—exists to serve both economic and educational goals.

Socialism demands greater effort by leaders in respect to economics than capitalism requires of its leaders. As a result, the economic task of socialist law is significant. Of course, law can come to the aid of capitalist economies also, but it presumably does so with its moral grounding intact (see David and Brierley, 1985). For example, law in a capitalist economy tells its citizens to observe the rules of justice and morality and, as a result, the society will enjoy economic order. Socialist law says it will help provide the desirable economic order and the result will be justice and morality for the citizens. The complete reversal of attitudes toward law brings a total transformation of fundamental ideas about law.

More than once, Lenin identified the educational nature of socialist law (see Terebilov, 1973). Law must be used in a socialist state to educate citizens in a spirit of new, socialist relations and in the new rules of the community. Judges should ensure the success of government policy by actively participating in educating the people. As David and Brierley (1985) put it, socialist law, and the decision of judges, should be so reasonable that every honest citizen, including the person losing the case, must support and agree with the law that served as the basis for the decision.

Since law is an aspect of policy, the courts do not exist just to interpret and apply socialist law. They also must help ensure the success of government policies by educating people. Socialist law does not establish a rule of order by providing a principle for use in solving disputes. Instead, it is a means of guiding society toward the communist ideal. This position is clearly held today in the People's Republic of China, as we will see in later chapters when discussing public legal education in China.

With the economic and educational assistance of law and the legal system, the socialist state could progress to communism. Once the goal of communism is achieved, crime ceases and there is no need for law or the legal machinery. Until that time, laws, police, courts, and prisons are necessary to ensure that everyone faithfully observes and obeys government instructions (Terebilov, 1973). The government policy and instructions (that is, socialist law) to be obeyed have their main source in legislation, since that is the simplest and most straightforward way to express the will of the people. Generally, this was accomplished via the deputies of the various soviets. More specifically, it was secured by legislative actions of the Supreme Soviet.

Socialist Legal Tradition after the USSR's Demise.
As noted earlier, we are discussing a socialist legal tradition, not a Soviet legal tradition. Other countries falling within the socialist legal family share aspects of the Soviet tradition. Specifically, the Marxism–Leninism perspective of law being subordinate to policy, and of the economic/educational functions of law, is common throughout the socialist tradition. In 1990, for example, two Chinese Public Security officials wrote of ways to "prevent and punish law-breaking criminal offences (*sic*) by comprehensively employing political, economic, administrative, educational, cultural and legal means" (Bo and Yisheng, 1990, p. 1). The placement of "legal means" at the end of that list was probably not accidental. Not because the pref-

erence is for extralegal or even illegal means, but rather because legal means under the socialist tradition is merely one of several social forces to be used for keeping order.

The role Russian law played in creating a socialist legal tradition is relevant to other socialist countries only to the extent that it helped form Soviet law. The view of law as artificial was not as entrenched in many post-World War II socialist countries as it had been in pre-1917 Russia. As a result, the legal systems of some of those new socialist countries were anything but duplicates of the Soviet legal system. However, the philosophical base in Marxism provides sufficient similarity to assign membership in a socialist legal tradition.

The term *legal tradition* refers to cultural aspects of law as well as to the technical attributes. For example, Louisiana's historical link to civil law and her reliance on codification is not enough to place her in the civil legal tradition. Similarly, even dramatic political and economic changes in a country will not automatically move the country from one legal tradition to another. For example, Warsaw Pact nations did not undertake an unrestricted adoption of the Soviet legal system after World War II. Poland, Hungary, and the German Democratic Republic retained technical aspects from their civil law heritage. Just as Soviet law considered the civil law history of those countries while getting them to accept socialist legality, any subsequent political and economic changes in those nations cannot dismiss the 50-year heritage of socialism. Movement away from Communist party monopoly does not require, nor could it achieve, complete disregard for the role socialism played in each country's legal history. Therefore, identification of a separate socialist legal tradition remains necessary for the future not only so that we can understand existing socialist nations, but also so that we can appreciate both the changes occurring and those that are necessary as other countries try to leave the socialist legal tradition.

Islamic Legal Tradition

With over 920,000,000 followers, Muslims comprise nearly 18 percent of the religious population of the world. As a base of comparison, Roman Catholics are about 19 percent of the world's religious population (1991 *World Almanac and Book of Facts*). Muslims live all around the world but have their highest concentrations in the Middle East, Africa, and Asia.

With Christians and Jews, Muslims believe in one God whom Muslims call Allah. Allah's messenger was the prophet Muhammad (570?–632), who had been preceded by Jesus and the Old Testament prophets. The religion preached by Muhammad is Islam (Arabic for submission), and its followers are "those who submit to Allah" (Muslims).

Compared to the other three legal traditions, Islamic law is uncommon in its singularity of purpose. Islam recognizes no distinction between a legal system and other controls on a person's behavior. In fact, Islam is said to provide all the answers to questions about appropriate behavior in any sphere of life.

As a legal tradition, Islam is unique among the four discussed here. While each of the other three took some principles and techniques from religion, the traditions themselves remained distinct and separate from religion. Islamic law, however, is intrinsic to Islamic faith and life in Islamic countries. Like all religions, Islam has sects, the *Shi'ite* and *Sunni* branches being the primary ones. Even within the sects, different schools of thought developed regarding legal questions. As a result, Islamic law is not uniformly applied throughout Islamic countries any more than civil, common, or socialist law is consistent across nations following those traditions.

Islamic law is best discussed by referring to some of its primary components. Specifically, we review the role played by the *Shari'a*, the use of witnesses and oaths, and the *mazalim* and civil extensions (see Figure 4-2).

The Shari'a. Before Muhammad, Arabic tribes operated under customary law, drawing heavily on blood revenge. After the angel Gabriel called Muhammad to be a prophet, Muhammad preached about the need to replace old tribal loyalty with equality and brotherhood among all Muslims. In 622 he fled from harassment in Mecca to greater appreciation in the city of Medina. As his prophet status spread, Muhammad was asked to judge disputes between Muslims. Generally, he followed the customary law of the town, but in cases where that law was lacking, he turned to Allah for direction. Muhammad did not provide any twelve tables, ten commandments, codes, or digests. Instead, Allah's revelations and Muhammad's own behavior provided answers to the quarrels and questions of the townsfolk. In time, these events comprised the primary ingredients of Islamic law: the *Qur'an* and the *Sunna*.

Islamic law is called the *Shari'a*, the path to follow. In its purest form, it consists of the writings in the *Qur'an* (the holy book of Islam) and the *Sunna* (the statements and deeds of the Prophet). However, even taken together these two elements do not make up a comprehensive code of law. In fact, they hardly comprise the bare skeleton of a legal system (Coulson, 1969). Therefore, added to the primary sources were two secondary sources of law: analogical reasoning (*qiyas*) and consensus by jurists (*ijma*).

The *Qur'an*, as the word of God, was recorded by scribes and edited by scholars. It has little legislative material, with only about 10 percent of its 6237 verses containing rules. Only some 200 of those actually deal with legal issues in the strict sense of the term (Lippman, McConville, and Yerushalmi, 1988, p. 26). In any event, the *Qur'an* provides the laws as given by Allah. Islamic law, then, is the divinely ordained system of God's commands; to deny that point would be to renounce the Islam religion.

The second basic source of the *Shari'a* contains the collected actions and sayings of Muhammad. This *Sunna* includes reports (*hadith*) that explain, clarify, and amplify (but do not add to) the *Qur'an*. For example, in the area of procedural criminal law, the *Sunna* advises:

Three classes of offenders are not to be punished: the child before coming to age, the sleeper until he wakes up, and the insane until he becomes sensible (quoted in Lippman et al., 1988, p. 30).

In applying the *Qur'an* and *Sunna*, two camps formed. One side took a strict interpretation and believed that every rule of law must be derived from the *Qur'an* or the *Sunna*. The other camp believed that human reason and personal opinion should be used to elaborate the law. In the eighth century, the disagreement resulted in the first fundamental conflict of principle in Islamic jurisprudence (Coulson, 1969) and provided the foundation for one of two secondary sources of Islamic law.

In the early ninth century, the jurist Shafi'a proposed a compromise that some authors claim earned him the title "father of Muslim jurisprudence" (Coulson, 1969). Basically, Shafi'a sided with the strict interpreters while acknowledging that there were gaps which human reason was helpful in filling. But, to make sure it did not result in human legislative authority, human reasoning had to be subordinate to principles established by divine revelation. Cases not seemingly answered by the *Qur'an* or *Sunna* were handled by a process known as reasoning by analogy or *qiyas*. The decision here can make use of human reasoning, but that reasoning must have had divine law as its starting point. For example, Lippman et al. (1988) note that some judges have sentenced committers of sodomy (not mentioned in the *Qur'an* or *Sunna*) to the same penalty the *Qur'an* provides for adultery by reasoning that sodomy and adultery are similar offenses.

The next secondary source of the *Shari'a* draws upon the knowledge of legal scholars. Following Muhammad's death, the caliphs (leaders of the Muslim community) made use of consultants to help in the proper interpretation of the *Qur'an* and *Sunna*. Not surprisingly, some scholars became more prominent than others, and each had supporters for his interpretations. Schools of legal thought developed around four particular jurists (Malik, Hanifa, Shafi'i, and Hanbal). By the end of the ninth century, the four schools had developed documents telling how their school interpreted questions or solved unique cases. This was arrived at through the doctrine of consensus or *ijma*. When qualified jurists had unanimous agreement on a given point, their opinion was considered binding and having absolute authority. Recall the use of English juries to identify custom and common usage. Similarly, Muslims used a "jury" of scholars to identify the appropriate meaning of a *Qur'anic* text. Since there was consensus among jurists about how to resolve a unique problem, an opinion by an individual judge was transformed to a statement of divine law.

With the *Qur'an* and *Sunna* serving as primary sources, and *qiyas* and *ijma* as secondary, the *Shari'a* was complete. But, while the law was God-given, its application fell to humans. A feature Muslims developed to apply the law was a reliance on witnesses and oath taking. Their importance under Islamic law and uniqueness among the world's legal traditions allow them to be highlighted as a basic component of Islamic law.

Witnesses and Oaths.   The mechanism for administration of *Shari'a* is the *qadi's* court. Originally, there were no provisions for courts with many judges, for counsel by lay people, nor for any system of appeals. Instead, the single *qadi* sat in judgment over the facts of the case and how the law should apply. The facts were created primarily through oral testimony as substantiated and validated by reliable witnesses. In fact, a *qadi's* primary task was to certify a person as having the necessary qualities to assure the truthfulness of his statements.

Significant importance of witnesses and oaths has been a hallmark of Islamic law since its earliest development. The *hadith* in the *Sunna* was validated by naming the line of respected men through whom the stories about the Prophet had passed. In other words, a recollection about Muhammad's statements or actions is true because trusted and reliable men passed the recollection from generation to generation. The tradition of Islamic law, then, is to seek truth through statements made by reliable people.

The *Shari'a* does not distinguish between private and public law. Therefore, for purposes of *Shari'a*, there are no public wrongs to which the "state" must respond. Actions common law people see as "crimes" (public wrongs) are handled in the same manner as actions called "torts" (private wrongs) in common law. If accusation of a *Qur'anic* or *Sunna* violation is made under *Shari'a*, the accuser is responsible for initiating the action. Consequently, upon being assaulted or stolen from, for example, it becomes your responsibility to bring a complaint against the offender. You show the truthfulness of your complaint (that is, prove your case) by presenting witnesses in your behalf and/or taking appropriate oaths. The *Qur'an* and *Sunna* set down the number of witnesses and type of oath required. For example, proof of adultery requires four witnesses while theft can be proved with just two (see Lippman et al., 1988, pp. 42–45).

Accusers must always shoulder the burden of proof. They do this by calling witnesses who give oral testimony to the truth of the accuser's claim. The witnesses must be male adult Muslims (some *qadis* allow two women to count as one man) of high moral character. The witnesses must testify directly about their personal knowledge of the truth. Upon presenting the required number of qualified witnesses, the *qadi* rules in favor of the accuser. This is done without cross-examination of the witnesses or even presentation of evidence for the defendant. The problem, as you can well imagine, is that few offenses occur in the presence of two or more witnesses. Unless four devout male Muslims were watching while the defendant committed adultery, or two such witnesses observed the defendant burglarize a home, it will be difficult to win a case via witnesses alone.

Without any real evidence, judgment is for the defendant. More often, however, the evidence is simply incomplete. At this point, the tradition of oath taking steps in. As Rosen (1989) describes it, the oath under *Shari'a* is very different from its quaint ritual status in western jurisprudence. Under Islamic law, witnesses are not sworn before testifying, nor is there any punishment recognized for perjury. In fact, given the nature of the proceeding, the law assumes that a person may well make statements that do not bear on the truth. Rosen (1989) compares the process to bartering in the marketplace. Statements are tossed out in court to get a reaction in the same manner that one tosses out a price at the bazaar just to see how the merchant responds. In the courtroom, witnesses speak freely, and judges inquire cleverly, but no one is held to the implications of truth until truth is attached via an oath.

Oaths are taken either toward the character of the parties or the actual occurrences in the case. But the key oath in *qadi* court is the decisory oath. If neither side can present adequate support for its claim, one party may challenge the other to take an oath in support of the latter's assertions. If the opponent does so, he automatically wins. Or he can refer the oath back to the challenger, who may achieve victory by then swearing as to his own truthfulness.

At this point, the power of the *qadi* comes into play and makes this oath-taking process different from similar procedures in other systems. In Islamic law the *qadi* decides which party will first challenge the other to take an oath. This is important, because the first to swear wins the case without the other having opportunity to rebut or in any way continue. In other systems the priority is determined by who is the plaintiff or defendant in the case. Here, the *qadi* designates. He does so by looking for the person presumed most likely to know what is true about the matter at hand, or the one presumed to have been carrying out his or her tasks correctly. That person is then designated as the one first to be challenged to take the oath (Rosen, 1989).

The oath works under *Shari'a* because false swearers will suffer the consequences on judgment day. The seriousness with which Muslims approach oath taking is shown by many cases in which persons have maintained their testimony right up to the moment of oath taking only to stop, refuse the oath, and surrender the case (Lippman et al., 1988).

Extensions of Islamic Law. The core of Islamic law is relatively inflexible. Conservative Islamic jurists claim that God, through the texts of Islamic law, offers the solution to every contemporary problem. Others have not always found Allah's guidance to be clear, consistent, and current. In fact, the idealistic scheme of procedure and evidence under *Shari'a* has required, since medieval times, alternative jurisdictions.

The non-*Shari'a* jurisdictions have taken many forms over the centuries. Petty commercial affairs were handled by the old inspector of the marketplace. Petty criminal cases went before the chief police officer. A "Master of Complaints" heard cases that the *qadi* failed to resolve (Coulson, 1969). Starting in the eleventh century, the collective description for these jurisdictions has been *mazalim*, or complaints court. The common feature of these courts was the significant discretion allowed in matters of procedure and evidence. Their charge was to resolve cases in the most effective way by using the best available evidence (Coulson, 1969; Lippman et al., 1988).

Mazalim jurisdictions provided a way for the ruler to have criminal and civil cases settled without submitting to the rigid requirements of *Shari'a*. These new "secular" courts were acceptable under Islamic law because the *Shari'a* gives the ruler power to enforce the law, to direct public security, and to maintain social order. The *mazalim* courts expanded to the point that their *qadis* were seen as representing the law of the ruler while *qadis* in *Shari'a* courts were regarded as representatives of Allah's law (Lippman et al., 1988).

As contact with western nations increased in the nineteenth and twentieth centuries, Islamic countries saw a need to make increased use of non-*Shari'a* courts and procedures. In areas like commerce, the ancient *Shari'a* simply could not respond to modern developments. In criminal law, the severe punishments demanded by *Shari'a* were regarded as antiquated and more appropriate for a tribal society. Modernization took the form of adopting European-style codes in many Islamic countries. By the end of the nineteenth century, *Shari'a* law had been generally abandoned in areas of commercial law, general civil law, and criminal law (Coulson, 1969). With the creation of new court systems (like the earlier *mazalim* jurisdictions) law became openly secular. The *Shari'a* remained responsible primarily for family law.

The westernization of Islamic countries and law continued with minimal complaint until the 1970s. In the last quarter of the twentieth century, Muslim traditionalists clamored for a return to the purity of Islamic heritage. The wealth and influence of some Muslims allowed them to realign their business practices with their religious beliefs and laws. The changing pattern of world wealth meant that Western businessmen could no longer dictate all the specifics of trade relations. The Iranian revolution and the growing strength of more fundamental strains of Islam in Egypt, Syria, and elsewhere meant considerable pressure for tighter adherence to Islamic orthodoxy (Tomkins and Karim, 1987).

Despite movement toward affiliation with other legal traditions, it appears that Islamic law will enter the twenty-first century as a separate tradition. Like the other three, the Islamic legal tradition will encompass diverse legal systems and undoubtedly be influenced by civil, common, and socialist countries. However, it gives all appearances of maintaining a footing in the traditions of *Shari'a*, oaths and witnesses, and some modern version of *mazalim*.

COMPARING THE LEGAL TRADITIONS

Legal traditions can be classified into the four categories of common, civil, social-ist, and Islamic. The discussion of elements basic to each tradition provides important information about the history and development of that legacy. Since a goal of this text is to use classification strategies to provide a sense of order to diverse institutions and procedures, it is appropriate to identify more carefully the similarities and differences among the four traditions. Our classification strategy choices, you will recall, are either synthetic or authentic in nature. The former, resulting in artificial groups, requires knowledge of only one or two aspects of the groups being classified. The latter, which provides natural groups, depends on extensive investigation of the objects.

Many legal scholars and comparative criminal justicians have written about legal traditions (see Cole et al., 1987; David and Brierley, 1968; Terrill, 1982), but not as many have attempted a comprehensive analysis comparing the traditions based on some common criteria (see Ehrmann, 1976; Ingraham, 1987). The shortage of detailed information means that any current classification of legal traditions is most accurately described as synthetic rather than authentic. This means that the categories of common, civil, socialist, and Islamic should be seen as artificial groups arrived at based on some one or two criteria of interest to the scientist.

Predictivity is the main thing lost by not having authentic classification resulting in natural groups. With natural groups, we could be told that a country's legal system falls in the civil legal tradition and immediately predict characteristics of that system. With synthetic groups, the best we can do is assume that the country had cultural similarities or links to Western Europe, and suggest that the country's system shares ideas about such things as the appropriate source of law and the correct role of judges. The great variability of systems within each tradition means that we cannot yet (and maybe never will) achieve an authentic classification of legal families. A much more extensive investigation of the various systems and a clearer understanding of their characteristics must precede any movement toward identifying natural groups of law systems. Until then, we must rely on artificial groups like the four presented here.

Because artificial groups depend on the criteria chosen by the person doing the classification, the resulting categories reflect his or her interests. My interests are threefold: the values and attitudes supporting legal systems (cultural component), the characteristics of law in each system (substantive law), and procedures by which each system enforces the law (procedural law).

Chapter 3 explained that two essential ingredients of any justice system are substantive law and procedural law. With these components, law is delineated (substantive law) and the manner of enforcement is specified (procedural law). The cultural component is also important, because it often provides the key ingredient distinguishing legal systems between, and even within, legal traditions. For example, the state of Louisiana has specific substantive and procedural elements linking it to the civil legal tradition. However, the cultural elements of law in Louisiana are undoubtedly closer to those of Arkansas and Texas than to France.

In this chapter, certain items have already been mentioned under each legal tradition. Several of these speak of cultural elements relevant to the historical development of a legal tradition. However, so far discussion has not addressed specific areas of substantive and procedural law. To place comments about the four traditions in a broader context, we will compare and contrast each in terms of cultural, substantive, and procedural aspects. Since remaining chapters provide country-specific information, this chapter continues its general discussion of the four traditions and saves individual treatment for later chapters.

Cultural Component

Although the role of culture is often noted as indispensable to understanding a country's legal system (cf. Friedman and Macaulay, 1969; Merryman, 1985; Rosen, 1989), it remains one of the least researched areas. Custom in common law, codification in civil law, the Russian view of law as artificial, and the importance Muslims place on oath taking are examples of cultural elements that help us appreciate each legal tradition. Sometimes the cultural differences hide similarities among the traditions. For example, Lippman et al. (1988) suggest that the Islamic restrictions on what evidence is allowable shows a shared belief with the common law principle that it is better to release a guilty person than to punish one who is innocent.

Similarly, the civil law tradition and the Islamic tradition share a religious heritage. But canon law under the civil tradition operated in a highly civilized world where law enjoyed great prestige. Christianity lacked interest in the actual organization of society, so there was no need to have church law replace, for example, Roman law. Roman law spread throughout the West without conflicting with the Christian religion (David and Brierley, 1968). The same was not true for Islamic law. By its very nature, Islam is all encompassing. Its relevance to all aspects of the individual's life includes the organization of society, the role of social institutions, and the norms appropriate for human behavior. Islamic law had to replace any existing legal system as it spread from Medina.

By drawing attention to points such as these, the comparative justician seeks to identify similarities and differences among legal traditions. As examples, we will briefly consider the cultural components concerning "public and private law," and the "balance/separation of powers" (see Figure 4-3).

Private and Public Law.   The idea of private law and public law is a useful distinction in comparing legal systems. In the sense used here, the terms refer to a "legal personality." That is, where do legal rights and obligations lie? Under civil law the question requires two answers. Some matters are the sole concern of the individuals involved. Those individuals come as equals before the judge, who serves as referee in the matter. The legal rights and interests lie with the private individuals and, in its truest form, the right to sanction rests with the individual as well. Public law, in the civil tradition, refers to rules governing activities of the state or of persons acting in the public interest. A separate system of laws, of courts to hear such cases, and of procedures regulating the whole process is a feature of the civil tradition.

Under common law, the distinction between public and private law is not

	Common Tradition	Civil Tradition	Socialist Tradition	Islamic Tradition
Do legal rights and obligations lie with the individual (private law) or the state (public law)?	Public law, with both the individual and the state having a legal personality.	Public law when concern is with the state's legal personality; private law when concern is with the individual's legal personality.	Public law, since the state has an interest in all transactions.	Private law, since the concern always centers on the individual's legal personality.
What is the position of the judiciary in relation to other government branches?	Courts share in balancing power.	Courts have equal but separate power.	Courts are subordinate to the legislature.	Courts and other government branches are subordinate to the Shari'a.

Figure 4-3. Some cultural components of legal traditions.

so clear. Common law does not provide separate systems for handling private and public disputes. Both types of questions go before the same courts of law, are heard by the same judges, and are governed by similar rules. Cases involving state action are placed in the same position as those involving the action of ordinary citizens (Schwartz, 1956).

The absence of a distinction between public and private law in the common tradition is historically based. Essentially, English common law is predominantly public law, since the courts were justified in settling disputes only because of the lord's (finally, the Crown's) interest in the case. In this manner, the public or state was given a legal personality. In the capacity of a "personality," the state could bring claims against an individual. Civil law also recognized a legal personality of the state, but claims initiated by that "personality" progressed through the separate legal system set up for that purpose.

The idea of the state's having a legal personality is not present under the Islamic tradition. The *Shari'a* took no steps to define the interests of the community or public. Consistent with the Arabic emphasis on the individual, the Islamic legal tradition gives primacy to private law (Lippman et al., 1988). As noted above, the *Shari'a* exists to orient the private lives of Muslims and their relations with each other. Like the common tradition, a single legal system appropriately hears all types of disputes. But, instead of justifying this as resulting from a widespread interest by the state, Muslims justify it as a general concern with the individual.

The socialist tradition is more like common law when law is regarded as primarily public rather than private. In fact, Lenin proclaimed that all law is public law. By that he meant that there is a state interest in every transaction, even those traditionally private in nature (Hazard, 1969). Because the interests of a private person are of secondary importance under socialism, there is no role for private law in the socialist tradition. At this point the socialist and common traditions part ways. Although the common tradition may emphasize public law, it still recognizes private law as relevant and appropriate. It simply does not need a separate system of justice as required by the civil tradition. For the socialist tradition, public law is not just emphasized; it is singular.

Balance/Separation of Powers. One of the more important cultural changes in modern times was the eighteenth-century political and intellectual revolutions in most Western nations. Especially significant were documents like the American Declaration of Independence and the French Declaration of the Rights of Man and of the Citizen. These manuscripts offered ideas about human equality and the relationship between state and citizen. We quickly notice political, economic, and intellectual aspects of the revolutions, but there were important legal ramifications as well. Consider first the impact events had in the civil and common law countries.

The French judicial aristocracy were targets of the Revolution because of their tendency to identify with the landholders. Repeated efforts toward reform had been obstructed by courts refusing to apply new laws, interpreting them contrary to their intent, or hindering attempts of officials to administer them (Merryman, 1985). The situation differed from the one found in England (and America), where judges had more often been on the side of the individual against a power-wielding ruler. English citizens did not have the French fear of judicial lawmaking and of judicial interference in administration.

Another reason for targeting French judges was their failure to distinguish clearly between applying law and making law. Montesquieu and Rousseau had argued for the importance of establishing and maintaining a separation of governmental powers. Especially important was a clear distinction between legislative and executive duties on the one hand, and the duties of the judiciary on the other. In the French Revolution, this emphasis on separation of powers led to a system designed to keep the judiciary from intruding into areas reserved for the other two powers: lawmaking and execution of the laws. Again, this situation differed from that found in the American colonies. The system of checks and balances developed in the United States does not try to isolate the judiciary, nor does it try to approximate the sharp division of powers typically encountered in civil law countries. Essentially, the judiciary was not a target of the American Revolution in the way it was in France (Merryman, 1985).

Following the French lead, European countries moved to separate the three governmental powers so that the judiciary could be isolated. In America and England, a system of checks and balances was used without any particular interest in isolating the judiciary.

While the common law tradition operated with a judiciary that balanced the power of the legislature and the executive, the civil tradition functioned with a judiciary separated from the other two branches of government. This separation of powers is one explanation for the development of a separate legal system for public law. It also, of course, reflects a greater suspicion of the judiciary under the civil tradition than was present in the common legal tradition (Merryman, 1985). Despite the different paths taken, both civil and common law traditions rely on each government part as a source of law. As explained below, there are important differences with regard to which government area is emphasized as the primary source of law, but for now we need only point to the expectation that each part has a role to play. The socialist legal tradition rejects the separation of powers principle and instead invests all power in the hands of the legislature (for example, the National People's Congress in China). As a result, socialist courts are not the equal of the legislature either by isolation from that branch or by serving as a check and balance to that branch. The implications of this for the duties of a judge and the function of the court are discussed below.

Like socialist courts, Islamic courts do not operate as a counterbalance to the legislature and executive. Instead, consistent with its emphasis on private law, the Islamic court serves as a stabilizing device among contending persons (Rosen, 1989). Actually, under classic Islamic theory, neither the state nor the courts were instruments for the application of law. Instead, each was to focus on the individual and perform its respective duties in a way that allowed individuals to carry on with their own affairs.

There are other intriguing and important questions about the cultural component of legal traditions. It would be good to know such things as the attitude of people toward their courts, what type of people and cases go to court, the extent to which courts are used or avoided, and so on. But such questions still await an interested scientist. Preliminary information on cultural views, like the role of the state in human affairs and the positioning of various parts of government, provides good data to start the journey.

With even basic information about the cultural component, we can propose a rudimentary design for the structure of each legal tradition. The cultural suspicion of the judiciary in many pre-French Revolution civil law countries has already helped explain the civil tradition's preference for separate public and private law systems. Similarly, the lack of distrust of common law judges explains that tradition's satisfaction with a single system hearing both public and private disputes. The trust/distrust distinction also suggests that the common law may be more willing to provide judges with lawmaking powers.

The Islamic emphasis on private law emanating from a divine source means that we should not be surprised to find the Muslim judge playing a restricted role in lawmaking (he cannot take Allah's place) or law-applying (he is there to assist individual rather than state interests). At the other extreme, cultural aspects of socialist law suggest that those judges will actively represent state interests, since all law is public law. Still, like the Islamic *qadi*, we would not expect the socialist judge to be involved in lawmaking, not because law comes from God, but because lawmaking falls to the socialist legislature, which operates at a governmentally superior level. Keeping points like those in mind, we turn to the substantive and procedural components of the legal traditions.

Substantive Component

In its broadest sense, substantive law concerns where laws come from (see Figure 4-4) and how they are defined. More specifically, as explained in Chapter 3, substantive law is composed of internal and external characteristics. Chapter 5 provides detailed information about the internal and external characteristics of criminal law in several countries, so here we can concentrate on a broader question of substantive law: Where do the laws come from?

Any legal tradition must consider the role local custom plays as a source of law. The *Qur'anic* part of Islamic law is of divine origin, but, besides its divine inspiration, the *Sunna* certainly reflects Muhammad's understanding of local custom. Socialist law began in the Soviet Union by taking advantage of the customary view of law as artificial and using existing courts to initiate implementation of the new tradition. In the civil legal tradition codes substituted for prior custom. Under common law, decisions by judges reflected custom and provided it with legitimacy. Unfortunately, a summary like this is misleading. Custom

	Common Tradition	Civil Tradition	Socialist Tradition	Islamic Tradition
The primary source of law is	Custom	Written code (Provided by rulers or legislators)	Principles of the socialist revolution	Divine revelation

Figure 4-4. A substantive component of legal traditions.

played a role in all four traditions, but the actual source of law in each does not equally reflect custom.

The primary source of law in the civil tradition is the written code. The code, which is complete and self-sufficient, is provided by the ruler or the legislature. Of course, completeness is a problem, since the codes would become unreasonably extensive if they anticipated all possible acts and the specifics of every case. Instead of offering direct and specific solutions to particular problems, codes supply general principles from which logical deduction provides a resolution in each case (Sereni, 1956). In this manner, civil judges need only identify the applicable code principle to decide a particular case. The solution should be reached through an independent process of legal reasoning that the judge can identify and explain. This process allows the judge to apply the law, but not to make it—exactly what the cultural tradition of separation of powers had in mind. Therefore, under the civil legal tradition, the solution to each case is to be found in the provisions of the written law, and the judge must show that the decision is based on those provisions.

For the common legal tradition, the primary source of law is custom. Law is a public expression of society's entrenched vision of right and wrong, good and bad (Postema, 1986). Like the civil law, common law rests on certain principles. The difference between the two is that for common law the principles exist as generally accepted tradition instead of through writing. Writing them down, reveals, not creates, the principles. Since the traditional way of identifying custom was through the court, rather than legislative, process, judges came to play a pivotal role in common law. A decision by a judge was accepted as legal recognition of a custom. In this sense, the judge "made law" by accepting the custom as binding in a particular case. The absence of a cultural suspicion about judicial actions, and the tradition of accepting principles other than those specifically written by rulers and legislators, gave the common law judge lawmaking and law-applying authority.

Islamic law is of divine origin. Its primary sources, the *Qur'an* and the *Sunna*, specify the legal principles linked to right and wrong behavior. Its authority is based on God's commands instead of long-held traditions or directives by state power. In fact, its divine nature means that no worldly authority can change it, let alone supplement it. So, like civil law judges, Islamic *qadis* must turn to written documents for solutions to disputes. Also like their civil counterparts, *qadis* cannot do any more than identify the correct principle for use in a particular case. The difference lies in the source of that principle.

The socialist legal tradition shares with the civil tradition a view of law as stemming from written codes. The difference is that civil codes are the work of special interest groups (rulers and the bourgeoisie), while socialist laws represent the ideals of the socialist revolution. In that sense, the revolution (more correctly, the principles of the revolution) is the primary source of socialist law. Further, since socialism does not regard law as an absolute value (whether divine, state, or tradition in nature), it is merely a means to achieve socialist and communist ideals. Since law is just an instrument, it stands to reason that judges have a similar role and therefore cannot be a source of law. So, like the judges under civil and Islamic traditions, socialist law judges are expected to apply—not make—the law.

Procedural Component

If law under each tradition really came only from the source identified above, few legal systems of any type could remain effective. The belief that state authorities anticipate every nuance of each potential dispute is just as unreasonable as trusting that ancient custom provides useful guidelines for contemporary behavior. Similarly, believing that God's pronouncements for appropriate behavior today are the same as those provided in the sixth century requires as much faith as accepting utopian theories of a nineteenth-century philosopher and a twentieth-century revolutionary. Obviously, each system had to provide ways to update, modify, fill in the gaps, and supplement the various sources of law in their respective legal traditions. The ways in which that was done brings us to the final topic for this chapter: the procedures for solving problems of flexibility (see Figure 4-5).

The concept of *stare decisis* has the potential to tie common law to the vestiges of the past. When judges are expected to decide the present case similarly to the way like cases were decided in the past, it seems unlikely that much change can occur. Maybe even more important, what happens when the court is presented with a case that seems very dissimilar to preceding ones? Luckily for the judge, and therefore for nations under this tradition, common law provides for flexibility by empowering judges to develop solutions to unique cases by "making law" (Postema, 1986). The only restraint requires the solution to be built from a base of existing law. The result is law established by judicial decision and precedent rather than issuing from statutes, codes, or divine proclamation.

Another technique to achieve flexibility under common law is the practice of "particularization." A review of U.S. Supreme Court holdings in any subject area quickly exemplifies this point. The common legal tradition limits court decisions to very particular facts. Two cases may involve stopping a suspect and searching the suspect's person and surrounding area. But in case A, the suspect was *walking* away from the reported scene of the crime, whereas in case B the suspect was *running* away. The particular behavior of the suspect may well make the cases different in the court's eyes. As a result, the judge in case B may decide that the decision in case A did not set a precedent for the situation now before her. So the case B judge has the flexibility to make law for this "unique" case.

The civil legal tradition faces a similar problem but for different reasons. The idea of a state authority (for example, legislature, parliament, and the like) reducing to writing all the necessary components of substantive and procedural law cannot be seriously proposed. But that is the objective under civil law. Ideally, the civil law judge must simply extract the facts in the case, find the

How is flexibility pro-vided?	Common Tradition	Civil Tradition	Socialist Tradition	Islamic Tradition
	Judge-made law	Variation in reasoning and definition	Principle of analogy	*Mazalim* courts
	Particularization	Identification of issues as either questions of law or of fact	Directives from higher-level courts	The process of *ijtihad*

Figure 4-5. A procedural component of legal traditions.

appropriate provision as provided by the legislature, and apply it to the problem. As Merryman (1985) explains, if a relevant provision is not found, the fault lies with either the judge (who obviously cannot follow clear instructions) or the legislator (who failed to draft clearly stated and clearly applicable legislation). Unfortunately, the ideal is just that. Relevant provisions often cannot be found, so where is the flexibility needed to handle those situations?

One way to provide flexibility in civil law is the recognition that deducing a solution from a necessarily general legislative provision may lead judges to different conclusions. That is, different reasoning can lead to different results (Sereni, 1956). As long as the judge shows how the decision proceeds logically from the rule stated by the legislature, the solution is acceptable. Similarly, the civil tradition allows for changes in meaning over time. Earlier civil courts may have correctly ruled in their time, but subsequent modification in the meaning attached to words in the written law allows and requires contemporary courts to arrive at different findings with sound reasoning.

The civil legal tradition gains flexibility by giving judges authority to characterize issues as either problems of law or problems of fact. Particularization in common law and the characterization of judicial precedents as law have resulted in more law in common law countries than in civil law countries (Sereni, 1956). The result is the designation of many issues as points of "law" instead of simply issues of "fact." This is an important distinction, since a legal issue, once recognized as such, must be followed. A factual issue is presented at face value and without authoritative connotation.

Whereas common law requires many issues to be considered questions of law, civil law provides courts with the discretion to view those same issues as questions of fact. Consider, for example, issues about evidence and testimony. A civil court judge may find it strange to keep an important piece of evidence or relevant testimony out of court. But for that judge these are issues of fact—Did this person commit this offense? For the common law judge, the same issues may be legal ones—Was this evidence or testimony gathered in the appropriate (legal) manner? Obviously, providing the civil court judge discretion to decide whether an issue is a factual or legal question gives that tradition a degree of flexibility not found under common law.

An early technique for flexibility used in the socialist tradition was the principle of analogy. Article 10 of the Soviet Union's 1922 Criminal Code instructed judges (and prosecutors) to punish, by analogy, any acts deemed socially dangerous even if they were not defined as criminal by the code (Hazard, 1969; Reshetar, 1978). This open-ended provision of substantive law provided the court with great flexibility to define something as criminal and determine the necessary punishment. As long as the act being prosecuted was analogous to one prohibited in the code, socialist law could prosecute and sanction the offender.

The usefulness of punishment by analogy is highlighted upon discovering how loosely drafted were some code definitions of crime. For example, the crime of hooliganism referred to intentional acts that seriously disturbed public order and showed clear disrespect for society (Chaldize, 1977). With a definition like that, it was easy to argue that a particular offense was analogous to something prohibited in the code. Use of the principle became excessive, and in 1932 the courts were chastised for applying the law to acts not prohibited by the code. In 1936, Stalin (of all people) brought a temporary lull in use of the principle when he demanded stability of laws (Hazard, 1969). After regaining vigor in 1941, the use of analogy was finally dismantled with revision of the Soviet criminal code in 1958.

Importantly, the Chinese code still incorporates the principle of analogy (McCabe, 1989). Under Article 79 of the code, a person committing a socially dangerous act not specifically prohibited by law may still be punished if the act is analogous to something that is specifically prohibited. McCabe (1989) reports an example of analogy's application when a Chinese citizen sold his passport to another person. Selling a passport was not explicitly prohibited by the code, so the offender was punished under the prohibition against forgery.

Today, flexibility in socialist law, even in China, also relies on more widely accepted procedures. Especially important is the role played by the higher-level courts. Like the civil court judge, the judge in the socialist tradition is expected to decide by reference to principles recorded in a set of codes. To aid in that process, the supreme court in socialist countries watches over the ways in which judges interpret laws and administer justice. When the supreme court deems something inappropriate, it issues directives that lower-court judges must follow. The flexibility, then, lies not so much with the ordinary court judge, but is still found in the court system.

The rigidity of the *Shari'a* required Islamic law to develop procedures for flexibility very early. The importance of flexibility procedures for the development of Islamic law was highlighted earlier in this chapter where we discussed *mazalim* courts. The *mazalim* courts gave flexibility to Islamic law by providing opportunities for rulers to make law. Of course, it was not called lawmaking, since only Allah could do that. Instead, the rulers' "laws" were seen as administrative and enforcement requirements. These rules supplemented and enforced the *Shari'a* in a way that essentially provided secular legislation.

The closest thing the *Shari'a* itself has had to flexibility was the early process of *ijtihad*. During the first several centuries of its growth, Islamic law allowed jurists to interpret independently the *Qur'an* and *Sunna* when deliberating a case. This process provided significant flexibility, because each judge could arrive at a decision based on his understanding of the law as it related to the current case. By the tenth century, it was determined that sufficient opinions had been written regarding interpretation of the *Qur'an* and *Sunna*. The door of *ijtihad* was closed, and future generations of jurists were denied the right of independent inquiry (Coulson, 1969). Instead, jurists had to follow the doctrine of their predecessors. Why close a procedure allowing flexibility? Coulson (1969) believes that Muslim lawyers, like those the world over, were creatures of precedent who saw law as primarily a way to stabilize social order. Each legal system has periods when law remains static with settled rules in line with the temper of society. If Islamic law remained settled and stable for an extremely long time, it was because Islamic society itself remained relatively unchanged. Importantly, since the mid-twentieth century, Muslim jurists and judges in some countries have been allowed to determine the rule of *Shari'a* by independent interpretation of the basic texts. Though not widespread, reopening the door of *ijtihad* would provide a flexibility that may allow *Shari'a* law to retain important influence as part of the Islamic legal tradition.

SUMMARY

Four legal traditions are identifiable today. Although there is considerable variety of legal systems within each tradition, it is possible to distinguish a common heritage making up each legal family. The common legal tradition is familiar to American students, because it developed in England and had significant impact on the legal system of the United States. Important aspects of its development include feudal practices, the importance of custom, and the concept of equity. The civil legal tradition is the oldest of the four contemporary families; its roots extend back to Roman law and canon law as it emphasizes codification. Getting its start in the Soviet Union, the socialist legal tradition built upon Russian law and a view of law as artificial, but took its specific form from Marxist–Leninist philosophy. Finally, the Islamic legal tradition has a divine source in the ingredients making up the *Shari'a* and customary Arabic reliance on oaths and witnesses. Various extensions of Islamic law have allowed it to continue in modern circumstances, and, given the acendency of Islamic fundamentalists, will continue to be a force in Muslim countries.

Attempts to compare the four traditions are most appropriately handled by considering certain cultural, substantive, and procedural components. In that manner, we identified how law is emphasized as either public or private, the relationship between the judiciary and other organs of government, the primary source of law, and how each tradition responds to the problem of flexibility. With this basic understanding of four categories of legal traditions, we are ready to tackle more specific topics concerning particular countries.

SUGGESTED READING

Clark, John P. (1989). Conflict management outside the courtrooms of China. In R. Troyer, J. Clark, and D. Rojek (Eds.), *Social control in the People's Republic of China* (pp. 57–69). New York: Praeger.

David, Rene, and Brierley, John E. C. (1985). *Major legal systems of the world today (3rd ed.)*. London, England: Stevens and Sons.

Lippman, Matthew R., McConville, S., and Yerushalmi, M. (1988). *Islamic criminal law and procedure: An introduction*. New York: Praeger.

Merryman, John H. (1985). *The civil law tradition* (2nd ed.). Stanford, CA: Stanford University Press.

Wigmore, John H. (1936). *A panorama of the world's legal systems* (library edition). Washington, DC: Washington Law Book Company.

REFERENCES

Bo, Jiang, and Yisheng, Dai. (1990). Mobilize all possible social forces to strengthen public security—A must for crime prevention. *Police Studies, 13,* 1–9.

Chalidze, Valery. (1977). *Criminal Russia.* New York: Random House.

Clark, John P. (1989). Conflict management outside the courtrooms of China. In R. Troyer, J. Clark, and D. Rojek (Eds.), *Social control in the People's Republic of China* (pp. 57–69). New York: Praeger.

Cole, George F., Frankowski, Stanislaw J., and Gertz, Marc G. (Eds.). (1987). *Major criminal justice systems: A comparative study* (2nd ed.). Newbury Park, CA: Sage.

Coulson, Noel J. (1969). *Conflicts and tensions in Islamic jurisprudence.* Chicago: University of Chicago Press.

David, Rene, and Brierley, John E. C. (1968). *Major legal systems of the world today.* London, England: Collier-Macmillan Ltd.

David, Rene, and Brierley, John E. C. (1985). *Major legal systems of the world today (3rd ed.).* London, England: Stevens and Sons.

Deloria, Vine Jr., and Lytle, Clifford M. (1983). *American Indians, American justice.* Austin, TX: University of Texas Press.

Ehrmann, Henry W. (1976). *Comparative legal cultures.* Englewood Cliffs, NJ: Prentice Hall.

Friedman, Lawrence M. (1973). *A history of American law.* New York: Touchstone Book.

Friedman, Lawrence M., and Macaulay, Stewart. (1969). *Law and the behavioral sciences.* Indianapolis, IN: Bobbs-Merrill.

Hazard, John N. (1969). *Communists and their law.* Chicago: University of Chicago Press.

Kolbert, C. F. (Trans.). (1979). *The digest of Roman law.* New York: Viking Penguin.

Lippman, Matthew R., McConville, S., and Yerushalmi, M. (1988). *Islamic criminal law and procedure: An introduction.* New York: Praeger.

Markham, Edward Lee, Jr. (1951). The reception of the common law of England in Texas and the judicial attitude toward that reception, 1840–1859. *Texas Law Review, 29,* 904–930.

McCabe, Edward J. (1989). Structural elements of contemporary criminal justice in the People's Republic of China. In R. Troyer, J. Clark, and D. Rojek (Eds.), *Social control in the People's Republic of China* (pp. 115–129). New York: Praeger.

Merryman, John H. (1985). *The civil law tradition* (2nd ed.). Stanford, CA: Stanford University Press.

Plucknett, Theodore F. T. (1956). *A concise history of the common law* (5th ed.). Boston: Little, Brown and Company.

Postema, Gerald J. (1986). *Bentham and the common law tradition.* Oxford: Clarendon Press.

Prassel, Frank. (1972). *The western peace officer.* Norman, OK: University of Oklahoma Press.

Quigley, John. (1989). Socialist law and the civil law tradition. *The American Journal of Comparative Law, 37,* 781–808.

Ingraham, Barton L. (1987). *The structure of criminal procedure: Laws and practice of France, the Soviet Union, China, and the United States.* New York: Greenwood, an imprint of Greenwood Publishing Group, Westport, CT.

Reshetar, John S., Jr. (1978). *The Soviet polity: Government and politics in the U.S.S.R.* (2nd ed.). New York: Harper and Row.

Rosen, Lawrence. (1989). *The anthropology of justice: Law as culture in Islamic society.* Cambridge, England: Cambridge University Press.

Ruiz, Manuel, Jr. (1974). *Mexican American legal heritage in the southwest* (2nd ed.). Los Angeles, CA: Author.

Russia's system on trial, too. (1992, April 25). *The Denver Post.* P. 10A

Schwartz, Bernard. (1956). The code and public law. In B. Schwartz (Ed.). *The Code Napoleon and the common-law world* (pp. 247–266). Westport, CT: Greenwood Press.

Sereni, Angelo P. (1956). The code and the case law. In B. Schwartz (Ed.). *The Code Napoleon and the common-law world* (pp. 55–79). Westport, CT: Greenwood Press.

Spanish History Museum. (1988). *Spanish law enforcement in New Mexico: From the baston de justicia to the billy club,* (Spanish History of the United States Series, number 5). Albuquerque, NM: Spanish History Museum.

Terebilov, V. (1973). *The Soviet court* (M. Saifulin, Trans.). Moscow: Progress Publishers.

Terrill, Richard J. (1982). Approaches for teaching comparative criminal justice to undergraduates. *Criminal Justice Review, 7*(1), 23–27.

Tomkins, Cyril and Karim, Rif`at Ahmed `Abdul. (1987). The Shari`ah and its implications for Islamic financial analysis: An opportunity to study interactions among society, organization, and accounting. *The American Journal of Islamic Social Sciences, 4,* 101–115.

Tucker, John H., Jr. (1956). The code and the common law in Louisiana. In B.

Schwartz (Ed.). *The Code Napoleon and the common-law world* (pp. 346–377). Westport, CT: Greenwood Press.

Ullman, Walter. (1975). *Law and politics in the Middle Ages*. Ithaca, NY: Cornell University Press.

Vernadsky, George (Trans.). (1947). *Medieval Russian laws*. New York: Columbia University Press.

Watson, Alan. (1970). *The law of the ancient Romans*. Dallas: Southern Methodist University Press.

Wigmore, John H. (1928). *A panorama of the world's legal systems* (Vol. 1). Saint Paul, MN: West Publishing.

Wigmore, John H. (1936). *A panorama of the world's legal systems* (library edition). Washington, DC: Washington Law Book Company.

Zigel (Sigel), Feodor F. (1974). *Lectures on Slavonic law*. Gulf Breeze, FL: Academic International Press. (Original work published 1902).

Chapter 5

Substantive Law and Procedural Law in the Four Legal Traditions

KEY TOPICS

- Aspects of substantive law in the four legal traditions
- Aspects of procedural law in the four legal traditions
- Three ways to implement the process of adjudication
- Contrasting the adversarial and inquisitorial adjudication process
- Supporting the rule of law through judicial review

KEY TERMS

adversarial adjudicatory process
common law crime
concentrated model of judicial review
diffuse model of judicial review
inquisitorial adjudicatory process
Islamic adjudicatory process

judicial review
mixed model of judicial review
private law
public law
Rechtsstaat

COUNTRIES REFERENCED

Argentina	Greece	Portugal
Austria	Italy	Russia
Brazil	Mexico	Scotland
England	Morocco	United States of America
France	New Zealand	Venezuela
Germany	Poland	

The discussion of law in this chapter continues the general theme begun in Chapter 4. The similarity in topics means that there is no reason to change classification schemes. The four legal traditions are reviewed in terms of their substantive and procedural aspects. This chapter includes more detailed reference to particular countries as means of explanation, but its focus remains broad.

SUBSTANTIVE CRIMINAL LAW

You will recall that substantive law deals with creating and defining behavior as criminal. With its general characteristics, substantive law provides citizens with information about what behavior is required or prohibited (*specificity*) and explains what may happen to people who misbehave (*penal sanction*). Further, substantive law assures citizens that the law comes from a legitimate authority (*politicality*) and will be applied by that authority in an unbiased manner (*uniformity*).

Those four general characteristics of substantive criminal law admittedly reflect a Western bias. But they also are presented as ideals rather than reality. Similarly, the seven major principles of criminal law (that is, *mens rea, actus reus,* concurrence, harm, causation, punishment, and legality) are criteria linked to Western law. There is a danger in applying the general characteristics and major principles to non-Western systems if we insist that they are in any way superior to other legal standards. However, if they serve merely as a point of contrast, the characteristics and principles can provide a useful comparative technique. Therefore, as an aid to comparison, we use traditionally Western aspects of substantive criminal law to describe law in other legal traditions.

General Characteristics and Major Principles

Every known legal system relies on some version of politicality to create and define criminal behavior. The authority may take forms like a tribal chief, a monarch, a supernatural force, a court official, or an elected body of citizen representatives. Whatever its form, it has the authority (either granted by the citizens or taken by force) to make laws. Similarly, every legal system provides some type of punishment or penal sanction to people who misbehave. Sanctions might range from a required apology to execution of the offender, but in each instance the offenders should understand that they have misbehaved and must suffer the consequences.

Providing citizens with specific information about their obligations is difficult but remains a universal ideal. American vagrancy laws and hooliganism in the former Soviet Union show the existence of laws lacking specificity. The intent is not necessarily to trick the citizen. Political authorities in both countries agreed that specificity is a desirable attribute of criminal law. It is also, however, difficult to achieve.

Similarly, American and Russian citizens can provide examples of the law's being applied with prejudice. Some citizens in each country seem above the law, whereas others have the law applied to them with obvious vigor. Such absence of uniformity does not mean that citizens and authorities in each country see it as an undesirable characteristic of law; it is simply an ideal quality we should strive toward (or at least give the appearance of doing so) even if we have fallen short in certain circumstances.

Extensive discussion of how different legal traditions or systems view the four general characteristics of substantive law is unnecessary. The ideal nature of the characteristics and their universal appeal as something to strive for provide few areas for differentiating countries. Simply stated, what country would not describe their laws as demonstrating, or striving toward, politicality, specificity, uniformity, and penal sanction? We must find more debatable and identifiable aspects of criminal law if we wish to distinguish between legal traditions or systems.

The major principles of substantive law also present ideals, but the seven internal requirements have the advantage of being more applied than their four philosophical cousins under the general characteristics. *Mens rea*, *actus reus*, concurrence, harm, causation, punishment, and legality are used to identify a particular behavior as criminal. As such, they can provide a mechanism to compare legal systems on points like the requirements each uses to show criminality. We will provide a brief example of how a few countries deal with the idea of criminal responsibility, since that concept incorporates several of the principles.

The penal code of the Federal Republic of Germany, which provided the base for unified Germany's penal code, assigns criminal responsibility to persons acting intentionally (*mens rea* and *actus reus*) to violate a criminal statute, but Germans do not assign criminal capacity to anyone under age 14. Further, if the act is the result of a mistake of fact or necessity, the actor is not criminally responsible. Similarly, persons acting in self-defense do not act unlawfully. Those modifications of criminal responsibility by defenses and justifications should look familiar to Americans (Penal Code of the Federal Republic of Germany, 1987).

In a comparable manner, the Italian penal code says that no one may be punished for an offense unless at the time it was committed the actor was responsible. For the Italians, one is "responsible if he has the capacity to understand and to will" (Italian Penal Code, 1978, p. 32). As do the Germans, the Italians require a person to be age 14 before criminal responsibility is attributed. The Italians further specify that offenders from ages 14 through 17 shall be responsible, but subject to reduced punishment, if the person had capacity to understand and to will. Other justifications and excuses for criminal responsibility in Italy include accidents, physical compulsion (similar to duress in American jurisdictions), self-defense, and necessity (Italian Penal Code, 1978).

Islamic law requires the presence of both criminal conduct and criminal intent to show criminal responsibility. As part of criminal conduct, Muslim jurists say that criminal responsibility also demands causation. However, recall the example in Chapter 3 wherein Bob, having been poisoned by John—who had intended to kill Bob—dies from the poison's antidote rather than from the poison. Since Bob's death was not the direct cause of the poison administered by John, John cannot legally be charged with murder. Had the Bob and John story occurred in an Islamic law jurisdiction, the outcome could be quite different. Sanad points out that under Islamic law; "A person is held criminally responsible even if some contributing factors intervene to assist in bringing about the criminal result as long as these factors are insufficient to bring about the result by themselves and do not break the causal relationship between the result and the act or omission, which remains the principal cause" (1991, p. 86).

Criminal intent, as Islam's second requirement for criminal responsibility, is taken to mean an evil state of mind (that is, *mens rea*). Muslim scholars distinguish between general and specific criminal intent by viewing the former as inferred whenever someone voluntarily participates in criminal conduct, but general intent is not always sufficient to show criminal responsibility. There are times when specific intent must be proven. In this sense, specific intent seems to refer to the need to prove that the person intended to commit the particular act under question and did so without justification or excuse. Since Islamic law will withhold criminal responsibility in such circumstances as coercion and necessity, it is possible for a person to have committed an illegal act with general intent (for example, he knowingly hit another person) but without specific intent (for example, he did so only to protect himself from the assailant).

Some of the Islamic reasons for withholding responsibility add an interesting twist on similar ones found in other countries. For example, infancy is a defense to crime under Islamic law, but Muslims believe that criminal capacity increases with age. As a result, criminal capacity is not possible until age 7 is reached, since younger children are not viewed as able to reason. Children between age 7 and the onset of puberty have partial criminal capacity and therefore have some criminal responsibility—though not for *hudud* or *qisas* crimes. After the onset of puberty, a person can be held fully criminally responsible as long as she is of sound mind. Since puberty plays such an important role in assigning responsibility, we might expect it to be well defined by Muslim jurists. Actually, Sanad (1991) reports considerable disagreement. Some scholars say that it is determined by age (either 11 or 12, depending on the scholar), while others say it varies in males and females, and still others argue that some signs of puberty should be used in making the judgment.

That brief review of how some countries view criminal responsibility reminds us that the similarity among countries can be just as interesting as the differences. As a final example, before moving to a discussion of substantive law in each legal tradition, let us look at how Germany and Italy handle the insanity defense. As Chapter 3 pointed out, the insanity defense has generated considerable debate in the United States regarding its most appropriate phrasing. Maybe other countries have come up with wording we may wish to borrow.

Section 20 of the Penal Code of the Federal Republic of Germany excuses those suffering from a mental disorder. Specifically:

A person is not criminally responsible if at the time of the act, because of a psychotic or similar serious mental disorder, or because of a profound interruption of consciousness or because of feeblemindedness or any other type of serious mental abnormality, he is incapable of understanding the wrongfulness of his conduct or of acting in accordance with this understanding (Penal Code of the Federal Republic of Germany, 1987, p. 55).

The code goes on in section 21 to also excuse persons of "diminished capacity." Here, if the perpetrator's ability to either understand the wrongfulness of his conduct or to act in accordance with that understanding is substantially diminished (rather than absent as in section 20), he is still criminally responsible but subject to a reduced penalty.

The Italian Penal Code distinguishes between total and partial mental deficiency. For the former, Article 88 states:

Anyone who, at the time he committed the act, was, by reason of infirmity, in such a state of mind as to preclude capacity to understand and to will shall not be responsible (Italian Penal Code, 1978, p. 32).

On the other hand, partial mental deficiency is

Anyone who, at the time he committed the act, was, by reason of infirmity, in such a state of mind as to greatly diminish, without precluding, his capacity to understand and to will, shall be liable for the offense committed; but the punishment shall be reduced (Italian Penal Code, 1978, pp. 32–33).

These two codes seem to leave the definition of mental deficiency as unmanageable as have the legislators in the United States. That does not, of course, give Americans a basis for gloating, but instead emphasizes the difficulty of attempts to be fair when assigning criminal responsibility. Such issues in the area of substantive criminal law present worldwide problems. And while specific examples like those just given are useful in showing both similarity and difference, it is necessary to move to a more general discussion as we consider substantive law in the four legal traditions.

Substantive Law in the Common Legal Tradition

As the historical home of the common law, England presents an excellent example of that tradition's substantive law. Since common law was unwritten law, there was no source to which one could turn and read a list of crimes and their punishments. Instead, identifying what was criminal relied on earlier decisions by judges and through reference to community folkways. As a result, the earliest common law offenses, called *felonies*, included crimes like murder, robbery, rape, arson, and larceny. These serious transgressions were punishable by death or mutilation and by loss of property. The judiciary could also identify other offenses, called *misdemeanors*, which were deemed less serious.

It seems that crimes under common law were essentially "pulled out of a hat" held by the judge. Even if the judge were a political authority applying penal sanction in a uniform manner, where was the specificity? If the judge got to decide what was criminal, how could citizens have any advance warning? The answer relies on the concept of immemorial custom. The "hat" from which a judge pulled the crimes was the norms guiding people in that community. Since everyone shared the same norms (see the consensus approach), everyone well knew what behavior was acceptable. Custom provided specificity.

Scotland provides a good contemporary example of substantive criminal law in the common legal tradition. Along with England, Wales, and Northern Ireland, Scotland helps comprise the United Kingdom. These four countries operate under a single government but have three separate legal systems. The systems of England, Wales, and Scotland share more in common than they do with Northern Ireland, but even the Scottish system differs from that of England and Wales. At this point, our general discussion need only note that Scotland is considered a member of the common legal family. More particularly, Scottish courts continue to take an active role in judge-made substantive law.

While most common law countries view legislation as the appropriate task for lawmakers (as discussed below), Scotland continues the common law traditions of judge-made law. This position may be related to the absence of a specifically Scottish parliament. The Scots rely on their representatives in the Parliament of the United Kingdom to provide necessary laws. But that body "has never shown much interest in the substantive criminal law of Scotland" (Jones, 1990). As a result, the traditional flexibility common law allows the court is embraced by the Scots as a strength of the system.

The High Court of Justiciary has a "declaratory power" which allows the Court to punish obviously criminal acts even though such behavior was not punished in the past. That power has not been explicitly used since 1838, but the High Court continues to create new crimes but without citing its declatory power as authority. Jones (1990) cites the cases of *Khaliq* v. *H. M. Advocate* (1983) and *Strathern* v. *Seaforth* (1926) as examples where the High Court invoked the power. The latter case, though older, provides the better example of this technique.

In the *Strathern* v. *Seaforth* case, the accused had used another person's automobile without permission. However, he had no intention of permanently depriving the owner of his property; hence there was no intent to "steal" under existing Scottish law. Nevertheless, the High Court decided it was wrong to secretly take and use any property belonging to another. With that phraseology, the Court created a new crime.

In addition to creating new crimes, the Scottish judiciary can also decide if an old crime has simply been perpetrated in a new way. This is done in the court's role of applying common law principles to new circumstances. Again, Jones (1990) offers an interesting example. At common law, malicious mischief identifies acts that involve serious and willful damage to another's property. All relevant precedents before 1983 involved physical damage to the property in question. However, in *H. M. Advocate* v. *Wilson* (1983) Scotland's High Court extended the crime of malicious mischief to cover economic loss as well as property damage. The Court did not believe it was creating a new crime; it was simply applying existing law to new circumstances.

The perseverance with which Scotland holds to the tradition of judge-made substantive law is not repeated in most other common law countries. With expanding populations and increased heterogeneity, common law countries found it increasingly difficult to rely on custom to inform citizens of their obligations. The problem was intensified in colonies, where the ancient ways of English villages provided little support for handling unique problems in the new surroundings. In America, for example, criminal law became essentially a matter of statute. By 1900, most states technically recognized the possibility of common law crime, but other states had specifically abolished the concept (Friedman, 1973). In the latter states, statutes said all crimes were listed in the penal code. If the code did not require or prohibit the behavior, it was not a crime—even if a judge believed such behavior was customarily abhorred. We return to this movement toward codification in America in this chapter's Impact section.

IMPACT

Codification in Common Law Systems

Today, almost half the American states have abolished common law crime in their jurisdiction (Gardner, 1989). Since all state legislatures have enacted hundreds of statutory criminal offenses, it is unusual for a person to be charged with a common law crime even in states where they have not been abolished. In a 1972 New Jersey case, a woman charged with the common law crime of being a "common scold" argued her innocence. Under common law, a scold was a quarrelsome, brawling, troublesome woman who broke the public peace and was a neighborhood nuisance. The woman based her defense on three points: the common scold offense was sexist, the offense lacked specificity, and being a scold was no longer a crime in New Jersey. The New Jersey Superior Court agreed with the woman on all three points (see Gardner, 1989, p. 31). In order, the court said the crime violated the equal protection requirement of the U.S. Constitution, since it applied only to women; the meaning of the term has been lost over the years; and most of the elements of being a scold are now found in the statutory crimes of disorderly behavior. The last point is important, because it reminds us that legislators have kept the common law crime intact by restating it in statutory form. Beyond that, legislators have also modified common law crimes and have required or forbidden other acts that were not crimes at common law.

It is very important to note that abolishing common law crime is not the same as abolishing the common law. American jurisdictions have definitely moved to the civil legal tradition's example of penal codes under statutory criminal law; but that is not a rejection of the common legal tradition. Not only are the codes developed in common law countries different from those under civil law (see Chapter 4), but the common law is also distinguished by its procedure. Common law rules of criminal procedure are developed by judges and deal with such subjects as investigation, arrest, evidence gathering, and testimony. Certainly, legislators have passed statutory rules of procedure, but some common law rules remain in effect in all states, so the abolition of common law crimes does not mean that the common law is abolished. Not only are the resulting codes distinguishable from penal codes in the civil legal tradition, but the common law rules of criminal procedure remain even where the common law crimes are gone.

The United States is not the only member of the common legal family to move toward statutory law. Canada revised her criminal code in 1987 and even England presented a draft code for England and Wales in 1985—though she entered the 1990s with the code still awaiting adoption. The codification of common law has never been easy, as Canada and England will attest, but New Zealand's 1989 attempt to revise her criminal code is particularly useful in showing the difficulties inherent in codifying the common law.

The New Zealand effort is interesting because it directs our attention to the internal characteristics of substantive law. New Zealand has had a criminal law statute since 1893, but its current version remains a partial code. It defines the major offenses, some defenses to crime, and identifies certain police powers and protections. Missing topics include things like guilty intent (*mens rea*) and voluntariness. In his report on the 1989 proposed reforms, France (1990) explains how new statutes might fill such gaps. The proposed definition of "intention" (currently undefined in New Zealand statute) is

(a) meaning to bring about that consequence; or

(b) knowing or believing that the consequence is highly probable (quoted in France, 1990 p. 832).

The problem lies in various interpretations of words like "highly probable." The proposed criminal code in England uses "almost certain," while the United States Model Penal Code prefers "practically certain." At least under common law the judge could simply use the words in their ordinary meaning. Of course, since their ordinary meaning was not written down, one could never be sure just how the judge was interpreting the words. But there lies the vicious circle!

Similar problems accompany the desire to punish only conscious, voluntary acts. Does impaired consciousness provide a defense to the act? If so, what constitutes impaired consciousness—intoxication, insanity? In their attempts to answer such questions, New Zealanders are finding that common law provides no meaning for the most basic concept of intention, and attempts to codify it are bursting with problems. Americans struggling with modification of the insanity plea (for example, guilty but mentaly ill) can sympathize with the people of New Zealand and with other citizens under a common legal tradition. How do you suppose the civil legal tradition, presumably more adept at putting things in writing, handles the dilemma?

Substantive Law in the Civil Legal Tradition

It may surprise you to learn that some people, mostly in civil law countries, find the common law to be crude, unorganized, and culturally inferior to civil law. In fact, Merryman (1985) suggests that the civil law lawyer's attitude of superiority over common law lawyers has become part of the civil law tradition. As he puts it, a lawyer from a relatively undeveloped Central American country may recognize the United States' advanced economic development and standard of living, but will find comfort in thinking of our legal system as undeveloped and of common law lawyers as relatively uncultured people (Merryman, 1985).

One basis for the civil lawyer's lack of appreciation for the common law concerns the substantive law. Even though common law jurisdictions have moved more toward statutory crimes and procedures, the civil law holds more closely to the principle that every crime and every penalty must be embodied in a statute enacted by the legislature. The civil lawyer sees common law courts violating this principle every time people are convicted of common law crimes and whenever judges prohibit relevant evidence and make rules regarding criminal procedure.

As we saw in Chapter 4, an early emphasis on the idea that crime existed only through statute enacted by a legitimate authority was a prime characteristic of the civil legal tradition. Add to that the belief that average citizens should be able to easily find, read, and understand the law, and you have the reasoning behind codification. The French saw this point as especially true in the areas of criminal law and procedure. In fact, a criminal code was the first object of codification in revolutionary France.

As England is home to common law, France can argue for a similar heritage regarding civil law. France, like most civil law countries, has divided her various laws into public law and private law. The criminal laws are under the public law category and, as expected in a civil law system, they are the result of specific legislation resulting in a written document. The two primary documents are the Code of Criminal Procedure and the Penal Code. The former specifies how to investigate a case and how to try a person charged with a criminal offense.

Substantive law is prescribed in the Penal Code, which identifies the types of offenses and their respective punishments. There are other sources of substantive law, but a written law defines all criminal offenses.

The Penal Code has four Books, identifying available punishments (Book I), explaining criminal liability and responsibility (Book II), defining the various offenses and punishments (Book III), and specifying the category of offenses called violations (Book IV). Criminal offenses divide into the three categories of *crime* (serious felonies), *delit* (less serious felonies and misdemeanors), and *contravention* (violations). This distinction not only refers to the seriousness of the offenses, but also indicates which court will hear the case. Offenses classified as *crimes*, heard before the highest-level court (Assize Court), are punishable by life imprisonment or a prison term of over five years. A Correctional Court hears *delits*, which are punishable by fine or a prison term between two months and five years. *Contraventions* can result in a fine or a prison term under two months and are heard before a Police Court (Tomlinson, 1983).

Such organization of crimes and jurisdiction is exactly what proponents argue is the advantage of codification over common law. The presumption is that criminal codes under civil law are clear, have no conflicting provisions, and are without gaps (see Merryman, 1985). With those features, citizens would know their rights and obligations, and judges could simply apply the appropriate provision of the code as cases came before the court. One result of this approach would be an extremely comprehensive code book that tries to anticipate all possible actions to prohibit. Another approach is to develop codes that express general principles to guide judges when they try cases.

Common law jurisdictions have increasingly relied on statutes (that is, codes) to express substantive law. As a result, there are fewer differences today between the ways common and civil law countries define crime and prescribe punishment. However, some illustrations may still prove instructive. Consider, for example, how the state of Colorado and the countries of Italy and Germany define the crime of theft.

As an example of a common law jurisdiction, the state of Colorado provides a standard definition of theft:

(1) A person commits theft when he knowingly obtains or exercises control over anything of value of another without authorization, or by threat or deception, and:

(a) Intends to deprive the other person permanently of the use or benefit of the thing of value; or

(b) Knowingly uses, conceals, or abandons the thing of value in such manner as to deprive the other person permanently of its use or benefit; or

(c) Uses, conceals, or abandons the thing of value intending that such use, concealment, or abandonment will deprive the other person permanently of its use and benefit; or

(d) Demands any consideration to which he is not legally entitled as a condition of restoring the thing of value to the other person (Colorado Revised Statutes, 1986, p. 142).

The statute then specifies theft as either a misdemeanor or felony (hence subject to the appropriate punishment) depending on the value of the thing involved. In additional subsections (numbered 2 through 8) the statute addresses such issues as thefts committed two or more times within six months and the increased penalty when the victim of theft is elderly or handicapped.

It seems unlikely that theft codes under a civil legal tradition could be much more complete or precise than that offered by Colorado. In fact, as noted earlier, codification can be either very comprehensive or can rely on general principles. While Colorado legislators seem to prefer a code that tries to anticipate most contingencies, some countries of the civil legal tradition are more comfortable with providing guiding standards rather than specifics. As a result, their codes are comparatively short.

The German code on theft has two subsections:

(1) Whoever takes moveable property not his own from another with the intention of unlawfully appropriating it to himself shall be punished by up to five years' imprisonment or by fine.

(2) The attempt is punishable (Penal Code of the Federal Republic of Germany, 1987, p. 190).

Two other sections of the German code define the related crimes of aggravated theft and armed theft/gang theft, but in each instance the code explains the terms "aggravated," "armed," and "gang," rather than modifying or elaborating the term "theft."

The Italian Penal Code defines theft as follows:

Whoever takes possession of the movable property of another, by taking it away from the person who holds it, for the purpose of deriving benefit from it for himself or for others, shall be punished by imprisonment for up to three years and by a fine of from 12,000 to 200,000 lire.

For purposes of penal law, electric power and any other form of energy which has economic value also shall be deemed to be movable property (Italian Penal Code, 1978, p. 212).

Like the German code, this one is relatively concise. In both examples, it is apparent that these countries of the civil legal tradition do not see the goal of codes to be providing specific solutions to particular problems. Instead, codes supply general principles from which logical deduction provides a resolution in each case. So, as described in Chapter 4, civil judges need only identify the applicable code principle to decide a particular case. The principle expressed regarding theft in Germany and Italy seems to be the idea that it is illegal to take something that doesn't belong to you. When a theft case is brought to court, German and Italian judges should use logical deduction to determine if the circumstances of the case are such that the defendant took something that didn't belong to him.

Interestingly, it is the code (statute) from the common legal tradition that provides greater detail and specificity. Are Colorado legislators trying to limit judicial discretion by providing such detail that the law is not open to interpretation by the judge? Since Colorado, as a common law jurisdiction, follows the concept of judicial precedent, did the codification process require more elaboration to incorporate various case law relating to theft? Such questions as these are intriguing but lie outside the scope of our present discussion. Instead, the statute and codes relating to theft merely provide examples of substantive law in both the common and civil legal traditions. With that background we are ready to look at substantive law in the socialist and Islamic traditions.

Substantive Law in the Socialist Legal Tradition

The socialist tradition owes much to the language and structure of the Criminal Code of the Russian Soviet Federated Socialist Republic. Borrowing from its civil legal tradition roots, socialist law is codified. However, the resulting code may not provide citizens with much information about what they may or may not do. Article 6 of the Russian Republic Code defined a crime as "any socially dangerous act or omission which threatens the foundations of the Soviet structure. . . ." (quoted in Terrill, 1984, p. 333). Specific description of criminal acts did not have to be provided, since anything "socially dangerous" was criminal. This version of civil law's codification principle set socialist law apart from its European heritage. After revisions and added specificity in the 1920s and 1950s, Soviet law remained comparatively ambiguous.

The 1958 revision of Soviet criminal law attempted to clarify the laws and eliminate their erratic enforcement. The Fundamentals of Criminal Legislation became the primary source of substantive law (Savitsky and Kogan, 1987). Also developed were the Law on Criminal Responsibility for Crimes against the State, the Law on Criminal Responsibility for Military Crimes, and the Fundamentals of Criminal Procedure. Each republic in the Soviet Union had to modify its criminal code to conform with the basic principles of the new legislation, and again the Russian Republic provided the model. A new definition described crime as "A socially dangerous act (an action or omission to act) provided for by the Special Part of the present Code which infringes the Soviet social or state system . . ." (quoted in Terrill, 1984, p. 335). This improved definition increases specificity by reference to the Special Part of the Code. That "special part" lists the major criminal acts, specifies the elements constituting each, and indicates the punishment that can be imposed.

Also serving to set socialist law apart from its civil cousin is the large number of government agencies with authority to enact law. Under 1977 Soviet guidelines, law was enacted by the popularly elected legislative bodies (that is, the soviets), but also by the Presidium of the Supreme Soviet, the Council of Ministers, and local organs of state administration.

As in the United States, each Soviet republic had its own criminal code, so variation in substantive law occurred. Criminal responsibility generally required reaching age 16; however, in six republics the age was 14. Persons 14 to 16 years old were subject to criminal responsibility in cases of murder, intentional bodily harm, rape, robbery, theft, malicious hooliganism, intentional destruction or damage to state, social, or personal property; theft of firearms, munitions, or explosives; theft of narcotics; and intentional acts which may result in a train accident. Similarly, criminal responsibility was absent if the accused's actions were a result of a permanent mental illness, temporary mental derangement, mental deficiency, or other pathological condition. Here, the court could impose compulsory medical measures and commit the subject to a psychiatric hospital (Savitsky and Kogan, 1987).

The Polish Example of the Change in Direction. Specific information is lacking, but it appears that the former Soviet republics are holding to the basic aspects of substantive law as they have known it for over 80 years. In all likelihood, they will approach change in a manner similar to that of Poland as it made the break with socialism. Even under its previous government structure, Poland exemplified a country operating under a socialist legal tradition that openly acknowledged a role for *stare decisis*. Since 1969 legislation, Poland has operated under substantive and procedural laws found in the Penal Code, the Code of Penal Procedure, and the Code on the Execution of Penalties. Reliance on this codification expressed Poland's civil legal heritage even while functioning as a socialist system. Also relevant is the historical importance that Poles gave judge-made law via directives from the Supreme Court (Frankowski, 1987). While not as prominent between 1970 and 1989, the directives are again influencing sentencing decisions.

The state's direct involvement in running the economy, prior to the change in government, means that work-related crimes are more comprehensive than in capitalist countries. For example, serious losses as a result of mismanaging a state firm subjected a person to criminal liability. On the other hand, the state did not get involved in questions of public morality in Poland. Acts such as adultery, prostitution, and homosexual behavior between consenting adults in private were decriminalized even before socialism took control.

Criminal responsibility begins at age 17, and persons aged 13 to 17 are handled differently, though not separately, from adults. *Mens rea* is a basic requirement of Polish substantive criminal law, and, as a result, it distinguishes between intentional and reckless offenses. Reckless and negligent offenses are punished only when the law specifically requires it, and the Code recognizes only a few such instances (Frankowski, 1987).

Defenses to criminal responsibility include acts of necessity, insanity, justified risk, and, as noted above, insignificant social danger. The justified risk defense applies to managers of state-owned enterprises who reasonably undertake risky business decisions resulting in economic losses. As long as they intended positive results, they bear no criminal responsibility.

Substantive Law in the Islamic Legal Tradition

Substantive law in the *Shari'a* identifies three categories of crime: *Hudud*, *Quesas*, and *Ta'azir* (Bassiouni, 1982; Lippman et al., 1988). *Hudud* crimes are offenses against God and require mandatory prosecution. The *Qur'an* and *Sunna* specify the punishment. The seven *Hudud* crimes are adultery or fornication, defamation (slander), use of alcohol, theft, highway robbery, apostasy (rejection or abandonment of Islam by one who professes Islamic faith), and rebellion and corruption of Islam (transgression of Islam).

The notoriety given the Islamic response to theft suggests that we should choose that crime to expand upon. With Morocco as an example, theft refers to the taking of property belonging to another when the value equals or exceeds 10 dirhams, or about $1.25. The property taken must have been under guard or in a place of safekeeping. This element is important because of the harshness of the penalty—amputation. Islamic jurists, especially of the Hanafi School, believe that a thief's hand should not be cut off for the theft of something that is not worth guarding. Siddiqi (1985) exemplifies items not worth guarding as dry wood, hay, game, fish, and other things found in great quantity in the land. Similarly, there is no amputation for stealing items like milk and fruit, which quickly spoil, or for theft of prohibited items (for example, alcohol), since the offender need only claim his intent was to destroy the harmful item.

For a first offense of theft, the thief's hand is cut off at the wrist and, with a second offense, he or she loses the other hand. Subsequent offenses are punished by amputating the feet, or imprisonment until the offender repents (Lippman et al., 1988). This harsh penalty reflects the belief that theft not only deprives the owner of property, but it also creates fear, distrust, and apprehension in the community. For a society to be truly Islamic, all men and women have the right to protection of their spiritual, intellectual, and physical needs. This right is attached to a corresponding duty (accompanied by a liability to punishment) that obligates each person to respect the person and property of everyone else. In that context, when an offender fails to show such respect, the *Qur'anic* punishment is not so harsh as it is appropriate and necessary.

Quesas are not always given a specific and mandatory criminal definition in the *Qur'an*, so the behavior constituting these offenses has evolved through academic, judicial, and political supervision. They include: voluntary homicide, involuntary homicide, intentional physical injury, and unintentional physical injury. The last two categories include crimes of assault, battery, and other acts not resulting in death.

Ta'azir offenses, for which prosecution and punishment is discretionary, are those not encompassed by either of the other two categories and result in tangible individual or social harm. Examples include giving false testimony, insulting another person, gambling, and neglect of prayers. The penalty for *Ta'azir* offenses is to be rehabilitative rather than retributive, which is the guiding principle for *Hudud* and *Quesas* offenses. A rehabilitative penalty under Islamic law could be imprisonment, infliction of physical punishment, or the imposition of compensation.

The severe penalties for *Hudud* crimes (for example, amputation of the thief's hand), result in defenses to criminal responsibility that are rather unique. For example, *Had* penalties (fixed penalties for *Hudud* crimes) cannot be imposed if there is any doubt or uncertainty regarding the accused's guilt. That doubt, however, does not necessarily lead to acquittal. Instead, the indictment may be reformulated to convict the accused of a crime other than the one that brought him to trial (al-'Awwa, 1982).

Similarly, criminal responsibility has a different twist. Besides the typical requirements of conditions like *mens rea* and *actus reus*, through mistake or neglect a person also may be responsible for criminal acts of another. Specifically, Islamic law may hold an employer responsible for work-related actions of employees, a property owner responsible for harmful consequences of the property, and animal owners for injuries committed by that animal (Bahnassi, 1982).

Defenses to criminal responsibility include the typical insanity, coercion, necessity, immaturity, self-defense, and unconsciousness. While this latter circumstance includes the common condition of involuntary intoxication, it also contains fainting, sleep, and forgetfulness.

PROCEDURAL CRIMINAL LAW

As you can see, issues of substantive law do not vary much among the four legal traditions. Each considers similar acts to be criminal, and they all debate questions such as criminal intent and responsibility while struggling with defenses to crime. The real differences among the traditions fall in the area of criminal procedure.

Chapter 3 presented two models of procedural law: one of due process and another of crime control. Since neither model corresponds to reality, nor represents an ideal, they are offered simply as techniques to understand how the legal process operates. Each model seeks to guarantee social freedom, but the crime control version does so by emphasizing efficient processing of wrongdoers, whereas the due process model emphasizes restrictions on government invasion into citizens' lives.

Consider, for example, the topic of public and private law in terms of the crime control and due process models. While the civil legal tradition distinguishes private and public law, a similar separation is not found in the other three legal families. The division of public and private law presents interesting problems when the civil legal tradition deals with criminal matters. Private law, which deals with disputes between individual citizens, has been the primary concern of civil law since Roman times. Public law, under the civil legal tradition, deals with relations between citizens and public officials or agencies. Its focus on public matters makes it more administrative than legal in nature. It provides a way for citizens to complain about the way social institutions and officials are acting.

Distinguishing between public and private law presents a problem when criminal law is categorized. Originally crime was considered the concern of private law, since the wronged person was expected to initiate action against the offender. When crimes came to be seen as also affecting the whole society, the public began to share an interest in what had been a solely private area. As the state (public) developed a legal personality, criminal law came to have a public component with two aspects. First, in addition to the victim, the public at large was harmed and had the right to sanction the wrongdoer. Second, the state took from the wronged citizen the obligation to investigate, prosecute, and punish the offender. That development was not a problem under common law, since the same courts handled both public and private law. However, civil law countries were presented with the dilemma of leaving crimes a matter of private law or switching them to the jurisdiction of public law courts.

The dilemma was resolved by keeping crimes in the private law domain. However, that means the officials in private law courts are asked to judge the actions of government officials (for example, police officers and prosecutors), a matter more comfortably handled by the administrative judges hearing public law complaints. This positioning of criminal law as part of public law but managed by the regular (that is, private law) courts helps explain why civil law systems seem to emphasize the crime control model.

The French, for example, do not view public law as law in the strict sense. Instead, public law is essentially administrative law useful to help keep society operating. The "true" law, for French citizens, concerns relations between individuals where the state simply serves as an impartial arbitrator. The public and administrative aspect of criminal law requires the state to play a more active role. French citizens allow their government a degree of discretion, and even arbitrariness, since society's interest is directly involved in catching and punishing the criminal. As long as officials like police and prosecutors act in a spirit respecting the liberty and equality of citizens, it is not so important that the law is strictly followed. "After all, criminal law is public, and public law is different from private law" (David, 1960/1972, p. 121). The result, to return to the metaphor in Chapter 3, is an assembly line where workers are able to complete their task with minimal interference from suspicious supervisors concerned with the ways in which workers do their job.

There are many aspects of procedural law and unlimited points to use for comparing legal systems. We will concentrate on just two general topics: the adjudicatory process and judicial review. In each instance you will find examples of legal systems following what seems to be one or the other of Packer's models. Just remember, Packer (1968) presents them as being different—not as one being better than the other. We should do the same.

Adjudicatory Processes

The process of adjudication is typically either adversarial (also called accusatorial) or inquisitorial in nature (see Figure 5-1). The former is often considered a substitute for private vengeance. As societies evolve, the power to initiate action first lies with the wronged person (the accuser). That power eventually extends to relatives of the "victim," then to all members of the person's group, and finally to the government responsible for the well-being of the person. In time, then, the accuser moves from being the individual to being the state (as in the State of Texas v. Jones). The setting for the accusation is before an impartial official serving as referee (judge). Because the disputing parties (the state and the accused) behave in a manner similar to a contest, they are considered adversaries.

The inquisitorial process also shows societal evolution, but along a different path. Here the wronged person is eliminated as private accuser and replaced with a public official. Unlike the development of the adversarial process, in replacing the private accuser the public official does not continue in that role. Instead of accusation, there is now investigation. Since the parties are not engaged in a contest, a referee is not necessary. Instead, the impartial official (judge) serves as an inquisitor actively seeking to determine what transpired.

In general terms, the common legal tradition makes use of the adversarial process, while the civil legal tradition follows one of inquisition. Because of its civil roots, the socialist tradition also exemplifies the inquisitorial process. The Islamic legal tradition offers a unique combination relying on private accusation in an inquisitorial-type setting. Because these distinctions provide one of the most common comparisons of legal systems, we should consider them in greater depth.

Inquisitorial Process. One of the first things necessary to an understanding of the inquisitorial process is to dissociate it from the term "inquisition." The Spanish Inquisition of the late fifteenth century was notorious for its use of torture to compel cooperation in its religious investigations. The only thing it had in common with the inquisitorial process was the prominent role given the judges. The judge is at the center of the fact-gathering process in the inquisitorial system, but torture is not.

By the mid-sixteenth century, the inquisitorial method was standardized and required for all French courts. Terrill (1984) identifies the major characteristics of that process as: (1) the positioning of the king's prosecutor as a party to the suit in every criminal case, and (2) the use of two magistrates during the course of the investigation and the trial. The first point is important because it recognized the

	Adversarial Systems	Inquisitorial Systems
Who plays the role of the accuser?	Role of accuser moves from the individual to the state in an evolutionary continuation of private vengeance.	The state as accuser replaces the individual in a developmental substitution for private vengeance.
How is truth determined?	Truth is said to arise from competition between opposing sides, so the emphasis is on the trail phase.	Truth is said to arise from a continuing investigation, so the emphasis is on the screening process.
Where does power lie?	Power is shared by the prosecutor, defense, judge, and jury, so the judge exerts influence indirectly in the role of referee.	Power is concentrated more in the judge, so the judge's influence is more direct in the role of investigator
What level of cooperation is expected of the defendant?	Defendant is neither expected nor required to cooperate with the investigation or court officials.	Defendant is expected, but not required, to cooperate with investigation (including court) officials as truth is sought.

Figure 5-1. The adjudicatory process.

state's (that is, the king's) interest in the case, and abolished the accusatory idea of trials as duels between two parties. The second point highlights the primary and active role judges, instead of attorneys, play in a civil law system.

Rather than a competition between opposing sides, a trial under the inquisitorial system is more like a continuing investigation. The parties in the case must provide all relevant evidence to the court. The judges, not the attorneys for the plaintiff or defendant, then call and actively examine witnesses (Abadinsky, 1988).

Trials play an important role in civil proceedings, because the inquisitorial procedure does not include a guilty plea as Americans know it. A defendant's confession of guilt is not the same as a guilty plea, and instead serves as additional evidence to be evaluated (Ingraham, 1987). However, we cannot conclude that civil law systems have nothing similar to the plea bargaining of adversarial systems. It is possible in such countries as France, Italy, and Germany to have "uncontested trials." In such cases, defendants confirm the validity of charges and take up as little as 15 minutes of the court's time in the process of becoming convicted (Ingraham, 1987).

While civil and socialist legal traditions both use the inquisitorial process, they implement it in slightly different ways. For example, an independent judiciary typically performs the inquisitorial function in civil law systems. Under socialist law, an agent of the police or prosecution often takes the role. Despite such variation, the inquisitorial process involves a procedurally active judge and rather passive lawyers. This situation is nearly the opposite of that in the adversarial process, which has a procedurally passive judge and rather active advocates.

Adversarial Process. The adversarial process assumes that truth will arise from a free and open competition over who has the correct facts (Samaha, 1988). The struggle is between the state on one side and the defendant on the other. This "sporting" or "fighting system of justice" developed from the trial by ordeal wherein a battle settled disputes between parties. The victor was assumed to have "truth" on his side, so a triumphant accused was cleared of the charges while a defeated one was obviously guilty.

As trial by combat grew in popularity (tenth to thirteenth centuries), procedures for conducting the ordeal received increased attention. The language setting forth the rules of the proceeding and the language used in that proceeding became very exacting. Procedure became so important that, some authors believe, the adversarial process became a system emphasizing procedure over substance. As a result, each side plays a game in which the players use the law (especially procedural rules and rights) to gain an advantage or act as a bargaining chip (Ingraham, 1987).

Waldron (1989) identifies two safeguards of the adversary system. First, it uses *cross-examination* (in place of swords) to challenge or destroy a witness's testimony. Each side has a chance to question the honesty of witnesses, search for biases, and figure out what witnesses actually know instead of what they think they know. Second, instead of granting power to a single position, the prosecution, defense, judge, and jury, share it. The prosecutor represents the state in trying to prove the defendant's guilt. The defense attorney argues the client's innocence and ensures that the accused has all the legal protection possible. The judge serves as the referee in this contest and guarantees that the players abide by the rules. This system of checks and balances differs from the inquisitorial process, which concentrates more power in the judge's position.

Importantly, just as variation exists among countries using the inquisitorial system, the adversarial process is not the same in all common legal traditions. One of the clearest examples of such differences are the ways in which American and British defense counsels approach a jury trial. Americans who are used to hearing emotional and dramatic orations by a lawyer on behalf of the client would be quite surprised at the apparent detachment, lack of interest, and absence of aggressiveness displayed by an English solicitor or barrister.

When representing the client, English barristers do not see their function as obtaining an acquittal by using procedural rules in the hope the prosecution will stumble. Of course, it is not fair to say that American defense attorneys see their duty as constantly erecting procedural barriers. But one does not have to be especially cynical to believe that such action occurs in the American courtroom. Some authors (see Graham, 1983) are convinced that it occurs much more frequently than in the British courtroom.

The English barrister tends to approach a trial as something to be decided on the basis of contested facts. The jury should inflict punishment on the defendant only if the jury is sure that the prosecution's story is true. As a result, some (especially Americans) may see the barrister as detached and uncommitted to the defense of the client.

Graham (1983) wondered why English barristers do not become more aggressive during the trial. He believes much of the behavior is explained by the barrister's working conditions. Unlike the American defense counsel (especially a privately hired one working in a large law firm), barristers usually work alone. They prepare much of their own cases and appear in court with the frequency of an American public defender in a large city. Such factors make it difficult to maintain an aggressive posture with each new case. As a result, the appearance of the adversarial process looks rather different in two common law countries. But the contrast between the adversarial and inquisitorial methods are still more pronounced than any differences within the two systems.

Contrasting Adversarial and Inquisitorial Processes.   Barton Ingraham developed an intriguing and helpful model of criminal procedure that allows him to compare and contrast procedures in a variety of nations. The application of his model to procedural criminal law resulted in the identification of four areas where inquisitorial and adversarial procedures differ:

> 1. The inquisitorial systems emphasize the screening phase of the criminal process so that a careful investigation ensures the correct determination of factual guilt. The adversarial systems emphasize the trial phase, where complex rules of evidence to produce substantive results ensure the defendant a fair trial.

> 2. The adversarial systems are much more likely to restrict the involvement of the judiciary in both the investigatory and adjudicatory process. The direct involvement of the judge in inquisitorial systems is replaced in adversarial systems by an ability to exert influence only indirectly.

> 3. Because the inquisitorial system assumes that all involved persons are seeking the truth, the defendant is expected (but not required) to be cooperative. That cooperation includes expectations of supplying information to investigators and answering questions at trial. The adversarial systems, on the other hand, neither expect nor require the defendant to assist investigators. The burden of proof is on the prosecutor, who assumes that the defendant will maintain silence.

> 4. The role of the judge in adversarial proceedings is primarily one of referee. The attorneys may develop and present their respective cases, and then a jury decides between the versions of the facts. The court in an inquisitorial system is another investigator with the added power of being able to decide the case. The judges ask most of the questions and develop the facts, while the attorneys exist more to argue the interpretation that the court should give those facts (see Ingraham, 1987, p. 121).

Ingraham believes that the main objectives of the inquisitorial system are a search for truth and the achievement of procedural justice. Is that different from the objectives of the adversarial system? The adversarial approach may differ in the sense that the search for truth officially begins at the trial stage. That occurs because information from the investigation is not considered until presented in court. Then each side presents its own private version of the truth, and the judge or jurors must decide who is the most convincing. As a result, the importance of *how* a person is adjudicated seems a more important objective in the adversarial process than determining whether the accused actually did it. This point is similar to the distinction made in Chapter 3 in terms of legal guilt versus factual guilt. One might argue that while each system seeks both types of guilt, the inquisitorial emphasizes the latter while the adversarial highlights the former. We return to this question of emphasis in the Impact section of this chapter.

Just as common law and civil law systems borrowed aspects of codification and precedent from each other, so too, have the inquisitorial and adversarial systems exchanged procedures. For example, the common law systems adopted a public prosecutor to file criminal charges without relying on a grand jury. Rules of discovery compel some sharing of evidence between the opposing sides, resulting in a "search for the truth" more similar to an inquisitorial than adversarial process. Also, the role of the common law judge has increased in areas like plea negotiation and what evidence the jury will be allowed to hear. The results of this cross-pollination are systems where each contain elements of the other (Ingraham, 1987; Merryman, 1985). The resulting mixture is not, however, as complete as that found in Islamic law.

IMPACT

Could the Inquisitorial System Work in the United States?

For a class lesson in my Introduction to Criminal Justice class, students had to read scenarios describing police interaction with crime suspects. The specific assignment was to determine if the police acted in a lawful manner when undertaking search and seizure. In her written report, a young woman from Japan expressed great dismay that her answer ("the search and seizure was reasonable"), was explained as incorrect given the circumstances. As she put it: "It is clear the person had drugs. This is the fact. The person should not be able to claim the search was unreasonable. I will never be able to understand this way of thinking, never!" There were, of course, many American students who had similar answers and were equally startled at the legal finding. But the student from Japan brought with her a different perception of how the search for truth is best undertaken. By the end of that chapter the American students seemed to have accepted the legal "technicalities" as either appropriate or inevitable, but Ms. Yahiro was still shaking her head in wonder at the American system.

Japan basically follows an inquisitorial approach in the search for truth. As a result, the search is undertaken by all participants in the process. This cooperative effort at determining exactly what happened is actually appealing to many people—even American students in an Introduction to Criminal Justice class. After all, shouldn't "justice" have priority over protecting the "rights" of some joker who is probably guilty anyway? I don't pretend to answer that question in class, and I am not prepared to answer it here. Yet it is a legitimate and thought-provoking question, similar to Packer's (1968) "due process" versus "crime control" contrast.

In this chapter we distinguished between the adversarial and inquisitorial process by referring to what Cole (1989) calls "legal guilt" versus "factual guilt." Similarly, Savitsky and Kogan write about stressing "objective truth" over "formal truth." In this manner, the Soviet inquisitorial system was described as one where the court's conclusions were to fully correspond to what has taken place (Savitsky and Kogan, 1987). Tomlinson (1983) also expressed interest in the possible benefits of an inquisitorial justice system. But, unlike others, he undertook a comprehensive comparative analysis to answer the questions. His work provides a useful response to questions about advantages the inquisitorial system may have over the adversarial one.

An appealing aspect of the civil law tradition is the active role played by an impartial judiciary that controls the investigation, trial, and sentencing. The result is a system with efficient and generally fair trials dispensing equal justice to all defendants. The absence of adversaries makes trials uncomplicated and brief (seldom longer than one day) affairs specifically aimed at determining the truth (that is, factual guilt or innocence). This strong point of the civil law occurs, in part, because of a coinciding weak point. That is, the absence of significant limitations on the pre-trial gathering of evidence lets police and prosecutor provide the judges with a comprehensive report specifying the facts in the case.

The French version of civil law results in what Tomlinson (1983) believes is a standoff between the chief weakness of that system—police and prosecutor domination of the investigation and charging stage—and its primary strength—judicial control of the disposition of the case.

The original design of the French Code of Criminal Procedure was to prevent any one official from dominating the criminal process. Authority was divided among the prosecutor, the examining magistrate, and the trial judge. The professional prosecutor is responsible for directing the investigatory activity of the police. Unlike civil law application in Germany, the French prosecutor does not have a mandatory prosecution duty and instead has considerable discretion in charging decisions.

Constraints on conducting an investigation come from a different source than in America. While police and prosecutors in the United States must follow procedural law as noted in statutes and interpreted by judges, their

French counterparts are not similarly restricted. The French legal system specifies what the prosecutor and police are allowed to do instead of recognizing individual rights of suspects. When either authority behaves in a manner not specified, their actions are extralegal or even illegal. Also, as noted above, partitioning of duties among prosecutor, magistrate, and judge should provide a system of checks and balances preventing any single official from controlling the process.

In this manner, the French system tries to protect citizens by specifying the actions government authorities may take to investigate a crime. The American version, on the other hand, seeks to protect citizens by granting them certain rights that government authorities cannot violate. Presumably the end result is the same, but the means to that end differ with regard to the trust placed in the government's representatives. The problem, as Tomlinson sees it, is that French prosecutors (and the police) have found ways to avoid these restrictions. "The separation of functions principle has not proved strong enough to prevent the prosecutor and the police from acquiring coercive investigatory powers similar to those of the examining magistrate" (Tomlinson, 1983, p. 150).

While the office of examining magistrate still exists in France, the position no longer plays an influential role. Instead, the police, under the prosecutor's supervision, investigate most offenses and prepare trial dossiers. Using their discretion, prosecutors can evade judicial investigation of their actions by charging the suspects of *crimes* with a *delit* or *contravention* which do not require judicial investigation. In this manner, defendants come before a *tribunal correctionnel* without the prosecutor's decision being subjected to any screening device. This power of the prosecutor to control how a defendant comes to trial has significant consequences for the individual's rights.

The French attempt to limit prosecutorial authority by specifying the prosecutor's powers and by giving the judiciary authority over investigation has proved ineffective in Tomlinson's eyes. The result, he argues, "is a criminal justice system in which the defendant's pre-trial rights are eroded to a degree many . . . (American's would find unacceptable)" (Tomlinson, 1983, p. 164). He concludes with the thought that despite faults in the American system, the French nonadversarial system is less favorable when we compare the balance each achieves between individual rights and state authority. Or, to put Tomlinson's argument in the words of Packer (1968), a "due process model" is preferable to a "crime control model." Do you agree?

A Mixed System. Islamic procedural law is a mixed system combining adversarial and inquisitorial aspects. Since the *Shari'a* is a religious law based on divine command and revelation, it did not develop through judicial precedent or legislative codification. Further, the *Shari'a* does not require the administration of justice to be a combined office (for example, the inquisitorial judge) or divided into many (for example, the adversarial attorneys, judge, and jury). Identifying Islamic procedural law is not so easy. Though the sacred law prescribes penalties for criminal acts, it does not specify the means used to apprehend the offender and bring him to justice. The matter is left to the discretion of the state (Awad, 1982).

Because of this discretion, Islamic law has features of both procedural types. The inquisitorial process seems to predominate, since historically there has been little division between the judge and the investigator. In addition, the defense attorney's role is not so adversarial as it is one of presenting favorable evidence, safeguarding against improper incrimination, and overseeing the criminal judgments. Simultaneously, such adversarial provisions as the right to confront accusers, maintain silence, and a modified presumption of innocence reflect adversarial interests.

A peculiar twist given procedural law by Islamic justice is the differing provisions for separate categories of offenders and its impact on the presumption of innocence. *Shari'a* judges place suspects into one of three categories: "(1) the accused is from the pious and righteous group; (2) he is among the disobedient and immoral; or (3) his character is unknown though neither righteous nor immoral" (Awad, 1982, p. 100). These categories help judges decide the appropriate procedures to follow when a person is accused of a crime. When presented with a person of the first category, jurists usually give no credibility to the accusations. After all, the person is pious and righteous and therefore deserves the benefit of doubt. Since accusations against the sinful and immoral person are more likely to be true, given their life-style, limiting their rights and freedoms in the quest for truth is permissible. Persons in the third category are generally placed with the immoral and subjected to the same restrictions.

As these examples from several countries show, there is greater diversity among nations in terms of procedural criminal law than we found on issues of substantive criminal law. But this focus on the adjudicatory process might lead us to believe that procedural law issues are essentially differentiated on the basis of which legal tradition a country follows. That assumption would be incorrect, since there are differences in procedural law both among and between the legal traditions. One area of variation is linked to the concept of judicial review. As we consider that topic, we will see that procedural criminal law shows variation beyond that which is explained by legal tradition affiliation.

Judicial Review

The phrase "laws change but the Law must remain" is commonly used to express the concept of *Rechtsstaat*, or the rule of law. That point reduces to the question of whether a country views its law, or its government, as supreme. The Soviet journalist Feofanov expressed it this way: "Putting people to death, the English king broke the law; by putting people to death, the Russian Tsar created the law . . . It is one thing when lawlessness tramples right, living in the con-

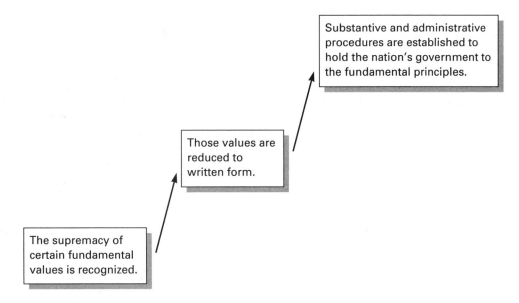

Figure 5-2.   Flow chart for achieving Rechtsstaat.

sciousness of society, and quite another thing when lawlessness becomes right" (1990–1991, p. 21).

As Figure 5-2 shows, reaching a position of *Rechtsstaat* requires a nation to first recognize the supremacy of certain fundamental values. Those values may have either secular or divine origin as long as they are understood to reflect basic and ultimate principles. After being recognized, the fundamental values must be reduced to written form. A country's constitution often accomplishes this task. Finally, the trip to *Rechtsstaat* requires a nation to provide procedures that hold its government to the tenets of this higher law. If citizens cannot challenge laws made by the country's legislature or ruler, the concept of a higher law is lost. For example, say that the legislature in a country whose constitution assures freedom of religion passes a law prohibiting Muslims from operating a place of worship. If citizens cannot challenge the substance of such a law as violating fundamental values (recorded in the constitution), the concept of *Rechtsstaat* is emasculated.

The procedures supporting the rule of law need to be of two types: those related to questions of substance, and those related to questions of administration. Questions of substance are similar to the example of the Muslims prohibited from worshiping in a country guaranteeing freedom of religion. Questions of administration, on the other hand, deal with how the government enforces its statutes and is itself subject to the law. Consider, for example, a case of Soviet pre-trial detention.

A Soviet journalist (Feofanov, 1990–1991) became aware of a defendant who had been kept in prison for five years and eleven months while awaiting his trial. The journalist asked the USSR Procuracy if such action was consistent with the principles of law and justice. The response was basically one of surprise that someone believed that a thief should be set free just because the term of pre-trial confinement was violated. The government official explained that the defendant was accused of a crime that stipulates a 15-year sentence. From the official's point of view, if six years are subtracted from that sentence, nothing so terrible has happened. The situation is worsened by the fact that the Procuracy is the very agency that the Soviets used to monitor such behavior. When the law is deemed inapplicable to certain citizens or agencies, it cannot have an independent value and there is no *Rechtsstaat*.

Of the three steps to a rule of law (that is, recognizing supremacy of certain values, reducing them to writing, and providing a way to hold the government to those laws), the third is particularly interesting. That is because the first two steps are rather well accomplished today and show little differentiation—at least in the common and civil legal traditions. A rule of law, if it exists, in the socialist and Islamic traditions must be approached differently. Consequently, we review ways to hold the government accountable in common and civil legal families and then turn to the question of *Rechtsstaat* under socialist and Islamic law.

The process by which governments are held accountable to the law is called *judicial review*. The term refers to the power of a court to hold unconstitutional, and hence unenforceable, any law, any official action based on a law, or any other action by a public official that the courts deem in conflict with the country's basic law (see Abraham, 1986). One of two models can be used to accomplish judicial review (see Brewer–Carias, 1989; Cappelletti, 1989). The *diffuse model* is decentralized and allows a wide variety and large number of courts in the country to rule on issues of constitutionality of laws. The *concentrated model* is centralized by restricting issues of the constitutionality of laws to a specific state agency (see Figure 5-3).

The diffuse model had its origin in the United States and is now found primarily in Britain's former colonies (for example, Canada, Australia, India). It is not, however, confined to countries following the common legal tradition. European countries such as Norway, Denmark, and Sweden have procedures that are very similar to the American prototype, as do the Latin American countries of Argentina and Mexico. The concentrated model was first established in Austria in 1920, and then spread to such European countries as Germany, Italy, and Spain. Not surprisingly, some countries fail to fit neatly into one of these two models. These "mixed-model" countries (for example, Venezuela, Colombia, Brazil, and Switzerland) offer interesting variations of judicial review and as a result they also warrant our attention (see Figure 5-3).

The Diffuse Model for Judicial Review.   The diffuse model gives a country's entire judiciary the duty of constitutional control. This approach follows the assumption that the judiciary functions to interpret the laws in order to apply them in concrete cases. When two laws conflict, the judge must determine which of the two prevails and then apply it. In countries with a rigid constitution, the judge should decide by deferring to the higher law, since a constitutional norm prevails over an ordinary legislative norm. Therefore, in countries following a diffuse model of judicial review, any judge having to decide a case where an applicable legislative norm conflicts with the constitution must disregard the former and apply the latter. As a result, even low-level courts can rule a statute unconstitutional or declare police action as violating a suspect's fundamental rights.

Providing all judges and courts the general power to act as constitutional judges is a consequence of the principle of the supremacy of the constitution (Brewer–Carias, 1989). For example, the Constitution of the United States includes a supremacy clause that makes clear the link between the principle and the diffuse model. A clause in Article 6, section 2 states:

> This Constitution, and the laws of the United States which shall be made in pursuance thereof; and all Treaties made, or which shall be made, under the Authority of the United States, shall be the supreme law of the land; and the judges in every State shall be bound thereby, anything in the Constitution or laws of the State to the contrary nonwithstanding.

After establishing the Constitution as supreme, and empowering judges at all levels to act as a constitutional court, the diffuse model countries are left with a potential problem. Since judges at all court levels and regions can rule on constitutionality, the potential for conflicting opinions and rulings is great. How does a system of diffuse judicial review respond to the danger of different judges reaching inconsistent results on close questions? For countries in the common legal tradition, the problem is responded to with the aid of *stare decisis*.

An emphasis on *stare decisis* reduces the danger of inconsistent rulings by requiring judges to follow their own prior decisions and the precedents of higher courts. In the United States, the presence of a single supreme court, and the requirement that lower courts follow its superior precedents, insures the uniformity of constitutional adjudication. The civil legal tradition countries using a diffuse system of judicial review cannot, customarily, rely on *stare decisis*. Instead, as we see below, they use related concepts (for example, Mexico), set up special procedures (for example, Argentina), or establish special courts (for example, Greece). In such ways, countries with a civil legal tradition and a diffuse system of judicial review are able to resolve problems of uncertainty and conflict arising when numerous judges make decisions on constitutionality of laws (Brewer–Carias, 1989). An overview of judicial review in three countries highlights these modifications while elaborating on the system of diffuse judicial review.

Like many other Latin American countries, Argentina and Mexico were influenced by the constitutional system of the United States. This presented some problems in the area of the judiciary, since those same countries had modeled their legal system after the civil legal tradition of European countries. In the area of judicial review, many Latin American countries eventually moved from the American diffuse system to a mixed system combining this common law feature with their civil law system. Argentina and Mexico, however, remained faithful to the American system (Brewer–Carias, 1989). Understandably, each country also added its own modifications, but they clearly follow a diffuse model of judicial review.

Article 31 of the Constitution of the Republic of Argentina says, in part, the Constitution and the laws passed by Congress are "the supreme law of the Nation" (quoted in Brewer–Carias, 1989, p. 156). Further, Article 100 makes the Supreme Court and the various inferior courts competent to hear cases related to the Constitution and congressional laws. As in the United States, therefore, all Argentinian courts can declare legislative acts, as well as executive and administrative acts and judicial decisions, to be unconstitutional.

In its appellate jurisdiction, the Argentinian Supreme Court of Justice hears two kinds of appeal. For ordinary appeals, the Supreme Court reviews particular decisions made by the National Chamber of Appeals and serves as a court of last resort for such matters. It is the second type of appellate jurisdiction, extraordinary appeals, which provides Argentina's special procedure for judicial review.

Any party having direct interest in a case decided at the provincial superior court or at the National Chambers of Appeals level can bring the case before the Supreme Court of Justice. The primary restriction for such access is that the case must involve a constitutional issue. In this manner, the Supreme Court provides final interpretation of the Constitution. For that reason, extraordinary appeal is the most important means for judicial review of state acts.

Judicial review in Mexico is directly linked to the *judicio de amparo* (trial for protection), which in turn comes from the Mexican Constitution. The trial for *amparo* (constitutional protection) comprises five different aspects: protection of fundamental constitutional rights; procedures against judicial decisions that incorrectly apply legal provisions; judicial review of administrative action; protection of the agrarian rights of peasants; and reviews on the constitutionality of legislation.

In addition to covering similar topics, Mexican and American judicial review share an appreciation for the concept of judicial precedent. As noted earlier, the absence of *stare decisis* in civil law countries makes it difficult to use a diffuse system of judicial review. Mexico integrated diffuse judicial review into its civil legal tradition by developing *jurisprudencia* as a procedure similar to *stare decisis*.

In cases when the law of *amparo* is at issue, precedents from previous federal court decisions are considered binding for lower courts. This process is similar to *stare decisis* in common law, but differs in an important respect. Whereas *stare decisis* relies on a single decision, Mexican *jurisprudencia* (precedents from previous decisions) require five consecutive decisions to the same effect (Brewer–Carias, 1989).

These similarities with judicial review in the United States are balanced by other aspects that set the Mexican system apart. Possibly most important is the restriction of *amparo* jurisdiction to federal level courts. Therefore, judicial review is not a power of all courts in Mexico as it is in America.

A country's entire judiciary has the duty of constitutional control with the potential inconsistency of decisions being lessened through *stare decisis* or a structural equivalent.

A specific government entity rules on the constitutionality of laws, and problems of inconsistent decisions are accordingly minimal.

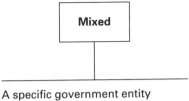

A specific government entity reviews the constitutionality of laws, and all courts in the country have the power to ignore laws they deem unconstitutional.

Figure 5-3. Models for accomplishing judicial review in common and civil traditions.

In addition to the Latin American countries that followed the American lead on diffuse judicial review, the model also caught on in a few European countries. Greece is especially noted for having a judicial review process that is very similar to that of the United States.

The 1927 Greek constitution expressly established judicial review powers of all courts, and the idea has remained through the present 1975 constitution (Brewer–Carias, 1989). There are three primary areas of difference between Greek and American judicial review. First, in common law countries, the constitutional issue must be raised by one of the parties in the case. In Greece, the courts have power to review the constitutionality of legislation even when there is no case before them which challenges that legislation. Second, neither the *stare decisis* doctrine nor the Mexican version of *jurisprudencia* exists in Greece. Therefore, decisions of the higher-level courts are not made obligatory for those at the lower level.

The third distinction between Greek and American versions of diffuse judicial review is the Greek addition of a special court to rule on constitutional matters. Greek courts are organized in three separate branches, which hear, respectively, civil and criminal cases, administrative cases, and public audit and financial matters. Since all courts in each branch have the power of judicial review, it is possible that the court of last resort for each branch will render contradictory and conflicting judgments on constitutional issues. To resolve such problems, the 1968 constitution established a Constitutional Court. The 1975 constitution reconstructed that court into a Special Highest Court, which provides a corrective measure to a judicial review process operating in three different court branches.

The Concentrated Model for Judicial Review. The alternative to diffuse judicial review is a concentrated approach. The distinguishing feature of the concentrated system of judicial review is the use of a single state organ to act as a country's constitutional judge. That entity can be the Supreme Court of Justice, acting as the highest court in the judicial hierarchy, or a specialized court organized outside the ordinary court hierarchy. In either situation, the country's constitution expressly creates and regulates the agency responsible for upholding the supremacy of that constitution.

The idea that a constitution should create and specify the process of judicial review is a distinguishing feature between the diffuse and concentrated models. For example, neither the United States nor the Argentinian (as examples of the diffuse models) Constitution conferred judicial review power on the courts. Instead, both constitutions simply note the supremacy of the constitution, and the duty of all courts to make decisions consistent with that document. By default, not by decree, all courts in the United States and Argentina are constitutional courts. In the concentrated model of judicial review, there is no doubt concerning which agency decides constitutional questions. As seen below, that duty falls to a very specific state organ, which was identified in the country's constitution itself.

Most adherents of this position are civil law countries, but some socialist countries either adopted the model (for example, Yugoslavia) or are flirting with the procedure. The archetype is Austria, but the concentrated model was also adopted by Italy (1948) and West Germany (1949). More recent followers include Cyprus (1960) and Turkey (1961). The countries following this model tend to believe more strongly in the separation of powers (rather than simply checks and balances) and the supremacy of statutory law. As such, the concentrated model refuses to grant judicial review power to the judiciary generally. The ordinary judge must accept and apply the law as he finds it; judicial review is undertaken by a specialized court or tribunal.

Austria provided the model for concentrated judicial review when its 1920 constitution created a constitutional tribunal (*Verfassungsgerichtshof*). This 14-person court was reinstituted in 1945. Members are appointed by the president of the republic after recommendations from the Parliament. They have life tenure to age 70 and possess the power to review the constitutionality of legislation and decide jurisdictional disputes (Abraham, 1986). Since 1920 Austrian citizens have been able to file complaints when they feel their constitutional rights have been violated by an act of administration. Since 1975, complaints are also allowed when they believe their rights have been violated by an act of legislation.

Germany's federal constitutional court, the *Bundesverfassungsgericht*, was created in 1951 (for West Germany). It consists of 16 judges, all of whom have considerable past judicial, legal, professional, or other high public experience. Half are elected by the lower house (*Bundestag*) and half by the upper house (*Bundesrat*) of Parliament. The judges serve a nonrenewable 12-year term. They hear cases brought by agencies, institutions, and certain individuals. The court decides the constitutional validity of any federal or state statute and protects the fundamental rights and privileges of citizens on both substantive and procedural issues.

Italy's constitutional Court (*Corte Costituzionale*) was established in 1948 and began functioning in 1956. This 15-member body is staffed with distinguished persons having at least 20 years experience as practicing lawyers, experienced judges, or professors of law. The judges are appointed for staggered nine-year terms with five selected by the president of the republic, five by three-fifths vote of Parliament, and five by the ordinary and administrative judiciary. The *Corte Costituzionale* is the final interpreter of the constitution and has the power to declare both national and regional laws unconstitutional.

With constitutional courts like those in Austria, Germany, and Italy, the concentrated model of judicial review achieves the same goal as the diffuse model: to provide procedures for holding the government to certain fundamental values. France offers another way to achieve the same end. In France, the belief that courts should not engage in any lawmaking at all prevented placement of "judicial review" within the judiciary. Instead, in 1958 the French created the Constitutional Council (*Counseil Constitutionnel*). Unlike the constitutional courts of other European countries, this entity lies outside the judicial system (Abraham, 1986). Neither individuals, groups, nor courts of law can appeal to it. The Council is composed of all the ex-presidents of France plus nine other persons selected (three each) by the president of the republic, the president of the senate, and the president of the National Assembly. The nine appointed members serve one nonrenewable nine-year term of office, while the ex-presidents serve for life.

The council has wide-ranging duties (see Brewer–Carias, 1989), only one of which is judicial reveiw. It accomplishes the judicial review duty by striking down laws or declaring them unconstitutional after they are drafted by the parliament but before the president signs them into law. A single opinion is delivered, without concurring or dissenting opinions, and that judgment is final and binding. However, since the council is not a court of law, its decisions can be enforced only by the council's ability to persuade the courts. Two things especially keep the council from representing an example of judicial review (Abraham, 1986). First, private individuals cannot challenge the constitutionality of a law, so, for example, there can be no French equivalent to America's Clarence Earl Gideon and his challenge to the absence of defense counsel for indigents. In addition, when challenges are authorized, they can be only on the law's substance, not on its procedural application. As a result, challenges like those in the United

States on search and seizure procedures are not considered by the French Constitutional Council.

The Mixed Model for Judicial Review.

Because the concentrated and diffuse systems of judicial review can exist in countries with either a common or civil legal tradition, it is not suprising that mixed systems of judicial review sometimes occur. Brewer–Carias (1989) believes that countries like Portugal and Venezuela exemplify mixed systems.

The Portuguese constitution of 1976 and its 1982 revision established a complete system of judicial review which has elements of concentrated (including the French version) and diffuse models. The Constitutional Court, created by the constitution as part of the judicial hierarchy, represents the concentrated aspect. Along with the establishment of the Constitutional Court, the Portuguese constitution authorizes all courts in the country to avoid implementing any law deemed by the court to be unconstitutional. This, of course, imitates the diffuse model. Similarly, building on a 100-year tradition, Venezuela's 1961 constitution established the Supreme Court of Justice as competent to review the constitutionality of laws. Simultaneously, the Civil Proceedings Code allows all courts in Venezuela to declare inapplicable laws the court deems unconstitutional. These combinations of diffuse and concentrated systems of judicial review provide Venezuela and Portugal with two of the most extensive systems of judicial review in the world (Brewer–Carias, 1989).

Brazil's new constitution (1988) places it among countries with mixed systems of judicial review (Dolinger, 1990). Although Brazil originally followed the United States and used a diffuse model, constitutional reforms over the years kept adding aspects of a concentrated model. As a result, any Brazilian judge at any court level can today ignore law that he or she considers unconstitutional for the current case (Dolinger, 1990). Additionally, the Brazilian *Supremo Tribunal Federal* not only rules on the constitutionality of laws related to the case immediately before it, but also can declare unconstitutional any action initiated by the office of the attorney general of the republic.

Judicial Review in the Islamic and Socialist Traditions.

As noted earlier, discussion of a *Rechtsstaat* in Islamic and socialist law must differ slightly from its discussion under common and civil legal traditions. Countries in the common and civil families usually (France being an exception) follow one of two judicial review models to hold their governments accountable to fundamental values. In all cases, those values have been reduced to written form through a constitution. Under Islamic law, the fundamental values are presented in the *Qur'an* and *Sunna*. Under socialism, law is subordinate to policy.

Islam very clearly accepts the supremacy of fundamental values or laws. Those laws preceded the state, and the state exists solely to maintain and enforce the law. The *Shari'a* records the fundamental values, so Islamic law meets the first two criteria for achieving a *Rechtsstaat*: recognition of the supremacy of fundamental values and reducing those values to written form. For those viewing the rule of law as desirable, the problem with the Islamic tradition is that it goes no further than the first two steps.

The *Shari'a* does not visualize any conflict between the interests of the ruler and of the citizen. As a result, there are no procedures (judicial or otherwise) to review the actions of government. Substantive questions cannot be brought by citizens, because the law is of divine origin and valid for all time. To question the legitimacy of a law would mean that a Muslim is questioning Allah. Similarly, questions regarding the procedures used to enforce the law are inappropriate because Muslims are told to give allegiance to the existing authority, regardless of the nature of that authority (Coulson, 1957). Unjust rulers and their inappropriate procedures will be punished by Allah in the next world.

The absence of any system to provide a remedy against the abuse of individual rights by government agents means that Islamic law does not completely operate under a rule of law. The recognition and written account of fundamental values is not backed up with formal procedures by which citizens can hold their government accountable to those values. Instead, the Islamic tradition simply counsels against abuse and relies on faith that rulers will hold themselves answerable. "To the power of the ruler who is supported by adequate physical force the *Shari'a* sets no other limits than those which he finds in his own conscience" (Coulson, 1957).

In terms of achieving a *Rechtsstaat*, Islamic law is similar to the common and civil legal traditions in recognizing and reducing to writing certain fundamental values. It differs from the other two by having incomplete mechanisms for judicial review to force the government to abide by the same values it requires of the citizens. Socialist law differs from the other three by failing to even recognize fundamental values, let alone reducing them to writing or providing procedures to hold the government accountable. The term "failure" is actually inappropriate, since socialism rejects the notion of law as an absolute value. Instead, socialist policy is the absolute and law is the subordinate. In other words, a *Rechtsstaat* is absent in the socialist tradition by design, not mistake.

Since socialist legality exists to advance the interests of the state, there has been only indirect interest in protecting the welfare of individual citizens. The possibility of inappropriate government behavior is recognized, but the judiciary is certainly not viewed as the appropriate monitor. Instead, the procuracy (in, for example, the People's Republic of China) is the agency responsible for supervising the activities of administrative agencies. Since this is not part of the judiciary, examinations of violations of law by state officials is initiated by this investigative body rather than by individual citizens.

Under the Soviet system, however, there were occasions where courts could investigate the legality of administrative decisions (Markovits, 1989). All socialist law systems had a few instances where citizens could take their administration to court. In some countries (for example, Rumania and Bulgaria) laws on the books provided opportunities for citizens to sue the administration if their rights were invaded by public authority. However, even in countries with the appearance of judicial review opportunities, socialist states preferred to enforce administrative legality through state-controlled institutions and procedures (Markovits, 1989). A prime example was (and still is in existing socialist systems) the procuracy, which investigates misuses of public authority at the state's own initiative. These procedures are informal, cheap, and easily accessible (compared to cumbersome lawsuits), but they have no bite and provide no legal entitlement to the citizen.

The philosophy, however, is consistent with the socialist perspective. When investigation of public authority is at the initiative of private individuals, societal interests may be compromised by the greed of a private plaintiff. Consequently, administrative justice is a matter of public concern more than of private importance. As such, it requires a public solution rather than provocation by private citizens.

The socialist rejection of law as an absolute value seems to be changing. One indication of that change was reflected even before the USSR's breakup in arguments made by Soviet citizens who sought recognition of a *Rechtsstaat*. In one example (Feofanov, 1990–1991), a Soviet newspaper is told of a collective farm chairman who took a section of land from the private plot of an elderly widow. A reporter went to the countryside and confirmed the complaint; there seemed no doubt that the chairman illegally took the widow's land. The newspaper took the position that the landlord acted illegally and supported that argument by noting how the widow's late husband was one of the first organizers of the collective, her eldest son had bravely died in war, and she participated in the farm workers collective.

The reporter was asked if it would have been illegal to take the widow's land had her husband and son been criminals and she a discontent. The action was clearly illegal, but the Soviet newspaper argued the woman's case on the basis of her, and her family's, clearly outstanding biography. Feofanov (1990–1991) wonders why the act was not censured because it was illegal, rather than because it harmed a good Soviet citizen. The Soviet newspaper agreed that the act was illegal regardless of the citizen's character. But, the paper argued, the readers are more understanding when worthy people are treated unlawfully than when the "victim" is deemed unworthy. The result denies the absolute value of law, but it is consistent with the supremacy of socialist policy over legal norms.

Actually, a drifting toward a rule of law started occurring in some socialist countries as early as 1980, when Poland established a separate administrative court system. Even today, with Poland's move toward democracy, the High Administrative Court in Warsaw adjudicates citizens' grievances against the executive. Hungary made similar reforms and by 1986, both Poland (Constitutional Tribunal) and Hungary (Council of Constitutional Law) developed a judicial review system to cover the constitutionality of legislation (Markovits, 1989). Importantly, these new procedures were not just paper placation. The legal controls over socialist executives gained momentum as more and more citizens took advantage of the courts to seek action against the state. And the citizens were winning! The new Polish Constitutional Tribunal, for example, came out in favor of the plaintiff in all of its first nine decisions.

Some former socialist countries in Eastern and Central Europe, while achieving versions of democracy and capitalism, are moving toward a rule of law very similar to that in common and civil legal traditions. However, some proponents of the supremacy of law now argue that such a concept is not inconsistent with socialism. The October Revolution proclaimed equality of all before the law, and Lenin spoke of the priority of law over expediency. From this perspective, law as an absolute value returns to the basic socialist perspective rather than rejects it (Feofanov, 1990–1991). The USSR disbanded before achieving *Rechtsstaat*, but arguments that socialism does not reject a rule of law may provide remaining socialist countries an opportunity to move in the direction in which the Soviet Union seemed headed.

Despite the apparent increased appreciation by some socialist theorists for law as an absolute value, Markovits (1989) hesitates to interpret such activity as indicating a birth of a socialist *Rechtsstaat*. She prefers to see the movement as another medicine being tried to treat socialist ills. Whatever form it ends with, countries currently or previously under the socialist legal tradition must confront the question of a *Rechtsstaat* and determine how citizens will hold their government accountable.

SUMMARY

Every legal system must address issues of substantive and procedural law but each system may approach the terms differently. This chapter takes the admittedly Western-linked perspective on substantive and procedural law as first presented in Chapter 3, and uses these concepts as a comparative aid in discussing legal systems.

Looking at substantive law in each of the four legal traditions, we found that defining what was criminal and specifying the punishment included reliance on judges (common legal tradition), legislators (civil legal tradition), a variety of government agencies (socialist legal tradition), and on God (Islamic legal tradition). Regardless of who or what is doing the defining, it is apparent that each legal tradition has some difficulty with several or all of the general characteristics and major principles associated with substantive law.

Procedural law was addressed with specific attention to the issues of the adjudicatory process and judicial review. Adjudication typically follows an adversarial or inquisitorial model. Both models seek the truth in claims made by the state against an individual. The inquisitorial process (civil law systems and socialist law systems) seems like a continuing investigation with all parties cooperating to determine what happened. The adversarial process (common law systems), on the other hand, is more obviously a contest between competing sides, where truth is said to lie with the victor. This is especially true in the United

States' version of the adversarial process. Adjudication under Islamic procedural law seems a combination of the inquisitorial and adversarial models.

The procedure of judicial review was introduced as an important way to ensure that a government abides by the fundamental values of a nation. In this way a *Rechtsstaat*, or rule of law, can be achieved because the government, like its citizens, is made accountable. One model of judicial review is the diffuse design, wherein all courts in a country have authority to find laws unconstitutional. This decentralized model is used in the United States and in some civil law countries, so it is not attached to particular legal traditions. The concentrated model for judicial review follows a centralized design and invests all constitutional review power in a single state organ. Some countries have successfully adopted aspects of both diffuse and concentrated models and as a result are said to have a mixed model for judicial review. Still other countries (for example, some under the Islamic and socialist legal traditions) do not seem to operate under a rule of law and as such have incomplete or nonexistent procedures for judicial review.

The chapter's Impact sections address two issues that are particularly relevant to United States citizens. The first considers the meaning that increased codification of laws has for America's placement among the common law families. The second asks if aspects of the inquisitorial system could be applied in the United States.

SUGGESTED READINGS

Ingraham, Barton L. (1987). *The structure of criminal procedure: Laws and practice of France, the Soviet Union, China, and the United States.* New York: Greenwood, an imprint of Greenwood Publishing Group, Westport, CT.

Sanad, Nagaty. (1991). *The theory of crime and criminal responsibility in Islamic law: Shari'a.* Chicago: Office of International Criminal Justice.

REFERENCES

Abadinsky, Howard. (1988). *Law and justice.* Chicago: Nelson-Hall.

Abraham, Henry J. (1986). *The judicial process: An introductory analysis of the courts of the United States, England, and France* (5th ed.). New York: Oxford University Press.

al-'Awwa, Muhammad Salim. (1982). The basis of Islamic penal legislation. In M. C. Bassiouni (Ed.), *The Islamic criminal justice system* (pp. 127–147). London, England: Oceana Publications.

Awad, Awad M. (1982). The rights of the accused under Islamic criminal procedure. In M. C. Bassiouni (Ed.), *The Islamic criminal justice system* (pp. 91–107). London, England: Oceana Publications.

Bahnassi, Ahmad Fathi. (1982). Criminal responsibility in Islamic law. In M. C. Bassiouni (Ed.), *The Islamic criminal justice system* (pp. 171–193). London, England: Oceana Publications.

Bassiouni, M. Cherif (Ed.). (1982). *The Islamic criminal justice system.* London, England: Oceana Publications.

Brewer-Carias, Allan R. (1989). *Judicial review in comparative law.* Cambridge, England: Cambridge University Press.

Cappelletti, Mauro. (1989). *The judicial process in comparative perspective.* Oxford: Clarendon Press.

Cappelletti, Mauro, Merryman, John H., and Perillo, Joseph M. (1967). *The Italian legal system: An introduction.* Stanford, CA: Stanford University Press.

Cole, George F. (1989). *The American system of criminal justice* (5th ed.). Monterey, CA: Brooks/Cole.

Colorado Revised Statutes. (1986). Englewood, CO: Colorado District Attorneys Council.

Coulson, Noel J. (1957). The state and the individual in Islamic law. *International and Comparative Law Quarterly, 6,* 49–60.

David, Rene. (1960/1972). *French law: Its structure, sources, and methodology* (M. Kindred, Trans.). Baton Rouge, LA: Louisiana State University Press. (Original work published 1960).

Dolinger, Jacob. (1990). The influence of American constitutional law on the Brazilian legal system. *The American Journal of Comparative Law, 38,* 803–837.

Feofanov, Iurii. (1990–1991). A return to origins: Reflections on power and law. *Soviet Law and Government, 29*(3), 15–52.

France, Simon. (1990). Reforming criminal law—New Zealand's 1989 code. *The Criminal Law Review,* December, 827–838.

Frankowski, Stanislaw J. (1987). Poland. In G. F. Cole, S. J. Frankowski, and M. G. Gertz (Eds.), *Major criminal justice systems: A comparative study* (2nd ed.) (pp. 221–261). Newbury Park, CA: Sage.

Friedman, Lawrence M. (1973). *A history of American law.* New York: Simon and Schuster.

Gardner, Thomas J. (1989). *Criminal law: Principles and cases* (4th ed.). St. Paul, MN: West.

Graham, Michael H. (1983). *Tightening the reins of justice in America.* Westport, CT: Greenwood Press.

Ingraham, Barton L. (1987). *The structure of criminal procedure: Laws and practice of France, the Soviet Union, China, and the United States.* New York: Greenwood, an imprint of Greenwood Publishing Group, Westport, CT.

Italian Penal Code (E. Wise, Trans.). (1978). Littleton, CO: Fred B. Rothman.

Jones, Timothy H. (1990). Common law and criminal law: The Scottish example. *The Criminal Law Review,* May, 292–301.

Lippman, Matthew, McConville, Sean, and Yerushalmi, Mordechai. (1988). *Islamic criminal law and procedure.* New York: Praeger.

Markovits, Inga. (1989). Law and glasnost: Some thoughts about the future of judicial review under socialism. *Law and Society Review, 23,* 399–447.

Merryman, John H. (1985). *The civil law tradition* (2nd ed.). Stanford, CA: Stanford University Press.

Packer, Herbert L. (1968). *The limits of the criminal sanction.* Stanford, CA: Stanford University Press.

Penal Code of the Federal Republic of Germany (J. Darby, Trans.). (1987). Littleton, CO: Fred B. Rothman.

Samaha, Joel. (1988). *Criminal justice.* St. Paul, MN: West.

Sanad, Nagaty. (1991). *The theory of crime and criminal responsibility in Islamic law: Shari'a.* Chicago: Office of International Criminal Justice.

Savitzky, Valery M., and Kogan, Victor M. (1987). The Union of Soviet Socialist Republics. In G. F. Cole, S. J. Frankowski, and M. G. Gertz (Eds.). *Major criminal justice systems: A comparative study* (2nd ed.) (pp. 191–220). Newbury Park, CA: Sage.

Siddiqi, Muhammad I. (1985). *The penal law of Islam* (2nd ed.). Lahore, Pakistan: Kazi Publications.

Terrill, Richard J. (1984). *World criminal justice systems: A survey.* Cincinnati, OH: Anderson.

Tomlinson, Edward A. (1983). Nonadversarial justice: The French experience. *Maryland Law Review, 42,* 131–195.

Waldron, Ronald J. (1989). *The criminal justice system: An introduction* (4th ed.). New York: Harper and Row.

Chapter 6

An International Perspective on Policing

KEY TOPICS

- Centralized and decentralized supervision of police forces
- Singular and multiple number of police forces to be supervised
- Examples of centralized single systems of policing
- Examples of centralized multiple coordinated systems of policing
- Examples of centralized multiple uncoordinated systems of policing
- Examples of decentralized multiple coordinated systems of policing
- Examples of decentralized multiple uncoordinated systems of policing
- Canada's contracting system for providing police services
- How permanent is a nation's police structure?

KEY TERMS

Carabinieri	*Gendarmerie Nationale*
centralized policing	*Guardia Civil*
contract policing	*Police Municipale*
Cuerpo Nacional de Policia	*Police Nationale*
decentralized policing	*Policia Municipal*
Department of Justice	*Polizia di Stato*
Department of Treasury	Royal Canadian Mounted Police

COUNTRIES REFERENCED

Belgium	Nigeria
Canada	Poland
Denmark	Saudi Arabia
Finland	Spain
France	Switzerland
Germany	Union of Soviet Socialist Republics
Italy	United States

In Japan, Seicho Matsumoto's fictional Inspector Imanishi travels throughout the nation to investigate a case. No one seems to mind the fact that Imanishi-san is with the Tokyo Metropolitan Police Force yet is interviewing witnesses, asking questions of local police officers, and apparently having the run of the country with no regard for jurisdictional boundaries.

A continent away, Georges Simenon has his French Inspector Maigret investigate crime scenes under the watchful eye of deputy public prosecutors and upstart examining magistrates. Meanwhile, further north in the Netherlands, police Commissaris Van der Valk (courtesy of Nicholas Freeling) must deal with an Officer of Justice who operates as an amalgam of a French public prosecutor and examining magistrate. Also in the Netherlands, but operating at lower ranks, Detective Adjutant Grijpstra and Sergeant de Gier (from the pen of Janwillem van de Wetering) work the Amsterdam streets, making decisions on such matters as the distance between a prostitute and the bar down the street. Since prostitution is illegal within 200 feet of a public place selling alcohol, police (who may actually be looking for drugs) may want to stop and question the streetwalker.

Police procedure novels showing officers with nationwide jurisdiction, having to work under the direction of an examining magistrate, reporting to a combination prosecutor–judge, or dealing with laws that allow prostitution only on certain parts of the street, may raise questions of credibility from American readers. But upon realizing that United States police structure and organization, as well as procedures followed, are just one of several models available, the reader may find such novels to be doubly intriguing.

In fact, the American model of policing is more unique than common compared to that in other countries. A basic principle of the American republic was the notion that the states and federal government would share power. In terms of maintaining law and order, the power was to be primarily at the state level. As if to emphasize the point, the United States Constitution mentions only two crimes (counterfeiting and treason) and avoids any mention of a national police force to protect federal property and enforce federal laws (Johnson, 1981). Taking their cue from the federal government, the states avoided direct involvement in law enforcement and delegated such duties to the local communities. This seemed appropriate, since crime was a local phenomenon and presumably local authorities would best know how to respond to violators.

A result of this assignment of responsibilities was the absence of federal and state law enforcement agencies and a general decentralization of policing throughout the country and within each state. Even when the federal government increased its involvement in law enforcement, Congress, instead of investing all authority in one agency, divided enforcement responsibilities, so each federal department has investigative units responsible for enforcing laws relevant to that department's jurisdiction. The result ranges from U.S. Department of Agriculture agents, enforcing specific legislation like food stamp regulations, to the Federal Bureau of Investigation (Department of Justice) with responsibility for investigating over 200 different types of cases, such as robbing a federally insured bank, interstate racketeering, and transporting stolen property across state lines.

It may surprise many Americans that citizens of some countries see our decentralized system of policing as unusual and inefficient. That would be particularly true of countries operating under a single law enforcement agency with responsibility for policing the entire country. This chapter describes the various types of police structure so that we can better appreciate what alternatives are available.

CLASSIFYING POLICE STRUCTURES

David Bayley (1985) used the concepts of centralization and decentralization as a base for his typology of worldwide police structures. The following analysis and discussion borrow heavily from Bayley's work. Two dimensions of analysis are necessary to describe adequately the structure of police systems: the type of supervision or command (either centralized or decentralized) and the number of forces to be supervised (either singular or multiple). The use of these dimensions results in a categorization of police systems as falling into one of three cells (see Figure 6-1). A fourth cell, "singular—decentralized" is not logically possible, so it can hold no system.

Bayley's criterion to identify a system as either centralized or decentralized is the *stated* locus of control. The emphasis is on "stated," since it is possible for a system to be one way in principle but another in actuality. This situation means that the resulting categorization may not always reflect the actual condition. France, for example, has multiple police forces whose day-to-day operations are decided at the unit level. Structurally, however, command is from Paris, though it is seldom applied. Using the criterion of stated locus of control, France has a centralized police command. Bayley realizes that this criterion is deceptively simple, because it ignores the reality of informal command relationships (1985). But until there are more comparative studies, this provides a sensible option.

Type of Command

	Centralized	Decentralized
Singular	Denmark Nigeria Poland Saudi Arabia	Not possible*
Multiple — Coordinated	Austria France Finland	Canada Germany Great Britain
Multiple — Uncoordinated	Italy Soviet Union Spain	Belgium Switzerland United States

*No countries can be placed in this cell, since a single decentralized police system is not logically possible.

Figure 6-1. Classification of types of police structures. *Source:* From *Patterns of Policing* by David H. Bayley. Copyright © 1985 by Rutgers, the State University of New Jersey.

Bayley's typology is especially helpful for understanding relationships among the countries in a particular cell and between countries in different cells. It also provides a concise way to describe policing in many different countries by emphasizing the similarities rather than being confused by the differences. In other words, like all good classification schemes, Bayley's typology of police structures summarizes and makes sense of diversity.

Upon understanding the characteristics of each category for police structures you can assign immediately a new structure to the appropriate category. For example, Kurian says: "Mexican police forces exist at the federal, state and municipal levels through many overlapping layers of authority" (1989, p. 258). We also know that Mexico's main federal police is part of the Ministry of Government; that each state and the Federal District has its own police force; and that police delegations, headed by a *comandante*, operate in large urban areas. Applying Bayley's classification scheme to these characteristics should result in your assignment of Mexico to the cell containing "decentralized" (a different authority supervises the force at each level) "multiple" (there are at least three types of police) "uncoordinated" (there are apparently overlapping layers of authority) police structures.

With the aid of Bayley's categorization, we now move to a description of police systems falling into each major type found in Figure 6-1. Since the United States uses a police system that is less often found, it seems fitting that we better understand what most countries are doing. We do that by describing the police systems in countries that fall into each of five cells in Bayley's typology. Under each cell heading, policing in several countries is discussed, but only one nation is described in detail. The five countries receiving a more thorough report are France (centralized multiple coordinated), Spain (centralized multiple uncoordinated), Germany (decentralized coordinated), and the United States (decentralized multiple uncoordinated). Denmark, Nigeria, and Saudi Arabia receive brief attention as centralized singular systems, but that cell is covered more completely near the chapter's end in a discussion of Poland's police.

CENTRALIZED SINGLE SYSTEMS

The idea of one national police force responsible for enforcing a single set of laws throughout an entire country sounds alien to Americans. As Fig. 6-1 shows, however, that system is perfectly acceptable to the citizens of several countries.

Denmark

The kingdom of Denmark covers some 16,630 square miles (not counting the province of Greenland) and has a population near 5 million but is policed by one national force. The Ministry of Justice has administrative authority over the police force but is also the central command for the prosecution, the judiciary, and the prison and probation services (Bro, 1988).

Two components make up the Danish police force: the national commissioner of police and the 54 police districts. This provides a dualistic system in which a central command assures general and efficient standards for the entire force, while independent police districts allow for a deployment of resources that considers the needs of the local communities.

The national commissioner is responsible for the administration of police personnel and clerical staff, the allocation of workers to districts, and the general organization of police work in the districts, and can issue codes of practice and general regulations for police performance throughout Denmark (Bro, 1988; Baun, 1978). Although the commissioner is under the authority of the Ministry of Justice, he exercises independent control over the district force, since on only rare occasions will the ministry interfere with the local chief's performance or management style. However, remember Bayley's (1985) focus on the *stated* locus of control; supervisory authority lies with the Ministry of Justice, so Denmark is a centralized single system.

The police districts vary in size from the 2000-officer force in Copenhagen to the smallest district, where 60 officers serve a population of 33,000. A chief of police (*politimester*) is responsible for law enforcement in each district. Besides directing district police operations, the chief of police also serves as the local prosecuting authority. In this role he conducts proceedings for civil and criminal offenses and initiates action in most criminal cases. These duties require that police chiefs have law degrees. In addition, the two to four assistant chiefs in each district also must be law graduates, since they occasionally must answer legal questions (Baun, 1978).

Prosecution is hierarchically organized, so the 54 police chiefs are subordinated to the seven regional prosecutors and the state prosecutor. Even in the major cases, which are the responsibility of the regional prosecutor, the police chief typically presents the case in court. The regional prosecutor's court appearances are mostly limited to serious cases (for example, murder, rape, robbery) where the defendant does not plead guilty. Presumably the Danish police are not as likely as their American counterparts to be frustrated with the prosecutor's refusal to take action in a case where they worked hard to make an arrest. If criminal proceedings are not initiated, it is the police chief's decision, not some prosecutor's who police may feel does not appreciate their efforts. Another possible benefit of "police as prosecutor" is suggested by Baun (1978), who believes local level integration of police and prosecutor allows the two functions to work smoothly and rationally together.

Saudi Arabia

Denmark's centralized police system works well because the 54 districts are divided completely and without any overlapping of authority. As a result, any police-related incident occurring in Denmark is the sole responsibility of a single police chief. The situation is not so clear-cut in Saudi Arabia. Although its police system is considered a centralized single type (cf. Alobied, 1989), Saudi Arabia has jurisdictional pockets of tribal authority (cf. Kurian, 1989). As a result, local efforts may be used before calling the formal police. Also, the Saudis use an autonomous religious police (*mutawwiun*), organized under the king's authority, to help ensure strict compliance with Islam. However, since we are primarily concerned with the legitimate and formally recognized police, Saudi Arabia serves as another example of a centralized single system.

All formal policing in Saudi Arabia links to the Ministry of Interior. The conduit to the minister is the Director of Public Safety. This director, appointed by the king, is responsible for all the police forces in Saudi Arabia. The Director of Public Safety controls the police system and is ultimately responsible for everything from murderers to traffic problems (Alobied, 1989). Specialized units like the Coast Guard, Frontier Force, and National Guard have specific duties as suggested by their names. The Public Security Police, however, provide general policing throughout the country and in every province. These uniformed officers are essentially a national police force.

Nigeria

A final example of policing with a single force under a centralized command is provided by Nigeria. Thirty years before gaining independence from the British in 1960, Nigeria had merged its Northern Constabulary, the Southern Police

Force, and the Lagos Police Force, into the Nigeria Police Force (Kayode, 1976). The continued existence of independent regional police departments and community police forces alongside that national force provided a decentralized system. But, given the local conditions and political climate of the time, decentralized law enforcement provided a sense of autonomy and stability for each administrative area.

As independence took hold during the 1960s, Nigeria moved toward a very centralized police model. A turning point occurred in 1964, when the first Nigerian head of the Nigeria Police Force took office. Before that date, every inspector-general of the national police was British (Kayode, 1976). The next step to complete centralization and Nigeriazation of law enforcement was the gradual integration of remaining local police forces into the Nigeria Police Force. The first group of local officers reported for training at the federal police college in 1968. By 1980, the merging of local police into the federal force was completed for all Nigeria.

The Nigeria Police is headquartered in Lagos and operates under the leadership of an Inspector General of Police (see Figure 6-2). Nigeria's military leadership suggests that the police force would be under the supervision of the Ministry of Defenses. But it actually exists as a separate body that is part of the military administration. Reflecting that link, the Inspector General of Police is a member of the Supreme Military Council, the Federal Executive Council, and the Council of States (Iwarimie-Jaja, 1980). Five assistant inspector generals each supervise one of the five departments at central headquarters (Igbinovia, 1989). These departments, labeled A through E, have responsibility for such activities as general administration (department A), communications and transportation (department B), general financial matters (department C), criminal records and investigation (department D), and a special branch (department E) responsible for internal security and countersubversive activities.

Below central police headquarters in the organizational hierarchy are police commands in each of Nigeria's 19 states. A commissioner of police heads each of the police commands, which are located in the 19 capital cities. Below the commissioner are the provincial police officers, then the district police officers, and finally the station officers.

The tasks of policing and the manner in which they are carried out are similar to any other modern nation. Patrol, either foot or automobile, is handled by uniformed officers, who are usually unarmed except for a billy club or baton. Foot patrol officers walk their beat during both day and evening hours. Two-way radios provide contact with police headquarters, the nearest police station, or patrolling police cars. Igbinovia (1989) says that these patrols are very effective in preventing crime, detecting certain types of street crime, and providing positive contact with the public.

Motorized patrol is of four types: roundabout, antirobbery, highway, and police accident (Igbinovia, 1989). The roundabout patrol involves the assignment of officers to the important traffic circles (roundabouts) in the cities. This posi-

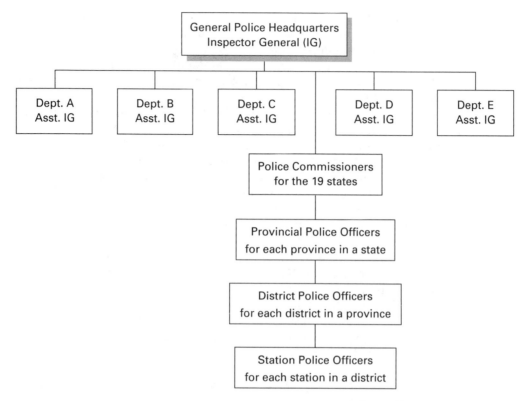

Figure 6-2. Nigeria's police organization.

tioning allows police officers to watch all movements in the area, report suspicious behavior, and to respond quickly to instructions from the police station. Antirobbery patrol teams, as their name implies, are mobile units charged with apprehending persons caught in the act of robbery or intercepting those believed ready to commit a robbery. The highway patrol units have access to ambulances, motorcycles, and sophisticated communications equipment. These officers enforce traffic laws, aid accident victims, and respond to crimes committed on highways. The police accident patrol responds to instances of hit-and-run driving and tries to prevent or reduce deaths from road accidents.

The centralized single police forces of Denmark, Saudi Arabia, and Nigeria show us just one way of providing law enforcement in a country. The fact that these countries vary considerably in size (Denmark is about the size of Massachusetts and New Hampshire combined, whereas Saudi Arabia is one third the size of the United States), and population density (Nigeria has 322 people per square mile, but Saudi Arabia has 15 people per square mile) suggests that geography alone is not a likely variable to explain the occurrence of this type of police structure. Since two of the countries are monarchies (Denmark is a constitutional monarchy; Saudi Arabia is a monarchy with a council of ministers) and Nigeria is a federal republic under military leadership, some explanation may be provided by government type. However, we also could have used Ireland (a parliamentary republic) or Israel (a parliamentary democracy) to exemplify a centralized single police force.

A country's preferred police structure is not easily explained as the result of one or two clearly identifiable features. A people's history, culture, traditions, and links to other people are only some topics to be considered in trying to understand a country's social institutions. Such disciplines as political science, history, sociology, psychology, and anthropology are among those that attempt to provide answers. For our purposes, we must be content with appreciating the variety and forgoing the analysis. In presenting the other examples of police structures, we continue to rely on descriptive accounts rather than analyzing the reasons that various countries share a similar police structure.

CENTRALIZED MULTIPLE COORDINATED SYSTEMS

Bayley (1985) distinguishes between multiple coordinated and multiple uncoordinated systems to demarcate situations where several forces operate within defined jurisdictions from those where several forces have overlapping authority. As a warning, however, he reminds us that all national governments create police agencies with authority for areas that transcend the concerns of subordinate government units. Examples include the FBI in the United States, Canada's Royal Canadian Mounted Police, and the National Police Agency in Japan. So technically all multiple-force countries have uncoordinated systems, since there is inevitably a national level agency with overlapping authority.

Bayley assigns a country to a coordinated or uncoordinated cell according to his personal judgment about the level of importance attached to the central government's responsibilities in the total view of policing. In a coordinated police system, enforcement by the central government is deemed relatively unimportant. Central authority is curtailed by such techniques as limiting its jurisdictional area and allowing it to intervene only at the request of local authorities. Alternatively, uncoordinated forces are independently active, have responsibility for many offenses, and can act without prior approval of local authorities. So, while recognizing that multiple force countries are necessarily uncoordinated, we follow Bayley's lead and for purposes of description and education distinguish some as coordinated.

Finland

The police in Finland are organized on three levels, but the Ministry of the Interior is ultimately responsible for each level (Laento, 1988). Specifically, the Police Department (a department in the Ministry of the Interior) acts as the central administrative body. The head of that department is commander in chief of all police forces in Finland.

At the first, or central, organizational level is the Ministry's Police Department itself. Operating at this tier are the Security Police, the Mobile Police, and the Central Criminal Police. The Security Police investigate crimes against the state, offenses against the law and order of the state or the community, and crimes that may endanger public safety. The Mobile Police assist other police units, maintain public order and safety, aid in crime prevention and traffic control, and operate as the national police reserve. The Central Criminal Police officers have jurisdiction throughout Finland, so they can investigate complex crimes too difficult for local police.

Administration of these three forces at the second (regional) level is handled by a provincial administration board in each of the twelve provinces. But it is at the third organizational level, the local police district, where much of the actual "street" police work occurs. Actually, there are two types of local police authorities (Laento, 1988): the town police departments headed by police chiefs, and the rural police districts headed by sheriffs. Crime investigation is initially directed by local authorities, but difficult cases are typically handled in cooperation with the Central Criminal Police at the provincial and central levels.

Besides their regular police duties, provincial and local police officials also have prosecutorial responsibilities. Sheriffs and police chiefs serve as prosecutors in lower courts, while the provincial superintendent of police is also the provincial prosecutor dealing with serious crime cases.

Das (1992) draws on his field research experience to provide interesting insight into the working environment and attitudes of Finnish police. In general, he found them to have high morale, minimal corruption, and a positive image among the public. Any complaints they had about police work related to such seemingly universal concerns as the difficulties associated with shift work, the shortage of important resources (for example, personnel, cars, computers), an inadequate salary at the junior levels, and the hazardous working conditions. This last point is worth elaboration, since it reminds us of the relative nature of such concerns. Crime in general, and even drug and organized crime more specifically, are well under control in Finland. The Finnish police point with satisfaction to the low crime rate, but that does not mean that they avoid concern on topics like the adequacy of official issue firearms, the availability of bulletproof vests, and the restrictions placed on their use of guns. With these issues as conversation points it seems likely that a Finnish police officer would have much to discuss with police in many other countries.

France

French policing dates back at least to 1666 and Louis XIV's creation of a Lieutenant-General of Police for Paris. The holder of that position had both administrative and judicial tasks ranging from controlling prices, weights, and measures, and inspecting markets to apprehending criminals and developing surveillance of suspected traitors. This office was abolished after the French Revolution, and Napoleon appointed a Minister of Police, who initially focused on information gathering and state security (Roach, 1985).

Nineteenth-century changes finally settled down when the Municipal Code of 1884 set the terms of commune (France's smallest division of local government) organization. The office of mayor was created, and the holder of that office was given control over police services (Kania, 1989). The result was a system of local policing operating in conjunction with the national police, or *Gendarmerie*.

In 1941, the Vichy government established the basic structure of French policing with the *Gendarmerie* policing the rural areas and a *Police Nationale* having responsibility for urban policing. In this manner, French policing reflects the multiple coordinated type, since each force has separate jurisdictions. Actually, each is also under a different ministry, as described below, but since the ministries make up the central government the police system is centralized.

The French are proud of their forked version of centralization (see Figure 6-3). Since Napoleon's time they have consistently refrained from placing control of the police under a single authority. In fact, Stead (1983) suggests the absence of a Minister of Police is a conspicuous strategy to avoid the concentration of force in the hands of a single person. The chosen alternative gives the Minister of the Interior administrative control over the civil police (the *Police Nationale*), while the Minister of Defense has similar control over the *Gendarmerie Nationale*. The Minister of Justice even gets into the act with its judicial control of the civil police and the *gendarmes* in the investigation of crime.

Gendarmerie Nationale. The *Gendarmerie* is the older of the two police forces. It is responsible for enforcing the law in the rural areas of France and in communities of fewer than 10,000 people. The fact that there are few densely populated metropolitan areas means that the over 85,000 *gendarmes* police some 95 percent of the national territory.

A Director-General, who is responsible to the Minister of Defense, controls the *Gendarmerie*. The military linkages should not, however, detract attention from its sophisticated and highly successful style. The policing of France's road traffic and smaller towns is carried out by personnel meeting high recruitment and training standards using quality equipment that would be the envy of most police forces. There is a *Gendarmerie* Regional Headquarters in each of France's six Defense Zones. All the *gendarmes* in the region serve to make up a Legion. The Legions, in turn, are composed of either *Departmentale Gendarmerie* or *Gendarmerie Mobile*. The *Departmentale Gendarmerie*, the larger of the two components, resides in and operates from fixed points in the main town of the district. The *Mobile Gendarmerie*, found throughout the country, is responsible for maintaining or restoring public order. These highly trained riot police operate on a regional or departmental basis, and are made "mobile" with their tanks, armored vehicles, and light aircraft (Roach, 1985; Stead, 1983).

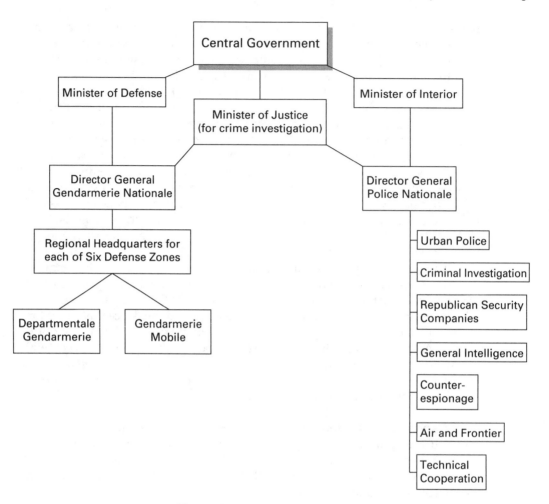

Figure 6-3. France's police organization.

Police Nationale. Stead (1983) points out that most foreigners seem to assume that all French police are *gendarmes*. The similarity of uniforms fosters that confusion, and the high visibility of *gendarmes* (constantly in uniform and on patrol throughout the country) makes the assumption understandable. The *Police Nationale* is the larger of the two forces with over 150,000 personnel (Kania, 1990). Operating primarily in urban centers over 10,000 in population, the *Police Nationale* is administrated by a Director-General under the Ministry of the Interior.

Seven directorates control and coordinate the operational work of the police. Several of these are similar to departments found in Anglo–American policing. For example, the Directorate of Urban Police uses patrol officers and plain-clothes *inspectors* for policing the cities. The Directorate of Criminal Investigation (*Police Judiciaire*) controls and coordinates the *Police Nationale's* detective work. Through subdirectorates it has responsibility for such things as forensic investigation, criminal statistics, banditry (for example, gang crime, aggravated theft, kidnapping), and white-collar crime activities like counterfeiting and art forgery. Importantly, the Central Directorate of Criminal Investigation also controls the Regional Crime Services. These 19 services make inquiries into organized, professional, and transient crime by coordinating efforts of the urban police, over which they have authority in more serious criminal matters (Stead, 1983).

The *Police Nationale* has its own version of the *Gendarmerie Mobile*. The military style (they are based in barracks and their officers have military rank) of the Republican Security Companies (CRS) disguises their civil nature. While not armed to the level of the *Gendarmerie Mobile*, the CRS can move equally fast, wherever needed, as they fulfill their duties of maintenance and restoration of public order.

The remaining four directorates have such duties as collecting and interpreting public opinion data for use by the government (Directorate of General Intelligence), repressing activities harmful to the interests of France (Directorate of Counterespionage), controlling the movement of people and foreign publications to and from French territory (Central Service of the Air and Frontier Police), and training, in France, of police officers from other countries (Service of International Technical Cooperation).

A presumed benefit of a centralized police force is an increase in cooperation and efficiency. As described above, the two great French police forces seem to embody those characteristics and well illustrate what is good about centralization. A prime example would be the urban police turning serious cases over to the regional crime service. As Stead describes it:

> Here one sees the value of a national police system: the urban police inform the regional crime service, which in turn transmits any important intelligence to the Central Directorate in Paris. The latter, in certain cases, circulates it throughout the country, and this can lead to cross-checks and association of data. Thus, the usefulness of centralization, coordination, and cooperation becomes clear (Stead, 1983, pp. 121–122).

Americans are more used to seeing police agencies at odds with one another than engaging in such a spirit of cooperation. The local police complain that the FBI takes credit for breaking a case, or a city police department withholds evidence from the sheriff's department in the hopes of making its own unaided arrest. Those examples seem more typical of America's version of interagency cooperation. However, we should not be too quick to assume that France avoids similar problems. As Stead points out, police everywhere and throughout time have been reluctant to share their hard-won knowledge. "It is hardly to be avoided that when two distinct organizations, heirs to very different traditions, are pursuing the same ends, there will be competition and rivalry" (Stead, 1983, p. 127). A source of friction, for example, centers on the inevitable growth of towns and the expansion of suburbs. When a town of 9000 expands to over 10,000 the policing should pass from *gendarmes* to the Police Nationale. Yet the *gendarmes* have policed the area for as long as anyone can remember and see no reason that they should suddenly leave. Similarly, as city suburbs extend to the countryside, the *Police Nationale* come to regard the new area as their jurisdiction despite the presence of the *Gendarmerie Nationale*. It appears that despite the tranquility of force coordination on paper, there is less harmony in practice.

Further indication that the French system is not as synchronized as they would like is suggested by a January 1983 law authorizing locally controlled police. Kania (1990) estimates that over 25,000 men and women are employed by various local governments as members of these "mayors' police forces" (*la garde des maires*, or *police municipale*). The units seem to have come into existence as President François Mitterrand and his Socialist party sought to carry out their campaign promise of decentralization and increased local control over governmental services. Some cities, Kania (1989) believes, were displeased with the policing services provided by the national government and took advantage of the opportunity to create their own force.

The existence of the local police units presents a problem for our placement of France with the police systems under a centralized command. If the *Police Municipale* is under local, rather than central, authority, that suggests a decentralized system. At this time, however, there are several reasons to downplay the importance of the mayors' police and to keep France among the countries with a centralized police system. These reasons include the municipal police forces' typical size, duties, and authority.

Police Municipale units are usually small and have police powers primarily in general crime prevention, direct deterrence of criminal elements, and the arrest of persons caught in criminal acts (Kania, 1990; Kania, 1989). Because the mayors have considerable latitude in developing their police agencies, substantial variation exists in the duties given each force. In towns with significant tourist traffic, the *Police Municipale* are primarily order-maintenance personnel. In other cities, they are weapons-carrying, crime-fighting, traditional cops. In both instances, however, these Municipales are supplements to—not replacements of—the *Police Nationale*. The municipal police have only limited enforcement powers and no general investigative powers. In cases of serious crime and for criminal investigations, they are expected to call the *Police Judiciaire*, the *Gendarmerie*, or the *Police Nationale*.

Despite their autonomous authorization, the municipal police are linked to the *Police Nationale*. Their selection, educational, and training requirements are similar to the National Police, and their uniforms are so alike that French citizens are easily confused about their distinction. Although empowered by the city, the *Police Municipale* must comply with the regulations and laws of the national government.

For these reasons, and because most French cities have not formed municipal police units (Kania, 1989), it seems appropriate to retain France among the countries operating a centralized multiple coordinated police structure.

CENTRALIZED MULTIPLE UNCOORDINATED SYSTEMS

After reviewing the rivalry between the *Police Nationale* and the *Gendarmerie*, you may question the claimed cooperation between the two French police forces. However in the true spirit of comparative criminal justice, a review of uncoordinated forces quickly shows us that any problems encountered between the French police groups pale in comparison to those in uncoordinated systems like Italy, Spain, or the former Soviet Union.

Union of Soviet Socialist Republics

The classic example of centralized multiple uncoordinated policing was offered by the Union of Soviet Socialist Republics. Since its breakup, the USSR no longer exemplifies a policing type. But its one-time prominence in this category and the precedent it set for such independent countries as Russia requires that it receive brief attention.

Law enforcement in the Soviet Union was the responsibility of two central government agencies: the Ministry for Internal Affairs (*Ministerstvo Vnutrennikh Del*, MVD) and the Committee for State Security (*Komitet Gosudarstvennoy Bezopasnosti*, KGB). These agencies, operating with various names and under different organizational structures over the years, shared responsibility for law enforcement within the Soviet Union. Primary responsibility for internal security was with the MVD, which handled most routine functions related to a national police force. The KGB, on the other hand, dealt with internal security tasks, such as investigation of major crimes and both internal and external threats against the state.

The Soviet system was considered uncoordinated because MVD and KGB functions overlapped. The KGB, however, was the more powerful agency because of its direct links to the Central Committee of the Communist Party and its power to carry out policies and programs above the law. One of Boris Yeltsin's first moves as president of the new Russian Republic was to abolish the KGB. The organization was succeeded by the new Russian Agency for Federal Security, which will apparently have as one of its duties the cooperation with foreign police agencies (see Wines, 1992).

Before the Soviet Union's collapse, the policies of *glasnost* and *perestroika* had already impacted the structure and function of the Soviet militia, which operated under the MVD. In addition to being subordinate to the MVD, the militia was also under the authority of local government units. With this dual accountability, the militia operated with consistent law enforcement principles (national) while taking local (regional) considerations into account. The Soviets found this situation desirable because it guaranteed the "unity of the militia's practical activity in accordance with the law and . . . it enables the local authority to guide the work of the militia, to supervise its activities and to strengthen its authority and links with the public" (Karpets, 1977, p. 34). In practice, there is little doubt that primary control over the militia was by the MVD (which also controlled the prison and labor camp system, the fire troops, and the guard units). But Shelley (1990) was impressed with reports gathered during her research on the militia that the local government commissions kept watchful eye over law enforcement personnel.

With policing and investigative functions divided among the militia, the KGB, and even the prosecutor to some extent, there was the inevitable competition and confusion regarding jurisdiction. The result was occasional situations like that described in *Gorky Park* at the beginning of this book when two police forces and the prosecutor's office challenged each other for control of the investigation. Because each agency was ultimately responsible to the central government, and because they shared some areas of jurisdiction, the Soviet system exemplified a centralized multiple uncoordinated system. Independent nations of the former USSR have this heritage for their own police system. The type of command structure and the number of police forces they set up will be influenced by that Soviet history and by the systems in other parts of the world. If the new countries wish to stay with a centralized multiple uncoordinated structure, both Italy and Spain provide models they can follow.

Italy

Italy's Interior Ministry has the basic responsibility for peacekeeping and law enforcement throughout the country. This is done, in theory, through direct links from the minister to the local prefect in each of the nation's 92 provinces. Since the minister often has other important duties, the actual supervision of this state police (*Polizia di Stato*) is through the minister's chief of police, who provides detailed instructions to senior police officials (*questors*) in each province. Proceeding through the supervisory levels of chief superintendent (*commissario*) and several junior officers, we finally reach the street-level patrol officers, the Public Security Guards.

Each province is subdivided several times until reaching a geographical area similar to an American police precinct. Mobile squads, operating under direct orders from Rome, can be assigned anywhere in the country to handle major disorders or other emergencies. Special units within the State Police are responsible for offenses in such areas as highways, railways, and the postal service. Using the officers assigned to the geographical areas, the mobile squads, and the special units, the *Polizia di Stato* provides administrative, security, and investigative services. The investigative duties differ from the other two because state police officers performing those tasks are serving as judicial police and take orders from prosecutors in the Ministry of Justice. Consequently the judicial police are organizationally part of the Ministry of the Interior, but become functionally subordinate to the Justice Ministry (Cammett and Gibson, 1989).

To this point, Italian policing seems straightforward and very similar to the centralized single systems. The distinguishing feature of Italy's system is the addition of a separate police force operating under centralized supervision. But even the presence of that second force, the *Carabinieri*, may only make Italy more like France than like Denmark. The specific feature setting Italy apart from centralized single and the centralized multiple coordinated systems is conflict between her two police forces.

We recognized that the French *Police Nationale* and *Gendarmerie* are not always in complete agreement, but the rivalry between the *Carabinieri* and the *Polizia di Stato* is structurally and historically more pronounced. The *Carabinieri* is part of the Ministry of Defense, and its officers hold military ranks. The typical commander of the *Carabinieri* is a three-star general on leave from the regular army. Being modeled on the French *Gendarmerie*, the *Carabinieri's* duties have focused on rural law enforcement. Constitutionally, when engaged in police duties, *Carabinieri* units in a given province are supposed to follow Interior Ministry instructions. But institutional rivalry, competition, and a somewhat high degree of animosity between the two police forces persuade the *Carabinieri* to be more responsive to orders from Ministry of Defense (Collin, 1985). The resulting lack of coordination between Italy's two primary police forces makes it a prime example of a centralized multiple uncoordinated structure.

Brief mention also must be made of Italy's other law enforcement units (Cammett and Gibson, 1989; Collin, 1985). The Finance Police, operating out of the Ministry of Finance, enforce customs regulations, investigate tax fraud, protect the borders, and block contraband. The Forest Police (Ministry of Agriculture) protect the forests, perform reforestation, and assist mountain residents. Even Italy's prison guards, reporting to the Justice Ministry, are considered police officers. This militarized corps is responsible for order in the prisons and serving as personal guards or drivers for judges and Ministry of Justice officials.

The only police forces not subordinate to a ministry of the central government are the Municipal Police, operating under local control. Their organization and duties vary from region to region, but they are most frequently used to enforce local traffic laws. The existence of these local police units could be sufficient to move Italy from exemplifying a centralized command type to a decentralized one. However, their primarily traffic-related duties (Cammett and Gibson, 1989) and their tendency toward inefficiency and corruption (Collin, 1985) make them only marginal law enforcement units. Despite their presence, and that of the specialized units under centralized command, Italy is best described as a centralized multiple uncoordinated system consisting of two police forces often operating at cross purposes.

Spain

Spanish police forces can trace their history to the twelfth century, but the first modern versions were formed in 1829 with the *Carabineros* and in 1844 with the *Guardia Civil*. Today Spain has three major law enforcement systems: the *Cuerpo Nacional de Policia* (National Police Corps), the *Guardia Civil* (Civil Guard), and the *Policia Municipal* (Municipal Police). The system is considered centralized because all forces operate under the authority of the national government. The Minister of the Interior has responsibility for policing in Spain, but within the ministry the task specifically falls to the Director of State Security. Even the Municipal Police are ultimately linked to the central government, since those local forces are governed by the same 1986 law that regulates the two national forces (see Figure 6-4).

Guardia Civil. The oldest national police force in Spain is the Civil Guard. This force was patterned after the French *Gendarmerie* and has always considered itself part of the army. The Civil Guard has defended government policy over the years and has successfully prevented challenges to have it demilitarized. Today it has responsibility for policing the rural parts of Spain, patrolling the highways between cities, controlling firearms and explosives, guarding certain installations, and protecting such areas as the coast, the frontiers, ports, and airports (Kurian, 1989; Macdonald, 1987).

The Civil Guard is headed by a director general (always an army lieutenant general) who is responsible to both the Ministry of the Interior and the Ministry of Defense. Some problems arising from this dual accountability are considered below, but here we can note that the 1986 law tries to respect the Civil Guard's military character while shifting power toward the Interior Ministry.

The Civil Guard's history and military links have given it an ultraconservative perspective that Morn and Toro (1989) describe as providing a remaining symbol of Franco's dictatorship (1939–1975). In fact, the Guard seems to be having a hard time moving into the new era of policing. Incidents of corruption have marred its public image, and there is fear among liberals that increased crime and terrorism may inspire the rise of neo-authoritarianism in the Guard (Morn and Toro, 1989).

Terrorism by Basque and Cataluna separatists is a particular problem for the Guard, since the Guard is considered to represent the national government against which these separatist movements are fighting. The Guard's base of operation in the countryside and smaller towns also increases its vulnerability to attack.

Cuerpo Nacional de Policia. If the Civil Guard is a symbol of Spain's past, the National Police Corps represents a new order and provides a symbol of democracy (Morn and Toro, 1989). The National Police is a combination of two earlier forces: the Armed and Traffic Police (*Policia armada y de trafico*) and the Superior Police Corps (*Cuerpo general de policia*). The former was a uniformed

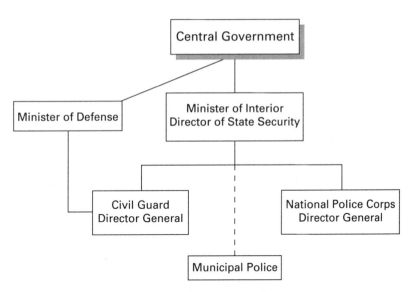

Figure 6-4.   Spain's police organization.

urban force under military control. The latter served as a plain-clothes investigative police with a highly political purpose and was accused of repressive gestapo-like tactics (Macdonald, 1987; Morn and Toro, 1989). When the two were united in 1986, the new National Police Corps took responsibility for policing Spain's urban areas. Today, the National Police Corps (with the Superior Corps as its detective component) operates in all provincial capitals and in municipalities with over 20,000 residents. Its responsibilities include issuing identity cards and passports, supervising private security forces, and enforcing gambling and drug laws.

The National Police Corps is headed by a Director General of the Police who reports to the Minister of the Interior through the Director of State Security. The separate and distinct nature of the two police forces before their combination has caused some turmoil as Spain tries to improve police efficiency and eliminate rivalry between the previously divided units. Attempts to reduce such problems have included common training and entrance procedures, and a clean break with any military links formerly held by the Armed and Traffic Police.

Other obstacles confronting the National Police include relatively weak relations with the public, new crimes for which the National Police seem unprepared, and problems with recruiting and deployment of personnel.

Response to the public relations problem has included attempts at more friendly contact with the people, but the citizens remain resistant. New offenses like international drug trafficking and organized crime seem to have grown with little interference from the National Police in general and the Superior Corps (as the detectives) more specifically. And, were those difficulties not sufficient to keep reformers busy, current recruitment and deployment practices receive criticism. The force draws heavily from the southern provinces and Madrid, so the northern provinces, already expressing strong feelings in favor of independence, are given tacit support for their contention that they are an occupied zone. In addition, as police officers gain experience and seniority they typically earn transfers to less hostile areas of the country. In a manner reminiscent of deployment practices in the United States (see Cole, 1986, p. 251), the younger, less experienced officers are assigned to the most unruly areas (Morn and Toro, 1989). That inexperience may lead to a public perception (possibly an accurate perception) of ineffective policing.

Despite problems and growing pains, the National Police Corps represents an important aspect of Spain's move toward democracy and greater police accountability (Morn and Toro, 1989). Also, though it is an even more recent arrival than the National Police, the Municipal Police provides another step away from the repressive police tactics of Spain's past.

Policia Municipal. Municipal Police officers are recruited locally, are typically unarmed, and wear uniforms that vary in design from city to city. Since every municipality, from the largest cities to those under 100 people, is authorized to create its own police force, these units would seem to make Spain's system decentralized. However, as mentioned earlier, the Municipal Police are regulated by the same 1986 law that governs the National Police and the Civil Guard. That law restricts the Municipal Police duties to protecting city buildings, traffic control, and assisting other police forces in such tasks as crowd control.

The Municipal Police are prominent figures on the streets of larger towns and cities. The largest of these local forces, the Security and Municipal Police Delegation of Madrid, is substantial enough to have two specialized units: the Citizens' Protection Patrol and the Ecological Patrol (Kurian, 1989).

Uncoordinated Policing. Spain's 1986 law attempted to improve police efficiency by eliminating parallel structures, dual command systems, and intercorps rivalry (Macdonald, 1987). The endeavor was successful to a great extent, but Spain's police system remains correctly classified as uncoordinated rather than coordinated. Macdonald (1987) identifies several areas of conflict among the three law enforcement units. First, both the National Police Corps and the Civil Guard have some authority to operate anywhere in the nation despite the presumed urban/rural jurisdictional division. The National Police can go anywhere their criminal investigation and intelligence operations take them, and the Civil Guard can follow any lead their inquiries may present. That national authority becomes especially troublesome when the crime areas for each police force overlap. For example, drug trafficking falls in the National Police Corps' concern with drug crime but is also linked to the Civil Guard's charge to protect ports and airports and to halt smuggling operations. When both national police forces investigate the same criminal activity, and can conduct that investigation throughout the country, the potential for confusion is considerable.

The lack of coordination is not just between the two national forces. Under the Spanish system, every member of any police force is automatically a member of the "Judicial Police." In that role, the police assist the judges and prosecutors as they investigate a crime. Prior to 1986 this provision caused some problems, because the police often took a leadership role in investigations while the court personnel simply followed. The 1986 law reasserts judicial power and makes units of Judicial Police functionally responsible to the courts while still administratively linked to the Ministry of the Interior. Since Municipal Police officers can act as judicial police where necessary, criminal investigation under court direction may at times rely on police from three different forces. Again, the possibility of confusion and working at cross purposes is increased by such an arrangement.

The 1986 law takes specific interest in trying to avoid disorder and create cooperation among the police forces. The law stipulates that police units must act in accordance with the principle of reciprocal cooperation and even sets penalties of dismissal or suspension for officers not so behaving (Macdonald, 1987). If both national forces find themselves involved in the same action, the first force committed is to continue its operation until the Civil Governor or the Ministry of the Interior rules on jurisdiction. The fact that the law must include these provisions reinforces the characterization of Spain's policing system as involving a centralized command with multiple uncoordinated forces. It is now time to see how decentralized policing handles the problem of supervising its multiple forces.

DECENTRALIZED MULTIPLE COORDINATED SYSTEMS

Of the countries that we could use to discuss the decentralized multiple coordinated type of structure, I have chosen Canada and Germany. Not only is Canada a good example of this type, but it is also good for us to understand how our northern neighbor approaches policing. Germany provides an interesting example because of the way post-World War II occupation forces influenced German policing, and because it offers a level of decentralization less pronounced than that in the United States.

Canada

Classification of Canada as a decentralized system could be confusing for tourists arriving in certain Canadian provinces and cities. Canada clearly has three levels of law enforcement (federal, provincial, and municipal), with control and supervision decentralized to the government at each level. But the differences may not always be apparent. For example, during a visit to North Vancouver you will find Royal Canadian Mounted Police (RCMP) officers providing police services to that city. Should you need a police officer as you leave North Vancouver and travel across the rural parts of British Columbia, you will be directed to the provincial police, whom you will easily recognize, because they are still the

RCMP. Of course, if the federal police stop you anywhere in the province, you will again see the now familiar RCMP uniform.

Just as you think you have this system figured out, you fly from Vancouver to Toronto. After renting a car at the airport, you drive to your hotel and pass a police car with "Metro Toronto Police" painted on the door. Inside the car is a police officer wearing a non-Mountie uniform. The next day you decide to drive to Ottawa. With a concern for the provincial police, who you correctly assume are responsible for catching speeders on the highway, you look for officers like the ones you saw in British Columbia. Unfortunately, while concentrating on remembering the Mountie uniform, you are pulled over by a policeman wearing an Ontario Provincial Police uniform.

Canada's police structure is not as strange as your visit may lead you to believe. In fact, it is very straightforward. As noted above, there are three distinct levels operating under the supervision of federal, provincial, and municipal authorities. The different experiences in British Columbia and Ontario are simply the result of Canada's provision for contract policing. The province of British Columbia and its city of North Vancouver have each contracted with the Royal Canadian Mounted Police (the federal agency) to provide the province and some cities with police services. The province of Ontario and its city of Toronto have chosen to provide their own provincial and local law enforcement.

Federal Police.   The Royal Canadian Mounted Police is a force as familiar to people as is the FBI. Like its American counterpart, the RCMP is a federal agency dedicated to the enforcement of federal statutes and executive orders. The RCMP was formally established in 1920 but has precursors dating to 1845. With headquarters in Ottawa, the RCMP is headed by a commissioner, who reports to the solicitor general of Canada. Although it is the federal police force, Mounties provide contract policing in eight of Canada's provinces and in its two territories. Only in the provinces of Quebec and Ontario are RCMP responsibilities strictly federal.

RCMP duties at the federal level include narcotics control, smuggling, customs and excise work, marine and aviation services, antiterrorism, and forensic science (Kurian, 1989). Close relations exist between the FBI and the RCMP. The Mounties have a liaison office in Washington, D.C., and the FBI has one in Ottawa. Computer links between the two agencies assist in their joint efforts to combat terrorism and counterfeiting, to stop the flow of narcotics, and to prevent or apprehend offenders trying to flee across international borders.

Provincial Police.   The responsibility for administration of justice in Canada lies with the provinces. However, a province can fulfill that duty by contracting with the federal government to provide policing services. Eight of Canada's 10 provinces have chosen to contract with the federal government and have the RCMP operate as the provincial police. In these cases, the RCMP is under the direction of the provincial attorney general but under administrative control from the Ottawa headquarters (Kurian, 1989). The exceptions to federal contract policing for the province are Ontario and Quebec. In those provinces, the Ontario Provincial Police and the Quebec Police Force provide law enforcement.

Provincial police forces (whether in the form of RCMP or separate forces) are responsible for policing all areas of a province not covered by a municipal police force. These areas are typically rural and semirural. Each province is usually divided into subdivisions that are further divided into detachments of one to 30 officers.

Municipal Police. Municipal forces include those in cities, towns, villages, and townships. Like their counterparts in the United States, these local police departments, when grouped together, make up the country's largest body of police. As the "street cops," they handle most of the crime and are the primary enforcers of the law. However, the Canadian municipal forces differ from their American neighbors in two important ways: (1) The local Canadian officer may actually be a member of the RCMP with whom the city has contracted for policing; (2) the local Canadian officers have the authority to enforce all laws in their jurisdiction. That includes certain federal statutes, the Criminal Code and the statutes of their province, and municipal bylaws. Local police officers in the United States enforce city codes and state laws, but do not have the authority to enforce federal statutes.

This overlapping jurisdiction of municipal police directs our attention to an important point. Presumably, countries falling into the multiple coordinated category were "coordinated" because they avoided overlapping jurisdiction. Bayley (1985) noted the problematic nature of designating Canada as multiple coordinated or multiple uncoordinated for exactly this reason, but I agree with Bayley's decision to place Canada with the coordinated systems. Despite the overlap of authority, Canada's police forces seem remarkably well coordinated and not subject to the complaints of jealousy and rivalry that we are more likely to find in the uncoordinated systems. Also, and this may be a reason for that cooperation, the contract system means that the municipal police officer is likely to be a Mountie, just like the federal officer.

Municipal contracting for police services is done with the province. Since the RCMP serves as the provincial police for eight provinces, the local police officer ends up being a Mountie if the municipality contracts with the province to provide police services. Quebec lacks a legal provision for contracting with its municipalities to provide policing, so Ontario is the only province where non-RCMP provincial police do contract policing for municipalities (Kurian, 1989). This process explains how you could visit cities like North Vancouver, travel around British Columbia, and see three levels of police officers, each wearing his or her RCMP uniform.

The contracting system, which helps set Canada's police system apart from that of other countries, is very cost effective for both provinces and municipalities. The procedure began for economic reasons during the 1930s (Talbot, Jayewardene, and Juliani, 1985) and continues today for similar reasons. The province is charged a percentage of the actual per capita cost for RCMP expenses. That charge is low enough that provinces and municipalities can maintain a highly efficient police system for a reasonable cost.

IMPACT

A key point of this chapter regards the structure of police systems as being either centralized or decentralized. The United States' version of extreme decentralization places us in the minority among nations and is a procedure that some authors have freely criticized. Is it possible that other countries structure their police system in a way we should consider? This Impact section looks first at the question of decentralization, and then considers the direction American policing seems to be taking.

The Question of Decentralization

The advantage of decentralized policing lies primarily in its acknowledgment of the right of local and state authorities to organize and manage their own affairs (Reid, 1987). The need for independence, allowing response to unique local conditions, may be more important than resolving the overlapping and duplication of services that decentralization produces.

It is unlikely that America will turn away from her closely held belief in decentralization of police. However, Pursley (1987) notes three problem areas that may lead local American jurisdictions to consider alternatives to the present system. First, the rapid growth of cities has created problems in governmental management, an increased demand for urban services, and problems in social adjustment. Consider, for example, that metropolitan Chicago has 1113 governments, Philadelphia has 876, Pittsburgh has 704, and New York has 551. Second, communities that have incorporated to avoid annexation to central cities or to provide tax relief have created such problems as overlapping and fragmented jurisdictions. Finally, the outdated governmental framework found in most counties does not allow them to respond effectively to urban problems.

Because many local units of government in metropolitan areas have their own police department, there is a definite fragmentation of police services in those parts of the country with the highest crime rates. A reasonable response to that fragmentation may be the combining of police services. Police consolidation in metropolitan areas may result in better police service at less cost than maintaining many small independent departments.

Despite the advantages of consolidation, communities in the United States have so far resisted the attempt to move away from locally independent police.

The preference for decentralization of police departments is obviously a closely held one. However, it seems unlikely that America's version of law enforcement structure will remain in its present form for another 175 years. When we are ready to consider alternatives or modifications, the experience of other countries will provide a useful information base. Consider, for example, what options we can generate just by reviewing the systems covered in this chapter.

Alternatives/Modifications to American Policing

Canada's system of contracting for police services may be appealing to many Americans. We already contract for things like defense counsel and correctional services, and some communities contract with their state police/patrol for law enforcement. Expansion of this option for police services would not violate the American preference for decentralization, but would require greater coordination of effort and may mean giving up some local control.

If increased contracting occurs, who will be the contractor? Communities combining resources for joint policing already happens, as does county and city governments working together to provide law enforcement. To what level of government involvement can we go before citizens become fearful of centralization? The occasional agreements between towns and the state police/patrol suggest that government involvement at the state level is at least a possibility. But would states be willing to let the federal government enforce state laws under a contract arrangement? What do you see as the various problems and potentials for increased contracting among the different government levels?

Another possibility could be contemporarily unique yet historically based. Policing in many countries, including colonial America and the United States, was provided by private citizens. This was often done as a civic obligation, but there were also instances of citizens receiving pay for their services. Increased reliance on private citizens would not have to be unorganized and on a small-time basis. The large number of private security companies could provide traditional police services for some communities. Maybe the future structure of American policing will include a variety of both private and public police forces under command structures that are centralized in one case (for example, a national private police corporation) and decentralized in the other (for example, traditional city, state, and federal agencies). Even if that would be too extreme, can you think of alternatives or modifications that could use private policing in the traditionally public arena?

Germany

The occupation of Germany by Allied forces after World War II provides an interesting recent history for German policing. The Potsdam agreement of 1945 provided the Allies with the task of decentralizing, democratizing, and demilitarizing areas of public life in each country's zone of occupation. While there was agreement on the need to decentralize the police, the Allies had different ideas about what decentralization was. Achieving this goal was approached differently by the British, French, and Americans (Fairchild, 1988; Thomaneck, 1985).

To the British, decentralization meant regionally organized police under the watchful eye of civilian Police Authorities. The system was remarkably similar to that found in Great Britain. Also, as in Britain, the police function in this occupation zone was limited to the maintenance of law and order and the detection of crime. This meant that the traditional administrative functions of German police (for example, registration of all residents, environmental health, building permits and regulations, road supervision) were abolished.

The police administrative functions were retained in the French zone. Also, the French saw nothing inherently bad in centralized control of the police, so that structure was essentially retained, with a concession to decentralization being the granting of some police functions to small town mayors. Again, the similarity to the structure of policing in France is not well hidden.

Americans retained central police control as an organizational principle, but only in communities with fewer than 5000 inhabitants. Larger communities had locally controlled communal police in much the same way that American cities have their own local police. This plan represented the greatest difference from the traditional German organization. In the American zone, mayors were made responsible for setting up police forces and providing for weapons, clothes, and supervision.

Not surprisingly, Germans found the mixture of police structures to be inconvenient, inappropriate, and ineffective. By 1949 German officials complained that communal police forces in small towns were impractical. In 1950, the Allied High Command decided that each state government (in then West Germany) could centralize their police at the state level. Gradually, cities gave up their local police force until each state passed police laws regulating the activities and organization of the newly centralized police. By 1955 all northern German states had completed the reconstruction of their police. In 1975, Munich ceased its communal police force, and the reconstruction was finally complete for all West Germany.

Today, the day-to-day operations of German policing is decentralized to the state (*Länder*) level (see Figure 6-5). Federal forces exist, but policing is essentially a state matter. The two primary federal agencies are the Federal Office of Criminal Investigation and the Federal Border Police. The former has a broad range of federal and international duties and operates under the Federal Ministry of the Interior. The Federal Border Police, also out of the Federal Ministry of the Interior, guards the frontiers of the republic—except in Bavaria, which has its own border police (Fairchild, 1988).

Each German state controls its own police force, with the federal government acting as a liaison and coordinating agent. Despite the ability to have great divergence, there is considerable similarity among the various state police. The

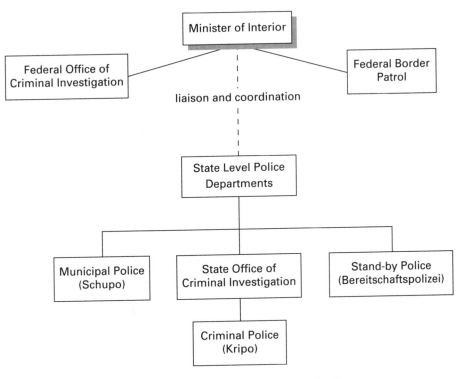

Figure 6-5. Germany's police organization.

glue providing the similarity is made from tradition and because the laws enforced in each *Land* are primarily federal laws (Thomaneck, 1985). The trend is toward even greater similarity. For example, before 1976 the police in each state wore different uniforms. In that year, a standard uniform (with different state sleeve patches) was introduced and, in 1980, made mandatory (Kurian, 1989).

The typical structure of policing in the *Land* involves a three-part division (Kurian, 1989; Thomaneck, 1985). The Municipal Police, called the *Schutzpolizei* (typically shortened to *Schupo*), are the uniform-wearing police and have the highest visibility and broadest range of duties. They are the first to arrive on the scene of all types of crimes and are initially responsible for all aspects of enforcement and investigation.

Soon after the *Schupo* have determined that a crime has occurred, or have identified a suspect, the criminal police or *Kriminalpolizei* (*Kripo*) are called in. The *Kripo* are plain-clothes officers similar to detectives in the United States. They have the authority to search and seize and are responsible for developing a case and initiating charges against suspects. Linked to the *Kripo* in every *Land* is a State Office of Criminal Investigation. This central headquarters for the *Kriminalpolizei* is responsible for gathering all significant information and documents used for the prevention and investigation of criminal offenses (Kurian,

1989). Personnel at this central crime-fighting headquarters analyze information, conduct crime lab activities, and notify police throughout the *Land* about the current crime situation.

The third police organization is the *Bereitschaftspolizei*, or Stand-by Police. The officers in this paramilitary force are quartered in barracks and act only in units rather than as individual police. Traditionally their function has been the training of young police officers. As the name suggests, their public function is to support the *Schupo* when large numbers of police are needed for crowd control, emergency activities, serious accidents, and the like.

Changes Brought by Reunification.
In August 1990 the People's Assembly of the German Democratic Republic voted overwhelmingly to set October 3, 1990 as the date to unify with the Federal Republic of Germany. This decision to dissolve the GDR brought, understandably, considerable confusion and apprehension to those people responsible for GDR law enforcement. Nancy Travis Wolfe (1992) provides an excellent review of policing in the GDR and how events leading to reunification affected that policing. She identifies two fundamental changes in the fall of 1990 that had major impact on policing in the GDR. The first, obviously, was the unification with the FRG. The second was the transformation of the GDR from a unitary to a federal system of government.

In anticipation of what was becoming the inevitable unification, GDR police officials began in the spring of 1990 to bring administrative structures and legal regulations into conformity with FRG police practices and law. FRG and GDR police officials examined the two systems to determine points of similarity and difference, and GDR police began preparing themselves to operate under FRG law. This latter activity was made difficult not only because of the differing role that law played in the two countries, but also because 40 years of separation had resulted in some German words coming to have different meanings for the GDR or FRG. As one GDR police supervisor put it: "I have gotten a copy of the Basic Law [the FRG 'constitution'] and from a legal-political standpoint I have problems in reading it, because the principles are, in part, different" (quoted in Wolfe, 1992, p. 215).

Transformation from a unitary to a federal system of government presented difficulties in areas like police organization, supervision, and jurisdiction. Under their unitary political system, the German People's Police (*Deutsche Volkspolizei*, VP) followed a highly centralized administration directed by the Ministry of the Interior. Further, as part of a socialist legal system, the VP's mission was essentially political and intent on furthering progress toward a true communist state (Wolfe, 1992).

In this national policing system, the VP was divided into districts, then into county agencies, and finally into sections and subsections. At this last level were police similar to their FRG cousins. As in West Germany, the East Germans called their vehicular and patrol officers the *Schutzpolizei*, the detective branch were the *Kriminalpolizei*, and a paramilitary force was called the *Bereitschafts-*

polizei. But the similarity between each country's force went little beyond sharing common names. The socialist principles and institutions influencing the GDR *Schupo*, for example, gave that force a more proactive role in crime prevention at one end of the process and in social reintegration of released convicts at the other end. As Wolfe (1992) explains it, the VP divisions had roles that extended beyond those of western police.

The reunited city of Berlin offers a particularly good opportunity to watch the progress of unified Germany's progress toward consolidated policing in two formerly separate jurisdictions. Berlin has the unique status of being reunified Germany's capital city as well as one of the German states. In this manner its situation is similar to that of Washington, D.C.

The changes brought by reunification of both the city and the countries have presented several problems for the *Polizei Berlin*. The former FRG police have added territory, with which they are unfamiliar, to patrol, and the former VP of the GDR have new laws and a totally new country to patrol. The initial response has been for the former East German police to patrol (enforcing the unified German laws) what had been East Berlin while the *Polizei Berlin* move to integrate those former VP officers into their new agency (Bernsdorff, 1992). The resolve of Berliners to unite the formerly distinct police forces in the same manner in which their city was united is summed up by a *Polizei Berlin* Police Lieutenant who said, "After all, we're Berliners!" (quoted in Bernsdorff, 1992, p. 7). Similar optimism is likely expressed by German citizens throughout the reunified country as they continue their efforts to change the centralized GDR police into the decentralized FRG model.

The Respectful German Citizen. In addition to the organizational problems that Germany faces as it consolidates two police systems, there is an additional problem of public perception of the police. Despite the *Volkspolizei*'s proclaimed mission of service to the farmers and workers (presumably the only class in the GDR), they were not popular with those citizens. Their negative standing with the public stood in stark contrast to the generally well-liked FRG *Schupos*. Whether the East Germans can easily come to like, let alone respect, the *Schupos* of reunited Germany remains to be seen. To help them along, they are now subject to German laws that provide an interesting twist on police–citizen relations. In addition, their German ancestry may provide them with a heritage that attaches respect to authority figures.

German culture provides certain national character traits that, when not presented in their extreme fashion as stereotypes, generalize citizen behavior. Such traits include an emphasis on order, authority, discipline, and the rule of law (Griswold and Massey, 1989). With attributes such as these, it may not be surprising that German citizens hold their police in higher esteem than do citizens of countries not so supportive of law and order. Griswold and Massey (1989) present an interesting type of support for this position in their analysis of German laws against insulting the police. They argue that insults to the police not only threaten the social order but also the authority of the state. Since free-dom of speech is a highly valued and constitutionally protected right in the United States, insults to police are not easily identified as criminal by Americans. It may not be polite and probably can increase the likelihood of arrest for another infraction, but is it a crime to call a police officer "pig"?

While it would be unfair to suggest that German citizens value free speech any less than do Americans or citizens of other countries, the Germans are more protective of the police officer's authority and position. To that end, calling a German police officer a pig, bear, clown, or joker, or suggesting that the officer is ugly or stupid may result in a fine ranging from the equivalent of $250 to over $1000. Of course, we cannot make too much of the point, since some Germans obviously are not respectful to their police. If German citizens were completely respectful, they would not insult the officers and there would be no need for such fines. But the implications of such laws are intriguing for what they suggest about police community relations in Germany, the likelihood that the former East Germans will come to view police differently than they did the old *Volkspolizei*, and the questions they raise for police community relationships in other countries.

DECENTRALIZED MULTIPLE UNCOORDINATED SYSTEMS

The United States, with more separate police forces than any country in the world, is easily the most extreme case of a multiple uncoordinated system (Bayley, 1985). Belgium's 2359 separate units are impressive, given the size of the country, but the estimated 20,000 public agencies in the United States is unsur-passed. Switzerland, another multiple uncoordinated system, has police at the federal, cantonal, and municipal level, all with concurrent jurisdiction. Still, the Swiss example pales by comparison with the United States. Because of its promi-nent position as an example of the multiple uncoordinated type, we include dis-cussion of the United States in this section.

Switzerland and Belgium

Switzerland has a decentralized police force with most police powers delegated to the self-governing cantons (Kurian, 1989). Each canton has its own police force, and most cities have their own municipal police. Federal government police powers are mostly in the area of criminal justice legislation, but the cen-tralized Federal Police are responsible for enforcing certain laws against treason, counterfeiting, forgery, and election fraud.

The Cantonal and Municipal Police perform all police functions outside the jurisdiction of the federal agencies. There is no central coordination of police operations, but there are ways in which the 23 cantonal and over 100 municipal police forces can cooperate. For example, in cases of serious crime involving two or more cantons, three agencies provide a means to collaborate: the Conference of Swiss Police Commanders, the Swiss Association of Police Chiefs, and the Swiss Police Technical Commission. With the intercantonal links provided by these agencies, the decentralized Swiss system can engage in successful teamwork when necessary.

Belgium has three primary kinds of police: the *gendarmerie*, the criminal police, and a number of commune police forces. There is also a parish constable system operating in the rural areas, providing at least one constable to each of the 245 small towns and villages. The *gendarmerie* reports to the Ministry of the Interior when dealing with police matters, but to the Ministry of National Defense on military matters, and to the Ministry of Justice on matters relating to the judiciary (Kurian, 1989). The primary function of the *gendarmes* is investigating crimes, escorting prisoners, performing preventive police work, enforcing traffic laws, and military police duties. Its jurisdiction extends over the entire country, but it normally operates only in those areas outside the jurisdiction of municipal police forces.

The Criminal (or Judicial) Police operates under the authority of the Ministry of Justice and deals only with the most serious crimes. Each of the 22 Judicial Police brigades is headed by a chief commissioner in charge of all criminal investigations assisting the public prosecutor in preparing evidence for the courts.

Each of Belgium's 345 major towns and municipalities has a Communal Police force. These are usually under the control of the mayor, but in larger towns there may be a police commissioner who is also an officer of the Judicial Police. The commune police have responsibility for all general police functions within the municipal boundaries.

United States of America

Now that you are familiar with many types of police structure, it may not surprise you that the system used in the United States is looked upon with curiosity by citizens of many other countries. For example, in his book on Australian police forces, O'Brien refers to the many American law enforcement agencies as operating on five levels (federal civil, federal military, state, county, and local) with a ". . . correspondingly bewildering variety of organizational and administrative patterns, having little or no formal or informal coordination with each other" (1960, p. 77).

As noted above, the United States is the model of a decentralized multiple uncoordinated police structure. There are over 20,000 (Champion, 1990; Senna and Siegel, 1987) public law enforcement agencies operating in the United States. Besides the multiple forces, decentralization means that police structure can vary among and within the federal, state, and local levels. As a result, it is difficult to make any summary statement about the typical police structure in this country.

Textbooks in an Introduction to Criminal Justice course valiantly struggle to describe the organization and structure of American policing within the confines of a chapter or two. It is neither necessary nor appropriate that we attempt to replicate those efforts. Instead, after a brief comment on local and state level police structure, we will describe in more detail the structure of federal level enforcement.

Both city and county forces are usually considered local policing in the United States. While city police chiefs typically owe their position to a mayor or city council, the sheriff is an elected official responsible for policing the unincorporated areas of a county. Local police officers enforce the laws of their state and the laws and ordinances passed by the city and county governments. As a county force, sheriff's deputies have authority throughout the county, including the ability to enforce state and county laws being violated in towns and cities. As a courtesy, sheriff's deputies are unlikely to operate in a municipal police jurisdiction without being invited by the police chief.

Since the primary enforcement of state laws is the responsibility of local police, the police agencies at the state level tend to have specific duties. For example, states may have police agencies responsible for patrolling the highways in the state, providing police services to state colleges and universities, enforcing state regulations on items like alcohol, and policing the state's parks and recreation areas. In many states these duties are divided among several agencies with names like Highway Patrol, University Police, Public Safety Officers, Bureau of Investigation Agents, and Park Rangers. In other states many tasks are consolidated and assigned to one agency, often called the State Police, who provide services ranging from highway patrol to criminal investigations.

Even federal level law enforcement reflects America's commitment to decentralization of policing. Command authority in federal law enforcement splits in two ways. First, policing divides between military and civilian agencies. Their authority is further apportioned within the military and civilian agencies themselves. Military law enforcement, for example, typically rests with traditional police-type agencies like the Military Police and three investigative agencies: the Naval Investigative Service, the Air Force Office of Special Investigations, and the Army Criminal Investigation Command (McGuire, 1988). These agencies are responsible for the investigation of crimes committed against U.S. military personnel or property, and crimes committed by military personnel.

Command authority within federal civil law enforcement is divided among various federal departments, agencies, and bureaus, but rests primarily in the Department of the Treasury and the Department of Justice (see Figure 6-6). In the spirit of decentralization, division of authority does not even stop at the department level.

Department of Treasury.   Four law enforcement agencies in the Treasury Department handle crimes ranging from the manufacture, sale, and possession of firearms and explosives to the protection of the President, Vice President and their families. A brief review of the four agencies will provide an example of the decentralization process.

The Internal Revenue Service is responsible for enforcement of federal revenue laws except those relating to alcohol, tobacco, and firearms. Agents in the

Criminal Investigation Division of the IRS are primarily concerned with attempts to evade a tax or the willful failure to file tax returns. Importantly, IRS special agents are also responsible for investigation into organized crime activities. Since income from even illegal sources (for example, bootlegging, prostitution, narcotics sale) is subject to tax, these agents are primary figures in the investigation and prosecution of big-time criminals.

Special agents in the Bureau of Alcohol, Tobacco, and Firearms have two primary responsibilities. First, they enforce federal laws concerned with the sale, transfer, manufacture, import, and possession of firearms and explosives. Of particular concern to them are the activities of organized crime and of terrorists groups operating in this country. The second major responsibility concerns enforcement of federal liquor and tobacco regulations. Illicit distillery operations, cigarette smuggling, and bootlegging of untaxed tobacco products occupy a significant portion of their investigative duties.

The United States Secret Service was created in 1865 as a bureau of the Treasury Department to combat widespread counterfeiting. The investigative duties of the Secret Service remain in the area of counterfeiting, forgery, and securities fraud. It is probably better known, however, for its protective responsibilities. After the 1901 assassination of President William McKinley, the Secret Service was assigned to protect President Theodore Roosevelt. In 1906 Congress enacted legislation authorizing the Secret Service to protect the president of the United States, and after the 1908 election they also began to protect the president-elect. Those responsibilities expanded to include the protection of the president, the vice president, the president and vice president elect, former presidents, and the immediate families of all those persons.

In 1927 Congress created the Bureau of Customs as an agency of the Treasury Department. In 1973 it was redesignated the U.S. Customs Service and its agents are responsible for enforcing not only customs laws and regulations, but also those of some 40 other federal agencies. Specific responsibilities center on ensuring that the government receives revenue on incoming goods and making certain contraband and controlled substances do not enter or leave the country illegally.

Department of Justice. The Justice Department also has four agencies, including both the oldest federal law enforcement department, and the best known. From the first 13 appointed by George Washington, the U.S. Marshals have grown to over 90 in number and have responsibilities throughout the United States and its territories. Those marshals and their over 1500 deputies are assigned to the federal courts for which they make arrests, take custody of property, execute warrants, protect court officials and witnesses, and help investigators in other federal departments.

The most well-known Department of Justice enforcement agency is the Federal Bureau of Investigation (FBI). This principal investigative arm of the Justice Department was created in 1908, when Attorney General Charles

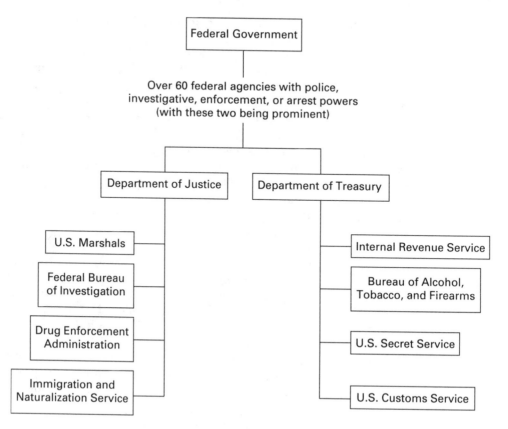

Figure 6-6.   United States federal police organization.

Bonaparte succeeded in getting eight agents transferred from the Secret Service to a new Bureau of Investigation to investigate charges of corruption and business violations of the law. The bureau expanded in 1910 when Congress passed the White Slave Traffic Act (Mann Act), which prohibited interstate transportation of women for immoral purposes, and gave the bureau responsibility for enforcing the act. The most rapid expansion occurred in the 1930s. Johnson (1981) suggests that three things caused that expansion. The first was the kidnapping in 1932 of Charles Lindbergh's son. Given the national hero status of Lindbergh, the kidnapping brought a national demand for action, and in 1932 Congress passed legislation creating a special unit of the FBI to handle kidnapping. Within four years the kidnapper, Bruno Hauptmann, had been captured and executed, and the FBI was well on its way to gaining national prestige.

In 1933, Pretty Boy Floyd and two companions tried to rescue a friend from being returned to federal prison (Johnson, 1981). The resulting hail of machine gun fire left the friend and four officers (including one FBI agent) dead. This "Kansas City Massacre" resulted in unprecedented maneuvering by the FBI, which was now under the direction of J. Edgar Hoover. The public response to such activities by the FBI was very positive, so Hoover continued to involve his agents in bringing gangsters to justice. The third event Johnson cites to explain the growth of federal law enforcement was the behavior of President Franklin Roosevelt. With the strong support of Roosevelt, and the positive publicity gotten by Hoover, in 1934 Congress passed a series of laws expanding the area of federal responsibilities. For example, it became a federal offense to "rob a national bank; to flee across state lines to avoid prosecution; to engage in interstate racketeering; to transport stolen property across state lines; and to resist a federal officer" (Johnson, 1981, p. 174). Enforcement of these laws was assigned to the FBI. Today the FBI is responsible for investigating over 200 types of cases resulting from violation of federal laws.

The two other law enforcement agencies in the Justice Department are the Drug Enforcement Administration (DEA) and the Immigration and Naturalization Service (INS). The DEA was the result of a 1973 merger of several drug enforcement units, including the Bureau of Narcotics and Dangerous Drugs. Agents of the DEA are responsible for enforcement of federal laws concerning narcotics and dangerous drugs. Their duties require undercover work, surveillance, interviewing, examination of records, and assisting local law enforcement officials. The best-known unit in the INS is the Border Patrol. This enforcement agency is responsible for patrolling the over 8000 miles of land and coastal areas marking the continental United States' boundaries. Border Patrol agents seek to prevent illegal entry of persons into this country and investigate violations of federal immigration and naturalization laws.

A NOTE ON THE PERMANENCE OF STRUCTURE

Bayley says "the structure of public national police systems displays remarkable permanence over time. Structural characteristics have remained the same in most contemporary countries since they became recognizable as states" (1985, p. 60). That statement seems cavalier considering the dramatic political and economic changes that occurred around the world in the late 1980s. By all indications the rest of the 1990s is going to be a time of almost monthly change in social-political-economic spheres of nations around the world.

Attempts to describe how things operate in a country have always been complicated by the chance that the description will eventually become obsolete. The likelihood of obsolescence has simply been increased as events unfold in Europe, the Middle East, Asia, and on most other continents. Obviously, a country's criminal justice system is as likely to be influenced by change as is any other part of the country. Yet the speed and content of that change is often overrated. As we think about it, that statement is not really surprising, since a country's criminal justice system is closely tied to the history and traditions of its people. Just as the Bolsheviks had to adapt carefully their socialist view of law to the traditions of peasants in places like the Kazakstan, the reformists in former Warsaw Pact countries must make revisions with an eye toward the traditions built up under more than forty years of socialism.

Few people would consider it either possible or desirable to change dramatically a country's political or economic system overnight. As such countries as Czechoslovakia and East Germany showed us in the late 1980s, the potential for dramatic change can occur very rapidly. But to take that potential to fruition is a longer process. The same is true for a country's legal system. The potential for change may occur after a short battle (whether in city streets or the aisles of a parliament), but the actual laws, the structure by which those laws are enforced, and the procedure for handling violators of the laws will change more slowly.

We began this section with a quotation from Bayley, who believes that police structures display remarkable permanence over time. In support of that idea, we will take a quick look at the structure of policing in Poland. In his 1985 book, Bayley used Poland as an example of a country with a centralized single police structure. With its change in government, Poland also changed its policing. The question is, Did Poland's dramatic movement in the political and economic areas result in a dramatically different police structure?

Policing in Poland. June 1989 marked the election of Poland's first noncommunist, democratic government. Some 14 months later, the Polish Police Force officially replaced the Citizens' Militia as the political changes brought reorganization across Poland. We begin our discussion with the pre-1990 police structure.

Before the change in government, Poland's basic police force was the *Milicja Obywatelska* (MO), or Citizens' Militia. The MO was responsible for maintaining public order, protecting state and private property, controlling traffic, maintaining identification cards and residence locator information, and countering criminal activity (Kurian, 1989). The MO was organized at the regional level (*voivodship*), but command was centralized out of the Ministry of Internal Affairs. Local government authorities were used on a consultation and coordination basis, but the militia units operated under the sole authority of the ministry. The MO operated as a paramilitary force and shared equipment and facilities with the armed forces.

Citizens' Militia officers typically worked in the Criminal Investigation Section, the Traffic Control Section, or as patrol officers at local stations. There were, however, two specialized militia units that were quite noticeable, and often hated, by the Poles. The Motorized Units of the Citizens' Militia (*Zmotoryzowane Oddzialy Milicji Obywatelskiej*, ZOMO) were initially established in 1956 after the Poznan riots emphasized the need for specially trained riot troops. After surviving severe reorganization in 1970, ZOMO began expanding in the early 1980s and was a primary enforcer of martial law regulations (Kurian, 1989). Besides controlling riots and pro-Solidarity demonstrations, ZOMO controlled crowds at sporting events and coordinated relief efforts during natural disasters. As part of the Citizens' Militia, ZOMO was also responsible to the Ministry of Internal Affairs.

A second notable section of the MO was the ORMO (*Ochotnicza Rezerwa Milicji Obywatelskiej*), or Volunteer Reserve of the Citizens' Militia. This section was formed in the early 1960s and by the mid-1980s was the largest of the militia forces. Its members served unpaid as they patrolled designated areas in a manner supposedly similar to organized neighborhood groups in the United States.

Poles during the 1980s were often critical of the personnel and tactics employed by their Citizens' Militia. The ZOMO were the target of particularly bitter comments, since they were responsible for dispersing popular demonstrations. With the change in government, Poles also found an opportunity to reorganize the police and modify public perception of its role in society. Both efforts seem to have been successful. By April 1991, police reorganization was essentially complete and, according to police officials, the new Polish Police Force was more popular among Poles than were members of the parliament.

Our specific interest in modification of Polish policing is to decide if the dramatic political changes brought significant structural changes in law enforcement. For example, did the structure of Polish policing change from a centralized single one to an example of another structure in Figure 6-1?

On April 6, 1990, the Polish Parliament passed a Police Act that created a new Polish Police Force. The Police Force is a civilian organization replacing the paramilitary Civilians' Militia. The Polish Police Force is charged with undertaking the fight against crime under conditions of a democratic state. The key factor for the Poles in accomplishing that objective is to respect fully the legal system and the rights of citizens (Research Division, 1990).

The basic police structure in the new Polish system remains centralized with general authority still coming from the Ministry of Internal Affairs. Of the specialized offices operating under the minister, the chief commander of police is of specific interest to us. As the supervisor for all Polish police officers, the chief commander reports directly to the Minister of Internal Affairs. However, the Polish prime minister can nominate or discharge the chief commander after accepting advice from the Minister of Internal Affairs and the Prime Minister's Political Advisory Committee.

The Polish Police Force operates at three geographical levels. At the largest area, each of Poland's 49 voivodships (provinces) has a voivodship police headquarters administered by a commander of police and located in the capital cities of the voivodships. In turn, voivodships are divided into territories with their own territorial police commanders. Police at the territorial headquarters make up the majority of the Polish Police Force and provide the primary policing duties for Poles. The smallest geographical area policed by the Police Force are the police stations with their respective commanders.

To this point, the actual structure of policing in Poland cannot be said to have changed with the new government. What has just been described is still a centralized single system; although it operates with a different self-, and public, perception. But there are indications that true structural changes may yet emerge. Two particular items are worthy of note: the decentralization of decision making down to the voivodship headquarters level, and the emergence of local police stations under a separate administrative authority.

The 1990 Police Act authorizes voivodship commanders to change the policing structure as provided by general police headquarters, if the commander believes a different model will be functionally or economically better (Research Division, 1990). Since the most important function of the voivodship headquarters is to organize, coordinate, and supervise the territorial and police station units, this option may have important consequences. Many voivodships took immediate advantage of this opportunity, so it is not even possible to describe a typical voivodship headquarters structure. Importantly, however, the Chief Commander of Police still has veto authority over the voivodship commander's proposals. Centralized command is still present, and this new decision-making authority is not yet sufficient to claim that Poland now has a new police structure.

The emergence of local police units, separate from the Polish Police Force's police stations, is another new opportunity accompanying the 1990 Police Act. Many local communities had expressed concern about operational problems of local policing. Because of this citizen input, the Police Act authorizes the *Gmina* (Poland's smallest administrative unit) to establish local police stations. As a result, *Gmina* authorities have significantly more autonomy in policing. At present, these local police can only patrol their particular area, maintain public order, protect a crime scene, and assist in reporting crimes.

As with the increased decision-making authority provided the voivodship commanders, the existence of local police is not yet sufficient to claim that the Poles have a new police structure. Not only are the local police restricted in their duties, they are also supervised by the territorial police commander. That supervision places the local police in the chain leading to the Ministry of Internal Affairs, so it is part of the centralized policing structure.

The political and economic changes in Poland since 1989 are undoubtedly dramatic and far-reaching. And, in a sense, it is reasonable to expect a similar shakeup of the police system. But recall Bayley's quotation, "The structures of public national police systems display remarkable permanence over time" (1985, p. 60). While the Polish Police Force is noticeably, even remarkably, different from the Citizens' Militia and its accompanying ZOMO and ORMO units, it remains a centralized single system.

This detour on Polish policing was taken to lend credence to the classification scheme used in this chapter, but it has bearing on other chapters as well. With the constant changes occurring on the world scene it is too easy to suppose that all social institutions in a country are tossed aside and built anew when a country changes government types or economic systems. Changes in the social institutions of countries will certainly occur, and should not be downplayed! But Bayley is right; system structures, and not just those for policing, display remarkable permanence.

SUMMARY

This chapter was organized around the concept of variation in police structure. Building from Bayley's (1985) classification scheme, we categorized police structures according to their type of supervision or command (centralized or decentralized) and the number of forces being supervised (singular or multiple). When multiple forces are supervised, Bayley realized that some would work well together (coordinated) while others seemed to operate at cross purposes (uncoordinated). Upon putting these conditions together, a typology was created yielding five possible cells, each containing a different police structure.

Three types of structures occurred under a centralized command type. Countries like Denmark, Saudi Arabia, and Nigeria each have a single police force reporting to a centralized command. The simplicity of such an arrangement has not, however, made the singular centralized police structure a worldwide favorite. Other countries accept the central government as appropriate for supervision purposes but show a preference for having multiple police forces to report to that central authority. France was highlighted as a country falling into this division, since both her *Gendarmerie* and *Police Nationale* report to ministries of the central government. While some conflict exists between the French forces, they are considered coordinated since they basically respect their assigned jurisdictions. In Spain, on the other hand, the multiple forces of *Cuerpo Nacional de Policia*, *Guardia Civil*, and *Policia Municipal* have overlapping responsibilities and jurisdiction. The result is an uncoordinated system.

Countries that have decentralized police services also provide examples of both coordinated and uncoordinated efforts. Canada was highlighted as a coordinated multiple police system, since her federal, provincial, and municipal police forces seem able to work very well with each other even if there is some overlapping jurisdiction. Importantly, that cooperative effort in Canada may be the result of a contracting system that has one agency (the Royal Canadian Mounted Police) providing police services at municipal, provincial, and federal levels. Where such contracts occur, it is not surprising that the Mounties are able to work well with the Mounties.

The United States presents the most extreme form of decentralized multiple uncoordinated policing, and as such was the highlighted country in this cell. Policing in America exists at the federal, state, and local levels, and the estimated 20,000 resulting forces understandably step over and on each other at times. Only the federal agencies were featured here, but even at that level we saw significant decentralization.

Finally, the chapter included a comment on the permanence of structure. The rapid and dramatic changes with which the 1990s began provide good reason to be skeptical about how permanent social institutions might be. Poland was used as an example of a country that experienced tremendous change but seemed to maintain a police structure similar to what it had under the previous political and economic system. The changes were more ones of philosophy than of command and force number. We cannot infer from this that police structures never change. Instead, we are simply reminded that social institutions are not easily or quickly made anew.

SUGGESTED READINGS

There are a number of interesting police procedure novels set in foreign countries and often written by authors of that country. Some, like Georges Simenon's Inspector Maigret series and the Inspector Imanishi stories by Seicho Matsumoto, are popular enough to be translated into English. Other are written in English and are widely available. From Britain, the works by P. D. James and her Commander Dalgliesh are more linked to police procedures than are Agatha Christie's mysteries using private investigators. James Melville's series about Inspector Otani provides easier access to the Japan scene than do the less available (in English) works by Seicho Matsumoto. From France, in addition to Simenon's Inspector Maigret, consider Nicholas Freeling's Henri Castang mysteries. The Netherlands provides the setting for Inspector Van der Valk (Nicholas Freeling) and for Janwillem van de Wetering's intriguing stories featuring Detective Adjunct Grijpstra and his assistant Sergeant de Gier.

Bayley, David H. (1985). *Patterns of policing: A comparative international analysis.* New Brunswick, NJ: Rutgers University Press.

Fairchild, Erika S. (1988). *German police.* Springfield, IL: Charles C. Thomas.

Kurian, George T. (1989). *World encyclopedia of police forces and penal systems.* New York: Facts on File.

Stead, Philip J. (1983). *The police of France.* New York: Macmillan.

REFERENCES

Alobied, Abdullah. (1989). Police functions and organization in Saudi Arabia. *Police Studies, 10,* 80–84.

Baun, Arne. (1978). The Danish police system. *Police Studies, 1,* 47–54.

Bayley, David H. (1985). *Patterns of policing: A comparative international analysis.* New Brunswick, NJ: Rutgers University Press.

Bernsdorff, O. Thomas. (1992). The Berlin police: An overview. *C. J. Europe, 2*(2), 5–7.

Bro, Jorn. (1988). Denmark. *C. J. International, 4*(4), 9–12.

Cammett, John, and Gibson, Mary. (1989). Italy. In G. T. Kurian (Ed.). *World encyclopedia of police forces and penal systems.* New York: Facts on File.

Champion, Dean J. (1990). *Criminal justice in the United States.* Columbus, OH: Merrill.

Cole, George F. (1986). *The American system of criminal justice* (4th ed.). Monterey, CA: Brooks/Cole.

Collin, Richard O. (1985). The blunt instruments: Italy and the police. In J. Roach and J. Thomaneck (Eds.), *Police and public order in Europe*. London, England: Croom Helm.

Das, Dilip K. (1992). The Finnish police: A model of conformity and uprightness. *C. J. International, 8*(4), 11–18.

Fairchild, Erika S. (1988). *German police*. Springfield, IL: Charles C. Thomas.

Griswold, David B. and Massey, Charles R. (1989). Legal infractions for insulting the police in the Federal Republic of Germany: A note. *American Journal of Police, 8*, 123–132.

Igbinovia, Patrick E. (1989). Nigeria. In G. T. Kurian (Ed.). *World encyclopedia of police forces and penal systems*. New York: Facts on File.

Iwarimie-Jaja, Darlington. (1988). The police system in Nigeria. *C. J. International, 4*(3), 5–7.

Johnson, David. (1981). *American law enforcement: A history*. St. Louis: Forum Press.

Kania, Richard R. E. (1989). The French municipal police experiment. *Police Studies, 12*, 125–131.

Kania, Richard R. E. (1990). The return of the municipal police. *C. J. International, 6*(2), 3–4.

Karpets, Igor. (1977). Principal directions and types of activity of the militia in the Soviet Union. *International Review of Criminal Policy, 33*, 34–38.

Kayode, Oluyemi. (1976). Public expectations and police role concepts: Nigeria. *Police Chief, 43*(5), 56–59.

Kurian, George T. (1989). *World encyclopedia of police forces and penal systems*. New York: Facts on File.

Laento, Toivo. (1988). Finland. *C. J. International, 4*(4), 12–14.

Macdonald, Ian R. (1987). Spain's 1986 police law: Transition from dictatorship to democracy. *Police Studies, 10*, 16–22.

McGuire, Phillip C. (1988). American law enforcement: A decentralized system with a central purpose. *C. J. the Americas, 1*(1), 13–16.

Morn, Frank, and Toro, Maura. (1989). From dictatorship to democracy: Crime and policing in contemporary Spain. *International Journal of Comparative and Applied Criminal Justice, 13*, 53–64.

O'Brien, C. M. (1960). *The Australian police forces*. Melbourne, Australia: Oxford University Press.

Pursley, Robert. (1987). *Introduction to criminal justice*. New York: Macmillan.

Reid, Sue Titus. (1987). *Criminal justice: Procedures and issues*. St. Paul, MN: West.

Research Division. (1990). *Polish police forces: 1990*. Warsaw, Poland: General Police Headquarters.

Roach, John. (1985). The French police. In J. Roach and J. Thomaneck (Eds.), *Police and public order in Europe*. London, England: Croom Helm.

Senna, Joseph J., and Siegel, Larry J. (1987). *Introduction to criminal justice* (4th ed.). St. Paul, MN: West.

Shelley, Louise I. (1990). The Soviet militsiia: Agents of political and social control. *Policing and Society, 1,* 39–56.

Stead, Philip J. (1983). *The police of France*. New York: Macmillan.

Talbot, C. K., Jayewardene, C. H. S., and Juliani, T. J. (1985). *Canada's constables: The historical development of policing in Canada*. Ottawa: Crimcare.

Thomaneck, Jurgen. (1985). Police and public order in the Federal Republic of Germany. In J. Roach and J. Thomaneck (Eds.), *Police and public order in Europe*. London, England: Croom Helm.

Wines, Michael. (1992, January 18). 'Gorky Park 2': FBI, Soviets foil extortion. *The Denver Post*, p. 7A.

Wolfe, Nancy T. (1992). *Policing a socialist society: The German Democratic Republic*. New York: Greenwood Press.

Chapter 7

An International Perspective on Courts

KEY TOPICS

- The primary actors in the criminal justice process
- Differences in legal training and career tracks
- Different ways prosecution is carried out
- Different ways counsel for defense is provided
- The role of professional judges and lay people in the adjudication process
- The need for an independent judiciary
- Lay people serving as judges or jurors
- Examples from each continent of variation in court organization
- Questions on the presumption of innocence and the concurrent consideration of guilt and sentence

KEY TERMS

adjudication continuum	presumption of innocence
jurors	presumption of guilt
law in action	private prosecutor
law on the books	professional judges
lay judges and people's assessors	public prosecutor

COUNTRIES REFERENCED

China	Germany
England	Nigeria
France	Saudi Arabia

On May 28, 1987, West German teenager Mathias Rust flew his Cessna 172 over the Soviet border and into Moscow's Red Square. Public reaction ranged from laughter at such a stunt to empathy for the men losing top Soviet positions because of the defense system breach. At another level, there was curiosity about how the Soviet legal system would handle the case. Under the Russian Republic's criminal code, Mathias faced a sentence of up to 10 years or a fine approaching $1600 for his act of "malicious hooliganism." Citizens of the world, especially those in the West, followed the case with a sense of confusion. What is hooliganism? they asked. Does he have a right to a defense attorney? Why are they having a trial, since he already confessed?

Rust's trial brought even more questions. Why was there no jury? What are the two people doing up there with the judge? When the judge (and those two other people we still were not sure about) sentenced Rust to four years in a "light regime" (a what?) Soviet labor camp, many Americans believed that the poor guy would not survive the assumed horrible conditions. Imagine the surprise when the Soviets expelled Rust about one year later and Mathias spoke of gaining weight in prison and working for the prison library. Many Americans were expecting to hear horror stories of adverse conditions and torture (Chua-Eoan, August 15, 1988).

The legal system confronting Rust was less alien to him than it was to Americans following his story. For example, he knew who those two people with the judge were, and in fact would have been more surprised at seeing 12 people off to the side receiving all the attention of the attorneys.

The concern of this chapter is with the institutions that different countries establish to bring a defendant to justice. Of course, when looking at particular social institutions, we also must consider the people who work there. Recall that Chapter 1 distinguished between a functions/procedures strategy and an institutions/actors one. The former highlights the similarities among legal systems but in doing so masks their differences. In several ways, Chapters 3 through 5 followed a functions/procedures approach, since they presented general material about legal systems according to separate traditions. As a result, you now have general information about the function of law in four legal families and some specific information about legal procedures in countries representing each family. You do not, however, have much understanding of who's carrying out those functions and procedures or in what setting they are working. That is what the actors/institutions strategy provides. Of course, it is not possible to speak of the "who" and "where" without occasional reference to the "what." Therefore, as we learn about the actors and institutions in various countries, we must be intermittently reminded of the functions and procedures.

We approach these topics by looking first at the actors Americans know as the prosecutor and defense counsel. We then turn to the players responsible for deciding the outcome of a case. These adjudicators can be either professionals or lay persons. Finally, we consider the stage upon which these performers carry out their duties.

PROFESSIONAL ACTORS IN THE JUDICIARY

The primary actors in the criminal process are the advocates (prosecutor and defense counsel) and the judge. These three positions indicate possible career tracks in the legal profession. Other choices might include legal scholar, corporate attorney, notary, or other forms of public and private legal work. The ease with which a law school graduate can move among these occupational areas helps show whether a country has a unified or separated legal profession. In the former, all legal professionals are considered to have the basic knowledge and training to participate in any of the fields. In the latter, each field has distinct entrance requirements that restrict horizontal movement by the legal professionals. Part of the difference results from how a country educates its law students.

Variation in Legal Training

Americans tend to associate legal education with graduate work undertaken after the student has completed a general college or university education. This process is actually uncommon from the world perspective, since civil law countries, and even legal studies in England, provide training in law at the undergraduate level.

Like college training almost everywhere, legal studies under the civil law tradition is usually general and interdisciplinary rather than professional (Glendon, Gordon, and Osakwe, 1985). As a result, civil law graduates are not trained to begin immediately the practice of law. Instead, those wishing to enter a legal profession need further practical training. The American law school graduate, on the other hand, is expected to be prepared to do any type of legal work with only a minimal apprenticeship.

The type and duration of training in the civil law vary by country, and according to the kind of legal career the new graduate wants to pursue. Shortly after receiving the university degree in law, new civil lawyers are given the option of being a private lawyer, a judge, a government lawyer (basically a public administrator), or a legal scholar. Entrance into each legal profession typically depends on the applicant successful passing an exam and completing a period of apprenticeship. With different educational backgrounds, occupational choices, and career entrance requirements, it is not surprising that countries vary regarding the role and social position of their legal professionals.

Lawyers in America often find themselves in the peculiar position of being in a prestigious occupation (Hodge *et al.*, 1964) while also serving as the butt of many jokes. Actually, jokes and negative comments about lawyers have been around since the late sixteenth century. Shakespeare's Dick the butcher said, "The first thing we do, let's kill all the lawyers" (*King Henry VI, Part II*), as he was making suggestions in support of Jack Cade's promise of a better society. In colonial America outright belligerence often took the form of hostile legislation. McDonald (1983) reminds us of the pre-Revolutionary dictum that it was not deemed necessary, or even advisable, to have judges learned in law. The hostility came primarily from the landed gentry and the clergy, both of whom feared the loss of their power and status to a lawyering class. The role of lawyers in England and the United States continues to occasion feelings of both respect and contempt among the citizens.

Lawyers in civil law countries seem to fare better in some respects. Their occupation is not so commonly the catalyst for jokes, but neither is it the representation of someone who is an obvious success. Part of the public perception of civil law attorneys results from the variety of distinct professional careers from which they choose. Graduates not wanting to become judges can follow a path leading to positions like public prosecutor, government lawyer, defense advocate, or private attorney. The specific career decision is made early and places the young graduate on a rather precise path.

The distinctions among the various legal careers in civil law countries may seem unusual to Americans. In the United States, the legal profession is more unified and allows lateral movement by lawyers from one type of position to another. For example, recent law school graduates may initially serve in a district attorney's office, or as a public defender, to get some experience and a reasonable starting salary. After a few years in that field, they may set up an independent practice where criminal law plays only an insignificant role.

The legal fields in civil law countries are much less unified. Civil lawyers often develop separate skills, images, and professional associations as they follow their chosen legal path. This process results in knowledgeable and rather efficient personnel, but also causes some problems. Results of the early career decision and separation of professions include isolation, inflexibility, professional rivalries, jurisdictional problems, and communication difficulties (Merryman, 1985). In an attempt to lessen the chances that a new university graduate will make an uninformed career choice, some countries (for example, Germany) require law graduates to engage in a period of practical training. Over a period of many months or several years, the "interns" experience the work of judges, government lawyers, and private attorneys. Drawing on those experiences, the still rather recent graduate can choose a legal profession with a better idea of what the career will involve.

Advocates in the socialist tradition tend to follow the same process as those in civil law countries. The law degree, offered at the undergraduate level, is essentially under the control of the universities rather than the legal profession itself. The members of the legal profession are primarily state employees with a status similar to that of other civil servants (Glendon *et al.* 1985).

Differences between the socialist and civil legal professions are primarily in terms of integration. Instead of having distinct and separate legal fields, the socialist legal profession is highly integrated. As in the United States, this means that socialist lawyers have horizontal mobility to move from one branch of the profession to another without facing additional entrance requirements. The term *jurist* designates all members of the legal profession for most socialist countries just as the term *lawyer* is applicable to the members of America's legal profession.

A notable exception to the socialist format is Poland. Both under socialism and now under the movement to democratization, university law graduates choose one of several legal professions. After passing relevant exams and working in the area for the required time, the person is accepted into the ranks of government attorney, private attorney, and so on. As a result, the Polish model follows the civil law tradition more closely. Each branch of the Polish legal profession has specific postlaw school training requirements that restrict, without totally foreclosing, horizontal mobility.

Just as Poland's separated legal profession varied from the socialist tradition, England departs somewhat from the common law practice of a unified legal profession. The positions of barrister and solicitor provide the basis for a bifurcated system of advocates in England. Terrill (1984) compares them to physicians who are general practitioners (solicitors) and those who are specialized surgeons (barristers). For example, when members of the public need general legal advice or assistance, they usually turn to a solicitor.

Barristers, the more specialized practitioners, can make arguments before higher-level courts where solicitors have restricted access. The solicitor's right to full audience in lower courts, but only limited hearing in higher courts, means that after preparing a case for the higher level, the solicitor must employ a barrister to make the arguments. The British legal system relies on the presenting of oral arguments, so his verbal skills and specialized talents make the barrister a respected figure in that system.

General comments about Islamic advocates are difficult to make. The parties in legal disputes are infrequently represented by counsel (Lippman, McConville, and Yerushalmi, 1988) and legal training typically results in scholars instead of practitioners. In Saudi Arabia, for example, persons wishing positions as advocates or judges follow a religious rather than traditional legal education (Amin, 1985). After five years in a preparatory religious school (similar to a secondary level education), potential legal actors attend a *Shari'a* law school in Mecca, Riyadh, Jeddah, or Medina. Those law schools do not have university status, but after graduation, persons wishing advocate status can request a practicing certificate from the Ministry of Justice. The necessary license to practice before the *Shari'a* courts is issued in each locality by a committee presided over by a chief justice of that locality (Amin, 1985). Persons wishing a judicial appointment must be selected by the appropriate committee in the Ministry of Justice. After such selection, the aspirants must complete a three-year course of judicial training at the Higher Judicial Institute.

In other Islamic countries, advocates follow a path closer to that in the civil legal tradition. In Iraq and Sudan, for example, aspirants to the legal profession must be law graduates of recognized universities (one of three in Iraq and one of two in Sudan). Graduates must then be accepted to the Iraqi or Sudanese bar, and then serve as an apprentice for one (Sudan) or two (Iraq) years with a practicing advocate.

IMPACT

The Presumption of Innocence

This Impact section concerns the broad issue of how a defendant is viewed as he or she comes before the court to interact with the various players. More specifically, does a legal system presume that the accused is innocent or guilty upon arrival at the court stage of the justice process? This topic also provides an opportunity to distinguish between "law in action" and "law on the books" as we describe the justice system in different countries.

Merryman (1985) notes that some people believe the civil law systems operate under the assumption that the accused is guilty until proven innocent. As with all generalizations, that belief ignores the practical application of law in some common law systems. That is, even if the law on the books says the accused is presumed innocent, it does not mean that the law in action will behave in that manner. Consider, for example, the common law system of Nigeria.

This chapter's discussion of Nigerian courts includes a dialogue reported by Cole (1990) from his ethnographic research on the Nigerian criminal process. Two other illustrations from Cole speak to the question of presumption of innocence:

(1) Magistrate: Why did you steal these bicycles?

Defendant: I did not steal them sir.

Magistrate: Look here . . . go and beg the police and tell them how you got the bicycles (Cole, 1990, p. 307).

(2) Magistrate (to defendant): You must have been speeding.

Defendant: No sir.

Magistrate: Then, you must have been drunk . . . people like you take drugs and smoke marijuana.

Defendant: No sir.

Magistrate: Shut up . . . Liar! (Cole, 1990, p. 307).

Of course, two examples from one Nigerian court do not indict the entire Nigerian justice system nor do they mean that common law systems throughout the world show similar disregard for presumption of innocence. The point is simply that courts are not always inclined to operate as the laws on the books specify. That is true not only for a concept like the presumption of innocence, but also for most other topics covered in this text. But we must first understand how a legal system is supposed to operate before we can tell when, where, how, and why it proceeds differently. To that end, this chapter and all the others concentrate on the proclaimed organization and operation of criminal justice systems. Occasionally that description will not be entirely correct, as we would discover upon proclaiming that Nigeria's judiciary operates under the presumption that a defendant is innocent. However, had we not known how the Nigerian magistrate was supposed to behave, we would not understand that his behavior contradicted the law on the books. In other words, a knowledge of both the law in action and the law on the books is necessary when we seek to understand any country's legal system. I just happen to believe that we should start with a knowledge of what is supposed to be and then study how things actually are.

For example, Chinese law seems at first glance to reject a presumption of innocence. The 1979 Chinese Code of Criminal Procedure does not specifically provide for a presumption of innocence, and historically the Chinese courts have placed great emphasis on confession. In fact, Berman *et al.* (1982) note that the accused in China is not told in advance what evidence will be used against him. He is not allowed to see the entire record of the preliminary investigation and even his lawyer, who can see the record, is not to give the defendant any details. The reason offered for this seemingly strange rule is that full disclosure of the evidence would tend to taint the voluntary character of a confession. That is, a confession following full realization of the evidence against a person cannot be as sincere as one given before the accused knows what the prosecutor knows.

Legal theorists in the PRC claim that the presumption of innocence principle simply creates confusion, ties the hands of law enforcement personnel, and leaves criminals unpunished (Leng, 1982). Such opinions, coupled with the pressure for confession and the absence of statutory claims that an accused should be presumed innocent, seem clearly to indicate that China has no presumption of innocence. However, this example of law on the books (more accurately, law omitted from the books) may be another instance where law in action suggests something different. For example, Gelatt (1982) says that the Chinese legal system claims not to presume anything. Instead, he quotes the legal scholar Zhang Youyu as saying Chinese procedure simply "seeks truth from facts" (quoted in Gelatt, 1982, p. 261). Chinese judges need only investigate the facts and evaluate the evidence with an open mind and from all sides of the issue (Leng, 1982). In this way, the accused's culpability or purity can be rightfully proved without the court officials having first presumed either guilt or innocence.

We covered the distinction between presumption of guilt and presumption of innocence in Chapter 2, but a brief review is in order, since it relates to this discussion as well. To the extent that civil law systems follow a crime control model one could argue that they presume the guilt of a defendant. Or, as Packer (1968) might put it, the investigation by civil law system officials is assumed to identify any accused person who is probably innocent. Similarly, people whom the investigation does not exclude are probably guilty. Therefore, subsequent action against those people proceeds under a presumption of guilt. On the other hand, if the common law systems emphasize a due process model, one could argue that they presume the innocence of a defendant. But that assumption is required, civil law system proponents might argue, because the investigatory stage is not as complete nor intensive as it is under civil law. As a result, common law officials cannot be so sure they have already excluded the "probably innocent." Maybe instead of trying to view one legal system as presuming guilt while another presumes innocence and a third presumes nothing, it is best to try and appreciate how a country's legal system tries to avoid prosecution of probably innocent people. Some choose to weed out in the early stages with intensive investigation of suspects, and others believe that the procedures themselves can be used to do the weeding as the suspect/defendant moves through the system.

It is difficult not to ask which system is more just. Merryman (1985) tells of a comparative scholar who said that if he were innocent he would prefer to be tried in a civil law court, but if he were guilty he would rather be tried by a common law court. Merryman (1985) believes that comment considers criminal procedure in civil law to be more likely to distinguish accurately between guilty and innocent. Do you agree?

Variation in Prosecution

Prosecution of criminal cases is accomplished either through private or public prosecutors (see Figure 7-1). The oldest process (private prosecution) allows the victim or victim's relatives to initiate action against the offender. As crime became seen as a wrong against society, as well as against the victim, prosecution also became the responsibility of the government (public prosecution). The United States, England and Wales, and France provide examples of the primary ways public prosecution is handled today.

United States.   As noted earlier, colonial Americans were not keen on the idea of lawyers. Because of that, private prosecution, rather than public prosecution by a governmental attorney, dominated the colonial system of criminal justice. For example, in colonial Pennsylvania, victims with a criminal complaint against another person were responsible for initiating action against that person. The victim informed the justice of the peace (whose fees the victim would pay) about the charge. The victim then attended pretrial hearings, ensured the appearance of witnesses, and hired an attorney to plead the case if the victim did not wish to argue it himself (Steinberg, 1984). It was the private citizen who pursued the case to its conclusion.

As the authorities before whom all prosecutions were initiated in colonial Pennsylvania, the aldermen (members of the municipal legislative body) and justices of the peace (judicial magistrates with limited jurisdiction) were the most important criminal justice officials. Procedures for prosecuting criminal cases were so simple and informal that by 1802 the justices complained that all the criminal cases left no time for more important civil matters (Steinberg, 1984). A solution to this problem allowed juries, in misdemeanor cases resulting in dismissals or acquittals, to charge the private prosecutor all the court costs. Felonies were not, however, included for fear that doing so would discourage private citizens from prosecuting serious crimes.

Since the early 1800s were times without an organized, modern police force, the enforcement of the law was still primarily the responsibility of a community's residents. The method used by the citizens involved the private citizen's starting criminal action against someone by initiating procedures at the office of the neighborhood alderman. A portion of the alderman's income was from a fee attached to each case. All criminal cases began in these offices. While the alderman did not have the power to make the final disposition, it was here that decisions were made about how far a case would proceed in the criminal justice process.

Either the alderman or the grand jury screened most of the private criminal cases out of the judicial system. If an alderman accepted a case, it had to be given to the grand jury for formal indictment. As can be seen, there was very little for a public prosecutor to do in this system of law enforcement. Most cases were resolved at the citizen–alderman level, and although aldermen were officers of the state, they were noticeably dependent on the private citizens who provided their fees (Steinberg, 1984). Because their role was judicial, the aldermen could not independently initiate a case. Therefore, if the private citizen did not start things rolling, the alderman (even if he knew of the wrong committed) could not prosecute the case for the private citizen.

None of this should be taken to suggest that public prosecutors did not exist during this time period. Until 1850 the official title for such persons was "deputy attorney general," and they had responsibility for prosecuting serious offenses or "great public wrongs." However, since most cases were minor offenses that were fully resolved by the aldermen, the public prosecutor was seldom called upon. The obvious question becomes, What did the public prosecutors actually do? In cases where an alderman chose not to go to a grand jury, the public prosecutor did nothing. For the rest of the cases he served as a clerk, organizing the court calendar and presenting cases to grand and petit juries. He conducted the prosecution's case in many but not all trials of serious crimes. For most cases, he could be, and perhaps was even expected to be, replaced by a private attorney. Essentially, the public prosecutor had very limited freedom to decide how a case would be handled (Steinberg, 1984).

The idea of a public prosecutor with minimal discretion strikes Americans as very strange today. Contemporary public prosecutors in the United States have significant discretion. They decide whether a case will be carried forward, what the formal charges will be, and even if the charges should later be dropped. It seems unlikely that such discretion was a twentieth-century creation. Steinberg (1984) suggests that the existence of discretion has not changed, but its location has. In these early years of American justice, discretion was in the hands of the alderman, grand jury, petit jury, and private citizens. Citizen discretion was especially overwhelming at each stage of the process, compared with the powerlessness of the public prosecutor. For example, at any point the parties could end the proceedings by simply settling their dispute and not making court appearances.

The public prosecutor's role began changing as the private citizen's role in law enforcement began to decline. According to Steinberg (1984), public disturbances could not be effectively quelled or prosecuted by private citizens. During the 1840s and 1850s the problem of public order reached crisis proportions. Philadelphia responded to these problems by increasing her police watch in 1850 and then consolidating the police force in 1854. Also in 1854, "the prosecuting attorney's title was officially changed to district attorney, the office was made elective, and the officer was required for the first time to `sign all bills of indictment and conduct in court all criminal or other prosecutions in the name of the commonwealth'" (Steinberg, 1984, p. 580).

The discretionary power of the district attorney increased slightly over the next 25 years, but private prosecution remained popular and served to limit that discretion. The end was in sight, however. Complaints grew about private settlements between aldermen and the parties, irritation at the failure of private prosecutors to appear before grand or petit jurors, and aggravation with the petty content of the cases themselves. Finally, in 1874 Pennsylvania set in motion changes that effectively altered the relationship between citizens, police, and the courts. The main characters in the criminal justice system became officers of the state (police and public prosecutors) instead of private citizens. Equally important, neither police officer nor prosecutor were officers of the court. Instead, they were independent law enforcement agencies whose purpose was to channel some cases into the courts while resolving others in alternative ways. The effect of the change occurred almost immediately. The percentage of felonies heard by the courts rose, and conviction rates increased, while the number of dismissed cases declined dramatically. This shift from a criminal justice process relying upon citizen initiation to one dominated by state initiation provided the power and discretion now housed in the office of public prosecutor.

It is important to note that private prosecution was not completely abandoned in the United States. In some jurisdictions (for example, Arkansas, Kentucky, North Carolina, Tennessee) victims may retain, at their own expense, private prosecutors to move a case through the criminal justice system (Robin and Anson, 1990). The private prosecutor acts under the supervision of the local public prosecutor's office, but provides victims an opportunity to take criminal legal action in cases (for example, misdemeanors) for which the public prosecu-

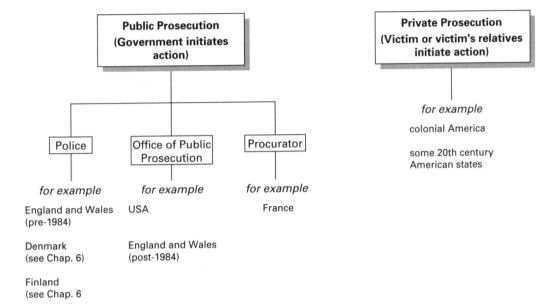

Figure 7-1.   Variation in prosecution.

tor gives low priority. Despite those few jurisdictions holding to the private prosecution concept, public prosecution is well entrenched in the American system of justice. The result is a person said, at the least, to have broad discretionary power (Newman, 1986) and at the extreme, to be the most influential person in America in terms of the power he or she has over the lives of citizens (Reid, 1987).

   England and Wales.   The role of a public prosecutor with primary responsibility for taking action against criminal offenders is even a more recent idea in England. Before 1984, the decision to prosecute rested with the police, not a public prosecutor. In this manner, England and Wales were similar to Denmark and Finland (see Chapter 6) where police take responsibility for prosecuting their cases. To initiate action against a suspect, the police in England and Wales hired solicitors and barristers who would present the police (that is, public) complaint in court. To help fulfill their prosecutorial duties, most police forces had solicitors on staff to handle the most serious cases (Hughes, 1984; Emmins, 1988). These solicitors were simply employees of the Police Authority and lacked decision-making power regarding the nature of eventual charges. When an "in-house" person was not available, police hired solicitors from the community. As with the private citizen, when a police case went to a higher court, a barrister was hired.

   In 1879, England created the office of the Director of Public Prosecutions. However, the office's growth was remarkably slow until the mid-1980s. Before 1985, the DPP's role was limited to only exceptionally important or difficult cases. That limited role was dramatically changed when the Prosecution of

Offenses Act of 1985 transformed the position by requiring the DPP to prosecute all criminal proceedings initiated by the police.

Because the increased responsibility and duties thrust upon the DPP would be too much a burden for the existing structure of the office, the Prosecution of Offenses Act also created the Crown Prosecution Service. Chief Crown Prosecutors (who are distributed in 31 geographical areas of England and Wales) are responsible for the operation of the Crown Prosecution Service in their area. Branch offices in each area handle prosecutions for a grouping of magistrates' courts—the CPS does not provide prosecutors in the Crown Court. A senior crown prosecutor heads the branch office and oversees the activities of the crown prosecutors and other staff (Emmins, 1988; Spencer, 1989).

Creation of the CPS was intended to allow an internal staff (the crown prosecutors) to handle most of the prosecutorial work necessary at magistrates' courts. Emmins (1988) notes that the great volume of work and the difficulty in recruiting staff means that much of the advocacy is still handled by solicitors and barristers in private practice. The primary difference from pre-CPS days is that those private attorneys are hired as agents of the CPS rather than working directly for the police.

The relatively new Crown Prosecution Service seems to bring British prosecutions more in line with American procedures. Once a person is charged by the police, the relevant papers are sent to the local CPS branch office, where the evidence is reviewed. The CPS lawyer reviewing the evidence decides if the charges are justified and can discontinue proceedings when prosecution seems unwarranted. If additional or alternative charges are needed, the CPS lawyer can have them added when the accused appears in court.

The ability of the CPS lawyer to discontinue proceedings is one of the primary changes from the pre-1985 system. When police were solely responsible for determining charges and initiating prosecution, advocates simply followed the wishes of the police. Today, the CPS still does not really initiate prosecution. But it does determine if that prosecution will continue and, if so, with what charges.

An area where the CPS has not encroached upon police duties is the investigation of a crime. Following the pre-CPS tradition, investigation of a crime remains the responsibility of the police. Of course, the idea that the prosecutor will be an active member of the investigative team seems unusual to Americans. But such a role is expected of the prosecutor in many countries, and that point brings us to a final example of structuring public prosecution.

France. Discussing public prosecution in countries of the common legal tradition is fairly straightforward—you describe the office of public prosecutor. When attention turns to prosecution in countries of the civil tradition, it is a bit more complicated. The main reason for that is the civil tradition's (more accurately, the inquisitorial process's) emphasis on the investigative stage and the office of procurator. The procurator is a person acting in the place of someone else. In this case, a government attorney takes action for a private citizen who has been wronged. France provides a good example of the prosecutorial role under a civil legal tradition, so we will briefly describe prosecution in that country.

There are three key players in the French prosecution process: the judicial police, the procurator, and the examining magistrate. Recall from Chapter 5's discussion of the inquisitorial procedure that the trial is essentially a continuation of the investigatory process. Further, judges play a more active role and attorneys a more passive one compared to those positions under an adversarial procedure. As we recall these circumstances, the idea of prosecution involving three players (police, prosecutor, and judge), representing three seemingly distinct (at least for Americans) stages, makes a bit more sense. We begin with a brief description of each player.

The role of judicial police can actually be taken by a member of the *Police Nationale*, the *Gendarmerie Nationale* (see Chapter 6), a prosecutor, or a few specific government officials (for example, mayors). The judicial police operate (regardless of the force or office they are under) at one of three levels: officers, agents, and assistant agents. Judicial Police Officers have the most authority and can investigate the most serious offenses, order a suspect detained for investigation, and be given even broader authority by an examining magistrate. Judicial Police Agents and Judicial Police Assistant Agents have more restricted authority (though agents obviously have more than their assistants) and function primarily to assist the Officers in carrying out their duties.

French procurators are part of a civil service hierarchy headed by the Minister of Justice. Below the Minister is the Attorney General for the Court of Cassation and the Attorneys General for each court of appeal. The Attorneys General supervise their own staff and the prosecuting attorneys (*Procureurs de la Republique*) for each court of General Jurisdiction in that appellate district (Frase, 1988). The prosecuting attorneys determine appropriate charges against the accused, prosecute less serious felonies and most misdemeanors, and direct the work of the judicial police. They also handle serious felonies that fall outside the jurisdiction of the Attorneys General.

Examining magistrates, who are chosen from among the court judges, serve three-year renewable terms. Article 81 specifies, "The examining magistrate shall undertake, in conformance with law, all acts of investigation that he deems useful to the manifestation of the truth" (French Code of Criminal Procedure, 1988). In this manner the judiciary has the role of an investigation director who assigns and supervises activities of the judicial police and the prosecutor. The examining magistrate cannot, however, open an investigation unless requested to do so by the prosecuting attorney or the victim (Frase, 1988).

Four types of investigations are anticipated by the French Code of Criminal Procedure: (1) investigations of flagrant offenses, (2) formal judicial investigations, (3) preliminary investigations, and (4) identity checks. All investigations are conducted under two general principles. First, official investigation of the facts should be fair in the sense that they attempt to uncover both favorable and unfavorable evidence, and that brutal or deceptive methods will be avoided. Second, all investigatory steps are to be thoroughly documented in writing (Frase, 1988). Although all four types of investigation are important, the first two allow the broadest investigatory powers and the last two the narrowest. To exemplify the process we will consider just the first two, since they are more involved. In doing so, we can come to understand the role of the French prosecutor.

Flagrant offenses are defined by Article 53 of the Code of Criminal Procedure as those that are in the process of being committed or have recently been committed. In such cases, the judicial police, prosecutors, and examining magistrates are given extensive search, seizure, and detention authority. There are procedural safeguards over that authority (for example, house searches must be witnessed by persons independent of the searching authorities), but there are no legal standards similar to probable cause under common law regarding, for example, where police may look for evidence (Frase, 1988). After considering the results of the investigation of a flagrant offense, a prosecuting attorney determines whether to charge the accused with a *contravention* (up to two months of incarceration possible), a *delit* (up to five years, sometime more, of imprisonment possible), or a *crime* (five years or more of imprisonment possible). The eventual charge will determine whether the accused is simply released on a promise to appear or held in custody to await (within two working days) court arraignment. In addition, the prosecuting attorney may decide that a judicial investigation is needed (if the charge is for a *contravention* or *delit*) or required (when the charge is for a *crime*).

A formal judicial investigation, which is conducted by an examining magistrate, is mandatory when the prosecution charges a serious felony (*crime*) and optional when *delit* or *contravention* charges are filed (Frase, 1988). During the judicial investigation, the magistrate can issue arrest warrants and detention orders and can initiate interrogations of the accused and the victim. When the judicial investigation is deemed complete, the accused is either released or formally charged.

Later in this chapter the French court system is described and reference is again made to the French prosecutor. At that point you will be reminded that the prosecutor has a rather limited role in the actual conduct of the trial. Despite differences in the role of French prosecutor as compared to one in the United States, we must remember that both exemplify public prosecution. That is a key point, since the existence of public, rather than only private, prosecutors reaffirms the idea that "crime" is a public wrong.

Variation in Defense

Variation in the way nations go about prosecuting cases is continued in the procedures countries develop to defend those citizens being prosecuted (see Figure 7-2). In the *Shari'a* courts of Saudi Arabia and other Islamic countries, professionally trained lawyers do not have a monopoly on legal representation. In fact, Muslims traditionally acted for themselves or nominated others, relatives or

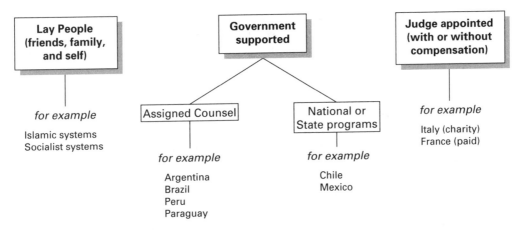

Figure 7-2. Variation in defense. (Keep in mind that variation exists within as well as among countries. The countries identified as exemplifying each general type may be accurately placed under another type as well. For example, Mexico also has an Assigned Counsel government-support system, and most countries under a socialist legal tradition also provide legally trained defense counsel.)

character witnesses, to act for them. Today, restrictions on representation by non-professionals have reduced the lay person's use, but lawyers still are not required personnel in the Islamic justice process.

The former Soviet Union provided an active role for nonprofessionals in the prosecution and defense of criminal defendants. If a person was accused of a crime, co-workers could secure a colleague of the accused to go to court as a "social defender" to testify about the defendant's good moral character and work habits. On the other hand, if the accused's work habits and other characteristics were not appreciated, colleagues could send a "social accuser" to speak against the defendant. In this manner, the public's interests were represented in court on a level equal to those of the defendant.

Despite these examples of lay people helping in the defense of an accused, most countries rely on legally trained professionals to help defendants present their case. Before the mid-nineteenth century, legal protection for people unable to hire an attorney was primarily the result of charitable acts. Men such as Saint Yves of Brittany—"'a lawyer and yet not a thief, to the wonder of the people'—were canonized for their work in representing the impoverished" (Cappelletti and Gordley, 1978, p. 516). Even the more organized programs faded in and out of use with changes in monarchs. When legal assistance programs were in use, it was not always clear just who benefited from the assistance, under which circumstances it would be provided, and by what process the assistance would be carried out.

More modern programs in the West began in 1851 with French legislation designed to remove financial barriers that the poor encountered during litigation. A 1901 act established a national system of *bureaux* to determine eligibility in that program. Italy (in 1865) and Germany (in 1877) also initiated programs that allowed judges to appoint lawyers, serving without pay, to assist in the defense of an impoverished defendant (Cappelletti and Gordley, 1978).

In the twentieth century, provisions for the defense of poor people around the world have continued to improve, but not always quickly. A 1972 French reform substituted a system of aid paid by the state for the previous "charity" with unpaid lawyers providing legal assistance to the poor. However, the nineteenth-century Italian innovation of judge-appointed lawyers providing uncompensated legal assistance remains essentially unchanged some 130 years later (Cappelletti, 1989).

Latin American countries provide examples of the slow movement toward establishing adequate means of legal assistance to poor defendants. Following their historical roots, the legal systems of most Latin American countries borrowed defense provisions from Spain, France, and Portugal. As a result, the assigned counsel (typically serving without pay) system was adopted throughout Latin America by the end of the nineteenth century.

Today, two basic kinds of assigned counsel operate in Latin America (Knight, 1978). In the first, a judge appoints lawyers from a list of practicing attorneys in the area. Lawyers appointed in this manner typically serve without pay as they fulfill their charitable obligation. The second type of assigned counsel involves the use of lawyers paid by the state. These "public defenders," operating in the criminal courts of such countries as Mexico, Argentina, Brazil, Peru, and Paraguay, work full time for the court or part time for both court and private clients.

Besides the assigned counsel system, some Latin American countries have national or state legal assistance programs. In Chile's national plan, the Ministry of Justice gives money directly to the Chilean Bar Association to finance the judicial assistance service (*Servicio de Asistencia Judicial*). The other popular Latin American alternative to assigned counsel is law school legal assistance clinics (Knight, 1978). For example, besides Mexico's government employed lawyers (*Defensores de Oficio*), some law schools provide free legal service through neighborhood legal assistance offices. Besides providing needed legal assistance to poor citizens, these programs give law students, and recent graduates, important practical training.

General comments about the legal assistance systems in continental and Latin American countries provide the necessary overview of worldwide options. Even in these brief remarks you should see similarities with the primary legal assistance procedures in the United States. We have government-supported programs similar to those in such countries as France, Chile, and Mexico. Like many European and Latin American countries, we also have programs that depend on judges to assign counsel from lists of available attorneys. In addition to those assigned counsel programs, American states also have jurisdictions where defense attorneys are full-time government employees. A review of defense systems on other continents would reveal few variations from these themes. But it is still instructive to highlight the defense system of a particular country.

THE ADJUDICATORS

Soviet journalist Iurii Feofanov relates an Eastern parable as he reflects on the idea of a state governed by law.

> A certain youth was sent to a sheik, famous for his wisdom, to study the laws. For ten years, the youth wrote down the pronouncements of the holy sheik on his scrolls. When he returned to his native land, now a mature man, he took along an ass loaded down with bales. In them were the scrolls of wisdom. This man then began to judge his countrymen. Whoever came, he would immediately unfold a scroll and read off a dictum. People marveled at the learning of their countryman. But they did not understand what to do; they would ask again, and he would give them a new dictum, even wiser than the first. And so they stopped going to the wise man. One time, he traveled into the mountains to teach people about the laws. Crossing a stream, the ass sank with all his load. The wise man was in despair: how could he now issue judgments? And when people came to him, being without his scrolls of wisdom, he would now for the first time ask again: `What did you say your problem was?' And when he looked into the matter carefully, he would begin to remember what he had been taught and he said what had to be done. He spoke so clearly and wisely that people could only marvel. From that time on, the fame of the learned man spread. And they would say about him: `Earlier, a wise ass would teach us, now it is the wise man himself' (Feofanov, 1990–1991, pp. 15–16).

From the perspective of the common legal tradition, that parable might be interpreted as criticizing the civil tradition's reliance on codes (the scrolls carried by the ass) for dispensing justice. But Feofanov used the parable to support the civil legal tradition's belief that law is best envisioned as general principles instead of specific rules. He interprets the parable in this way: "the ass with the `scrolls of laws' sank in the mountain stream but the principles of law remained in their original sense within the memory of the wise man and judge" (Feofanov, 1990–1991, p. 17). In this manner, the common legal tradition is disparaged as loaded down with so many specific rules covering every individual problem that the legal system sinks from its own weight.

A distinguishing feature between the civil and common legal traditions is the former's preference for codes that clearly set forth general principles for judges to follow as they dispense justice. The latter's preference is for judges to follow specific guidelines as set down in similar cases handled by the same or other judges. A goal of both traditions is to provide uniformity of justice. The common tradition sees that as best achieved when judges follow decisions in similar cases, whereas the civil tradition feels that the goal is reached by judges following the same general principles. In either case, however, achieving the goal is linked to the behavior of an adjudicator.

In a sense, the adjudication process is the *raison d'être* for a justice system. Citizens and agencies of the government make use of the justice system when they seek resolution of some dispute. Whether the dispute concerns a private or public wrong, some process for adjudication must be part of the resolution. The parable above highlights the role that a judge plays in the decision, but in some justice systems others are recruited to assist the judge.

Plato was among the first to champion a role for lay persons in the criminal process. As he explained it: "In the judgment of offenses against the state the people ought to participate, for when anyone wrongs the state all are wronged and may reasonably complain if they are not allowed to share in the decision" (quoted in Ehrmann, 1976, p. 95).

Today, the United States is among only a few countries that take Plato's suggestion to the extreme. In the infrequent case where a jury is used, Americans are relying on lay people to decide the defendant's guilt or innocence while a judge, separate from those lay people, controls the proceedings. The seriousness of the task before these members of the public, acting without legal training, is highlighted daily by judges across the country. Although a fictional account, the words of Judge Larren L. Lyttle in Scott Turow's best-selling novel, *Presumed Innocent*, give a feel for the role and mission of American jurors.

Murder defendant Rusty Sabich watches as the prospective jurors for his case are brought into the courtroom. Of the 75 people, 12 will be chosen to decide his fate. As a former prosecutor, Sabich knows that most jurors are going to begin the trial with a proprosecution bias. After all, jurors must tell themselves, the police and prosecutor think the guy is guilty, so who am I, a mere citizen off the street, to say he isn't guilty? The only way Sabich can maintain hope is his knowledge that Judge Lyttle has a reputation for emphatically explaining to the jury such concepts as the presumption of innocence. Sabich listens carefully as the judge begins by telling the potential jurors what the case is about.

> (Judge Lyttle) has probably seen a thousand juries chosen during his career. His rapport is instantaneous: this big, good-looking black man, kind of funny, kind of smart. . . . He is skilled in addressing juries, canny in divining hidden motivation, and committed to the foundation of his soul to the fundamental notions. The defendant is presumed innocent. Innocent. As you sit here you have gotta be thinking Mr. Sabich didn't do it.
>
> `I'm sorry, sir. In the first row, what is your name?'
>
> `Mahalovich.'
>
> `Mr. Mahalovich. Did Mr. Sabich commit the crime that he is charged with?'
>
> Mahalovich, a stout middle-aged man who has his paper folded in his lap, shrugs.

`I wouldn't know, Judge.'

`Mr. Mahalovich, you are excused. Ladies and gentlemen, let me tell you what you are to presume. Mr. Sabich is innocent. I am the judge. I am tellin you that. Presume he is innocent. When you sit there, I want you to look over and say to yourself, There sits an innocent man' (Turow, 1987, pp. 234–235).

The parable of the "wise ass/wise man" and the story of Judge Lyttle's speech to potential jurors suggest extremes in the assignment of people to adjudicate a dispute. At one extreme is a professionally trained judge with sole responsibility for hearing the dispute, determining guilt or innocence, and assigning appropriate sanctions. At the other extreme, carrying out the same duties, is a panel of citizens, minimally knowledgeable in the law. Using these extremes as ideal types for purposes of analysis suggests the continuum in Figure 7-3.

Notice that we are referring only to decisions of fact when speaking of the adjudication process. Courts will often decide questions of law as well as ones of fact. In those instances, the court will rule on such things as the legality of police procedures in the arrest, or the constitutionality of the law that the accused supposedly violated. When dealing with questions of law, courts invariably rely only on professional judges. Those judges may be at the mercy of political or religious leaders when making their decisions, but the decision is given by the judge. For questions of fact (that is, did the accused commit the offense?), however, several countries provide input from lay people. It is to this process we refer when speaking of the adjudication continuum. After considering the players at the continuum's ends and middle, we will look at country-specific examples along that continuum.

Professional Judges

During the 1980s, some 300 judges and court workers were killed in Colombia. That number includes half the 24-member Colombian Supreme Court, who were killed on a single day in 1985. Most of the murders were linked to drug traffickers and their attempts to stall government repression of their activities. Since they were an essential link in the punishing or extradition of the drug dealers, being a Colombian judge became a high-risk occupation.

In 1991, Colombia tried to provide greater safety to those persons still willing to serve as a judge. Under the "anonymous judge" program (Marcus, 1991), armed guards took accused drug smugglers, for example, into a small courtroom. Instead of facing a judge, the defendant sat with his lawyer and a court reporter while staring into a bulletproof one-way mirror. Behind the mirror, the judge, known to the defendant only by a number, watched the proceedings in the safety of anonymity. When it was necessary for the judge to speak, his voice was electronically disguised in a further attempt to lengthen his career and life.

Stories of killing judges and court officials are unusual but not lacking. Between January 1988 and June 1989, a report on harassment and persecution of judges and lawyers identified 145 such officials who had been attacked or threatened with violence, detained, or killed (United Nations, 1990). The countries with the most cases reported were the Philippines (28), Colombia (23), and Peru (15). Colombia received particular attention because of groups like the "Extraditables" that threatened to murder 10 judges for every Colombian extradited to the United States.

Harassment and persecution of judicial officials is of greater concern than just a humanitarian interest in the well-being of these people. When the judiciary does not feel free to function, the law cannot operate. The Colombian legal system faced severe problems when judicial officials were executed, compelled to resign, or forced to leave the country. In the face of violence, those judges trying to hold court found few people willing to testify. Colombia's reliance on oral testimony meant that cases made little progress. Combine that with a shortage of technical facilities for crime investigation, and the result is an ineffective court system. The problem may not be as stark in other countries, but a judiciary subject to manipulation by others is a well-recognized problem. We will take a look at procedures used in various countries to ensure their judiciary is able to act independently.

An Independent Judiciary. In 1986, the General Assembly of the United Nations passed a resolution for the Basic Principles on the Independence of the Judiciary. Those principles emphasize that the independence of the judiciary should be guaranteed by the state and enshrined in the constitution or law of each country. This position was taken in the belief that an independent judiciary is indispensable for implementing everyone's right to a fair and public hearing before a competent and impartial tribunal (United Nations, 1988).

It is hard to imagine that any country would take a stand against an independent judiciary. In fact, most governments claim that the United Nations Basic Principles are already embodied in the constitution or laws of their countries. But after seeking information from nongovernment agencies, the United Nations found that the Basic Principles were not always fully respected, despite the public stance taken by government officials.

The judicial system of the former Soviet Union provided an example of a judiciary with questionable independence. The Soviet judiciary fell under the political leadership of the Communist Party of the Soviet Union (CPSU) and the various agencies of state power. Despite its political placement, the USSR constitution declared the Supreme Court to be independent and subject only to the law. The Party and state agencies were categorically prohibited from interfering in the examination of specific cases before the court. Yet in practice the Soviets were not able to end the intervention of Party and Soviet organs in judicial activity. In the early 1980s, 25 percent of people's judges polled by the USSR Academy of Sciences said that they were subjected to unlawful influence. By 1986, the chairman of the USSR Supreme Court suggested that "'the main reason for judicial error is the violation of the principle of the independence of judges'" (quoted in Petrukhin, 1988–1989).

The frustration of the USSR Supreme Court chairman correctly identifies the importance of an independent judiciary. A country's judiciary can only deal with all crimes (including abuse of power by government agents) when it exists separate and independent from the legislative and executive branches. How do countries seeking an independent judiciary go about finding people to serve as judges? Strange as it might seem, some countries rely on the legislature and executive. Other nations use committee recommendations, and still others hold public elections. Of course, various combinations of these approaches are also possible. Some countries seek a more clear-cut separation of government powers and have made the judicial service a bureaucratic career that can be chosen by persons formally educated in the law.

The variability by which judges arrive at their positions deserves closer attention. After all, every country's goal (or at least the publicly stated one) is to provide citizens with an independent judiciary. Only in this way can judges be free to decide in an impartial manner the disputes brought forward by citizens and government officials.

Becoming a Judge.   The people who adjudicate legal disputes typically come to their position in one of two ways: selection by others or self-selection. When the selection of judges is by others, it takes the form of either appointment or election. The people chosen usually have already gained experience as attorneys and, especially when chosen for higher courts, may have attained a certain level of distinction in the legal profession.

Appointment to the magistracy can be by the executive or by a special committee. For example, the President of the United States appoints (with the consent of the Senate) federal judges, and the British Prime Minister selects judges for the House of Lords. Special committees sometimes appoint judges through recommendations to the executive (for example, Israel) or a member of the executive's cabinet (for example, Germany). In some Latin American countries (for example, Bolivia, Honduras, and El Salvador) judges of the highest court appoint members of the lower courts (Hitchner and Levine, 1981).

Election of judges by the people is not frequently found in countries of the world. The United States provides an exception; the majority of American states select judges through some form of popular election. But even in this country, several states are moving toward a combination appointment/election process (see discussion of the Missouri Plan in introductory criminal justice texts like Schmalleger, 1991; Senna and Siegel, 1987).

Judges also can be elected by a country's legislature. Hitchner and Levine (1981) say that this process is used to free judges from executive control (for example, some Central American states), ensure political reliability (for example, the former USSR), or to provide appropriate distribution of desirable characteristics (for example, judges on the Swiss Federal Court must reflect the German-, French-, and Italian-speaking aspects of Swiss culture).

In the self-selection process, judicial service is chosen as a career after the completion of one's formal legal education. In countries with this process, graduates with law degrees choose among such careers as prosecutor, defense counsel, private attorney, or judge. When choosing a judicial career, the aspirant typically takes a state examination and, if successful, begins serving as an adjudicator. In some countries the new judge will attend a special school, but more often will immediately be sent to a remote part of the country to begin service at the lowest-level courts (Merryman, 1985). Promotion in the court hierarchy and transfer to more desirable locations result from some combination of seniority and proved ability.

Self-selected judges are most often found in countries following the civil legal tradition, but the process is also found in Islamic countries (for example, Saudi Arabia). Since civil law judges have the duty of applying rather than making law, their function is essentially a mechanical one. Judges in the common law tradition are more involved in lawmaking and are often expected to be knowledgeable enough in the law to render creative decisions. One result of this distinction is the perception that common law requires experienced and renown persons to serve as judges, whereas the civil law operates well with a civil servant or expert clerk. After all, the judicial process in civil law should be a fairly routine activity (Merryman, 1985). The judge is presented with a fact situation, and his duty is merely to link that situation with the appropriate legislative provision and then to pronounce the solution that the union automatically produces. That process, one could argue, can as easily be completed by a young law school graduate as by a celebrated lawyer with many years of legal experience.

Lay Judges and Jurors

When Americans think of lay people participating in the court process, the picture that typically comes to mind is of 12 citizens sitting off to one side of the courtroom. The right to a trial by jury has been a cherished one for quite some time in America's history. As was often the case, Thomas Jefferson provided the reasoning for such a procedure:

> Were I called upon to decide, whether the people had best be omitted in the legislative or judicial department, I would say it is better to leave them out of the legislative. The execution of the laws is more important than the making of them (quoted in Moore, 1973, p. 159).

Participation of lay people as jury members is only one way that citizens take part in the adjudication process. In some countries lay people sit at the court bench with professional judges and enter into the decision-making process from that location. These two means of participation (juror or lay judge) identify the primary ways in which citizens provide a judiciary with input from the common folk. After an overview of each strategy we will look at country-specific examples of how these techniques operate.

Juries.   Although similar assemblies existed in continental Europe before the eleventh century (see Moore, 1973), England is considered the birthplace of the jury. The first type of jury, as it developed after 1066 in England, was to decide if an accusation against a person was well founded. Sometimes that accusatory jury determined guilt or innocence. But eventually two types of juries were separated with the accusatory one called the grand jury and the verdict one becoming the petit or trial jury.

The early trial juries either assembled and stated what they knew about a particular crime, or were told to go into the countryside and establish facts about the alleged crime. To accomplish that duty the jurors talked to neighbors, picked up hearsay information and rumors, and spoke with the accused and the accuser. After gathering their evidence they would reassemble and draw a conclusion about guilt or innocence (Stuckey, 1986). If the accused was found guilty, he was given the punishment prescribed for the crime. Soon not only the jurors expressed what they had learned about the crime, but witnesses might even appear before the jury and relate what they knew about the accusation.

The witnesses' knowledge, like that of the jurors, was often no more than rumor or hearsay, so the jury might give little weight to their testimony. This was particularly true if the witnesses portrayed the accused as innocent. The reason for discounting witness testimony and deciding contrary to what appeared to be the facts rested in the jurors' fear of the king (Stuckey, 1986). The jurors knew that the king's justices often had advance information about a crime because of reports from the sheriffs and the coroners. If the justices believed that the jurors presented a false verdict, the jurors were required to make atonement (a payment of property or money) or be punished.

The bias toward conviction in a trial by jury meant that many accused preferred other systems for exoneration. For example, before its abolishment in 1215, many an accused opted for trial by ordeal. Here the accused had to do some physical feat as a call to the deity for help in determining guilt or innocence. Presumably, God would enable the innocent to do the required ordeal, while the guilty would fail in his performance. Such required feats included holding a red-hot iron or removing a large rock from a boiling pot of water. After the test, the accused's hand was wrapped, and after three days he appeared before a priest who unwrapped the wound and determined if it had healed. The healed hand showed innocence, while those not healed belonged to the guilty.

Trial by compurgation was another alternative. This system used "character witnesses" for both the accused and the accuser to take oaths asserting the truthfulness of their respective statements. The technical language of the required oath (an error when repeating it meant guilt) and the general unreliability of the oath helpers (compurgators) did not make this option especially popular. The remaining choice was trial by battle. The accused and the accuser would go into actual combat with each other, usually using battle axes. Like trial by ordeal, the "winner" in the battle was said to have had the assistance of God and therefore must be innocent (Stuckey, 1986).

Efforts to "encourage" the accused to submit to trial by jury included the placing of weights on his chest in increasing amounts until he submitted to a jury trial. Even then, the accused often preferred being crushed to death in an effort to save his possessions for his family, rather than having them confiscated by the king should the jury convict him.

As time passed the king could no longer confiscate property as payment for crimes. Equally important, jurors were no longer punished or required to make atonement for possible erroneous verdicts, and the testimony of witnesses received greater consideration. It was this concept of the jury trial that the colonists brought with them to America. By 1673 trial by jury had become an important procedure in Virginia, the Massachusetts Bay Colony, New York, and Pennsylvania (Moore, 1973). Jury trials continued to play a major role in the development of the American republic as the colonists prepared for the Revolution. The Declaration of Rights of the First Continental Congress (1774) included trial by peers as a "great and inestimable privilege." In the Declaration of Causes and Necessity of Taking Up Arms (1775) the colonists claimed that they had been deprived of "the accustomed and inestimable privilege of trial by jury in cases affecting both life and property." And the Declaration of Independence (1776) gave as one reason requiring separation: "For depriving us, in many cases, of the benefits of Trial by Jury." The place of honor American revolutionaries gave jury trials continues today in the hearts of Americans, although very few cases ever get to the jury stage.

Lay Judges. During the late eighteenth and early nineteenth centuries, the appeal of jury trials influenced legal developments first in France and then other European countries. It became obvious that the jury trial was not suited to criminal proceedings in civil law systems (Ehrmann, 1976). Instead, the "mixed bench" provides a functional equivalent to the jury trial. This process is common today in both civil and socialist law systems. Private citizens and professional judges combine into a single body responsible for deciding questions of fact, and occasionally law, while determining guilt and punishment. As full participants in the trial process, lay judges on mixed tribunals seem to provide another use of the public in civil legal systems.

Germany's use of lay judges is discussed below, but before considering that rather effective use of the mixed bench we can note how lay judges can be more show than substance in some cases. In the former Soviet Union, for example, lay participants in the adjudication process were called *people's assessors* (as they are still called in China). Their role was criticized by foreigners, and even some Soviets, as being little more than puppets to the professional judge with whom they sat.

Being a people's assessor was not a full-time responsibility, since the assessor usually spent no more than two weeks per year hearing cases. Because of the limited involvement, assessors often had an understanding of the law only to the extent that they either read the handbook provided them or listened to lectures presented by jurists. Officially, the lay judges were on an equal footing with the professional judge (Terebilov, 1973). If one of the three tribunal members disagreed with the other two, the dissenting member had to sign the judgment and provide a written minority opinion. However, Soviets themselves complained that judges occasionally suppressed assessor activity in the deliberation room and frequently determined a sentence without consulting the assessors (Petrukhin, 1988–1989).

The role of people's assessor seemed most simply a way to ensure civilian participation (Terrill, 1984) and to represent the voice of peers (Barry and Barner-Barry, 1982). Despite such laudable motives, the Soviet judicial system was criticized for judges putting pressure on people's assessors to come to a particular decision. Petrukhin (1988–1989) notes that contrary to the law, assessors were summoned at the judge's discretion instead of in a sequential order. This meant that judges hearing controversial cases could summon the more submissive and obedient assessors to ensure agreement with the judge's position. Even when given the opportunity to participate actively, the assessors' lack of training suggested that they were not likely to challenge the advice and counsel of the professional judge unless that assessor was especially assertive.

The more typical use of lay judges is exemplified by such countries as Germany. And, when used in accordance with the original intent, the lay judges provide an intriguing alternative to the jury system as a means of providing citizen input to the trial process. But there are some law systems that prefer to rely almost totally on professional judges and avoid any active participation by lay people. And that point brings us back to the adjudication continuum (see Figure 7-3).

Examples along the Adjudication Continuum

Before we consider country-specific examples of the continuum types it is important to emphasize the continuum's analytic purpose. As with all ideal type constructs, the extremes are not represented by any real-life example. Still, for purposes of analysis we can identify examples that are closer to one end or the other. Similarly, whenever you have two ends, there must be a middle; there should be mid-range examples that show a sense of balance between the extremes. Below the continuum line in Figure 7-3 are names of countries that

Figure 7-3. Variation in adjudication: An adjudication continuum.

Heavy Reliance on Professional Judges	*Mixed Reliance*	*Heavy Reliance on Lay People*
for example	*for example*	*for example*
Saudi Arabia	Germany	England

arguably exhibit characteristics running from one ideal type to the other. To provide structure for our discussion of adjudicators, we will consider these countries as they relate to either a heavy reliance on judges or on lay people in the adjudicating process. To set the boundaries, we will look at the extremes and then move toward the middle.

Saudi Arabia. It may seem strange to have Saudi Arabia toward the "judge heavy" end of an adjudication continuum. During the discussion of judicial review (Chapter 5), this same country exemplified the absence of complete judicial review, and that might imply the absence of judicial power. But we must remember that judicial review concerns the ability of the judiciary to rule on actions of the legislature and the executive. For purposes of an adjudication continuum, we are looking only at the more traditional role of the judge as he or she decides disputes between citizens or between the government and a citizen. In other words, does the adjudication process rely more heavily on a single judge or a group of lay people in deciding the question of guilt?

Chapter 4 discussed the importance of witnesses and oath taking in the Islamic court. It is apparent from that review that adjudication in a *qadi's* court relies on that judge's ability to direct independently the activities of the accused, the defendant, and any witnesses. Granted, the *qadi* is in turn directed by the *Qur'an*, which stipulates the number of witness and types of oaths necessary for conviction. But it is still the *qadi*, without the assistance of any lay people, who decides if the witnesses and oaths are acceptable. The *qadi* may not have judicial independence and may lack the power of judicial review, but in the courtroom he, and he alone, adjudicates the cases brought before him.

The procedure in *Shari'a* courts of Saudi Arabia is very straightforward (Solaim, 1971). When both plaintiff and defendant are present, the *qadi* listens first to the plaintiff and then to the defendant. Each side may refute the other's arguments and may bring witnesses to support their side. The *qadi* is responsible for determining that the witnesses are of good character, and is also charged with cross-examining the witnesses. At the conclusion of testimony, the *qadi* renders his decision, which must include a summary of the facts and the legal reasoning supporting the decision.

England. Figure 7-3 places England at the "heavy lay people" end of the adjudication continuum. Actually, English courtroom policy allows a much more active role for the judge than does American procedure (Hughes, 1984). In the English tradition, the court will often question witnesses and take a rather active role in the proceedings. At the conclusion of prosecution and defense presentations, the judge may deliver a summary and instructions to the jury. Those comments may include the judge's opinions on witness credibility and may express a particular view of the case.

Judges must be careful with this opportunity to influence the jury via the summary, since the defense could appeal on the grounds the judge went too far in trying to persuade the jury. But Zander (1989) believes that judges can normally make the summing up "appeal-proof" while at the same time indicating (for example, through body language) his or her true opinion of the facts. Since the judge in criminal cases knows of any criminal record the accused may have (a fact the jurors do not know) there is likely a temptation to exert improper influence on the jury. In the United States such a temptation is avoided by having judges sum up only on the law and not on the facts. Despite the temptation and opportunity, English judges seem not to abuse their power (Zander, 1989).

Although judges have a fairly involved role, it remains for the English jury to adjudicate questions of fact. On that basis, England is correctly placed on the continuum, since lay people have an active role as jurors. Additionally, as discussed later in this chapter, lay people in England are used as magistrates and in that role have an even more active role in the justice process.

While the English jury trial would look more familiar to Americans than would the process in countries outside the common legal tradition, it would still seem unusual. A first impression would likely be surprise at the placement of the key courtroom actors. In the English courtroom, the opposing barristers sit next to each other and wear identical wigs and robes. Instead of being at his barrister's side, the accused sits in the dock at the rear of the courtroom. The jury never sees the defendant talk directly with the defense counsel (Graham, 1983).

Before 1972, English jurors were selected from a group of persons occupying a dwelling with a certain taxable value. This procedure did not provide much of a cross section of the population and tended to exclude women and low-income people. Acts of Parliament in 1972 and 1974 required jury panels to be chosen at random from the voter registration list. Hughes (1984) notes that there are still some problems, because the people who end up on the list of possible jurors for a specific case are not randomly selected. He cites several reports of court officials purposefully selecting more men than women, few minority group members, and even avoiding persons with certain family names (Hughes, 1984).

The "randomness" of the eventual jury is further ensured by avoiding the American practice of *voir dire*. In that procedure, the American adversaries question potential jurors to identify possible biases for or against the defendant. The English jurors arrived at their position without having to suffer such questioning by prosecutor and defense counsel.

While the *voir dire* process has been absent in the English jury trial since 1973, the defense maintained a version of "peremptory challenges" until the Criminal Justice Act of 1988. Criminal Justice Acts in 1925, 1948, and 1977 progressively reduced the number of peremptory challenges an accused was allowed from a high of 25 to the three allowed by the 1977 Act. Opponents of these challenges without cause complained that defense counsel improperly manipulated the composition of the jury by excluding potential jurors simply because they may have appeared proprosecution (Emmins and Scanlan, 1988). Retentionists argued that a person on trial should have confidence in the jury and that may mean an occasional objection on grounds as obscure as the way a potential juror looks.

After considerable debate, the abolitionist position prevailed and the 1988 Act abolished peremptory challenges with the simple statement that: "The right to challenge jurors without cause in proceedings for the trial of a person on indictment is abolished" (Section 118.-(1) as quoted in Emmins and Scanlan, 1988, p. 302). Interestingly, the right to "stand a juror by," which is the prosecutorial parallel to peremptory challenges, was not similarly abolished. There are technical differences between the defense's challenge without cause and the prosecutor's standing a juror by, but the practical impact of each is to remove a potential juror from the jury without showing cause. The argument that prosecutors use the right of stand-by only sparingly and seldom improperly (supposedly unlike the defense use of peremptory challenges) conviced Parliament to leave the right of stand-by intact (Emmins and Scanlan, 1988). The impact that these decisions will have on jury trials in England is yet to be determined. Since challenges for cause (unlimited in number but requiring the judge to accept counsel's explanation as to why a person will not make a good juror) are still possible, it seems likely that they may be requested more often.

Following closing speeches by prosecuting and defense counsels (defense always having the last word), the judge summarizes the evidence for the jury and, as noted earlier, may even comment on the credibility of witnesses. For example, Emmins (1988) reports a 1917 case that was upheld on appeal although the judge had called the defendant's story a "remarkable" one and contradictory to his previous statements. Basically, the judge is allowed to express an opinion about the defense as long as questions of fact are left to the jurors. Such action by the judge would be distressing to American defense counsels, who are given considerably more leeway in their attempts to win over the jury with emotion and oratory when the facts of the case may not be enough.

Germany. The enthusiasm that American revolutionaries had for jury trials was repeated by revolutionaries in the French Revolution and the nineteenth-century bourgeois European revolutions. The rising middle classes saw participation in criminal proceedings as a weapon in the fight against aristocracy, the professional judiciary, and overpowering monarchs (Ehrmann, 1976). The idea caught on in France, and spread to most civil-law countries, but proved to be a disappointing experiment.

The Europeans tried to incorporate the common legal tradition of a jury into their civil legal tradition system without otherwise modifying their system. The inquisitorial trial format, the importance of the investigatory stage, and the active role of the judge made it difficult for jurors to follow the evidence presented under civil legal procedure. In their confusion regarding their role, European jurors often asked the judge for advice. The advice was provided in forms that would be totally inadmissible in an Anglo-American jury trial (Ehrmann, 1976).

Today, the classical jury system is primarily a common law tradition. There are still some civil law country exceptions like France, where nine lay jurors (initially chosen from voting rolls) hear cases involving serious criminal trials before the Courts of Assize. But even the French version seems unusual to those familiar with the English and American juries, since the French jurors join three professional judges upon whom the jurors are dependent for explanations of both law and facts (Terrill, 1992).

The French use of both professional judges and lay people signals, but does not illustrate, the more typical direction of courts following the civil law. That is, instead of using lay people who independently and bindingly determine guilt or innocence, countries of the civil legal tradition are more likely to use a "mixed bench," wherein two or three lay people work with professional judges to adjudicate criminal cases. This approach seems better suited to the inquisitorial process, since the lay people and professional judges are expected to work together toward sound verdicts and sentences. Germany provides a particularly good example of the mixed-bench approach.

The German people used the jury system in the 1840s and briefly in Bavaria after World War II. For the most part, however, recent German history has involved the use of citizens as lay judges rather than as jurors. Specifically, the community chooses fellow citizens to serve on the bench with professional judges. These lay judges have full powers of interrogation, deliberation, voting, and sentencing.

As described by Wolfe (1983) and Weigend (1983), lay judges serving in criminal courts are called *Schoffen*. They serve in courts of limited jurisdiction and the higher-level courts with general criminal jurisdiction. An accused criminal will be tried in a court with professional and lay judges, unless it is for a petty offense. In those cases the trial is before a single professional judge; the defendant has a right to a second hearing before a combined bench.

There are three types of mixed tribunals in the courts with general criminal jurisdiction. The *Kleine Strafkammer* (with one professional and two lay judges) is a court of second hearing. Its cases come on appeal from the lower-level court of limited jurisdiction, where trial was before a single professional judge. A *Grosse Strafkammer* (with three professional and two lay judges) has original jurisdiction for more serious crimes. The *Schwurgericht* (also with three professional and two lay judges) hears the most serious crimes such as murder and aggravated assault.

The lay judges are assigned to sessions over a period of four years. Usually they serve an average of one day per month. If their service ever exceeds 24 days in one year, they can ask to be stricken from the list of lay judges. Because a defendant lacks choice between a bench or jury trial, it is easier than it would be in the United States to figure out the number of lay judges needed over a four-year period. In addition, the date and length of a German trial is more predictable. This is because the judge in the inquisitorial system determines the evidence to introduce, the witnesses to summon, and the general nature of the proceedings. As a result, German trials tend not to be as long as those in America. There are other time-savers as well. Since there is no jury, the rules of evidence are uncomplicated and there is never a need to remove a jury while attorneys make motions and arguments the jurors should not hear. Finally, "hung juries" are eliminated, since decisions on guilt can be made with less than a unanimous vote.

As in the United States, the participation of the lay public is the result of efforts to ensure representation of the average citizen. Selection of the *Schoffen* begins with a list of nominees drawn up by the community council. That list goes to the local county court, where a committee chooses, by two-thirds vote, *Schoffen* for the next four-year period. *Schoffen* may repeat their service as long it has been at least eight years since they last served. The state courts determine via formula the number of citizens required and call the necessary principal lay judges (*Hauptschoffen*) and a number of alternates (*Hilfschoffen*).

Notably absent from this process is a procedure similar to American *voir dire*, where either prosecution or defense challenge lay judges. Although there is no German counterpart to the *voir dire* process, it is possible to challenge the persons on the nomination list and the chosen lay judges. Such challenges are rare, however. Since the lay judges are not screened for particular cases, the possibility exists that a certain *Schoffe* could be inappropriate for a specific hearing. The presiding judge has responsibility for the composition of the court, but a *Schoffe* must inform the judge if he or she does not feel completely free in considering the case.

We now have a better understanding of the actors involved in the judicial process of different countries of the world. It is time to move on to the second part of the actors/institutions strategy and consider the stage on which these actors play. We do this by considering the assorted ways in which that stage can be arranged.

IMPACT

Concurrent Consideration of Guilt and Sentence

We often hear complaints that the American system of justice cares more about the way a suspect is handled (procedural criminal law) than with determining if a crime was in fact committed (substantive criminal law) and the accused was the actual offender. Weigend (1983), in his review of sentencing in Germany, presents an interesting perspective on an alternative way to conduct a trial. As you read about this simultaneous consideration of guilt and sentence, consider whether the German system has any advantages over the United States' system.

Under the American system of justice, sentencing hearings typically follow trials—sometimes by as much as several weeks. One reason for this procedure is to provide time to gather information about the defendant for use by the judge in determining the appropriate sentence. The Probation Department, for example, will need time to complete a pre-sentence investigation. Because determination of guilt and determination of sentence are separate procedures, the rules governing trials in the United States differ greatly from those controlling sentencing hearings. The law of evidence, for example, limits the nature and sources of information to be considered during the guilt phase of a trial. However, there are few such limits at the time of sentencing. The restriction on evidence about the defendant's prior criminality, for example, vanishes after conviction. As a result, there are few evidentiary or other restraints placed on the court during the sentencing phase. German law, on the other hand, does not separate the guilt-finding and sentencing functions. The trial court finds the facts, decides upon the verdict, and determines the sentence, all in one proceeding. Since the two aspects are not separate activities, there is no need to distinguish, as in America, between evidence admissible relevant to guilt and other types of evidence. The German trial court must gather simultaneously the information necessary to reach a verdict and to arrive at an appropriate sentence.

The standards used in Germany to collect evidence about guilt and sentencing may seem rather loose to many Americans. For example, hearsay evidence may be introduced, and the closest thing to an exclusionary rule is the barring of evidence gathered in such extreme situations as deception, illegal threats, and hypnosis. Evidence about the defendant's character, including prior convictions, can be introduced even if the defendant refuses to testify! The Code of Criminal Procedure recommends introducing evidence of prior offenses only "as far as necessary." But in practice the defendant's criminal record is usually read into the court record just before the closing arguments of the trial (Weigend, 1983).

Germans do not view the unified trial (that is, simultaneous determination of guilt and sentence) and the unstructured manner of gathering evidence as at all unjust. Their confidence in the fairness of the procedures comes from two sources: the absence of an unsupervised lay fact-finder (an American jury), and a tradition of inquisitorial procedure. Together, these result in a different approach to truth-seeking. First, the German court system, unlike the American, does not have to control the deliberations of lay jurors through complicated rules of evidence. The lay judges discuss and decide cases with the professional judge and are under that judge's continuous guidance and advice. "The German system relies on the professional judge's ability to explain the relevance and the weight of the evidence to the lay judges to prevent them from confounding the issues. Professional judges, due to their training and experience, are presumed to know how properly to assess evidence without the guidance of formal rules" (Weigend, 1983, p. 62).

The long history of inquisitorial procedures has given the German people confidence in their unified trial. For over 300 years the court was responsible for investigating the case, pronouncing the verdict, and imposing the sentence. During the nineteenth century, investigatory duties were transferred to the *Staatsanwalt*, but not since the Middle Ages has there been a separate determination of guilt and sentence.

Consideration of this different way of conducting a trial highlights distinctions between the inquisitorial and adversarial systems. In America, truth emerges in an indirect fashion from a contest between the people involved. Therefore, as in any other "competition," procedural rules to guide and regulate the contest are of foremost importance. In Germany, the truth comes directly to the court through questioning of persons most likely to know it. That does not mean that the truth can be sought at any cost, but the German system does put less emphasis on formality and rules of evidence. "A German judge would think it absurd to limit testimony from a witness who is about to convey useful information on the defendant's need for rehabilitation because the witness was called to testify about the offense. The loss of 'truth' would be regarded as much more harmful than any disturbance in the intended sequence of taking proof" (Weigend, 1983, p. 63).

VARIATION IN COURT ORGANIZATION

A review of court organizations around the world reveals a strange combination of similarity and uniqueness. The similarity comes from the seemingly universal use of a basic organizational structure composed of lowest-level, mid-level, and highest-level courts. We find uniqueness when we look more closely and see many possible variations on that basic theme. Attempts to classify the various organizations into only a few categories would be fruitless. In some countries a dual system operates with courts at the state or province level coexisting with courts at the federal level. In other countries, the system is so centralized that a simple three-tiered structure handles criminal, civil, and administrative cases in the same courts with the same judges. Criminal, civil, and administrative disputes may be under the jurisdiction of three separate court hierarchies in other countries. Some countries include a system of religious courts with an autonomous system of secular courts.

Obviously, finding three or four common variables to use in categorizing the systems is an unwieldy assignment. The most reasonable approach for handling the profusion of organizations is simply to describe some variations to show the different ways in which a basic theme can be played. In the absence of a reasonable classification scheme, we will simply consider examples from some countries covered in other chapters and a few new nations to ensure a broad-based representation.

France

The courts of France are organized into two major court systems: the ordinary or regular courts, and the administrative courts (Abraham, 1986; Glendon *et al.*, 1985). The simplicity of the French system stops at this point, however, because each system has separate and distinct hierarchies that even the French authorities consider quite complex. Confusion regarding court jurisdiction required the creation of the eight-member *Tribunal des Conflits*. This tribunal, headed by the Minister of Justice, makes unappealable decisions regarding the system to which a case will be assigned.

Since the ordinary courts handle both civil and criminal cases, our discussion will be restricted to that area. Further, as seen in Figure 7-4, there are different lower- and intermediate-level courts for civil and criminal cases. We will follow the hierarchy for criminal cases. First, since there are some common features of trials at each court level, an overview of court procedures will be helpful before we tackle the inevitable differences.

In the most general sense, French defendants do not enter pleas in their courts. In principle, all cases go to trial and whether the accused agrees with or fights the charges is simply another piece of evidence for the court to consider.

Figure 7-4. Ordinary courts of France.

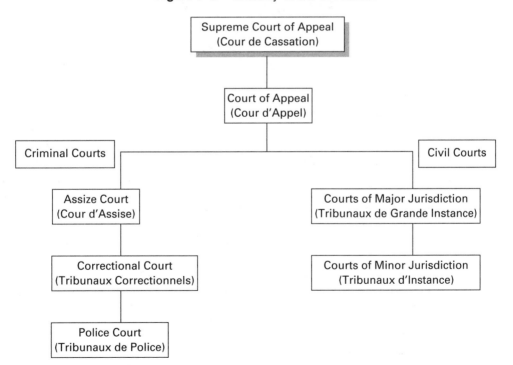

Obviously a full-fledged trial in all instances would be too burdensome for almost any country, but especially an industrialized nation like France. As a result, there are several procedures and practices (especially at the lower court levels) that are designed to save time and discourage unnecessary litigation (Frase, 1988). At the lowest tier (police court) trials can be completely avoided through trial substitutes. At the next higher tier (correctional court) there are several ways (see the discussion below) to condense the process.

During a trial, regardless of the court level, any prior convictions of the accused are admissible as relevant evidence. In fact, from an American perspective, French trial courts seem bound by few restrictions on the kind of evidence that can be introduced. This apparent permissiveness may be explained by three factors (see Frase, 1988):

1. Fact-finding in France is dominated by professional judges rather than lay jurors, so procedural safeguards need not be as stringent as in systems where lay persons have a significant role.

2. Since there are not separate guilt-finding and sentencing phases to French trials, all evidence relevant to sentencing must be admitted at the same time as that relevant to guilt.

3. For both guilt and sentence, the French believe it is better to judge the whole person (including past behavior and character) rather than just the current charges.

The trial itself is conducted by the presiding judge at each court level. The accused is given an opportunity to provide a statement to the court after which the attorneys can pose questions (usually through the judge) to the defendant. The accused, who is not put under oath, is not required to answer any of the questions; but they cannot prevent the court from drawing unfavorable conclusions from that silence (Frase, 1988). After interrogating the accused, the court calls in the witnesses, places them under oath, and asks them to provide information that they have regarding the offense and the accused. The presiding judge may interrupt the witnesses' narrative to clarify ambiguities and encourage relevance. The attorneys can also question the witnesses, but they do so under restricting guidelines. Following the last witness, the prosecution and the defense attorneys (always in that order) make their closing arguments. With that brief overview, we can look more closely at the different types of French courts.

Trial Level: Police Court. The basic tribunal for minor (for example, parking violations) criminal offenses is the Police Court (*Tribunaux de Police*). Over 450 of these courts are spread throughout the country and are presided over by justices of the peace, who are required to live in the tribunal's jurisdictional area. While several judges may be assigned to the court, a single judge makes the decision.

When trials occur in police court they are invariably brief and simple. More typically, adjudication occurs without an actual trial and even away from the actual courtroom (Frase, 1988). A substitute for the trial is used when the prosecutor sends information on the case to the court and the judge believes that the matter can be handled simply with a fine. The court notifies the prosecutor of the fine's amount, and the prosecutor (if he or she does not object to foregoing the trial) informs the accused. The accused has 30 days to either pay or object. If either prosecutor or accused objects to this procedure, the case is set for trial in police court.

Trial Level: Correctional Courts. Criminal or Correctional Courts (*Tribunaux Correctionnels*) are above the Police Courts in the hierarchy. These courts have jurisdiction over lesser criminal offenses and can assign penalties of up to five years' imprisonment. A panel of three or more (but always an uneven number) judges hears the cases and reaches a decision by majority vote.

The accused appearing before this court has the right to counsel (either retained or appointed), but counsel is not required unless the accused suffers from some disorder that could compromise the defense (Frase, 1988). Because witnesses are allowed, the trial process could be rather time-consuming. However, both defense and prosecution typically rely on pretrial statements and information from any judicial investigation, instead of bothering with witnesses.

The proceedings are further consolidated by having rather permissive rules of evidence. As Article 427 of the Code states it: "Except when the law provides otherwise, offenses may be established by any manner of proof, and the judge shall decide according to his thorough conviction" (French Code of Criminal Procedure, 1988). When the Correctional Court (to which Article 427 specifically applies) can use any manner of proof to find the accused guilty, the proceedings are not prolonged by many questions of law.

The court can announce its verdict and sentence immediately after closing arguments, later the same day, or even at a later date. Whenever announced, the judgment must include both the disposition and the reasons for that decision.

Trial Level: Assize Court. The Assize Court (*Cour d'Assise*) has original jurisdiction in serious felony cases, and can assign penalties ranging from fines to life imprisonment. An interesting aspect of the Assize Court is its use of a lot-chosen jury of nine citizens who sit with three judges to hear cases of original jurisdiction (Abraham, 1986). Jurors chosen by lot are not automatically impanelled, since the prosecution has four peremptory challenges and the defense has five (Frase, 1988). The three judges include a presiding judge who is always a member of the *Cour d'Appel* (the next higher-level court) and two other magistrates who may come from the *Cour d'Appel* or a local lower court.

During the trial, and with the presiding judge's approval, the jurors and other two judges can question the accused and the witnesses. Also, the prosecution and defense can submit questions for the presiding judge to ask.

After hearing the last witness and the closing statements, the presiding judge instructs the jurors on their duty to determine the accused's guilt or innocence. Rather than a standard of proof like "beyond a reasonable doubt," the Assize Court jurors and judges are told that for determination of guilt: "The law asks them only the single question, which encompasses the full measure of their duties: `Are you thoroughly convinced?'" (French Code of Criminal Procedure, 1988; Article 353). The law does not ask them how they became convinced but instead requires them to ask themselves what impression the evidence and the defense made on their reason. If those impressions "thoroughly convinced" the juror or judge that the accused is guilty, then they are obligated to vote accordingly.

Voting by judges and jurors is by secret ballot, with conviction requiring at least eight of the twelve members. A vote for conviction is followed by a vote on the penalty. From the penalties proposed by the members, the one imposed will be that receiving a majority vote.

Appellate Level: Courts of Appeal.   At the level of the Courts of Appeal (*Cour d'Appel*) both the previously separate civil and criminal systems come together. These courts not only take appeals from the civil and criminal courts below, but also from such special courts as the Commercial Court and Juvenile Court. Each of the 27 judicial districts (*Chambres*) has a Court of Appeal. Each Court has three to five judges (seven in the Parisian court) who hear the case and make decisions on both points of law and points of fact (Abraham, 1986; Rhyne, 1978). Decisions on points of fact are final, whereas those on points of law can be appealed to the *Cour de Cassation*.

Appellate Level: Supreme Court of Appeal.   The court of last resort in the French hierarchy is the Supreme Court of Appeal (*Cour de Cassation*). This highest-level court has five chambers (only one hearing criminal cases) with 15 judges in each. The court, which lacks original jurisdiction, is headed by a president and must have seven judges present to hear a case.

The term "cassation" derives from the French *casser*, which means "to break" or "to smash" (Abraham, 1986). The term is appropriate for this tribunal, since the court's power is limited to voiding the legal point of a case. When the *Cour de Cassation* decides that the lower court inappropriately applied a point of law, the case is returned for retrial to a different court at the same rank and of similar category. However, if the new court disagrees with the Court of Cassation's position (and the new court has the right to do that), the case goes once again before the *Cour de Cassation* (David, 1972). At this second appearance, the full Court hears the case. This opinion, now considered an authoritative interpretation on the point of law, must be followed by the lower tribunal.

England

The English court design includes a rigid structural segregation between the country's criminal and civil courts. In fact, a separate criminal jurisdiction has existed for over 700 years (Abraham, 1986). But the two separated judicial hierarchies typically make use of the same judges to hear the cases brought forward. For our purposes, only the criminal court hierarchy is of concern (see Figure 7-5).

Trial Level: Magistrates' Court. At the lowest level of the criminal court hierarchy are Magistrates' Courts. Unpaid lay magistrates (also called Justices of the Peace or JPs) preside over these highly visible tribunals that Edward II (1307–1327) established near the end of his reign. Over 27,500 JPs now work in more than 500 magistrates' courts throughout the country. In larger cities, Stipendiary Magistrates are more likely than JPs to be found at the helm of the magistrates' courts. London, for example, can have up to 60 of these officials. As the title suggests, the Stipendiary Magistrate receives a regular salary. Also, unlike the Justice of the Peace, the Stipendiary Magistrate must be a full-time professional lawyer (Abraham, 1986; Zander, 1989).

The magistrates' courts serve as the workhorse for the English criminal jurisdictions. About 80 to 90 percent of the criminal cases begin and end in this court (Abraham, 1986; Hughes, 1984). The trials at this lowest-level court are conducted without a jury and before two or three justices of the peace. When a Stipendiary Magistrate heads the court, he or she hears the case alone.

Defendants before the magistrates' court are typically unrepresented by counsel and find themselves subjected to proceedings that are conducted at a dazzling speed. The rapid action is surprising, since the JPs are lay magistrates both in the sense of being unpaid and in terms of not needing a legal background. It might be expected that such a person would run a rather deliberate and time-consuming courtroom. Luckily, since magistrates' courts have such a heavy workload, that situation does not occur. The court's efficiency may come in part from the presence of lawyers volunteering as magistrates (there is no prohibition against legally trained people becoming JPs), but is more clearly the result of the management by the court's clerk.

Figure 7-5. English court organization.

The magistrates' clerks often are, but are not required to be, legally trained. They are assigned to the magistrates' courts, where their duties range from helping unrepresented defendants present a case to advising the magistrates on points of law or procedure (Emmins, 1988). Although the JPs receive basic legal training, they are typically pleased to accept their clerk's advice on matters of law.

Trial Level: Crown Court. Immediately above the magistrates' court level is the Crown Court, which the Courts Act of 1971 established. This court, which has both appellate and original jurisdiction, is the first level at which an accused is entitled to a trial by jury. The Crown Court, authorized to sit anywhere in England and Wales, is typically presided over by a professional circuit judge. On occasion, the presiding official is a Recorder who has been selected from barristers with at least five years' experience and has agreed to be available on a part-time basis to hear cases.

The Crown Court hears cases involving serious offenses and carries out its duties with great pageantry and fanfare. All contested trials take place before a jury. In such cases, the jury alone decides whether the defendant is guilty or not guilty. The Criminal Justice Act of 1967 provides for nonunanimous verdicts (for both conviction and acquittal) when jurors vote 11 to 1 or 10 to 2. Despite this allowance for a majority verdict, a unanimous one is still preferred. To that end, the judge will accept a majority decision only after the jury has had two hours (or longer if the judge thinks the case requires it) to reach a unanimous verdict (Emmins, 1988).

Appellate Level: Court of Appeal. The Court of Appeal hears appeals from defendants at the two lower-level courts. The prosecution may not appeal a verdict of acquittal. The defendant's appeals, which can be either on points of law or on fact, come to the Criminal Division of the Court of Appeal. Sitting without a jury, this court hears appeals based on the transcripts of the evidence taken at the trial (Abraham, 1986). The court is typically composed of three judges from the Queen's Bench Division of the High Court of Justice (a court primarily responsible for civil cases) and possibly one or two members of the Lords Justices (from the legal section of the House of Lords).

Only a few convicted persons actually attempt the appeals process (Zander, 1989). The system discourages appeals, because it is assumed that defendants had their day in court and appeals are justified only in exceptional circumstances. Putting some teeth in this philosophy, the Court of Appeal has the power to add up to three months to the sentence of a convict whose application is deemed frivolous. Zander (1989) reports that the court used this authority in only 60 to 65 cases per year out of the over 6000 heard. Further, the time penalty ranged from 7 to 64 days and had a modal average of 28 days.

Appellate Level: House of Lords. The House of Lords provides the accused with a court of last resort, but access is very restricted. If the appeal is on

a point of law involving "general public importance," and the appeal is supported by the Court of Appeal, the Divisional Court of the Queen's Bench Division of
the High Court of Justice, or by the House of Lords itself, the case may proceed
to this final stage.

Nigeria

Nigeria is located on the West African coast near its namesake river the Niger. As
they did in several other parts of Africa, the British began colonizing important
areas of Nigeria in the late 1800s. The important port of Lagos was taken as a
British colony in 1861 and then incorporated with the rest of southern Nigeria in
1906 as the Colony and Protectorate of Southern Nigeria. Independence was won
in 1960, but in 1966 the fairly new Federal Republic of Nigeria was placed under
a federal military government that held all executive and legislative power. In
1989 the military lifted a ban on political activity, and efforts to reestablish a civilian government began.

Before 1861 Nigeria's courts consisted primarily of village officials hearing
cases involving the government or community, and family elders handling family disputes. The system seems to have worked fine for the Nigerians, but the
British found it ineffective for their purposes. British merchants had trouble
using the existing courts to enforce payment of debts by their local customers. To
assist in this process, the British government established a judicial system wherein a resident agent (British consulate) regulated trade between British merchants
and their local customers (Iwarimie-Jaja, 1988). With this foothold, an English
court system began to spread throughout Nigeria.

Today, Nigeria's court system is hierarchically organized with a federal
Supreme Court sitting atop a structure that includes other federal courts and systems of state courts, customary courts, and *Shari'a* courts (see Figure 7-6). The
federal and state courts comprise Nigeria's modern court system, but also suggest some of the problems that can arise when courts are imposed upon a people
rather than developing within the culture itself. Iwarimie-Jaja (1988) notes that
the modern court system has spread to all aspects of life in contemporary
Nigeria, but the Nigerians do their best to avoid the courts.

Efforts to bypass the formal courts may result from the delays typical in the
modern system. Oloruntimehin (1992) notes that such delays keep many people,
who are presumed to be innocent, in terrible, overcrowded, unhygienic prisons.
In addition, the people hesitate to serve as prosecution witnesses because of their
aversion to the court. Whether the Nigerians' efforts to shun the modern court
are a result of the delays in getting a complete judgment in a case, or because the
people have little confidence in modern courts, the typical Nigerian prefers more
common ways to settle a dispute.

The preference for traditional justice systems over modern ones provides
an opportunity, before we consider the modern system, to look at a level of
court operation that is often neglected. The customary and *Shari'a* courts, specif-

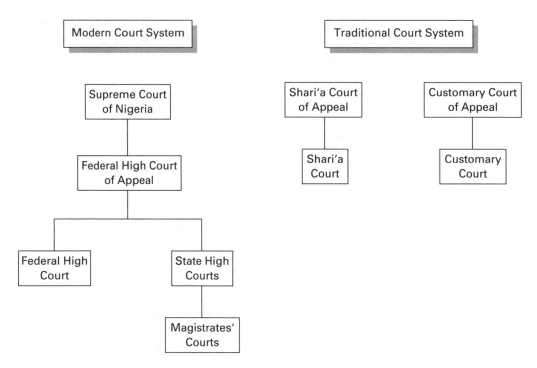

Figure 7-6. Nigeria's modern and traditional courts.

ically, provide Nigerians the chance to use more traditional ways to resolve conflict. These traditions can involve the intervention of chiefs and elders or can include consulting with oracles, juju (amulet), shrines, and the like. (Iwarimie-Jaja, 1988). Cases dealing with personal injury and those involving crimes can all be handled from a perspective of traditional customs and religious beliefs. The specific mechanisms used to deal with these situations are the customary and *Shari'a* courts.

Nigerian customary courts are especially popular in the southern states, where they dispose of cases by reference to established customs, beliefs, and values. In the northern states, with a primarily Islamic population, Islam encompasses all aspects of the people's life. *Shari'a* courts give these Nigerians a means to decide cases on the basis of Islamic law. Both types of courts play a very important role for the Nigerian people, and Iwarimie-Jaja (1988) believes that they continue to exist because the modern courts are considered ineffective for many issues, irrelevant for others, and lack credibility on issues where they could be relevant.

The Magistrates' Courts are the workhorse of Nigeria's modern court system. It is here that most felony cases are tried, so it is this court that provides the average Nigerians with most of their knowledge about how modern courts operate. Unfortunately the present operation is not one that impresses or instills trust.

Crucial facilities, from accommodations to secretarial assistance, are lacking, and magistrates may have to take notes and write judgments in longhand. Additionally, the high level of discretion given magistrates results in considerable sentence variation from judge to judge (Oloruntimehin, 1992). As a result, Nigerians are provided few reasons to find legitimacy in the formal court setting.

Upon considering Cole's (1990) description of cases before the Magistrates' Court, it becomes easy to understand why many Nigerians seem disillusioned with movement away from tradition. For example, Cole relates the following exchange between a defendant and court officials:

> Court Clerk: Are you guilty or not?
>
> Defendant: Let me explain, I . . .
>
> Clerk: Stop wasting our time; are you guilty or not?
>
> Defendant: (silent)
>
> Clerk: The . . . accused person, not guilty, my lord.
>
> Defendant: No . . . I was just . . .
>
> Clerk: Shut up!
>
> Magistrate (to defendant): You are either guilty or not guilty.
>
> Defendant: (silent)
>
> Clerk: Defendant pleads guilty, my lord.
>
> Magistrate: I find the accused person guilty as charged.
>
> Clerk: As your lordship pleases (Cole, 1990, p. 306).

The proceedings in this defendant's trial would not continue without a plea being duly recorded, but one wonders how freely (or accurately) that plea was entered. Cole (1990) also reports instances of defendants being ridiculed in court, called a liar, and subjected to police misbehavior. If Nigerians are told that such behavior symbolizes a modern court system, it is little wonder that many prefer the traditional justice systems over those imposed by a foreign power.

China

With the formation of a communist dictatorship in 1949, the People's Republic of China (PRC) began a path that would join her with those countries following a socialist legal tradition. The Chinese Communists sought to modernize the legal system by looking to the Soviet Union for ideas. While a Soviet pattern was followed in the ensuing decades, the PRC was not quick to put her new legal system in writing. Comprehensive codes of substantive and procedural law were generated only in 1979, but they (that is, the Criminal Law of the PRC and the

Criminal Procedure Law of the PRC) reflect the influence of the USSR as the birthplace of socialist legal systems. China's versions have much in common with such counterparts as the USSR's 1960 Code of Criminal Procedure and the Criminal Code (Berman, Cohen, and Russell, 1982). One explanation for the delay in producing codes of criminal law and of criminal procedure rests on the viability of China's preexisting informal judicial system. That system is important enough in the PRC that our discussion of China's courts must include the informal processes.

Victor Li (1978) titled his book comparing law in China and the United States *Law Without Lawyers*. That title nicely characterizes the informal justice structure that some consider the lowest tier of the PRC's criminal justice system (Rojek, 1985). A main benefit of the informal system is the absence of lawyers—an occupation that the Chinese have never awarded much prestige. Although lawyers are becoming more prominent in today's China, it remains to be seen if they will become more acceptable to the public. There is, after all, a well-entrenched dislike for attorneys dating at least to Imperial China, when one could receive a three-year sentence for helping litigants prepare documents (McCabe, 1989). An 1820 imperial edict referred to lawyers as "litigation tricksters" and "rascally fellows (who will) entrap people for the sake of profit" (Li, 1983, p. 103). Such attitudes are hard to turn around, so it should be of little surprise that in the mid-1980s there were still only 12,000 lawyers in this country of one billion people (McCabe, 1989).

In the absence of reliance on legally trained professionals to handle disputes, Chinese citizens turned to each other (see especially Clark, 1989, but also Li, 1978 and Rojek, 1985). The foundation for the resulting informal justice structure is the small groups (essentially, mediation committees) of 10 to 20 people to which everyone in China, except small children, belongs. The units are organized at places of work, neighborhoods, schools, and the like, so each person is likely to belong to several such groups (especially one at work and one in the neighborhood). The resulting peer pressure from these constant companions provides the glue holding together an informal sanctioning process.

In the tradition of socialist legality, China believes that education must play a primary role in the justice system. The mediation committees serve as a conduit for the norms and values that upper levels of government believe are appropriate. Government officials use the mass media to spread such information as legal norms, and then the mediation committees furnish a setting to discuss and enforce those norms. Importantly, the norms provided by the central government are simply general policies indicating priorities and directions (Li, 1978). Actual application of those general principles is, government officials believe, more appropriately done at the local level. One obvious result is that different local groups will interpret the general principles differently. Such variation is not considered bad. Central authorities issue a single general policy, and then local units adapt that policy to suit local needs and conditions (Li, 1978). Since there are few lawyers in China to serve as intermediaries between the cen-

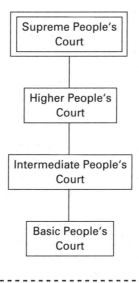

Figure 7-7.   China's court organization.

tral government and local units, "law" is neither clarified nor confused by professional decipherers.

Through a process of discussion and persuasion the small groups respond to everything from misbehavior and outright deviance to questions of health care and family planning. Justice is provided in this informal way without the use of lawyers or courtrooms. But the utopian ideal of pure communism has not been achieved in the PRC, or anywhere else, so there is also the need for a more formal justice system.

China's formal justice system uses four layers of courts organized along territorial lines (see Figure 7-7). The Supreme People's Court serves as the highest tribunal in the country. Below it in the hierarchy are the Higher People's Courts, Intermediate People's Courts, and the Basic People's Courts. Court officials at each level are elected and recalled by the people's congress relevant to each court level. The courts are essentially agencies of the central government and do not have judicial independence in a manner similar to courts in Western countries (McCabe, 1989). Central government supervision is not direct, but instead is routed through judicial committees appointed by the various people's congresses. The judicial committees review court activities, discuss major difficult cases, and concern themselves with other court-related issues.

The Supreme People's Court, which is made up of several subcourts or branches, handles cases impacting the entire country. It interprets statutes and provides explanations and advisory opinion to the lower courts. The Higher People's Courts are found at the province level and in some large cities (for example, Beijing and Shanghai). This is the court of first instance for criminal cases in which a sentence of death or life imprisonment is possible, and such special cases as those involving counterrevolutionaries or non-Chinese citizens. The Intermediate People's Courts handle cases similar to those at the Higher People's Court level, but they perform their duties at the district or multicounty level (Felkenes, 1989).

The workhorses in China's formal court system are the Basic People's Courts. Operating at the county level, these courts have original trial jurisdiction over ordinary criminal and civil cases. Discussion of their activities gives us a chance to look more closely at some of the players and procedures in Chinese courts.

Since the Chinese system is more inquisitorial than adversarial, the trial is essentially a continuation of the investigation. In fact, the Chinese Criminal Procedure code identifies four stages in a criminal trial: investigation, debate, appraisal by the judges, and the judgment (Leng, 1982). The investigation was begun by the procurator before the trial. Following the Soviet model of the 1950s, China developed a national procuracy responsible for investigating and prosecuting cases at each government level. While similar in concept to prosecution systems in countries following the civil legal tradition, the Soviet and Chinese models differed by setting the procurator (prosecutor) apart from the court. That is, whereas the French and German (for example) prosecutors are subordinate to the court, the Chinese procurator is attached to a separate agency with no accountability to the court. From this independent position, the procurators approve arrests by police, direct case investigations, initiate prosecution of cases, and then conduct that prosecution in court.

At the investigation stage of the trial the judges take control of the proceedings. Before 1983, the Chinese code provided for tribunals consisting of a professional judge and two lay assessors. Changes in 1983 still permit lay assessors but also allow decisions by a panel of three professional judges (McCabe, 1989). The three adjudicators hear the evidence and question the parties (the investigation stage); listen to assertions by the parties (the debate stage); share their opinions with each other (the appraisal stage); and then render, by majority vote, a decision in each case (the judgment stage).

The debate stage, or what Felkenes (1989) calls the contending part, does not have an counterpart in the United States, so it needs some elaboration. As described by Felkenes (1989), at this stage the procurator speaks first and reviews the facts, comments on the evidence, concludes that the defendant is guilty, and recommends a sentence. The defendant then speaks for herself and is followed by the defense advocate (who may or may not be an attorney), who may claim that the facts show the defendant to be innocent but is more likely to simply acknowledge guilt and claim mitigating factors that the court should consider. Following these comments, the defendant is given a final chance to address the court (usually with a plea for leniency) before the judges recess to discuss the case.

Saudi Arabia

The Saudi Arabian judiciary is actually dual in nature. A hierarchy of *Shari'a* courts exercises general and universal jurisdiction, while a separate system of specialized tribunals has jurisdiction over specific issues. Our concern, however, is with the *Shari'a* courts. Chapter 5 noted that while *Shari'a* law has aspects of both inquisitorial and adversarial procedures, the former seems to predominate. An example of this is the absence of any dividing line between the investigation and trial stages. However, the result is not a pure inquisitorial process, since there is no investigating magistrate supervising the investigation. Instead, interrogation of suspects is conducted by designated officials whose positions fall either above or below that of the judge. Specifically, the interrogation is conducted by the *wali al-mazalim* or the *al-mohtasib* (Sanad, 1991). The former's post is traditionally higher than that of judge, and its holder can actually rule on cases outside the judge's jurisdiction. The *al-mohtasib*, on the other hand, is inferior to the judge but has the duty of assuring correct enforcement of Islamic *Shari'a*.

The interrogation phase obviously has significant influence on the eventual trial outcome, so Islamic law provides several safeguards to the accused at this stage. One of these relates to Chapter 4's discussion of the basic features making up the Islamic legal tradition. As noted in that chapter, the oath plays an important role in the judicial process—so important that its impact is felt as early as the interrogation. Sanad (1991) explains that in cases of *hudud* and *qisas* crimes, the authority in charge of interrogation is not allowed to require an oath from the accused. The concern is that an accused who actually committed the crimes might be tempted to state untruths, thereby compounding his misconduct by false swearing. The duty of proving *hudud* and *qisas* acts falls on the accuser, and Muslim jurists are told that silence of the accused is not considered evidence.

When a case moves on to actual trial, the Saudi Arabian system provides a three-tiered court structure with trial and appellate level courts (see Figure 7-8). The king, who heads the Saudi judicial system, may act as a source of pardon and can serve as the final court of appeals to determine if the verdict conforms to the *Shari'a*. At a more practical level, the Ministry of Justice presides over the *Shari'a* judicial system.

The *Shari'a* courts are ones of general jurisdiction and as such may hear civil and criminal matters. In fact, a single judge might hear a criminal case immediately after hearing a civil one. In the hierarchical structure, ordinary courts are at the bottom and, progressing upward, we find the High Courts and then the Courts of Appeal.

The ordinary courts (*Musta'galah*), presided over by a single Islamic judge (*qadi*), are the lowest-level *Shari'a* court, and exist in nearly every town. They deal with minor domestic matters, misdemeanors, small claims, *ta'azir* crimes

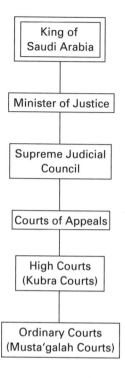

Figure 7-8. Saudi Arabia's courts.

allowing discretionary penalties, and with *hudud* offenses of intoxication and defamation.

The high courts of *Shari'a* law (*Kubra* courts) have exclusive jurisdiction over *hudud* and *qisas* crimes and general jurisdiction to hear cases on appeal from the lower courts. A single judge hears the case unless a sentence of death, stoning, or amputation is called for, since that requires a three-judge panel (Amin, 1985; Moore, 1987).

Before moving to the appellate level court, we should look briefly at some aspects of the trials in the ordinary and high courts. The right to defense, for example, is definite if not specific. *Shari'a* includes many admonishments favoring an opportunity for the accused to tell his or her side of the story. One caliph cautioned his judges: "If an adversary whose eye had been blinded by another comes to you, do not rule until the other party attends, for perhaps the latter had been blinded in both eyes" (quoted in Sanad, 1991, p. 81). The right to defend oneself against accusations by another does not necessarily require the services of a professional lawyer. In fact, although the accused has a right to retain an attorney, the presence of a defense attorney does not eliminate the defendant's right to defend himself or herself. The attorney is merely the defendant's agent.

Chapter 5 noted that Islamic procedural law is not easily identified, since the sacred law does not specify what means should be used to bring offenders to justice. Sanad (1991) elaborates this point in his discussion of the rules of evidence in criminal trials. He believes that the majority of Muslim scholars maintain that evidence in criminal cases must be restricted to testimony and confession. Judges cannot base a criminal conviction on other kinds of evidence (for example, prior personal knowledge). Within these two types of evidence are more specific rules for their use. Regarding testimony, for example, at least two witnesses (one legal school says a single witness) should provide consistent testimony before a conviction on *hudud* and *qisas* crimes can be rendered.

Just any witness is not acceptable when testimonial evidence is given. For the evidence to be condoned, the witness must, for example, be an adult male (one school accepts two females as equivalent to one male) known to have good memory, sound mind, and good character (Sanad, 1991). Even with these characteristics, a witness's testimony may not count if they are family members or have feelings of either animosity or partiality toward the accused or accuser.

Confessions, the second kind of evidence, are more complicated than simply saying that the accused admits to the charges. To be valid the confessor must be a mature, mentally sound person who gives, with free will, a confession that is neither doubtful or vague. A coerced confession is not only inadmissible, but requires the coercer to be punished (Sanad, 1991). Despite that seemingly straightforward statement, Moore (1987) notes that flogging and long detention of suspects refusing to confess does occur in Saudi Arabia. This point reminds us that not all cultures agree on what might constitute coercion.

Once a judgment is given, the appeals process may come into play. The Islamic systems view the appealing of decisions to higher courts somewhat differently than do other legal traditions. *Shari'a* is not case law, so the judge is not bound by decisions of other judges, whether in a higher court or not, or even by his decisions in the same court. More important than the absence of case law is the Islamic rejection of generalized legal reasoning.

When deciding a case, the *qadi* was traditionally limited to highly particularized legal rules instead of general legal concepts. His task was to decide which of the very specific and detailed rules most closely fit the particular facts before him (Shapiro, 1981). Since a major purpose of appeals courts is to provide uniform legal rules to make justice similar throughout the country, the Islamic approach has little use for the appellate process. In the absence of a need for uniformity of law, appellate courts become unnecessary.

Despite the lack of a historic need for an appeals process, many Islamic countries now provide some type of appeals court. Although this may show an interest in providing some uniformity to the law, it also reflects the influence of Western legal ideas and a need to accommodate activities in the growing secular areas of law.

Two Courts of Appeal operate in Saudi Arabia; each hears appeals from a specific part of the country. Each court divides into departments to hear cases of criminal law, personal status, or complaints not falling into either of those two categories. Three-judge panels hear appeals except, once again, sentences of death, stoning, or amputation. Panels of five judges hear those cases.

The Supreme Judicial Council is the highest judicial authority in the *Shari'a* system. The Council's 11 members do not actually serve as a court. It can review decision by the Courts of Appeal, but in cases of disagreement can only refer the case back to the court of appeals for reconsideration.

SUMMARY

This chapter looked at the judiciary from an institutions/actors perspective. Beginning with how the primary actors in a judicial system arrive at their positions, we considered various processes of legal training. Since every system has some type of prosecutor and defense attorney, we then looked at the different ways those positions are implemented. In addition to prosecution and defense, each legal system has actors responsible for adjudicating the case brought to court. An adjudication continuum illustrated the variation in adjudicator types by identifying systems that rely heavily on a professional judge (for example, Saudi Arabia), while others emphasize a role for lay people (for example England). Still other countries prefer a mixed bench wherein professional judges and lay people sit together to judge the facts of a case (for example, Germany).

Since these actors must have a setting for their performance, we next looked at different ways courts can be structured. Since the diversity here does not lend itself to easy classification into types, I simply took examples from several countries to show the variation. The formal structure was typically emphasized, although the informal justice system in some countries (for example, China and Nigeria) was pertinent to a more complete understanding of that country's judiciary.

SUGGESTED READINGS

Emmins, Christopher J. (1988). *A practical approach to criminal procedure* (4th ed.). London, England: Blackstone Press Limited.

French Code of Criminal Procedure (G. L. Kock and R. S. Frase, Trans.). (1988). Littleton, CO: Fred B. Rothman.

Li, Victor H. (1978). *Law without lawyers: A comparative view of law in China and the United States.* Boulder, CO: Westview.

Lippman, Matthew, McConville, Sean, and Yerushalmi, Mordechai. (1988). *Islamic criminal law and procedure.* New York: Praeger.

Rand, Robert. (1991). *Comrade lawyer: Inside Soviet justice in an era of reform.* Boulder, CO: Westview.

Simenon, Georges. (1961). *Maigret in court* (Robert Brain, Trans.). New York: Avon Books.

REFERENCES

Abraham, Henry J. (1986). *The judicial process: An introductory analysis of the courts of the United States, England, and France* (5th ed.). New York: Oxford University Press.

Amin, Sayed H. (1985). *Middle East legal systems.* Glasgow, UK: Royston Limited.

Barry, Donald D., and Barner-Barry, Carol. (1982). *Contemporary Soviet politics: An introduction.* Englewood Cliffs, NJ: Prentice Hall.

Berman, Harold J., Cohen, Susan, and Russell, Malcolm. (1982). A comparison of the Chinese and Soviet codes of criminal law and procedure. *Journal of Criminal Law and Criminology, 73,* 238–258.

British Information Services. (1984). *Justice and the law in Britain* (No. 9/84). London, England: Central Office of Information.

Brown, Douglas and Allen, Peter A. P. J. (1968). *An introduction to the law of Uganda.* London, England: Sweet and Maxwell.

Cappelletti, Mauro, and Gordley, James. (1978). Legal aid: Modern themes and variations. In J. H. Merryman and D. S. Clark, *Comparative law: Western European and Latin American legal systems.* Indianapolis: Bobbs-Merrill.

Cappelletti, Mauro. (1989). *The judicial process in comparative perspective.* Oxford: Clarendon Press.

Chua-Eoan, Howard G. (1988, August 15). Coming home to roost. *Time, 132,* 45.

Clark, John P. (1989). Conflict management outside the courtrooms of China. In R. J. Troyer, J. P. Clark, and D. G. Rojek (Eds.), *Social control in the People's Republic of China* (pp. 57–69). New York: Praeger.

Cole, Bankole A. (1990). Rough justice: Criminal proceedings in Nigerian magistrates' courts. *International Journal of the Sociology of Law, 18,* 299–316.

David, Rene. (1972). *French law: Its structure, sources, and methodology* (M. Kindred, Trans.). Baton Rouge, LA: Louisiana State University Press.

Ehrmann, Henry W. (1976). *Comparative legal cultures.* Englewood Cliffs, NJ: Prentice Hall.

Emmins, Christopher J. (1988). *A practical approach to criminal procedure* (4th ed.). London, England: Blackstone Press Limited.

Emmins, Christopher J. and Scanlan, Gary. (1988). *A guide to the Criminal Justice Act 1988.* London, England: Blackstone Press Limited.

Felkenes, George T. (1989). Courts, sentencing, and the death penalty in the PRC. In R. J. Troyer, J. P. Clark, and D. G. Rojek (Eds.), *Social control in the People's Republic of China* (pp. 141–158). New York: Praeger.

Feofanov, Iurii. (1990–1991). A return to origins: Reflections on power and law. *Soviet Law and Government, 29*(3), 15–52.

Frase, Richard S. (1988). Introduction. In G. L. Kock and R. S. Frase (Trans.), *The French code of criminal procedure* (rev. ed.). Littleton, CO: Fred B. Rothman.

French Code of Criminal Procedure (G. L. Kock and R. S. Frase, Trans.). (1988). Littleton, CO: Fred B. Rothman.

Gelatt, Timothy A. (1982). The People's Republic of China and the presumption of innocence. *Journal of Criminal Law and Criminology, 73,* 259–316.

Glendon, Mary Ann, Gordon, Michael W., and Osakwe, Christopher. (1985). *Comparative legal traditions.* St. Paul, MN: West Publishing.

Graham, Michael H. (1983). *Tightening the reins of justice in America.* Westport, CT: Greenwood.

Hitchner, Dell G., and Levine, Carol. (1981). *Comparative government and politics* (2nd ed.). New York: Harper and Row.

Hodge, Robert W., Siegal, P. M., and Rossi, Peter. (1964). Occupational prestige in the United States, 1925–1963. *American Journal of Sociology, 70,* 286–302.

Hughes, Graham. (1984). English criminal justice: Is it better than ours? *Arizona Law Review, 26,* 507–614.

Iwarimie-Jaja, Darlington. (1988). On the bench in Africa: The Nigerian court system. *C. J. International, 4*(6), 13–20.

Knight, C. Foster. (1978). Legal services projects for Latin America. In J. H. Merryman and D. S. Clark, *Comparative law: Western European and Latin American legal systems.* Indianapolis: Bobbs-Merrill.

Leng, Shao-Chuan. (1982). Criminal justice in post-Mao China: Some preliminary observations. *Journal of Criminal Law and Criminology, 73,* 204–237.

Li, Victor H. (1983). Introductory note on China and the role of law in China. In J. H. Barton, J. L. Gibbs, Jr., V. H. Li, and J. H. Merryman, *Law in radically different cultures* (pp. 102–136). St. Paul, MN: West Publishing.

Li, Victor H. (1978). *Law without lawyers: A comparative view of law in China and the United States.* Boulder, CO: Westview.

Lippman, Matthew, McConville, Sean, and Yerushalmi, Mordechai. (1988). *Islamic criminal law and procedure.* New York: Praeger.

Marcus, David L. (1991, June 23). Justice goes underground: Colombia's judges scared, faceless. *The Denver Post,* pp. 17A, 19A.

McCabe, Edward J. (1989). Structural elements of contemporary criminal justice in the People's Republic of China. In R. J. Troyer, J. P. Clark, and D. G. Rojek (Eds.), *Social control in the People's Republic of China* (pp. 115–129). New York: Praeger.

McDonald, William F. (1983). In defense of inequality: The legal profession and criminal defense. In W. F. McDonald (Ed.), *The defense counsel* (pp. 13–38). Beverly Hills, CA: Sage.

Merryman, John H., and Clark, David S. (1978). *Comparative law: Western European and Latin American legal systems.* Indianapolis: Bobbs-Merrill.

Merryman, John H. (1985). *The civil law tradition* (2nd ed.). Stanford, CA: Stanford University Press.

Moore, Richter H., Jr. (1987). Courts, law, justice, and criminal trials in Saudi Arabia. *International Journal of Comparative and Applied Criminal Justice, 11,* 61–67.

Moore, Lloyd. (1973). *The jury: Tool of kings, palladium of liberty.* Cincinnati, Ohio: W. H. Anderson.

Moore, Sally F. (1978). The legal system of the Incas and its judicial functions. In J. Merryman and D. Clark, *Comparative law: Western European and Latin American legal systems.* Indianapolis: Bobbs-Merrill.

Newman, Donald J. (1986). *Introduction to criminal justice* (3rd ed.). New York: Random House.

Oloruntimehin, Olufunmilayo. (1992). Crime and control in Nigeria. In H. Heiland, L. Shelley, and H. Katoh (Eds.), *Crime and control in comparative perspective* (pp. 163–188). New York: Walter de Gruyter.

Packer, Herbert. (1968). *The limits of criminal sanction.* Stanford, CA: Stanford University Press.

Parnell, Philip. (1978). Village or state? Competitive legal systems in a Mexican judicial district. In L. Nader and H. Todd, Jr. (Eds.), *The disputing process— law in ten societies.* New York: Columbia University Press.

Petrukhin, I. L. (1988–1989). Justice and legality. *Soviet Law and Government,* 27(3), 19–30.

Reid, Sue T. (1987). *Criminal justice: Procedures and issues.* St. Paul, MN: West.

Rhyne, Charles S. (Ed.). (1978). *Law and judicial systems of nations* (3rd ed.). Washington, DC: World Peace Through Law Center.

Robin, Gerald D., and Anson, Richard H. (1990). *Introduction to the criminal justice system* (4th ed.). New York: Harper and Row.

Rojek, Dean G. (1985). The criminal process in the People's Republic of China. *Justice Quarterly, 2,* 117–125.

Sanad, Nagaty. (1991). *The theory of crime and criminal responsibility in Islamic law: Shari'a.* Chicago: Office of International Criminal Justice.

Schmalleger, Frank. (1991). *Criminal justice today.* Englewood Cliffs: Prentice Hall.

Senna, Joseph J., and Siegel, Larry J. (1987). *Introduction to criminal justice* (4th ed.). St. Paul, MN: West.

Shapiro, Martin. (1981). *Courts: A comparative and political analysis.* Chicago: University of Chicago Press.

Solaim, Soliman A. (1971). Saudi Arabia's judicial system. *The Middle East Journal, 25,* 403–407.

Spencer, J.R. (Ed.). (1989). *Jackson's machinery of justice.* Cambridge, England: Cambridge University Press.

Steinberg, Allen. (1984). From private prosecutor to plea bargaining: Criminal prosecution, the district attorney, and American legal history. *Crime and Delinquency, 30,* 568–592.

Stuckey, Gilbert. (1986). *Procedures in the justice system* (3rd ed.). Columbus, OH: Charles E. Merrill.

Terebilov, Vladimir. (1973). *The Soviet court* (M. Saifulin, Trans.). Moscow: Progress Publishers.

Terrill, Richard J. (1984). *World criminal justice systems: A survey*. Cincinnati, OH: Anderson.

Turow, Scott. (1987). *Presumed innocent*. New York: Farrar Straus Giroux.

United Nations. (1990). *Implementation of the basic principles on the independence of the judiciary* (A/CONF.144/19). Vienna, Austria: UN Crime Prevention and Criminal Justice Branch.

United Nations. (1988). *Basic principles on the independence of the judiciary*. New York: UN Department of Public Information.

Weigend, Thomas. (1983). Sentencing in West Germany. *Maryland Law Review, 42*, 37–89.

Wolfe, Nancy T. (1983). Participation in courts: American jurors and German lay judges. In I. L. Barak-Glantz and E. H. Johnson (Eds.), *Comparative criminology* (pp. 121–134). Beverly Hills: Sage.

Zander, Michael. (1989). *A matter of justice*. Oxford: Oxford University Press.

Chapter 8

An International Perspective on Corrections

KEY TOPICS

- Problems in determining imprisonment rates
- Corrections in Australia
- Racially disproportionate incarceration rates
- Corrections in Poland
- Corrections in Japan
- Types of community corrections

KEY TERMS

assignment	severe rigor
rehabilitation	lenient rigor
deterrence	transportation
diversion	ordinary rigor
retribution	volunteer probation officers
incapacitation	

COUNTRIES REFERENCED

Australia	Poland
Japan	United States

It is always dangerous to make statements implying universal agreement. We do not, however, go too far out on a limb by saying that all societies want social order. It would be more dangerous to say that they all agree on what social order means. This chapter avoids the dangerous position and concentrates instead on how societies view social order's form and attainment.

Social order's form may vary from one country's desire to have extreme conformity and consistency among its people, to another country's view of order as allowing as much individuality and diversity as reasonable. It is neither possible nor appropriate to identify one view as correct. It is, however, necessary to see the difference if we want to understand how each country tries to achieve social order.

Some countries develop strategies to achieve social control by emphasizing conformity to a cultural standard for behavior. Japan is offered in this chapter as an example of this type of response. Other countries, like Poland in this chapter, seek social control by appealing to each person's sense of civic obligation. Still others (the United States may be an example) believe that social control is best gotten by penalizing misbehavior to encourage the scoundrel, and others considering disobedience, to behave themselves.

With such different social control strategies it is not surprising that countries often develop distinct techniques to control misbehaving citizens. The effect of capital punishment is always the death of the offender, but how that penalty is achieved varies considerably. Consider, for example, the French execution of Damiens.

In 1757, as punishment for assaulting King Louis XV, Robert François Damiens was condemned to make the *amende honorable* before the main door of the Church of Paris. Foucault (1977) quotes the account left by an observer of the punishment as follows:

> The sulphur was lit, but the flame was so poor that only the top skin of the hand was burnt, and that only slightly. Then the executioner, his sleeves rolled up, took the steel pincers, . . . especially made for the occasion, . . . and pulled first at the calf of the right leg, then at the thigh, and from there at the two fleshy parts of the right arm; then at the breasts. Though a strong, sturdy fellow, this executioner found it so difficult to tear away the pieces of flesh that he set about the same spot two or three times, twisting the pincers as he did so, and what he took away formed at each part a wound about the size of a six-pound crown piece. After these tearings . . . the same executioner dipped an iron spoon in the pot containing (molten lead, boiling oil, burning resin, and sulphur melted together, and he liberally poured it) over each wound. Then the ropes that were harnessed to the horses were attached with cords to the patient's body; the horses were then harnessed and placed alongside the arms and legs, one at each limb. . . . The horses tugged hard, each pulling straight on a limb, each horse held by an executioner (Foucault, 1977, pp. 3–4).

Today, France does not even have the death penalty. In fact, just 80 years after Damiens's execution, France was looking at a very different form of punishment. In 1837, also in Paris, Leon Faucher drew up rules for a facility housing young prisoners. The rules included a nine-hour workday; two hours per day devoted to instruction in reading, writing, drawing, and arithmetic; several recreation periods; and two full meals with several rationings of bread throughout the day (Foucault, 1977, p. 6). Within an 80-year span in the same city, punishment included gruesome torture and enlightened reformation.

Most countries experience a similar variation in preferred forms of punishment. Within 35 years of Damiens's execution in France, Americans had established Philadelphia's Walnut Street Jail as the country's first true correctional institution. For 15 years before Faucher designed his Paris facility for young offenders, Americans had debated the benefits of two correctional philosophies. Both the Pennsylvania and Auburn systems provided imprisonment as a humane alternative to corporal and capital punishment.

Whether ironic, or just further indication of the variability in punishment, we must note that while France abandoned the death penalty as a punishment, the United States has made increased use of it since 1977. However, compare a newspaper reporter's account of a more recent American execution to the description of Damiens's:

> I folded my arms across my chest and said to myself I was ready. . . . At the instant White pulled the switch and sent 1,900 volts burning into Evans, who clenched his fists and arched his body rigidly into the restraining straps, the folly of being prepared was gone.
>
> A moment later, as spark and flame crackled around Evans' head and shaven, razor-nicked left leg, white smoke seeped from beneath the veil and curled from his head and leg. Midway through the surge of electricity his body quivered, then fell back into the chair as the current ended. . . . We thought that was it—bad enough, but expected and bearable. . . . (The nod from the prison doctor meant a heartbeat had been found when Evans was checked, so the electric jolt was repeated). . . . Evans' chest rose against the straps the first time. It rose evenly once, twice, maybe again. A stream of saliva ran down the front of the white prison smock . . . . I had been told a body might continue to spasm after taking a massive electric charge. I strained to figure out if this was convulsive movement in Evans' strap-crossed chest, and concluded absolutely not. This was too measured. Just slow deep breathing . . . . I said (to another witness) "He survived" (Harris, May 1, 1983, Reprinted with the permission of United Press International, Inc.).

On the third try, the state of Alabama successfully executed convicted murderer John Louis Evans III.

These examples of variation in capital punishment show the vast array of techniques countries use to control misbehavior and achieve social order. This chapter describes some of those differences. The problem is deciding which one or two of the various punishment forms best shows country differences. Similarly, countries vary by the justifications they emphasize for administering punishment and the goals they perceive punishment serving. While they are not mutually exclusive, reasons for punishing offenders have included protection of society, the seeking of revenge, securing an orderly society, and changing the offender. Before identifying the primary thrust of this chapter, we must familiarize ourselves with these different perspectives.

VARIABILITY IN JUSTIFICATION

The classic justifications and goals for punishment are retribution, deterrence, rehabilitation, and incapacitation. Retribution, possibly the oldest of these, is considered by some to reflect a basic human tendency toward vengeance. The argument is that punishment is a necessary and natural response to persons violating social norms. Its most explicit depiction is in the "an eye for an eye, a tooth for a tooth" dictum of biblical times. A goal of retribution is to retaliate for the wrong done in a manner that allows the punishment to reflect the offense (Newman, 1978). For example, the germanic tribes in northern Europe of the middle ages were very protective of their forests. In fact, the penalty for illegal cutting down trees was execution. In an effort to have the "punishment fit the crime," the offender was executed in a manner that would reflect the crime itself. So persons taking the life of a tree by cutting off its top were buried in the ground from the shoulders down. A plow was then taken across the offender's head and his life was lost by topping just as the tree had been topped.

The deterrence fork has two prongs: specific and general deterrence. When the offender is punished for the expressed purpose of deterring his or her future wickedness, specific deterrence is operating. When an offender is punished in the belief that the penalty will prevent other people from misbehaving, the punishment serves a general deterrence function.

Rehabilitation was recognized as a legitimate goal of punishment as early as the eighteenth century, when the Quakers encouraged the reforming of offenders into productive members of society. During its peaks and valleys of acceptance over the last several centuries, rehabilitation has taken a variety of forms. In one version, it follows a medical model wherein the offender (or patient) is classified (or diagnosed) according to his or her problems (or illness). The classification committee (or physicians and pathologists) composed of psychologists, social workers, clergy, health workers, educators, and the like discuss the offender's needs and develop a treatment plan. Successful completion of the treatment plan should make the offender "better" and able to operate as a law-abiding member of society.

Incapacitation as a punishment goal refers, in its most general sense, to restricting an offender's freedom of movement. Presumably, society is protected when the offender's ability to move about in society is restricted. Historically, incapacitation was achieved almost solely through incarceration in jails and prisons. Other techniques included corporal punishments (for example, the stocks in colonial America) and the pre-1991 Soviet Union's use of a passport system to control movement of Soviet citizens throughout the country (Shelley, 1990). Incapacitation of the future is likely to rely on technology to restrict the offender's movement. The increased popularity of electronic monitoring devices (Schmidt, 1989) probably foretells twenty-first century gadgets that allow constant monitoring of a person's movement and immediate analysis of blood and urine samples.

Retribution, deterrence, rehabilitation, and incapacitation are not always mutually exclusive, but it is often difficult for several of them to operate together. While a penal system may be effectively based on a combination of retribution and deterrence, it may be more difficult to merge, for example, rehabilitation with retribution. Also, the location where the punishment is administered may affect the ability to realize each goal. General deterrence may be possible only in an open society where the public is kept informed of the application of punishments. Restricting movement may be more easily accomplished in a prison than in an open community. Rehabilitation, which may be achieved in a community setting, may be out of reach in the confines of a secure prison. All these suggest a variety of ways for a country to implement one or more of the justifications for punishment.

The punishment systems in three countries are described in this chapter. All four justifications for punishment are found in each country, but they vary in terms of the emphasis that one or two are given over the others, and in terms of the location deemed appropriate for achieving punishment's goals. Our point of departure for discussing each country is the prison system. With this focus, we can find examples of countries that make minimal use of imprisonment, others that rely heavily on their prisons, and still others that seem to portray a middle point.

Discussion of legal systems and aspects of criminal law fell nicely into four legal families (Chapters 4 and 5). Describing differences among police forces was aided by reference to the number of forces and their type of command (Chapter 6). The variation in forms, justifications, and goals of punishment among countries makes it difficult to categorize nations around a specific topic. Still, remember Ehrmann's dictum that "all comparison proceeds from classification" (1976, p. 12); it is important to highlight one form. Despite some problems noted below, our basis for categorization of countries is their use of imprisonment as punishment.

IMPRISONMENT AS PUNISHMENT

Imprisonment as punishment, rather than as a way to detain someone for trial or to hold them for other punishment, has become popular around the world. It is certainly not the only form social control has taken in the twentieth century, but it is common enough to warrant close attention. Imprisonment as punishment occurs in most societies and provides one way to categorize countries.

Determining Imprisonment Rates

A popular way to compare countries on their use of imprisonment is to measure their respective incarceration rates as shown in Figure 8-1, which presents the basic formula to determine a country's rate of imprisonment (Ir).

Using this formula, we find that the imprisonment rate for the United States in 1988 was 295 [(627,402/246,100,000) × 100,000 = 295]. It is easy, then, to figure an imprisonment rate for any country, providing that their total population and the number of persons in their prisons on a particular date are known. Unfortunately, the simplicity is deceiving!

There are definitional and methodological problems when we figure imprisonment rates in this manner. Definition problems come from differences about what counts as a prison and who counts as a prisoner. For example, Canadian prisons include federal penitentiaries, provincial prisons, some jails, and community correctional centers (Rahim, 1986). In the United States, state and federal prisons are counted, but inmates in jails and community corrections facilities are typically excluded. The 295 rate arrived at by using the formula in Figure 8-1 excludes the American jail population. When the jail population is included (as it is in Figure 8-2), the incarceration rate becomes 394. As a result, comparing Canadian and American imprisonment rates means that Canada will have a more broadly defined numerator in the equation than will America with her usually provided "prison only" figure. Similarly, are juvenile facilities prisons or are prisons places holding only adults? Should countries that send mentally ill criminals to hospitals include those hospitals among their prisons?

Besides problems of deciding what constitutes a prison, there is not universal agreement about who are prisoners. In some countries, pre-trial detainees spend months or years awaiting trial. In other countries, the average stay in an unconvicted status is comparatively short and may not count as prisoner status. Also, some persons may be in prison for civil rather than criminal offenses. Is it appropriate to count persons serving time for nonpayment of fines with others who are truly criminal offenders? Since neither the establishment (that is, the prison) nor the unit (that is, the prisoner) of count is universally defined, any comparison of countries concerning prison population is problematic (Rahim, 1986).

There are also methodological problems with incarceration rates as defined above. The first comes from having a numerator and denominator that do not correspond. For example, the numerator comes from the adult population (where juveniles are not counted as prisoners) of a country, but the denominator includes persons of all ages living in that country. The result, therefore, reflects a

Figure 8-1.   Determining imprisonment rates (Ir).

$$Ir = \frac{\text{The number of persons in prison}}{\text{The total population of the country}} \times 100,000$$

downward bias, since a country with a high proportion of juveniles shows a low incarceration rate even with a high prison population. For example, the Philippines had a 1988 estimated general population of 63,200,000 (*Information Please Almanac*, 1988) and a 1988 prison population of 26,884 (Australian Institute of Criminology, 1988), yielding an incarceration rate of 43 per 100,000 general population. However, since 39 percent of the Filipino population is under age 15 (*World Almanac*, 1989), the incarceration rate per 100,000 adults is 70. Countries wishing to use incarceration rates as a political or public relations tool can conveniently manipulate both numerator and denominator when presenting information on their use of imprisonment.

Other problems come from using the number of persons in prison on a specific date rather than the number of admissions to prison over a certain time. Lynch (1988) calls the former figure "stock design" and notes that the likelihood of an offender's being in prison on a given day is a function of sentence length. Therefore, stock designs overrepresent more serious offenders with longer sentences. Lynch prefers the "flow design," since it takes the number of admissions over time and thereby separates the tendency to incarcerate from the length of sentence served. However, the "flow design" risks double-counting inmates who may be released and then returned during the time period for technical reasons rather than having committed a new crime.

Both Rahim (1986) and Lynch (1988) offer alternative formulas to find a country's use of imprisonment. Rahim thinks the rate should be the number of persons sentenced to prison divided by the number of persons convicted during the same year. Lynch prefers dividing the number of persons admitted to prison by the number of arrests made during the same year. Each of these suggestions has its own problems, but the authors provide a service by increasing our appreciation of the difficulty in doing comparative research.

Despite the appropriate criticism offered by Rahim (1986) and Lynch (1988) we will still use the traditional method to find incarceration rates. The primary reason for this is the absence of necessary numbers to compute rates as suggested by critics of the traditional method. Further, incarceration rates are difficult to come by, and those few sources providing them use the old "total prisoners divided by total population" method. Therefore, we must heed the warnings of the critics and proceed cautiously. Despite its problems, the traditional incarceration rate is best for comparing the largest number of countries. As such, it becomes the means for our categorization of countries (see Figure 8-2).

Using Prison

Figure 8-2 lists the incarceration rates for selected countries around the world, and Figure 8-3 orders those countries from high to low rates of imprisonment. Note that there does not appear to be any pattern based on which legal tradition the country belongs to. Statistics are mostly unavailable for countries in the socialist and Islamic families, but civil and common law countries are well dis-

Country	1988 Prison Population		1988 General Population*	1988 Ir		Data Source
Australia	11,519		16,500,000	70		1
Austria	5,862		7,600,000	77		5
Botswana	2,424	(1986)	1,300,000	222	(1986)	7
Denmark	3,469		5,100,000	68		5
England	48,595		50,000,000	97		5
France	46,423		55,900,000	81		5
Ireland	1,953		3,500,000	55		5
Italy	34,675		57,300,000	60		5
Japan	54,558		122,700,000	44		2
Korea, South	44,696		42,600,000	105		1
Netherlands	5,827		14,700,000	40		5
New Zealand	3,197		3,300,000	97		1
Nigeria	60,000		111,900,000	54		3
Norway	2,041		4,200,000	48		5
Philippines	26,884		63,200,000	43		1
Poland	67,824		38,000,000	180		8
South Africa	119,682		35,978,284	333		6
Spain	29,344		39,000,000	76		5
Sudan	9,336	(1986)	24,000,000	42	(1986)	7
Sweden	4,716		8,400,000	56		5
Tanzania	19,164	(1986)	24,300,000	86	(1986)	7
Thailand	76,903		54,700,000	141		1
Turkey	51,810		52,900,000	96		5
United States	969,295		246,100,000	394		4
			Average =	106.9		

*General population statistics for 1988 are from *Information Please Almanac* 1988.

1. Number of adults in prison in 1988 from: Australian Institute of Criminology (1988). *Corrections in Asia and the Pacific*. Canberra: Author.

2. Number of adults in prison in 1988 from: Correction Bureau (1990). *Correctional Institutions in Japan*. Tokyo: Ministry of Justice.

3. Number of adults in prison from: D. Iwarimie-Jaja (1989). "Corrections: A System in Need of Reform." *C. J. International*, 5,5, pp 13–19.

4. Number of adults in jail in 1988 from: Bureau of Justice Statistics (June, 1990). *Jail Inmates in 1989*. Washington, D.C.: Department of Justice. Number of adults in prison in 1988 from: Bureau of Justice Statistics (April, 1989). *Prisoners in 1988*. Washington, D.C.: Department of Justice.

5. Number of adults in prison in 1988 from: Council of Europe (December, 1988). *Prison Information Bulletin* (Report #12). Strasbourg, France: Author.

6. General population statistics and number of adults in prison in 1988 from: M. Mauer (1991). *Americans Behind Bars: A Comparison of International Rates of Incarceration*. Washington, D.C.: The Sentencing Project.

7. Number of adults in prison in 1986 and 1986 imprisonment rate from: A. Rzeplinski (1988). *Prison Labour in African Countries*. (Report UNSDRI 407 231 369). Rome, Italy: United Nations Social Defense Research Institute.

8. Number of adults in prison in 1988 from: T. Bulenda, Z. Holda, and A. Rzeplinski (1990). "Human Rights in Polish Law and Practice: Arrest and Preliminary Detention." Unpublished manuscript.

Figure 8-2.   1988 prison populations and imprisonment rates (Ir).

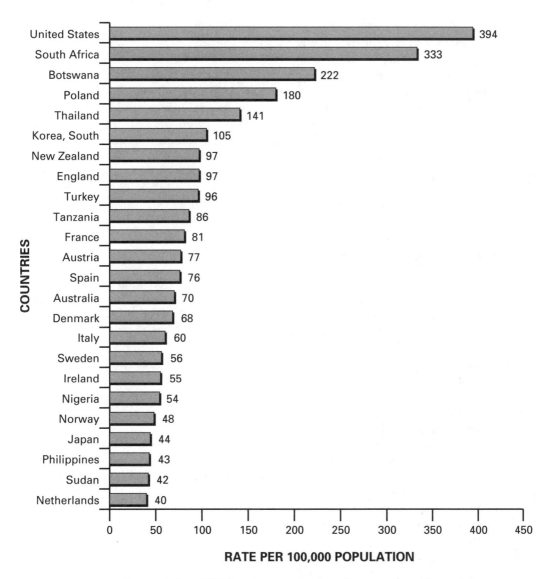

Figure 8-3. 1988 imprisonment rates. *Sources:* See Figure 8-2.

persed throughout the list. It would be difficult to argue that use of imprisonment is a function of the legal family of a country.

Given the definitional and methodological problems noted above, it seems unwise to try to make distinctions between countries with somewhat similar rates. It probably is not safe, for example, to claim that Australia uses imprisonment less than does France and more than Italy. The rates in the three countries are just too close together to discuss reasons for differences that may not exist—

or may exist in a different order if measured otherwise. On the other hand, it seems unlikely that definitional and methodological problems account for Poland's standing in comparison with Japan's. A difference of nearly 100 suggests, at the very least, that one country imprisons its citizens more than does the other country. Similarly, a country like Australia, whose rate falls midway between the two, probably really does provide a middle example.

This chapter describes the prison system of Poland, Australia, and Japan, but prison is only one side of the coin. If Japan is not incarcerating its offenders, what happens to them? Similarly, Poland cannot keep everyone locked up, so what happens to those released from prison or who are never sent there? Answering these questions requires a look at the alternatives to prison each country uses. We begin in the middle, with Australia.

CORRECTIONS IN AUSTRALIA

To paraphrase a Down Under saying, "Australia is such a different place because God made it last and he was tired of doing the same old thing." Australia's penal strategy is not the platypus of the world's corrections systems, but it does have interestingly unique aspects. The unusual features are balanced by more common characteristics that make Australia similar to her common law cousin, the United States. To emphasize both the unique and the ordinary, this discussion of Australian corrections highlights historical and contemporary issues. In the process, the stage is set for discussing Poland, a country where corrections seems to imply prison, and Japan, a country where corrections apparently suggests more than just imprisonment.

Some of Australia's unique correctional characteristics include: (1) its history as a penal colony, (2) its racially disproportionate incarceration rate, (3) the wide variation in the incarceration rates among its states, and (4) its creativity in using alternatives to prison. Interestingly, those same characteristics show the similarity between Australia and the United States. We begin with the shared heritage of serving as a receiving port for England's banished criminals.

A History of Transportation

Australia provides a unique example in studying imprisonment, because it is the only continent settled as a penal colony. For that reason, a discussion of corrections in Australia is a discussion of that nation's most fundamental historical roots (Chappell, 1988). One of the reasons that England turned to Australia to send some of her criminals was the growing resentment in the American colonies to this British practice. This shared correctional heritage between the United States and Australia warrants brief attention.

During medieval times a popular way to relieve a village of the burden of misbehaving citizens was to force them to leave the village. The problems those people might cause at the next village was of little concern to the first village. This banishment was desirable from the perspective of the sending village because: (1) there was no need to worry about the future behavior of the offender; (2) the procedure was cheap compared to other means of social control; and (3) the exiling village could ignore the opinions of the receiving village. Eventually this practice of banishment led to the punishment response known as *transportation*.

In setting up a system of transportation, the British Parliament passed an act in 1598 which provided that persons be sent to "such parts beyond the seas as shall at any time hereafter" be assigned (quoted in Shaw, 1966, p. 23). Like banishment, transportation allowed a society to get rid of troublemakers, but it had the added advantage of providing people to carry out dangerous and unpleasant work. It was this new advantage that provided a link between transportation and colonization. A motherland could get rid of her misfits and at the same time provide her colonization efforts with a labor pool. By the early seventeenth century, the American colonies were receiving a rather steady stream of English convicts, who would provide labor for the fledgling settlements; just as later convicts would assist with the eighteenth-century development of Australia. While recognizing the human misery associated with transportation, twentieth-century authors often make the argument that transportation was a penal practice that worked by helping the economic development of colonies (Chappell, 1988; Shaw, 1966).

In 1615 the English Privy Council ordered persons found guilty of robbery or any felony other than willful murder, rape, witchcraft, or burglary to be transported to either the East Indies or the American plantations as laborers. Despite these early beginnings, it was not until the eighteenth century that transportation became a major part of English law. The Transportation Act of 1718 declared its purpose as being to deter criminals and to supply the colonies with labor. Transportation was possible as a substitute for execution, an act of royal mercy, a reprieve or commutation of punishment, or as a form of punishment itself.

The possibility that a convict could choose transportation over execution was not a choice required only on an infrequent basis. In 1797, for example, crimes punishable by death included: counterfeiting gold and silver coins, murder, arson, rape, sodomy, piracy, burglary, highway robbery, picking pockets, shoplifting, stealing horses, cutting down trees in a garden, sending threatening letters, and a host of other offenses. Crimes for which transportation was itself a possible punishment included: grand larceny, receiving or buying stolen goods, stealing letters, theft under one shilling, assault with intent to rob, stealing fish from a pond or river, stealing children with their apparel, bigamy, and others.

The actual process of transporting the convicts was contracted out to individuals. The contractor was given the rights to the convict's labor in the colonies, and he could sell those services to the planters. If the convict had enough of his own money, he could buy off his servitude and basically turn his punishment into mere banishment. All the American colonies except those in

New England received some convicts at some time; most went to Maryland and Virginia, where agriculture was more labor intensive. While many settlers benefited from the extra labor, not all colonists were pleased with the policy of transportation. Maryland tried to banish it in 1676, and by 1697 several other colonies had expressed their displeasure. For a time, England sent most of her transportees to the West Indies, but in 1718 the Transportation Act revived mainland trade, and the convicts were sent to America in even greater numbers. In 1722 Pennsylvania prohibited the receiving of transported convicts and a year later, Virginia did the same (Shaw, 1966). In fact, Virginia even went one more step and in 1740, when England asked the colonies for troops for the Spanish war, Virginia enlisted ex-cons!

While there are no official figures, historians estimate that some 50,000 convicts were transported to the American colonies prior to 1775. In 1775, the rising resentment of the colonies toward England led, not surprisingly, to refusing to serve any longer as the dumping ground for English convicts. Undaunted and patient, the English found a replacement colony in a new continent Captain James Cook had claimed for Great Britain a mere five years earlier.

In January 1788, after eight months at sea, 11 British ships landed in Sydney Cove. Of the more than 1000 people going ashore, nearly 750 were prisoners being transported from England as punishment for a variety of offenses. From that date and until 1840, English prisoners were continually transported to New South Wales, and until 1867, to other parts of Australia (O'Brien and Ward, 1970). They represented both men and women who had been convicted of a wide range of offenses. The typical transportee was sentenced for theft, had been a propertyless laborer, and averaged 26 years of age (Hughes, 1987). In all, about 160,000 prisoners were transported to Australia.

Hughes (1987) suggests that the System (as convict transportation to Australia was called) passed through four stages. During the first stage (1787–1810), transportation was primarily used to clear out the English jails and to help declare a new English presence in the Pacific. Only about seven percent of the total number of transportees were sent to Australia during these first 23 years.

The second stage, lasting from 1811 through 1830, saw a significant growth of social problems in England. Population increases, runaway unemployment, and the growth of slums were stirred together in a caldron brewing crime. To this stew, the British Parliament finally authorized the new police force championed by Sir Robert Peel. The success of the "peelers" provided an ever-increasing supply of felons for the British courts to handle. When these conditions in Britain were matched with Australia's post-1815 demand for convict labor, the resulting push–pull connection furnished some 31 percent of the eventual total of transportees.

From 1831 through 1840, the System peaked and then began its decline. Nearly 32 percent of the 160,000 transportees arrived during these nine years. Alternative ways of handling British criminals were still at the discussion level. The former colonists in America were experimenting with penitentiaries as an alternative to corporal and capital punishment, but similar suggestions in

England developed very slowly. Reformists in England were increasingly out-spoken in their complaints about the slavery aspects of transportation. And opposition by Australians was taken more seriously. After all, 50 years of settlement provided the Australian colonists with a voice to be reckoned with. The Australians increasingly disliked the competition that convict labor presented for jobs and came to resent the continuous dumping of fresh convicts on their soil. As a result, in 1840 all transportation to New South Wales ceased.

With a lingering death from 1841 to 1868, the System provided convict labor primarily to Van Dieman's Land. When that reception point dried up in 1853, a last dribble of convicts were sent to Western Australia to help colonists settle that difficult part of the continent. By 1868, transportation was all over (Hughes, 1987).

In his fascinating and detailed account of the transporting system in Australia, Hughes (1987) suggests that proponents had hoped it would do four things: sublimate, deter, reform, and colonize. Sublimation would remove the criminal class, or a good slice of it, from England and put it where it could do no further harm. The cause of crime was found in the individual—not in society or social structure—so it made sense to amputate this sickness.

By the 1830s proponents' hopes centered more on general deterrence. It was assumed that banishment across the seas would terrify the innocent away from crime. Interestingly, the problem became one of convincing Great Britain's lower class that Australia was a terrible place to go. Verses written as early as 1790 suggested that Botany Bay might be a paradise compared to the drudgery of Mother England. The bravado in letters the transportees sent home, the wishful thinking of those at home, and the often true examples of ex-cons prospering in Australia all made it difficult to portray transport to Australia as something to be feared.

Reformation was a distant third among the aims of transportation. But at least one author suggests that the System provided the "most successful form of penal rehabilitation that had ever been tried in English, American or European history" (Hughes, 1987, p. 586). Hughes takes this position because of the benefits seemingly linked to the assignment system. Despite its inherently exploitative nature, assignment may have provided transportees with a sense of value in work and a motivation to obey the law. This, in turn, is directly related to the fourth purpose of transportation: colonization.

Most convicts were assigned (lent out) by the government as laborers to private settlers. A few (maybe one in 10) were kept by the government to labor on public works projects. Opulent British settlers were enticed to the distant colony with offers of free land and free labor. Assigned labor was not simply something to do with people who had been punished by transportation; the labor was, in fact, the punishment.

Assignment was the early form of today's open prison. Instead of herding men together in gangs, assignment dispersed them throughout the bush and kept them in working contact with the free. It fostered self-reliance, taught them jobs, and rewarded them for proper completion. The work was hard, but not really harder than what the settler had to do for himself. It was not slavery, since the assigned man worked within a watchful set of laws and rights. For example, convicts exiled to Australia served a fixed term and then became free. All had, within limits, the right to sell some portion of their labor on the free market, and could bring their "master" to court for ill-treatment. While the situation should not be romanticized, there were aspects to it that contradict the horror stories reformists told in the 1830s.

Contemporary Australian Corrections

Chappell (1988) believes that the legacy produced by Australia's convict past had specific influence on the eventual structure of its criminal justice system. The responsibility of controlling a largely disobedient population led to an early reliance on centralized authority. Individual settlements, villages, and even small cities were not able to support the necessary organizations to provide police, court, and correctional services. That initial dependence on the larger government unit established a pattern that became formalized with the 1901 creation of a Commonwealth of Australia.

The new commonwealth provided a federal government, but, following the traditional pattern, each of the member states was charged with administering their own criminal laws and criminal justice systems. In fact, the federal (commonwealth) government gave state courts the power to adjudicate and determine cases involving federal criminal laws. The Australian Federal Police enforces commonwealth criminal laws (and are responsible for policing in the Australian Capital Territory), but prosecution and sentencing of those offenders falls to the states. Further, when a state court system sentences a federal law offender, the sentence is carried out in state prisons or by other state correctional services. Basically, the Australian correctional system is entirely the responsibility of the six states (New South Wales, Victoria, South Australia, Queensland, Tasmania, and Western Australia) and the Northern Territory.

Australia's nine major systems of criminal justice administration (six states, two territories, and the federal system) clearly fall in the common legal tradition. But its decentralization to the state level makes it closer to the United States model than to either Canada or England (Sallmann and Willis, 1984). Instead of a single unified system applicable to all counties (see England) or one giving the national government responsibility for criminal law (see Canada), Australia entrusts her state bodies with criminal justice administration (see the United States). The primary difference from the American system is Australia's limited federal involvement in criminal justice.

Prisons

There are nearly 80 state prisons throughout Australia, with New South Wales having the most (21) and Tasmania the least (3). The pattern in most states is to place about one-half the prisoner population in one large prison and disperse the remaining half among a number of smaller prisons.

Of the total prisoner population, about 3.5 percent are federal convicts serving their sentence in a state prison. The absence of any prisons operated by the commonwealth means that people sentenced to prison for violating a federal law are subject to the discretion of judges for the state in which the federal law was breached. One result of this practice is discrepancy in the sentences that federal offenders receive when convicted of the same offense but in different jurisdictions. For example, offenders of the federal drug and fraud laws (the most common convictions for federal criminals) may receive different sentences in New South Wales than they would in Western Australia. The argument supporting such inconsistency says that state and federal prisoners should receive similar treatment for similar offenses. If a New South Wales drug conviction brings a three-year sentence, so should a federal drug conviction when the crime occurred in New South Wales. Further, since the states are required to provide places in prison for federal offenders, and since the commonwealth does not pay the cost of housing their prisoners in state prisons, the states understandably believe they have much to say about how those offenders will be sentenced.

Intra-Country Variation in Incarceration rates. The decentralization to the state level makes it difficult to describe an "Australian" corrections system. We would rightfully balk at a suggestion that American corrections can be described by reference to one, or even several, of the 50 states. Similarly, a discussion of Australian corrections in general, and imprisonment more particularly, is hampered by the variation among the states and the Northern Territory. But just as authors write textbooks on American police, courts, and corrections— without having to do a different book for each state—there are similarities that allow some general comments about Australian corrections. In the interest of fairness, however, occasional reference to the situation in different jurisdictions is appropriate.

An early reliance on community corrections (in the form of assignment) made Australians familiar with, if not accepting of, an alternative to imprisonment. Correspondingly, the knowledge of experiments with penitentiaries in the United States and in England provided an impetus for building similar facilities for offenders not suitable for assigned labor positions. This combination seems to have given Australian states a rather mid-road perspective on the proper place to achieve penal goals: a mixture of both prison and community. The result is Australia's middle placement in a listing of incarceration rates around the world (see Figure 8-3).

While Australia's incarceration rate places her around the middle among countries of the world, there is actually considerable variation within the country itself (see Figure 8-4). For example, in 1985 Australia's imprisonment rate was 70.5, but the rate for individual states varied from 47 in Victoria to 119 in Western Australia (Biles, 1986). Similar intracountry differences have been con-

Ir (per 100,000 population)		
Australia (1985)	70.5	(includes "jail" population)
Northern Territory	269	
Western Australia	119	
Queensland	85	
New South Wales	69	
Tasmania	63	
South Australia	62	
Victoria	47	
Aust. Capital Terr.	30	
United States (1991)	303	(does not include jail population)
South	326	
High = D.C.	1160	
Low = W.Va.	87	
West	288	
High = Nev.	481	
Low = Utah	141	
Midwest	248	
High = Mich.	378	
Low = N.Dak.	69	
Northeast	243	
High = N.Y.	313	
Low = Vt.	121	

Figure 8-4. Imprisonment rate (Ir) variation in Australia and the United States. *Source:* Australia data from D. Biles (1986). "Prisons and their problems." In D. Chappell and F. Wilson (eds.). *The Australian Criminal Justice System: The Mid-1980s* (p. 239). Sydney: Butterworths. United States data from Bureau of Justice Statistics (1992). *Prisons and Prisoners in the United States* (p. 1).

sistently reported since 1961, while the country's average rate has remained relatively stable.

Similar variation is found in the incarceration rates among states in the United States. In 1991 the prison (that is, not including persons in jails) incarceration rate for the United States was 303. But, as in Australia, that rate masks considerable diversity, ranging from the District of Columbia's unbelievable 1160 to North Dakota's rate of 69 (see Figure 8-4).

Explaining differences in the incarceration rates among jurisdictions within a country is as difficult as explaining rate differences among a grouping of countries. As we discovered when working with comparison of crime rates (Chapter 2), it is not possible to identify one, or even a few, variables to adequately explain differences in crime among countries. Methodological, definitional, and cultural problems mean that we can only make best guesses in this area of comparative criminal justice. Similar problems explain the difficulty of drawing conclusions about the differing incarceration rates among nations. The best we can do is remember Chapter 2's warning that conclusions drawn on rate comparisons are tentative and possibly misleading. That caution applies, though certainly less so, to comparison of jurisdiction within a country as well those among countries.

With the warning in mind, one explanation offered for the differences among Australian states draws on Australia's disproportionate rate of Aboriginal imprisonments. As you will see, researchers believe that this situation has little impact on the intracountry variation, but it highlights an important aspect of Australian corrections and deserves closer attention.

Racially Disproportionate Incarceration rates. In discussing Australian imprisonment rates, Biles (1986) refers to claims that Australian Aboriginal people are the most imprisoned race in the world. In the United States, African Americans comprise 12 percent of the general population but are 46 percent of the prison population. This 4 to 1 ratio indicates a serious problem in America, but consider the 10 to 1 ratio of Aboriginal prisoners (14.5 percent) to the total Aboriginal population (1.4 percent) in Australia (excluding Queensland, where Aboriginal population figures are unreliable). Ratios of 15 to 1 in South Australia (Aboriginals are 1.0 percent of the state population and 15 percent of the prison population) and 3 to 1 (23 percent of the general population and 67 percent of the prison population) in the Northern Territory reflect the extent of the problem in Australia (Chappell, 1988). Despite the importance and implications of those numbers, they cannot explain Australia's intracountry variation in imprisonment. As Biles notes, "even if the Aborigines in prison and in the general population were not counted, considerable differences in imprisonment rates would still exist" (1986, p. 240).

Although the disproportionate imprisonment rates for Aborigines cannot explain different rates among the jurisdictions, they do highlight a dilemma for Australian criminal justice by showing the problems of forcing a foreign justice system upon an native population. Aborigines were officially recognized as British subjects in 1837 and were thereby afforded the protection and rights accompanying such status. Unfortunately, British justice was not always understood, appreciated, or even wanted by the Aborigines. Midford (1992) suspects that local Aborigines had a lack of comprehension or sense of justice about the whole process. A news report from 1842 relates a conversation between a government official and an Aborigine convicted of murdering a fellow Aborigine and thereby sentenced to life in prison. The Aborigine could not understand why the Governor punished him so severely: "If a White man kills a White man, we never interfere—some time back, the White men killed many of the natives and the Governor took no notice, now why should the Governor take any notice of me, if I kill a fellow native, that steals my wife, or kills my brother, when it is according to our law?" (quoted in Midford, 1992, p. 12).

The Aborigines' experiences in the Australian justice system remain problematic today. Improvements have been made since the late nineteenth century, when a newspaper noted that the run-down collection of wooden sheds where Aboriginal prisoners were kept was a place where "the nigger is both happy and comfortable" (quoted in Midford, 1992, p. 14). Certainly problems of prejudice and discrimination remain, but also troublesome are the ever-present cultural barriers that work against equal treatment for Aborigines. Consider, for example, difficulties arising from Aboriginal concepts of time, name, and social relations.

Tribal Aboriginals seldom use clocks or calendars and may not even know their date of birth. Prisoners have had their length of sentence explained to them by the number of dry seasons they will be locked up. Police are frustrated in their investigation of deaths when trying to interview people who cannot speak the dead person's name. In a ripple effect, living relatives with the same name as the recently deceased person must use another name for the appropriate time. Inappropriately, the police may record such a name change as using an alias (Midford, 1992; Palmer, 1992). And there is always the danger that police will use a taboo name when speaking to a victim, witness, or suspect and thereby violate Aboriginal custom and reduce the Aborigine's community standing.

Social relations among Aboriginals also make their incorporation into this imposed justice system very difficult (Midford, 1992; Palmer, 1992). Avoidance relationships, wherein people may not normally speak or even look at each other, make it difficult for some prisoners to work or live together. Obligation relationships, wherein one shows duty and respect to a kin, present problems for Aboriginal prison officers and police aides, since their official status does not override kinship requirements. And since the term *family* has a broad meaning for Aboriginals, prison administrators must try to be fair to all prisoners yet recognize cultural differences when deciding about family visits and leaves for family emergencies.

Cultural differences and the prejudice and discrimination they engender are not, of course, limited to relations between Aboriginals and other Australians. It is difficult to find a country anywhere in the world where charges of institutionalized racism and discrimination are not levied. Blacks in South Africa; Turks in Austria; Koreans and *Burakumin* in Japan; Hispanos, African Americans, and Native Americans in the United States; and the list, unfortunately, goes on. Australia's response to the problems of its minority population is an unhappy combination of informal and formal policies.

The informal (some say, paternalistic) handling of Aboriginals is especially apparent at sentencing. In Queensland, for example, a 1965 law allowed judges to order Aboriginal offenders to reserves rather than sentencing them to prison. Since this could be done even if the accused had not been convicted, it was possible for Aborigines to be compulsively detained on settlements or reserves. Even today, an Aborigine living in Australia's more remote areas is occasionally punished according to tribal law rather than in the formal courts. The comments of one judge choosing to release a juvenile to "the traditional ways of his people" rather than a state facility, illustrates this philosophy: "It is, I think, sad but true that to many aboriginal children a term of imprisonment tends to be regarded as a sign of manhood and a much more comfortable experience than those designed over the centuries by their own people as the transition from childhood to manhood" (quoted in Gifford and Gifford, 1983, p. 121).

Despite the use of informal methods, Aboriginal offenders are still most likely handled by the formal machinery and are overrepresented at each stage of the criminal justice system. Their disproportionate number in Australia's prisons is especially problematic, since it seems to indicate discrimination in the use of community-based alternatives. Their typical poverty status means that many Aborigines lack the necessary funds to gain access to nonprison sentences like fines. Further, community service work or compliance with probation orders may be difficult, since the required behavior may not be culturally acceptable (Leivesley, 1986). But Australia's willingness to try a variety of community-based programs suggests that more opportunities for placement of Aboriginal offenders may be possible in the future.

Community-Based Corrections. Despite the considerable difference in incarceration rates, Australia and the United States make similar use of community-based corrections. When all types of correctional supervision in both countries are totaled, Australia and the United States each have about 25 percent of their convicted adults in prisons and the remaining 75 percent under some form of community-based supervision (see Chappell, 1988; Zawitz, 1988).

Since the mid-1980s, Australia has pursued the principle that prison should be a sentence of last resort (Zdenkowski, 1986). That perspective was influenced by the growing cost of prisons and by the disillusionment with prison either as a place for rehabilitation or as a means of deterrence. But just as the use of imprisonment varies by state and territory, so too does the use of community alternatives to prison.

Despite the variation among jurisdictions, three types of community corrections are common in the Australian states and territories: probation (sometimes called supervised recognisance), community service/work orders, and parole (Walker and Biles, 1986). Probation, or supervised recognisance, is possible for any conviction where imprisonment may be imposed. A court releases adult offenders to a fixed time period under a probation order. The time period ranges from about three months to over five years, but around 60 percent of the probationers serve a two- or three-year sentence. While under a probation order, the offender receives supervision, guidance, support, and referral services from paid and volunteer staff.

For Australia as a whole, probation is the most frequently used community-based corrections procedure (see Figure 8-5). Within each jurisdiction, except South Australia, probation is the most common form (Walker and Biles, 1986). But even in South Australia, nearly half the people under community corrections are sentenced to a supervised suspended prison sentence, which is in fact an order under the Offenders Probation Act. In South Australia, probation—or a first cousin to it—still provides the most used form of community corrections.

(Percentage of persons serving orders by state and type order)*

Order type	New South Wales	Victoria	Queensland	Western Australia	South Australia	Tasmania	Northern Territory	Australian Capital Territory	Australia (country average)
Probation/ Supervised recognizance	74.5	65.5	66.5	66.2	29.8	69.5	52.3	64.6	66.3
Community service/ Work order	13.7	7.5	15.4	25.9	9.0	20.9	12.2	n/a	14.1
Parole/ License	14.6	16.1	6.2	23.1	16.5	3.5	15.3	23.0	13.6
Supervised suspended prison sentence	n/a	n/a	n/a	n/a	46.8	23.5	29.3	8.9	5.5
Fine option order	n/a	n/a	11.0	n/a	n/a	n/a	n/a	n/a	2.2
Attendance center order	n/a	9.1	n/a	n/a	n/a	n/a	n/a	n/a	1.5
Pre-sentence supervision	0.5	n/a	0.0	n/a	0.0	n/a	n/a	0.9	0.2

*Percentages within jurisdiction do not necessarily sum to 100 because of other options available but not reported here and/or due to receiving overlapping orders.

Adapted from: J. Walker & D. Biles (1986). *Australian community-based corrections: 1985-86* (Table 1A). Australian Capital Territory: Australian Institute of Criminology.

Figure 8-5. Australian community-based corrections.

Community service or work orders are alternatives to imprisonment; the court requires offenders to make restitution by performing a set number of hours of community service work. The required hours range from around 25 to over 500, but national statistics show about 75 percent falling between 100 and 300 total hours (Walker and Biles, 1986). Because this is an alternative to imprisonment, a wide variety of offenses have been committed by persons under this sentence. In Victoria, for example, all persons other than those convicted of treason or murder are eligible for community service/work orders.

Parole [called *release on licence* (sic) if the person is being released from a life imprisonment sentence] refers to early release from prison. At the discretion of a parole board, the prisoner can serve the difference between his minimum and maximum sentence (that is, the parole period) under supervision in the community. Nationally, about 14 percent of the persons in community-based corrections are under parole or licence (see Figure 8-5). Over 60 percent of the parolees serve a parole period of over 18 months but under five years.

While probation, community service, and parole are common to the eight Australian jurisdictions, some of the unique community-based options are worth noting. For example, New South Wales makes use of pre-sentence supervision orders, which apply to persons convicted but awaiting sentence. They are used to assess the offender's performance under community-based supervision before a penalty is actually imposed. After this short (usually less than 12 months) trial period, the sentencing judge presumably has more information useful in determining an appropriate sentence for the offender.

In Victoria, *attendance centre* (sic) *orders* provide the court with a noncustodial sentencing option where the period of imprisonment can be served in the community. This penalty combines restitution in the form of community work with a requirement of regular attendance at an attendance centre. During the 1- to 12-month time period, the offender goes to the center to participate in a variety of personal development activities.

The willingness of Australian state governments to support community-based programs has pleased criminologists who favor substituting community alternatives for prisons. They see the resulting situation as one where government policy runs in parallel with criminological theory. Others suggest that the government support for prison alternatives has more to do with economic concerns than humanitarian ones, but even these cynics are pleased with Australia's innovations in community corrections.

From her origins as a penal colony to her contemporary standing as a modern industrialized nation, Australia has maintained an intriguing combination of the standard and the unique. Its mid-range use of imprisonment, and its development of community alternatives provide an appropriate position from which to view other countries falling toward the extremes on the incarceration continuum.

IMPACT

What would you consider an appropriate governmental response to persistent increases in a country's crime rate? How about locking more criminals up for longer periods of time? A "get tough" policy like that would not be unreasonable or unexpected as citizens and politicians worry about public safety. After all, deterrence and incapacitation are sensible grounds for building a punishment philosophy. The effect on the crime rate is not, however, as predictable as the effect on the prison system.

Since the 1960s such countries as Great Britain, France, and the United States have gotten tough on crime and increased both sentence lengths and the number of persons placed in prison. Great Britain experienced a 60 percent increase in the average length of prison sentences between 1961 and 1980. Within the same period, the number of probation orders fell by 17 percent. In France, prison terms under four months increased by over 500 percent between 1960 and 1977, and the number of juveniles detained in adult prisons nearly doubled from 1974 to 1981. While more persons were sentenced to prison, fewer were leaving, since parole commutations fell dramatically in the same time span (Jenkins, 1987). In the United States, tougher sentencing policies, lengthened sentences, and increased use of imprisonment help explain a 115 percent increase in inmate populations between 1980 and 1989 (Bureau of Justice Statistics, May 1990).

Prison overcrowding is a condition without national boundaries. Even countries with low imprisonment rates like Japan have expressed concern about anticipated increases in the number of persons placed in prison. Countries at the other extreme like Poland recognize the problem and seek solutions. Jenkins (1987) highlights the similar problems experienced by Great Britain, France, and the United States over the last several decades. Each country experienced enormous growth in prison populations. That surge was considered the result of rising crime rates and increased use of penal measures as the countries tried to "get tough" on crime.

Increasing Prison Capacity

The problem of too many people in prisons has obvious solutions. You can reduce the number going into prison, or increase the number leaving! Unfortunately, obvious solutions are not always easily achieved. This Impact section considers techniques used in various countries to respond to overcrowded prisons by influencing entry and exit numbers.

Prison capacity can be expanded by increasing the physical space into which inmates are placed. Countries like the Netherlands and the United States have certainly taken that course. Other countries, like those in Eastern Europe, cannot afford construction costs even if they wanted to build more prison space. So for economic, humanitarian, rehabilitative, and other reasons, most countries try to reduce overcrowding by manipulating the people rather than the space. This process is often referred to as *diversion*.

The term *diversion* is often used to refer to redistributing offenders away from prisons and into other correctional agencies and programs. Or an argument can be made that diversion requires the offender to be detoured completely away from the justice system and handled outside that system. By either usage, diversion is an effort to achieve a level of least restrictive control. This goal can be sought under several punishment philosophies. For the rehabilitation-minded, diversion away from prison, or from the justice system as a whole, may provide better opportunities to modify offender behavior and reintegrate the offender into society. Proponents of incapacitation may believe that society can be adequately protected when the freedom of movement of some offenders is restricted only by mandatory visits to treatment centers instead of placement in a prison. Deterrence may be achieved simply by having offenders' names printed in the local newspapers. Even retribution can be exacted through required community service work or a public apology.

Since this chapter is specifically concerned with imprisonment and its alternatives, I will emphasize diversion from prison as the focus for this Impact section. The United States' extremely high incarceration rate suggests that we need to be aware of all the possible ways to redistribute offenders. To that end, we will review some programs and techniques not yet familiar in most American jurisdictions. As we do that, we must remember that only 25 percent of the American population under correctional supervision is actually in prison. The 75 percent majority are supervised in the community. Therefore, the United States already makes significant use of alternatives to prison, but our severe problem of overcrowding requires us to consider boosting that already high percentage of persons under supervision in the community.

Reducing the Number of Persons Entering Prison

If correctional goals can be achieved without the use of prison, public opinion and government policy will likely be supportive of such options. In the United States various jurisdictions typically avoid imprisoning offenders through fines, sentences to community service work, placement in halfway houses, and suspended sentences with supervision provided by a probation officer. Other countries do not provide radically different options, but when and how they are used make them distinct from their American cousins. Consider, for example, the use of fines.

Fines.   A financial punishment providing compensation to either the victim or society is one of the oldest forms of punishment. In the United

States, fines are used extensively across the country. State penal codes usually set maximum amounts of fines for particular classes of crimes, and judges frequently impose a fine alone or in combination with another penalty (Hillsman, Mahoney, Cole, and Auchter, 1987). Fines are linked to minor offenses like loitering and shoplifting, but also to such serious crimes as assault and robbery. Similar statements can be made concerning the use of fines in many countries. The primary difference is that American jurisdictions are not using fines as an alternative to prison or to probation (Hillsman *et al.*, 1987). The primary example of fines as an alternative to incarceration is the European "day fine."

The day fine system, which is especially popular in Germany and Sweden, is based on the idea that punishment should be proportionate to the severity of the crime but equal across individuals with differing financial resources (Hillsman *et al.*, 1987). In other words, the seriousness of the offense and the offender's income level determine the amount of fine. The court sets the number of day fine units according to the type of offense. Then the offender's daily net income (after deducting an amount for family support and other necessary expenses) is determined. The daily net income (for example, $16.00) is multiplied by the number of day fines (for example, 85 for burglary) to determine the amount owed (for example, $1360.00). Since the number of day fine units is consistent by crime, another offender charged with the same crime (for example, 85 units) but having a lower daily net income (for example, $12.00) would be punished proportionately differently (for example, $1020).

The day fine is the most frequently applied punishment for the majority of criminal and traffic offenses in Sweden (Amilon, 1987) and for most adult sentences in Germany (Feest, 1981; Weigend, 1983). In both countries, the fine becomes a jail sentence if the offender does not pay. When that occurs, the number of day fines imposed and unpaid equals the number of days to be spent in jail. In this manner, the jail sanction is the same for all offenders of a particular crime, since the jail time is based on the number of units, not the monetary amount.

Hillsman *et al.* (1987) surveyed American judges to determine the possibility of implementing a day fine system in the United States. They concluded that day fines could be used in state jurisdictions if judges had access to accurate information about the offender's economic status. Even welfare recipients, the working poor, and the temporarily or seasonally unemployed could be punished by day fine instead of incarceration. The amount may be minimal by many economic standards, but if it is substantial enough to be a punishment for that specific offender, the fine serves its purpose.

Suspending the Sentence. The classic way to reduce the number of people entering prison has been the suspended sentence. Two types are possible: suspended sentence with supervision (typically known as probation) and suspended sentence without supervision. The latter type was exemplified by the Japanese example of suspended execution of imprisonment without supervision. Similarly, Sweden uses "conditional sentencing," wherein the court finds the defendant guilty but places no supervision requirements on that person (Amilon, 1987). Germany also provides for suspended sentences without supervision, but the actual process yields what seems to be a mid-range between the absence and presence of supervision. As a result, Germany presents an interesting twist on the traditional dichotomy of suspended sentence with supervision and suspended sentence without supervision.

Germany's Penal Code actually requires suspension of a sentence to imprisonment in some instances. For example, a suspended sentence must be given if the sentence is for one year or less, and if the court believes that the sentence itself sufficiently warned an offender who is not likely to commit additional offenses. According to Teske and Albrecht (1991), the court can impose two types of requirements on sentenced persons whose sentence is then suspended. The requirements known as "conditions" oblige the offender to: (1) pay money to an organization or the state, (2) perform community service duties, or (3) provide victim restitution.

The second type of requirement involves "orders." These directives are attempts to structure the sentenced person's life in hopes of preventing further criminal behavior. They sound very similar to conditions of probation in American jurisdictions, since they affect things like place of residence, use of work time, financial matters, associates, required reporting to court officials or representatives, and voluntary participation in treatment programs.

The important difference between the German and American versions is that the German conditions and orders neither imply nor require supervision (Teske and Albrecht, 1991). In other words, German offenders under a suspended sentence are held to similar requirements as American offenders under probation, but the German is not under the formal supervision of a court official. It is possible that Germans with a suspended sentence can have attached to their conditions or orders the requirement for supervision by a probation worker. But even then German probation differs from the American version, since probation "workers" in Germany lack the enforcement powers of American probation "officers" (Teske and Albrecht, 1991).

Variations in the use of fines and suspended sentences to reduce the number of persons entering prison suggest possible modifications in American procedures. Increased use of suspended sentences but without conditions or supervision, or with stipulations but without assignment to a probation officer are strategies worthy of our consideration. Even greater potential may lie in the increased use of fines in United States jurisdictions. Morris (1987) expresses amazement that this capitalist country does not make better use of fines. The European use of day fines as punishment, even for a poor individual, suggests an alternative to imprisonment that would seemingly fit very nicely with some American values. But other American values lean more toward retribution and incapacitation via the tradition of imprisonment. Even in that area there are ideas to be gleaned from other countries.

Increasing the Number of Persons Leaving Prison

Just as the suspended sentence is the classic way to reduce the number of persons entering prison, parole illustrates the typical exit pattern. Sometimes, early release from prison is mandatory and therefore does not require a decision about the prisoner's release date. In Sweden, for example, persons with prison sentences between two months and two years receive a mandatory conditional release after serving one-half their sentence. In countries where early release requires a decision, it is typically made by either the judicial (for example, Austria) or executive (for example, Canada) branch of the government.

In Austria, 18 prisons are attached to regional criminal courts and each court has jurisdiction over the possible early release of an inmate. Eligibility for such release requires two-thirds (a minimum of six months) of the sentence to be served (or one-half under favorable circumstances). The court must believe that the inmate shows good prospects for the future and can oppose the early release out of concern for protection of society. If early release is granted, it can be either with or without supervision. However, Austria uses conditional release very cautiously, and accounts for only 10 percent of the prisoners released each year (International Symposium on Parole, 1986). Another glance at Figure 8-2 shows that Austria has a somewhat high incarceration rate. Presumably, the reluctant use of early release provides some explanation for that high rate.

Canada also provides for conditional release of inmates, but leaves the decision making to the National Parole Board rather than to the courts. The federal government is responsible for all prisoners sentenced to over two years. In addition, seven of the provinces and two territories rely on the National Parole Board to provide paroling authority. Eligibility for parole in Canada occurs after serving one-third, or seven years (whichever is the lesser) of the sentence. Nearly 85 percent of the cases undergo a gradual release program of day parole, and even persons denied parole are released under mandatory supervision after serving about two-thirds of their sentence (International Symposium on Parole, 1986). This more frequent use of parole is likely reflected in Canada's mid-range standing in Figure 8-3.

CORRECTIONS IN POLAND

During nearly 45 years as the Polish Peoples Republic, Poland's imprisonment rate never dropped below 100 per 100,000 general population (see Figure 8-6).

Moving from a 1945 low of 107, it peaked at 372 in 1973. Between 1980 and 1988 it stayed in the 200 range with a low of 205 in 1984, and a high of 295 in 1985.

One reason for the fluctuating imprisonment rate was the use of general amnesties, which often released large numbers of prisoners. Thirteen amnesties since 1945 resulted in a lowered imprisonment rate 12 times (see Figure 8-6). The exception, 1983, involved a partial amnesty to imprisoned Solidarity leaders and to other Solidarity leaders willing to turn themselves in before October 31. The net result was an insufficient number to affect the overall imprisonment rate.

The year 1986 marks the active return of Solidarity in Poland. As such, it also marks the start of dramatic changes culminating in the 1989 transformation of Polish government and the election of Poland's first noncommunist prime minister since 1945. An indication of the importance of this change is seen with another look at Figure 8-6. The 1986 amnesty is one of the few since 1945 in

Figure 8-6. Imprisonment rates (Ir) in Poland from 1945 to 1990* (including both unconvicted and convicted persons). *A = Amnesty given during this year. *Source:* Z. Holda and A. Rzeplinski (eds.) (1992). "Zatrzymanie i Tymczasowe Aresztowanie a Prawa Czlowieka" (*Arrest and Preliminary Detention and Human Rights*). Adapted from Table 4, p. 58. Lublin, Poland: Maria Curie-Sklodowska University Press.

Year	Total confined	Ir per 100,000 inhabitants	Year	Total confined	Ir per 100,000 inhabitants
1945-A	24,702	107.4	1968	98,685	304.6
1946	61,365	256.8	1969-A	64,952	198.6
1947-A	56,554	233.7	1970	82,436	190.9
1948	77,116	313.5	1971	102,902	312.8
1949	92,786	377.2	1972	115,343	347.4
1950	98,046	392.2	1973	124,685	372.8
1951	93,064	356.0	1974-A	81,075	239.9
1952-A	87,460	336.4	1975	96,691	282.7
1953	84,603	319.3	1976	97,748	283.3
1954	91,197	337.8	1977-A	85,262	244.3
1955	80,920	293.2	1978	97,849	278.8
1956-A	35,879	127.7	1979	106,243	300.1
1957	61,248	214.9	1980	99,638	279.1
1958	70,348	242.6	1981-A	74,807	207.2
1959	92,595	313.9	1982	79,783	219.0
1960	98,250	329.7	1983-A	85,295	232.4
1961	98,506	327.3	1984-A	76,164	205.3
1962	95,863	314.3	1985	110,182	295.4
1963	105,444	341.2	1986-A	99,427	266.6
1964-A	71,448	228.3	1987	91,140	241.1
1965	80,026	253.2	1988	67,824	179.9
1966	94,193	296.2	1989-A	40,321	106.3
1967	97,867	303.9	1990	46,606	122.4

which the imprisonment rate did not return to the preamnesty level within two or three years. However, after declining in 1987, 1988, and 1989, the rate was inching back up again in the first eight months of 1990.

Despite a declining imprisonment rate since the mid-1980s, Poland is not likely to soon fall below 100 prisoners per 100,000 general population. After 45 years without any significant institutionalized system of alternatives to incarceration, it will be difficult during the 1990s to change radically Poland's reliance on imprisonment. The 1988 rate used in Figure 8-2 may not be reached again, but even with a rate of 110, Poland will be among the heavy users of imprisonment. Despite the dramatic political and economic changes in Poland during the end of the 1980s, we can reasonably expect it to remain a 1990s example of a country with heavy reliance on prisons as a form of punishment. Let us look more closely at the Polish system.

Sentencing Options

The 1970 Penal Code provides for sentence types ranging from fines to incarceration. The primary nonfine options are conditional discontinuance of proceedings, deprivation of liberty, conditional suspension of a prison sentence, and limitation of liberty. In the first of these four, conditional discontinuance of proceedings, petty offenders identified as good risks can have the proceeding against them ended. The action is suspended on the condition that the offender meets requirements like abstaining from alcohol, finding work, or going to school. Since this strategy does not actually involve a sentence, we will concentrate on the remaining three nonfine sentencing options (see Figure 8-7).

Deprivation of Liberty. As the most incapacitative sentence, deprivation of liberty (that is, imprisonment) can be for as little as one month or as long as 15 years. Some 25-year sentences are possible but not typical. A life sentence is not available, but the penal code provides for the death penalty. Figure 8-7 shows a declining use of the deprivation of liberty sentence in recent years, but we must remember that even with only 29,120 people added to its prisons in 1990, Poland still had an imprisonment rate of 122 (see Figure 8-6), which is high compared to the rate in other counties. Nevertheless, Polish judges are making increased use

Figure 8-7. Sentence types in Poland (percent of total sentences). *Source:* Ministerstwo Spvawiedliwosci (Ministry of Justice) (1991). *Statystyka Sadowa 1990* (c2 III). Warszawa (Warsaw): Author (Translation provided by Monika Platek).

Year	Total Sentences	Deprivation of Liberty	%	Sentence Suspended	%	Limitation of Liberty	%
1988	89,760	39,071	44%	29,675	33%	21,014	23%
1989	65,740	24,733	38%	31,249	48%	9,758	15%
1990	81,150	29,120	36%	46,800	58%	5,230	6%

of nonprison options by suspending the prison sentence and either requiring that certain conditions be met or limiting the offender's liberty.

Conditional Suspension of a Prison Sentence. Conditional suspension of imprisonment includes sanctions, which demand that the offender do certain things but do not require reporting to any court official (see suspended sentence in some countries). However, this same sentence may also place the offender under supervision of a court official (see probation in some countries). Conditional suspension of a prison sentence is used for cases of "intentional" offenses where the sentence would not exceed two years of deprivation of liberty. It is also applicable in cases of "unintentional" offenses where the sentence would not exceed three years of deprivation of liberty. The judge sets the term of suspension between three and five years.

With the suspension, the court can impose a fine, demand an apology to the victim, require obligations like abstaining from alcohol or submitting to medical treatment, and can have the defendant perform community service, find work, go to school, or report to a supervising authority. Should the person commit a new offense or not abide by the conditions of suspension, the judge may send him or her to prison.

Limitation of Liberty. Some of the conditionally suspended sentences include specific limits to the person's liberty. This sanction (more accurately, this type of conditional suspension of a prison sentence) is referred to as "limitation of liberty." As with the broader conditional suspension of sentence, limitation of liberty can include placing the offender under supervision. Limitation of liberty can be for three months to two years and requires specific behavior while the offender retains freedom of movement in the community.

The penalty typically takes one of three forms: supervised community work for 20 to 50 hours per month; wage deductions of 10 to 25 percent for employed persons; and compulsory employment for those offenders without a job. If the conditions are not met, the court can impose a fine. Should the fine not be paid in time, the judge can change the sentence to a maximum of three years in prison.

Ostrihanska *et al.* (1985) cite the educative (emphasizing work) benefits of the limitation of liberty penalty, but claim that it is less popular today than in the 1970s. Those authors do not provide data on its use in the 1970s, but in 1983 only six percent of those found guilty received this sentence (Ostrihanska *et al.*, 1985). Great variation is found in recent years with limitation of liberty comprising 23 percent of the sentences in 1988, but down to 15 percent in 1989, and only 6 percent in 1990 (see Figure 8-7).

In recent years the total use of the conditional suspension of a prison sentence (that is, the sum of sentence suspended and limitation of liberty in Figure 8-7) has stayed between 56 and 64 percent of all prison sentences. Those numbers make the suspended sentence the most frequently applied penal measure in

Poland. Before looking more closely at community placement of offenders, we must become familiar with the custody option.

The Use of Imprisonment

About 160 prison facilities exist in Poland with most of the buildings being acquired and converted by the prison service at the end of World War II. Nearly 70 percent of these buildings were constructed before World War I, and some of them date to the nineteenth, and even eighteenth, century.

The living conditions for prisoners has improved since the mid-1980s, but remain austere. Prior to the reforms, prisoners were sometimes kept in the semi-darkness of dirty and stifling cells. Inspectors found prisoners sleeping on wooden boxes instead of beds, living without running water, made to use sanitary buckets in the absence of toilets, and being fed at irregular times (Bulenda et al., 1990). With the start of noticeable reforms in 1986, problems in prisons were openly discussed. Prison staff began conscientious efforts to make real improvements in the prison environment (Platek, 1990). Indication of success is found in a more relaxed daily routine for prisoners, access to more recreational activities, reduction in the amount of time the prisoner must stay in a locked cell, and increased use of furloughs to visit family members. But these changes are best considered in the context of Poland's current use of imprisonment.

Prisoners in Poland, as is true in most other countries, include both convicted and unconvicted people. As explained in the earlier discussion of imprisonment rates, the category of prisoner typically includes persons in detention while the charges against them are investigated or while they await their trial. In the United States, people in this situation who are not on some form of pre-trial release are kept in jails operated by city or county governments. We do not often think of persons awaiting trial as "prisoners" (although we may use the term "inmate"), since they have not been found guilty of anything and are not serving time in a prison. However, our perspective and our usual elimination of people in detention from our imprisonment statistics is not shared by most other countries.

While both convicted and unconvicted (that is, detained) persons share the prisoner label, they are not treated in the same manner. Our discussion of imprisonment in Poland would be incomplete if the situation of the detainees was omitted, so we begin at that point.

Preliminary Detention

Preliminary detention is a procedure initially authorized by the prosecutor or, in a few instances, by the court. In general, preliminary detention can be used when the collected evidence is sufficient to indicate that the accused committed the crime and at least one of the following is also present: (1) it is feared that the accused will go into hiding; (2) it is believed that the accused will try to get others to commit perjury or will otherwise try to obstruct the criminal proceeding;

(3) the charge is for a felony or for activities which will amount to recidivism charges against the accused; or (4) the accused is charged with acts which suggest that he or she presents considerable danger to society (Bulenda *et al.*, 1990).

Regardless of those criteria, preliminary detention is required when the accused faces a sentence of imprisonment for more than two years if the crime was premeditated, or three years if the crime was without premeditation. On the other hand, preliminary detention is prohibited when the accused's identity has been established and the offense carries a penalty of less than one year in prison. More vaguely, preliminary detention is also prohibited when it would create serious danger to the life or health of the accused or would create hardship for the family.

After determining that the appropriate criteria exist, the prosecutor can set a term of preliminary detention at a period of three months. Continued detention, in periods of three months, can be assigned by the court of first instance. Although there does not appear to be a clear maximum, the assumption is that no one should spend more than one year in detention. In 1991, academics and practitioners believed that the more serious cases were being handled within the one-year time frame. The less serious cases were taking a longer time, since officials did not feel so compelled to get them through the process.

Since mid-1990, preliminary detention is conducted only in the houses of detention under the direction of the Minister of Justice (Bulenda *et al.*, 1990). However, unlike American jails, the detention houses are sometimes physically attached to regular prisons and under the same administration as the prisoners. One hundred fourteen of the facilities in the department of prisons are set up to handle persons under preliminary detention. In 1990, 48 of the prisons had sections for detainees.

The presence of both convicted and unconvicted persons in what appears to be the same physical structure makes it difficult to identify some facilities as prisons or detention houses. For example, in 1991 at the Bialoleka facility near Warsaw, some 1700 persons under preliminary detention were being housed in four buildings, each having four units or floors. In a physically distinct section of the compound, separated by gates and walls, another 450 prisoners were housed in a similar setting. The only way for an uninitiated observer to distinguish between the groups is the knowledge that detainees get to wear their own clothes, whereas convicted prisoners must wear prison uniforms.

The difficulty of differentiating detainees and prisoners is not lost on Polish academics and officials. Some (for example, Bulenda *et al.*, 1990) express concern that the use of the same buildings and personnel for both convicted and unconvicted persons provides an undesirable organizational symbiosis. There should be, critics argue, noticeably different conditions for persons in the two situations.

Prisons

Polish officials believe that work, education, and cultural activity provide the means by which offenders can be resocialized (Platek, 1990). Of the three, work was especially emphasized under socialism. The 1970 Penal Code said the purpose of a prison sentence is to: "'accustom the prisoner to work and observe the legal order, thus preventing his relapse into crime'" (Ostrihanska et al., 1985, p. 61). Even after the change in government, work remains a desirable goal and is considered a way to instill socially desirable attitudes in the prisoner.

Fewer jobs are available for prisoners today, since the economic changes have, among other things, meant that prison industries cannot keep pace with the outside competition. On the prison grounds are workplaces ranging from inmates making gloves in converted cells, to furniture workers in regular buildings, and including outside construction work, where prisoners make prefabricated sections for buildings. These areas are not as busy as they were before 1989, but every effort is made to provide work, and an accompanying fair wage, to all prisoners.

The Penitentiary Service, operating out of the Ministry of Justice, is responsible for nearly 160 prison facilities throughout Poland. The prisons fall into seven general categories: work centers, ordinary prisons, prisons for recidivists, transition prisons, special care prisons, military prisons, and prisons for youth. The specialized nature of the last three means that they need only brief comment.

Prisons for offenders needing special care are set up to handle persons with mental diseases and handicaps, drug and alcohol addicts, and prisoners with physical handicaps. The military prisons house all offenders sentenced as a result of a military arrest. Prisons for youth guard offenders aged 17 through 20. The 1970 Penal Code said that these people should receive more lenient treatment than adult offenders. Actually, according to studies conducted in the 1970s, sentences given to young offenders did not differ much from those imposed on adults. Ostrihanska et al. (1985) suggest that young offenders were actually imprisoned more often than were adults. The physical condition of prisons for youth, and the structure of activities therein do not differ much from the typical adult prisons discussed below.

The rehabilitation of prisoners and their restoration to society are primary goals of imprisonment in Poland (Ostrihanska et al., 1985; Platek, 1990). The basic means by which those goals are achieved is through activities related to work, education, and cultural endeavors. The principal location for providing the activities is a prison facility rather than a community setting. Since assignment to the facilities and activities is linked to the process of classification, initial attention must be directed to that term.

Classification in the Polish Penitentiary Service refers to the severity of a prisoner's penalty. Factors influencing assignment to lenient, ordinary, and severe rigors include the prisoner's age, prior record, degree of demoralization, and his attitude toward rehabilitation (Rozalicz, 1989). After initial classification, the inmate is assigned to a specific institution and a particular control level, or regimen. Transfer between prisons and movement among regimens is accomplished through a process of progression in the inmate's treatment plan.

Prisoners typically start at the ordinary rigor, and with good progress (that is, behaving adequately and realizing progress in social rehabilitation) are promoted to the lenient regimen with its increased rights. Similarly, poor progress may bring transfer to the severe rigor and the loss of rights.

Work centers are semi-open facilities using lenient and ordinary rigors. These labor sites hold prisoners serving sentences of less than 5 years for unintentional offenses, first offenses, and failure to pay a fine. Frankowski (1985) suggests that the work centers actually house most of Poland's prisoners regardless of the offense type or sentence length, but the heavy use of work centers may be more the result of transfers from other prison types than an indication of the prisoner's initial assignment. Prisoners under the lenient regimen while at a work center may be granted up to 24-hour furloughs and can participate in cultural, educational, and sport activities outside the prison.

The ordinary prisons are closed facilities housing inmates with long-term sentences and those convicted for hooligan-type offenses. All three control levels operate in ordinary prisons, but the ordinary and severe are most frequent. Under the ordinary regimen, prisoners receive 30 percent remuneration for their work (that is, 30 percent of the set wage for a certain type of labor). They also are allowed two contact visits per month and can receive food packages once every three months. Should they progress to the lenient rigor while at an ordinary prison, they receive 35 percent remuneration, three visits per month, and food packages every two months. Inmates under the severe rigor get 25 percent remuneration, can have one noncontact visit each month, and may receive food packages only at six-month intervals (Rozalicz, 1989).

For prison classification purposes, recidivists are persons who have either been sentenced once before for a similar offense (for example, crimes against property) or have been sentenced two or more times before with at least one prior offense in the same crime category as the current offense (Z. Lasock, personal communication, April 1991). Such offenders are sent to prisons for recidivists, which primarily follow a severe regimen. Under these conditions of limited liberty, the inmates are encouraged to follow the progression system through ordinary and lenient rigors with the accompanying transfer to other prisons.

Transitional prisons are the newest type of facility in Poland's Prison Service. These open institutions house inmates who have served at least two years of their sentence in another type of prison and are within six months of finishing their sentence.

Community Placement

Community supervision in Poland can be either obligatory or optional. As noted earlier, supervision is possible for sentences of conditional suspension of a prison sentence, but it is also used in other cases where the court believes the offender needs supervision. When supervision is required instead of a prison term, it operates like probation in other countries. The person reports to a professional supervision officer, but lay volunteers augment the professional staff. The use of lay citizens lends an informality to supervision and shows offenders that they have a friend. The Polish system assumes that the volunteers also will benefit from this process. Because of their interaction with offenders, the volunteers will presumably come to understand better the role society plays in the development of criminal behavior.

The Polish version of "parole" allows for release from incarceration after serving two-thirds of the sentence, achieving the aims of punishment, and receiving a favorable prognosis. The minimum time to serve before parole is one-half the sentence for young adults, and three-quarters of the sentence for recidivists. The time spent on "parole" cannot be less than one year (three years for recidivists) nor longer than five years. As noted earlier, the penitentiary court makes the "parole" decision at the request of the warden, prisoner, and prisoner's counsel. The release may require direction by the community supervision officer, but such supervision is mandatory only for recidivists.

Earlier in this chapter we noted that countries differ in their opinions about the appropriate location for achieving punishment goals. Poland's high imprisonment rate suggests that, at least for its years under socialism, the goals were best achieved in an institutional setting. Even since the change in government, Poland still makes greater use of prisons than do most other countries. Rapid changes cannot be expected, since no infrastructure existed as the 1990s began for an alternative location to administer punishment. While probation and parole (to use American terms) existed under socialism, they were not fully used or formally integrated into the country's penal philosophy. Even if Poles want to change the location for achieving penal goals from prisons to the community, the process will be long and controversial. Platek, who says that it is hard to find Polish examples of community supervision and community-based corrections, suggests two reasons for Poland's delayed development in this area: (1) the courts are not willing to share power with the people, and (2) Poles believe it is the court's role, rather than the public's, to devote time to wrongdoers (Platek, personal communication, January 12, 1992). Such attitudes will not only limit the involvement of citizen volunteers in working with offenders, but will also hinder development of paid professionals to supervise persons receiving suspended sentences.

After 45 years without any significant institutionalized system of alternatives to incarceration, it will be difficult during the 1990s to change radically Poland's reliance on imprisonment. The incarceration rates approaching 200 (see Figure 8-2) may not be reached again, but even with ones just over 100, Poland will be among the heavy users of imprisonment. Despite the dramatic political and economic changes in Poland during the end of the 1980s, we can reasonably expect it to remain a 1990s example of a country with heavy reliance on prisons as a form of punishment. That situation will remain until the Poles change their attitudes about community supervision of offenders and develop an infrastructure for community-based corrections.

Poland's persisting view of institutions as legitimate places for offender rehabilitation and restoration into law-abiding society is certainly not unique amoung countries of the world. As Empey (1982) points out, the beginning stages of a rehabilitation philosophy in America included the belief that institutions were the most effective means for preventing a child's movement into criminality and for rehabilitating those already engaged in crime. From the late nineteenth century through the mid-twentieth century Americans had great faith in institutions as places where social ills could be alleviated.

Obviously, Polish officials have not given as much thought to alternatives to imprisonment as they have to prison itself. The result is a high incarceration rate. At the other extreme on the incarceration continuum is Japan. Unlike Poland—in fact, unlike most countries—Japan does not have problems with overcrowded prisons. One reason, as we see below, is Japan's willingness to use alternatives to imprisonment.

IMPACT

Nontraditional Responses to Prison Overcrowding

High incarceration rates are often considered to be undesirable because they typically mean overcrowded prisons. That, in turn, suggests high operating costs, control problems in the prison, and potentially unsanitary and inhumane conditions. What if citizens of a country cannot be convinced that alternatives to imprisonment are the best or the only way to respond to large numbers of prisoners? Maybe it is more appropriate to identify ways to handle, efficiently and economically, large numbers of prisoners under humane conditions.

Prison labor systems have been used for decades to fulfill assorted goals in prison environments. While providing additional punishment for prisoners, they also furnish job skills, promote control within the prison, and can even help offset the cost of maintaining the prison. It is possible that rather than actively reducing the prison population by placing fewer people in prison or providing early release of those already there, governments can use labor systems to better manage those in custody. Suggestions for effectively using prison labor systems when confronted with large numbers of prisoners come from several countries.

The Beijing Municipal Prison and the Shandong Provincial Prison in Jinan place heavy emphasis on industrial production in the People's Republic of China. This stress reflects Mao's belief that prisons should be run like a school, factory, or farm (Miller, 1987). As a result, working conditions in the prisons are similar to those in community factories. Inmates must put in a full day's work and meet various production quotas. The purpose of prison industries, as far as the Chinese government is concerned, is to contribute to the national economy—not simply as a way to keep inmates busy.

As a fully integrated part of the national economy, prison industries in China receive necessary technical support and advice that help the prisons show a net operating profit. All inmates physically able to do so must work. Their eight-hour days over six days per week allow the prison industries to operate at full production capacity (Miller, 1987). The job assignments relate more to institutional than inmate needs, but the skills learned are typically applicable to employment after prison. The inmates receive money to purchase personal care and luxury items and can earn bonuses each quarter for exceeding production quotas. Positive psychological sanctions of praise and merits from supervisors can combine with consistently strong work records to gain the inmate a sentence reduction or even parole.

When reporting on his visit to Chinese prisons, Miller (1987) summarized the experience as exemplifying a prison labor system with realistic working conditions that imitate those found in the community. By considering prison industries an integral part of the overall economy, the Chinese more efficiently and effectively handle their prison population. Miller (1987) notes the irony that a socialist country is developing a quasi-capitalistic approach to correctional administration based in prison industries.

If Americans continue placing more people in prison and keeping them there for longer periods of time, changing prison industries may provide a humanitarian means to control inmates while providing job skills and earning the prison a profit. Unfortunately, while our prison industries history is possibly the oldest in the world, it currently cannot claim advantages like "rehabilitative," or "profitable."

As Beaumont and Tocqueville discovered during their journey to America, many nineteenth-century industrial prisons of the North were competitive and successful in marketing products like soap, clothing, and twine. In 1929, however, Congress responded to complaints of rival industries and of labor unions regarding the low prices that prisons charged for goods made with low-cost prison labor. That reaction came in the Hawes–Cooper Act passed in 1929 and effective in 1934. Basically it prohibited or restricted the sale of prison-made products according to the laws of the state into which the products were shipped. This legislation was the first of several to respond to complaints from industry and labor officials. The Sumners–Ashurst Act, first (1935) forbade interstate transportation of prison-made products without the consent of each state through which they would pass. An amendment (1940) banned all but agricultural prison products from one state from being sold to other states. Congress modified the interstate selling prohibition in 1979 in an attempt to increase financial support for what had become the ailing prison industries across the country.

Today, American prison work programs can be viewed in terms of the pyramid whose base is occupied by a large number of inmates engaged in such institutional maintenance activities as food service, laundry, painting, and cleaning (Demos and Lucas, 1986). Institutional maintenance activity is the type of "work" done by the largest percentage of the inmate work force. One level up is the growing work activity of traditional prison industries. Here, prisoners engage in work with a vocational aspect. They may receive an hourly wage for their efforts (for example, 50 cents), although some states still provide no financial compensation. The two top tiers of the pyramid are occupied by new work programs created after Congress authorized up to 20 prison industry projects that would be exempt from legislation prohibiting prison industries from moving goods in interstate commerce and from selling to federal agencies.

The largest of the two new systems is the free-venture or private-sector prison industries that attempt to adapt contemporary business and marketing practices to the prison setting. Included in such practices are a full work week for the inmate employees and wages based on productivity. At the top of the pyramid are a few prison industries that have been certified to participate in the Prison Industries Enhancement Certification Program (PIE). This experimental program tries to operate prison work programs in a nonprison fashion. Under the PIE program, wages paid to inmates must be comparable to those in the private sector and require deductions for such things as taxes, room and board, family support, and victim compensation. The PIE program is not for all states, since it requires a willingness to operate a prison industry like a private sector business. The involvement of the private sector can be in capital, management skills, planning and design of business, or even the actual operation of certified businesses in prison.

As the United States moves toward integrating prison labor systems into the economy, it is desirable to consider the experiences of countries like China, which have already followed such a path. As with ideas borrowed from any country, however, appropriate modification must occur in light of different cultures.

CORRECTIONS IN JAPAN

The Penal Code of 1907 has served, with consistent modification, to orient Japanese corrections for nearly 90 years. The designated goals of retribution and rehabilitation are reflected in the treatment of prisoners. While a goal of retribution might suggest imprisonment as the typical punishment, Japan actually has a very low incarceration rate. After reaching a peak in 1950 of 102 convicted prisoners per 100,000 population, the rate dropped to 35 in 1978 (Correction Bureau, 1985). A slight but steady growth to a rate of 37 in 1984 was officially attributed to increased gangster-group members and stimulant abusers (Correction Bureau, 1985). Even with the estimates of a prison population increase of three to ten percent by the mid-1990s, Japan will still have one of the lowest incarceration rates in the world.

Number sentenced with percent of all sentences		(A) Total number sanctioned (B)+(C)	(B) Total number imprisoned	(C) Total number noncustody	(D) number noncustody under supervision
Poland	1990	81,150	29,120 (36%)	52,030 (64%)	21,784 (42%)
Japan	1988	57,095	21,071 (37%)	36,024 (63%)	4,547 (13%)

Figure 8-8. Custodial and noncustodial sentences in Japan and Poland. *Sources:* Poland data from: Minesterstwo Spvawiediwosci (Ministry of Justice) (1991). *Statystyka Sadowa 1990* (c2 III). Warszawa (Warsaw): Author. (Translation provided by Monika Platek). Japan data from: Research and Training Institute. (1990).

A common sense explanation for Japan's low incarceration rate would suggest that it uses imprisonment sentences less frequently than do other countries. However, Figure 8-8 shows that both Poland and Japan, despite being at opposite extremes on incarceration rates, impose prison sanctions in about 36.5 percent of the cases receiving sentences in one year. Japan's low incarceration rate is not, therefore, the result of her judges refusing to sentence offenders to prison.

If minimal use of prison sentences does not explain Japan's low rate, we must consider other reasons. One possibility is that the Japanese people are simply more law-abiding than citizens of other countries and as a result a small proportion of the population is incarcerated. Another explanation suggests that Japanese officials have found alternative ways of handling offenders so that those who do get in trouble are not subjected to eventual prison sentences. Actually, both these solutions seem to play a role. The first, the well-behaved Japanese citizen, is a topic more appropriate to Chapter 10's elaboration on Japan. The second, alternative handling, is also discussed in Chapter 10, but deserves brief attention here as well.

Looking again at Figure 8-8, we see that judges in Japan and Poland both gave noncustody sentences about 63.5 percent of the time. However, while 42 percent of the Poles under a noncustody sentence were being supervised by a court official, only 13 percent of Japanese offenders were similarly supervised. In our earlier discussion of community corrections in Poland, I noted that Poland does not have the necessary infrastructure to operate a community-based corrections program. With only 13 percent of her noncustody offenders being supervised, we might suppose that Japan is even worse off than Poland.

Actually, the meager use of supervision for noncustody offenders is a very purposeful and central aspect of the Japanese criminal justice system. As Chapter 10 explains, informal (from an American perspective) handling of offenders begins with Japanese police officers and continues through the Japanese courts. The result is a constant diverting of offenders away from formal processing. However, of those offenders actually reaching the formal sentencing stage, over one-third will be sentenced to prison (see Figure 8-8). Until we can explore these points more fully, it may help to think of the Japanese process in the following manner: (1) Japan's low incarceration rate means that it imprisons a low proportion of its citizens; (2) Japan is likely to divert many offenders away from any kind of correctional supervision, but (3) when official supervision is deemed necessary, it will likely be in a prison setting rather than in the community. These three points orient our discussion of corrections in Japan and allow us to look at the country's sentencing options, prison system, and community-based alternatives.

Sentencing Options

Nakayama (1987) identifies Japanese sentencing options as including execution, imprisonment (both with and without labor), major and minor fines, penal detention, and suspension of sentence. Execution is imposed only in the rare case of aggravated homicide or homicide resulting from robbery. Imprisonment is reserved for serious offenses, persons dangerous to society, and recidivists who previously failed in institutional or community treatment (Tsuchiya, 1984). Whether sentenced to prison with or without labor, Japanese inmates typically serve a fixed term from about one month to 15 years. Exceptions include an occasional life sentence (parolable after 10 years) or a 20-year sentence when aggravating circumstances accompanied the crime. Imprisonment with labor is the most typical type (98 percent of the imprisonment sentences), but even inmates sentenced without required labor may request a work assignment. Since most inmates request work assignment, there is little distinction between the two types.

Penal detention involves a short (1 to 30 days) deprivation of liberty to be served in a house of detention. Persons convicted of minor offenses, like insult or public indecency, are the most likely candidates for this sanction (Nakayama, 1987). Fines (about $20 and up) and minor fines (under about $20) are monetary punishments that may result in imprisonment if not paid.

The enforcement of sentences to imprisonment can be suspended for a period of one to five years. In fact, this suspended sentence of imprisonment is the most widely imposed sentence by Japanese judges (Westermann and Burfeind, 1991). It is usually considered for offenders lacking any prior incarceration or whose period of imprisonment occurred more than five years earlier. Suspended execution of sentence can occur either with or without supervision. When accompanied by supervision, this is essentially a sentence to probation.—However, in recent years only 13 to 18 percent of the defendants actually had supervision stipulated as part of their suspended sentence (see Research and Training Institute, 1990; Parker, 1986; Westermann and Burfeind, 1991). More often, supervision is not required, and the offender is simply under his or her own recognizance.

Prisons

The supervision and treatment of inmates in all Japanese correctional institutions is the responsibility of the Correction Bureau of the Ministry of Justice. A result of this highly centralized structure is a unified and coordinated corrections system. The Correction Bureau operates seven detention houses with 109 branches, 59 adult prisons and their eight branches, and eight juvenile prisons (Correction Bureau, 1990). Six of the adult prisons and branches are designated for women prisoners, while five of the facilities are medical prisons treating prisoners with mental or physical disorders. Other specialized units handle only traffic offenders, prostitutes, or foreign prisoners (Archambeault and Fenwick, 1988).

While rehabilitation is considered more effective in a community setting, it is not ignored in the institution. Persons sentenced to adult prisons will first go to one of eight regional classification centers. While there, the inmate is oriented to prison life, tested, and classified according to needs (Terrill, 1984). Central coordination of the classification process (described more fully in Chapter 10) makes the decision-making consistent and enhances general stability of prison operations.

Upon arrival at the assigned institution, inmates are placed in a progressive grade system that varies treatment according to the prisoner's level. This system was first carried out in 1934 in response to the Ordinance for Prisoner's Progressive Treatment. Movement begins at the lowest grades (fourth and third), where prisoners are, in principle, confined in communal cells. Through motivation and reform the prisoner moves to second and first grades, where they enjoy single cells at night, more extensive self-government, and increased privileges (Correction Bureau, 1990; Nakayama, 1987).

Japanese prison industries are more productive and progressive than those in America. Divided into the three areas of production, vocational training, and maintenance work, prison industry lacks restrictions regarding competition with private sector. The Japanese prisoners work an eight-hour day, five days a week, with a half-day Saturday (Parker, 1986). They receive minimal wages (about $12 per month in 1981) for their labor. Money the prisoners do not use for necessities while in prison is saved and given to them at their release.

Community-Based Services

Our discussion of Japan began by noting that its low incarceration rate is accompanied by a low percentage of persons under community supervision. This was surprising since one explanation for a low use of imprisonment might be the diversion of offenders into community-based programs rather than into prisons. But, as Figure 8-8 shows, Japan actually sentences 63 percent of her offenders to noncustody alternatives. The catch, as described above, is the number of offenders released to the community under a suspended sentence but without any required supervision.

Since the majority of offenders were returned to the community without correctional supervision, it is not really fair to say that they are in a community-based program. But clearly they have been given a community-based alternative! Chapter 10 suggests reasons why Japan can rely on nonsupervision alternatives to prison, so in this chapter we focus on the more traditional programs of probation and parole.

Probation and Parole in Japan. Given the Japanese shared sense of shame and embarrassment when a group member misbehaves, it is not surprising that family and neighbors may resent offenders. Parker (1986) tells of an 1880s case where a discharged prisoner committed suicide after being rejected by family and community members. That incident moved the philanthropist Meizen Kinbara to establish a private aftercare halfway house to provide shelter, employment, and guidance to released offenders with no place to return in the community. Other private individuals and organizations, following Kinbara's lead, established a number of hostels throughout Japan. Halfway houses remain an important part of Japan's corrections system, but its probation and parole service is considered the primary means for keeping the imprisonment rate low.

Japanese probation officers provide what Americans know as both probation and parole. As noted earlier, the Rehabilitation Bureau of the Ministry of Justice administers rehabilitation services for the entire country. Despite the centralized administration, Japanese probation facilities are dispersed, with 50 main offices and 25 branch offices throughout the nation.

Prisoners may be considered for parole after serving one-third of a fixed prison term, or 10 years of a life sentence. In either instance, they must show genuine reformation (Parker, 1986). One of eight regional parole boards, sitting in panels of three, reviews parole nominations completed by the inmate's warden. Successful candidates remain under parole supervision for the unexpired portion of their original sentence. As in the United States, parole may be revoked should the parolee commit a new offense or violate conditions of the parole. Conditions of parole, which are essentially the same as those for probation, include:

1. Living at a specified residence and engaging in a lawful occupation;

2. Avoiding bad conduct;

3. Refraining from association with criminal types;

4. Seeking prior approval for changing residence or taking a long journey;

5. Abiding by any additional conditions set by the parole board (Parker, 1986, pp. 61–62).

Japanese Probation/Parole Officers. Because of the large number of volunteer probation officers (see below), Japanese officers perform a different function from those in America. The professional probation officer in Japan is a coordinator, counselor, investigator, and personnel officer. Most importantly, however, he or she supervises volunteer workers, who handle most of the face-to-face contact with probationers and parolees. Because the large-scale use of government-appointed volunteer probation officers (V.P.O.s) is the most unique feature of the Japanese system (Parker, 1986), we turn our attention directly to those citizens.

Japan's ratio of one professional officer to every 205 offenders is not unlike the situation in the United States. However, after including the V.P.O.s, Japan's ratio becomes 1 to 1 (Parker, 1986). Because they live and work in the same community as their clients, the volunteers develop close working relations with the offenders.

Volunteer officers must be healthy, active, and financially stable citizens with the enthusiasm and time necessary for probation work. The ranks are filled with housewives, Buddhist and Shinto priests, and businessmen volunteering their service for two years. Reappointments are possible and occur so frequently that over 40 percent of the V.P.O.s in 1983 had over 10 years experience (Parker, 1986).

The lengthy experience of many volunteers represents a problem with the system. Most volunteers are older than their clients, and some consider this generation gap a major problem. Despite the age difference, V.P.O. and client often develop a trust and confidence not possible between the professional officer and the client. After all, as in America, professional probation officers have a "cop" role requiring them to investigate and report violations of probation/parole conditions. The V.P.O. lacks such authority and can devote all his or her attention to the helping role.

When compared with the variety of community-based alternatives available in Australia, Japan seems to have a rather undeveloped program. Similarly, Japan's prison system is not noticeably different from Poland's, so neither can really be offered as examples of innovation in imprisonment. Essentially, Japanese community corrections consists of halfway houses, probation, and parole. These are certainly not imaginative concepts and, except for the significant use of volunteers, are not implemented in a unique fashion. The commonness of Japanese corrections would not be notable except for the fact that the country uses them so infrequently and yet has one of the world's lowest crime rates. Do the traditional corrections systems typified by prisons, halfway houses, probation, and parole work only in Japan? The answer, not surprisingly, is more complicated than a simple yes. In Chapter 10, Japan is looked at in greater detail as we consider explanations for its seemingly effective criminal justice system.

SUMMARY

This chapter's classification scheme relied on the use of imprisonment in countries throughout the world. The resulting incarceration rate provides one indication of a country's preference for incapacitation as a punishment philosophy. Working only with extreme cases to lessen the problems of definition and methodology, we considered the situation in countries with a high rate (Poland), a low rate (Japan), and one with a rate at the middle range (Australia). The Australia example was especially relevant to Americans, since we share some of Australia's correctional history (for example, receiving prisoners from England) and some contemporary problems (for example, intracountry variation and racially disproportionate incarceration rates).

Poland's high incarceration rate seems partially explained by its belief that positive change can be achieved in an institutional setting, but also by the relative absence of any infrastructure for community corrections. Japan, on the other hand, uses imprisonment rather infrequently, but is also unlikely to use formal community corrections agencies. Instead, Japan seems to prefer informal sanctioning in the community setting but without relying on a bureaucratic structure.

In the Impact sections, ideas were offered for ways to respond to the worldwide problem of prison overcrowding. Essentially, a country can either reduce the number of persons entering prison or increase the number leaving. With brief reference to procedures in a variety of countries, ideas were presented that may be useful as American prison systems seek ways to solve the problem of prison overcrowding.

SUGGESTED READINGS

Hughes, Robert. (1987). *The fatal shore*. New York: Alfred A. Knopf.

Parker, L. Craig, Jr. (1986). *Parole and the community based treatment of offenders in Japan and the United States*. New Haven, CT: University of New Haven Press.

Whitfield, Dick (Ed.). (1990). *The state of the prisons—200 years on*. New York: Routledge.

REFERENCES

Amilon, Clas. (1987). The Swedish model of community corrections. *International corrections: An overview* (Monograph number 11, 11–15). College Park, MD: American Correctional Association.

Archambeault, William G., and Fenwick, Charles R. (1988). A comparative analysis of culture, safety, and organizational management factors in Japanese and U.S. prisons. *The Prison Journal, 68*, 3–23.

Australian Institute of Criminology. (1988). *Corrections in Asia and the Pacific* (Record of the Ninth Asian and Pacific Conference of Correctional Administrators). Canberra, Australia: Author.

Biles, David. (1972). Australian prisons and their use. In D. Chappell and P. Wilson (Eds.), *The Australian criminal justice system* (pp. 623–655). Sydney, Australia: Butterworths.

Biles, David. (1986). Prisons and their problems. In D. Chappell and P. Wilson (Eds.), *The Australian criminal justice system: The mid 1980s* (pp. 238–254). Sydney, Australia: Butterworths.

Bulenda, T., Holda, Z., and Rzeplinski, A. (1990). *Human rights in Polish law and practice: Arrest and preliminary detention.* Unpublished manuscript.

Bureau of Justice Statistics. (1990, June). *Jail Inmates 1989.* Washington, DC: Department of Justice.

Bureau of Justice Statistics. (1989, April). *Prisoners in 1988.* Washington, DC: Department of Justice.

Bureau of Justice Statistics. (1990, May). *Prisoners in 1989.* Washington, DC: Department of Justice.

Chappell, Duncan. (1988). International developments in corrections: Australia in a bicentennial year. *The Prison Journal, 68*(1), 34–40.

Correction Bureau. (1985). *Correctional institutions in Japan.* Tokyo, Japan: Ministry of Justice.

Correction Bureau. (1990). *Correctional institutions in Japan.* Tokyo, Japan: Ministry of Justice.

Council of Europe. (1988, December). *Prison information bulletin* (Report number 12). Strasbourg, France: Author.

Demos, Nicholas, and Lucas, Louise. (1986). PIE: Inmates work free-world style. *Corrections Today, 48*(7), 62–65, 73.

Ehrmann, Henry W. (1976). *Comparative legal cultures.* Englewood Cliffs, NJ: Prentice Hall.

Empey, LaMar T. (1982). *American delinquency: Its meaning and construction* (rev. ed.). Homewood, IL: Dorsey Press.

Feest, Johannes. (1981, May). *Cross national study of correctional policy and practice, country profile: Federal Republic of Germany.* (Available from National Institute of Corrections Information Center, Longmont, CO).

Foucault, Michel. (1977). *Discipline and punish: The birth of the prison* (A. Sheridan, Trans.). New York: Pantheon Books.

Frankowski, Stanislaw. (1987). Poland. In G. F. Cole, S. J. Frankowski, and M. G. Gertz (Eds.), *Major criminal justice systems* (pp. 221–261). Newbury Park, CA: Sage.

Gifford, D. J. and Gifford, Kenneth H. (1983). *Our legal system* (2nd ed.). Sydney, Australia: Law Book Company.

Harris, Mark D. (1983, May 1). Viewing execution nets mixed feelings. *Augusta (GA) Herald,* pp. 1B, 5B.

Hillsman, Sally T., Mahoney, Barry, Cole, George F., and Auchter, Bernard. (1987). *Fines as criminal sanctions* (NIJ Research in Brief). Washington, DC: Department of Justice.

Hughes, Robert. (1987). *The fatal shore.* New York: Alfred A. Knopf.

International Symposium on Parole. (1986). *International perspectives on parole.* Symposium conducted April 6–9 in Austin, TX. (Report available from National Institute of Justice Information Center, Longmont, CO).

Iwarimie-Jaja, Darlington. (1989). Corrections: A system in need of reform (Nigeria). *C. J. International, 5*(5), 13–19.

Jenkins, Philip. (1987). Prison crowding: A cross-national study. *International corrections: An overview* (Monograph number 11, 17–25). College Park, MD: American Correctional Association.

Johnson, Elmer H., and Hasegawa, Hisashi. (1987). Prison administration in contemporary Japan: Six issues. *Journal of Criminal Justice, 15*, 65–74.

Katoh, Hisao. (1992). The development of delinquency and criminal justice in Japan. In H. Heiland, L. Shelley, and H. Katoh (Eds.), *Crime and control in comparative perspective* (pp. 69–81). New York: Walter de Gruyter.

Leivesley, Sally. (1986). Alternatives to imprisonment. In D. Chappell and P. Wilson (Eds.). *The Australian criminal justice system: The mid 1980s* (pp. 255–273). Sydney, Australia: Butterworths.

Lynch, James P. (1988). A comparison of prison use in England, Canada, West Germany, and the United States: A limited test of the punitive hypothesis. *Journal of Criminal Law and Criminology, 79*, 180–217.

Mauer, Marc. (1991). *Americans behind bars: A comparison of international rates of incarceration.* Washington, DC: The Sentencing Project.

Midford, Richard. (1992). Imprisonment: The Aboriginal experience in Western Australia. In M. Carlie and K. Minor (Eds.), *Prisons around the world* (pp. 11–23). Des Moines, IA: Wm. C. Brown.

Miller, E. Eugene. (1987). Corrections in the People's Republic of China. *International corrections: An overview* (Monograph number 11, 65–71). College Park, MD: American Correctional Association.

Morris, Norval. (1987). Alternatives to imprisonment: Failures and prospects. *Criminal justice research bulletin* (Vol. 3 No. 7 of a monograph series). Huntsville, TX: Sam Houston State University.

Nakayamma, Kinichi. (1987). Japan. In G. F. Cole, S. J. Frankowski, and M. G. Gertz (Eds.), *Major criminal justice systems* (pp. 168–187). Newbury Park, CA: Sage.

Newman, Graeme. (1978). *The punishment response.* Philadelphia: J. B. Lippincott.

Nomura, Yukio. (1987, July). Recent trends in the Japanese prison service. *Prison Service Journal*, 6–10.

O'Brien, Eris, and Ward, John. (1970). *The foundation of Australia.* Westport, CT: Greenwood Press.

Ostrihanska, Z., Balandynowicz, A., Jasinski, J., Kolakowska-Przelomiec, H., Kossowska, A., Porowski, M., Rzeplinska, I., Rzeplinski, A., and Wojcik, D. (1985). *Ordinary crime prevention and control in Warsaw.* Unpublished manuscript. Polish Academy of Sciences, Department of Criminology, Institute of State and Law, Warsaw.

Palmer, Michael J. (1992). Policing remote areas: Difficulties and initiatives. *C. J. International, 8*(2), 9–24.

Parker, L. Craig, Jr. (1986). *Parole and the community based treatment of offenders in Japan and the United States.* New Haven, CT: University of New Haven Press.

Platek, Monika. (1990). Prison subculture in Poland. *International Journal of the Sociology of Law, 18*: 459–472.

Rahim, M. A. (1986). *On the issues of international comparison of "prison population" and "use of imprisonment."* (Report No. 1986–41 from the Statistics Division, Programs Branch). Ottawa, Canada: Ministry of the Solicitor General.

Research and Training Institute. (1990). *Summary of the white paper on crime.* Tokyo, Japan: Ministry of Justice.

Rozalicz, Jacek (Trans.). (1989). *The penitentiary system in Poland.* Warsaw, Poland: Wydawnictwo Prawnicze.

Rzeplinski, Andrzej. (1988). *Prison labour in African countries* (Report UNSDRI 407 231 369). Rome, Italy: United Nations Social Defence Research Institute.

Sallman, Peter, and Willis, John. (1984). *Criminal justice in Australia.* Melbourne, Australia: Oxford University Press.

Schmidt, Annesley K. (1989). *Electronic monitoring of offenders increases* (Research in Action Report). Washington, DC: National Institute of Justice.

Shaw, A. G. L. (1966). *Convicts and the colonies.* London, England: Faber and Faber.

Shelley, Louise I. (1990). The Soviet militsiia: Agents of political and social control. *Policing and Society, 1,* 39–56.

Terrill, Richard. (1984). *World criminal justice systems: A survey.* Cincinnati, Ohio: Anderson.

Teske, Raymond H. C., Jr. and Albrecht, Hans-Jorg. (1991, March). An overview of probation procedures and statistics in the Federal Republic of Germany. Paper presented at the meeting of the Academy of Criminal Justice Sciences, Nashville, TN.

Tsuchiya, Shinichi. (1984, June). *Japan.* (Available from National Institute of Corrections Information Center; Longmont, CO)

Walker, John and Biles, David. (1986). *Australian community-based corrections: 1985–86.* Australian Capital Territory, Australia: Australian Institute of Criminology.

Weigend, Thomas. (1983). Sentencing in West Germany. *Maryland Law Review, 42,* 37–89.

Westermann, Ted D., and Burfeind, James W. (1991). *Crime and justice in two societies: Japan and the United States.* Pacific Grove, CA: Brooks/Cole.

Zawitz, Marianne W. (Ed.). (1988). *Report to the nation on crime and justice* (2nd ed.). Washington, DC: U.S. Department of Justice.

Zdenkowski, George. (1986). Sentencing: Problems and responsibility. In D. Chappell and P. Wilson (Eds.), *The Australian criminal justice system: The mid 1980s* (pp. 212–237). Sydney, Australia: Butterworths.

Chapter 9

An International Perspective on Juvenile Justice

KEY TOPICS

- Four models of juvenile justice
- The problem of juvenile offenders throughout the world
- Special panels for juveniles in Australia
- Children's hearing in Scotland
- Delay as a characteristic of Italian juvenile justice
- How corporatism moves decision making from the courts to administrative agencies
- China's educational response to young offenders

KEY TERMS

Children's Aid Panels

Children's Hearing

corporatist model

help and education teams

Juvenile Suspended Action Panels

Juvenile Liaison Bureau

la dottrina

legalistic model

net-widening

parens patriae

participatory model

peer juries

welfare model

COUNTRIES REFERENCED

Australia	Italy
China	Indonesia
Cuba	Scotland
England and Wales	Yugoslavia
Fiji	

On November 12, 1934, Charles Maddox was born out of wedlock to 16-year-old Kathleen Maddox in Cincinnati, Ohio. For the first several years of Charles's life, Kathleen would disappear for days and weeks at a time. Charles would ricochet between the homes of his grandmother and aunt. In 1939, Kathleen received a five-year penitentiary sentence after she and her brother were arrested for armed robbery in West Virginia. While his mom was "away," Charles stayed with an aunt and uncle until Kathleen's release. Now back with his mother, Charles lived in run-down hotel rooms visited by a long line of "uncles" who, like his mother, drank heavily.

After a year with foster parents, Charles was sent for by Kathleen, who had moved to Indianapolis. Again, he received minimal attention, but still had visits from a number of "uncles." In 1947 Kathleen tried unsuccessfully to place Charles with foster parents. Instead, Charles became a ward of the county and was sent to the Gibault Home for Boys in Terre Haute, Indiana. His stay at the home was not beneficial, as his record showed poor institutional adjustment, only a fair attitude toward school, moodiness, and a persecution complex. After ten months, Charles ran away to his mother, but she rejected him again.

Burglary and theft became part of Charles's life, and eventually he was sent to the Juvenile Center. After escaping, then recapture, he was placed at Father Flanagan's Boys Town. After only four days there, he stole a car and made it to Johnsonville, Iowa with stops for two armed robberies along the way. After "training" from a friend's uncle, Charles tried burglary but was arrested in his second attempt. Now age 13, Charles went to the Indiana Boys School, where he ran away 18 times during his three-year stay. His nineteenth attempt was successful, but it was not escape from his final prison. (This account adapted from Kenneth Wooden, *Weeping in the Playtime of Others*, © 1976 by McGraw-Hill, Inc. Reproduced by permission of McGraw-Hill, Inc.)

Charles's story highlights the classic conflict confronting society's response to juveniles. With its inception in 1899, the juvenile court in America reflected a concern for the care, protection, and treatment of children. Eventually, citizens expressed concern about the informal juvenile court as a violator of due process and called for greater attention to legal procedure. More recently, the philosophy of just deserts questions the basic concept of a juvenile justice system geared toward treatment instead of punishment. Juveniles like Charles were sent, presumably with good intentions, to institutions that responded to neglected (Charles's first stay) and delinquent (his later stays) youths.

One question his case brings up is whether a social welfare or treatment orientation is the most desirable societal response to neglected and/or misbehaving children. The sympathetic reader may well believe that a more compassionate societal response may have prevented Charles from falling into a pattern of delinquent and criminal behavior. That is, the justice system should have the welfare and protection of the juvenile foremost in its process.

On the other hand is the argument that the welfare and protection of society must be of predominant concern in the juvenile justice system. After all, kids like Charles may have unfortunate circumstances, but response to their misbehavior should still follow the process used to deal with any offender.

Both positions are reasonably argued. Sometimes a spectacular case influences a preference for one position. For example, I failed to mention that several years after Charles's birth, Kathleen married William Manson, who adopted Charles and gave him his name. The idea that the juvenile justice system should have ever expressed more concern about the care and protection of Charles Manson, over the welfare of society as a whole, is likely to send shivers up the back of people who remember the gruesome murders committed by Manson's "family" in 1969. However, it is just that type of philosophical difference now discussed throughout the world. What is the best way to respond to the inevitable problem youth, and to youths with problems?

Four models of juvenile justice are readily identified: the welfare model, the legalistic model, the corporatist model, and the participatory model. These models are taken from several sources (Binder, Geis, and Bruce, 1988; Pratt, 1989; United Nations, 1985), and are used here to provide a categorization format to allow description and discussion. The principles of each model are not mutually exclusive, so we must be careful not to suggest a country following one format will disagree with the tenets of the other schemes. We will review country-specific examples falling into each model but must first appreciate the problem that juvenile offenders present throughout the world.

Delinquency as a Worldwide Problem

At the Eighth United Nations Congress on the Prevention of Crime and the Treatment of Offenders, delegates from all regions of the world reported on the problem of juvenile offenders (United Nations, 1990a). Reports from the Arab region indicated that juvenile delinquency appeared less serious than in other parts of the world, but it was still cause for concern in several of those nations. For example, prosperous countries like Kuwait (prior to the Iraqi invasion), Saudi Arabia, and the United Arab Emirates were experiencing more difficulty than other Arab countries. Their problems were attributed to factors like the impact of migrants seeking employment, continued urbanization, sudden affluence and a rapidly changing economy, and a heterogeneous population.

More typically, delegates reported that delinquency was a problem throughout the countries of their region. When variation occurred, it was more likely to be within a country than between countries of the same region. For example, both the African and the Asian/Pacific regions reported juvenile crime and delinquency as being primarily an urban problem. In the African region, crimes of theft, robbery, smuggling, prostitution, and drug abuse/trafficking were linked to hunger, poverty, malnutrition, and unemployment factors more prevalent in the urban than rural areas. In the Asian/Pacific region urban areas received most of the youthful offenders' attention. Young people statistically constituted the most criminally active portion of the population and were especially involved in violent acts and drug-related offenses.

The problem of juvenile delinquency was reported as particularly acute in Latin America, where young people constituted a very high percentage of the population. This high proportion of juveniles (for example, 60 percent of Nicaraguans are under age 19) is also among the hardest hit by economic problems in the region. The turn to crime by this large and economically deprived portion of the population is disappointing but not particularly surprising.

The North American and European regions reported increases in delinquency since World War II and continue to view juvenile offenses as a serious problem. Stabilization and even decline in delinquency rates during the 1980s are not viewed as indication that the problem is really lessening. Demographics in both regions certainly had some role in the stabilization and decline, but the European region delegates countered that good news with concern over the region's increase in delinquency by females.

Obviously, crime by young people presents a problem for countries throughout the world. Not surprisingly, each country's response reflects the history and culture of its citizens. One area of historical and cultural differences that makes it difficult to compare how countries respond to juvenile offenders lies in the definitions related to the term *juvenile*.

Americans can appreciate the problem of varying definitions for the minimum age of criminal responsibility, because each of the 50 states can choose its own age limits. Actually, most states use 18 as the cutoff, so there is at least consensus if not uniformity. Of course, what appears to be agreement on that point conceals the dissension on other points. For example, there is considerable variation in how the states define the circumstances under which a juvenile's case can be heard in adult court (Rogers and Mays, 1987; Siegel and Senna, 1991). In some jurisdictions transfer to adult court is possible between the ages of 14 and 17, but in a few states a child of any age can be processed by the criminal courts. There are other jurisdictions where the determining factor is the type of crime being charged, with more serious offenses being excluded from juvenile court jurisdiction.

Not suprisingly, the variation seen in how American states handle juveniles is a microcosm of the variation found in countries of the world (see Figure 9-1). As an example, in Nigeria the age of criminal responsibility is fixed at 7 years,

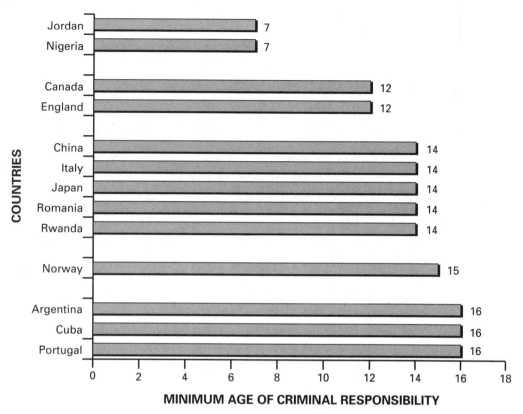

Figure 9-1. Age of criminal responsibility in selected countries.

but application of penal sanction to persons under age 17 is restricted by the Children and Young Persons Act. The Penal Code of another African country, Rwanda, sets the minimum age of criminal responsibility at 14 and considers offenders between 14 and 18 as having diminished responsibility (United Nations, 1990b).

While age 18 is popular in the United States, the ages 14 and 16 seem to be the preferred cutoff points in other countries. Just what they distinguish is not, however, always clear. In Argentina persons under age 16 cannot be charged under any circumstances, and in Cuba they cannot be tried by ordinary courts. But in China and Romania, 16 is the preferred limit but it can be dropped to 14 (so 14 is the absolute lower limit) if the offense is very serious (China) or if the juvenile is found to be capable of discernment (Romania). Obviously, just because a particular age is frequently mentioned by several countries does not mean that it is consistently applied.

In attempting to develop rules for the administration of juvenile justice, the United Nations was frustrated in its effort to define a minimum age of criminal responsibility (United Nations, 1985). Since some legal systems do not even recognize the concept of the age of criminal responsibility, the United Nations settled for broad statements and general guidelines. Rule 4.1 of the Standard Minimum Rules for the Administration of Juvenile Justice states:

> In those legal systems recognizing the concept of the age of criminal responsibility for juveniles, the beginning of that age shall not be fixed at too low an age level, bearing in mind the facts of emotional, mental and intellectual maturity (United Nations, 1986, p. 4).

One intention of this rule was to encourage countries where the age reached down to the level of infancy to raise that age so that the notion of responsibility would have more meaning.

The variation among countries regarding what age distinction will orient the justice system is repeated when attention turns to the procedures used to handle juveniles. This point brings us back to the models of juvenile justice noted earlier in the chapter.

MODELS OF JUVENILE JUSTICE

It is reasonable to suspect that the four major legal traditions would each produce a subsystem for handling juvenile offenders. Things are not that simple. In fact, there is often considerable variation among countries in the same legal family regarding their response to, and even definition of, delinquents. In the common legal tradition alone, we find countries emphasizing treatment (for example, Australia), justice (for example, South Africa), or administrative efficiency (for example, England and Wales). It is also important to note that juvenile justice models, like legal traditions themselves, undergo change over the years. A country's preference for a treatment approach to juveniles may be exchanged for a "get-tough" approach as citizens want young offenders to receive their just deserts.

The four models reviewed here (see Figure 9-2) should be considered classification aids allowing for description and discussion of approaches to juvenile justice. The countries used to exemplify each model will likely have aspects of the other types as well, and at some other point in time may even have been a prime example of another model. For present purposes, however, these countries follow certain procedures that highlight features of either a welfare, legalistic, participatory, or corporate model.

Welfare Model

The development of America's juvenile justice system was built on the doctrine of *parens patriae*. Following this teaching, the state is obliged to serve as guardian over children who are in such adverse conditions that their health and/or basic

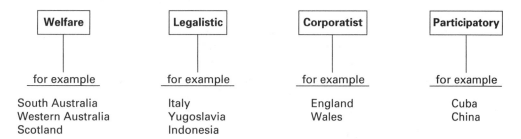

law-abiding nature may be in jeopardy. As a result, the juvenile court had jurisdiction over young people who were dependent or neglected (protection of the juvenile's health) or who had violated the penal code (protection of the juvenile's law-abiding nature). This emphasis on the child's general well-being is at the heart of the welfare model of juvenile justice.

The universal impact of the welfare model is best seen in the work of the United Nations. Rule 5.1 of the Standard Minimum Rules for the Administration of Juvenile Justice states:

> The juvenile justice system shall emphasize the well-being of the juvenile and shall ensure that any reaction to juvenile offenders shall always be in proportion to the circumstances of both the offenders and the offense (United Nations, 1986, p. 5).

When the United Nations takes the position that the aim of a juvenile justice system should be the well-being of the juvenile, it lends credibility to the welfare model and serves warning to the competing strategies. The Australian states of South Australia and Western Australia and the country of Scotland provide contemporary examples of the welfare model in action.

South Australia and Western Australia. From its claim of having established the world's first juvenile court in 1890 (Nichols, 1985; Sarri and Bradley, 1980) to its more recent use of Children's Aid Panels, South Australia portrays a long tradition of progressive juvenile justice. The basic principle underlying legislation for juveniles in South Australia is a concern for the protection and welfare of the child. Officials recognize, but do not accept, the claim that interests in protecting society and in protecting the child are contradictory. A 1968 government report concluded that "the aims of protecting society from juvenile delinquency, and of helping children in trouble grow up into mature and law abiding persons, are complementary and not contradictory" (quoted in Althuizen, 1977, p. 195).

To carry out this welfare-oriented approach, troubled youth proceed through a system of successive filters consisting of the nonjudicial Children's Aid Panels, through the Children's Courts, and to community-based intervention and residential care facilities. A review of these stages will exemplify the welfare and treatment emphasis of this approach.

The Children's Aid Panels (originally called Juvenile Aid Panels) were established in 1971 to achieve several goals. As a nonjudicial response, they provide an alternative to court action that: (1) supports and helps the child and family, (2) provides an opportunity for growth and development within the family and community, and (3) provides consistency and uniformity in handling youths in a way that does not forfeit flexibility (Sarri and Bradley, 1980).

The panels handle first offenders between the ages of 10 and 18 who are accused of fairly minor offenses. Cases not handled by the juvenile aid panel include children accused of homicide, those currently under a court order, and youths arrested by the police (Althuizen, 1977; Murray and Borowski, 1986; Sarri and Bradley, 1980). The police have an important role in determining whether a juvenile will go before a panel or the court. Arrested youths go directly to the juvenile court for processing. If the police do not make an arrest, they may refer the youth to a local Children's Aid Panel.

The panel proceedings are initiated by the local community welfare department, which has a welfare worker serving as panel secretary. The secretary arranges a panel meeting and invites the youth and his or her parents to attend. If the parents or child refuse the panel hearing, or if the youth denies the charges, the matter goes to the Children's Court.

The panel has two members: a senior police officer (sometimes a justice of the peace) and an experienced community worker from the welfare department. The panel's primary objective is to figure out a course of action that all participants can accept. They do this by questioning the child and parents and encouraging their comments on the situation. The options available to the panel include issuing a warning to the child and/or the parents, counseling sessions for the child and/or parents, the drawing up of a written agreement signed by the parties and stipulating specific action, and referral to juvenile court for further action (Sarri and Bradley, 1980).

In their evaluation of the South Australian panels, Sarri and Bradley (1980) found that youths processed through the panels had a reappearance rate similar to that of youths going through the Children's Court. While that seems faint praise for the panels, the authors point out that the panels have the advantage of achieving similar results with a more benign and less stigmatizing (no conviction is recorded) method. Nichols (1985) found other advantages to include handling cases within three to eight weeks of the offense instead of the three- to four-month wait for a Children's Court appearance; a fairly harmless way to warn juveniles and their parents about the danger of repeated offenses; and increased cooperation between police and welfare workers.

Of course, the panels present some problems as well (Nichols, 1985). Juveniles who are in fact innocent of the charges may be compelled to admit to them just to avoid a court hearing and possibly more severe punishment. The child and the parents subject their family to rather close inspection for what may actually be a rather minor offense. The question is how much intervention by welfare workers is actually needed, given the nature of the offense? Finally, some wonder how much impact the panelists can have in the 20 to 45 minutes they have with the family. Skilled and cooperative though they might be, there will be differences in the panelists' perception, approach, and influence.

Western Australia also uses children's aid panels and has found similar kinds of success, with claims that 83 percent of the children appearing before their panels do not reoffend (Murray and Borowski, 1986). The Western Australia version is called a Juvenile Suspended Action Panel and was first established in Perth in 1964. That initial model dealt only with children from age seven through 12. Since 1971 the upper age has been at 16 and the panels have spread throughout the state. Like their South Australia counterparts, the Juvenile Suspended Action Panels consist of a police officer and an officer of the Department of Community Welfare. The young person must plead guilty to the charges, and both the child and his or her parents must agree to a panel hearing (Murray and Borowski, 1986).

The Children's Courts in the Australian states also reflect a welfare orientation. If precourt options like children's aid panels are not appropriate or successful, the young offender is liable for more formal action in the juvenile court. In South Australia the revised legislation guiding the Juvenile Court since 1971 states the philosophy of the court as one placing foremost importance on the interests of the child. The appearance of a child in court suggests personal, family, or social problems (Althuizen, 1977). A variety of options are available to the court, including: dismissal of charges, placement under care and control of the welfare department (essentially probation), commitment to a residential center, imposition of a fine and/or compensation, or revocation of the juvenile's driver's license.

Postcourt programs in the Australian states show as much diversity for juveniles as Chapter 8 indicated is present for adults. In Victoria, for example, Youth Welfare Service programs accept male offenders age 14 to 17 who have at least one prior probation sentence (Murray and Borowski, 1986). The youths must attend the Youth Welfare Service facility three evenings per week and on Saturday are required to perform eight hours of community service work. Following a guided group interaction strategy, the programs also use peer group counseling as one of their core features.

In South Australia, supervision by community welfare workers has combined activities formerly divided between probation officers and welfare officers. The entire thrust is away from one-to-one counseling and family support by a court officer, to establishing a link between available community resources and the offender's needs. Following the lead of Victoria's Youth Welfare Service programs, South Australia also uses a program that allows closer supervision for some juveniles. The Children's Court may require attendance at a local Youth Project Center, which provides nonresidential care and control for juveniles needing closer supervision. On specified days and times, juveniles participate in group counseling and various activities. The Youth Welfare Service and Youth

Project Center are similar in concept and operation to the Community Treatment Centers popular in the United States during the 1970s.

For those juveniles unable or unwilling to respond to any of the early levels of societal response, the court can commit them to residential care. At these facilities the juveniles engage in work-training, education, and recreation with increased attention to such treatment methods as token economies.

Scotland. The South Australia and Western Australia systems provide a good example of the welfare model's philosophy but, except for the Children's Aid Panels and Juvenile Suspended Action Panels, the general structure is rather traditional. In Scotland, the welfare model does not simply provide precourt alternatives, but instead modifies the entire procedure for responding to youths. Most notable is the Scottish view that societal response to troubled juveniles should not concern only those youths who violate laws. Instead, assistance should be available for young people with a wide range of problems, including law violation. Moreover, that response should be a treatment-oriented one carried out in a nonlegalistic manner.

Scotland's Social Work Act of 1968 provided for that type of approach when it replaced juvenile courts with a system of children's hearings. These hearings provide a way to handle any "children in need of compulsory measures of care" (Wilson, 1974, p. 252). The identification of whom this process serves is intentionally broad to emphasize that the clientele is more than just juvenile offenders. Instead, the hearings would be for any person up to age 16 (or 18 if already under supervision) exhibiting or suffering from such circumstances as persistent truancy, incorrigibility, moral danger, or domestic disorder. Most youths do, however, enter the system as a result of committing an offense (Binder *et al.*, 1988).

Although the 1968 Act abolished juvenile courts, Scottish youths are not totally exempt from court reaction to their misbehavior. Serious cases like offenses against the person, weapons cases, or when a juvenile is jointly charged with an adult go before a regular criminal court (Jones and Murray, 1978; Martin, 1978).

Appearance at a children's hearing is determined by a *reporter* charged with investigating the allegations, and determining if the child needs care beyond what the parents can offer. The reporter, with a background in either law or social work, receives referrals from any agency or private individual, but most are the result of police or school concerns. The three options available to the reporter are (1) to take no further action; (2) referral of the child to the social work department for a voluntary supervision program; and (3) to refer the case to a children's hearing (Binder *et al.*, 1988; Jones and Murray, 1978). Before choosing the third option, the reporter must be satisfied that there is evidence of at least one ground for referral and that the child is in need of compulsory measures of care.

If a hearing seems appropriate, it is scheduled and organized by the reporter. Three members for a specific hearing come from a regional pool of volunteers. These volunteers, who responded to advertisements and then under-went interviews and preservice training, are to represent a cross section of community members with a variety of ages, incomes, and occupations. In practice, however, they tend to be homogenous and primarily middle class (Binder *et al.*, 1988; Jones and Murray, 1978).

The hearings are dispositional instead of adjudicatory. If a child accused of an offense denies the charge, the case first goes to the local criminal court (the Sheriff Court in Scotland) for determination of guilt or innocence. Typically, however, even cases going to trial return to the panel for disposition. Legal aid is not available at hearings, but parents and/or child can have a friend or representative (including legal) at the hearing.

While the reporter has a dominant role before the hearing, the social worker is the key figure during the hearing. The panel's main source of information is the social background report prepared by the social worker who visited the family before the hearing. As a person knowledgeable of treatment possibilities, the social worker may have and make particular recommendations regarding treatment.

Panel members rely on information from a variety of sources to make their decision regarding the diagnosis and treatment of juveniles. Reports from social workers and the child's school may be supplemented with accounts from psychiatrists, child guidance agencies, and other professionals. Information about the child's family background, prior experiences with social agencies, school habits, and clinical assessments provide details for panel discussion. Dispositions available to the panel include: to decide that compulsory care measures are not necessary and to discharge the youth; to order the child placed under community supervision; or to commit the child to a residential establishment (Jones and Murray, 1978).

Despite the sincere conviction that this action serves the child's best interests, serious injustices can result from the wide discretionary power of this non-judicial system. For example, some people worry about children and parents being pressured to accept grounds for referral to avoid public stigma and appearance before a trial court. Also, there is question about how adequately advised children and parents are of the right to appeal (Martin, 1978).

As noted earlier, similar concerns are expressed by critics of the Australian juvenile aid panels. In fact, Victoria decided in 1982 not to follow South Australia and Western Australia in establishing juvenile aid panels out of concern for possible negative impact on youths (Murray and Borowski, 1986). Victoria was troubled by the possibility that aid panels would result in the dilemma of net-widening. That problem, which has been a concern with diversion programs for some 20 years (Nejelski, 1976), refers to a phenomenon wherein a program actually serves to bring more people into the system rather than lowering the number through diversion. The state of Victoria feared that since the process appears rather benign, juvenile aid panels might be viewed as a good response to even low-risk youth. As a result, children who might never have come before any court official could be subjected to the control of a government agency.

	Welfare	Legalistic	Corporatist	Participatory
Key personnel	Child care experts	Lawyers	Administrators and bureaucrats	Community members
Use of formal process	Partial; prefers nonjudicial process	Full	Partial; prefers nonjudicial process	Scarce; prefers extralegal process
Prime objective	Protection and well-being of the juvenile is emphasized, with treatment taking priority over due process.	Due process and formal action take priority over treatment, since the emphasis is on applying the law.	Emphasis is on operating an effective juvenile justice system with increased efficiency and decreased delays.	Education of all citizens and the full integration of misbehaving youth into law-abiding society is emphasized.

Figure 9-3. Four juvenile justice models compared.

Specific concern in Victoria was over the question of legal protection. Since the panels require suspected youth to admit guilt before a case can be heard, juveniles may take what they perceive as a lenient option rather than maintaining their innocence and risking a harsher penalty. Further, once in front of the panel, juveniles stand without benefit of due process, which would be granted in the Children's Court. As the Victoria Legislative Review Committee put it, "'(we are concerned that) the juvenile aid panel is merely a court by another name, but lacking the advantages of legal protection normally afforded by court'" (quoted in Murray and Borowski, 1986).

Interest in ensuring that juveniles' rights are adequately protected when they enter the juvenile justice system has taken a dominant role in some countries. The resulting legalistic approach does not replace concern for the child's welfare with a preoccupation on due process, but the latter point is given priority (see Figure 9-3).

Legalistic Model

The legalistic approach to juvenile justice emphasizes applying the law instead of treating the juvenile. This strategy is not necessarily less humanitarian than the welfare model; it simply stresses when and how the law is used if a juvenile is involved. Indonesia provides an extreme example of this approach, since its penal code does not yet provide for any juvenile court structure (United Nations, 1990b). Instead, Indonesian juveniles are granted certain privileges within the framework of the adult criminal justice system. In this manner, juveniles are accorded all the due process requirements given to adult offenders. However, unfortunate results of this policy include the mixed occupancy of penal facilities by juveniles and adults and the difficulty of providing discretionary justice for youthful offenders.

More typical examples of a legalistic model are offered by Yugoslavia and Italy. Both countries recognize the important role for treatment of juveniles, but each relies on a criminal justice model for dealing with young offenders.

Yugoslavia. In 1992 the republics of Serbia and Montenegro proclaimed a new "Federal Republic of Yugoslavia." Since Serbia had a dominant role in determining the policies of the "old" Yugoslavia, the following discussion (although based on pre-1992 information) is likely to hold true for the "new" Yugoslavia. Even if it does not, the pre-1992 Yugoslavia provides an excellent example of the legalistic model and deserves our attention.

The first indication of the legal nature of Yugoslavia's juvenile justice system is the specification of offenses and age categories under court jurisdiction. Judicial intervention occurs only if the juvenile commits an offense defined by the Criminal Code. That means that petty offenses like minor traffic violations and public disorder are exempted from court control. Similarly, the Criminal Code does not contain something similar to status offenses in America. In other words, the Yugoslavian court hears cases only when the young person has committed an act that would have been a crime if committed by an adult. This does not mean that Yugoslavia lacks concern about other forms of juvenile misbehavior. However, the working assumption is that "agencies other than the courts should deal with minors who have manifested their deviance, not by committing a criminal offense, but by other kinds of deviant behavior" (Selih, 1978, p. 112).

Just as the court deals with specific offenses, it also has a particular clientele. Court jurisdiction does not begin until the minor has reached age 14. In fact, no court deals with a child under 14. People 14 to 16 at the time of the offense are "younger minors" and comprise the first age category heard by the court. Offenders in this age category can be responded to only through educational measures. "Older minors" are 16 to 18 years old and may receive an additional penalty of imprisonment.

Probably the most obvious aspect of Yugoslavia's legalistic approach is the absence of a separate juvenile court. As a result, juveniles receive the same protection given adults. There are, however, special sections for juveniles in the communal and district court systems (United Nations, 1990b). The communal courts hear cases where the penalty can be up to five years of imprisonment, and the district court has jurisdiction over all other cases.

Only public prosecutors may initiate proceedings against a minor between 14 and 18 years of age. This prosecutor has the discretion to dismiss a case against the juvenile during pretrial proceedings. Selih (1978) says this might be done upon the prosecutor's belief that the minor's personal traits, past conduct, and circumstances of the offense warrant dismissal. In addition, minor cases of "insignificant social danger" also may be dropped. Making this determination requires significant data collection about the juvenile's personality, family background, school performance, and the like. As in America's version of the medical model, more importance is theoretically attached to the offender than to the offense.

While officials compile the social history, the juvenile is returned to an observation center, referred to a social welfare agency, placed in a school, or, most likely, released to the parent's custody. In exceptional cases, the judge can hold the juvenile in preventive detention. But Selih (1978) suggests that it is hardly an exceptional measure, since some 20 percent of all juveniles get preventive detention.

If the prosecutor decides to proceed with the case, the judge makes plans for either a main trial or a session of the juvenile panel. The main trial, from which the public is excluded, is handled by the same judge who heard the pretrial proceedings. The goal of that requirement is to increase the judge's understanding of the history of the case and characteristics of the juvenile. The purpose of the trial is to prove that the accused juvenile was the offender, and to introduce the already gathered social information about the juvenile's rehabilitation and society's protection.

Less often used is the juvenile panel, which has a judge (as chairperson) and two lay judges (assessors) experienced in working with youth. The panel may apply only noninstitutional measures. Since the juvenile is absent during a panel session, Selih (1978) appropriately asks what becomes of the principle that juveniles should be present for adjudication.

The Yugoslav Criminal Code provides two special responses for dealing with juveniles: noninstitutional measures and juvenile imprisonment. The noninstitutional approaches are closely linked to educational measures. Examples include the reprimand, for cases not needing extended care. As the first measure typically applied, critics complain about its frequent use and its lack of any special effect (Selih, 1978). Commitment to a disciplinary center for minors for several hours per day over a one-month period is another noninstitutional measure. The final one is strict supervision in the community. That supervision can be assigned to parents, to a foster family, or to social agencies, and will last between one and three years.

Four kinds of institutional measures are possible:

1. Commitment to an educational institution
2. Commitment to an educational reformatory home
3. Commitment to an institution for defective minors
4. Juvenile imprisonment

The educational institutions are divided between those housing neglected children under age 14, and others housing minors over age 14. Educational reformatories receive delinquent minors, while institutions for defective minors house the handicapped, mentally ill, and physically underdeveloped.

In principle, juvenile imprisonment is close to the philosophy of educational measures. This sanction is used only for senior minors found guilty of an offense that could gain an adult more than five years of strict imprisonment. During their imprisonment (sentences range from one to 10 years), the minors undergo reeducation and receive vocational training.

Italy. In his exhaustive review and analysis of juvenile justice in Italy, Lemert (1986) explains how the formal tradition requires strict procedural legality in criminal justice for minors as well as for adults. He attributes this emphasis on legality to Italian doctrine (*la dottrina*), which features such things as a commitment to legal certainty, strict procedural legality, and the priority of enacted law.

Consistent with the civil legal tradition, *la dottrina* is not comfortable with situations wherein a single judge has wide discretionary power. As a result, Italy hesitated to follow the lead of early juvenile justice models (like that of the

*Sections of this discussion are taken from Lemert, Edwin W. (1986). Juvenile justice Italian style. *Law and Society Review*, 20:4, pp. 509–544. Reprinted by permission of the Law and Society Association.

United States) giving one judge, operating outside the traditional due process procedures, considerable discretion in handling youthful offenders. This did not mean, however, that Italy failed to recognize a need for differential response to juvenile offenders of the criminal code. In fact, as early as the thirteenth century, Italian cities were declaring children immune from punishment for murder and providing for placement in houses of correction instead of prisons (Lemert, 1986).

Despite its early start, Italy was among the last of the Western European nations to set up a juvenile court. This 1934 formal achievement was preceded by developments like the 1929 creation of special sections in the Courts of Appeal which provided prosecutors with instruction and judgment on juvenile cases. Also, 1930 brought a penal code revision that raised the age of minimum responsibility from nine to 14 while lowering the age of full responsibility from 21 to 18. The 1934 law solidified these prior actions and gave the new juvenile court jurisdiction over youths who are shown to have strayed (*traviamento*) and are in need of correction.

Lemert (1986) argues that the formal establishment of an Italian juvenile court presented an intriguing conflict which continues today. Since the court has jurisdiction over minors who have "strayed" and are in need of correction, Italy essentially follows the traditional American emphasis on the offender and individualized treatment of delinquent youth. However, Italy has not rejected *la dottrina's* emphasis on the offense and its accompanying dislike for variability in sanction where similar offenses were committed. The result is an awkward alliance between legality's consistency and individualization's variability. New provisions for juvenile procedures which were implemented in 1989 provide juvenile court judges with more options for handling defendants under age 18 (United Nations, 1990b), but the context of legality remains. The resulting mixture provides Italy with a juvenile justice system offering formal rigidity tempered by informal adaptability.

Formally, Italian juvenile justice requires strict procedural legality in criminal justice for both minors and adults. That means that prosecution is not waived, plea bargains are not made, and juvenile diversion programs or informal probation are not possible. Of course such requirements are difficult to enforce. Lemert (1986) provides reports from police and court officials who use such tactics as informal arrest, withholding of charges, and referral to family members, in lieu of formal action. In this fashion, the appearance of strict legality is maintained, since cases handled in the official manner do indeed follow the formal procedures. This situation is exemplified even more clearly by looking at informal maneuvering in the juvenile court.

The Italian penal code specifies that minors 14 years old and over can be found guilty and punished like adults. Simultaneously, the juvenile court is charged with correcting the behavior of youth who have strayed. As Lemert says, "The task the judges confront is one of maintaining the appearance of legality while doing something else" (1986, p. 532). The "something else" takes several forms, each of which avoids the formal requirement of strict procedural legality.

For example, juveniles found to be "immature" can be released, while others may receive a judicial pardon or a suspended sentence. Suspended sentences can be accompanied by dispositions like fines, placement with social services, or even partial institutionalization, but even these are more individualized than the formal legality requires.

Where finding of immaturity, pardon, or suspended sentence is not appropriate, the use of delay is often beneficial. As one of the major characteristics of Italian juvenile justice, delay is often explained as the result of inadequate staff and facilities, and of pressures for postponement made by police, prosecutors, and even judges. Since delay often results in a magistrate's granting of a pardon, Lemert (1986) suggests that some juvenile courts may actually use delay as a means of treatment. With this strategy, judges use continuances rather deliberately while the youth matures out of his delinquency.

These techniques to provide individualization under the constraints of strict legality let Italy remain true to *la dottrina* while providing individual sanctioning of juvenile offenders. As we saw with the Yugoslav example, a legalistic approach to juvenile justice does not require a country to avoid attention to the child's welfare in the interest of ensuring the child's legal rights.

The welfare and legalistic models of juvenile justice present the horns of a dilemma. If the legalistic approach seems to lack compassion and flexibility, the welfare approach may go to another extreme in lack of concern for legal protection. When speaking of the Scottish system, Murray expresses concern about "welfare totalitarianism, in which we take control of people's lives and liberties with no better justification than the belief that we know what is best for them" (1978, p. 86). It is not surprising that some countries have tried to balance desirable aspects of the legalistic and welfare models. One such attempt has resulted in what Pratt (1989) calls the *corporatist approach*.

Corporatist Model

It is possible that conflict between the welfare and legalistic models could lead to a symbiotic relationship wherein the goals of each are reached through cooperation by various institutions in a country. In fact, we might argue that some countries, Italy for example, may have the cultural and bureaucratic base to achieve a success of this type. Unfortunately, just when a solution between conflicting issues seems within grasp, another variable often presents itself. This seems to be the situation giving rise to our third model of juvenile justice: corporatism.

England and Wales seemed well on the way to combining the welfare and legalistic approaches in their juvenile justice systems. In fact, Binder *et al.* (1988) offer these countries as examples of a combined approach. A problem with this example is suggested by Pratt (1989) when he draws attention to the importance England and Wales have given to a "justice model" of juvenile justice since the early 1970s. An important part of the justice model is increased attention to due process, right to counsel, visible and accountable decision making, and other procedures typically linked to the legalistic model. But the justice model goes beyond the legalistic approach, because it also requires punishment of the juvenile offender. In this manner, the public's interest in seeing juveniles get their "just deserts" is the new variable making difficult the combination of welfare and legalistic approaches.

The movement from a welfare orientation to a legalistic one, with the additional concern for punishment, provided England and Wales with a new juvenile justice approach best described as "corporatism" (cf. Pratt, 1989). Before explaining the meaning of this term, it will be helpful to review the developmental path that juvenile justice followed in this part of the United Kingdom.

In 1908, England and Wales established separate courts for juvenile law violators from ages seven to 16. These courts were actually special sittings of magistrates' courts held at a separate place or at a different time from adult hearings (Marshall, 1978). Besides those criminal duties, the juvenile courts had civil jurisdiction in cases of neglected or destitute children. Over the years, the initial English reaction to youths has become more specific and well defined. In 1933, the minimum age for criminal responsibility increased to eight, and a system of "approved schools" developed to treat juveniles between ages 10 and 17. A 1963 Act encouraged diversion of young offenders from the juvenile courts and again raised the age of responsibility—this time from eight to 10 (Binder *et al.*, 1988).

A significant legislation affecting juvenile justice in England and Wales was the 1969 Children and Young Persons Act. The act was important because it represented a compromise between the welfare and legalistic approaches so that a juvenile's welfare was assured, but within the context of procedural safeguards.

The 1969 Act raised the minimum age of criminal responsibility from 10 to 12, and allows a young person to be taken to juvenile court on criminal charges only when a "qualified" person (a police officer) brings a formal charge. Before bringing those formal charges, the police officer must see if the complaint can be handled by another means. One possibility is a formal "police caution" administered at the police station in the presence of parents by a uniformed officer (Emmins, 1988). If the juvenile admits to the offense, a senior police officer administers the caution by explaining to the juvenile that prosecution will not occur this time but similar acts in the future will likely result in a court appearance. Since the caution is an official formal action (but not a conviction), it can be referred to in any later juvenile court proceedings.

For jurisdictional purposes, a juvenile in England is a person who has not reached age 17. However, simply being a juvenile does not ensure an appearance before the juvenile court. The juvenile court, which remains a special form of magistrates' court, hears cases when juveniles are charged by themselves or with other juveniles. If a juvenile is charged with an adult, both juvenile and adult come before the adult magistrates' court. Even in that adult court, however, the juvenile can be tried summarily (determined by the magistrates or by statute) instead of being subjected to the regular adult court proceedings. Upon reaching age 17, all persons are treated the same for purposes of criminal procedure.

However, persons aged 17 through 20 can receive sentences that are not available to offenders age 21 and older (Emmins, 1988).

Should the youth end up in juvenile court, the focus is on guilt or innocence. If found guilty, the court then determines the proper disposition. In concurrence with the legalistic model, the fundamental legal basis of the British juvenile court is the same as that of the adult court (Thornton *et al.*, 1987). As such, youths have such procedural protection as legal representation, legal aid, specification of charges, proof beyond a reasonable doubt, rights to appeal, and so on.

Children under age 12 go before the juvenile court only for purposes of "care" proceedings. A criminal offense can be a circumstance resulting in a care proceeding, but this is also the means by which the court hears cases of neglect, abuse, incorrigibility, and the like.

Whether brought before the juvenile court or, as necessary, the magistrates' court, for care or criminal proceedings, the youth is subject to similar dispositions. After deciding that a child has committed an offense or needs care, the court can (Emmins, 1988; Emmins and Scanlan, 1988):

1. Discharge (either conditionally or absolutely) the case.
2. Issue a hospital order.
3. Fine the juvenile or parent.
4. Issue a care order.
5. Issue a community service order.
6. Issue a community supervision order.
7. Issue an attendance center order.
8. Place the juvenile in a Young Offender Institution.

We will look briefly at each to provide an idea of what they entail. The first several are rather straightforward. When a case is *discharged*, the offender is either let off completely and suffers no adverse effects at all (an absolute discharge), or the offender is warned not to commit an offense during a specified time period (not exceeding three years) and upon successful completion will never suffer an actual penalty (a conditional discharge). *Hospital orders* are used, for both juveniles and adults, in cases where medical evidence suggests that an offender charged with an imprisonable offense needs treatment for a mental disorder. In such cases the offender (either juvenile or adult) is placed in a hospital in lieu of an actual sentence. *Fines* can be ordered against juveniles (with higher limits for those 14 to 17 than for those under 14), with the parent actually directed to pay the sum. The expectation of the court is that the parents will be reimbursed from the child's pocket money.

The *care order*, which essentially removes the juvenile from the home, is to be used only for serious offenses that could be punishable with imprisonment.

One can be discharged early from a care order, but the order is assumed to be in force until the child reaches age 18 (19 if the juvenile was 16 or over upon receiving the care order). Many children are sent to community houses, which include those providing education on the premises (hence the juvenile need not leave the "home") and those where the childern are sent to regular schools. Other placement options include foster homes and residences operated by volunteer agencies.

Courts dealing with offenders aged 16 and older who are charged with an imprisonable offense may impose a *community service order*. Offenders so sentenced must perform, without pay, work of value to the community. The required hours range from a minimum of 40 to a maximum of 240 (120 for 16-year-olds).

Upon receiving a *supervision order*, the juvenile is placed under the guidance of the local social services department (under 12 years old) or probation service (age 12 and over). This order may include specific requirements, like place of residence, curfew requirements, and school attendence, but the intent is to provide flexible social welfare support for up to three years or until the eighteenth birthday.

Attendance centers are for persons guilty of an offense but not committed to a career of crime. Boys under 17 have been the primary candidates for this disposition, but recent efforts have increased involvement of girls. The punishment is basically "loss of leisure" (Marshall, 1978), since the youth must attend sessions at facilities run by volunteer police officers or teachers. The sessions run for at least two hours, typically on Saturday afternoons, and are often purposely made to conflict with more enjoyable activities like sporting events the youth may have wanted to watch. The person in charge determines the regime, which will include firm discipline as well as handicrafts and physical activity.

Prior to 1988 custodial sentences for young offenders were of two types. Detention centers received 14- to 17-year-olds found guilty of offenses for which adults could be imprisoned. These full-time facilities provided education, work, and short-term treatment over a period of about three months. For longer-term confinement, youths age 15 and older were sentenced to youth custody if they were guilty of an offense for which an adult could be imprisoned. The sentence was indeterminate and ranged from six months to two years.

The Criminal Justice Act of 1988 abolished the distinction between youth custody sentences and detention center orders. Now the only custodial orders a court may give offenders under age 21 is a sentence of detention in a young offender institution (YOI). The result is a merging of youth custody and detention sentences and centers. Juveniles sentenced to a YOI must be age 14 (15 for girls) through 20. The maximum term of imprisonment varies depending on the juvenile's age (that is, 4 months for 14 year olds and 12 months for those 15 to 21), but in any case the sentence is considered only for the more serious crimes when a noncustodial sentence cannot be justified.

At this point it would be appropriate to explain how the 1969 Children and

Young Persons Act or the 1988 Criminal Justice Act achieved the historic compromise between the apparently conflicting welfare and legalistic models. Unfortunately, that report cannot be made, since full implementation of the 1969 Act never took place and the 1988 Act only incidentally dealt with juveniles. The problems with fulfilling the 1969 Act's provisions included lack of funding, and ideological quarreling between more punishment-oriented magistrates and rehabilitation-minded social workers (Binder *et al.*, 1988; Thornton *et al.*, 1987).

The ideological quarreling was reflected in the 1982 passage of a Criminal Justice Act whose provisions show that the justice model had achieved considerable influence. That influence continued with the Criminal Justice Act of 1988 and, for example, the merging of custodial sentences. While still recommending diversion from the juvenile justice system, the primary means for diversion is now the police caution. The general thrust of legislation has been a return to a custodial model that sees more youth accused of crime going to court, and greater use of institutionalization for those found guilty (Binder *et al.*, 1988; Pratt, 1989). Despite the emphasis on just deserts, it is not appropriate to view England and Wales as typifying a justice (that is, punitive or retributive) approach to juvenile offenders. Both countries still hold too many welfare approach ideals and implement extensive legalistic model procedures to claim primary adoption of a just deserts philosophy. Instead, the trends in England and Wales brought those countries to a corporatist approach toward juvenile justice.

Corporatism is a tendency found in advanced welfare societies when society itself creates social institutions that accept the duties and responsibilities formerly held by the government. As a process, corporatism does not have to occur throughout society affecting all of its institutions simultaneously. Instead, it can occur in particular areas including, according to Pratt (1989), the juvenile justice system. From this position, Pratt argues that juvenile justice in England and Wales moved from a welfare approach to what he calls a corporatist model.

Pratt uses the term *corporatism* to refer to a tendency to reduce conflict and disruption through "centralization of policy, increased government intervention, and the cooperation of various professional and interest groups into a collective whole with homogeneous aims and objectives" (1989, p. 245). He argues that corporatism is becoming the predominant approach in juvenile justice in England and Wales. To support that argument he highlights the increased administrative discretion encouraged by the various diversion programs. Movement of decision making from the courts to the administrative agencies increases efficiency and decreases delay, so the juvenile justice system can operate more effectively (see Figure 9-3).

As administrative discretion grows, so too do the extralegal sanctions available to these agencies. Minor breaches by juveniles in community programs can be handled by the program staff without requiring appearance before the juvenile court. Social workers and other treatment personnel, who were already co-opted into the welfare approach's adjudication and decision-making process, are now involved in constructing and devising the penalty itself.

While the decision making for "what to do" is moving from the court the administrative agencies, corporatism also affects "how to do it" concerns moving emphasis from due process to policy. This is seen in the Northam Juvenile Liaison Bureau, which acts as a body designed to divert cases juvenile court and deliver instead a form of administrative justice (Pratt, The members of the liaison bureau represent the agencies respons responding to offending youths. In consultation with each other, the members are able to avoid the delays inherent in the traditional juver The Bureau is not so quick to point out if delays resulting from du guarantees, which youths receive when taken before a magistrate avoided! In other words, corporatism is more interested in guara desired way of management (that is, policy) than in ensuring that th was accorded appropriate due process.

The bureaucratic-administrative form of law, seemingly brough ratism, is acceptable to policy makers and government officials because it operates as only one side of the juvenile justice coin. As mentioned earlier, the advent of a just deserts punishment model made it difficult for England and Wales to simply combine welfare and legalistic approaches to juvenile justice. The public also wanted the offender to be punished for the wrongdoing. Importantly, however, this retributive philosophy was not applicable to all juvenile offenders. Instead, the pound of flesh was demanded of only the most serious, violent, and dangerous youths. The corporatist model developed in England and Wales because it allows the secure custody sanction to remain in effect for the hard-core offenders. As long as the noncustodial alternatives are used for offenders deemed safe to have in the community, corporatism is likely to move forward as a juvenile justice model.

Even more so than the welfare model, corporatism relies on members of the community to assist in meeting the needs of youthful offenders. In both approaches, however, the noncourt personnel are professionals in areas like social welfare, medicine, probation, and law enforcement. A final model to juvenile justice expands on the role of the community to the extent that it becomes very participatory in nature.

IMPACT

This chapter's review of four models of juvenile justice allows us to appreciate better both the overlap and contrasts among the approaches. Each model seems genuinely interested in addressing the child's needs in balance with community interests. Admittedly, the scale's balance often tips toward one side or the other, but each approach recognizes that juveniles require different handling than do adults. What impact do these models have on the justice response to juveniles in the United States? Can we categorize juvenile justice in each American state as typifying one of the four approaches? Are there programs used in other countries, regardless of the model followed, which can be transferred to this country? If we argue that American juvenile justice began with a welfare approach, do we also claim that we have since moved to a legalistic model? Does the participatory model work only in countries oriented around a socialist political economy, or can increased reliance on community members be effective under democratic capitalism? Is the movement in England and Wales toward a corporatist model, built around bureaucratic administrative law, the likely direction for juvenile justice in the United States?

Obviously there are many intriguing and important questions having possible impact on America's version of juvenile justice. We will look at only two. The first concerns an American twist on aid panels. The second suggests the potential for a fifth approach, which may be the best of all: benign neglect.

An American Twist

A consistent theme in several countries reviewed here is the use of community members or professionals to decide the appropriate disposition for a young person in trouble. The children's aid panels in South Australia, the children's hearing panels in Scotland, Yugoslavia's infrequently used juvenile panel, and China's help and education teams either replace, or provide assistance to, a single judicial authority charged with disposing of juvenile offenders. Adherence to the principle of a jury system makes the use of similar citizen panels in the United States likely. However, since the U.S. Supreme Court ruled that juveniles do not have the right to trial by jury (*McKeiver* v. *Pennsylvania*, 403 US 528, 1971), there is no existing structure to provide for citizen input in American juvenile justice. As I have tried to emphasize throughout this book, the absence of an existing structure in this country does not mean that valuable examples are also absent. Maybe the various forms of citizen panels used in other countries can provide ideas useful in America. In fact, an experiment in a Georgia county has already made use of ideas similar to citizen panels in South Australia and Scotland. The American "twist" to those citizen panels is the use of other juveniles rather than adults in determining what the response to a misbehaving juvenile should be.

Columbia County (Georgia) Peer Juries. Peer juries are informal adjustment programs where age peers make recommendations regarding the disposition of adjudicated youth who have volunteered to go before the jury. One peer jury that has received the attention of researchers (Reichel and Seyfrit, 1984; Seyfrit *et al.*, 1987) is in Columbia County, Georgia. In January 1980 a program was drawn up under the authority of the "Informal Adjustment" section of the Georgia Juvenile Court Code. That program provided a peer jury to serve in the capacity of advisor to the court. Potential jurors must be under age 17 (the same age cohort as youth under juvenile court jurisdiction in Georgia), may not currently be under supervision by the court, must not have any pending offenses, must be working to potential in school (or have gainful employment), and must undergo training by the Youth Services staff. In addition, the juveniles wishing to serve as peer jurors must return a parental permission form showing that parents are aware of, and consent to, the child's participation.

The Columbia County Peer Jury hears cases meeting the following criteria:

1. The complaint is within the jurisdiction of the juvenile court, and is of a nonviolent nature.

2. The youth admits the complaint.

3. It appears that it is in the best interest of the youth and the community to handle the complaint informally.

4. The youth and parents or guardians are in agreement to participate in the peer jury program, and abide by the conditions set.

5. The length of time the youth can be supervised cannot exceed six months.

The presumed benefit of peer juries lies in the ability of age peers to understand the problems and behaviors of other youths and to make recommendations that can positively influence the misbehaving youngster. To this end, peer jurors are encouraged to use their imaginations when making recommendations. Their recommendation cannot set any conditions that involve physical punishment, detention, or restrictions extending beyond six months. Examples of recommendations made by the peer juries include: curfew restrictions, making oral or written apologies, better school attendance, restitution either financially or in terms of community work, and, possibly the most effective, surrendering of a driver's license.

The success of the peer jury program has been measured in several ways. First, researchers sent questionnaires to peer jurors, youth who went before the peer jury, and parents of the offenders. Results of the questionnaire suggest that all participants felt the peer jury set conditions that were fair and appropriate. Importantly, these conditions were seen as coming from a supportive and understanding environment by persons who could empathize with the offender. The offenders made comments like:

"They were more my age so I guess they understood me."

"It made me feel like I was among friends who understood how adults could pressure you."

"You get a better chance because they are about your age and think the same way you do."

The results of the qualitative analysis of the peer jury supported the program's efforts, but researchers needed quantitative data to determine if the effort helped change the offender's behavior. To that end, researchers evaluated the effectiveness of the Columbia County Peer Jury as determined by its success in reducing later involvement in delinquency by youth who had gone before the peer jury.

After the creation of the Peer Jury, few Columbia County juveniles went through the more traditional informal adjustment procedure. Therefore, there were not enough incidents to allow a comparison within the county of peer jury cases and traditional cases. The alternative was to compare the Columbia County peer jury cases with traditional cases in another Georgia county. Liberty County had enough similarities to justify its selection as a comparison sample, so researchers analyzed records for 52 Columbia County youths and 50 in Liberty County. Information sought included the offense for which the juvenile was first committed, the number of prior offenses, and the number of offenses after informal adjustment. The data show the peer jury handled more serious crimes and more serious offenders but the percentage of youths committing later offenses was slightly (not significant) lower than in Liberty County. The researchers conclude (Seyfrit *et al.*, 1987) that the peer jury can handle more serious offenses and second offenders as effectively as the traditional system and, for that reason, may be a desirable diversion technique.

The evaluations of Columbia County's Peer Jury and of South Australia's Aid Panel were consistent in finding that such welfare approach programs posed no increased risk to the public (Sarri and Bradley, 1980; Seyfrit *et al.*, 1987). Neither program, however, is without its critics. Under both procedures there remain concerns about the potential for net-widening effects and for violating the juvenile defendant's due process. It seems the justice personnel cannot please everyone.

No approach seems to allow a formal response to juvenile offenders which simultaneously meets the juvenile's needs (while providing community security) and protects the juvenile's due process concerns (while avoiding the negative stigma brought by legal action). The frustration of being unable to please everyone may convince some people that no response at all is the best reaction. In fact, with tongue only partly in his cheek, Hackler (1991) suggests that juvenile justice in the United States and Canada might benefit from Fiji's more casual way of handling juvenile offenders.

A Benign Neglect Approach

Hackler (1991) offers the juvenile justice system in Fiji as an example of one that is superior to those in North America in meeting the goal of reintegrating young people back into the community. This position is built on the idea that "countries with more developed social control agencies, particularly those heavily influenced by legal traditions, can unwittingly create bureaucracies that hurt clients more than they help" (Hackler, 1991, p. 104). In contrast, countries without similar "development" may be more successful in assisting their juveniles through a period of delinquency and into a position as law-abiding adults.

The country of Fiji is composed of more than 800 islands, but two, Viti Levu and Vanua Levu, account for over 80 percent of its land area. The capital city of Suva, located on Viti Levu, has about 70,000 people. As a port city Suva has its share of crime, much of which is attributable to juveniles. But upon inspecting the statistics for juvenile court cases, one would think that Fiji is either crime free or her criminals are all adults. Hackler (1991) reports that only 12 juveniles had been charged during 1989 in the Suva magistrate's court. The combination of a port city crime rate with a very small number of juvenile cases suggests that Suva may be diverting problem juveniles from a formal court appearance.

After a 1975 recommendation that police screen more juvenile cases from the court system, the Fijian police force established the Police Juvenile Bureau in 1979. Under the new program, the Police Juvenile Bureau received information about a case and conducted an investigation before any charges were made. The process involved visits with victims, the accused juvenile, and the juvenile's family. The investigating police officer could caution the juvenile, and this happened in a large majority of the cases, but also operated as a liaison with other social and government organizations in the community (Hackler, 1991).

A military coup, and accompanying economic problems, forced the abolishment of the Police Juvenile Bureau in 1987. But Hackler (1991) reports that the communication links established between police and community agencies continue to operate. Police officers still bring formal charges against only a few juveniles, and rely instead on police connections with court alternatives.

When formal charges are brought, the juvenile is taken before a chief magistrate at a regular court of law. There is no specialized juvenile court in Fiji, but the use of an adult court system does not require Fiji to mimic Yugoslavia's legalistic approach. In fact, the lack of concern for due process would likely disturb many observers. Consistent with the informality of police–juvenile encounters, court–juvenile confrontations in Fiji offer only casual protection of due process. For example, like the concurrent consideration of guilt-finding and sentencing in Germany (see Chapter 7), Fijians do not strictly separate issues of guilt and punishment. A juvenile brought before a Fijian judge is just as likely to be asked about the circumstances of his life as the circumstances of his offense. The judge responds less to concerns about the proving of guilt than to the problem of how to handle juveniles in trouble.

The informality at police and court levels is repeated in the type of facilities used to house the few juveniles who are formally processed at those earlier stages. The Suva juvenile detention center, now located in buildings at a former leper colony, houses the approximately 35 delinquents who were not successfully handled at the police or court levels. While these are presumably the most difficult juvenile offenders, they are not kept locked up. Most attend school outside the center, while others enroll in vocational training programs or work as apprentices (Hackler, 1991). The freedom of movement means that the youths occasionally abscond, but even that is responded to in a casual manner by having police contact detention center staff if they determine a runaway's location.

Admittedly, economics may be directing juvenile justice policy in Fiji. The absence of specific courts for juvenile offenders may result in greater efforts to avoid formal processing. Similarly, the lack of money for a fence and reliance on a rusty jeep to chase runaways may require a nonchalant response to detention center escapes. A stronger economic base may encourage Fiji to respond more formally and legalistically to juveniles, but that will not necessarily be an efficient or effective response. As Hackler (1991) argues, Fiji's consistently informal response to misbehaving juveniles avoids the trappings of presumably advanced systems which rely on legal tradition and government bureaucracies. It may be unfair to identify Fiji's juvenile justice system as a benign neglect approach; but is it possible that doing less is actually better than doing more?

Participatory Model

The participatory model of juvenile justice requires active participation by community agencies and citizens in a concerted effort to contain the harmful behavior of young people (United Nations, 1985). The primary goal of this approach is the full integration of misbehaving youths into the mainstream of society without any significant use of formal legal intervention. The model is especially popular in countries following a socialist political–economic philosophy. In Cuba, for example, youths under age 16 cannot be tried by ordinary courts nor be subject to penal sanctions (United Nations, 1990b). Instead, juvenile offenders participate in education and treatment programs at "schools of good conduct" operated by the Ministry of Education. Also available is placement at reeducation centers operated by the Ministry of Interior. It is possible that the setting and impact of these schools and centers are equivalent to institutional placement in other countries, but Cuba's stated policy toward juvenile offenders is one of educational evaluation and treatment.

The People's Republic of China also emphasizes a participatory approach and, more clearly than does Cuba, makes specific use of citizens and agencies outside the legal arena. China provides the primary example of the participatory model, and its system suggests interesting differences from the welfare, legalistic, and corporatist approaches.

People's Republic of China.   Between its founding (1949) and the 1960s, the People's Republic of China did not regard juvenile delinquency as especially troublesome. Young criminals made up only 20 percent of the criminal population in the 1950s and some 30 percent in the early to mid-1960s (Zu-Yuan, 1988). However, the increased economic growth and higher standard of living since 1976 brought steadily increasing delinquency rates. The Deputy Director of the Research Institute for Public Security in Beijing reported young offenders as now making up 70 to 80 percent of the criminal population in big and medium cities, and 60 to 70 percent in the countryside (Zu-Yuan, 1988).

China's system of responding to juvenile offenders has a legalistic aspect similar to Yugoslavia's. For example, the Chinese Criminal Code provides that persons who have reached 16 years of age shall bear criminal responsibility for their acts. Persons aged 14 to 16 who commit the crimes of murder, serious injury, robbery, arson, habitual theft, or other crimes seriously undermining the social order also shall bear criminal responsibility. But persons between 14 and 18 who commit a crime should receive a lesser or mitigated punishment (Myren, 1989; United Nations, 1990b; Zhao, 1990).

Rather than having a specific juvenile court, basic-level people's courts can create special courts to handle peculiarities of various cases. With juvenile offenses presenting "peculiar cases," the People's Court in Shanghai in 1984 developed a specialized children's criminal court that has served as a model for the country. By the end of the 1980s, more than 100 of these special tribunals had been established to consider offenses committed by youths between ages 14 and 18 (United Nations, 1990b). These courts comply with the procedural law set down in the Chinese Code, but they operate under a dual philosophy of education and punishment. The emphasis is on education for younger children committing minor offenses, and then shifts to punishment for older children engaged in serious offenses.

Since China's educational response to young offenders is especially representative of the participatory model, we begin discussion with this younger group. The basic assumption is that juvenile offenders, like their adult counterparts, fail to understand and embrace socialism. If society can simply convince the offenders that a socialist perspective and life-style is desirable, the craving for crime will pass. Given this conviction, it is not surprising that response to juvenile offenders is scattered among many agencies and organizations (see Figure 9-3). Programs that focus on raising the moral character and sense of legality of youth as a whole, and delinquents in particular, are carried out through economic, cultural, educational, administrative, and legal means (Zu-Yuan, 1988).

Chinese authorities seem to have taken their lead from the classical school of criminology when they place great emphasis on the doctrines of rationality, free will, and deterrence. Actually, their position is based in their own culture through the values of Confucian philosophy (Troyer, 1989). That philosophy believes that humans are basically good and that we act only after thinking (that is, humans are rational). Further, humans are educable, so proper education and training will produce virtuous citizens. From that perspective, intense reliance on educating the public about laws is less a twentieth-century socialist notion than a pre-Christian native one.

Regardless of its ancestry, since 1979 the Chinese have made concerted efforts toward a public legal education campaign that teaches virtually every citizen about law and the legal system. Troyer (1989) describes two phases of the campaign as being routine legal education (1979–1985) and special legal education (1985 to the present). During the first stage, "propaganda (in the Chinese sense of educate and inform) workers" were assigned to teach people about the constitution, the criminal code, and other laws. The print media also played an important role in disseminating information, as did the judges and the police. In fact, some claim that legal education became the major task for patrol officers in China (Troyer, 1989). The goal in each of those efforts was to make sure young people knew what behavior was legal and illegal, and what punishment would be imposed for violating the law.

The second stage, or the special legal education campaign, builds on the groundwork laid from 1979 to 1985. To implement this new stage, the Ministry of Justice established legal education offices throughout the country. From these offices, seven million "legal advocators" help citizens learn, understand, and use the laws and legal system (Troyer, 1989). The mass media, judges, and police still play an important role in the education process, but for young people the schools have an especially prominent position.

To achieve a goal of universal citizen knowledge of law, all types of schools include law education courses. Elementary schools emphasize common legal knowledge and traffic regulations. Middle school and high school students study the constitution and criminal law. Colleges and universities emphasize legal theory and legal specialties as well as offering course work in public legal education. While school teachers provide some information, officials especially like using police officers who can encourage observation of laws by telling young people of graphic criminal cases (Zu-Yuan, 1988). General deterrence is sought through the public display of crime evidence or confiscated spoils. Zu-Yuan (1988) suggests that such action can increase the citizen's attentiveness to crime while showing the power of the police in combatting it.

Young people 12 to 17 years old who have shown minor criminal activity (for example, stealing, fighting, incorrigibility) may go to special work/study schools administered by the educational departments in cooperation with public security agencies. Because parental permission accompanies the assignment, the schools become a special educational measure instead of a criminal or administrative punishment. While at the school, students undergo a "strict disciplinary and ideological education, while studying the same subjects taught in the regular schools" (Zu-Yuan, 1988, p. 10). They spend about half the day in academic study and the other half in practical work at a school-operated factory or workshop (Myren, 1989). After two years of study, during which the students go home only on Sundays and holidays, the young people return to their original school or advance to a higher educational level.

The preferred response to juvenile offenders makes use of the "help and education team" system (Zhao, 1990; Zu-Yuan, 1988). With the close cooperation of government agencies and private citizens, young people are placed under the constant care of the help-education teams until they reform. Each help-education team has three to five members who take responsibility for helping one individual. Team members can represent teachers, parents, police officers, neighbors, government officials, or other interested citizens. They are chosen, however, because they know the person and will be able to influence by example. The constant contact with families, neighbors, and police keeps everyone informed about the "client's" progress. The team's work is not finished until the result satisfies the leaders, parents, or neighbors.

While the participatory approach is especially exemplified in China's reaction to younger, less serious offenders, a similar philosophy appears even when the offender is older and the crime is more serious. Young persons 14 to 18 who commit serious crimes go to the Surveillance and Rehabilitation Centers for Juvenile Delinquents. While education is the tool for reform of younger offenders, labor is the device used by Surveillance and Rehabilitation Centers to reform the older delinquents. These juvenile reformatories receive older offenders committing such serious offenses as stealing, fighting, rape, robbery, and damage to public property. Both boys and girls go to the same facility but stay in separate sections. Commitment is either directly by public security agencies, or through the juvenile court. The average stay is about two years and upon release the juvenile returns home to the parents and begins either school or a job (Myren, 1989).

SUMMARY

This chapter began with a sketch of how juvenile justice agencies in America responded to Charles Manson, eventually the instigator of at least eight murders. The dilemma facing juvenile justice agencies around the world is the same regardless of the legal tradition to which the system is linked. There is, on the one hand, an interest in doing what is best for the child, and on the other hand, responding so that society is protected. These goals are not necessarily mutually exclusive, but is seems difficult to simultaneously give each equal weight. Four models of response to juvenile offenders are presented to show the variation in how countries respond to problem youth and youths with problems.

Some response to misbehaving young people is necessary because delinquency is a worldwide problem. United Nations data were used to show how all regions of the world report problems and concerns with misbehaving youth. Nations do not agree on what constitutes delinquency or who comprises the delinquents. Similarly, there is diversity regarding the appropriate way to respond to a country's misbehaving youth.

The United Nations seems to encourage countries to use a juvenile justice system that concentrates on the well-being of the child. This is a basic feature of systems following a welfare model, as exemplified in Australia and Scotland. The states of South Australia and Western Australia include juvenile aid panels in their system as an alternative to court action against the juvenile. Scotland takes the welfare approach a bit further and provides assistance to any troubled youth, with law violators being just one group in that category. Children's hearings in Scotland allow community members to participate in determining the appropriate disposition for misbehaving youth. The nonjudicial response in Australia and in Scotland are followed in the belief that the best interests of the child are being served.

The welfare approach is criticized by some, however, for its apparent absence of concern with the rights of the juvenile. Countries following a legalistic model are also concerned about the well-being of the child, but here there is equal or more concern about protecting juveniles' rights. Yugoslavia and Italy illustrate this legalistic approach in their use of the traditional court system (Yugoslavia) or the strict adherence to formal requirements of due process (Italy). Importantly, each country has procedures (both formal and informal) that allow attention to the individual's needs despite the appearance of rigid formality or a legalistic approach.

Tension between welfare and legalistic models were said to push England and Wales into a new approach toward juvenile justice—a corporatist model. An increased public interest in punishing juveniles who committed serious crimes made it difficult for those countries to achieve their initial goal of combining welfare and legalistic models. Instead, they moved to a model wherein decision making has been moved from the courts to administrative agencies in cases where the public opinion still favors a treatment response to juveniles. Cases of "hard-core" delinquents are handled in the traditional court setting and impose increasingly harsh penalties. The more sympathetic cases are handled under a bureaucratic-administrative form of law wherein social service employees identify a way to manage the juvenile outside the justice system.

The participatory model provides the fourth approach to juvenile justice. China's system is a particularly good example of this approach, since it emphasizes an educational response to young offenders. A wide variety of agencies and organizations are responsible for the "correction" of misbehaving youth. While a traditional judicial process also operates in China, the overall philosophy for juvenile offenders is one of getting them to accept socialist principles through the power of community persuasion.

The Impact section highlighted an American version of aid panels by describing the Peer Jury in one juvenile court system. It is appropriate to consider how ideas and aspects from each model might operate in the United States. The second Impact section uses Fiji to ask if the absence of any formal response might be the best response of all.

SUGGESTED READINGS

Emmins, Christopher J. (1988). *A practical approach to criminal procedure* (4th ed.). London, England: Blackstone Press.

Lemert, Edwin M. (1986). Juvenile justice Italian style. *Law and Society Review, 20,* 509–544.

Myren, Richard A. (1989). Juvenile justice: People's Republic of China. *C. J. International, 5*(3), 5–6, 22–23.

Troyer, Ronald J. (1989). Publicizing the new laws: The public legal education campaign. In R. Troyer, J. Clark, and D. Rojek (Eds.), *Social control in the People's Republic of China* (pp. 70–83). New York: Praeger.

Zhao, Peter. (1990). Violent crime and its countermeasures in China. *C. J. International, 6*(3), 11–18.

REFERENCES

Althuizen, F. (1977). Juvenile offenders in South Australia. In P. R. Wilson (Ed.), *Delinquency in Australia: A critical appraisal* (pp. 198–228). St. Lucia, Australia: University of Queensland Press.

Binder, Arnold, Geis, Gilbert, and Bruce, Dickson. (1988). *Juvenile delinquency: Historical, cultural, legal perspectives.* New York: Macmillan.

Emmins, Christopher J. (1988). *A practical approach to criminal procedure* (4th ed.). London, England: Blackstone Press.

Emmins, Christopher J., and Scanlan, Gary. (1988). *A guide to the Criminal Justice Act 1988.* London, England: Blackstone Press.

Hackler, Jim. (1991). Using reintegrative shaming effectively: Why Fiji has a juvenile justice system superior to the U.S., Canada, and Australia. In J. Hackler (Ed.), *Official responses to problem juveniles: Some international reflections* (pp. 103–120). Onati, Spain: Institute for the Sociology of Law.

Jones, Beti, and Murray, G.J. (1978). The Scottish rejection of the juvenile courts. In V. L. Stewart (Ed.), *The changing faces of juvenile justice* (pp. 87–110). New York: New York University Press.

Lemert, Edwin M. (1986). Juvenile justice Italian style. *Law and Society Review, 20,* 509–544.

Marshall, Peter. (1978). As the pendulum swings in England and Wales. In V. L. Stewart (Ed.), *The changing faces of juvenile justice* (pp. 87–110). New York: New York University Press.

Martin, F. M. (1978). The future of juvenile justice—English courts and Scottish hearings. *Howard Journal of Penology and Crime Prevention, 17,* 78–90.

Murray, James M., and Borowski, Allan. (1986). Perspectives on juvenile crime and justice in Australia. In D. Chappell and P. Wilson (Eds.), *The Australian criminal justice system: The mid 1980s* (pp. 165–192). Sydney, Australia: Butterworths.

Myren, Richard A. (1989). Juvenile justice: People's Republic of China. *C. J. International*, 5(3), 5–6, 22–23.

Nejelski, P. (1976). Diversion: The promise and the danger. *Crime and Delinquency*, 22, 393–410.

Nichols, Helen. (1985). Children's aid panels in South Australia. In A. Borowski and J. Murray (Eds.), *Juvenile delinquency in Australia* (pp. 221–235). North Ryde, Australia: Methuen.

Pratt, John. (1989). Corporatism: The third model of juvenile justice. *British Journal of Criminology*, 29, 236–254.

Reichel, Philip, and Seyfrit, Carole. (1984). A peer jury in the juvenile court. *Crime and Delinquency*, 30, 423–438.

Rogers, Joseph W., and Mays, G. Larry. (1987). *Juvenile delinquency and juvenile justice*. New York: John Wiley and Sons.

Sarri, R., and Bradley, P. (1980). Juvenile aid panels: An alternative to juvenile court processing in South Australia. *Crime and Delinquency*, 26, 42–62.

Selih, Alenka. (1978). Juvenile justice in Yugoslavia. In V. L. Stewart (Ed.), *The changing faces of juvenile justice* (pp. 111–134). New York: New York University Press.

Seyfrit, Carole L., Reichel, Philip L., and Stutts, Brian L. (1987). Peer juries as a juvenile justice diversion technique. *Youth and Society*, 18, 302–316.

Siegel, Larry J., and Senna, Joseph J. (1991). *Juvenile delinquency: Theory, practice and law* (4th ed.). St. Paul, MN: West.

Thornton, William E., Jr., Voigt, Lydia, and Doerner, William G. (1987). *Delinquency and justice* (2nd ed.). New York: Random House.

Troyer, Ronald J. (1989). Publicizing the new laws: The public legal education campaign. In R. Troyer, J. Clark, and D. Rojek (Eds.), *Social control in the People's Republic of China* (pp. 70–83). New York: Praeger.

United Nations. (1990a). *Prevention of delinquency, juvenile justice and the protection of the young: Policy approaches and directions* (A/CONF.144/16). Vienna, Austria: UN Crime Prevention and Criminal Justice Branch.

United Nations. (1990b). *Implementation of the United Nations standard minimum rules for the administration of juvenile justice* (A/CONF.144/4). Vienna, Austria: UN Crime Prevention and Criminal Justice Branch.

United Nations. (1985). *Youth and crime* (A/CONF.121/7). Vienna, Austria: UN Crime Prevention and Criminal Justice Branch.

United Nations. (1986). *Standard minimum rules for the administration of juvenile justice*. New York: UN Department of Public Information.

Wilson, Andrew. (1974). New approaches in the handling of juvenile delinquents in Scotland. *International Journal of Offender Therapy and Comparative Criminology, 18,* 247–259.

Wooden, Kenneth. (1976). *Weeping in the playtime of others.* New York: McGraw-Hill.

Zhao, Peter. (1990). Violent crime and its countermeasures in China. *C. J. International, 6*(3), 11–18.

Zu-Yuan, Huang. (1988). Juvenile delinquency and its prevention: China. *C. J. International, 4*(5), 5–6, 8, 10.

Chapter 10

Japan: Examples of Effectiveness and Borrowing

KEY TOPICS

- In what way can Japan's criminal justice system be considered effective?
- How has Japan used ideas from other countries to build her criminal justice system?
- Japanese cultural traits that help explain how and why her system operates as it does.
- The use of bureaucratic informalism in Japanese criminal justice.
- The structure and operation of policing in Japan.
- The judiciary in Japan.
- Corrections in Japan.
- What may and what may not work in America.

KEY TERMS

chuzaisho	National Police Agency
collectivism	National Public Safety Commission
contextualism and harmony	order
homogeneity	prefectural police
honne	Summary courts
koban	*tatemae*

COUNTRIES REFERENCED

Japan	United States

Japan offers an excellent opportunity to highlight the benefits of comparative study. Its example is so perfect because much of Japan's criminal justice system is borrowed; yet the adaptation was done to fit in the context of Japan's cultural heritage. The Japanese have a long history of identifying key elements of the social institutions in other countries and modifying those ingredients so that they become workable in Japan. I believe this is an important point to remember as we conclude this tour of comparative criminal justice. Just because something works well in one country does not mean that it is appropriate for other countries. But the procedures and experiences a country has with the components of its justice system may suggest useful modifications in the systems of other countries. As long as the receiving country remembers to adapt rather than adopt the idea, comparative studies will benefit individual countries and the world.

To drive home the point, this concluding chapter concentrates on the criminal justice system of Japan. After showing why Japan is an appropriate example for such concentrated attention, we will review its history as a borrower of ideas, identify some relevant cultural traits important in what ideas were adapted and how they were adapted, and then describe Japan's criminal justice system through review of its criminal law, police, courts, and corrections.

WHY STUDY JAPAN?

Japan is an island nation perceived by many people (the Japanese included) to be quite small. But as Reischauer (1988) points out, size is a relative matter. Japan is admittedly dwarfed by such neighbors as China to its immediate left, Australia to the south, and by the United States and Canada to its far right on the globe. A more accurate perspective is to compare Japan to some of the European countries. Doing so reveals that Japan's nearly 146,000 square miles of land area is considerably larger than Italy (116,000 square miles) and half again the size of the United Kingdom (94,000 square miles). Were it superimposed on a map of the United States, Japan's northern island of Hokkaido would begin just north of New York state (almost to Montreal, Canada) and the other main islands (Honshu, Shikoku, and Kyushu) would extend south into the Florida panhandle. Similar latitudes on America's west coast would take Japan from Oregon's border with Washington to California's border with Mexico.

Since the post-World War II era, Japan has operated as a parliamentary-cabinet system. The Diet (parliament) serves as the sole lawmaking organ of the state, while the Cabinet (the Prime Minister and other ministers of state) operates as the government's executive branch. The majority of Cabinet ministers are Diet members, serving simultaneously as heads of government departments and directors of civil servants. The Cabinet, then, combines politics (the Diet) with administration (government departments). Japan's constitution identifies the emperor as the symbol of the state and the unity of the people, but his position does not include powers related to government.

Japan provides an interesting and appropriate case study for our purposes because: (1) its criminal justice system seems to provide an effective response to the crime problem, and (2) its effective criminal justice system owes much to the policies and procedures of criminal justice systems in other countries.

Japan's Effective Criminal Justice System

Between 1950 and 1989, Japan's crime rate dropped from 1756 per 100,000 population to 1358. During the same time period, its imprisonment rate dropped from 139 to 42 (see Figure 10-1). The decline in both sets of figures occurred while Japan was undergoing postwar industrialization, population increases (especially in the younger category), and continued urbanization. Since these factors are among those often cited as causing crime, Japan presents a contradiction that criminologists find intriguing.

Keeping in mind the cautions in Chapters 2 and 8 about cross-cultural comparison of crime and imprisonment rates, it is still instructive to see how Japanese officials view their response to crime in comparison with other countries. Comparing their own statistics with those issued by the United States, the United Kingdom, the Federal Republic of Germany (West Germany prior to the 1990 unification), and the Republic of France, Japan finds itself to be in an enviable position. Japan's crime rate in 1988 was the lowest of the five countries, and its clearance rate was the highest (Research and Training Institute, 1990). Looking only at the violent crime of homicide and the property crime of larceny, Japan remained the winner. For example, Japan's homicide rate of 1.2 and larceny rate of 1158 compared to the respective United States rates of 8.4 and 5027 per 100,000 population. Homicides and larcenies cleared by police in the United States in 1988 stood at 70.0 percent (homicide) and 17.5 percent (larceny) compared to Japanese clearance rates of 96.6 percent and 55.7 percent, respectively (Research and Training Institute, 1990).

When crime does occur, and after the police—nearly inevitably, it appears—catch the offender, the Japanese criminal justice system continues to stand apart. Over 99 percent of the offenders eventually coming before a judge are convicted. Further, nearly 99 percent of those convicted are sentenced to prison. As this chapter shows, such statistics are potentially misleading, since informal control mechanisms are used at each stage regardless of the formal terminology. A 99 percent conviction rate hides the fact that the vast majority of these cases are not contested by the defendant. Similarly, saying that 99 percent of those convicted receive a prison sentence seems impressive until we realize that over half those prison sentences are suspended; and in most of those cases the offender is not even placed under supervision. But, as described below, even the significant use of informal sanctioning separates the Japanese system from most others in the industrialized world.

Scholarly attention on Japan as a comparatively safe industrialized urban society has resulted in many interesting works. Some emphasize the police role

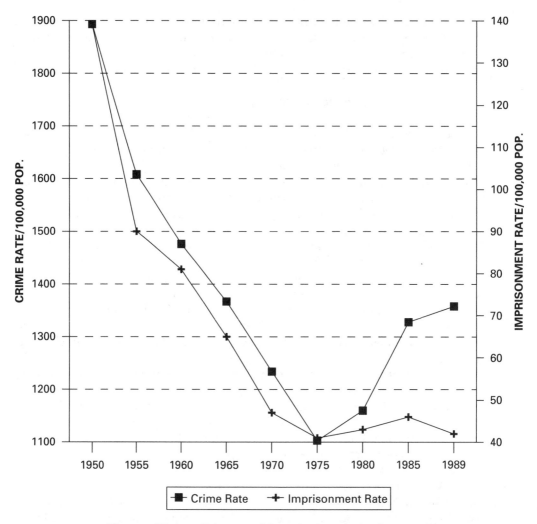

Figure 10-1. Crime and inmate trends in Japan. *Sources:*
Correction Bureau (1990). *Correctional Institutes in Japan.* Tokyo:
Ministry of Justice. Research and Training Institute (1990).

(for example, Ames, 1981; Bayley, 1991; Parker, 1984), others concentrate on law
or the courts (for example, Castberg, 1990; Upham, 1987), and some look particularly at corrections (for example, Clifford, 1976; Parker, 1986). A common theme,
at least among those scholars who actually visited Japan for their research, is an
appreciation for the apparent absence of crime and the perception of safety that
produces. Bayley (1991) presents the feeling most succinctly by titling his first
chapter "Heaven for a Cop." He also wonders, as have many other researchers
and authors, how Japan's justice system operates, why it is so effective and effi-

cient, and whether some of its features are transferable to other countries. In this chapter we will see how some scholars have attempted to answer such questions.

Borrowing in a Cross-Cultural Context

Diffusion is a classic way by which innovation is shared. This is true in the broad areas of science and humanities, as well as specific areas, such as systems of justice. The way modern policing operated in early nineteenth-century America was heavily influenced by happenings and experiences in other countries. Prison construction in European countries was influenced by America's experiment with the Pennsylvania system. Roman law had specific and long-lasting impact on the legal systems of countries ranging from Europe to South America. Sometimes the influence of one country is imposed on another, but there are also occasions when ideas are freely and willingly imitated. Japan's system of criminal justice, as well as many of its other social institutions, have both imposed and imitated aspects.

In a fascinating manner, Westney (1987) provides detailed information on how Japan's Meiji Era transformation (1868–1912) relied on the deliberate emulation of Western organizations. The Japanese navy was modeled on the British; the army on the French and then on the German; the educational system on the French, the American, and the German; and the banking system on the American. But even this nineteenth-century willingness to look beyond its own boundaries was simply a continuation of earlier disposition to view foreign ideas with favor.

Japan's first sources of influence (around 300 B.C. to A.D. 500) were from the Asian continent and included important developments such as agriculture and metalworking. The fourth and fifth centuries brought specific influences from China (via Korea), and the Japanese became familiar with the philosophies of Confucianism and Buddhism, and with the Chinese written script. China continued to play the role of primary model into the eighth century and provided Japan with the basics of a centralized bureaucratic state that moved Japan into an aristocratic age.

Contacts with the West did not occur until 1543, when a Portuguese ship drifted ashore on a small southern island in the Japanese archipelago. These sailors, who brought the first firearms to Japan, were followed six years later by the arrival of the Spanish Jesuit, Francis Xavier, who introduced Christianity. By the 1630s, the Tokugawa shogunate became increasingly concerned that Christian missionaries were intent on political conquest of Japan. A rigid isolationist policy was adopted and Portuguese ships could not enter Japanese ports nor could Japanese people take trips abroad. The only countries continuing contact with Japan were China and Holland. Despite their European placement, the Dutch were acceptable to the shogunate because they made it very clear that their interest in Japan was financial rather than spiritual or political. Through the Dutch, Japan received information about the outside world, but in many respects Japan missed the scientific and industrial revolutions of the eighteenth century.

By the early nineteenth century, Japan was confronted with internal pressure for political reform and external pressure for economic contacts. Russian and British ships made occasional approaches, but the real breakthrough came in 1853, when Commodore Matthew Perry and his fleet of ships forced the Japanese government to accept a letter from the president of the United States. The Tokugawa shogunate realized the opening of Japan was inevitable, so treaties of friendship and commerce were initiated with Western countries.

Japan's period of modern history begins in 1868, when control of the government moved from the shogunate back to the emperor. This Meiji (after the reign name of the emperor) Restoration and the resulting Meiji Era (1868–1912) brought dramatic political, economic, and cultural changes to Japan. Things Western came to be defined as good, and the Japanese once again turned to other countries for ideas. Among the more important innovations was the 1890 establishment of a constitutional government modeled in the European tradition. The United States government structure was not deemed suitable to the Japanese, because it did not provide for an emperor. Germany and Prussia, on the other hand, operated with a Kaiser, and this provided a version of parliamentary government more appealing to Japan.

Over the centuries, Japan has been remarkably skillful in its borrowing practices. Whether it was religion from China or a political structure from Germany, the Japanese took to heart Sakuma Shozan's (a Tokugawa reformer) phrase "'Eastern morals, Western science'" (quoted in Upham, 1987). It was desirable to import and adapt Western learning, but only while protecting the Japanese spirit. That philosophy continues today and provides the heart of this chapter's argument: Countries can and should learn for each other, but things borrowed must be adapted rather than adopted. To best understand the application of this argument, we must appreciate aspects of the "Japanese spirit" that have influenced the development of Japan's justice system.

JAPANESE CULTURAL TRAITS

With Japan's increased economic prowess in the 1980s and 1990s came great interest among business people around the world in everything from Japanese management techniques to Japanese language. Similar interest was sparked among justice officials, who were intrigued with Japan's apparent success in responding to the crime problem. But Japan's accomplishments must be considered in light of its cultural heritage. Notehelfer (personal communication, June 14, 1990) uses the analogy of the bonsai to make a similar point. Americans admire the bonsai tree for its simple elegance, its sense of harmony, and the serenity imparted by its miniaturization. In some ways the bonsai is considered a metaphor for Japanese society itself: orderly, efficient, peaceful, with citizens acting in unanimity. But before foreigners covet the bonsai or, by analogy, Japanese society, it is important to see how they got this way. The bonsai's beauty is the result of wiring and molding the limbs of the tree so that it does not develop beyond certain limits. The aesthetics of Japanese society may result from similar wiring and molding. We should not ignore the wires when admiring the tree.

The wiring and molding of Japanese society is provided by its cultural heritage. Every society has been shaped by its own peculiar heritage. The analogy of the bonsai can be repeated for every society in the world by merely choosing an object linked to the particular country. The danger in undertaking a discussion of any country's "wiring and molding" is to avoid going so far that cultural traits become stereotypes. Japan, especially, exemplifies this problem because it presents as many paradoxes as parallels. For example, Japan is a conservative society with radical student groups; a contemplative self is admired by materialistic and consumerist citizens; the Japanese strive for a closeness with nature while surrounded by a serious pollution problem. Obviously it is unwise and unfair to make claims for specific traits to identify Japan or the Japanese.

Despite the danger involved, anthropologists and others realize that broadly stated cultural values help make sense of the complexity and variation found in all societies. If we approach the issue with an understanding of the potential problems (for example, developing stereotypes), the search for cultural values—and even cultural traits—can be beneficial.

With that warning, we shall look at the wires before admiring the tree. That is, before appreciating the apparent efficiency and success of Japan's criminal justice system, we will inspect the cultural mold in which that system operates. We do that by considering the impact some Japanese cultural values may have on the criminal act and on society's response. A number of cultural traits have been used to understand better the success of Japan's social control mechanisms. A nonexhaustive list would include a homogeneous society, emphasis on harmony, a reliance on collectivism, and a respect for hierarchy and authority.

Homogeneity

Japan is ethnically homogeneous, with over 99 percent of its population being Japanese. The largest single minority group is the Koreans, who comprise about 0.5 percent of the island nation's population. Also noteworthy are the *burakumin* (or people of the hamlet). Although fully Japanese, these physically and culturally indistinguishable citizens are the recipients of serious prejudice and discrimination. Presumably the *burakumin* comprised a social class during feudal times that was perceived as an outcast group (Hendry, 1989; Reischauer, 1988; Upham, 1987). The *burakumin* of Tokugawa times were those people engaged in defiling or dirty occupations like burying the dead or working with dead animals (for example, butchers and leather workers). Another name for this group is *eta*, meaning heavily polluted, since their work is considered contaminating in Shinto and Buddhist views.

The Emancipation Edict of 1871 granted the *burakumin* formal liberation from their feudal status of outcasts. But as minorities in other countries can attest, legal emancipation did not have much impact on *burakumin* status. Official government policy helped perpetuate prejudice and discrimination by registering *burakumin* as "new commoners" in the family registries maintained at each citizen's place of origin (Upham, 1987). Since descent from a Tokugawa outcast is the only distinguishing feature of *burakumin*, these public registries provided easy identification of, and discrimination against, *buraku* individuals. The estimated two or three percent of today's population who fall into this group continue to have underprivileged status (Upham, 1987) that forces substantial numbers into associations with *boryokudan* criminal gangs (Kaplan and Dubro, 1986). That process concerns Japanese justice officials, since *boryokudan* activity has increased in recent years. Later in this chapter we will look at the *boryokudan* more closely.

In apparent contradiction to Durkheim's ideas about homogeneity declining with increased division of labor (see Chapter 3), the Japanese continue to express similar values and hold tightly to common norms. When virtually all the country's inhabitants know and agree upon what it means to be Japanese, the job of social control becomes remarkably easier. But homogeneity in itself cannot explain low crime rates. Certainly there are many examples worldwide where citizens know and agree upon certain norms, yet continue to violate them. Japanese culture must provide more than simple similarity among its people.

Contextualism and Harmony

An important correlate to homogeneity is contextualism, or relativism. These terms refer to the Japanese belief that standards of morality and ethics are determined by reference to the group rather than to rigid legal codes or universal principles (Archambeault and Fenwick, 1988; Reischauer, 1988). Instead of there being absolute standards of morality, all behavioral standards are relative to the context in which people find themselves. That belief system helps explain atrocities (such as the 1937 Nanking massacre of Manchurians by Japanese forces) committed in the context of war (Becker, 1988b) by the same people who, in their own country, report more things being *found* than *lost* (Parker, 1984).

One way to view this apparent contradiction is through the concepts of *tatemae* (how things appear) and *honne* (the underlying reality). Early in the socialization process, Japanese children learn the importance of maintaining harmony (*wa*). But since complete and continual harmony can be only an ideal, Japanese become rather adept at portraying harmony even where it does not exist. Often the ideal harmony that primary groups display on the surface disguises the reality of conflict underneath. The observer will usually only see the *tatemae* face, because airing of dirty laundry to outsiders brings shame on the primary group. That is, the group (whether it be the family, neighborhood, workplace, or even sport team) is faulty, since it cannot maintain harmony.

Putting the concepts of contextualism and harmony together, we can appreciate some of the control techniques popular in Japan. It is possible that in certain situations (contextualism), a person's own internal motivations (*honne*) might lead to deviant behavior. But conventions require offender, victim, and control agent to handle the problem so that *tatemae* is achieved. Keeping this in mind will help us understand the Japanese preference for informal justice and a firm belief in social, over individual, rehabilitation. Control techniques that present harmony are more easily found outside the formal setting of justice agencies. Further, since misbehavior is contextual, hence social, the treatment must also be social. Put deviants in a nurturing social environment and they will get better.

Collectivism

From the earliest life stages, Japanese learn the importance of the group to their existence and well-being. There is probably no clearer way to express the point than by noting an aspect of Japanese child-rearing practices. Misbehaving children in America are often punished by being confined to the house and made to stay with the family. In Japan, parents are more likely to put the misbehaving child outside the house. The American child clamors to be let out; the Japanese child begs to be let in. As Bayley states it: "American mothers chase their children around the block to get them to come home; Japanese mothers are chased by their children so as not to be left behind" (1991, p. 143).

The family and group orientation of Japanese society continues a sense of collective responsibility present since pre-Confucian Japan. Individualism is present, but it takes a different form than in America. A sense of personal self-worth and identity in Japan stems from the groups to which one belongs. In this sense, individualism in Japan is achieved through one's ability to create, maintain, and guard relationships. Parker (1984) exemplifies this when he notes that a Japanese is likely to introduce himself as a faculty member at Tokyo University or a worker at Toyota. Secondarily, specific occupations such as psychologist or janitor may be offered, but the group affiliation takes precedence.

The sense of collectivism attaches to family, employer, school, and other groups. The accompanying close ties to both formal and informal groups result in a sense of obligation of one toward the others. Such associations give the individual strong emotional support, but those same close ties also bring a strong sense of shame and embarrassment when a group member misbehaves. It is still not uncommon to find a boss resigning for the employee's misconduct, or parents apologizing for the behavior of even a fully grown child (Becker, 1988b). Family members experience a sense of shame and embarrassment if a member's conduct brings dishonor on the family. Importantly, such group consciousness and family identity push most Japanese to avoid actions that may bring pain, shame, and punishment on the group (Archambeault and Fenwick, 1988; Becker, 1988b).

Finally, we must note that collectivism links to contextualism because the way a reference group interprets a standard is more important than the abstract standard itself. The group is placed above the individual. For purposes of criminal justice, this means that the goal of keeping society moral and crime-free must take precedence over a goal of protecting the letter of each individual's rights in Japan (Becker, 1988b). And, as we see later, a criticism of the Japanese system is its apparent preference for the crime control model over the due process model. In addition, the importance of collectivism means that threatened exclusion from the group is more likely to produce conformity that is a formal punishment.

Hierarchies and Order

An appreciation for hierarchial arrangements among people is the final element of Japanese culture to consider here. When discussing trends in American response to juvenile delinquents, Empey (1982) noted the importance of Americans' distrust in the 1960s of their social institutions. Japanese do not seem to have had a similar experience, and given their affinity for an ordered hierarchical society, it is not likely that they will.

The link between preferring hierarchies and faith in social institutions proceeds as follows: Japanese hierarchies, which are not just grounded in power, are of great variety and based on differing social prescriptions and social obligations. As Archambeault and Fenwick (1988) put it, group consciousness combines with a sense of order to force cooperative relationships between most segments of the Japanese community and their justice agencies. The respect for one's position leads citizens to honor and trust justice system employees. Police, courts, and corrections officials are seen as guardians of society's morals as well as enforcers of the law. As a result, the people's faith in the agents of the system, and the belief that decisions will be made according to what best serves society, allow the Japanese people to give extensive discretion to the criminal justice agents.

Because the values of contextualism, harmony, collectivism, and order are firmly grounded in Japanese culture, they help explain the Japanese response to criminal offenders and how that response differs from other countries. Importantly, however, the Japanese difference is more in the means to the end than in the end itself. For example, as with most Western systems, Japanese corrections is caught between the often conflicting punishment goals of rehabilitation and retribution. Western systems typically seek rehabilitation by encouraging the offender to become independent and responsible. The Japanese system, however, encourages the offender to integrate voluntarily into the structured social order. In addition, the Japanese see the community, rather than an institution, as the more likely place for getting that voluntary integration. Since imprisonment is not considered a useful means for achieving the rehabilitative goal, a low incarceration rate is not really surprising.

Similarly, retribution is seen as an appropriate and desirable goal. But rather than following an "eye for an eye" philosophy, Japan secures the goal through "disgrace" or "reintegrative shaming" (Braithwaite, 1989). This approach would not likely work in many Western heterogenous societies, but the value of collectivism makes retribution through disgrace very reasonable in Japan. The Japanese desire and need for group association and acceptance make alienation from the group a harsh and meaningful punishment. Since the impact of alienation and rejection does not increase over time, there is no need to have long prison sentences.

IMPACT

The emphasis in this chapter is on the general ideas of system effectiveness and borrowing. Japan has been cited for years as an example of a country with a low crime rate and apparently effective criminal justice system. It is all the more intriguing when we realize that much of Japan's system is the result of borrowing from other countries and either modifying the ideas to fit in Japanese culture, or modifying the culture to accept the new ideas. The result is a justice system looked upon by other countries, including some Japan has borrowed from, as a model for improving their own criminal justice procedures. This chapter concludes with a discussion of aspects of the Japanese system that may transport to the United States. As a contrast to that optimism, this Impact section provides a necessary caution. Cultural differences make the transfer of some Japanese procedures unlikely and even undesirable for many Americans. It is just as important for a country to realize what it cannot adapt as it is to understand what is adaptable.

Wires Around the Bonsai

As this chapter notes, the beauty, simplicity, and harmony of the bonsai tree is not achieved without stifling freedom of growth. Similarly, the unity, order, and safety of Japanese society is accomplished by, according to American values, some inhibiting of personal freedoms. Consider, for example, the values of privacy, the right to a public trial by an impartial jury, and protection against self-incrimination.

Privacy.   Reasons given for the effectiveness of Japanese police included their working relationship with citizens and their service orientation. Those sound innocent enough, but some Americans might be troubled by some of the techniques used to achieve those conditions. Remember, for example, the residential survey conducted by *koban* officers twice a year. Americans may not be so willing to share personal and neighborhood information with police officers. Kim (1987) believes that United States citizens would find this practice totally unacceptable. He even suggests that the resentment caused by the door-to-door inquiries would offset any gains made by the survey.

Parker (1984) writes about *koban* officers on patrol entering a home found unlocked and empty. The officer leaves a calling card with his name on one side and a possible comment on the reverse warning the occupants about their poor crime prevention habits. Since police behavior in Japan reflects a moral norm as much as a legal one, Parker (1984) argues, such paternalism is acceptable in Japan. Many Americans might find similar behavior by the police to be overly intrusive.

Intrusive behavior does not just take place in the citizen's home. Japanese law allows police officers to stop and question people only if there is reasonable ground for suspecting they have committed or are about to commit a crime, or have information about a crime. Despite that, Bayley (1991) found it to be standard patrol procedure to stop and question anyone whenever the officer considers it useful. The tactic's effectiveness is suggested by noting that 75 percent of all Penal Code arrests are made by *koban* and *chuzaisho* officers—and most of those are the result of field interrogations (Bayley, 1991, p. 35). Officers become very adept at on-street questioning (there are even prefectural and national competitions) and often elicit both information and even consents to be searched.

A Public Trial and Impartial Jury.
Japan's constitution gives all defendants in criminal cases the right to a public trial by an impartial tribunal. For the most part, both conditions are clearly offered. However, the summary proceeding does seem to present an exception. As Castberg (1990) points out, such proceedings probably violate due process provisions in a way United States citizens may find unacceptable. Summary procedures, although they include the defendant's signed consent form, are conducted in private without either the defendant or defense counsel present. The prosecutor, who admittedly is also absent, plays a quasi-magisterial role as the only court official to inform defendants of their rights. With a summary proceeding, the defendant does not appear before a judge and is not informed by a judge about the implications of opting for a summary procedure instead of a formal trial. The Japanese trust the prosecutor to perform that duty. Since over 50 percent of the cases disposed of by the prosecutor's office go to summary proceedings (Research and Training Institute, 1990), such due process concerns seem potentially relevant—at least from an American perspective.

For the 15 years between 1928 and 1943, Japan used a jury system for criminal cases (Shibahara, 1990). The Jury Trial Law was passed in 1923, but government officials believed time was needed to prepare the citizens for such direct involvement in the adjudication process. In its eventual format, the jury consisted of 12 literate male jurors over 30 years of age. Their verdict did not have to be unanimous—a simply majority was sufficient. During its 15-year existence, only 484 cases were tried by jury, while defendants in over 25,000 serious cases waived their right to a jury trial (Shibahara, 1990). Obviously, the idea did not catch on.

Several conditions acted to make the jury trial a failure in Japan. On a cultural level, the jury system did not appeal to the basic national characteristic of the Japanese people. As Shibahara says: "Japanese people prefer to be tried by a professional judge rather than by their neighbors" (1990, p. 28). But there were also some practical problems with the jury system as implemented in Japan. The primary one seems to be the limited power given the jurors. Specifically, their decision was not binding on the judge. Whatever the jury's decision, if the judge did not agree, he could put the case before a new jury with newly selected jurors. Not surprisingly, most defense counsels decided that it would make most sense to simply go before the professional judge.

This preference for professional judges over lay jurors means the Constitutional guarantee for an impartial tribunal results in a single judge, or a panel of three judges, deciding the facts and determining the sentence.

Protection Against Self-Incrimination. One of the primary reasons for the effectiveness of Japan's criminal justice system is the tendency of Japanese citizens to confess their misbehavior. That tendency is also seen by some foreign and some Japanese observers as one of the system's greatest problems. The predicament is outlined in Article 38 of Japan's Constitution: "No person shall be compelled to testify against himself. Confession made under compulsion, torture or threat, or after prolonged arrest or detention shall not be admitted in evidence. No person shall be convicted or punished in cases where the only proof against him is his own confession."

Confession has played an important role in Japanese criminal cases since the early part of the Meiji period, when defendants could not be found guilty without a confession (Tamiya, 1983). Unfortunately, the requirement for a confession was accompanied by an acceptance of torture as a means to encourage the admission. Article 38, then, presents a dilemma wherein one horn recognizes the importance of confession and the other horn recognizes the protection against self-incrimination. To date it appears that the tradition of confession takes precedence over the constitutional protection.

Toyoji Saito, a professor on the law faculty at Konan University in Kyoto, notes that "any efficient social or state system is apt to cause human rights infringements . . . (and) the Japanese criminal justice system is no exception" (1990, p. 399). His particular concern is with the process of pre-trial detention, which Saito argues is used for interrogation and to obtain a confession. Saito's position is supported by Hiroshi Hataguchi, a defense counsel in Japan, who argues that confessions are routinely admitted into evidence despite the likelihood that they are the result of police coercion (Hataguchi, 1990).

This chapter's earlier discussion of police activities during the pre-trial period noted the role of detention. To appreciate the concerns of people like Saito and Hataguchi, we need to understand more about this process.

The Criminal Procedure Code allows suspects to be detained for up to 23 days before a decision to prosecute is made. The police can detain a suspect for 48 hours. If the suspect is turned over to the prosecutor, an additional 24 hours detention is permitted. During that 24-hour period, the prosecutor can apply to the judge for an order that extends detention for 10 days. If the investigation is not completed during those 10 days, the prosecutor may request an additional 10 days. At the end of that extension, the prosecutor must make a decision about prosecuting the case.

The public prosecutor's office disposes of three-fourths of its cases within 15 days (Research and Training Institute, 1990), but the suspicion is that confession plays a significant role in how quickly the case is handled. Bail is guaranteed, except in a few cases, but only after the prosecutor files charges. During the potentially 23-day detention period, the suspect does not have the right to bail. Bayley (1991) suggests that since inducing confession is a key purpose of precharge detention, confession may well become a condition for bail.

Prior to initiation of prosecution, the detention is that of a suspect. Once the prosecutor files charges, a detention of the defendant begins. Of course, the prosecutor may simply release a newly charged defendant, or the defendant may be released on bail. But when confinement is desired, detention for up to two months from the day prosecution is initiated is possible. From that point, detention may be prolonged by a judge for a period of up to three months following initiation of prosecution. Saito (1990) lists the circumstances under which detention may exceed three months, but he also notes that there is no legal limit on the total period of detention.

As if the absence of release on bail were not bad enough, access to legal counsel during precharge detention is also problematic. In the United States, a person has the right to counsel (including counsel at government expense if the person is indigent) once investigation of a crime focuses on that person (*Miranda* v. *Arizona*, 1966). That means, for example, suspects being interrogated by the police (*Escobedo* v. *Illinois*, 1964) and suspects in a police lineup (*Gilbert* v. *California*, 1967) have the right to the presence of counsel during that questioning and at that lineup. Once the person moves from the status of "suspect" to "defendant" (that is, once formal charges have been brought), she or he continues to have the right to counsel at the preliminary hearing (*Coleman* v. *Alabama*, 1970) and during any trial that could result in the defendant's imprisonment (*Gideon* v. *Wainwright*, 1963 and *Argersinger* v. *Hamlin*, 1972). In other words, in the United States both "suspects" and the "accused" (that is, defendants) enjoy the right to counsel (at government expense when necessary) from the earliest stages of the arrest process through the final stages of trial.

The constitution of Japan distinguishes between the right to counsel for the suspect and the accused in a manner unfamiliar to Americans. Article 34 states: "No person shall be arrested or detained without being at once informed of the charges against him or without the immediate privilege of counsel. . . ." Article 38 reads: "At all times the accused shall have the assistance of competent counsel who shall, if the accused is unable to secure the same by his own efforts, be assigned to his use by the State." In this manner, anyone "arrested" or "detained" has the "privilege of counsel," but, since it is a privilege rather than a right, the state is not obligated to pay. Therefore, indigents at the suspect stage, which Hataguchi (1990) says is the majority of suspects, are not provided counsel during the investigation/arrest process.

Once a Japanese suspect becomes an "accused" or defendant, Article 38 kicks in, and the state is obliged to provide competent counsel to assist the defendant during the trial phase. One result of the suspect/accused distinction is that few people held in precharge detention have access to an attorney (Hataguchi, 1990). In fact, even suspects who can afford to hire a lawyer may not see their counsel very often, since attorney access to the suspect is controlled by the investigating authorities.

The Code of Criminal Procedure places the police and prosecutor in charge of a lawyer's access to the detained suspect. Arrested suspects whom the police wish to detain are placed in a police custody cell at the police station, or in a detention center. The detention centers are administered by the Ministry of Justice, but the police custody cells are under the control of police authorities. When these cells are used to detain suspects they are called *substitute prisons*. The substitute prisons are controversial because their connection to the police station gives police officials easy and continuous access to the suspect. If the suspect is sent to a detention center, police access is restrained by the rules and regulations of the center.

Fortunately for the police, most suspects are held under police control rather than by the Ministry of Justice. This gives police officials up to 23 days to interrogate the suspect. In addition, the interrogation need not be hampered by the presence of an attorney since the prosecutor and police can restrict and control communication between suspect and counsel. Since police believe that confession is the king of evidence (Bayley, 1991; Saito, 1990), it is not surprising that critics believe that unchecked interrogation may lead to coercive police tactics.

The restricted access to defense counsel, in those few cases where the suspect had the funds to hire an attorney, continues until the prosecutor files formal charges against the person. At that point, the place of detention typically changes to a detention center where, those already with attorneys get increased interaction while the indigent defendants can meet with counsel for the first time.

CRIMINAL LAW

Japanese law traces its foundation to the Seventeen Maxims issued in 604 by the government of Prince Shotoku (Ryavec, 1983; Wigmore, 1936). Like the Ten Commandments, the Seventeen Maxims are more accurately a short moral code rather than rules of law. The maxims included urgings that government officials behave with decorum (Law IV) and that judges respond to cases with impartiality (Law V). The first strictly legal code was made up of short enactments between

645 and 646 in the reign of Emperor Kotoku. This Decree of Great Reform established the Chinese-like administrative organization, fixed land titles, and reformed the taxation system. Actual codification of law began with the Code of the Taiho (701), which elaborated upon the Decree of Great Reform. The Taiho Code was in turn modified by the Yoro Code of 718.

Knowledge and appreciation of Chinese society was apparent in these early days of Japan's legal growth. Not only were Chinese models used in developing those early decrees, edicts, and codes, but the Japanese also borrowed a Chinese custom for direct access to the ruler (Wigmore, 1936). In essence, this was a "suggestion box" in the form of a bell and box placed outside the palace (China) or in the court (Japan). In a 646 edict, the Japanese emperor ordered citizens to place their complaints in the box so that the ruler might call the matter to the attention of his ministers. Should there still be neglect, lack of diligence, or bias on the ministers' part, the citizen was to strike the bell to so inform the Emperor. Wigmore (1936) compares this practice with the English right to petition, since it both enabled common people to seek personal justice from the ruler and kept the ruler in direct touch with public opinion.

During this early stage, Japanese law had little differentiation between civil and criminal aspects, followed an inquisitorial rather than adversarial procedure, and lacked any division between judicial and executive branches. The ruling class, being educated in the Confucian classics, was deemed morally superior to everyone else and therefore had the power to determine what constituted a crime and how serious it was. While the codes suggest similarities with the civil legal tradition, Ryavec (1983) notes that jurists of the time referred to Japanese custom and provincial precedents more often than citing from the criminal code. This interesting mixture of legal traditions, which Europeans of the time were keeping separate, continued to influence the development of Japanese law.

As this first period came to a close, rich military barons acquired semi-independence from the emperor. In the 1100s palace intellectuals lost their power, and the emperor in Kyoto was left playing second fiddle to a military feudal tenure system directed by the shogun (the commander-in-chief of the Japanese army). In theory, the emperor appointed each new shogun. But in fact the shogun position was as hereditary as that of emperor, and for nearly 700 years the shogun was Japan's real ruler.

The second period of Japanese law (1192–1603) begins with the military shogun, Minamoto Yoritomo (Ryavec, 1983; Wigmore, 1936). Minamoto's Kamakura Shogunate (1192–1333) consolidated the new centralized feudalism and took nationwide control over all police and military agents. He also set up a court of justice (actually, a board of inquiry) and issued a legal code which, with supplementary regulations, lasted from 1232 until the end of the medieval period. Minamoto's successor, Hojo Yasutoki, established the court more firmly by ordaining the first 15 days of each month to be devoted to justice. According to the old custom, a bell was hung at the court's door and, after striking it, a complainant had his petition immediately heard.

The Kamakura shogunate's code (*Goseibai Shikimoku*) and its supplements reflected the widening range of military jurisdiction in local economic and criminal matters. Interestingly, the tendency toward common law procedures with civil law codification continued into this stage. Precedent was increasingly relied upon rather than statute, and at times civil law cases were allowed to use adversarial instead of inquisitorial procedures (Ryavec, 1983).

The third period (1603–1868) saw political equilibrium introduced by Tokugawa Ieyasu, who began the Tokugawa dynasty (1603–1868). Both feudalism and military class domination continued, but now under the control of a central federalized government. Economic and social prosperity flourished, as did the development of the Japanese legal system. While the barons (*daimyo*) had jurisdiction in local matters in their own provinces, they were kept well informed of the shogun's expectations in legal affairs. Ieyasu required the great barons to spend alternate years with him at the new capital in Edo (Tokyo). This policy was most helpful in keeping the barons up to date with new legislation. The barons' judges often consulted the Supreme Court in Edo in attempts to achieve uniformity of law.

One of the features of Japanese law in Tokugawa times seems unusual in comparison to our knowledge of legal systems in other countries. The four legal traditions introduced in Chapter 4 shared a belief that citizens should know the laws. Whether that knowledge comes from clearly drafted codes, immemorial custom, or divine proclamations, the people were expected to know their obligations. The laws and decisions of Tokugawa times were not circulated to the public. Wigmore (1936) suggests that this may be a result of the Confucian principle that the responsibility for justice rests with the ruler, not with the people. Since Tokugawa rulers often repeated the Confucian caution to "Let the people abide by the law, but not be instructed in it" (quoted in Wigmore, 1936, p. 484), the link seems quite probable. The foregoing should in no way imply that the laws were kept secret from the public. The trial courts were open to the public, and penal laws were posted in public places. The point to remember is that the written laws were commands addressed to the officials—not the people.

The fourth period of the Japanese legal system (1868–1945) corresponds to Japan's period as an institutionalized monarchy beginning with the Meiji Restoration. The New Code of Laws was created in 1870 and then revised in 1873 to incorporate what was basically the current penal law in China (George, 1983). By the 1880s, increased contacts with America and Europe brought Japan additional ideas about legal systems. Those of France and Germany were particularly appealing. With the assistance of a French criminal law scholar, the 1873 code was replaced with an 1880 version heavily emphasizing French legal principles. But soon after the 1882 implementation of the 1880 code, the Japanese came to appreciate German law. The Germans seemed to share Japan's view of law as a system imposed by an absolute monarch (the German kaiser and the Japanese emperor), so the 1907 Japanese code was modeled on the German code of that time. But the Japanese were ever mindful of their own traditions. For example, the first three books of the new Civil Code (General Principles, Property Rights, and Obligations) resembled the German Civil Code, but the fourth and fifth books on Family and Inheritance Law were clearly based on Japanese custom (Oppler, 1977).

In its modern form (1946–present), Japanese criminal law received instruction from the United States during the Allied occupation after World War II. The 1947 constitution reflects Western influence by stipulating a separation of legislative, administrative, and judicial powers; extensive protection of civil liberties; and introducing the American system of judicial review (Hendry, 1989; Ryavec, 1983). The occupation lawyers who supervised the legal reforms had to remember that the Japanese legal system was built on a foundation using both civil and common legal traditions in the context of local custom (Oppler, 1977).

Fortunately, the occupying forces understood that the legal system could not simply be replaced with one that worked in England, the United States, or France. Using considerable input from Japanese lawyers (Oppler, 1977), a legal system was outlined which brought innovation yet maintained tradition. Hendry (1989) describes the result as another example of a Western-like exterior hiding a clearly Japanese interior. The Ministry of Justice in Tokyo serves as an analogy for itself: the brick front reflects the Western influence, but the interior of the building—like the core of the legal system itself—reflects the Japanese spirit. And, as we saw while discussing cultural values, part of that spirit is informality. Upham (1987) draws on the concept of informality to position the Japanese legal system in a different light than other systems. A brief review of his comments will provide a context within which we can view the specifics of Japanese police, courts, and corrections.

Law by Bureaucratic Informalism

In his excellent analysis of law's operation in Japan, Upham (1987) describes two hypothetical legal systems. The first, called rule-dominated, involves legal professionals using specialized techniques to find and apply unambiguous rules to certain kinds of controversy. Under this system, courts have a monopoly on dispute resolution, since only the court personnel are familiar with the specialized methods of legal reasoning. Important as these court actors are, their role is limited, since all they really need to do is find the correct rule governing the particular case before them and then apply that rule.

The second hypothetical legal system is judge-dominated. Here the emphasis is on judges as political actors, and the legal process becomes a forum for broad-based social controversies. Instead of simply identifying the proper rule and applying it, judges are involved in policy making. Now the court personnel, specifically the judge, have an extensive role that allows them to seek social change as they declare and form social values.

Although the rule-dominated system may remind us of the civil legal tradition, and the judge-dominated system brings the common legal tradition to mind, Upham is careful to note that his types are purely theoretical. Despite Upham's cautions, to the extent that they describe features representing existing legal systems, Upham's types provide a base from which Japan's system can be discussed. Upon searching for Japanese justice components that reflect either rule-dominated or judge-dominated aspects, Upham concludes that neither theoretical type approximates the Japanese system. Instead he suggests a model, unique to Japan, that he calls *bureaucratic informalism.*

As we saw earlier, Japanese society emphasizes, among other values, those of contextualism, harmony, collectivism, and order. Collectivism is of initial importance here because it points to a difference between the Japanese model and the rule- or judge-dominated models. Under the two latter types, individuals play a key role in either instigating the process or in having the process launched against themselves. In either event, the individual plays a central role in the judicial process. Such individuation would not set well with the Japanese. Taking individuals as the principal social unit denies that society is composed of groups, each of which is greater than the sum of its members.

The ideal characteristic of a legal system wishing to downplay the role of individuals is informality. Informal responses to misbehaving individuals confirm the view that Japanese society is harmonious and conflict-free. When sanctions are private, indirect, and ambiguous, they can be virtually invisible to society at large. In this manner, *tatemae* is securely harmonious and the group, including its disobedient members, maintains its respectable position. As we review the components of the Japanese criminal justice system, we will see several examples of justice personnel using informal sanctions. In fact, even when the

Figure 10-2. Flow chart of the adult system.

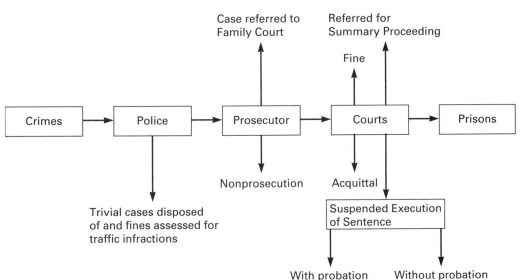

formal process is imposed, we will see prosecutors and judges preferring responses that are private and unceremonious.

The formal process of Japanese criminal justice provides the basis and structure for my comments in this chapter. As Figure 10-2 shows, the flow of adult cases is seemingly straightforward and rather reminiscent of flow charts for the United States. That similarity allows us to approach the Japanese system from the traditional police, court, corrections format. As we proceed through each of these stages, the informal system reinforcing the formal process is also discussed.

POLICING

Policing in Japan is not easily placed in one of the categorization cells discussed in Chapter 6. It is actually a combination of a pre-World War II reliance on centralization and the remnant of a decentralized format imposed by occupation forces after the war. If pushed to choose only one descriptor, it is best to emphasize the traditional and argue that Japan's police system is centralized.

The Tokugawa shogunate (1600–1868) provided for law enforcement through an elaborate system wherein town magistrates (or their delegates) served in roles we would today call police chief, prosecutor, and judge. Average citizens also played an important part, since they were grouped into organizations and made mutually responsible, and collectively liable, for any crimes or disorder caused by each other (Ames, 1983). The shogun provided a central authority over this policing arrangement through his links to town magistrates and the citizen organizations.

With the Meiji Restoration, Japan began gathering ideas about policing from the West. When Kawaji Toshiyoshi was sent to Europe in 1872, he was charged with investigating the police structures in several countries. Upon his return to Japan later that same year, Kawaji recommended police reorganization along the lines of France (Westney, 1987). The result was the 1873 establishment of the Home Ministry, which provided direct control over prefectural administration. The Police Bureau, within the Home Ministry, allowed the ministry to control police activities throughout Japan. It was centralization like this that the Allied occupation forces found potentially destructive to the newly established peace. As a result, like their counterpart in post-World War II Germany, Allied occupation forces in Japan decided to decentralize Japanese policing.

Ames (1983) describes how the American advisors made suggestions for a reorganized Japanese police that would closely follow the American model. With the new Police law of 1947, the Home Ministry was abolished, police were relieved of administrative duties (for example, issuing permits, regulating public health, construction, and similar businesses), and autonomous police units were established. All cities and towns with populations of 5000 and over were told to establish a police force and as a result some 1600 independent municipal police departments were organized. The smaller towns and villages were policed by a new National Rural Police, which was organized at the prefecture level with very limited national level involvement (Ames, 1983).

Like the citizens of the new West Germany, the Japanese had immediate problems with these structures imposed by the occupation forces. Difficulties in providing financial support for the local police and the presence of undesirable influence from politicians and gangsters were of particular concern. Finally, in June 1951, the Police law was amended to allow smaller communities to merge their police forces with the National Rural Police. Eighty percent of the communities with autonomous police forces quickly disbanded their independent force and joined with the rural police.

In 1954, a new Police Law abolished the dual system of municipal and rural police and integrated the two types into prefectural police forces (Ames, 1983; Kurian, 1989), which provided the base for today's structure.

The Structure of Japanese Policing

Japan now has three main law enforcement organizations (see Figure 10-3). The National Public Safety Commission, under the direct authority of the prime minister, is responsible for all police operations and activities in Japan. Ames sees this remnant from decentralization times as a relatively ineffective way to guarantee public control of the police. The typically elderly and conservative men serving on the commission "almost always defer to police decisions" (Ames, 1983, p. 199). As a result, the police are independent of effective formal external checks on their power and operation. However, informal checks, as discussed below, seem to serve very nicely.

The National Police Agency, the second of the three main organizations, serves as the central supervisory agency for the Japanese police system. The NPA is not a separate police force, and its officers perform strictly supervisory duties. This agency compiles crime statistics, furnishes criminal identification services, procures police equipment, and supervises police education and training (Ames, 1983). The NPA is headed by a commissioner general and consists of five bureaus: Police Administration, Security, Traffic, Communications, and Criminal Investigation. Also part of the NPA's organizational structure are seven regional police bureaus (RPB), which serve as a liaison with the prefectural police. In addition to the seven RPBs, there are two police communications divisions that also operate under the NPA (see Figure 10-3). These divisions provide structural integration of the country's largest city police force (Tokyo Metropolitan Police Communications Division) and for Japan's only region that is also a prefecture (Hokkaido Prefectural Police Communications Division).

The last law enforcement organization in Japan's structure is the only one to actually perform police work. Japan is divided into 47 prefectures which are similar in concept to American states and in size to large American counties. The organizational chart in Figure 10-3 indicates (in parentheses) the number of pre-

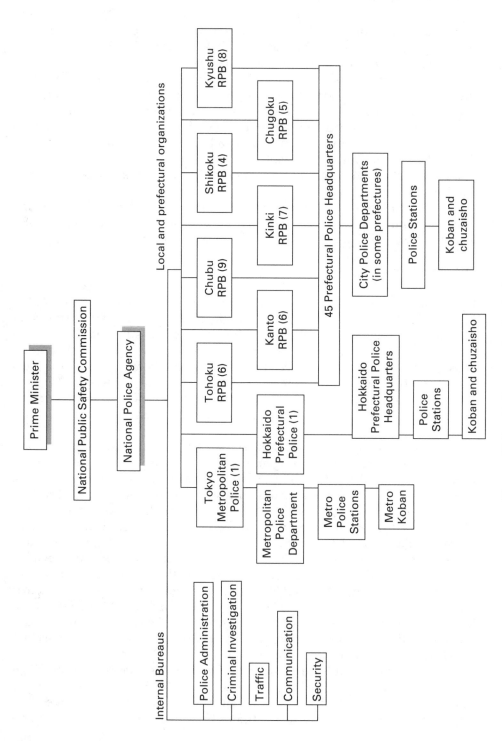

Figure 10-3. Police organization in Japan.

fectures in each of Japan's regions (for example, the Tohoku region has six prefectures). Each prefecture has one police headquarters from which chiefs and assistant chiefs control everyday police operations.

It is at the prefecture level that confusion arises regarding Japan as a centralized or decentralized police structure. The highest-level officials at prefectural police headquarters (for example, chief and senior police superintendents) are employees of the National Police Agency. All other officers (for example, police superintendent, police inspector, police sergeant, policeman), are employed by the prefecture and at the prefecture's expense. The prefecture-employed police are primarily found at the organizational levels below Prefectural Police Headquarters. Looking again at Figure 10-3, an assumption that police in the police station and *koban/chuzaisho* levels are prefectural employees would be correct in most cases. Further, each prefectural police department is supervised by the prefectural public safety commission under the prefectural governor's jurisdiction. In this manner, some authors believe the departments are autonomous and local police forces indicative of Bayley's (1985) decentralized coordinated type.

The stated responsibility given prefectures over local policing is not enough to convince all authors that the Japanese system is best described as decentralized. Ames (1981), for example, believes that the supervisory link from prefectural police headquarters to the National Police Agency (via the NPA officers in charge at the prefectural level) exemplifies *de facto* centralization of Japanese policing. While I am inclined to agree with the centralized argument, the more important point here is to emphasize Japan's ability to adapt a borrowed idea (or, in this case, an imposed idea) of decentralized policing to the centralized system of their prewar structure.

The 47 prefectures are themselves divided into districts. Each district has its own police station area under the direct control of prefectural police headquarters. Some of the police station boundaries correspond to city boundaries, but larger cities often have several police stations (Ames, 1983). Officers start their shift by reporting to the police station headquarters and are then deployed throughout the station boundaries.

The area covered by a police station further divides into small jurisdictions linked to police boxes called *koban* and *chuzaisho*. *Koban*, which are located in urban areas, are staffed by two to 12 officers in a single shift. The specific number varies according to the area covered by the *koban*. Ames (1981), Bayley (1991), and Parker (1984) provide interesting descriptions of *koban* based on their individual experiences in Japan. *Koban* vary in size and shape from kiosk-like structures at busy street intersections to a quaint house on the bank of a canal. Between these extremes are *koban* operating from a thin two-story building crammed among tall office buildings or a room sandwiched between the bar below and a restaurant above. Bayley (1991) identifies the only common features to the *koban* as a round red light globe hung over the front door and dull grey interior walls.

Chuzaisho are the *koban* of rural areas. These police boxes are more typically built like the houses of their village. The *chuzaisho* includes a living area for the assigned police officer and his or her family. Parker (1984) highlights the close ties that develop between an officer and the community by noting that the *chuzaisan* ranks with the village headman and school principal as top town officials.

Understanding the organizational structure of Japanese policing suggests reasons for its success but does not pinpoint specific topics. Since the basic theme of this chapter centers on "borrowing," we should take the opportunity to analyze why Japan's police are effective. After all, maybe there are some ideas for American policing!

Why Are the Japanese Police Effective?

The subheading for this section is somewhat misleading. It implies that the police are indeed effective, that we know why they are, and that the answer can be simply stated. It is hoped that you, the critical reader, will not be duped by a subheading. But the question is intriguing and important, so I will attempt an answer. If we accept Japan's comparatively low crime rate as a reflection of fact, and if we believe that the police play a role in that low rate, we can at least dismiss problems regarding the term "effective." Similarly, if we accept the idea that aspects of police organization and citizen response impact how the police anywhere complete their work, we can identify possible reasons for any police agency's effectiveness or ineffectiveness. With these cautions in mind, let us draw on studies of Japanese policing in an attempt to understand what impact the police officer may have in Japan's low crime rate. Specifically, we direct our attention to: (1) the deployment of police officers, (2) the working partnership with citizens, and (3) the police emphasis on a service role. These are not mutually exclusive categories, and all obviously work in concert to provide effective policing.

Deployment of Police Officers.   A long-time problem for law enforcement officials has been determining the best way to distribute their forces over a geographical area. That deployment problem impacts how the job is conducted and how supervision is carried out. Once police officers are dismissed from roll call, supervisors often lose any significant ability to monitor the officers' behavior. The supervision problem was a real concern to Henry Fielding when he initiated a patrol beat in mid-eighteenth-century England. A specified patrol area allowed more exact supervision of Fielding's men, since absence from their particular area meant either a crime problem or a personnel problem.

Just as supervisors must know where their officers are, the officers need to be able to contact the supervisors. The classic scattering of officers throughout a geographic area made communication with supervisors rather difficult. The result could be officers who felt isolated and vulnerable. Boston responded to this problem in the 1870s by modifying its telegraph system in such a way that police call boxes could be positioned on city street corners so officers could notify the supervisor that they were at their post (Rubenstein, 1973). The 1880 advent of two-way communication, via the telephone call box, meant that patrolmen could make hourly contact with the station house. But it remained difficult for the station to contact the officer. Rubenstein (1973) describes the horns, colored lights, and bells attached to the call boxes and activated from the station house when a supervisor wanted to contact the officer. The wireless radio and patrol cars provided the next technological advance. The cars allowed officers to patrol their territory more frequently, and the radio enabled the police station to quickly notify officers of a citizen's call for help.

Today, the use of patrol cars may seem not only the natural, but maybe even the only way for a modern society to deploy its police. Japan has not agreed. In fact, her deployment system via the *koban* is offered by some (see Bayley, 1991; Kim, 1987; and Rake, 1987) as an explanation for police effectiveness.

While the Japanese use patrol cars, it is the *koban* that provide the primary means of police deployment. In the city of Osaka, for example, one-fifth of all patrol officers work in cars while four-fifths operate from *koban* (Bayley, 1991). Tracing its origin to checkpoints the samurai established to protect the populace in feudal times (Kim, 1987), the *koban* now number about 6600 and the *chuzaisho* total over 9000 (Bayley, 1991).

Japan's reliance on static deployment through fixed posts rather than dynamic deployment via constantly moving cars occurs as much from necessity as from choice. Not only do the Japanese citizens strongly favor the *koban*, but the small proportion of Japanese land devoted to streets makes patrolling by car less feasible than in other countries. For example, only 15 percent of Tokyo's land area is composed of streets, compared with 27 percent in New York City and 43 percent in Washington, D.C. (Bayley, 1991). Highly congested cities and streets mean that *koban* officers on bicycle or foot often beat patrol cars to scenes requiring police response.

The *koban* is a community fixture physically representing the link between police and citizen. It operates, and is perceived, as much like an assistance office as a police post. *Koban* officials spend much of their shift providing information about locations and addresses of homes and businesses tucked away in the confusing maze of often unnamed Japanese streets. They also act as the neighborhood lost and found, distribute crime prevention circulars, provide initial response to calls for assistance, and offer other services benefiting the community and citizen. The character of each *koban* is influenced by its surroundings (Bayley, 1991); in some locations it may provide a community television set, while in others it serves as the primary time check and alarm clock. Essentially, the needs of the neighborhood determine any unique traits found in individual *koban*.

The services provided at the *koban* and by the *koban* officers truly reflect the concept of community policing. The *koban* officers, who are not even considered to know the area until after two years at the post, spend 56 hours on duty each week. This deployment system means that every part of Japan is continually under the supervision of a *koban* (or *chuzaisho*) officer who is familiar with, and known to, the residents of that area. Not surprisingly, *koban* officers and citizens develop a strong working relationship, which also seems to make the police effective.

The Citizen as Partner. During the informal stage of police development in England and the American colonies, policing relied on the efforts of individual citizens. Whether the citizen was issuing or answering the old "hue and cry," or was more actively serving as watchman or constable, policing depended on citizen participation. The growth of professional police work in the early twentieth-century United States was accompanied by a philosophy that citizen involvement in policing was inappropriate. Instead, law enforcement was the duty of professional police officers who only incidentally had to interact with the law-abiding citizen. By the 1960s and 1970s, the pendulum was swinging back, and American police officials were recognizing the need for active citizen participation in crime prevention and reduction activities. In Japan, the tradition of police–citizen cooperation was never forsaken.

Building from a base that may stretch back some 600 years (see Plath, 1964, p. 142), Japan has established formal and informal associations that include crime prevention activities now linking the citizen and the police (Bayley, 1991; Kim, 1987). Crime prevention associations exist from the central government level down to the neighborhoods, but the primary organization level is tied to police station jurisdictions. Association members cooperate with the police to maintain social order through activities like distributing crime prevention literature and maintaining "contact points" where information and police assistance is available. Some crime prevention organizations may even organize civilian watches, which help monitor juvenile behavior, patrol streets, and assist police during emergencies.

Police response to these civilian efforts is one of support and encouragement. As Bayley put it, the Japanese police and their public believe each has "to work through the other in order to make the society a civil place to live" (quoted in Rake, 1987, p. 151). That cooperation requires Japanese police to place significant emphasis on nonenforcement activities and to interact with people other than those acting illegally. The result is a service orientation, which may also explain police effectiveness.

Policing as Service. Monkkonen (1981) argues that prior to the 1890s, American policing had a strong service component. Police stations served many functions now handled by social welfare agencies, and police officers provided as much service as enforcement. Between the 1890s and 1920, the public service work of police departments disappeared or was substantially diminished. Couple that with the movement toward professionalism and the disinvolvement of a citizen-partner, and the United States was left with rather isolated police officers.

Mid-twentieth-century American police officers had few occasions to interact with the helpful law-abiding citizen or even the troubled resident who had fallen on hard times. Instead, daily association was (and essentially still is) primarily with society's riffraff. Even when they interact with a supposedly upstanding citizen, it is often because that citizen has crossed the boundary into deviance. No wonder police officers are accused of having a distorted image of John and Jane Citizen. When you constantly see people's misbehavior, it is easy to assume that people are basically bad.

The deployment system for Japanese police, and the citizen-police partnership provide the Japanese officer with a different view of people. Japanese police are called *Omawari-san* (the Honorable Mr. Walkabout), and their constant presence in the community gives them many opportunities to see people's good behavior. One result is a willingness to operate in a service capacity instead of constantly emphasizing their crime fighter role.

The Japanese police officer's presence in the community is fittingly described by Bayley, who compares policing styles in America and Japan. "An American policeman is like a fireman—he responds when he must. A Japanese policeman is more like a postman—he has a daily round of low-key activities that relate him to the lives of the people among whom he works" (Bayley, 1991, p. 86). The Japanese officer is consistently polite and businesslike during encounters with citizens (Kim, 1987), and the officer's presence is considered rather routine and personal. Police involvement in activities seemingly unrelated to law enforcement is accepted and expected by Japanese citizens.

One of the best examples of nonenforcement activities, and one that also emphasizes the citizen–police partnership, is the residential survey. Twice a year uniformed officers visit every residence in Japan to conduct a residential survey requesting general data about the occupants and the neighborhood (Bayley, 1991; Kim, 1987). Questions about the names, ages, occupations, and relationship of the residents are willingly answered by most people. Similarly, the respondent provides information about possible criminal activity in the area, may pass on rumors about neighborhood happenings, and might complain to the officer about municipal services. What might be considered an invasion of privacy in some countries is typically accepted in Japan as way for police to gain knowledge of an area and its people. The information, which is kept in large record books at the *koban*, is of great benefit in providing service and fighting crime.

The Japanese police officer's ability to play the potentially conflicting roles of authority figure and fellow citizen speaks well of both the officer and the citizen. Of course, it also reflects some of the cultural traits discussed earlier in this chapter. Police officers comprise one of the hardest-working groups among hardworking people, view their fellow officers and supervisors as an extension of their family, and take enormous pride in the successful performance of their roles. For their part, the citizens' respect for authority and orderliness coupled with an acceptance of responsibility for each other's behavior, provides an atmosphere supporting police efforts. But, of course, the police are not the extent of the criminal justice system. We must also understand the role played by the courts.

JUDICIARY

Just as Japan's policing exhibits an intriguing combination of tradition, innovation, and imitation, so too does its contemporary court system. First we will examine the historical base for the adjudication system, and then we will consider how the end result reflects aspects of Japanese cultural traits. Especially meaningful in this section is the preference for compromise and conciliation, and the importance of apology.

The Japanese judicial system certainly owes some of its features to the Chinese, but there seems always to have been a glimmer of features more typically associated with European legal traditions. For example, aspects of precedent and a role for adversaries have been present since the first developmental stage of Japanese legal process, but this does not appear to be the result of borrowing. Instead, the similarity to common law is an element that seems to have developed independent of outside influence. Since the 1600s, Japan's highly organized court system began developing a body of native law and practice based on judicial precedent. Though similar to the practice of *stare decisis* in English common law, its development in Japan cannot be attributed to borrowing from the common law tradition.

To see how judicial precedent operated it is necessary to describe the organization of courts. The Regency domain was divided into three jurisdictions: metropolitan, rural, and ecclesiastical. The Metropolitan Judge received all suits where the plaintiff was a townsman, the Exchequer Judge got those with a countryman plaintiff, and the Temple Judge accepted complaints from residents of church lands. When sitting as a single court, these three judges formed the Supreme Court, which had original jurisdiction in cases between parties from different jurisdictions. Actually, the men in these positions were not as busy as that description sounds. Each post was in fact held by two officials with each, in alternate months, sitting in the Supreme Court. At other times, he officiated in his own jurisdiction. Even in his home province, there were lower magistrates who heard most cases.

Within this structure, an independent system of case law developed without need to cite Chinese or any other foreign authority. Wigmore (1936) points out that this total reliance on native laws and precedents was a feature not found among any European people (except the Celtic) since Roman times. To make his point, he quotes at length a case that included formal and recorded consultation between judges, a search for precedent extending back nearly 100 years, the application of precedent, and the creation of new precedent. English case law had no advantage over this aspect of the Tokugawa legal system.

The Japanese desire to appease disputes is borrowed from the Chinese principle of conciliation as emphasized by Confucian philosophy. To achieve conciliation, each Japanese town and village was divided into *kumi*, or groupings of five neighboring families, with each responsible for the other's conduct. In times of disagreement the five family heads met to settle the matter. In a dinner-party type of atmosphere, agreement was achieved in the midst of eating, drinking, and a friendly spirit. On those occasions when settlement was not reached, the complaint could be passed to a higher authority. Such appeal occurred more often in larger towns and cities. In the villages, the seeking of settlement outside the *kumi* or beyond the chief village officials was considered a dishonorable last resort.

Once a magistrate received a case from either a village or city, it could still be treated in a manner Western eyes might see as something other than legalistic. Wigmore (1936) provides several examples of decisions which reflect a considerably flexible view toward the law. In an 1840 case the Magistrate of Komo County was asked to order a woman (Cho) and her four male family members to stop bothering Farmer Uhei and his son, Umakichi. Cho's family claimed Umakichi should marry Cho because prior relations (the exact nature of which are not specified) between the boy and girl made marriage the honorable thing to do. The magistrate investigated the case and apparently encouraged the two families to reach a settlement of their own accord. The records show that later in the same month as the first petition, Farmer Uhei asked the magistrate to dismiss the petition. Uhei explained that the affair turned out to be unimportant and based on foolish statements. All parties were at peace and Uhei credits the magistrate with bringing about the settlement. The petition asks the magistrate to shut his eyes to the case and not give it further consideration. Magistrate Shinomoto concurred and no legal action was ever taken.

A 1983 case (see Hendry, 1989, pp. 190–191) suggests that 140 years have not significantly modified Japanese aversion to litigation and court activities. In 1983 a family's three-year-old son drowned in an irrigation pond while he was in the care of a neighbor. The bereaved family filed a lawsuit claiming negligence by the neighbor, the contractor who had failed to fence in the pond, and against various levels of government. The District Court ordered the neighbors to pay five million yen, but the other parties were exonerated. The case received considerable media coverage, and the bereaved family soon received hundreds of anonymous phone calls and some 50 letters and postcards condemning them for taking legal action against their neighbors. The father lost his job, and the other children in the family were subjected to ridicule at school. The neighbors, meanwhile, appealed the court's decision. This action brought a similarly abusive response by the public toward the neighbors themselves. Apparently, appealing to the courts, even in self-defense, is regarded as being as inappropriate as are cases of disputes between neighbors.

The 1840 and the 1983 cases exemplify civil rather than criminal incidents, but the principle remains. Since the Tokugawa era, official conciliation procedures have provided alternatives to civil litigation and to criminal trials when the preferred informal conciliation efforts fail. The main difference between historical and modern procedures is the people playing the role of mediator. Where samurai and village officials served in the past, police officers and lawyers act today. As we review the formal system of handling criminal disputes, we will necessarily refer to some of the informal procedures reflecting conciliation ideals.

Pre-Trial Activities

There is a saying about the American criminal process that "in the Halls of Justice, justice is in the halls." The implication is that much of the everyday work by justice officials takes place away from the formal courtroom environment. Police deals with informants, prosecution favors in return for testimony, plea negotiations, sentencing arrangements, and other activities constantly take place in informal settings. At times those informal arrangements result in very formal activities (for example, a formal contract stating a plea bargain agreement), but they may also simply remain an informal transaction. Not surprisingly, Japan's aversion to courtroom activities means that their "hallway justice" is even more pronounced than our own. This is especially clear as we become familiar with the actors and actions involved at the pre-trial stage.

Police Role.   In 1989, Japanese police recorded contact with nearly 408,000 suspects (Research and Training Institute, 1990). They arrested and referred to the prosecutor 22 percent; arrested and released just over 1 percent; 77 percent of the suspects were not even arrested. At the start of this chapter I reported a very high clearance rate for Japanese police. You might reasonably wonder how 77 percent of the suspects can avoid arrest and yet the police can claim a clearance rate of 60 percent. Much of the explanation lies in terminology, but since it introduces the role of informal sanctioning by police, it is important to clarify.

The clearance rate for American police, as reported in the annual Uniform Crime Reports, reflects a suspect being arrested, charged with committing an offense, and turned over to the court for prosecution (Department of Justice, 1984). In Japan, a crime is reported as cleared when the police tell the prosecutor the crime has been solved. No arrest is necessary. Even when an arrest is made, the police need not turn the suspect over in order to "clear" the crime (Araki, 1985). By these definitions, Japanese police might well be expected to have a higher clearance rate than do their American counterparts.

Japanese police have three choices in initiating cases. They can: (1) "send only the evidence to the prosecutor leaving the suspect unarrested but still liable to prosecution, (2) arrest the suspect but decide not to detain him or her, or (3) arrest the suspect and recommend that the prosecutor detain him or her" (Araki, 1985, p. 609). The first situation (evidence forward, suspect not) contains most of the cases noted above, showing that 77 percent of the suspects were not even arrested. The procedure allowing police to clear a case and then discharge the suspect is established by the local prosecutor's office. Araki (1985) explains that each chief of the district public prosecutor's office develops criteria permitting police to discharge persons committing less serious offenses when the crime and criminal are determined to be nondangerous.

The institutionalization of informal sanctioning is only one indication of the significant discretion given Japanese police. Contextualism, as discussed earlier, plays an important role in understanding when and why police use their discretion to respond informally to offenses. Bayley (1991) reports that enforcement is influenced by where the offense occurred so that officers may respond according to the custom of each area (that is, contextualism). In other instances officers may believe that formal punishment would be inappropriately severe in a particular case, and respond with anything from friendly warnings to ignoring evidence.

It is apparent that those examples of police discretion can just as accurately describe American, and most any other, police officers as well. The difference lies more in the extent to which nonenforcement tactics are used than in their form or the situation provoking them. As the 77 percent "release without arrest" statistic indicates, Japanese police officers make liberal use of policing tactics that avoid the formal justice process.

One reason Japanese officers are likely to use informal tactics stems from the recognized importance of collectivism. Since the significance of the group is accepted by most Japanese, they are also aware of the obligations accompanying group membership. One of the most basic obligations is to refrain from embarrassing the group. If that obligation is not met, the dutiful group member should do his best to avoid public display of the misconduct. The police, being fully aware of this protocol, can use it to handle the situation informally. The primary method employed is to require an apology from the offender.

Americans may consider giving an apology to one's victim to be barely a slap on the offender's wrist. But this is where the cultural differences come into play. When a Japanese apologizes, he or she is admitting to having failed in his or her obligation to the group. Were that not bad enough, an apology also forces recognition of *honne* overcoming *tatemae*. It is no easy task to admit that one is responsible for disrupting the harmony, has failed in his duty to the group, or has jeopardized his group standing. The apology, in other words, can simultaneously be a punishment for the acutely embarrassed offender and an expression of remorse to compensate the victim.

Bayley (1991) relates several stories of observed police encounters that resulted in a formal apology as the police imposed sanction. The tactic, which is always at the discretion of the officer, is used for minor violations ranging from traffic offenses and wandering drunks, to inappropriate behavior toward fellow citizens. The apology as sanction is so commonly used that *koban* officers may keep a copy of an appropriate letter of apology to be used by remorseful offenders. But it is also taken so seriously by Japanese citizens and police that some offenders are simply warned instead of being required to make a formal apology.

The police preference for nonenforcement strategies in responding to offenders is not unique to this stage of the Japanese criminal justice system. Of course, there are situations that require the police to respond formally and send the case to the next stage. However, as we will see, prosecutors and judges continue both the process and the propensity for informal sanctioning.

Prosecutor Role. Prosecution in Japan falls under the authority of the Ministry of Justice and is under the direction of a prosecutor-general, who is appointed by the Cabinet. Neither the prefectural government nor any of the other subdivisions has any control of prosecution. So, unlike the police system, which has aspects of decentralization via prefectural involvement, prosecution is fully centralized.

Following a European model, law graduates choose career paths in prosecution, defense, or judgeships after receiving their law degrees. After initial entry, each area has some levels from which to choose and others to which one can aspire. Prosecutors, for example, work at one of four court levels: supreme, high, district, and local. The workload is greatest at the district level, since that is where most criminal cases are handled.

The prosecutor's primary activity is to gather information regarding the case, and to provide information about the suspect to assist the judge in sentencing. In fact, Castberg (1990) suggests that these two activities not only define the role of prosecutors, but of police, defense, and even the trial itself. This appeared to be true in our discussion of the pre-trial activities of police, and we will soon appreciate its pertinence to the defense and in the trial, but we must begin with the prosecutor.

Given the vigorous investigation by police, and the typical confession they were able to elicit, it may seem the prosecutor's job must require only minimum effort. Actually, there is still plenty to keep prosecutors busy since they must determine if there is sufficient evidence to prosecute, initiate specific charges, and decide if the prosecution should be suspended. Defendants in Japan cannot be found guilty solely on the basis of a confession, so prosecutors must have sufficient additional information to convince the judge of the defendant's guilt. Also, there is no plea bargaining in Japan, so determination of specific charges against the suspect is neither automatic nor always simple. Despite the time requirements for those activities, a spur-of-the-moment visit to a prosecutor's office is likely to find him pondering the appropriateness of suspending prosecution in a particular case.

The authority to suspend prosecution in a case is provided in Article 248 of the Code of Criminal Procedure:

> If, after considering the character, age, and situation of the offender, the gravity of the offense, the circumstances under which the offense was committed, and the conditions subsequent to the commission of the offense, prosecution is deemed unnecessary, prosecution need not be instituted (quoted in Castberg, 1990, p. 60).

Since prosecution is actually terminated in these cases, the term *suspension* is somewhat misleading. In any event, suspension of prosecution is an increasingly popular way for prosecutors to handle criminal cases. From a 1987 rate of 17 percent, suspension of prosecution increased to 21.8 percent in 1988, and was up to 24.3 percent in 1989 (Research and Training Institute, 1990).

Offenses ranging from homicide (a 1989 suspension rate of 5.1 percent) to gambling (a 1989 suspension rate of 37.9 percent) receive this prosecutorial

	Prosecuted	Suspended
Total*	73.6	24.3
Homicide	50.9	5.1
Robbery	71.8	6.9
Bodily injury	76.4	20.7
Extortion	65.9	26.8
Larceny	51.9	44.6
Fraud	61.7	30.1
Rape	65.2	15.2
Arson	53.3	16.4
Gambling	61.4	37.9
Violent acts	78.9	17.0
Traffic professional negligence	39.8	58.1

*Total includes more offenses than shown here. Percentages may not total 100, since options beside prosecution or suspended prosecution are also available.

Figure 10-4. 1989 prosecution and suspended prosecution percentages by penal code offense. *Source:* Research and Training Institute (1990). *Summary of the White Paper on Crime.* Tokyo:

response each year. However, as Figure 10-4 shows, suspension of prosecution is especially used in cases of larceny (44.6 percent) and traffic professional negligence (58.1 percent). This latter offense category, which would more likely end up in a civil court in the United States, involves injuries in traffic accidents caused by a person in the conduct of an occupation (see Araki, 1985).

Article 248 is very general in setting criteria for prosecutors to use when deciding if suspension of prosecution is appropriate. Castberg (1990) suggests that "circumstances under which the offense was committed" deal primarily with aggravating circumstances, like excessive force or cruelty, which accompanied the crime. The "conditions subsequent to the commission of the offense" generally refers to apology and restitution by the suspect and forgiveness by the victim or victim's family. It is at this point that the defense attorney can begin an active role.

Defense Attorney Role. There are no public defenders in Japan, but the Constitution assures anyone accused of a crime of the right to counsel, at state expense if the defendant is indigent. Indigents are represented by counsel appointed from the ranks of lawyers listed on the roll of the Japanese Bar Federation. The low crime rate and high confession rate suggests that there is little work for defense attorneys in Japan and, in fact, few lawyers do exclusively criminal defense work (Castberg, 1990). But, like the police and the prosecutors, defense attorneys assist in gathering information about the case and the defendant.

Use of the term *defendant*, instead of *suspect*, is important when we discuss defense attorneys, because appointment of counsel occurs after indictment. As we discovered when discussing police interrogation, a suspect's access to defense counsel at that stage is often problematic. Indigents wishing to have legal representation prior to arraignment must appeal to the Legal Aid Society or the Civil Liberties Union. Since nearly two-thirds of the criminal cases involving defense counsel are for indigents, the majority of defendants cannot receive legal advice during police interrogation (Hataguchi, 1990). So there is basically no role for the defense attorney prior to indictment.

Even between indictment and the trial, defense counsel has a more informal than formal role. For example, the attorney may accompany the defendant to contact the victim, or victim's family, so that appropriate apologies can be made and reparations offered. The defense attorney can advise the defendant regarding the proper way to show remorse and the appropriate restitution to offer. If counsel can obtain written statements of forgiveness, and maybe even a victim's request for leniency toward the defendant, the prosecutor might be inclined toward suspending prosecution. Should the victim's statements and requests for leniency not impress the prosecutor, defense counsel can always use them during the trial. In fact, since so many defendants have confessed, much of the defense role during trial is to present mitigating circumstances that might convince the judge to be sympathetic toward the defendant. But even when there is no confession and the defendant is contesting the charge, a prime defense counsel role is to provide the judge with reasons to be compassionate (Castberg, 1990).

The pre-trial activities of police, prosecutor, and defense attorney seem intent on avoiding formal sanctioning of suspects and defendants. This seeking of informal responses does not stop in those cases which actually do make it to a courtroom.

Trial Options

In 1989, the Public Prosecutor's Office handled over two million cases. After referring about one-half million to the Family Courts, the prosecutors disposed of the remainder through prosecution (74 percent) and either suspension of prosecution (24 percent) or simply nonprosecution (3 percent, with rounding errors making the total over 100 percent). Of those cases actually prosecuted, 92 percent were handled under summary proceedings and 8 percent went to formal trial. Of those going to formal trial, over 99 percent are convicted and, although nearly all those will receive a prison sentence, about 60 percent will have execution of that prison sentence suspended (Research and Training Institute, 1990).

To emphasize the reluctance to impose formal sanctions, consider the numbers we would get by using these percentages on a hypothetical cluster of 1000 offenders arriving at the prosecutor's office and not being transferred to Family Court (see Figure 10-5). Since about 260 of those would either have prosecution suspended or no action toward prosecution even attempted, only 740 would even continue in the process. Of those 740 people being prosecuted, about 681

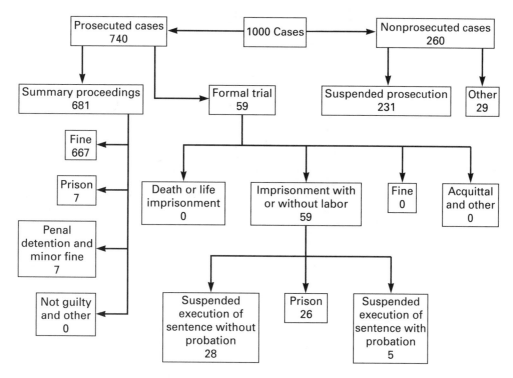

Figure 10-5. Dispositions by prosecutor's office of 1000 hypotheti-

will plead guilty and have their case quickly handled through summary procedures for which they are not even present. Of the remaining 59 people going to formal trial, at least 58 of them (and probably all 59) will be convicted and sentenced to prison. However, about 33 of those convicted and sentenced will have the execution of that sentence suspended. Only about 5 of those receiving a suspended execution of sentence will be placed on probation, while the other 28 live in the community without any court supervision. Of the original 1000 people, about 26 are sent to prison.

It appears that the formal trial process is an infrequent occurrence in the Japanese criminal justice system. Even when adjudication is required, most of the cases are handled summarily instead of in a formal court setting. Following a brief review of Japan's court structure, we will look more closely at the summary procedures and regular trials.

Court Structure. The Japanese court system has four levels composed of two trial courts and two appellate courts (see Figure 10-6). At the apex is Japan's Supreme Court, which was the primary judicial modification in the postwar constitution. The American influence is seen in the authority given the Supreme

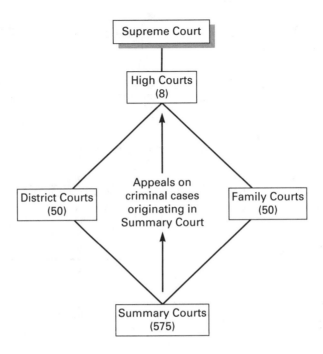

Court, which has administrative control over all other courts and has the right to determine the constitutionality of all laws. This latter point, the concept of judicial review, presents an awkward situation, since Japan's government is essentially parliamentary in nature. In most other such systems, nothing can override the parliament, but the right of judicial review gives Japan's judicial branch the authority to do just that. Reischauer (1988) notes that the Japanese Supreme Court has been reluctant to go against the Japanese Diet's political decisions and will typically defer to what the Diet majority voted. This is in contrast to the United States Supreme Court's vigorous use of judicial review to shape social and political developments.

The Supreme Court consists of one chief justice and 14 justices. Cases, which are received on appeal, are initially assigned to one of three petty benches composed of five justices each. If the case concerns a constitutional issue, it is transferred to the Grand Bench, where all 15 justices sit (Castberg, 1990).

Eight High Courts, with six branches, serve as intermediate appellate courts with cases typically heard by a panel of three judges. Most of the High Court cases come on appeal from the district or family courts, but criminal cases originating in summary court can also go directly to the High Court (Westerman and Burfeind, 1991).

The trial level court for both criminal and civil offenses are the 50 District Courts. Each of the 47 prefectures has one District Court, but Hokkaido's size requires it to have an additional three. Equal in level and number with the district courts, yet administratively independent, are the Family Courts. These courts handle most domestic and juvenile (persons under age 20) matters. The only criminal matters heard in Family Court are those involving adults who have violated a child's well-being (typically less than one percent of Family Court cases).

Summary courts, numbering 575, have original jurisdiction in minor criminal and civil cases (Westerman and Burfeind, 1991). Cases heard in summary proceedings range from larceny to bodily injury, but the penalties imposed are limited to fines or short-term detention (that is, no more than three years). The popularity of summary procedures with prosecutors and offenders makes the summary courts a good starting place in discussing Japan's adjudication process.

Summary Courts.   Japan has no grand jury system, so when the prosecutor decides to initiate formal proceedings the defendant is indicted through the filing of an information. There is no preliminary hearing, so the next step is for the prosecutor to choose between a summary procedure and a regular trial. If the summary procedure is used, the case is handled in one of the country's Summary Courts. These courts also conduct a few formal trials, but the vast majority (99 percent in 1988) of their activities are summary proceedings (Research and Training Institute, 1990).

If the defendant agrees (and that is required for this procedure), the prosecutor can dispose of the case by sending the Summary Court judge the defendant's consent form, the evidence related to the case, and the prosecution's sentence recommendation (Araki, 1985; Castberg, 1990). Neither party has the opportunity to appear before the Summary Court, since the judge reviews the case outside the presence of either the prosecutor or defendant. However, there is a level of protection for both sides, since defense or prosecution can apply for a formal trial if either is dissatisfied with the ruling under summary procedures. The sanctions resulting from summary procedures are fines (both regular and minor) and they are used in both violent (for example, bodily injury, assault) and nonviolent (for example, embezzlement, gambling, traffic violations) offenses.

Modified Public Trials.   If the charge is not a serious one (for example, larceny), and the defendant is not contesting the facts, it is possible to have a formal, yet streamlined, trial (Araki, 1985; Castberg, 1990). These modified public trials can be held in either Summary Court or District Court, but it is much more likely to be the former. Trial procedures are simplified and great reliance is placed on information provided by the prosecutor as being an accurate reflection of the facts in the case. The judge's written work is simplified, since this type of trial does not require written reasons for the decision, which can include fines or short-term (that is, less than three years) detention.

Regular Trials.   District and Family Courts serve as the court of first instance for most contested criminal cases and for cases where the defendant or prosecutor is not pleased with the result of a summary procedure. Criminal jurisdiction of Family Courts is limited to cases of domestic relations, juvenile delinquency, and cases where adults violated laws protecting a child's welfare. The 50 District Courts have jurisdiction over all criminal cases except insurrection (which must start in the High Court), Family Court adult criminal cases, and crimes handled in Summary Court. Hearings are conducted by one judge (most cases) or by a panel of three judges (the most serious offenses and those with the most severe penalties). In either format, the court handles two general types of cases: noncontested and contested.

The noncontested cases, which are the vast majority, are typically disposed of rather quickly. A single judge examines the written and documentary evidence presented by the prosecutor and hears challenges from the defense. Since the defendant has confessed, the judge's role is basically to protect the accused's rights by examining all submitted evidence, occasionally requiring submission of more evidence, and determining an appropriate sentence (Castberg, 1990). Even though this is a formal trial setting, there is considerable flexibility regarding the admissibility of evidence. Like many of the trials under the civil legal tradition, Japanese trials are not bifurcated. That is, determination of both guilt and sentence is done simultaneously. There is no pre-sentence investigation done for adult offenders, so the judge relies on information presented during trial to help determine an appropriate punishment for the defendant.

When the defendant contests the charges, the Japanese court system follows its most formal procedures. In this type of trial there is either a genuine dispute regarding the facts of the case or there is no confession. The judge, or judges, serve as impartial adjudicator and fact-finder (Castberg, 1990). As in countries following a civil legal tradition, Japanese judges play an active role during the trial as they decide the order of witnesses, frequently begin the questioning of those witnesses, and rule on admissibility of evidence. There are no clearly defined prosecution and defense phases in the trial, but each side may question witnesses, present closing arguments, and make sentencing recommendations.

One of the most striking differences between Japanese and American trials is the intermittent nature of hearings in Japan. Rather than having a single hearing stretching over a few hours or days, trials in Japan consist of several short separate hearings scheduled every few weeks or months. Seventy percent of the District and Family Court trials last less than three months, but over 20 percent last for three to six months (Research and Training Institute, 1990).

Judgments

Judges in District and Family Courts have several judgment types available. The defendant can, of course, be acquitted; but this occurs in less than 0.1 percent of the cases. The extremely high conviction rate in Japanese courts must be considered in light of the system's screening process and the defendant's tendency to confess. Over 80 percent of the suspects are not arrested at all, or are arrested and then released by the police; 24 percent of the cases reaching the prosecutor are suspended; only 5 percent of the cases that are prosecuted are heard in a formal trial (Research and Training Institute, 1990). Even among that 5 percent, most defendants are not contesting the charges. Given these circumstances, a 99.9 percent conviction rate is not quite so surprising.

Allowable sentences for convicted offenders include execution, life imprisonment, imprisonment with or without forced labor, a fine, and suspended execution of sentence. Neither the death sentence (10 of the 57,790 adjudications in 1988) nor life imprisonment (44 times in 1988) are handed down very often. Similarly, fines (including short-term penal detention) also account for only a small number of sentences (493 in 1988). By far the most frequent sentence from District and Family Courts is one of imprisonment with or without labor. The 1988 rate of 98.7 percent is typical of the norm (Research and Training Institute, 1990).

A prison sentence in nearly 99 percent of the cases suggests that Japanese judges are quite severe. People favoring a punitive response to offenders may say it is about time somebody in the Japanese criminal justice system got tough on criminals. Actually, the preference for informal justice that we found at the police and prosecutor levels still exists in the courtroom, despite the seemingly high imprisonment rate. This is because over half those prison sentences are suspended. And, as noted in Chapter 8, only about 13 percent of the suspended executions of sentences even require probation. All types of crimes can receive suspended execution of sentences. For example, prison sentences for homicide, robbery, and drugs are suspended with and without probation; just as are sentences for larceny, gambling, and road-traffic violations. When the sentence is for imprisonment, or involves probation on a suspended sentence, the corrections area in Japan's system takes over.

CORRECTIONS

Corrections in Japan received specific coverage in Chapter 8, so we need not duplicate information here. Instead, I will highlight those aspects of Japanese corrections which relate to this chapter's themes of effectiveness and borrowing.

History

Throughout the various shogunate periods, corrections (in its broadest sense) varied from the right of samurai to execute on the spot any misbehaving commoner (Westney, 1987) to the use of prisons (*royas*) built in the fourteenth century as both pre-trial holding facilities and as places of punishments (Eskridge, 1989). Some of the later efforts, like the early nineteenth century "Coolie Gathering Place" facility, even provided inmates with an opportunity to learn a trade (Correction Bureau, 1990). Despite that historical base, the modern era of Japanese corrections did not begin until the late nineteenth and early twentieth centuries. The push toward modernization resulted from efforts during the Meiji Restoration to increase Japan's contact with the Western world. Actually, one of the stipulations made when revising treaties with the West required Japan to improve prison administration. As they did for so many other areas in the late nineteenth century, Japan's response was to begin a search for a model to bring home.

By 1890 Japan had joined the International Penal and Penitentiary Congress and, with the assistance of Prussian penologist Kurt von Seebach, started the country's first national training institute for prison officers (Correction Bureau, 1990). However, concern about the prison employees was not matched with concern for the inmates until the 1920s and the efforts of Japanese jurist Akira Masaki. His reminiscences (Masaki, 1964) provide an interesting review of imitation and innovation while describing the development of modern corrections in Japan.

Masaki was sent abroad in 1928 to gather information on prison systems in other countries. Among his stops was the Hungarian farm prison, Kiss Halta, where Masaki was impressed with the absence of iron bars and walls. However, the feature he would dwell upon was the administrator's use of a prisoners' self-government policy controlled by a progressive stage system to modify prisoner behavior. A trip to the United States gave him an opportunity to see the classification system at Sing Sing prison (a system he found similar to the Belgian one he had earlier observed), and to visit the Elmira (New York) Reformatory, which he called "the Mecca for criminologists" (Masaki, 1964, p. 54).

American prisons at Sing Sing and Auburn (New York) and the naval prison at Portsmouth (New Hampshire) also provided Masaki an opportunity to gather more information on inmate self-government. He found the process, as used in these prisons, had several defects. But he believed when properly implemented, inmate self-government could be the core of a treatment system.

In 1933, Masaki was finally able to try out some of his ideas gathered while abroad. Under orders from the director of the Prison Bureau, Masaki began to set up a progressive stage system. He used the classification procedure from Belgium and the United States to set up four specific stages of inmate categorization. Following the mark system observed at Elmira Reformatory (which had come to America from Australia via Ireland), Masaki awarded prisoners marks based on their work habits, good behavior, and a showing of responsibility and firm will. The marks allowed inmates to progress through the stages; with each promotion they received more freedom and privileges.

At the second and first stages, self-government became an important aspect of the treatment plan. Inmates at these levels worked without the supervision of guards but instead under the leadership of a fellow prisoner they had selected. Unfortunately for Masaki, his program was criticized for being too lenient. Masaki admitted that some wardens forgot the need to instill a sense of responsibility in the prisoners, but he accepted the criticism and reported feelings of frustration with implementing a philosophy he believed to be correct. Today, the classification and progressive stage systems brought to Japan by

Masaki remain important aspects of Japanese corrections—the use of inmate self-government is not.

Aspects of Effectiveness

Determining the effectiveness of prisons and community corrections is difficult. One type of attempt, using the concept of recidivism, judges effectiveness by whether or not a person who has been through a corrections program returns to criminal behavior. It is difficult to establish, however, just who the recidivist actually is and which program, or program part, was apparently ineffective. Is probation effective as long as the probationer is law-abiding while under probation supervision but commits a new offense after being released from probation? Was imprisonment effective if the released person does not commit a new offense within three years of being released from prison, or do we have to wait five or more years before claiming success? Even if we claim that the prison experience was effective in this case, is it important to know which prison program (for example, academic education, vocational education, drug therapy) made the difference?

In addition to the definition problems associated with the term *recidivism*, there are practical problems related to data gathering. If John is released from prison in California and moves to New Mexico, where he commits a new crime, California is not likely to hear about John's recidivism. If Mary successfully completes probation in Weld County, Colorado, and then is sentenced to a Colorado prison two years later from a different county, Weld County officials probably will not know about Mary's recidivism. The decentralized corrections system operating in the United States makes it difficult to monitor the location and recurring misbehavior of persons going through the state or federal systems. This is especially true among the various states, but can also be true within a particular state. The absence of a nationwide record-keeping process prohibits effective sharing of information among all the different corrections agencies in the country.

In countries with a centralized corrections system the ability to keep track of current and former clients is obviously increased. As such, Japan's single system reduces some of the practical problems associated with measuring recidivism, but the definitional ones remain. The difficulty of playing with terms like *effectiveness* and *recidivism* can be seen with a brief look at Japanese suspended sentence numbers and United States probation numbers.

Each year the Research and Training Institute of Japan's Ministry of Justice publishes statistics on various aspects of the criminal justice process. Their *Summary of the White Paper on Crime* (Research and Training Institute, 1990) provides the data for this quick look at recidivism. During 1989, 36,091 convicted persons were granted suspended execution of sentence. Of that group, 12.3 percent (4429) had the suspension revoked either for committing another crime (98 percent) or for violating conditions of suspension (2 percent). Similar numbers are reported for earlier years, when 12.9 percent (1987) and 13.5 percent (1988) of the persons receiving suspended sentences had that sentence revoked. Since Japan uses a flow, rather than stock, system for keeping statistics, it is difficult to determine the revocation rate for all persons under suspension at any given time. Although we do not know the revocation rate for the entire suspended sentence population, we do know that of all those receiving that sentence each year, about 12 to 14 percent will have it revoked. If recidivism is defined as committing new offenses and technical violations while under a suspended sentence, Japan's rate is around 13 percent.

If we surrender to temptation and compare those figures to ones from the United States, we can see problems of cross-cultural comparison. On December 31, 1990 the number of adults on probation in the United States was 2,670,234. By the end of the 1990 year, 1,489,448 adults had been discharged from probation (Jankowski, 1991). Among those discharged, 31 percent had their probation revoked (Greenfeld, 1992). From these numbers it appears that Japan has a lower recidivism rate (13 percent) than does the United States (31 percent) when recidivism refers to committing new offenses and technical violations while under a suspended sentence.

Some dangers in drawing such conclusions are worth noting, since they remind us of problems when doing comparative research. For example, unlike the Japanese flow-type statistics wherein the discharges refer to the same people as the admissions, the United States stock-type numbers refer to the total number of adults on probation and the total discharges during the year as reported at the end of the year. If we looked only at the revocations for the United States adults going on probation in 1990, their percentage might well be under 31. Similarly, if we knew the total number of Japanese revocations for all people under suspended sentence in 1989, we might find a number above 13 percent. It is also possible, of course, that the percentages would be even higher in the United States and lower in Japan, or they could be exactly the same as those found when comparing the flow and stock types.

Potential confusion increases when we recall that a suspended sentence in Japan seldom includes supervision, whereas all United States probationers are under at least minimal supervision. As a result, we may not be comparing similar samples. The point is, we cannot comfortably compare statistics between countries when those countries keep records differently and do not share common status (for example, suspended sentence versus probation) definitions.

The problem of determining program effectiveness is difficult enough without adding the burden of cross-cultural comparison. At this point in comparative criminal justice studies, there are many times we should just report the numbers available in each country and leave comparison of things like recidivism rates until we can better match samples and definitions. So let us simply direct attention to aspects of Japan's prison system that some believe are effective procedures.

Initial decisions about how to respond toward a new prisoner are made on the basis of a classification process. The classification system, which takes about two months, allows effective treatment based on the prisoner's needs (the reha-

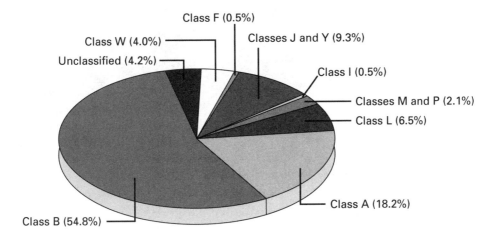

Class W = Females
Class F = Foreigners
Class I = Imprisonment without forced labor
Class J = Juveniles
Class Y = Young adults under 26

Class A = Those without advanced criminal tendency
Class B = Those with advanced criminal tendency
Class M = Those with mental disorder
Class P = Those with physical disorder

Figure 10-7. Inmates by allocation category (1988). *Source:* Correction Bureau (1990). *Correctional Institutions in Japan.* Tokyo: Ministry of Justice.

bilitative aspect), while the necessary level of supervision (the control aspect) is determined by the prisoner's personality.

The end result of the classification process is the prisoner's placement in one allocation category and one treatment category. The allocation category ascertains the appropriate institutional assignment as determined by the inmate's sex, nationality (there is one prison just for foreigners), kind of penalty, age, term of sentence, physical or mental disorders, and criminal tendency (see Figure 10-7 for the related classes). That last criterion (criminal tendency) is based on the frequency of imprisonment, degree of association with organized gangs, mode of committing offense, and social attitude (Nakayama, 1987; Nomura, 1987).

Some 80 different institutions are used to house prisoners by allocation category. In some cases the prison keeps several classes together, while other facilities receive only a single category of prisoner. For example, four prisons accept Class L and Class B inmates, while another three facilities receive only Class L. Similarly, two institutions accept Class J, Y, and A offenders, but all women prisoners will go to one of the six Class W specific facilities.

Especially notable among the offenders sent to Class B facilities (prisoners with advanced criminal tendency) are the *Boryokudan* (meaning violent gang) members. These organized crime groups constitute a serious problem for prison security and treatment programs. In 1989, *Boryokudan* members comprised 32

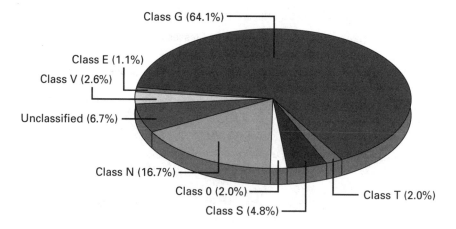

Class V = Those needing vocational training
Class E = Those needing academic training
Class G = Those needing social education (living guidance)
Class T = Those needing professional therapeutic treatment
Class S = Those needing special protective treatment
Class O = Those recommended for open treatment
Class N = Those recommended for prison maintenance work

Figure 10-8. Inmates by treatment category (1988). *Source:* Correction Bureau (1990). *Correctional Institutions in Japan.* Tokyo: Ministry of Justice.

percent of the prisoners placed in all penal facilities, and 45 percent of all inmates in Class B institutions are *Boryokudan* (Research and Training Institute, 1990). Their incorrigibility and misconduct set the *Boryokudan* apart from the typical Japanese inmate who exhibits much more compliance.

After selecting the most suitable institution, classification continues in an attempt to designate the appropriate treatment category. The seven possible categories to consider at this stage range from persons needing vocational or academic training to those needing special protective treatment (see Figure 10-8 for the related classes).

Regardless of an inmate's allocation and treatment categories, there is significant interest in providing all prisoners with a work experience. As a result, there is a nearly 95 percent prison industry employment rate (even for those sentenced to imprisonment without forced labor) in Japan's prison system (Correction Bureau, 1990).

The emphasis on work is seen as constructive in nature. Inmates are provided vocational knowledge and skills, and also have their will to work and spirit of cooperation through working together heightened. During a visit to some Oregon prisons, prison psychologist Takehiko Terasaki expressed surprise at the amount of free time American prisoners seemed to have (Ward, 1991). Japanese

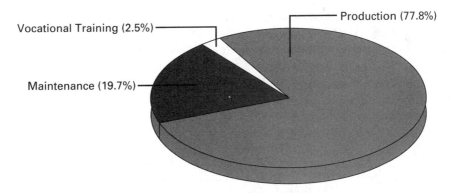

Figure 10-9. Prison employment categories. *Source:* Correction Bureau (1990). *Correctional Institutions in Japan.* Tokyo: Ministry of Justice.

prisoners spend 48 hours per week (8 hours a day, 6 days a week) either working or participating in counseling or academic programs. As a result, their free time is minimal. Because most prisoners have a sentence that includes forced labor, work-related activities take up 40 to 44 of those 48 hours. In fact, work is considered the core ingredient to the prison's rehabilitation and resocialization efforts.

Prison industry divides into the three categories of: maintenance work, production, and vocational training (Correction Bureau, 1990). Maintenance work (involving about 20 percent of the employed inmates) includes the jobs of cooking, washing, and cleaning in the facilities, as well as construction and repair work on prison buildings. The production (for example, printing, food processing, metal work) and vocational training (for example, plastering, welding, auto repair) areas are performed in two different versions. In one, the government provides all the raw materials and facilities needed to complete a product. Those products are then sold on the open market throughout the country. In the other form, a private contractor provides the raw material and facilities and then pays the government for use of the prisoners' labor. Figure 10-9 shows the percentages of inmates involved in each of the three broad work areas.

Profits from the prisons' work are transferred to the national treasury, but the prisoners are given a gratuity (neither called nor considered a wage) to encourage them to work. This money is set aside for the prisoner's release, but can also be accessed to buy necessities in prison or sent home for family support. Inmates wishing to do extra work are allowed to do "side jobs" for two hours a day after the normal working hours. All earnings from these jobs belong to the prisoner (Correction Bureau, 1990).

Coming Full Circle

Japan is unique among countries of the world because of her comparatively low incarceration rate. That characteristic is all the more unusual because Japan emphasizes the same correctional objectives as most other countries: rehabilitation and retribution. However, despite similar aims, Japan takes a somewhat different route to realize those goals. Whereas many Western countries seek rehabilitation by encouraging individualism, Japan secures it through an appeal to collectivism and social responsibility. Similarly, since association provides self-identity to Japanese, rejection and alienation from the group (that is, retribution) provide for society's revenge while making the offender lament.

Westerners often see the goal of retribution as conflicting with that of rehabilitation. The Japanese see it as a more harmonious relationship, since both can be accomplished in the community with the aid of other citizens. The group in Japan serves as the dispenser of guilt feelings (retribution) and the provider of social support (rehabilitation). The cultural values of contextualism, harmony, collectivism, and order make achieving correctional goals difficult and inappropriate in an institution. On the other hand, those goals are more easily and properly realized in the community. Not surprisingly then, the use of imprisonment is somewhat infrequent.

When imprisonment is required, its explicit goal is to develop in the prisoner a willingness and ability to return to society as a law-abiding and productive member. Given the general societal importance of the work group, and pride in one's work-related accomplishments, it is not really surprising that labor has a special role in Japanese prisons. Through work, prison officials believe, inmates can learn such values as harmony, respect for authority, and the importance of the group.

There is a sense of having come full circle with this philosophy, since these are the cultural traits identified at the start of this chapter. The homogeneity of agreed-upon values means, in the first instance, that citizens are not so likely to misbehave. But on those occasions when norms are broken, the various agencies of social control operate both informally and formally to emphasize and uphold those values. Even at the last stage in the process, prison officials respond to the offender in a manner designed to instill those cultural traits that seem to make a law-abiding citizen. But, one might argue, therein lies the essence and simplicity of Japan's seemingly low crime rate—and that brings us back to the bonsai tree.

Seductively simple and harmonious, the Japanese criminal justice system seems to call for imitation. But, like the gardener and her bonsai, criminal justice policy makers must consider the necessary role restraining wires play in making both the tree and the justice system attractive. This chapter's Impact section addressed that concern.

WHAT MIGHT WORK?

As this chapter's Impact section explains, the attractiveness of Japan's comparatively safe and orderly society seems partially achieved through tactics that citizens of other countries may find unacceptable. Intrusive police behavior toward law-abiding citizens, providing prosecutors with quasi-judicial duties, allowing judgments to be made without a public confrontation between defendant and judge, an apparent encouragement of self-incrimination, and severely restricted access to counsel for defense are some of the problems critics see in the Japanese justice system. Effective though they might be, proponents of due process (including those in Japan) are likely to express concern. But this is certainly not a dilemma found only in Japan. Recall Chapter 3's discussion of the Crime Control Model and the Due Process Model. Japan may well exemplify the type of due process concessions that are necessary to control crime.

It is inappropriate to finish a book that hopes to encourage cross-cultural research, understanding, and appreciation with a suggestion that countries cannot effectively borrow from each other. In fact, although the Impact section emphasized problems such borrowing might have, this whole chapter is built on the idea that borrowing is both possible and desirable. The question is not if countries can learn from each other; it is how unfamiliar ideas can be made effective in a different setting.

A number of authors have made a variety of suggestions about adapting aspects of the Japanese criminal justice system in the United States (for example, Bayley 1991; Becker, 1988a; Castberg, 1990; Chang, 1988; Fenwick, 1982; Parker, 1986). Some of the suggestions would require as much cultural as structural change, while others require primarily structural change. Of course the latter type is easiest to implement and has the greatest chance for success since such change would not pose significant challenges to cultural tradition.

For example, the centralization of policing would likely make law enforcement more efficient and effective. But that seemingly simple structural change directly opposes the long-held American values of decentralization and apprehension concerning a national police force. Some American communities are contracting with county or state officials to provide policing in their area, but even regional police forces in a particular state are not likely to be a popular tactic. If the United States moves away from its current decentralized multiple uncoordinated system, it seems more likely that we will turn to a country like Canada and its tendency to contract with a provincial or national agency to provide police services. Alternatively, we may inventively change American police structure through increased similarity brought by national police accreditation standards and regional training facilities.

There are, however, some aspects of Japanese policing which should be easily adapted to the American setting. Interestingly, one of the most importable tactics is the one some observers see as Japan's most effective police strategy—deployment via the *koban*. Bayley (1991) argues that Japanese-style deployment is possible in the United States since there is no compelling reason of culture inhibiting its use. Actually, several American cities have tried this approach and find it to be quite effective. Detroit has ministations in various neighborhoods, Houston uses community centers which its police chief compares with a *koban*, and the substations in Santa Ana's city core are credited with reducing that California city's street crime (Bayley, 1991; Brown, 1990; Rake, 1987).

Koban-like deployment is probably not appropriate throughout the United States. Differences in population density would make it uneconomical in some places. But even smaller cities can make use of the basic idea. Lake Worth, Florida, is comparatively small (28,000 population), but its proximity to West Palm Beach, and an influx of tourists, present it with many big-city problems. Lake Worth police turned an old recreation department building into a ministation acting as a community center for both police officers and residents (McLanus, 1991). The ministation stays busy with neighborhood kids hanging out, residents and vendors visiting, and patrol officers using it to eat their meals and complete their paperwork. The result is a decline in drug dealing for several blocks around the ministation, and a significantly more pleasant neighborhood.

With the occasional exceptions like Lake Worth, Florida, *koban*-like deployment is probably most likely to assist America's urban areas. Bayley (1991) recommends its use in places like public housing projects, major shopping malls, and around transportation and community centers. As the Santa Ana example shows, police deployment via fixed posts rather than constantly mobile patrol cars can be effective and efficient. The small storefront police posts, with Spanish-speaking officers walking downtown beats, are very similar in design and purpose to the *koban*. Similarly, Houston's police community centers are strategically placed for optimal access by neighborhood residents. At the centers, Houston police officers take complaints, write reports, give crime prevention tips, and assist residents who have questions about other city services (Brown, 1990). The programs in both cities receive the support of both citizens and police.

With *koban*-like deployment comes the opportunity to implement such other aspects of Japanese policing as foot patrol and increased community–police interaction. Houston's Victim Recontact Program has police calling recent crime victims to ask if they have any problems the police could handle or if they have additional information about their case. Similarly, Houston's Direct Citizen Contact Program used uncommitted officers (that is, those not responding to calls) to visit residents and business owners in a particular patrol area. During the visit, the officer introduces himself or herself and asks about any concerns the resident or business person might have. An evaluation of the programs in Houston found that the community center deployment strategy and the Direct Citizen Contact procedure were very successful in reducing citizens' fear of crime (Brown, 1990).

The unannounced visits by Houston police officers seem similar to Japan's residential surveys. Although some authors (for example, Kim, 1987) are skeptical about Americans' willingness to have this type of interaction with police, experiments in Houston, Detroit, Newark, and New York City show that most citizens react with surprised delight rather than hostility (Bayley, 1991).

This discussion emphasizes ideas related to Japanese policing that may be transferable to the United States. Obviously, there are aspects of Japan's court system and corrections process that can also be helpful. Increased use of mediation, conciliation, and compromise in pre-trial, and even precharge stages, could benefit from the Japanese experience. If greater use of volunteers in adult and juvenile probation, parole, and aftercare seems desirable, program directors may want to consider Japanese examples. Interest in providing productive work for prison inmates could benefit from examining prison labor procedures in Japan. The problem is not going to be finding alternatives to America's existing programs; it will be determining which, if any, foreign approaches are possible and appropriate in the United States.

The Japanese example is particularly relevant for Americans, since the United States played such an important role in structuring the contemporary Japanese system. In fact, as Castberg (1990) points out, the criminal justice provisions in both countries are essentially the same. Differences arise because the respective courts have not interpreted the provisions similarly. For example, each country's constitution protects against double jeopardy, but Japanese courts do not interpret that provision as preventing the prosecution from appealing not guilty verdicts. Similarly, search and seizure provisions are comparably stated, but Japanese courts do not require that arrest always precede search and seizure, nor are warrantless searches and seizures necessarily invalid as long as arrest takes place closely in time (see Castberg, 1990, pp. 80–81).

The point is that imitation and innovation go hand in hand. Japan borrowed from European, Asian, and North American countries but made sure that the new ideas were compatible with Japanese culture. Ensuring compatibility may require selective borrowing, or might necessitate modifying the borrowed practice to fit a new cultural context, or could even mean using culture to gain acceptance for the new scheme. Whatever the technique, an understanding and appreciation for one's own cultural traditions is necessary for successful borrowing. Further, as Japan's short-lived experiment with a jury system shows, there must be a willingness to admit when a imported idea is not working and move on to other tactics.

SUMMARY

This book followed a descriptive approach focusing on primary components of a large number of countries rather than providing a detailed description of a few countries. In this manner I was able to show the variability of systems but was not able to take a very close look at how any particular justice system operates. This chapter does look closely at a different system, but not just to provide detail about another country. Instead, Japan warrants specific attention for two reasons. First, by all indications Japan has an effective criminal justice system if we measure effectiveness by an item like low crime rate. Second, Japan's criminal justice system includes a blend of foreign ideas adapted to her particular cultural history. This borrowing is one of the goals that comparative criminal justice hopes to achieve. But the key to borrowing is to make something that may have a foreign origin work in the context of the adapting country. Some things that are very effective in one setting may not work at all in a new location. Concentrating on Japan provides an opportunity to see how cross-cultural borrowing can work and to consider what, if any, Japanese strategies might be effective in the United States.

Since peoples' cultural traits might impact the transferability of policy and procedures, we briefly considered some of the more agreed-upon features of Japanese culture. Things like homogeneity, an emphasis on harmony, a respect for hierarchy and authority, and a reliance on collectivism help explain why and how the police, courts, and correctional agencies are effective in Japan. Upon looking at the three primary components of a criminal justice system, we saw how police deployment via the *koban* is a key feature in Japanese policing. Also important was the informal justice process that police officers and court personnel used. In fact, the reluctance to impose formal sanctions is apparent throughout the criminal justice operation and is a feature that sets the Japanese system apart from many others in the world.

The chapter's Impact section considers some of the problems that might be encountered if parts of Japan's system were started in the United States. Even after such cautions, the chapter concludes by noting some things the Japanese do that may be worthy of continued and even increased study by American policy makers. That, after all, is what comparative criminal justice is all about: What can we learn from each other and how can we work together?

SUGGESTED READINGS

Ames, Walter L. (1981). *Police and community in Japan*. Berkeley: University of California Press.

Bayley, David H. (1991). *Forces of order: Policing modern Japan* (2nd ed.). Berkeley: University of California Press.

Castberg, A. Didrick. (1990). *Japanese criminal justice*. New York: Praeger.

Hendry, Joy. (1989). *Understanding Japanese society*. New York: Routledge.

Jankowski, Louis. (1991). *Probation and Parole 1990* (NCJ-133285). Washington, DC: Bureau of Justice Statistics.

Parker, L. Craig, Jr. (1986). *Parole and the community based treatment of offenders in Japan and the United States*. New Haven, CT: University of New Haven Press.

Parker, L. Craig, Jr. (1984). *The Japanese police system today: An American perspective*. Tokyo, Japan: Kodansha International Ltd.

Upham, Frank K. (1987). *Law and social change in postwar Japan*. Cambridge, MA: Harvard University Press.

Westermann, Ted D., and Burfeind, James W. (1991). *Crime and justice in two societies: Japan and the United States*. Pacific Grove, CA: Brooks/Cole.

Westney, D. Eleanor. (1987). *Imitation and Innovation: The transfer of western organizational patterns to Meiji Japan*. Cambridge, MA: Harvard University Press.

REFERENCES

Ames, Walter L. (1981). *Police and community in Japan*. Berkeley: University of California Press.

Ames, Walter L. (1983). Police system. In *Encyclopedia of Japan, Vol. 6* (pp. 198–201). Tokyo, Japan: Kodansha.

Araki, Nobuyoshi. (1985). The flow of criminal cases in the Japanese criminal justice system. *Crime and Delinquency, 31*, 601–629.

Archambeault, William G., and Fenwick, Charles R. (1988). A comparative analysis of culture, safety, and organizational management factors in Japanese and U.S. prisons. *The Prison Journal, 68*, 3–23.

Bayley, David H. (1991). *Forces of order: Policing modern Japan* (2nd ed.). Berkeley: University of California Press.

Bayley, David H. (1985). *Patterns of policing: A comparative international analysis*. New Brunswick, NJ: Rutgers University Press.

Becker, Carl B. (1988a). Old and new: Japan's mechanisms for crime control and social justice. *The Howard Journal of Criminal Justice, 27* (November), 283–296.

Becker, Carl B. (1988b). Report from Japan: Causes and controls of crime in Japan. *Journal of Criminal Justice, 16*, 425–435.

Braithwaite, John. (1989). *Crime, shame, and reintegration*. Cambridge, England: Cambridge University Press.

Brown, Lee P. (1990). A new style: Neighborhood oriented policing. In V. Kusuda-Smick (Ed.), *Crime prevention and control in the United States and Japan* (pp. 84–96). Dobbs Ferry, NY: Transnational Juris.

Castberg, A. Didrick. (1990). *Japanese criminal justice*. New York: Praeger.

Chang, Dae H. (1988). Crime and delinquency control strategy in Japan: A comparative note. *International Journal of Comparative and Applied Criminal Justice, 12*, 139–149.

Clifford, William. (1976). *Crime control in Japan*. Lexington, MA: Lexington Books.

Correction Bureau. (1990). *Correctional institutions in Japan*. Tokyo, Japan: Ministry of Justice.

Department of Justice. (1989). *Correctional Populations in the United States, 1987*. Washington, DC: Government Printing Office.

Department of Justice. (1984). *Uniform crime reporting handbook*. Washington, DC: Government Printing Office.

Empey, LaMar T. (1982). *American delinquency: Its meaning and construction* (rev. ed.). Homewood, IL: Dorsey Press.

Eskridge, Chris W. (1989). Correctional practices in Japan. *Journal of Offender Counseling, Services and Rehabilitation, 14*(2), 5–23.

Fenwick, Charles R. (1982). Crime and justice in Japan: Implications for the United States. *International Journal of Comparative and Applied Criminal Justice, 6,* 61–71.

George, B. J., Jr. (1983). Criminal law. In *Encyclopedia of Japan, Vol. 2* (pp. 47–51). Tokyo, Japan: Kodansha.

Greenfeld, Lawrence A. (1992). *Prisons and Prisoners in the United States* (NCJ-137002). Washington, DC: Department of Justice.

Hataguchi, Hiroshi. (1990). A few problems of criminal trial—A defense counsel's point of view. In V. Kusuda-Smick (Ed.), *Crime prevention and control in the United States and Japan* (pp. 41–44). Dobbs Ferry, NY: Transnational Juris.

Hendry, Joy. (1989). *Understanding Japanese society.* New York: Routledge.

Jankowski, Louis. (1991). *Probation and Parole 1990* (NCJ–133285). Washington, DC: Bureau of Justice Statistics.

Kaplan, David E., and Dubro, Alec. (1986). *Yakuza: The explosive account of Japan's criminal underworld.* Reading, MA: Addison-Wesley.

Kim, Yongjin. (1987). Work—The key to the success of Japanese law enforcement. *Police Studies, 10,* 109–117.

Kurian, George T. (1989). Japan. *World encyclopedia of police forces and penal systems.* New York: Facts on File.

Masaki, Akira. (1964). *Reminiscences of a Japanese penologist.* Tokyo, Japan: Japan Criminal Policy Association.

McLanus, Tina. (1991). Lake Worth, Florida: A small town with a big commitment. *Footprints: The Community Policing Newsletter, III,* (1 and 2), 9–11.

Monkkonen, Eric H. (1981). *Police in urban America 1860–1920.* Cambridge, England: Cambridge University Press.

Oppler, Alfred C. (1977). The reform of Japan's legal and judicial system under Allied occupation. *Washington Law Review,* (special edition), 1–35.

Parker, L. Craig, Jr. (1986). *Parole and the community based treatment of offenders in Japan and the United States.* New Haven, CT: University of New Haven Press.

Parker, L. Craig, Jr. (1984). *The Japanese police system today: An American perspective.* Tokyo, Japan: Kodansha International Ltd.

Petersilia, Joan M. (1985). *Probation and felony offenders.* Washington, DC: Department of Justice.

Plath, David W. (1964). *The after hours.* Berkeley: University of California Press.

Rake, Douglas E. (1987). Crime control and police-community relations: A cross-cultural comparison of Tokyo, Japan, and Santa Ana, California. *Annals of the American Academy of Political and Social Science, 494,* 148–154.

Reischauer, Edwin O. (1988). *The Japanese today: Change and continuity* (rev. ed.). Cambridge, MA: Belknap.

Research and Training Institute. (1990). *Summary of the white paper on crime.* Tokyo, Japan: Ministry of Justice.

Rubinstein, Jonathan. (1973). *City Police.* New York: Farrar, Straus and Giroux.

Ryavec, Carole A. (1983). Legal system. In *Encyclopedia of Japan, Vol. 4* (pp. 375–379). Tokyo, Japan: Kodansha.

Saito, Toyoji. (1990). "Substitute prison": A hotbed of false criminal charges in Japan. *Northern Kentucky Law Review, 18*(3), 399–415.

Shibahara, Kuniji. (1990). Participation of citizens in criminal justice in Japan. In V. Kusuda-Smick (Ed.), *Crime prevention and control in the United States and Japan* (pp. 26–31). Dobbs Ferry, NY: Transnational Juris.

Tamiya, Hiroshi. (1983). Confession. In *Encyclopedia of Japan, Vol. 1* (p. 350). Tokyo, Japan: Kodansha.

Upham, Frank K. (1987). *Law and social change in postwar Japan.* Cambridge, MA: Harvard University Press.

Ward, Jon. (1991). Japan: Prisons in U.S. don't compare. *C. J. International, 7*(4), 7.

Westermann, Ted D., and Burfeind, James W. (1991). *Crime and justice in two societies: Japan and the United States.* Pacific Grove, CA: Brooks/Cole.

Westney, D. Eleanor. (1987). *Imitation and Innovation: The transfer of western organizational patterns to Meiji Japan.* Cambridge, MA: Harvard University Press.

Wigmore, John H. (1936). *A panorama of the world's legal systems* (library edition). Washington, DC: Washington Law Book Company.

Appendix

Almanac Information
for Countries Referenced

Because the structure of this book uses a variety of countries to describe the variation in criminal justice across the world, it is not possible to provide much detail about the over 30 countries referenced. To make your search for more country-specific information a bit easier, this appendix provides almanac information on all the countries listed in the "Countries Referenced" section starting each chapter. Such information could prematurely date this text, but I have tried to choose data that are less likely to change dramatically over the years. Also, since this information comes from a widely available source published on an annual basis, the condensed version found in this appendix can remind you to check the current version of the *World Almanac and Book of Facts*.

The *World Almanac and Book of Facts*, 1993 edition, graciously granted permission to provide information from their almanac about the countries referenced in this text. All the following material comes from the almanac except for the Country Narratives, which combine almanac information with criminal justice details from the text. (*The World Almanac and Book of Facts*, 1993 edition, © Pharos Books 1992, New York, NY 10166)

Argentina

People. *Population* (1991 est.): 32,663,000. *Age distribution*: 0–14 (30.3%), 15–59 (56.8%), 60+ (12.9%). *Ethnic groups*: Europeans (Spanish, Italian) 85%, Indians, Mestizos, Arabs. *Languages*: Spanish (official), Italian. *Religions*: Roman Catholic 92%.

Geography. *Area*: 1,065,189 sq mi, 4 times the size of Texas, second largest in South America. *Location*: Occupies most of southern South America. *Neighbors*: Chile on west, Bolivia, Paraguay on north, Brazil, Uruguay on northeast. *Capital*: Buenos Aires. *Cities* (1990 est.): Buenos Aires, 10,500,000; Cordoba, 969,000; Rosario, 750,455; Mendoza, 597,000.

Government. *Type*: Republic. *Local divisions*: 22 provinces, 1 national territory (Tierra del Fuego), and 1 federal district (which includes Buenos Aires).

Communications. *Television sets*: 1 per 4 persons. *Radios*: 1 per 1 person. *Telephones in use*: 1 per 9 persons. *Daily newspaper circulation* (1986): 88 per 1,000 population.

Health and Education. *Life expectancy at birth* (1990): 67, male; 74, female. *Physicians*: 1 per 370 persons. *Literacy*: 92%. *School*: 21.5% attendance through secondary school.

Country Narrative. When the Spaniards, led by Juan Diaz de Solis, arrived in the early 16th century they found nomadic natives roaming the Pampas. The Spanish established permanent settlements in 1535. Independence from Spain was declared in 1816 but no national government was formed until the 1820s. In 1829, army officer Juan Manuel de Rosas took control of the government and ruled as dictator for over 20 years. The first constitutional president (General Bartolome Mitre) was elected in 1862 but the government was controlled essentially by wealthy Argentines into the late 1800s.

Modernization was spurred after 1880 by large-scale immigration of Italians, Germans, and Spaniards. Argentina became the most prosperous, educated, and industrialized of the major Latin American nations. General Juan Peron's ascension to the presidency in 1946 brought labor reforms but also suppressed speech and press freedoms. A 1955 coup exiled Peron but he returned in 1973 and again became president, only to die 10 months later. Peron's wife and vice president, Isabel, succeeded her husband, but she was ousted by a military junta in 1976. Democratic rule finally returned to Argentina in 1983 as Raul Alfonsin's Radical Civic Union gained an absolute majority in the presidential college and in the congress.

Argentina is used in Chapter 5 as an example of how a civil legal tradition country, with a diffuse system of judicial review, can resolve problems of uncertainty and conflict that arise when numerous judges rule on the constitutionality of laws.

Australia

People. *Population* (1991 census): 16,849,496. *Age distribution*: 0–14 (21.9%), 15–59 (62.6%), 59+ (15.5%). *Ethnic groups*: European 95%, Asian 4%, aborigines (including mixed), 1.5%. *Languages*: English, aboriginal languages. *Religions*: Anglican 26%, other Protestant 25%, Roman Catholic 25%.

Geography. *Area*: 2,966,200 sq mi, almost as large as the continental United States. *Location*: Southeast of Asia, Indian Ocean is west and south, Pacific Ocean is east. *Neighbors*: Nearest are Indonesia, Papua New Guinea on north, Solomons, Fiji, and New Zealand on east. *Capital*: Canberra. *Cities* (1991 est.): Sydney, 3,600,000; Melbourne, 3,000,000; Brisbane, 1,200,000; Adelaide, 1,000,000; Perth, 1,200,000.

Government. *Type*: Democratic, federal state system. *Local divisions*: 6 states, 2 territories.

Communications.   *Television sets*: 1 per 2 persons. *Radios*: 1 per 2 persons. *Telephones in use*: 1 per 2 persons. *Daily newspaper circulation* (1988): 405 per 1,000 population.

Health and Education.   *Life expectancy at birth* (1991): 73, male; 80, female. *Physicians*: 1 per 438 persons. *Literacy*: 89%. *School*: compulsory to age 15; attendance 94%.

Country Narrative.   Australia, which is the only continent that is also a country, received European visitors in the early 1600s, but the ancestors of today's aborigines arrived some 40,000 years ago from Southeast Asia. In 1770 English Captain James Cook claimed Australia's eastern coast for Great Britain and European "colonists" (in the form of convicts) began arriving in 1788. Today the population, or at least the European-ancestored majority, is highly educated and enjoys a generally high standard of living. Some of the remaining aborigines live on reservations, but the majority are detribalized and live in considerable poverty.

There are six states and two mainland territories comprising Australia's political divisions. The states, with their respective capitals, are: New South Wales (Sydney), Victoria (Melbourne), Queensland (Brisbane), Western Australia (Perth), South Australia (Adelaide), and Tasmania (Hobart). The mainland territories are the Northern Territory (Darwin) and the Australian Capital Territory (Canberra), which is a jurisdiction similar in concept to Washington, D.C.

Australia is mentioned in Chapter 1 and receives extensive discussion in Chapters 8 and 9. The system of bail in New South Wales is described in Chapter 1, while Chapter 8 reviews Australia's history as a penal colony and provides examples of contemporary corrections in several Australian states. South Australia's innovations in juvenile justice make that state an appropriate jurisdiction for discussion in Chapter 9.

Austria

People.   *Population* (1991 est.): 7,665,000. *Age distribution*: 0–14 (17.4%), 15–59 (62.1%), 60+ (20.5%). *Ethnic groups*: German 99%, Slovene, Croatian. *Languages*: German. *Religions*: Roman Catholic 85%.

Geography.   *Area*: 32,374 sq mi, slightly smaller than Maine. *Location*: In south central Europe. *Neighbors*: Switzerland, Liechtenstein on west, Germany, Czech Republic on north, Slovakia and Hungary on east, Slovenia, Italy on south. *Capital*: Vienna. *Cities*: (1988 census); Vienna 1,500,000.

Government.   *Type*: Federal republic. *Local divisions*: 9 Länder (states), each with a legislature.

Communications.   *Television sets*: 1 per 2.8 persons. *Radios*: 1 per 1.6 persons. *Telephones in use*: 1 per 1.8 persons. *Daily newspaper circulation* (1990): 389 per 1,000 population.

Health and Education. *Life expectancy at birth* (1991): 74, male; 81, female. *Physicians*: 1 per 356 persons. *Literacy*: 99%. *School*: compulsory for 9 years; attendance 95%.

Country Narrative. By 1300 the House of Hapsburg had gained control of Austrian lands and, over the next few hundred years, added vast territories in all parts of Europe to its realm. The Congress of Vienna in 1815 confirmed Austrian control of a large empire in southeast Europe populated by Germans, Hungarians, Slavs, Italians, and others. The dual Austro–Hungarian monarchy was established in 1867, giving authority to Hungary and beginning almost 50 years of peace. After World War I, Austria was reduced to a small republic with the borders it has today. Nazi Germany invaded Austria in World War II and the republic was not reestablished until Allied occupation in 1945. Full independence and neutrality were restored in 1955.

Austria is noted in Chapter 5 for its concentrated judicial review process. The Austrian Constitutional Tribunal, created in 1920, provided the model for the judicial review system that uses a single state organ to act as a country's constitutional judge.

Belgium

People. *Population* (1991 est.): 9,921,000. *Age distribution*: 0–14 (18.2%); 15–59 (61.7%); 60+ (20.1%). *Ethnic groups*: Fleming 55%, Walloon 33%. *Languages*: Flemish (Dutch) 57%, French 33%, Italian, German. *Religions*: Roman Catholic 75%.

Geography. *Area*: 11,799 sq mi, slightly larger than Maryland. *Location*: In northwest Europe, on North Sea. *Neighbors*: France on west, south, Luxembourg on southeast, Germany on east, Netherlands on north. *Capital*: Brussels. *Cities* (1988 est): Brussels, 970,000; Antwerp, 479,000; Ghent, 233,000.

Government. *Type*: Parliamentary democracy under a constitutional monarch. *Local divisions*: 9 provinces, 3 regions, 3 cultural communities.

Communications. *Television sets*: 1 per 3.2 persons. *Radios*: 1 per 2.2 persons. *Telephones in use*: 1 per 2.1 persons. *Daily newspaper circulation* (1990): 213 per 1,000 population.

Health and Education. *Life expectancy at birth* (1991): 74, male; 81, female. *Physicians*: 1 per 317 persons. *Literacy*: 98%. *School*: compulsory to age 18.

Country Narrative. The area now known as Belgium was conquered by the Romans in the 50s BC, then ruled for 1800 years by successive invaders from regions of Germany, France, Spain, Austria. After 1815 it was made part of the Netherlands, but it became an independent constitutional monarchy in 1830. The country served as a battlefield during both World Wars and suffered significant destruction as a result. One of the most densely populated countries in the world, Belgium is composed of two ethnic groups whose cultures often clash.

The Flemings, living in the north, speak Dutch, while the Walloons live in southern Belgium and speak French. Parliament has passed measures aimed at transferring power from the central government to three regions: Wallonia, Flanders, and Brussels (populated by both the Walloons and the Flemings).

Belgium's location on the borders of three major trading nations, and across a narrow strip of the North Sea from a fourth (Great Britain), has made it a prominent thoroughfare for criminals as well as the more welcome law-abiders. As Chapter 1 notes, such positioning has encouraged Belgium to take a leadership position in developing bilateral agreements on limited cross-border powers for national police forces. In addition, Belgium's 2,359 separate police units are used in Chapter 6 as an example of a decentralized multiple uncoordinated police system.

Brazil

People.   *Population* (1991 census): 148,000,000. *Age distribution*: 0–14 (35.2%); 15–59 (57.7%); 60+ (7.1%). *Ethnic groups*: Portuguese, Africans, and mulattoes make up the vast majority; Italians, Germans, Japanese, Indians, Jews, Arabs. *Languages*: Portuguese (official), English, German, Italian. *Religions*: Roman Catholic 89%.

Geography.   *Area*: 3,286,470 sq mi, larger than the contiguous 48 United States; largest country in South America. *Location*: Occupies eastern half of South America. *Neighbors*: French Guiana, Suriname, Guyana, Venezuela on north, Colombia, Peru, Bolivia, Paraguay, Argentina on west, Uruguay on south. *Capital*: Brasilia. *Cities*: (1989 met.): Sao Paulo, 16.8 million; Rio de Janeiro, 11.1 million; Belo Horizonte, 3.4 million.

Government.   *Type*: Federal republic. *Local divisions*: 26 states, federal district (Brasilia).

Communications.   *Television sets*: 1 per 4 persons. *Radios*: 1 per 2.5 persons. *Telephones in use*: 1 per 11 persons. *Daily newspaper circulation* (1988): 55 per 1,000 population.

Health and Education.   *Life expectancy at birth*: (1991) 62, male; 68, female. *Physicians*: 1 per 684 persons. *Literacy*: 81%. *School*: n/a.

Country Narrative.   The first European to explore Brazil is considered to have been Portuguese navigator Pedro Alvares Cabral. His arrival in 1500 found the area to be settled by various Indian tribes, only a few of which have survived to the present. Portuguese domination lasted until 1822 when independence was proclaimed and the son of the Portuguese king was acclaimed emperor. A Brazilian republic was proclaimed in 1889, but in 1930 a military junta took control. The dictator, Getulio Vargas, was forced out by the military in 1945 and a democratic regime lasted from 1945 to 1964, when military leaders ousted the president. Successive military leaders served as president until 1985, when democratic elections returned the nation to civilian rule.

Brazil's links to Europe and North America have given it some interesting combinations of common and civil law. An example of this is found in Chapter 5 where Brazil is offered as an example of the mixed system of judicial review.

Canada

People.   *Population* (1991 est.): 26,835,000. *Age distribution*: 0–14 (21.4%); 15–59 (63.6%); 60+ (15%). *Ethnic groups*: British 25%, French 24%, other European 16%, mixed 28%. *Languages*: English, French (both official). *Religions*: Roman Catholic 46%, Protestant 41%.

Geography.   *Area*: 3,849,000 sq mi, the largest country in land size in the Western Hemisphere. *Location*: stretches 3,223 miles from east to west and extends southward from the North Pole to the United States border. *Neighbors*: United States on south. *Capital*: Ottawa. *Cities* (1990 met. est.): Montreal, 3,068,000; Toronto, 3,751,000; Vancouver, 1,547,000.

Government.   *Type*: Confederation with parliamentary democracy. *Local divisions*: 10 provinces, 2 territories.

Communications.   *Television sets*: 1 per 1.7 persons. *Radios*: 1 per 1.2 persons. *Telephones in use*: 1 per 1.3 persons. *Daily newspaper circulation* (1989): 221 per 1,000 population.

Health and Education.   *Life expectancy at birth* (1991): 73, male; 80, female. *Physicians*: 1 per 449 persons. *Literacy*: 99%. *School*: n/a.

Country Narrative.   French explorer Jacques Cartier, who discovered the Gulf of St. Lawrence in 1534, is generally regarded as the founder of Canada, although English seaman John Cabot had sighted Newfoundland 37 years earlier. Of course, centuries before either of those events, Vikings are believed to have reached the Atlantic coast. The French preceded the English in establishing settlements, with Quebec City in 1608 and Montreal in 1642. Britain acquired Acadia (later Nova Scotia) in 1717 as part of its American expansion, and through military victory over French forces in Canada captured Quebec (1759), then obtained control of the rest of New France in 1763. The French Canadians, through the Quebec Act of 1774, retained the right to their own language, practice their religion, and establish their own civil law.

The Dominion of Canada was established by the 1867 British North America Act, which brought together Ontario, Quebec, and the former colonies of Nova Scotia and New Brunswick. That act became Canada's first written constitution and established a federal system of government on the model of a British parliament and cabinet structure under the crown. Canada was proclaimed a self-governing Dominion within the British Empire in 1931. In 1982 Canada severed its last formal legislative link with Britain by obtaining the right to amend its constitution.

Chapter 6 uses Canada as a prime example of a decentralized multiple coordinated policing system. With three levels of policing (federal, provincial, and local) Canada shares more than a national border with the United States. However, Canada's system of contract policing helps win it a placement in the coordinated cell of police types while the United States police agencies operate in a more uncoordinated fashion.

China

People.   *Population* (1991 est.): 1,151,486,000. *Age distribution*: n/a. *Ethnic groups*: Han Chinese 94%, Mongol, Korean, Manchu, others. *Languages*: Mandarin (official), Yue, Wu Hakka, Xiang, Gan, Min, Zhuang, Hui, Yi. *Religions*: Officially atheist; Confucianism, Buddhism, Taoism are traditional.

Geography.   *Area*: 3,696,100 sq mi, slightly larger than the contiguous United States. *Location*: Occupies most of the habitable mainland of east Asia. *Neighbors*: Mongolia on north, Russia on northeast and northwest, Afghanistan, Pakistan on west, India, Nepal, Bhutan, Myanmar, Laos, Vietnam on south, North Korea on northeast. *Capital*: Beijing. *Cities* (1989 est.): Shanghai, 7.3 million; Beijing, 6.8 million; Tianjin, 5.6 million; Canton, 3.4 million.

Government.   *Type*: Communist party led state. *Local divisions*: 22 provinces, 5 autonomous regions and 3 cities.

Communications.   *Television sets*: 1 per 8 persons. *Radios*: 1 per 9.1 persons. *Telephones in use*: 1 per 101 persons. *Daily newspaper circulation* (1989): 37 per 1,000 population.

Health and Education.   *Life expectancy at birth* (1991): 68, male; 72, female. *Physicians*: 1 per 643 persons. *Literacy*: 70%. *School*: 9 years compulsory, first grade enrollment 93%.

Country Narrative.   Considered one of the cradles of civilization, the first in China arose about 4,000 years ago. A succession of dynasties and interdynastic warring kingdoms ruled China into the 20th century. China became a republic in 1912 and, after World War II, came under domination of communist armies. The People's Republic of China was proclaimed in 1949 under Mao Zedong and in 1950 China and the USSR signed a 30-year treaty of "friendship, alliance and mutual assistance." Those relations deteriorated by the 1960s and the USSR canceled aid accords, to which China responded by launching anti-Soviet propaganda drives.

After the 1976 death of Mao Zedong the new ruling group modified Maoist policies in education, culture, and industry, and sought better ties with noncommunist countries. By the mid 1980s, China had enacted far-reaching economic reforms highlighted by the departure from rigid central planning and the stressing of market-oriented socialism.

With the collapse of the Soviet Union, China provides one of the best remaining examples of the socialist legal tradition. As a result, China is used in several chapters to exemplify the socialist tradition. In Chapter 1, China's Procedure Law is used to show one way to implement pre-trial detention. Chapter 4 draws more heavily on aspects of precommunist China to discuss the historical importance of Chinese law and the role of Confucius. That chapter also shows how China continues some socialist legal traditions first associated with the Soviet Union. For example, the principle of analogy is still used to provide flexibility to the law, and the justice system is seen as having specific economic and educational functions. Chapter 7 uses Chinese courts to exemplify court structure in a socialist legal tradition, and Chapter 9 presents China's educational response to young offenders as an example of a participatory model of juvenile justice.

Cuba

People.   *Population* (1991 est.): 10,732,000. *Age distribution*: 0–15 (23.3%); 15–59 (64.9%); 60+ (11.8%). *Ethnic groups*: Spanish, African. *Languages*: Spanish. *Religions*: Roman Catholic 42%, none 49%.

Geography.   *Area*: 44,218 sq mi, nearly as large as Pennsylvania. *Location*: westernmost of West Indies. *Neighbors*: Bahamas, United States on north, Mexico on west, Jamaica on south, Haiti on east. *Capital*: Havana. *Cities*: (1989 est.): Havana 2,077,000; Santiago de Cuba 397,000; Camaguey 274,000.

Government.   *Type*: Communist state. *Local divisions*: 14 provinces, Havana.

Communications.   *Television sets*: 1 per 5 persons. *Radios*: 1 per 3 persons. *Telephones in use*: 1 per 19 persons. *Daily newspaper circulation* (1988): 155 per 1,000 population.

Health and Education.   *Life expectancy at birth* (1991): 73, male; 78, female. *Physicians*: 1 per 303 persons. *Literacy*: 98%. *School*: 92% of those ages 6–14 attend school.

Country Narrative.   Some 50,000 Indians were living in Cuba when it was discovered by Columbus in 1492. Except for British occupation of Havana (1762–1763), Cuba remained Spanish until 1898. Spain gave up all its claims to Cuba after its 1898 defeat at the hands of the United States in the Spanish–American War. United States troops withdrew in 1902, but under 1903 and 1934 agreements the United States still leases a site at Guantanamo Bay as a naval base. In 1956 Fidel Castro assembled a rebel band to overthrow the harsh and corrupt dictatorship of Fulgencio Batista. In 1959 Castro took power and the government began a program of sweeping economic and social changes, without restoring promised liberties. By 1960 all banks and industrial companies had been nationalized and a system of cooperatives was in place.

Cuba has resisted the social and economic reforms that have taken place in the former USSR and Eastern Bloc countries and today remains an example of the socialist legal tradition. In Chapter 9, Cuba is noted as an example of the participatory model of juvenile justice.

Denmark

People.   *Population* (1991 est.): 5,134,000. *Age distribution*: 0–14 (17.1%); 15–59 (62.5%); 60+ (20.4%). *Ethnic groups*: Almost all Scandinavian. *Languages*: Danish. *Religions*: Evangelical Lutheran 90%.

Geography.   *Area*: 16,633 sq mi, the size of Massachusetts and New Hampshire combined. *Location*: In northern Europe, separating the North and Baltic seas. *Neighbors*: Germany on south, Norway on northwest, Sweden on northeast. *Capital*: Copenhagen. *Cities* (1988 met.): Copenhagen, 619,000.

Government.   *Type*: Constitutional monarchy. *Local divisions*: 14 counties and one city (Copenhagen).

Communications.   *Television sets*: 1 per 2.7 persons. *Radios*: 1 per 2.4 persons. *Telephones in use*: 1 per 1.2 persons. *Daily newspaper circulation* (1990): 361 per 1,000 population.

Health and Education.   *Life expectancy at birth* (1991): 73, male; 79, female. *Physicians*: 1 per 375 persons. *Literacy*: 99%. *School*: 9 years compulsory, attendance 100%.

Country Narrative.   The city of Copenhagen dates back to ancient times, but Bishop Absalon (1128–1201) is regarded as the actual founder of the city. Danes formed a large component of the Viking raiders in the early Middle Ages. The Danish kingdom was a major north European power until the 17th century, when it lost its land in southern Sweden. Norway, which had been united with Denmark under Queen Margrete in 1380, was lost to Sweden in 1815. After German occupation during World War II, Denmark and 11 other nations formed the North Atlantic Treaty Organization.

Denmark has a national police force and is offered in Chapter 6 as an example of a single centralized policing system. Interestingly, the chief of police in each district also serves as the local prosecuting authority in Denmark.

England and Wales
(See United Kingdom)

Fiji

People.   *Population* (1991 est.): 744,000. *Age distribution*: 0–14 (38.2%); 15–59 (56.9%); 60+ (4.9%). *Ethnic groups*: Indian 48%, Fijian (Melanesian–Polynesian) 46%, Europeans 2%. *Languages*: English (official), Fijian, Hindi. *Religions*: Christian 52%, Hindu 38%, Moslem 8%.

Geography.   *Area*: 7,056 sq mi, the size of Massachusetts. *Location*: In western South Pacific Ocean. *Neighbors*: Nearest are Solomons on northwest, Tonga on east. *Capital*: Suva. *Cities*: (1986 est.): Suva 69,000.

Government.   *Type*: Republic. *Local divisions*: 4 divisions, 1 dependency.

Communications.   *Television sets*: 1 per 73 persons. *Radios*: 1 per 1.7 persons. *Telephones in use*: 1 per 12 persons. *Daily newspaper circulation* (1988): 56 per 1,000 population.

Health and Education.   *Life expectancy at birth* (1987): 62, male; 67, female. *Physicians*: 1 per 2,649 persons. *Literacy*: 85%. *School*: 95% attend school.

Country Narrative.   A British colony since 1874, Fiji became an independent parliamentary democracy in 1970. Cultural differences between the descendants of laborers imported from India in the 19th century (comprising a majority of the population) and the less modernized native Fijians (who by law own 83% of the land in communal villages) have led to political polarization. In early 1987 a military coup ousted the government, but by December a civilian government was restored.

In Chapter 9, Fiji's response to juvenile offenders is presented as a good example of how to reintegrate misbehaving young people back into the community.

Finland

People.   *Population* (1991 est.): 4,991,000. *Age distribution*: 0–14 (19.3%); 15–59 (62.9%); 60+ (17.8%). *Ethnic groups*: Finns 94%, Swedes, Lapps. *Languages*: Finnish, Swedish (both official). *Religions*: Lutheran 97%.

Geography.   *Area*: 130,119 sq mi, slightly smaller than Montana. *Location*: In northern Europe. *Neighbors*: Norway on north, Sweden on west, Russia on east. *Capital*: Helsinki. *Cities* (1991 est.): Helsinki, 490,000; Tampere, 170,000; Turku, 160,000.

Government.   *Type*: Constitutional Republic. *Local divisions*: 12 laanit (provinces).

Communications.   *Television sets*: 1 per 2.7 persons. *Radios*: 1 per person. *Telephones in use*: 1 per 2.1 persons. *Daily newspaper circulation* (1990): 521 per 1,000 population.

Health and Education.   *Life expectancy at birth* (1991): 71, male; 80, female. *Physicians*: 1 per 503. *Literacy*: 99%. *School*: 9 years compulsory, attendance 99%.

Country Narrative.   The early Finns probably migrated from the Ural Mountains area at about the beginning of the Christian era. Swedish settlers brought the country into Swedish domination during the 12th and 13th centuries, then during the 16th through 18th centuries control of Finland was contested by Sweden and Russia. In 1809 it finally became an autonomous grand duchy of the

Russian Empire. In 1917 Finland declared its independence from Russia and in 1919 it became a republic. In 1948 Finland signed a treaty of mutual assistance with the USSR, then saw its economy suffer as a result of changes in the former USSR and Eastern Europe.

In Chapter 6, Finland provides an example of a centralized multiple coordinated police structure. The provincial and local police officials in Finland are interesting from American standards since they have prosecution duties in addition to their regular police duties.

France

People.   *Population* (1991 est.): 56,595,000. *Age distribution*: 0–14 (19.1%); 15–59 (61%); 60+ (19.9%). *Ethnic groups*: A mixture of various European and Mediterranean groups. *Languages*: French (official); minorities speak Breton, Alsatian German, Flemish, Italian, Basque, Catalan. *Religions*: Mostly Roman Catholic.

Geography.   *Area*: 220,668 sq mi, four-fifths the size of Texas. *Location*: In western Europe, between Atlantic Ocean and Mediterranean Sea. *Neighbors*: Spain on south, Italy, Switzerland, Germany on east, Luxembourg, Belgium on north. *Capital*: Paris. *Cities*: (1990 est.): Paris 2,152,000; Marseille 801,000; Lyon 415,000; Nice 342,000.

Government.   *Type*: Republic. *Local divisions*: 22 administrative regions containing 95 departments.

Communications.   *Television sets*: 1 per 2.6 persons. *Radios*: 1 per 1.1 persons. *Telephones in use*: 1 per 1.7 persons. *Daily newspaper circulation* (1990): 176 per 1,000 population.

Health and Education.   *Life expectancy at birth* (1991): 74, male; 82, female. *Physicians*: 1 per 403 persons. *Literacy*: 99%. *School*: Years compulsory 10.

Country Narrative.   Roman armies began invading the area they called Gaul about 200 BC. Julius Caesar conquered the entire region between 58 and 51 BC. Gaul prospered under Roman rule for 500 years. Under Emperor Charlemagne, Frankish rule extended over much of Europe. After Charlemagne's death, France emerged as one of the successor kingdoms. The monarchy was overthrown by the French Revolution (1789–1793) and the First Republic was established. Napoleon seized control of France in 1799 and he founded the First Empire in 1804. Louis XVIII came to power after Napoleon was exiled in 1814 and France again existed under a monarchy until 1848. Successive changes saw France establish the Second Republic (1848–1852), exist under the Second Empire (1852–1870) founded by Napoleon III, then return to the Third Republic (1871–1946). The Fourth Republic (1946–1958) helped France rebuild after World War II, but by 1958 French people saw the need for a new constitution and they established the Fifth Republic, which continues today.

The new constitution gave the new French president (then Charles De Gaulle) significant power while reducing the power of Parliament. In 1981 France elected François Mitterrand, a Socialist candidate, president. Four months later the government nationalized 5 major industries and most private banks. Mitterrand was elected to a second 7-year term in 1988.

Examples from the French justice system appear in Chapters 1, 4, 5, 6, and 7. Excluding the United States, those appearances make France one of the two (the other is England) most widely referenced countries in this book. From discussion of cooperative law enforcement efforts with England (Chapter 1), to its importance in the civil legal tradition (Chapters 4 and 5), and its interesting exception to the concept of judicial review (Chapter 5), France provides several justice examples from one of the world's great countries. Particularly in-depth information is provided on French policing (Chapter 6) which typifies the centralized multiple coordinated type. Detail is also provided for the French use of a procurator in the prosecution process and on the way French courts are organized (Chapter 7).

Germany

People. *Population* (1991 est.): 79,548,000. *Age distribution*: 0–14 (14.7%); 15–59 (64.7%); 60+ (20.6%). *Ethnic groups*: German 93%. *Languages*: German. *Religions*: Protestant 44%, Roman Catholic 37%.

Geography. *Area*: 137,838 sq mi, about twice the size of Washington state. *Location*: In central Europe. *Neighbors*: Denmark on north, Netherlands, Belgium, Luxembourg, France on west, Switzerland, Austria on south, Czech Republic, Poland on east. *Capital*: Berlin. *Cities* (1991 est): Berlin, 3.0 million; Hamburg, 1.6 million; Munich, 1.3 million; Frankfurt, 635,000.

Government. *Type*: Federal republic. *Local divisions*: 16 Länder (states) with substantial powers.

Communications. *Television sets*: 1 per 2.6 persons. *Radios*: 1 per 2.3 persons. *Telephones in use*: 1 per 1.5 persons. *Daily newspaper circulation* (1987 for then West Germany): 417 per 1,000 population.

Health and Education. *Life expectancy at birth* (1991): 73, male; 79, female. *Physicians*: 1 per 346 persons. *Literacy*: 99%. *School*: 10 years compulsory, attendance 100%.

Country Narrative. In ancient times tribes from northern Europe began to arrive in what is now Germany. Julius Caesar defeated those tribes between 55 and 53 BC, but Roman expansion north of the Rhine was stopped in 9 AD. In 843 the Treaty of Verdun divided Charlemagne's empire into three kingdoms. One of Charlemagne's grandsons, Louis II, received lands east of the Rhine River and his kingdom became what is now Germany. The Thirty Years' War (1618–1648) split Germany into small principalities and kingdoms. After Napoleon's defeat in

1815, Austria contended with Prussia for dominance. In 1866 Austria lost the Seven Weeks' War to Prussia and a year later Otto von Bismarck, Prussian chancellor, formed the North German Confederation. In 1870, after Prussia's victory in the Franco–Prussian War, the four southern German states agreed to join the northern confederation in a united German Empire under Prussian leadership. On January 18, 1871 Wilhelm I of Prussia was crowned the first *Kaiser* (emperor) and he appointed Bismarck to be the first chancellor.

The German Empire reached its peak before World War I in 1914, but after that war Germany ceded land to France, Poland, and Denmark. Between 1919 and 1933 Germany operated under the Weimar constitution, which established a democratic federal republic with a parliament and a president who could appoint the chancellor and cabinet members. In 1933 President Paul von Hindenburg named Adolf Hitler chancellor. After Hindenburg's death in 1934 the offices of president and chancellor were combined and Hitler was made leader (*Führer*). Following Germany's defeat in World War II the Allied Powers divided Germany into zones of occupation. The area administered by the French, British, and Americans was proclaimed the Federal Republic of Germany (West Germany) on May 23, 1949. The sector administered by the USSR was proclaimed the German Democratic Republic (East Germany) on October 7, 1949.

As communism was being rejected in East Germany, talks began concerning German reunification. In May 1990 NATO ministers adopted a package of proposals on reunification including the inclusion of the united Germany as a full member of NATO, and the barring of the new Germany from having its own nuclear, chemical, or biological weapons. The two nations agreed to monetary unification under the West German Mark beginning July 1990, and on October 3, 1990 the two Germanies were merged.

Germany's legal system provides examples in several chapters. In Chapter 5 Germany's penal code is used to show aspects of substantive law and its court hierarchy helps explain the concentrated model of judicial review. The decentralized multiple coordinated police structure of Germany makes it a prime example for Chapter 6. In addition, the changes required by unification of East and West Germany provide an opportunity to consider the impact such an event has on policing in a country. In Chapter 7 Germany provides a prime example of the use of lay judges in a civil legal tradition system. Also, in Chapter 7 Germany is used to consider the possible benefits of concurrent consideration of guilt and sentence.

Greece

People. *Population* (1991 est.): 10,042,000. *Age distribution*: 0–14 (20.5%); 15–59 (61.1%); 60+ (20.4%). *Ethnic groups*: Greeks 98.5%. *Languages*: Greek. *Religions*: Greek Orthodox 97% (official).

Geography. *Area*: 51,146 sq mi, the size of Alabama. *Location*: Occupies southern end of Balkan Peninsula in southeast Europe. *Neighbors*: Albania,

Yugoslavia, Bulgaria on north, Turkey on east. *Capital*: Athens. *Cities*: (1981 est.): Athens, 3,016,457; Thessaloniki, 800,000; Patras, 120,000.

Government. *Type*: Presidential parliamentary republic. *Local divisions*: 51 prefectures.

Communications. *Television sets*: 1 per 5.7 persons. *Radios*: 1 per 2.4 persons. *Telephones in use*: 1 per 2.4 persons. *Daily newspaper circulation* (1986 est.): 88 per 1,000 population.

Health and Education. *Life expectancy at birth* (1991): 75, male; 80, female. *Physicians*: 1 per 327. *Literacy*: men 96%; women 89%. *School*: 9 years compulsory.

Country Narrative. Greece fell under Roman rule in the 2nd and 1st centuries BC. In the 4th century AD it became part of the Byzantine Empire and, after the fall of Constantinople to the Turks in 1453, part of the Ottoman Empire. Greece won its war of independence from Turkey in 1829 then became a kingdom in 1833 and a constitutional monarchy in 1844. A republic was established in 1924 only to have the monarchy restored in 1935. In 1973 the monarchy was abolished and Greece was again proclaimed a republic.

Greece is noted in Chapter 5 as having a judicial review process that is very similar to that of the United States. However, the special Greek court set up to hear constitutional questions helps distinguish its version of a diffuse model of judicial review.

India

People. *Population* (1991 est.): 866,000,000. *Age distribution*: 0–14 (36.8%); 15–59 (56.4%); 60+ (5.8%). *Ethnic groups*: Indo–Aryan groups 72%, Dravidians 25%, Mongoloids 3%. *Languages*: 16 languages including Hindi (official) and English (associate official). *Religions*: Hindu 83%, Moslem 11%, Christian 3%, Sikh 2%.

Geography. *Area*: 1,266,595 sq mi, one third the size of the United States. *Location*: Occupies most of the Indian subcontinent in south Asia. *Neighbors*: Pakistan on west, China, Nepal, Bhutan on north, Myanmar, Bangladesh on east. *Capital*: New Delhi. *Cities*: (1991 est.): Calcutta, 10.8 million; Bombay, 12.5 million; New Delhi, 8.3 million; Madras, 5.3 million.

Government. *Type*: Federal Republic. *Local divisions*: 25 states, 7 union territories.

Communications. *Television sets*: 1 per 44 persons. *Radios*: 1 per 15 persons. *Telephones in use*: 1 per 280 persons. *Daily newspaper circulation* (1988): 21 per 1,000 population.

Health and Education. *Life expectancy at birth* (1991): 57, male; 58, female. *Physicians*: 1 per 2,471 persons. *Literacy*: 48%. *School*: compulsory to age 14.

Country Narrative.   India has one of the oldest civilizations in the world. Aryan tribes, speaking Sanskrit, invaded from the northwest around 1500 BC and merged with the earlier inhabitants to create classical Indian civilization. Buddhism, Hinduism, and Islam competed for the loyalty of the inhabitants. Western and northern areas were more influenced by Islam, while Hinduism predominated in the rest of India. Trading posts were established by the Portuguese, Dutch, and British in the 16th and 17th centuries. By the 19th century Britain had gained control of most of India and the British parliament assumed political direction in 1828. In 1935, due especially to the efforts of Mohandas (Mahatma) Gandhi, Britain gave India a constitution providing a bicameral federal congress. British India was partitioned into the dominions of India and Pakistan, with Pakistan identified as a Moslem nation. India became a democratic republic in 1950.

India's links to Britain provided it with a common legal tradition. In Chapter 1, India is used as an example of a common law country using recognizance as the primary process for pre-trial release.

Indonesia

People.   *Population* (1991 est.): 193,000,000. *Age distribution*: 0–14 (39.2%), 15–59 (56.5%), 60+ (5.3%). *Ethnic groups*: Malay, Chinese, Irianese. *Languages*: Bahasa Indonesian (Malay) (official), Javanese, other Austronesian languages. *Religions*: Moslem 88%.

Geography.   *Area*: 735,268 sq mi, about one and one fourth times the size of Alaska. *Location*: Archipelago southeast of Asia along the Equator. *Neighbors*: Malaysia on north, Papua New Guinea on east. *Capital*: Jakarta. *Cities* (1988 est.): Jakarta, 8.8 million; Surabaja, 2.5 million.

Government.   *Type*: Independent republic. *Local divisions*: 24 provinces, 3 special regions.

Communications.   *Television sets*: 1 per 24 persons. *Radios*: 1 per 8 persons. *Telephones in use*: 1 per 172 persons. *Daily newspaper circulation*: n/a.

Health and Education.   *Life expectancy at birth* (1991): 59, male; 63, female. *Physicians*: 1 per 7,427 persons. *Literacy*: 85%. *School*: 84% attend primary school.

Country Narrative.   Hindu and Buddhist civilizations from India reached the peoples of Indonesia nearly 2,000 years ago, taking root especially in Java. Islam spread along the maritime trade routes in the 15th century, and became predominant by the 16th century. The Dutch replaced the Portuguese as the most important European trade power in the area in the 17th century. They secured territorial control over Java by 1750. The outer islands were not finally subdued until the early 20th century, when the full area of present-day Indonesia was united under one rule for the first time.

Following Japanese occupation in 1942–1945, nationalists proclaimed a republic. The Netherlands ceded sovereignty in 1949 after four years of fighting. Indonesia's Communist Party tried to seize control in 1965 but the coup was smashed by the army. General Suharto, head of the army, was named president in 1968, reelected 1973, 1978, and 1988. The military retains a predominant political role.

The penal code of Indonesia does not provide for a juvenile court. This makes it a good Chapter 9 example of the legalistic model of juvenile justice.

Italy

People. *Population* (1991 est.): 57,772,000. *Age distribution*: 0–14 (17.8%), 15–59 (62.8%), 60+ (19.4%). *Ethnic groups*: Italians, small minorities of Germans, Slovenes, Albanians. *Languages*: Italian. *Religions*: Predominantly Roman Catholic.

Geography. *Area*: 116,303 sq mi, about the size of Florida and Georgia combined. *Location*: In southern Europe, jutting into the Mediterranean Sea. *Neighbors*: France on west, Switzerland, Austria on north, Slovenia on east. *Capital*: Rome. *Cities* (1989 est.): Rome, 2.8 million; Milan, 1.4 million; Naples, 1.2 million; Turin, 1 million.

Government. *Type*: Republic. *Local divisions*: 20 regions with some autonomy, 94 provinces.

Communications. *Television sets*: 1 per 3.8 persons. *Radios*: 1 per 3.9 persons. *Telephones in use*: 1 per 2.0 persons. *Daily newspaper circulation* (1989): 142 per 1,000 population.

Health and Education. *Life expectancy at birth* (1991): 75, male; 82, female. *Physicians*: 1 per 233 persons. *Literacy*: 98%. *School*: 8 years compulsory.

Country Narrative. Rome emerged as a major power in Italy after 500 BC, dominating the more civilized Etruscans to the north and Greeks to the south. Under the Empire, which lasted until the 5th century AD, Rome ruled over most of Western Europe, the Balkans, the Near East, and North Africa. After the Germanic invasions, lasting several centuries, a high civilization arose in the city–states of the north, culminating in the Renaissance. But German, French, Spanish, and Austrian intervention prevented the unification of the country. In 1859 Lombardy came under the crown of King Victor Emmanuel II of Sardinia. Other regions followed, and the first Italian parliament declared Victor Emmanuel king of Italy in 1861.

Fascism appeared in Italy in 1919, led by Benito Mussolini, who took over the government at the invitation of the king in 1922. Mussolini acquired dictatorial powers and joined Germany in World War II. After Fascism was overthrown in 1943, Italy declared war on Germany and Japan and contributed to the Allied victory. Victor Emmanuel III, whom Mussolini had proclaimed emperor, abdicated in 1946 and his son served as king until June 10, 1946, when Italy became a republic.

Italy's juvenile justice system is presented in Chapter 9 as a legalistic model. Italy is a particularly intriguing example since it seems able to counteract the consistency provided by legality without losing the variability required by individualization. A similar balancing act is not achieved in its policing system. Chapter 6 uses Italy to exemplify a centralized multiple uncoordinated police structure primarily because its two main police forces exhibit resentment, if not hatred, toward each other. Italy also provides some examples of substantive criminal law in Chapter 5's discussion of mental deficiency and ways to define the crime of theft.

Japan

People. *Population* (1991 est.): 124,017,000. *Age distribution*: 0–14 (18.0%); 15–59 (64.3%); 60+ (17.7%). *Ethnic groups*: Japanese 99.4%, Korean .5%. *Languages*: Japanese. *Religions*: Buddhism, Shintoism shared by large majority.

Geography. *Area*: 145,856 sq mi, slightly smaller than California. *Location*: Archipelago off east coast of Asia. *Neighbors*: Russia on north, South Korea on west. *Capital*: Tokyo. *Cities* (1990 census): Tokyo, 8.1 million; Osaka, 2.6 million; Yokohama, 3.2 million; Kyoto, 1.4 million; Kobe, 1.4 million; Sapporo, 1.6 million.

Government. *Type*: Parliamentary democracy. *Local divisions*: 47 prefectures.

Communications. *Television sets*: 1 per 1.8 persons. *Radios*: 1 per 1.3 persons. *Telephones in use*: 1 per 2.3 persons. *Daily newspaper circulation* (1990) 429 per 1,000 population.

Health and Education. *Life expectancy at birth* (1991): 76, male; 82, female. *Physicians*: 1 per 609 persons. *Literacy*: 99%. *School*: Most attend school for 12 years.

Country Narrative. According to Japanese legend, the empire was founded by Emperor Jimmu in 660 BC, but earliest records of a unified Japan date from 1,000 years later. Chinese influence was strong in the formation of Japanese civilization and Buddhism was introduced before the 6th century. A feudal system, with locally powerful noble families and their samurai warrior retainers, dominated from 1192. Central power was held by successive families of shoguns (military dictators) from 1192–1867. In 1868 central power was recovered by the Emperor Meiji.

In the late 19th and early 20th centuries Japan fought China (1884–1895) and Russia (1904–1905), annexed Korea (1910), took over German Pacific islands (World War I), and started another war with China (1932). Japan launched war against the United States by attack on Pearl Harbor on December 7, 1941. Japan surrendered on August 14, 1945. In a new constitution adopted May 3, 1947, Japan renounced the right to wage war, the emperor gave up claims to divinity, and the Japanese Diet became the sole law-making authority.

After World War II Japan emerged as one of the most powerful economies in the world, and as a leader in technology. Remarkably, in the face of dramatic growth, industrialization, and urbanization, Japan consistently has one of the world's lowest crime rates and imprisonment rates. These features make Japan an important country for detailed consideration in this book. As a result, Chapter 10 is devoted entirely to a review of the police, courts, and corrections aspects of Japanese society. In addition to that detailed coverage, Japan is also a prime example in Chapter 8's discussion of imprisonment. Further, the Japanese *koban* is briefly noted in Chapter 1 as an example of how a comparative perspective might provide ideas to improve a justice system.

Mexico

People.   *Population* (1991 est.): 90,007,000. *Age distribution*: 0–14 (36.5%); 15–59 (57.8%), 60+ (5.7%). *Ethnic groups*: Mestizo 60%, American Indian 29%, Caucasian 9%. *Languages*: Spanish (official). *Religions*: Roman Catholic 97%.

Geography.   *Area*: 761,604 sq mi, three times the size of Texas. *Location*: In southern North America. *Neighbors*: The United States on the north, Guatemala, Belize on the south. *Capital*: Mexico City. *Cities* (1988 est.): Mexico City, 20 million; Guadalajara, 3 million; Monterrey, 2.7 million.

Government.   *Type*: Federal republic. *Local divisions*: Federal district and 31 states.

Communications.   *Television sets*: 1 per 6.6 persons. *Radios*: 1 per 5.1 persons. *Telephones in use*: 1 per 7.6 persons. *Daily newspaper circulation* (1986): 142 per 1,000 population.

Health and Education.   *Life expectancy at birth* (1991): 68, male; 76, female. *Physicians*: 1 per 600 persons. *Literacy*: 88%. *School*: 10 years compulsory.

Country Narrative.   Mexico was the site of advanced Indian civilizations. The Mayas, an agricultural people, moved up from Yucatan, built immense stone pyramids, and invented a calendar. The Toltecs were overcome by the Aztecs, who founded Tenochtitlan (now Mexico City) in 1325 AD. Hernando Cortes, Spanish conquistador, destroyed the Aztec empire between 1519 and 1521.

After three centuries of Spanish rule the people rose and a republic was declared in 1823. Mexican territory extended into the present American Southwest and California until Texas revolted and established a republic in 1836. The Mexican legislature refused recognition but was unable to enforce its authority there. After numerous clashes, the United States–Mexican War (1846–1848) resulted in the loss by Mexico of the lands north of the Rio Grande.

Rule by monarch, then dictator, moved Mexico into the 20th century. A new constitution in 1917 provided social reform and, since then, Mexico has seen gains in areas of social services, agriculture, and industry.

As the southern neighbor of the United States, Mexico's justice system should be of interest to Americans. The influence of Mexican justice on the development of procedures in the American Southwest and California is reviewed in Chapter 4. On a more contemporary basis, Chapter 1 points to some of the problems shared national borders present to both Mexican and American authorities. Diffuse systems of judicial review are most typically found in countries following a common legal tradition. Mexico, as noted in Chapter 5, provides an example of a primarily civil law country that has developed a rather unique way to resolve problems of uncertainty and conflict arising when numerous judges make decisions on constitutionality of laws.

Morocco

People. *Population* (1991 est.): 26,181,000. *Age distribution*: 0–14 (41.2%), 15–59 (53.7%), 60+ (5.1%). *Ethnic groups*: Arab–Berber 99%. *Languages*: Arabic (official), Berber. *Religions*: Sunni Moslems 99%.

Geography. *Area*: 172,413 sq mi, larger than California. *Location*: On northwest coast of Africa. *Neighbors*: West Sahara on south, Algeria on east. *Capital*: Rabat. *Cities* (1984): Casablanca, 2,600,000; Rabat, 556,000; Fes, 852,000.

Government. *Type*: Constitutional monarchy. *Local divisions*: 37 provinces, 5 municipalities.

Communications. *Television sets*: 1 per 21 persons. *Radios*: 1 per 5.4 persons. *Telephones in use*: 1 per 68 persons. *Daily newspaper circulation* (1988): 12 per 1,000 population.

Health and Education. *Life expectancy at birth* (1991): 63, male; 66, female. *Physicians*: 1 per 4,873 persons. *Literacy*: 35%. *School*: n/a.

Country Narrative. Berbers were the original inhabitants of Morocco, followed by Carthaginians and Romans. Arabs conquered in 683; then, during the 11th and 12th centuries, a Berber empire ruled (from Morocco) all northwest Africa and most of Spain. Part of Morocco came under Spanish rule in the 19th century and France controlled the rest in the early 20th century. Tribal uprisings lasted from 1911 to 1933. The country became independent in 1956.

If an American has heard about any single aspect of Islamic law, it is quite likely the punishment of amputation for theft. Chapter 5 uses Morocco to review substantive and procedural law aspects of this particular crime under one Islamic legal system.

New Zealand

People. *Population* (1991 est.): 3,308,000. *Age distribution*: 0–14 (23.1%); 15–59 (61.9%); 60+ (15.0%). *Ethnic groups*: Europeans (mostly British) 87%, Polynesian (mostly Maori) 9%. *Languages*: English, Maori (both official). *Religions*: Anglican 29%, Presbyterian 18%, Roman Catholic 15%, others.

Geography. *Area*: 103,736 sq mi, the size of Colorado. *Location*: In southwest Pacific Ocean. *Neighbors*: Nearest are Australia on west, Fiji, Tonga on north. *Capital*: Wellington. *Cities* (1990 est): Auckland, 310,000; Christchurch, 290,000; Wellington, 148,000.

Government. *Type*: Parliamentary democracy. *Local divisions*: 93 counties, 12 towns and districts.

Communications. *Television sets*: 1 per 3.1 persons. *Radios*: 1 per 1.1 persons. *Telephones in use*: 1 per 1.4 persons. *Daily newspaper circulation* (1989): 306 per 100,000 population.

Health and Education. *Life expectancy at birth* (1991): 72, male; 78, female. *Physicians*: 1 per 373 persons. *Literacy*: 99%. *School*: Compulsory ages 6–15; attendance 100%.

Country Narrative. The Maoris, a Polynesian group from the eastern Pacific, reached New Zealand before and during the 14th century. The first European to sight New Zealand was Dutch navigator Abel Janszoon Tasman, but Maoris refused to allow him to land. British Capt. James Cook explored the coasts from 1769 to 1770. British sovereignty was proclaimed in 1840, with organized settlement beginning in the same year. The colony became a dominion in 1907 and is an independent member of the Commonwealth.

Codification of common law is an activity undertaken only with great difficulty and potential confusion. Chapter 5 uses New Zealand's 1989 attempt to revise its criminal code as an example of the problems inherent in codifying the common law.

Nigeria

People. *Population* (1991 census): 88,500,000. *Age distribution*: n/a. *Ethnic groups*: Hausa 21%; Yoruba 20%; Ibo 17%; Fulani 9%; others. *Languages*: English (official), Hausa, Yoruba, Ibo. *Religions*: Moslem 50% (in north), Christian 40% (in south), others.

Geography. *Area*: 356,667 sq mi, more than twice the size of California. *Location*: On the south coast of West Africa. *Neighbors*: Benin on west, Niger on north, Chad, Cameroon on east. *Capital*: Abuja. *Cities* (1991): Lagos, 1,300,000; Ibadan, 1,263,000.

Government. *Type*: Military. *Local divisions*: 21 states plus federal capital territory.

Communications. *Television sets*: 1 per 12 persons. *Radios*: 1 per 12 persons. *Telephones in use*: 1 per 240 persons. *Daily newspaper circulation* (1990): 12 per 1,000 population.

Health and Education. *Life expectancy at birth* (1991): 48, males; 50, females. *Physicians*: 1 per 6,900. *Literacy*: 51%. *School*: Primary school attendance 42%.

Country Narrative.   Early cultures in Nigeria date back to at least 700 BC. From the 12th to the 14th centuries more advanced cultures developed in the Yoruba area and in the north, where Moslem influence prevailed. Portuguese and British slavers appeared from the 15th to 16th centuries. Britain seized Lagos in 1861, during an anti-slave trade campaign, and gradually extended control inland until 1900. Nigeria became independent in 1960 and a republic in 1963. After 13 years of military rule, the nation experienced a peaceful return to civilian government in 1979. Military rule returned to Nigeria in 1983 as a coup ousted the democratically elected government.

Although it took a number of years and a degree of patience, Nigeria changed its formerly decentralized police with local forces into the single centralized structure of which it serves as an example in Chapter 6. Also, Nigeria's court system is reviewed in Chapter 7.

Panama

People.   *Population* (1991 est.): 2,426,000. *Age distribution*: 0–14 (35.5%); 15–59 (57.6%); 60+ (6.9%). *Ethnic groups*: Mestizo 70%, West Indian 14%, Caucasian 10%, Indian 6%. *Languages*: Spanish (official), English. *Religions*: Roman Catholic 93%, Protestant 6%.

Geography.   *Area*: 29,208 sq mi, slightly larger than West Virginia. *Location*: In Central America. *Neighbors*: Costa Rica on west, Colombia on east. *Capital*: Panama. *Cities* (1990 est): Panama City, 411,000.

Government.   *Type*: Centralized republic. *Local divisions*: 9 provinces, 1 territory.

Communications.   *Television sets*: 1 per 4.9 persons. *Radios*: 1 per 2.5 persons. *Telephones in use*: 1 per 9.3 persons. *Daily newspaper circulation* (1990): 60 per 1,000 population.

Health and Education.   *Life expectancy at birth* (1991): 72, male; 76, female. *Physicians*: 1 per 841 persons. *Literacy*: 87%. *School*: Primary school attendance almost 100%.

Country Narrative.   The coast of Panama was sighted by Rodrigo de Bastidas, sailing with Columbus for Spain in 1501, and was visited by Columbus in 1502. Vasco Nunez de Balboa crossed the isthmus and "discovered" the Pacific Ocean in 1513. Spanish colonies were ravaged by English explorer, Francis Drake, between 1572 and 1595, and by the English pirate, Henry Morgan, between 1668 and 1671. Two years after Colombia revolted against Spain (1819), Panama also broke away from Spain and became a province of Colombia. Panama declared its independence from Colombia in 1903 with United States naval forces deterring action by Colombia. That same year, Panama granted use, occupation, and control of the Canal Zone to the United States by treaty. In 1978 a new treaty provided for a gradual takeover by Panama of the canal, and withdrawal of United States troops to be completed by 1999.

In 1988 General Manuel Noriega, head of the Panama Defense Forces, was indicted by two United States federal grand juries on drug charges. Despite United States-imposed economic sanctions Noriega remained in power. Voters went to the polls to elect a new president in 1989. Noriega claimed victory but foreign observers said that the opposition had won overwhelmingly and that Noriega was trying to steal the election. The government voided the election. The United States invaded Panama in December 1989, with the chief objective being the capture of Noriega. Noriega surrendered to United States officials on January 3, 1990. He was convicted on 8 counts of racketeering and drug trafficking in a United States District Court in Miami on April 9, 1992.

Chapter 1 uses Panama to exemplify the type of material a political approach to comparative criminal justice would emphasize. Since the Panama Defense Forces, headed by Noriega, provided both internal and external security, Panama had no independent civil police system. To understand the "policing" problems resulting from action against Noriega, we must understand the political dealings in Panama.

Poland

People. *Population* (1991 est.): 37,799,000. *Age distribution*: 0–14 (25.7%); 15–59 (60.2%); 60+ (14.1%). *Ethnic groups*: Polish 98%, Germans, Ukrainians, Byelorussians. *Languages*: Polish. *Religions*: Roman Catholic 94%.

Geography. *Area*: 120,727 sq mi, about the size of New Mexico. *Location*: On the Baltic Sea in East Central Europe. *Neighbors*: Germany on west, Czech Republic and Slovakia on south, Lithuania, Byelorussia, Ukraine on east. *Capital*: Warsaw. *Cities* (1990 est): Warsaw, 1.6 million; Lodz, 851,000; Kracow, 748,000.

Government. *Type*: Democratic state. *Local divisions*: 49 provinces.

Communications. *Television sets*: 1 per 3.9 persons. *Radios*: 1 per 3.6 persons. *Telephones in use*: 1 per 7.5 persons. *Daily newspaper circulation* (1988): 217 per 1,000.

Health and Education. *Life expectancy at birth* (1991): 69, male; 77, female. *Physicians*: 1 per 480 persons. *Literacy*: 98%. *School*: attendance 97%.

Country Narrative. Poland was a great power from the 14th to the 17th centuries. In three partitionings (1772, 1793, 1795) Poland was apportioned among Prussia, Russia, and Austria. Overrun by the Austro–German armies in World War I, its independence, self-declared on November 11, 1918, was recognized by the Treaty of Versailles on June 28, 1919. Germany and the USSR invaded Poland September 1–27, 1939, and divided the country. Following Germany's defeat in World War II, a Polish government-in-exile in London was recognized by the United States, but the USSR pressed the claims of a rival group. The election of 1947 was completely dominated by the Communists.

Following 12 years of rule by Stalinists, a new Politburo, committed to a more independent Polish Communism, was named in October 1956. Collectivization of farms was ended and many collectives were abolished. Religious liberty was permitted and, in the 1970s, government relations with the Roman Catholic Church improved.

After two months of labor turmoil had crippled the country, the Polish government on August 30, 1980 met the demands of striking workers at the Lenin Shipyard in Gdansk. In 1981 the government feared Soviet intervention over the reforms occurring in Poland, so martial law was declared in December, then suspended one year later in December 1982. In April 1989 an accord was reached between the government and opposition factions on a broad range of political and economic reforms, including free elections. In the first free elections in over 40 years, candidates endorsed by Solidarity swept the parliamentary elections. On August 19, 1989 Tadeusz Mazowiecki became the first noncommunist to head an Eastern bloc nation when he became prime minister.

As the first Eastern bloc country to elect a noncommunist leader, Poland provides an interesting example in several of the chapters. Chapter 5 notes Poland's disregard for strict adherence to traditional socialist legality, even before the 1989 changes, by reviewing its approach to substantive law and its early interest in the concept of a "rule of law." In Chapter 6, Poland's police system is considered in an attempt to determine how dramatic changes in political and economic institutions in a country might affect the country's police structure. Chapter 8 highlights Poland's use of imprisonment as an example of a country with one of the highest imprisonment rates in the world.

Portugal

People. *Population* (1991 est.): 10,387,000. *Age distribution*: 0–14 (22.7%); 15–59 (59.9%); 60+ (17.4%). *Ethnic groups*: Homogeneous Mediterranean stock with small African minority. *Languages*: Portuguese. *Religions*: Roman Catholic 97%.

Geography. *Area*: 36,390 sq mi, including the Azores and Madeira Islands, slightly smaller than Indiana. *Location*: At southwest extreme of Europe. *Neighbors*: Spain on northeast. *Capital*: Lisbon. *Cities* (1987 est.): Lisbon, 2 million; Oporto, 1.5 million.

Government. *Type*: Parliamentary democracy. *Local divisions*: 18 districts, 2 autonomous regions, one dependency.

Communications. *Television sets*: 1 per 6.2 persons. *Radios*: 1 per 4.2 persons. *Telephones in use*: 1 per 4.2 persons. *Daily newspaper circulation* (1987): 76 per 1,000 population.

Health and Education. *Life expectancy at birth* (1991): 71, male; 78, female.

Physicians: 1 per 388 persons. *Literacy*: 83%. *School*: 6 years compulsory, attendance 60%.

Country Narrative. Portugal, an independent state since the 12th century, was a kingdom until a revolution in 1910 drove out King Manoel II and a republic was proclaimed. A strong, repressive government existed from 1932 to 1968 under Premier Antonio de Oliveira Salazar. The government was seized by a military junta in 1974 and in 1975 influence by the Soviet-supported Communist party brought nationalization of banks, insurance companies, and other industries. In 1989, Parliament approved a package of reforms that did away with the socialist economy and created a "democratic" economy and denationalized the industries.

Portugal has developed a system of judicial review that combines aspects of both the diffuse and concentrated models. The resulting mixed system is reviewed in Chapter 5.

Russia

People. *Population* (1991 est.): 148,542,000. *Age distribution*: n/a. *Ethnic groups*: Russians 82%, Tatars 3%. *Languages*: Russian (official), Ukrainian, Byelorussian, Uzbek, Armenian, Azerbaijani, Georgian, many others. *Religions*: Russian Orthodox 25%, nonreligious 60%.

Geography. *Area*: 6,592,800 sq mi, the largest country in the world. *Location*: Stretches from East Europe across North Asia to the Pacific Ocean. *Neighbors*: Finland, Poland, Norway, Estonia, Belarus, Ukraine on west, Georgia, Azerbaijan, Kazakhstan, China, Mongolia, North Korea on south. *Capital*: Moscow. *Cities* (1990 est.): Moscow, 8.8 million; St. Petersburg, 5.0 million; Samara, 1.5 million.

Government. *Type*: Republic. *Local divisions*: n/a.

Communications. *Television sets*: 1 per 3.2 persons. *Radios*: 1 per 1.5 persons. *Telephones in use*: 1 per 6.7 persons. *Daily newspaper circulation* (1989, for the former USSR): 383 per 1,000 population.

Health and Education. *Life expectancy at birth* (1991): 64 males, 74 females. *Physicians*: 1 per 259 persons. *Literacy*: 99%. *School*: Most receive 11 years of schooling.

Country Narrative. Slavic tribes began migrating into Russia from the west in the 5th century AD. The first Russian state, founded by Scandinavian chieftains, was established in the 9th century, centering in Novgorod and Kiev. In the 13th century the Mongols overran the country. It recovered under the grand dukes and princes of Muscovy, or Moscow, and by 1480 freed itself from the Mongols. Ivan the Terrible was the first to be formally proclaimed Tsar (1547). Peter the Great (1682–1725) extended the domain and in 1721, founded the Russian Empire.

Western ideas and the beginnings of modernization spread through the huge Russian Empire in the 19th and early 20th centuries, but political evolution failed to keep pace. Military reverses in the 1905 war with Japan and in World War I led to the breakdown of the Tsarist regime. The 1917 Revolution began in March of that year with a series of sporadic strikes for higher wages by factory workers. A communist coup on November 7, 1917 brought Vladimir Lenin to power.

After Lenin's death in 1924, Joseph Stalin emerged as the absolute ruler and led what had become the Union of Soviet Socialist Republics through World War II. Nikita Khrushchev was elected first secretary of the Central Committee of the Communist Party after Stalin's death in 1953. Khrushchev was deposed in 1964 and replaced by Leonid Brezhnev. In 1985 Mikhail Gorbachev was chosen General Secretary of the Communist Party. In 1987 Gorbachev initiated a program of reforms including expanded freedoms and the democratization of the political process through openness (*glasnost*) and restructuring (*perestroika*). On August 19, 1991 it was announced that the vice president had taken over the country due to Gorbachev's illness. A state of emergency was imposed for six months with all power resting with the State Committee on the State of Emergency. The Russian Republic's president, Boris Yeltsin, denounced the coup and called for a general strike. Some 50,000 demonstrated at the Russian parliament in support of Yeltsin. By August 21st the coup had failed and Gorbachev was restored as president. On August 24th Gorbachev resigned as leader of the Communist Party and recommended that its central committee be disbanded. Several republics declared their independence, including Russia, Ukraine, and Kazakhstan. On August 29th the Soviet parliament voted to suspend all activities of the Communist Party. The Union of Soviet Socialist Republics broke up on December 25, 1991 as Gorbachev resigned as head of state.

When part of the USSR, Russia played a prominent role in the development and direction of a socialist legal tradition. As a result, several of the USSR examples used in this book are more specifically from the Russian Soviet Federated Socialist Republic (Russian Republic), which is how Russia was identified while one of the 15 Soviet Republics. Chapter 5, for example, explains how the socialist legal tradition owes much to the language and structure of the Criminal Code of the Russian Republic. And, as Chapter 4 notes, even when the USSR was created the traditions of early Russian law played a prominent role in the development of the socialist legal tradition. In one instance, the former USSR is used as an example. That occurs in Chapter 6 when policing in the USSR provides such a good example of a centralized multiple uncoordinated type that it is used for historical purposes.

Saudi Arabia

People. *Population* (1991 est.): 17,869,000. *Age distribution*: n/a. *Ethnic groups*: Arab tribes, immigrants from other Arab and Moslem countries. *Languages*: Arabic. *Religions*: Moslem 99%.

Geography. *Area*: 839,996 sq mi, one-third the size of the United States. *Location*: Occupies most of Arabian Peninsula in Middle East. *Neighbors*: Kuwait, Iraq, Jordan on north, Yemen, South Yemen, Oman on south, United Arab Emirates, Qatar on east. *Capital*: Riyadh. *Cities* (1986 est): Riyadh, 1,380,000; Jidda, 1,210,000; Mecca, 463,000.

Government. *Type*: Monarchy with council of ministers. *Local divisions*: 14 emirates.

Communications. *Television sets*: 1 per 3.5 persons. *Radios*: 1 per 3.3 persons. *Telephones in use*: 1 per 13 persons. *Daily newspaper circulation* (1989): 49 per 1,000 population.

Health and Education. *Life expectancy at birth* (1991): 65, male; 68, female. *Physicians*: 1 per 852 persons. *Literacy*: 62%. *School*: n/a.

Country Narrative. Arabia was united for the first time by Mohammed, in the early 7th century. His successors conquered the entire Near East and North Africa, bringing Islam and the Arabic language. But Arabia itself soon returned to its former status. Jejd, long an independent state and center of the Wahhabi sect of Islam, fell under Turkish rule in the 18th century, but in 1913 Ibn Saud, founder of the Saudi dynasty, overthrew the Turks and captured the Turkish province of Hasa, took the Hejaz in 1925 and, by 1926, most of Asir. The discovery of oil in the 1930s transformed the new country.

Crown Prince Khalid was proclaimed king in 1975 after the assassination of King Faisal. Fahd became king following Khalid's death in 1982. The Kingdom of Saudi Arabia has neither a constitution nor a parliament. Instead, the king exercises authority together with a Council of Ministers.

The Islamic religious code is the law of the land, so Saudi Arabia provides an excellent example of the Islamic legal tradition. As a result, it is mentioned in several of this book's chapters. Because Islam saturates Saudi culture, some researchers have used Saudi Arabia crime statistics to consider possible links between religion and crime. Chapter 2 presents examples of such research. While pockets of tribal authority and examples of a religious police are found in Saudi Arabia, the country's formally recognized police is offered in Chapter 6 as an example of a centralized single system. Frequent reference is made to Saudi Arabia in Chapter 7 as Islamic court procedures, actors, and organization are reviewed.

Scotland
(Also see United Kingdom)

People. *Population* (1991 census): 4,957,000. *Age distribution*: (see United Kingdom). *Ethnic groups*: (see United Kingdom). *Languages*: About 90,000 persons speak Gaelic as well as English. *Religions*: (see United Kingdom).

Geography. *Area*: 30,405 sq mi, slightly smaller than South Carolina.

Location: Occupies the northern 37% of the main British island, and the Hebrides, Orkney, Shetland and smaller islands. *Neighbors*: England on southeast, Ireland, Northern Ireland on southwest. *Capital*: Edinburgh. *Cities* (1986 est.): Glasgow, 733,000; Edinburgh, 439,000.

Government.   *Type*: A kingdom united with England and Wales in Great Britain. *Local divisions*: 9 regions, 3 island areas.

Communications.   (see United Kingdom).

Health and Education.   (see United Kingdom).

Country Narrative.   Scotland was called Caledonia by the Romans who battled early Celtic tribes and occupied southern areas from the 1st to the 4th centuries. The Kingdom of Scotland was founded in 1018. William Wallace and Robert Bruce both defeated English armies in 1297 and 1314 respectively. In 1603 James VI of Scotland, son of Mary, Queen of Scots, succeeded to the throne of England as James I, and effected the Union of the Crowns. In 1707 Scotland received representation in the British Parliament, resulting from the union of former separate Parliaments. Its executive in the British cabinet is the Secretary of State for Scotland. The growing Scottish National Party urges independence. A 1979 referendum on the creation of an elected Scotland Assembly was defeated.

In Chapter 5 Scotland provides a contemporary example of substantive criminal law in the common legal tradition. While many countries of the common legal tradition move more toward legislature-made law, Scottish courts continue to take an active role in judge-made substantive law. In Chapter 9, Scotland's use of children's hearings provides an example of the welfare model of juvenile justice.

South Africa

People.   *Population* (1991 est.): 40,600,000. *Age distribution*: 0–14 (41.0%); 15–59 (52.8%); 60+ (6.2%). *Ethnic groups*: Black 75%, White 14%, Coloured 8%, Asian 3%. *Languages*: Afrikaans, English (both official), Nguni, Sotho languages. *Religions*: Mainly Christian, Hindu, Moslem minorities.

Geography.   *Area*: 472,359 sq mi, about twice the size of Texas. *Location*: At the southern extreme of Africa. *Neighbors*: Namibia (South West Africa), Botswana, Zimbabwe on north, Mozambique, Swaziland on east. *Capitals*: Cape Town (legislative), Pretoria (administrative), and Bloemfontein (judicial). *Cities* (1990 met.): Durban, 1 million; Cape Town, 1.9 million; Johannesburg, 1.7 million; Pretoria, 850,000.

Government.   *Type*: Tricameral parliament with one chamber each for whites, coloureds, and Asians. *Local divisions*: 4 provinces, 10 "homelands" for black Africans.

Communications.   *Television sets*: 1 per 11 persons. *Radios*: 1 per 3.0 persons. *Telephones in use*: 1 per 8.5 persons. *Daily newspaper circulation* (1988): 41 per 1,000 population.

Health and Education.   *Life expectancy at birth* (1991): 61, male; 67, female. *Physicians*: 1 per 1,340 persons. *Literacy*: 99% (whites), 69% (Asians), 62% (coloureds), 50% (Africans). *School*: n/a.

Country Narrative.   Bushmen and Hottentots were the original inhabitants of what is now South Africa. In the 17th century the Dutch began settling the Cape of Good Hope area only to have it seized by Britain in 1806. Many Dutch trekked north and founded two republics, the Transvaal and the Orange Free State. Diamonds were discovered in 1867 and gold in 1886. The Dutch (Boers) resented encroachments by the British and others and the Anglo–Boer War occurred in 1899 to 1902. Britain won and created the Union of South Africa which incorporated the British colonies of the Cape and Natal, the Transvaal and the Orange Free State. The Union became the Republic of South Africa in 1961 and withdrew from the Commonwealth.

Separate development of the races (apartheid) became the official policy in 1948. Under apartheid, Blacks were severely restricted to certain occupations, and paid far lower wages than whites for similar work. Only whites could vote or run for public office. A new constitution was approved in 1983 that extended the parliamentary franchise to the Coloured and Asian minorities. Laws banning interracial sex and marriage were repealed in 1985. Some 2 million South African Black workers staged a massive strike in 1988 to protest the government's new labor laws and the banning of political activity by trade unions and antiapartheid groups. In 1990 the government lifted its ban on the African National Congress, the primary Black group fighting to end white minority rule. The Separate Amenities Act was repealed in October 1990, thereby ending the legal basis of segregation in public places. In June 1991, the race registration law was repealed.

South Africa's links to Britain provided it with a common legal tradition. In Chapter 1, South Africa offers an example of bail procedures that use cash deposits but does not operate as a commercial bail bonding system.

Spain

People.   *Population* (1991 est.): 39,384,000. *Age distribution*: 0–14 (24.6%); 15–59 (59.5%); 60+ (15.9%). *Ethnic groups*: Spanish (Castilian, Valencian, Andalusian, Asturian) 72.8%, Catalan 16.4%, Galician 8.2%, Basque 2.3%. *Languages*: Spanish (official), Catalan, Galician, Basque. *Religions*: Roman Catholic 90%.

Geography.   *Area*: 194,896 sq mi, the size of Arizona and Utah combined. *Location*: In southwest Europe. *Neighbors*: Portugal on west, France on north. *Capital*: Madrid. *Cities* (1990 est.): Madrid, 3,120,000; Barcelona, 1,707,000; Valencia, 758,000; Seville, 678,000.

Government.   *Type*: Constitutional monarchy. *Local divisions*: 17 autonomous communities.

Communications.   *Television sets*: 1 per 2.6 persons. *Radios*: 1 per 3.4 persons. *Telephones in use*: 1 per 2.5 persons. *Daily newspaper circulation* (1990): 76 per 1,000 population.

Health and Education.   *Life expectancy at birth* (1991): 75, males; 82, females. *Physicians*: 1 per 275 persons. *Literacy*: 97%. *School*: compulsory to age 16.

Country Narrative.   Spain was settled by Iberians, Basques, and Celts, partly overrun by Carthaginians, and conquered by Rome. The Visigoths, in power by the 5th century AD, adopted Christianity, but by 711 had lost to the Islamic invasion from Africa. Christian reconquest from the north led to a Spanish nationalism. In 1469 the kingdoms of Aragon and Castile were united and the last Moorish power was broken by the fall of the kingdom of Granada in 1492. Spain became a bulwark of Roman Catholicism.

Spain obtained a colonial empire with the discovery of America by Columbus in 1492, as well as the conquest of Mexico by Cortes, and Peru by Pizarro. Spain lost its American colonies in the early 19th century, then Cuba, the Philippines, and Puerto Rico during the Spanish–American War in 1898.

After significant political turmoil in the 1920s and 1930s Army officers under Francisco Franco revolted against the government in 1936. War ended in 1939 and Franco was named leader of the nation. After Franco's death in 1975 Juan Carlos was sworn in as king. He presided over the formal dissolution of the institution of the Franco regime. In free elections in 1977 moderates and democratic socialists emerged as the largest parties. Catalonia and the Basque country were granted autonomy in 1980 following overwhelming approval in home-rule referendums. Basque extremists, however, have continued their campaign for independence.

Spain has three major police forces but since they operate under the authority of the national government, Chapter 6 uses Spain as an example of a centralized system. However, since the jurisdictional boundaries of the forces overlap and they do not cooperate very well with each other, they are a multiple uncoordinated example of centralization.

Switzerland

People.   *Population* (1991 est.): 6,783,000. *Age distribution*: 0–14 (17.0%); 15–59 (63.7%); 60+ (19.3%). *Ethnic groups*: Mixed European stock. *Languages*: German, French, Italian (all official). *Religions*: Roman Catholic 49%, Protestant 48%.

Geography.   *Area*: 15,941 sq mi, as large as Massachusetts. *Location*: In the Alps Mountains in Central Europe. *Neighbors*: France on west, Italy on south, Austria on east, Germany on north. *Capital*: Bern. *Cities* (1990): Zurich, 342,000; Basel, 171,000; Geneva, 161,000; Bern, 135,000.

Government.   *Type*: Federal republic. *Local divisions*: 20 full cantons, 6 half cantons.

Communications. *Television sets*: 1 per 2.9 persons. *Radios*: 1 per 2.6 persons. *Telephones in use*: 1 per 1.2 persons. *Daily newspaper circulation* (1990): 471 per 1,000 population.

Health and Education. *Life expectancy at birth* (1991): 75, male; 83, female. *Physicians*: 1 per 357 persons. *Literacy*: 99%. *School*: compulsory to age 9, attendance 100%.

Country Narrative. Switzerland, the Roman province of Helvetia, is a federation of 23 cantons. Three of the cantons had created a defensive league in 1291 and later were joined by other districts. In 1648 the Swiss Confederation obtained its independence from the Holy Roman Empire. The cantons were joined under a federal constitution in 1848 with large powers of local control retained by each canton. Switzerland has maintained an armed neutrality since 1815 and has not been involved in a foreign war since 1515. It is the seat of many United Nations and other international agencies.

Switzerland shares with Belgium and the United States the rather unique status of having a decentralized multiple uncoordinated police structure. As noted in Chapter 6, the Swiss use several different agencies to allow some cooperation among its federal, cantonal, and municipal police agencies.

United Kingdom of Great Britain and Northern Ireland

People. *Population* (1991 census): 55,486,800. *Age distribution*: 0–14 (19.2%); 15–59 (60.1%); 60+ (20.7%). *Ethnic groups*: English 81.5%, Scottish 9.6%, Irish 2.4%, Welsh 1.9%, Ulster 1.8%, West Indian, Indian, Pakistani over 2%; others. *Languages*: English, Welsh spoken in western Wales. *Religions*: Church of England, Roman Catholic.

Geography. *Area*: 94,226 sq mi, slightly smaller than Oregon. *Location*: Off the northwest coast of Europe, across English Channel, Strait of Dover, and North Sea. *Neighbors*: Ireland to west, France to southeast. *Capital*: London. *Cities* (1988 est.): London, 6,735,000; Birmingham, 993,000; Glasgow, 703,000; Leeds, 710,000; Edinburgh, 433,000.

Government. *Type*: Constitutional monarchy. *Local divisions*: England and Wales: 47 nonmetro counties, 6 metro counties, Greater London; Scotland: 9 regions, 3 island areas; Northern Ireland: 26 districts.

Communications. *Television sets*: 1 per 3 persons. *Radios*: 1 per 1 persons. *Telephones in use*: 1 per 1.9 persons. *Daily newspaper circulation* (1990): 388 per 1,000 population.

Health and Education. *Life expectancy at birth* (1991): 73, male; 79, female. *Physicians*: 1 per 611 persons. *Literacy*: 99%. *School*: 12 years compulsory, attendance 99%.

Country Narrative. Britain was part of the continent of Europe until about 6,000 BC, but migration of peoples across the English Channel continued long afterward. Celts arrived some 2,500 to 3,000 years ago. Their language survives in Welsh and Gaelic enclaves. England was added to the Roman Empire in 43 AD. After the withdrawal of Roman legions in 410 waves of Jutes, Angles, and Saxons arrived from German lands. They contended with Danish raiders for control from the 8th through 11th centuries. The last successful invasion was by French speaking Normans in 1066, who united the country with their dominions in France. Opposition by nobles to royal authority forced King John to sign the Magna Carta in 1215 and in doing so guaranteed right and the rule of law. In the ensuing decades, the foundations of the parliamentary system were laid.

A struggle between Parliament and the Stuart kings led to a bloody civil war (1642–1649) that resulted in the establishment of a republic under Oliver Cromwell. The monarchy was restored in 1660, but the "Glorious Revolution" of 1688 confirmed the sovereignty of Parliament. In the 18th century parliamentary rule was strengthened. The 13 North American colonies were lost, but replaced by growing empires in Canada and India. Though victorious in World War I, Britain suffered huge casualties and economic dislocation. The country suffered major bombing damage in World War II but held out against Germany single-handedly for a year after the fall of France in 1940. Industrial growth continued in the postwar period, but Britain lost its leadership position to other powers.

The United Kingdom of Great Britain and Northern Ireland comprises England, Wales, Scotland, and Northern Ireland. Each is represented in the British Parliament which consists of two houses. The House of Lords has a total membership over 1,000 and includes hereditary positions, certain judges, life peers and peeresses, and some archbishops and bishops of the Church of England. The House of Commons has 650 members elected by direct ballot.

Examples from the United Kingdom appear in chapters 1, 4, 5, 7, and 9. Except for Scotland's appearance in Chapter 9, the specific examples are from England (including a section of Chapter 9). Excluding the United States, those appearances make England one of the two (the other is France) most widely used countries in this book. It should be noted that justice examples for England are also examples for Wales since the two countries are administered as a unit.

England is of particular importance when the development of the common legal tradition is discussed (Chapter 4) and exemplified (Chapter 5). England's use of criminalization as an alternative to commercial bail bonding in noted is Chapter 1, but it receives detailed attention in Chapter 7 through discussion of the English courts and courtroom actors. In Chapter 9, England and Wales provide the prime example of the corporatist model of juvenile justice.

United States of America

People. *Population* (1990 census): 248,709,873. *Age distribution*: 0–14 (21.7%); 15–59 (61.4%); 60+ (16.9%). *Ethnic groups*: White nonhispanic 71.3%; Black 12.1%; Hispanic 9%; American Indian, Eskimo, or Aleut 0.8%; Asian or

Pacific Islander 2.9%. *Languages*: English. *Religions*: Protestant 35%, Roman Catholic 24%, others.

Geography. *Area*: 3,618,770 sq mi, slightly smaller than China. *Location*: Covers the full width of the North America continent from Atlantic Ocean to Pacific Ocean plus Alaska on the edge of the Arctic and Hawaii in the Pacific Ocean. *Neighbors*: Canada on north, Mexico on south. *Capital*: Washington, D.C. *Cities* (1990 census): New York City, 18,087,251; Los Angeles, 14,531,529; Chicago, 8,065,633; Atlanta, 2,833,511.

Government. *Type*: Federal republic. *Local divisions*: 50 states and District of Columbia.

Communications. *Television sets*: 1 per 1.3 persons. *Radios*: 1 per 0.5 persons. *Telephones in use*: 1 per 1.9 persons. *Daily newspaper circulation* (1990): 255 per 1,000 population.

Health and Education. *Life expectancy at birth* (1991): 72, male; 79, female. *Physicians*: 1 per 404 persons. *Literacy*: 97%. *School*: n/a.

Country Narrative. For purposes of comparison and explanation, examples from the United States are found throughout this book. Most often, those comments are fairly brief and not particularly detailed. Occasionally, however, the United States provides the best example of a category or model and discussion is therefore extended. For example, because of its unique status of having some 20,000 public law enforcement agencies operating an extremely decentralized police system, the United States is used in Chapter 6 to exemplify a decentralized multiple uncoordinated police structure.

Venezuela

People. *Population* (1991 est.): 20,189,000. *Age distribution*: 0–14 (38.3%); 15–59 (56.0%); 60+ (5.7%). *Ethnic groups*: Mestizo 69%, White (Spanish, Portuguese, Italian) 20%, Black 9%, Indian 2%. *Languages*: Spanish (official). *Religions*: Roman Catholic 92%.

Geography. *Area*: 352,143 sq mi, more than twice the size of California. *Location*: On the Caribbean coast of South America. *Neighbors*: Colombia on west, Brazil on south, Guyana on east. *Capital*: Caracas. *Cities* (1990 est.): Caracas, 1,290,000; Maracaibo, 1,206,000; Barquisimeto, 723,000.

Government. *Type*: Federal republic. *Local divisions*: 20 states, 2 federal territories, federal district, federal dependency.

Communications. *Television sets*: 1 per 5.6 persons. *Radios*: 1 per 2.4 persons. *Telephones in use*: 1 per 11 persons. *Daily newspaper circulation* (1989): 111 per 1,000 population.

Health and Education. *Life expectancy at birth* (1991): 71, male; 78, female.

Physicians: 1 per 576 persons. *Literacy*: 88%. *School*: 8 years compulsory, attendance 82%.

Country Narrative.   Columbus first set foot on the South American continent on the peninsula of Paria in 1498. Alonso de Ojeda found Lake Maracaibo in 1499 and called the land Venezuela, or Little Venice, because natives had houses on stilts. Venezuela was under Spanish domination until 1821. The republic was formed after secession from the Colombian Federation in 1830.

Military strongmen ruled Venezuela for most of the 20th century. They promoted the oil industry and implemented some social reforms. Since 1959 the country has had democratically elected governments.

Venezuela uses a judicial review process that combines aspects of the more typically found diffuse and concentrated models. The resulting mixed-model makes Venezuela an appropriate example for discussion of judicial review in Chapter 5. The country also appears in Chapter 2 in an interesting comparison of crime rates in Venezuela and the United States.

Yugoslavia

(Data prior to 1992 include former republics of Croatia, Slovenia, Bosnia and Herzegovina, and Macedonia)

People.   Population (1992 est.): 10,337,000. *Age distribution*: 0–14 (23.5%); 15–59 (63.7%); 60+ (12.8%). *Ethnic groups* (1990): Serbs 36%, Croats 20%, Bosnian Moslems 9%, Slovenes 8%, Macedonians 6%, Albanians 8%. *Languages*: Serbo–Croatian, Macedonian, Slovenian, Albanian. *Religions*: Eastern Orthodox 50%, Roman Catholic 30%, Moslem 9%.

Geography.   *Area*: 39,000 sq mi, slightly smaller than Virginia. *Location*: On the Balkan Peninsula in southeast Europe. Consists of the former republics of Serbia and Montenegro, and the autonomous regions of Kosovo and Vojvodina. *Neighbors*: Croatia, Bosnia and Herzegovina on west, Hungary on north, Romania, Bulgaria on east, Greece, Albania, Macedonia on south. *Capital*: Belgrade. *Cities* (1991 est.): Belgrade, 1,553,000.

Government.   *Type*: Republic. *Local divisions*: 2 republics, 2 autonomous provinces.

Communications.   *Television sets*: 1 per 3.6 persons. *Radios*: 1 per 6 persons. *Telephones in use*: 1 per 4.9 persons. *Daily newspaper circulation* (1990): 88 per 1,000 population.

Health and Education.   *Life expectancy at birth* (1991): 70, male; 76, female. *Physicians*: 1 per 511 persons. *Literacy*: 90%. *School*: Almost all attend primary school.

Country Narrative.   Serbia, which had since 1389 been a vassal principality of Turkey, was established as an independent kingdom by the Treaty of Berlin in 1878. Montenegro, independent since 1389, also obtained international recognition in 1878. In 1913, after the Balkan wars, Serbia's boundaries were enlarged by the annexation of Old Serbia and Macedonia. When the Austro–Hungarian empire collapsed after World War I, the Kingdom of the Serbs, Croats, and Slovenes were formed from the former provinces of Croatia, Dalmatia, Bosnia, Herzegovina, Slovenia, Voyvodina and the independent state of Montenegro. The name was later changed to Yugoslavia. In 1946 Yugoslavia became a federated republic and Marshal Tito, a communist, became head of the government. Tito rejected Stalin's policy of dictating to all communist nations. Instead Tito accepted economic aid and military equipment from the United States and received aid in foreign trade also from France and Great Britain. Beginning in 1965 reforms designed to decentralize the administration of economic development and to force industries to produce more efficiently in competition with foreign producers were introduced and considerable trade with the West was developed.

President Tito died in 1980, and the post of head of the Collective Presidency and head of the League of Communists became a rotating system of succession among the members representing each republic and autonomous province. In 1990 a Communist Party conference renounced its constitutionally guaranteed leading role in society and called on parliament to enact "Political Pluralism, including a multiparty system." Croatia and Slovenia formally declared independence in 1991. In Croatia, fighting began between Croats and ethnic Serbs. Serbia sent arms and medical supplies to the Serb rebels in Croatia. The republics of Serbia and Montenegro proclaimed a new "Federal Republic of Yugoslavia" on April 17, 1992.

Prior to the 1991 proclamations of independence in its former republics, Yugoslavia provided an example of the legalistic model of juvenile justice. Chapter 9 retains the Yugoslavia example since it appears the new Federal Republic of Yugoslavia will hold close to the justice system of the old Socialist Federal Republic of Yugoslavia.

Index

NAME INDEX

Only the first author in coauthored and multiauthored works is indexed.

SUBJECT INDEX

Locators followed by an asterisk (*) indicate figures.

Belgium, 5, 401
police, 200–201
victimization rates, 42*
Benefits of an international perspective, 3–6, 8
Bolivia, 233
Boryokudan, 47, 352, 387–88
Botswana, 272*–73*
Brazil, 164, 402
Burakumin, 282, 351–52
Bureaucratic informalism, 362–64
Burglary, 31, 34*

Canada, 140, 290, 403
age of criminal responsibility, 315
crime statistics, 38*, 40*
police, 191–94
victimization rates, 42*–43
Canon law, 101–2, 118
Children's aid panels (Australia), 317–19, 333
Children's hearings (Scotland), 320–21, 333
Chile
crime statistics, 40*
defense attorneys, 228
China, 349–50, 361, 372, 404
age of criminal responsibility, 315
court organization, 255
courts, 253–57
lawyers, 254
mediation committees, 254–55
participatory model of juvenile justice, 337–40
pre-trial detention, 11–12
presumption of innocence, 219
principle of analogy, 128
prison labor, 299–300
Chinese legal system (ancient), 94
Chuzaisho. See Japan.
Civil law (distinguished from civil legal tradition), 99
Civil legal tradition, 98*, 362
developmental elements (subtraditions), 99–102
flexibility of law, 125–27
inquisitorial process, 149
judges in, 229
lawyers in, 216
primary source of law, 123*–24
public versus private law, 119*–20, 148
substantive law, 141–44
Classification, 16–20, 23
groups:
artificial, 17, 23, 117
natural, 18, 117
strategies:
authentic, 18*, 23, 117
synthetic, 17–18*, 23, 117
Code Napoleon, 99, 102, 105
Code of Hammurabi, 93
Codification (of law), 102, 139–41
Colombia, 47, 231–32
Common legal tradition, 98*
adversarial process, 149, 150–51
bail types, 14*, 19
codification of law, 102, 105, 139–41
developmental elements (subtraditions), 95–99
flexibility of law, 125–26*
judges in, 229
lawyers in, 216

primary source of law, 123*–24
public versus private law, 118–19*, 148
substantive law, 137–41
Comparative criminology, 52–56. *See also* Crime;
Transnational crime
Conflict perspective (of criminal law), 61, 63
Confucius, 94, 338–39, 349, 353, 360–61, 372
Consensus perspective (of criminal law), 61, 62–63
Corpus Juris Civilis, 95, 99–102
Crime, 29–31. *See also* Transnational crime types;
specific country
comparative studies, 41, 53, 55–56
country rates, 38*, 40*–41, 53
specific types, 30–31, 34*, 39–40, 43, 54–56, 146, 347,
377*
theories, 52–56
worldwide trend, 41, 46–51
Crime control model, 66–67*, 77, 82–85, 147–48, 154–55,
391
Crime statistics, 31–33, 37–39. *See also* National Crime
Survey; Uniform Crime Reports
Criminal responsibility, 73, 75–77, 135–37, 147
Cuba, 405
age of criminal responsibility, 315*
participatory model of juvenile justice, 337
Cuerpo Nacional de Policia (Spain), 188–89
Custom, 96–97, 112, 122–24, 138, 362
Czechoslovakia:
crime statistics, 30
organized crime, 47

Day fines, 287–88
Defense, 226–29. *See also* specific country
Denmark, 406
crime statistics, 40*
imprisonment rates, 272*–73*
police, 175–76
Detention, investigative, 20. *See also* Pre-trial detention
Due process model, 66–67*, 77, 82, 84–85, 147, 154–55,
391

East Germany, 198–200. *See also* Germany
Egypt, 38*, 40*
Egyptian legal system (ancient), 93
El Salvador, 233
England, 6, 103, 140. *See also* United Kingdom
age of criminal responsibility, 315
bail, 15–16
corporate model of juvenile justice, 327–32
court organization, 249*
courts, 248–51
crime statistics, 38*, 40*, 347
development of common legal tradition, 95–99
imprisonment rates, 272*–73*
judges, 233, 238–40
lawyers, 151, 217
prosecution, 223–24
substantive law, 137
transportation of criminals, 274–78
victimization rates, 42*
Extradition, 5–6, 44–45

Factual guilt, 84, 153
Feudalism, 95–96, 361
Fiji, 335–37, 406